2022
Publishers Weekly®
Book Publishing
Almanac

T0306943

2022
Publishers Weekly®
Book Publishing Almanac

A Master Class in the Art of Bringing Books to Readers

Skyhorse Publishing

Skyhorse Publishing books may be purchased in bulk at special discounts for sales promotion, corporate gifts, fund-raising, or educational purposes. Special editions can also be created to specifications. For details, contact the Special Sales Department, Skyhorse Publishing, 307 West 36th Street, 11th Floor, New York, NY 10018 or info@skyhorsepublishing.com.

Skyhorse® and Skyhorse Publishing® are registered trademarks of Skyhorse Publishing, Inc.®, a Delaware corporation.

Visit our website at www.skyhorsepublishing.com.

BookLife® is a registered trademark of BookLife, LLC.
Publishers Weekly® is a registered trademark of PWxyz, LLC.

10 9 8 7 6 5 4 3 2 1

Library of Congress Cataloging-in-Publication Data is available on file.

This book is designed to provide accurate and authoritative information with respect to the subject matter covered. It is sold with the understanding that neither the publisher nor the author is engaged in rendering legal or other professional services. It contains information gathered at the time of publication such as telephone numbers, Internet addresses, and other contact information, including information gathered from third parties. While every attempt is made to provide accurate information, the author and publisher cannot be held accountable for errors or omissions. In addition, the publisher does not have any control over and does not assume any responsibility for author or third-party websites or their content.

Cover design by Matt See

Hardcover ISBN: 978-1-5107-6902-1
Paperback ISBN: 978-1-5107-6881-9
Ebook ISBN: 978-1-5107-6890-1

Printed in the United States of America

CONTENTS

INTRODUCTION: THE PUBLISHERS WEEKLY STORY

Publishers Weekly, now celebrating its 150th anniversary, is familiarly known in the book world as *PW* and "the bible of the book business." Focused on the international book publishing business, it is now a multimedia news platform with full horizontal coverage of book publishing beginning with the author-as-creator to publisher, printer, and distributor to the end consumer. Its varied products are targeted at publishers, booksellers, librarians, literary agents, authors, book lovers, and the media. It offers feature articles and news on all aspects of the book business, bestseller lists in a number of categories, and industry statistics, but its best-known service is prepublication book reviews, of which it publishes nearly 9,000 per year.

The magazine was born in 1872 as *The Weekly Trade Circular* and in 1873 renamed *The Publishers' Weekly* (the article and the apostrophe were later dropped), a collective catalog where publishers pooled their resources to create one common presentation of new books, issued each week. The aim was to keep booksellers and librarians informed of forthcoming titles, and an array of features and articles were added as years went by. The original creator of the magazine, and its first editor, was the German-born Frederick Leypoldt, a passionate bibliographer—so passionate and hardworking that he died prematurely, at the age of 49, in 1884. An early colleague in the enterprise was Richard Rogers Bowker, a literary journalist and also a keen bibliographer, who went on to create the R. R. Bowker Company. Bowker ultimately became the owner of *PW*, and later began to publish the massive annual *Books in Print* volumes and assign the International Standard Book Numbers (ISBNs) given to every published book. Another key player in *PW*'s history, who joined the magazine in 1918 and was active with it for over more than years, was Frederic G. Melcher, a polymath who served as secretary of the American Booksellers Association, helped create the National Association of Publishers, and launched such notable book awards as the Newbery Medal and Caldecott Medal for children's books and the Carey-Thomas Awards for distinguished publishing. He also created Children's Book Week and was responsible for the early extensive coverage of children's books that has remained a *PW* tradition. For the 150th anniversary, *PW* plans to relaunch the Carey-Thomas Awards in late 2022.

Owned for much of the 20th century by R. R. Bowker (which in turn was collectively owned by its staff since 1933), Bowker was sold to the Xerox Corporation at the end of 1967, and for the next 43 years *PW* was in corporate hands. Xerox sold the magazine (and its sister publications, *Library Journal* and *School Library Journal*) to Britain's Reed International in 1985, as part of its Cahners trade magazine division in the United States. Reed later combined with the Dutch giant Elsevier and in 2002 rebranded Cahners as Reed Business Information.

In 2008, Reed put its division of U.S. trade magazines up for sale and eventually began selling off individual magazines once it became clear that a deal for the entire portfolio could not be struck. In April 2010, *PW* was bought by George Slowik, Jr., a magazine and web entrepreneur who had been *PW*'s publisher from 1990 to 1993, and his partner, Patrick Turner. Slowik created a company called PWxyz LLC and moved the magazine from its Park Avenue South offices to its current location on West 23rd Street in New York City.

The magazine has enjoyed a succession of editors who have expanded the quality and range of its coverage, giving it in the process a remarkable preeminence in its field. Mildred Smith, who joined in 1920 just out of college and ran the magazine for more than 40 years, placed strong emphasis on its news coverage and demanded clear, concise writing from the many industry figures she persuaded to write for the magazine. It still, however, had many old-fashioned features: it ran the texts of speeches at industry occasions verbatim and was printed in a small format, only slightly larger than *Reader's Digest*. Smith was succeeded by Chandler Grannis, who was passionate about scholarly and university press publishing and book design.

But perhaps it was Arnold Ehrlich, who came from the world of consumer magazine publishing (*Holiday*, *Show*, and *Venture*) who did the most to make the magazine one that a lay reader could also dip into with interest. He created a series of author interviews, launched a news section, and hired an expatriate American in Paris, Herbert R. Lottman, as the magazine's first international correspondent. The bilingual Lottman became a household name in publishing circles in Europe, wrote dozens of penetrating features, interviews, and a regular column, and grew *PW* into a magazine that was genuinely international in its coverage.

As publishing activity extended beyond the metropolitan cities, Ehrlich also established a group of regional columnists, covering the West Coast, Southern, Midwestern, and New England scenes. (A West Coast correspondent for many years went on to become the bestselling novelist Lisa See.) A young editor who had joined *PW* straight from high school, Daisy Maryles, worked more than

40 years at the magazine and was largely responsible for the development of the magazine's influential bestseller lists and religious publishing coverage.

Ehrlich hired another figure from the consumer and news world as his managing editor in 1973, John Baker, an Englishman with a background at Reuters and Reader's Digest General Books. In 1977 Baker went off to edit a spin-off attempt at a consumer book magazine, *Bookviews*, which ran its own features and original reviews, plus reviews from *PW*. It folded after two years. Baker then returned to *PW* as editor-in-chief, where he remained for more than 25 years.

Among editors hired during Baker's tenure were editorial director Jim Milliot and his co-editorial director, Michael Coffey; Diane Roback, who heads up the magazine's extensive coverage of children's books; and Sybil Steinberg, now retired, who helped shape the reviews section as it is today.

As the power of the book chains grew, however, and the number of independent bookstores fell, the ad pages declined as publishers poured more of their promotional revenues into in-store promotions and ads in the chains' own catalogs. The upheavals in the early 1990s involved in the creation of Reed Business Information caused further turmoil, and Nora Rawlinson, a career librarian who had edited *Library Journal*, was brought in as editor in 1992, with Baker becoming editorial director. Rawlinson added coverage of the library market to *PW*'s mission and oversaw the development of *PW*'s first website. In another effort to shake things up, Sara Nelson was brought in to replace Rawlinson in 2005. Nelson, formerly a publishing columnist for the *New York Post* and *New York Observer*, ordered up an extensive redesign emphasizing color and shorter stories and features.

Despite all these efforts, the economics of the book business were working against the magazine. Advertising continued to decline, and circulation descended below 15,000. After a period of many rumors of a pending sale, the as-is purchase of *Publishers Weekly* was achieved by Slowik and Turner, over the weekend before Reed folded 23 other trade magazines, taking a final write-off on March 31, 2010. They brought the entire *PW* staff with them, including Jim Milliot (now senior vice-president) and Michael Coffey as co-editorial directors, Diane Roback as children's book editor (now senior vice-president), Louisa Ermelino as book reviews editor (now editor-at-large), Cevin Bryerman as publisher (now CEO), and Joseph Murray as ad director (now associate publisher).

Under Slowik's leadership, the editorial team's vision, and the business group's sales acumen, the magazine's online presence flourished. *PW* hired Mediapolis to reengineer the magazine's website and its electronic newsletters and blogs;

made the magazine available as an iPad app; added a section that reviewed and announced self-published titles entitled *PW* Select; and partnered with the BookScan service to quantify the magazine's extensive bestsellers lists. In 2019 *PW* acquired the popular online literary journal *The Millions*.

PW's international profile expanded with the creation of several digital tools for global publishers. They included PubMatch, a joint venture with Combined Book Exhibit, a title database and set of tools for selling international book rights, and the Global 50, a ranking of the world's largest publishers done in cooperation with *Livres Hebdo* and publishing consultant Dr. Rüdiger Wischenbart. An Arabic edition of *Publishers Weekly*, a translation of articles from the American edition, appears regularly through arrangement with the Sharjah Book Fair.

Bryerman increased *PW's* coverage of international publishing trade events. In 2016 *PW* spearheaded the U.S. Publishing Mission to Cuba for a two-day conference of U.S. and Cuban publishers.

In 2019 *Publishers Weekly en Español* was launched in partnership with Seville-based Lantia Publishing under the editorial leadership of Enrique Parrilla. The Spanish edition features original Spanish-language news of the Spanish publishing industry, original book reviews, and author interviews. It is distributed in selected Spanish-speaking countries and in the U.S.

One of Slowik's signature accomplishments was to digitize the physical archive of bound issues of the magazine, which are housed at the magazine's Chelsea office. The *Publishers Weekly* Digital Archive took several years to execute. The searchable archive is composed of 7,703 issues, with a total of 667,000 pages, in full color, including all advertising, covers and a Wiki-style correction function. It is sold and managed by Minneapolis-based East View Information Services, Inc.

For many years, the magazine's book review section, now helmed by Jonathan Segura, has been a key element in *PW*'s influence and success, and it occupies nearly half of every issue, covering nearly 9,000 titles a year in a dozen categories. These are advance reviews, written on the basis of early galleys of the book, published two to four months before a book's publication date. They are therefore of great importance in stimulating interest among booksellers and librarians, movie and TV studios, and foreign rights agents—and also acting as an early warning system for reviewers in consumer media, including print, broadcast, and online, as well as news segment producers. Many books receive their only review here, and favorable reviews are widely quoted in publisher promotions, in newspaper and magazine advertising, and on book jackets.

The first reviews appeared in the early 1940s and were called Forecasts, since early reviews included a line or two at the end that attempted to predict a book's likely success in stores. The label continued to be used long after the actual "forecasting" ceased, and it was not until 2005 that the name of the section changed to simply "Reviews." One of the feature's important innovations was that it made no distinction in the reviewing between hardcover and paperback books—this was at a time, in the 1950s and 1960s, when paperback books were seldom reviewed. *PW*'s review editors have numbered anywhere from six to a dozen, each with a specific area of coverage, and between them they call on the services of several hundred reviewers, many of them specialists in their fields. *PW*'s reviews are 200–250 words long and are anonymous (though reviewers' names are printed in the section, but without any indication of who wrote which review). Today's much-expanded reviews section includes boxed reviews, topical review roundups, author interviews, reviews by name authors, and more than 3,000 web originals. According to Books in Print, the *Publishers Weekly* reviews database includes more 715,000 reviews, making it the leading book review resource. Another 150,000 reviews reside in the *Publishers Weekly* Digital Archive. *PW*'s reviews are widely licensed to both consumer and business sites such as Amazon.com, Apple Books, Barnes and Noble, Google, LexisNexis, Proquest, EBSCO, Gale/Cengage, OverDrive, and Books in Print.

The reviews department has been led by a number of editors over the years, but two vastly different personalities left a lasting impact on it. Barbara Bannon, who was the chief fiction reviewer in the 1970s and early 1980s (and who became the magazine's executive editor), gave the reviews department an aura of power and high visibility as a result of her own extravagant persona and her acknowledged power to make or break a book with her published verdict. And it was a highly visible verdict, because she was the first and only *PW* reviewer to insist upon the use of her name in connection with any review quoted in an ad or promotion. Sybil Steinberg, whose star rose as Bannon's declined, had a keener, more sophisticated critical eye, and for a wider range of books. She also yearned to give more prominent attention to books she particularly admired, and it was under her aegis that *PW* began to award stars to books of exceptional merit, and later to create the lengthier and more prominent boxed reviews. Steinberg also created an annual Best Books list, which the magazine continues to this day. For many years she also edited the magazine's author interviews and, beginning in 1992, put together the first of four anthologies of them in book form, published by Pushcart Press.

For most of its life, the reviews section did not review books that were self-published, but in early 2012, *PW* introduced a regular supplement called

PW Select. The supplement included book listings, book reviews, author profiles, and news and feature coverage of the self-publishing industry. *PW* utilized the pool of submissions as a source for selecting titles to be reviewed, for the first time allowing all self-published titles to be submitted for review consideration at no cost. Those reviews appear in the more than 35 syndicated outlets where *PW*'s reviews are licensed.

On the heels of *PW* Select's success, in 2014 *PW* launched BookLife. This website, a joint venture with Mediapolis, is dedicated to serving as a resource for self-published authors and writers considering self-publishing their books. Simultaneously, *PW* hired Carl Pritzkat (now COO) from Mediapolis as president of BookLife and to handle *PW*'s business development. BookLife became a *PW* supplement, growing from quarterly to now weekly, subsuming *PW* Select, which remains as a marketing program for self-published authors to promote their books within BookLife. BookLife focuses on three main areas: a book's creation, including editing and cover design; publishing—the physical making of the book; and book marketing, including distribution, publicity, and sales.

In addition to the BookLife supplement, self-published titles selected for review are published within the review pages of *Publishers Weekly* magazine alongside reviews of traditionally published titles. In 2019, BookLife Reviews launched as a paid review service for self-published authors who wanted to pay to have their books reviewed.

The BookLife Prize, which is a $5,000 writing prize, launched as a fiction-only award in 2016 and added nonfiction as a separate contest in 2019. The BookLife Prize has had more than 6,000 entries to date.

In 2020, in conjunction with U.K.-based BookBrunch, BookLife launched the U.S. Selfies, an award carrying a cash prize for the year's best self-published book.

Notably, in recent years under the direction of Jim Milliot and Michael Coffey—and beginning in 2014 under the sole direction of Milliot as editorial director after Coffey's retirement—*PW* expanded its editorial perspective to include a broader time frame and to include more post-publication market coverage. In 2011 *PW* launched the *PW* Tip Sheet, a weekly newsletter that informs librarians, booksellers, and consumers about news of books currently on sale.

Other e-newsletters, which are all free, include:
- *PW* Daily, a daily roundup of publishing and bookselling news
- Children's Bookshelf, a twice-weekly look at children's book publishing

news, rights updates, children's and YA book reviews, and an original comic strip, *The Slush Pile.*
- Must Reads, highlights of the previous week's publishing news
- *PW* Preview for Librarians, a weekly newsletter for librarians featuring notable books publishing the coming week, printable PDF files of bestsellers lists, and book reviews
- The BookLife Report, published weekly, covers news of interest to self-published or "indie" authors
- Global Rights Report, weekly, covers the world of literary rights and deals
- The Fanatic, semimonthly coverage of graphic novels and comics
- School and Library Spotlight, a monthly newsletter covering issues of interest to K-12 librarians and educators
- Religion BookLine, published semimonthly, focuses on the business of publishing and new titles in religion and spirituality
- Book It!, a monthly newsletter from the *PW* publisher Cevin Bryerman, featured sales and marketing brand-promotion opportunities in *Publishers Weekly* and ran from 2013–2020

In 2012, *PW* entered the realm of podcasting:
- *PW's Week Ahead* is a weekly segment on the *Velocity of Content* podcast hosted at the Copyright Clearance Center by Chris Kenneally with *PW's* senior writer Andrew Albanese discussing the upcoming news of the week.
- *More to Come: PW Comics World*, a regular comics podcast, is hosted by editors Calvin Reid, Heidi MacDonald, and Kate Fitzsimons. With nearly 500 episodes, it is *PW's* longest-running podcast.
- *PW Radio*, an hour-long, weekly show featuring conversations about the week's bestsellers, author interviews and publishing news, ran for 296 episodes, followed by 29 episodes of *PW Insider*, its natural successor covering publishing news. *PW Radio* aired on SiriusXM's Book Radio until the station was canceled and is now available at PublishersWeekly.com/podcasts as well as at Apple Podcasts, iHeartRadio, SoundCloud, Mixcloud, and Stitcher. The author interviews are also available at Infobase.
- In 2019, *The Skillset Podcast* with R. David Lankes and Nicole A. Cooke began as an offshoot of a *Publishers Weekly* panel with librarians. The podcast is a conversation about important issues facing libraries and librarians.

PW also opened a new category of sponsored content:

- *PW KidsCast*, a sponsored podcast of children's and YA author interviews
- *PW LitCast*, a sponsored podcast hosted by various *PW* editors and featuring interviews with authors of new fiction and nonfiction books
- *PW FaithCast*, hosted by *PW* religion editors, features authors of religion and spirituality books. A variety of live, sponsored webcasts cover industry trends, plus video author interviews.

Subsequently, *PW* started PWxyz Studios, dedicated to sponsored, advertiser-driven products and newsletters. Grab-a-Galley promotions, while not technically part of PWxyz Studios, were another new initiative to engage advertisers and librarians. E-blasts were created for advertisers to reach *PW*'s burgeoning mailing list of well over 150,000 trade and consumer newsletter subscribers.

During this period, *PW*'s social media presence increased exponentially across all platforms, helping to draw traffic to the *PW* website, which sees 1.2 million unique visitors per month. In addition to frequent postings on nearly all social media channels, *PW* hosts a booksellers group on Facebook and, on Instagram, the "Picture of the Day" feature that is also published in *PW Daily*.

Publishers Weekly hosts regular live and virtual discussion series about current issues in book publishing as they evolve. Panel discussions cover an array of topics ranging from the annual *PW* Salary Survey, supply chain issues, diversity in publishing, global rights, and issues facing librarians.

PW Star Watch is an award to honor up-and-coming individuals in the publishing industry. The annual award was launched in 2015 with the stated intention "to identify and celebrate talented emerging leaders in the U.S. publishing community, bring recognition to them on a global stage, and provide them with additional mentoring and an expanded network." The inaugural winner was Helen Yentus, the art director for Riverhead Books in New York. The annual award is given in the fall in New York and offers a cash honorarium to five finalists, of which one is named the "Superstar."

Publishers Weekly entered the events realm in 2015. In association with the Bologna Children's Book Fair, Global Kids Connect was a conference to address issues of international importance to children's book publishers. The annual conference took place in New York and ran two years.

PubTech Connect was launched in 2016 with New York University's School of Professional Studies Center for Publishing (NYUSPS). The conference continues virtually on an annual basis.

The New York Rights Fair was a move to acknowledge the need for an annual gathering of literary agents that would be held in tandem with BookExpo America. In 2018, *Publishers Weekly* joined forces with BolognaFiere to create a fair rich with industry and author panels. The New York Rights Fair ran from 2018–2019.

The most recent opportunity arose with the Covid-19 pandemic and the demise of BookExpo. After ReedPOP announced the end of BookExpo, a hallowed U.S. book publishing tradition, *PW* determined that the need for an industry event far outweighed the pandemic-enforced closures of event spaces.

The U.S. Book Show was inaugurated in May 2021 to much acclaim, with an opening keynote by Oprah Winfrey and three days of editorial "buzz" panels, celebrity and literary author interviews, a special track for librarians, and a wealth of media coverage from the *New York Times*, the *Washington Post*, the Associated Press and others. With the U.S. Book Show's resounding success, *Publishers Weekly* announced the 2022 dates, May 24–26, 2022.

PW has grown from its historic print edition to include a wide array of products and brand extensions. For more information about *Publishers Weekly*, visit its FAQ at publishersweekly.com/pw/corp/faq.html.

PART I.
THE BUSINESS OF
BOOK PUBLISHING

PUBLISHERS, BOOKS, AND BOOKSTORES

TEN REMARKABLE PUBLISHERS

BY LARRY KIRSHBAUM

Note: It is impossible to cover the incredible growth and diversity of American-based publishers within a relatively brief chapter. I have chosen 10 hardcover houses that provide a taste of the unique strengths and entrepreneurial history of the industry. This exercise was aided by two prominent histories that I have shamelessly used as basic guides: *The Time of Their Lives* by Al Silverman, St. Martin's Press, 2008; and *Between Covers* by John Tebbel, Oxford University Press, 1987.

So here we go.

DOUBLEDAY

Frank Nelson Doubleday was one of the more colorful characters in publishing history. Born in 1862, he started out at the age of twelve as a "book and job printer" producing circulars and cards on a press he had bought for $15. When he was fourteen, his father's hat business failed, and Frank had to leave school and find a job.

He chose Scribner's as a superior firm "worthy" of his services and managed to convince a skeptical manager there that he would be a "good boy" to hire at $3 a week over Christmas. The manager liked his "cheeky" style and hired him for a week, which turned out to be 18 years. Scribner's gave him the opportunity to work in manufacturing, advertising, as business manager, and, most importantly, subscription selling of sets of uniform editions of famous authors' works as a premium for a year's subscription to *Scribner's Magazine*.

The first author was Rudyard Kipling, whose collection sold hundreds of thousands of copies and started a close friendship and future collaboration. It was Kipling who took Doubleday's three initials (FND) and nicknamed him "Effendi" which is a title meaning "lord" or "master" in Turkish. Frank played that role to the max; he was regarded by his peers with a sense of awe.

His ego asserting itself, Frank ultimately resented his subordinate roles at Scribner's and left to work at *McClure's Magazine*. In 1897, the publishing partnership Doubleday, McClure and Co. was formed, and Kipling was its first author. Frank was not an editor by nature; he believed that publishing should be "an intelligently conducted commerce, not a form of aesthetic bohemianism."

Through a series of partnerships, Frank Doubleday developed a number of firsts: he offered royalty statements to authors, he concentrated on advertising books in magazines where he believed the most readers could be found, he opened bookstores, and, of course, he built a substantial mail-order business that later became the largest book club, the Literary Guild. He even moved a large portion of the business to Garden City, Long Island.

Like Tom Guinzburg, Frank had a son, Nelson, who played a role in a successful children's book. In this case, Nelson read an abridgement of *Just So Stories* by Rudyard Kipling in a magazine and suggested to the author that he do a book of those stories devoted to animals. (Nelson also managed to insert into the contract a small royalty for himself on the book that lasted for years.)

Of course, Frank Doubleday started a tradition cultivating talent on the editorial side that persisted long after his son succeeded him as president in 1922.

Al Silverman tells the story of Judith Jones (ultimately destined for a great career at Knopf) sitting in a Doubleday outpost in Paris tasked with rejecting a pile of unsolicited manuscripts. One book in the pile was by a young Dutch-German diarist translated into French. Judith found herself in tears reading it most of the afternoon. *The Diary of Anne Frank* was published by Doubleday in 1952.

Nelson Doubleday Jr. sold the company to Bertelsmann in 1986, and in late 2008 and early 2009, the Doubleday imprint was merged to create the Knopf Doubleday Publishing Group, all part of Penguin Random House now.

FARRAR, STRAUS AND GIROUX

When John Farrar and Roger W. Straus Jr. published their first list at Farrar Straus in 1946, they wrote: "A new book imprint gathers character over the years, and it is our hope that readers will come to know ours and, perhaps, to feel a certain friendship for it."

Over the years, a better word from readers would be respect, for what became Farrar, Straus and Giroux in 1955 set a postwar standard for literary excellence with more Nobel prizes than Knopf and the sensibility of Roger Straus, which mixed family wealth, a powerful ego, and a sharp business mind with a deep love of and belief in his authors as a unique source of creativity. The current CEO, Jonathan Galassi, is a brilliant poet with the same business acumen for executing and sustaining Roger's creative and literary vision.

The union of Farrar and Straus at the outset was never a marriage made in heaven, but it set the stage for what was to come. John Farrar was a veteran in publishing. He had left Doubleday and cofounded Farrar and Rinehart in 1929 with the sons of Mary Roberts Rinehart, the popular mystery writer known as "the American Agatha Christie" and credited with originating the phrase "the butler did it."

In an autobiographical sketch, Farrar had declared, "Unlike my jolly partners, I have no sense of humor and a vile temper. . . . I take the publishing business with horrible seriousness. I'm sorry but I just can't help it." He and his partners, using their mothers' money, built a formidable company during the Great Depression, and he left two years before joining Straus.

Roger Straus attended Hamilton College and the University of Missouri School of Journalism (class of 1939), and edited magazines before launching a book packaging operation that supplied content to publishers. He was handsome, outgoing, and perhaps a bit self-conscious about his family wealth (his mother was a Guggenheim) and lack of a literary background.

According to Al Silverman, in Galassi's estimation, the hiring of Robert Giroux in 1955 was the seminal moment, "the beginning of the real FSG." Giroux had left Harcourt Brace when the management refused to let him publish "Jerry" or J.D. Salinger's first novel, *The Catcher in the Rye*. Without Salinger, Giroux had joined Roger and brought along relationships with a trove of poets and literary stars including T.S. Eliot (a Nobel Prize winner), Robert Lowell, Flannery O'Connor, Jack Kerouac, and Bernard Malamud. (The latter won a National Book Award for a short story collection, *The Magic Barrel*, and the same award again for a novel, *The Fixer*).

Roger's relationship with Giroux had some of the same issues as the friction with Farrar. Roger liked being the man in charge, and his antenna prickled when he felt one of his associates was trying to share the limelight. That was Roger with his enormous charm and an uncanny ability to woo authors—such as Edmund Wilson—using his great passion for their work.

Roger, like many publishing executives in the golden era in publishing before it became obsessed with profit, was a superstar luncher. In his later years he could be seen presiding as a gourmet impresario over the Union Square Cafe. Roger made Robert Giroux the chairman of the board in 1964 and officially renamed the company Farrar, Straus and Giroux,

Jonathan Galassi has maintained the great literary flavor set by Roger while nurturing cutting-edge commercial books such as Scott Turow's *Presumed Innocent* and Tom Wolfe's *Bonfire of the Vanities*.

Galassi could also use his poetic skill as a way of celebrating his authors. In the 1990s, Roger would lead a delegation of his associates to Chicago to celebrate the new Scott Turow publication with the author. Galassi would write a special poem, a very thoughtful one, for the occasion. Straus and Giroux might have had trouble sorting out who was the publisher and who was an editor, but Galassi has maintained control of both functions very successfully.

Roger Straus died in May of 2004 at the age of 87, and Silverman reports that while "poets die young . . . the heads of publishing houses live longer." There were numerous memorial services, and Silverman summed it up: "Roger's firm was often discussed as if it were an antique. . . . But as Mr. Straus knew and demonstrated, the only meaningful efficiency in publishing is excellent taste."

GROVE PRESS

In 1951, Barney Rosset acquired a tiny publishing house from two friends of his wife, the abstract expressionist Joan Mitchell. The entire inventory of this company was contained in two suitcases. Supported in part by his father, Rosset paid $3,000 to acquire the Grove Press and turned it into a haven for controversial titles that were often banned on the grounds of their sexually explicit content.

In a continual flurry of lawsuits, Rosset won the right to publish such works as D.H. Lawrence's *Lady Chatterley's Lover* and Henry Miller's *Tropic of Cancer*. Rosset had attended high school at the left-leaning Francis W. Parker School in Chicago (where the author of this article also matriculated), and had acquired an early passion for radical, avant-garde literature, much of it from Europe.

The Grove catalog (now in the capable hands of Morgan Entrekin, the CEO of Grove-Atlantic) came to include Samuel Beckett, Jean Genet, Frantz Fanon, George Luis Borges, Bertolt Brecht, Harold Pinter, successful American outliers such as William Burroughs, and Eric Berne, who wrote an early popular study of psychological relationships, *Games People Play*, which sold over five million copies.

Beckett was discovered by an American expat named Richard Seaver, who saw two Beckett titles in a French bookstore window and brought them back to Barney in New York. As translator and editor, Seaver became one of the most prominent fictional custodians from the mid-20th century through his death in 2009. His wife Jeanette now manages their joint imprint Arcade Books at Skyhorse Publishing.

Barney was never financially astute, and his company unraveled when he went on an acquisition binge of pornographic movies starting with *I am Curious (Yellow)*, which was a success, and then a series of color-themed sequels that failed. As Barney recalled, "I made most of my decisions in a second and spent many years regretting them."

HACHETTE BOOK GROUP

(Note: Reader be warned, the writer of this article worked for 31 years at the company that was bought by and became the Hachette Book Group in 2006.)

In the elite group of major global publishers, Hachette has been the only one to emerge from mass paperback roots, with the most recent founding as well.

The origin of this company dates to 1972, when the legendary Steve Ross founded Warner Communications with the intent of making it a media conglomerate built around Warner Brothers. On the book side, Warner bought a tiny entity called Paperback Library, which had a list of what are now called "genre" titles in romance, humor, and gothic novels.

A typical example was the Avenger series, priced at seventy-five cents, that had grown out of the pulp magazines from the late thirties and early forties. The first title had introduced Richard Henry Benson, a wealthy superhero who sought to avenge the murder of his wife and daughter.

Humor emerged in *Mad Magazine* titles under the direction of Bill Gaines that were turned into books and the eyebrow-raising *The Cunning Linguist*, written by Richard Lederer and described as "the naughtier side of wordplay."

Appropriately, the man at the helm of Warner paperbacks was Howard Kaminsky, whose first cousin was Mel Brooks. (Mel always kidded that Howard was the only direct relative of his that made it on his own merit.) Howard was a veteran of selling book rights at Random House, where he had developed water-cooler contests deploying the unique skill of firing crumpled paper into wastebaskets from long range. He turned marketing meetings into laugh-fests.

Behind and above him (literally much taller) was the chairman of the group, William Sarnoff, a relative of the legendary General Sarnoff of RCA fame. (Many of us worked for him over 25 years, and he was about 90% of the reason for our success since he let us take risks and protected us from corporate interference.)

There were some key purchases engineered by the Sarnoff-Kaminsky duo in the early years. The Richard Nixon memoir, *RN*, following his resignation, was bought with some controversy from Swifty Lazar for over $2 million in worldwide rights. And the first major paperback acquisition was *All the*

President's Men by Bob Woodward and Carl Bernstein, which had been published by Simon & Schuster in hardcover in 1974.

As it happened, Robert Redford and Dustin Hoffman were developing the Warner Brothers film version of the book in our building, and they would occasionally wander down to our offices. I jokingly instructed my assistant to tell "Bob" Redford that I was busy if he inquired. And she said, also in jest, "I hope you don't mind if I sit in his lap while he waits for you." (Note: Bob Redford never waited a second for the few brief encounters we had with him.)

It wasn't all fun and games and celebs. Howard and his editorial chief Bernie Shir-Cliff had great commercial instincts. Howard and Bill Sarnoff believed in heavy marketing support and introduced TV ads for major titles. The core of the company's future was developed over the next 20 years with authors such as James Patterson, Nelson DeMille, Sandra Brown, Scott Turow, David Baldacci, Michael Connelly, Stephenie Meyer, Brad Meltzer, Nick Delbanco, and Nicholas Sparks. Many of these authors produced books every year, sometimes more than one, so the Warner entity had a solid revenue-producing backlist.

The editorial publishing leader in the early 1990s, Maureen Egen snatched an unsold manuscript off an agent's shelves that was about an itinerant photographer and a lonely housewife in Iowa. *The Bridges of Madison County*, written by Robert Waller and published in 1992, was a multimillion-copy success as a book and a blockbuster film starring Clint Eastwood and Meryl Streep.

The merger of Time Inc. and Warner Communications in 1990 had brought one of the great jewels of publishing, Little Brown (founded in 1837), into the fold as part of what became the Time Warner Publishing Group. Its president, Charlie Hayward, was responsible for international expansion as well as bringing James Patterson into the fold. So now the youngest and one of the oldest publishers were together, and it made a great combination.

Yours truly was CEO from 1996 to 2006, when the company was bought by Hachette Livre, the largest publisher in France and a subsidiary of the Lagardere Group. The Hachette Book Group has had two brilliant CEOs: David Young, a British publisher who brought a global sensibility, "big data," and a lot of common sense to management and decision-making, and now Michael Pietsch, who is an editor's editor and a man with great business acumen as well. The latter's most recent coup was announcing a deal to purchase Workman Publishing, one of the best independent operations with an enormous backlist.

HARPERCOLLINS

The two major strands of HarperCollins originated two years apart, but it took over 170 years for them to be woven together. James and John Harper founded J.&J. Harper as a modest print shop in 1817 and were joined by two other brothers shortly thereafter. William Collins, Sons was a Scottish printing and publishing company founded by Collins, a Presbyterian schoolmaster in Glasgow, in 1819.

Rupert Murdoch's News Corp brought them together when it acquired what was then known as Harper & Row in 1987 and merged Collins into the company in 1990, to be known as HarperCollins. Their logo combined the torch of Harper and the fountain of Collins into a more stylized combination of flames atop waves.

Collins was initially a religious and education publisher, and its strength continues in education, reference, wildlife and natural history, and children's books, although its Collins Crime Club published the first six Agatha Christie novels starting in 1926.

By the 1850s, Harper & Brothers was the largest English language publisher in the world, printing over two million books and pamphlets per year. But the company suffered under the Harper heirs, and in the 20th century the family needed some outside blood. Cass Canfield and his son helped shape the modern-day company with a first-rate editorial approach. Jane Friedman, as CEO from 1997 to 2008, began bringing HarperCollins into the digital age.

The current president/CEO of Harper/Collins, Brian Murray, joined the U.S. company in 1997 and spent three years starting in 2001 as CEO of the Australia/New Zealand subsidiary and came back to the United States as group president and then president of Harper Collins Worldwide. He became CEO and president in 2008.

His global and digital experience are reflected in HC's current program of 10,000 annual new books in 16 languages and 24 countries (including China) with a print and digital catalog of over 200,000 titles. He has put together a top-tier management team that has driven the company into the #2 position as a consumer publisher in the United States. (The digital business alone is now approaching $400 million.)

The strategic success of Murray's team is due to focusing the corporate banner on strong market brands within the most popular consumer genres: Harlequin and Avon paperback romances, prizewinning Harper children's, William Morrow suspense, and Harper literary fiction, Thomas Nelson and Zondervan Christian publishing, edgy Harper One nonfiction for personal growth, and the overall expanding presence in digital. A recent acquisition, the Houghton Mifflin Harcourt trade group, brings a powerful backlist and tightly knit staff into the fold.

Of course, the bestseller list is still a major target, and Jonathan Burnham, president and publisher of the Harper Division, has a good eye as well as very good taste, backed by a strong editorial and marketing/sales team. All in all, HarperCollins will continue to be a major player and one of the crown jewels of the News Corp empire.

MACMILLAN

Many of today's best and biggest publishers were born outside of the United States. In 1843, the brothers Daniel and Alexander Macmillan formed a company in their name based in Cambridge, England. For nearly 100 years, under various ownerships, the American version of Macmillan was primarily a distribution channel for British titles. By 1931, an increasing mixture of American publications had made Macmillan the largest U.S. publisher. (One major domestic success originated in Atlanta: Margaret Mitchell's *Gone with the Wind*, which was published in 1936 and became a multimillion-copy seller as well as the basis for the highly successful film.)

Macmillan became American owned in 1951, but it had lost its earlier glory (and financial stability). Fortuitously, Sir Harold Macmillan, the future British Prime Minister, realized he still needed an American outlet and founded St. Martin's Press in 1952. It took until 1956 for St. Martin's to throw off the shackles of being a book colony and begin offering American books on its own.

Enter the George Washington of this story, Tom McCormack. He graduated from Brown in 1954 and spent the next 15 years tilling the paperback soil at Doubleday, Harper, and New American Library. In 1969 he was hired by St. Martin's, and within a year he had changed strategic direction and turned a $150,000 loss into a tiny profit.

Tom succeeded by continuing to import British titles—primarily in popular genres like romance and mystery—but with a twist. Other publishers were cutting back their lists to maximize profits, but Tom's philosophy was to expand his British list to cover his overhead and then develop more exciting titles elsewhere, such as James Herriot's *All Creatures Great and Small*. Of course, no one could believe that the 1930s adventures of a Yorkshire veterinarian would sell books in a contemporary market where big, sexy novels were the rage. Tom could and did, with great success. St. Martin's went on to publish the contemporary thriller *The Silence of the Lambs* by Tom Harris in 1988.

Tom McCormack was smart (and lucky) enough to rely on his unstoppable, high-energy rights director, Sally Richardson, who was a magician when it came to pulling dollars out of subsidiary rights. To this day, Sally is respected as one of the brightest lights in publishing who has been responsible for building the St. Martin's paperback lists among many achievements as a great ambassador for the company. Tom chose to retire on his 65th birthday in January 1997 to go back to his first love, writing plays.

On the editorial side, Tom Dunne has been a major force with his eponymous imprint, which brought in sleeper bestsellers like Dan Brown's first book, *Digital Fortress*, which earned him an advance of $4,000 and ultimately sold over four million copies in the wake of the success of his *The Da Vinci Code*.

Tom Doherty is another major figure in the company's history. He founded Tor Books in 1980 and sold it to St. Martin's in 1986. It has become the pre-eminent science fiction and fantasy imprint since that time, more recently adding Forge Books as an imprint with special focus on mysteries, suspense, and other popular genres.

Overall, St. Martin's has been a racehorse coming up on the rails and headed for the winner's circle as one of the five major companies in U.S. publishing. In 1999, the German company Holtzbrinck Publishing completed acquiring St. Martin's and other Macmillan imprints.

It was John Sargent, coming from a publishing family (his father had been a co-CEO of Doubleday), who turned Macmillan into one of the most successful publishers in the business. He started as chief of St. Martin's in 1996 and ascended to become CEO of Macmillan in 2012.

John was not flashy, preferring McDonald's to the Four Seasons Grill Room, and never seeming to possess a tie or a tux. But in his laid-back style, he could be very tough and stubborn when he believed his cause was right. He fought the e-book revolution, believing it was cutting into more valuable hardcover sales, and he had a very public skirmish with Amazon, but he was a great leader who sadly left Macmillan at the end of 2020 as the result of a dispute with Stefan von Holtzbrinck.

In announcing that the very capable and highly respected Don Weisberg, a Penguin and Macmillan veteran, would be taking over as head of the group, Stefan had this say about John Sargent.

"John's principles and exemplary leadership have always been grounded in worthy, essential causes, be it freedom of speech, the environment, or support for the most vulnerable. Since Holtzbrinck shares these ideals, they will live on."

RANDOM HOUSE

The story of Random House began when two bohemian brothers, Charles and Albert Boni, opened a bookstore in Greenwich Village in 1912. Their initial offering was the Little Leather Library, 30 pocket-sized classics that became the forerunner of the Modern Library.

Albert moved on to team up with the storied figure Horace Liveright, a young playwright. In 1917, Boni & Liveright was born, along with the first volumes of the Modern Library classics.

That partnership didn't last very long, and Liveright became the majority stockholder. He had great flair and wooed top talent, but he was also egotistical and reckless about finances.

Enter Bennett Cerf. Born in 1898, he graduated from Columbia Journalism School in 1920 and started his career on Wall Street. But publishing was in his blood, and he joined Liveright in 1924. The company was virtually bankrupt and selling off assets.

Bennett and the man who was to be a lifelong partner, Donald Klopfer, acquired The Modern Library for $200,000, named their firm after it, and began selling the line of classics in 1925. They quickly achieved $1 million in annual sales, but they wanted to broaden their editorial slate. Having wide-ranging literary tastes, they decided to sign up books "at Random." Thus was their legendary name born, and the famous designer and artist Rockwell Kent created a modest-looking house that cemented the name in our memories. John Tebbel called it "a cottage with pretensions of being a palace."

The first Random House book came out in January 1928, an elegant edition of Voltaire's *Candide*. While The Modern Library was growing to 400 regular-sized volumes and 150 thicker "giants," the book that put Random on the map was the controversial publication in 1934 of James Joyce's *Ulysses*, after a lengthy legal battle to have a judge declare the book "not obscene."

Meanwhile, Horace Liveright, who had been so critical to the Modern Library's founding, died a Gatsby kind of death, with only "a straggling handful" attending his funeral, according to Bennett Cerf.

Closer to the present, Bennett scored a front-page literary coup when Random House acquired the vaunted house of Alfred and Blanche Knopf in 1970. This brought together two of the most prestigious houses in the business, with greater emphasis from Knopf on European publishing.

With the Knopfs nearing retirement, in 1968, Bob Bernstein, who had succeeded Bennett Cerf as CEO, wooed Bob Gottlieb and a small team of colleagues from Simon & Schuster to run Knopf. Gottlieb has been one of the most successful publishers in the business and even after leaving the company remained the editor of a key Knopf author, Robert Caro.

The final (almost) act of Random House was its purchase by Bertelsmann and then its expansion by completing the purchase of Penguin in 2019. This brought Madeline McIntosh from Penguin under the Random House CEO Markus Dohle to form a flawless combination. Penguin Random House, now the largest publisher with an estimated quarter of the consumer market, is still on the hunt for more imprints. Its offer to buy Simon & Schuster, under review by the government, would take it to a few notches above one third of consumer market share.

SIMON & SCHUSTER

They were very different.

Richard Simon was tall and burly with a great flair for marketing along with other interests. He was an excellent musician, and his three daughters all pursued musical careers, Carly Simon being the most successful.

Max Lincoln Schuster was shorter and more intense, almost professorial in his approach. He might have become an academic publisher, but like his partner, he had a great sense of the popular pulse.

They both attended Columbia and met in 1921 when they were in their early twenties. Simon was selling pianos. Schuster was editing an equipment trade magazine and possibly interested in buying a piano. By the summer of 1923, they were planning to launch a book publishing company and did so in January 1924 with $8,000 in capital and a one-room office in midtown Manhattan.

Success came quickly. Simon's aunt was a crossword puzzle aficionado, and she had found there were no books on the subject. The first S&S crossword puzzle book came out in 1924 with an initial printing of 3,600 copies. The price was $1.35, and Simon, showing his marketing chops, attached a rubber eraser–topped pencil to every copy.

One year later, they had sold over one million crossword books. The S&S reputation as a bestseller publisher was born.

Enter Leon Shimkin, who had a solid business head and an interest in self-help books. His ideas blossomed in the 1930s. He told J.K. Lasser to keep the *Your Income Tax* book simple for readers perplexed by the IRS codes. At its peak, the title was selling one million copies a year, and many buyers were from the IRS itself.

To overcome his shyness, Shimkin took a course on public speaking from a man named Dale Carnegie. When Carnegie converted the lectures into a book, *How to Win Friends and Influence People*, it became the #1 nonfiction bestseller of 1937 and has sold millions of copies through the years. An association with Will and Ariel Durant created the 11-volume *Story of Civilization*, which became the Book of the Month Club's best premium for membership, another huge seller. (It is probably the greatest unread compilation of history on home bookshelves today.)

In 1939, S&S backed Robert Fair de Graff to found Pocket Books, the first paperback publisher. This led the company to release classic reprints in the educational market. In the 1960s, Richard Simon died of a heart attack. and Max Schuster sold his half of the company to Leon Shimkin.

The company flourished over the next 60 years with names like Dick Snyder, Jack Romanos, and Carolyn Reidy as CEOs. The editorial side was brilliantly led by Robert Gottlieb (who left for Knopf), Michael Korda, Susan Moldow (at Scribner's), and the recently anointed Jonathan Karp as the CEO who is charged with handling the company's acquisition by Penguin Random House for over $2 billion. The transaction is pending approval by the government.

Karp is more than up to the leadership task, having worked with a multitude of major authors such as Walter Isaacson, David McCullough, and the prolific media czar of Washington politics, Bob Woodward. Karp is, like S&S cofounder Dick Simon, a Renaissance man with musical and theatrical roots. (He further distinguished himself during the brief period in our employ at Hachette as founder of the imprint Twelve, by disregarding most of my advice and being inevitably right.)

VIKING PRESS

It's apt to say that in its origin, Viking was unfurled as well as founded under the colophon designed by Rockwell Kent. His famous ship became the symbol for the mission statement of founders Harold K. Guinzburg and George S. Oppenheimer in March 1925. "Our aims," they wrote, "are, briefly, to have the name a symbol of enterprise, adventure and exploration [and] to acclaim treasure when we find it, but avoid calling brass gold."

There was to be plenty of gold in Viking's illustrious history. Guinzburg had spent a year at Simon & Schuster, and Oppenheimer had spent three years as advertising and publicity manager at Knopf. Both were 25 years old.

Even before their first list was published, they acquired in August the firm of B.W. Huebsch, which brought in James Joyce's *A Portrait of the Artist as a Young Man* along with titles by D.H. Lawrence and Sherwood Anderson. Huebsch himself was to become one of Viking's great editors over the next four decades.

Another coup took place in 1938 when Guinzburg, now steering the ship, convinced Pascal Covici, an immigrant and former bookseller in Chicago, to join the team. He was described by one colleague as a "flamboyant Romanian with the shock of white hair on a poet's head, which in turn was set on a football player's six-foot-three body."

His prized author was John Steinbeck, who was to be joined later by Saul Bellow and Arthur Miller as part of a catalog of literary stars. Covici became their personal, passionate champion, always pressing management to increase their advertising budgets.

Like many of the great publishing houses started by powerful founders in the 1920s, Viking eventually had to recognize a passing of the guard. Al Silverman tells a wonderful anecdote about Harold Guinzburg bringing home a children's book in manuscript form when his son Tom was nine years old. Young Tom read the opening sentence: "Once upon a time in Spain there was a little bull and his name was Ferdinand."

Tom told his father how much he liked the story, and the book *Ferdinand the Bull* went on to sell millions of copies. It gave Tom the confidence that he might become a publisher like his father. Indeed, upon his father's death in 1961, Tom took over his father's house and invigorated it as one of the great independent publishers.

The quality of Viking's editorial staff never slackened as editors like Cork Smith brought in Thomas Pynchon's *Gravity's Rainbow* after signing it for a $5,000 advance without knowing anything about the book's subject. Aaron Asher, a Knopf alum, took over editing Saul Bellow, including *Mr. Sammler's Planet*, for which Bellow received his third National Book Award. Marshall Best, another legendary veteran Viking editor, was handling Graham Greene. Elisabeth Sifton edited Peter Matthiessen's *The Snow Leopard*, another National Book Award winner.

Lack of space precludes bringing the story up to the present except to point out that in 1975 the company merged into Viking/Penguin and thus began a more corporate life.

That life took on a fabulous new form with the growing partnership of Marcus Dohle and Madeline McIntosh after Bertelsmann, the German media giant, completed its final 25% purchase of the Penguin Random House assets in December 2019.

Madeline had been appointed CEO of the merged company in April of 2018, bringing one of the most versatile and impressive backgrounds to the combined company. She had been president of the Penguin Publishing group with a previous record of innovation and achievement on the Random House side in audio, adult sales, new media, and a two-year position as director of content acquisition for Amazon, based in Luxembourg. Under Markus's leadership, she had integrated Penguin and Random almost seamlessly, reinforcing the inherent strength of this huge company as a literary and cultural standard-bearer. Her next task will be, subject to government approval, bringing Simon & Schuster into the fold.

W.W. NORTON

William Warder Norton founded the company in 1923 and ran it with three employees (including his wife), from his living room. Now approaching its centennial anniversary, W.W. Norton has spread its wings, exemplified by its iconic seagull colophon, and established itself as the oldest and largest independent publisher owned entirely by its employees.

For a company that operates without the corporate resources of its competitors, Norton has become a major player in the industry with bestselling cultural mind-setters such as Michael Lewis, Stephen Greenblatt, Neil deGrasse Tyson, Jared Diamond, and Adrienne Rich, plus multiple Nobel Prize winners in its backlist. To more than 20 million college students, the company is best known for its Norton Anthologies, ranging in subjects from English literature to history. And its textbook list encompasses a who's who of liberal arts stars.

One of the company's smartest moves was resuscitating Liveright Publishing, an iconic firm that published its first list of Modern Library Classics at under a dollar in 1917 and became a major factor during the 1920s. (See Random House origins.) Norton revived its Liveright imprint (recently celebrating a 10-year anniversary) under the direction of one of the hardest working publisher/editors in the business, Robert Weil, who, in typical fashion, nurtured the prolific historian Peter Gay through his final productive years.

With Bob's golden touch, Liveright has established an iconic status in a relatively short time. Most recently, two of the Liveright titles won Pulitzer prizes: Les Payne's biography of Malcolm X, *The Dead Are Arising*, and Marcia Chatelain's *Franchise*, about the role that fast-food restaurant ownership has played in creating black wealth.

Of course, publishing greatness starts in collegiality and independence and a classic sense of literary taste honed by intuition, as a former Norton president, Donald Lamm, put it. Norton has all of the above.

Bestselling authors like Michael Lewis (*Liar's Poker* was definitely a royal flush) and Jared Diamond (*Guns, Germs, and Steel*) and or prizewinning poets like Adrienne Rich or Rita Dove may get the most notice, but the heart of Norton, as Al Silverman put it, is the "Prettiest Backlist in the Business."

That is the education machine that has been the profit foundation for Norton as far back as the 1950s when Norton's third president, George Brockway, began putting together Norton anthologies. Today, the Norton Critical Editions now number in the hundreds across every aspect of liberal arts. One example, originally created by George Tindall, now fully updated by David E. Shi, is *America: A Narrative History* (Full & Brief) in their twelfth editions. Norton touts Shi's "rich storytelling style, colorful biographical sketches, and vivid first-person sketches." In short, the book is a crowd-pleasing way to teach history through the diversity of American voices.

The more recent fourth, fifth, and sixth presidents, Donald Lamb, W. Drake McFeely, and currently Julia Reidhead, have all come through the college division. Lamb and McFeely started as college sales representatives. Reidhead has nurtured many of the legendary titles as in-house editor or publisher, including the flagship *Norton Anthology of English Literature.*

In introducing her as his successor, W. Drake McFeely made the following statement about the qualities of Norton's first woman president.

"Julia Reidhead, who has made her entire publishing career here at Norton, embodies all the values we hold dear: an abiding love of books and literature, pride in and dedication to the editorial process, a commitment to innovation . . . and above all, a passion for our status as independent publishers."

*

Larry Kirshbaum has spent more than 50 years in the publishing world as writer, agent and executive. He is the co-author of the 1970 title about student protest, Is the Library Burning? He spent over 40 years at the Time-Warner Book Group and he has been an agent since 2006.

ABA AND INDIE BOOKSELLING: THE PAST FORTY YEARS

BY OREN J. TEICHER

In early 2020, we were looking at a lot of very encouraging news about the state of indie bookselling. ABA membership was on the rise; sales across the network of indie stores were increasing; and, most important, a whole new generation of booksellers was taking over our business. The resurgence was not limited to our borders, either; reports from many of our international colleagues were also upbeat. It was a very heady time!

In fact, in my farewell message to ABA members—written in December of 2019 at the time of my retirement after more than thirty years at ABA—I was able to fondly look back on a period when all the predictions of the demise of indie bookselling had finally been put to rest. To be sure, we remained concerned about the growing influence of Amazon, the increasing costs associated with operating a retail bookstore, our low margins, and other issues. But overall, the astonishing resiliency of indie bookstores—their ability to remain competitive in the face of overwhelming odds—was the dominant theme of the day.

Of course, that wasn't always true. And though the reduction in ABA membership was never as bad as was often reported, many stores did close in the face of the massive chain expansion of the 1980s and '90s and, later, as a result of Amazon's staggering growth. In addition, stores faced growing competition from mass merchandisers, discounters, warehouse clubs, and, later, from e-commerce and the introduction of e-books.

Back in the '80s and '90s, putting a B. Dalton or Waldenbooks store in virtually every mall in America helped democratize consumer book buying and brought reading into millions of homes. Though many indie booksellers were at first unhappy with the growth of the chains, many Americans who had never before been in a bookstore now had access.

Other changes were afoot as well. From its modest beginnings in the garage of the Shoreham Hotel in Washington, D.C., the annual ABA Convention became one of the largest industry trade shows in the United States. It became so big that at its peak in the mid-'90s there were only a few convention centers in the country large enough to accommodate it. ABA's practice was to move the show around the country and while that was often a logistical challenge, it did serve to make the show far more accessible. Outgrowing the Shoreham garage, the show first moved to more traditional hotel venues before graduating to much larger convention centers. The show was held in New Orleans, Anaheim, Los Angeles, San Francisco, Las Vegas, Miami, Washington, D.C., Chicago, and New York. Its growth attracted the interest of Reed Exposition Services, one of the largest operators of trade shows in the world, who eventually purchased the show from ABA, renamed it Book Expo America, and settled the annual event in either Chicago or New York. The sale of the show was a watershed moment for ABA, as it allowed the association to focus on its core purpose: to help indie stores become profitable and successful.

Another significant change was the evolving wholesale environment. While there had always been third-party wholesalers—operating between publishers and retailers—they began to grow in importance. For a time, in addition to the two national companies, Baker & Taylor and Ingram, there were vibrant regional wholesalers operating in virtually every part of the country. The wholesalers played an indispensable role in getting books to market both quickly and efficiently. A network of regional booksellers' associations providing an array of services to help stores also flourished and grew.

On the legal front, after many years of investigation, the Federal Trade Commission in the early '90s abruptly halted an investigation into anticompetitive behavior in the book business resulting in ABA deciding to pick up that torch. Through a series of lawsuits—first against a select group of publishers in 1994 and, later against Barnes & Noble and Borders in 1998—ABA argued that many publishers engaged in a range of trade practices that unfairly benefited the large chains at their members' expense. The cases were ultimately all settled out of court. But many publisher practices did change significantly, and a heightened awareness of antitrust guidelines became an everyday part of the book business.

There were also multiple skirmishes over First Amendment and free expression issues in the '90s. Booksellers—with strong allies in the publishing and library communities—became fierce opponents of any effort to suppress constitutionally protected speech. Most notably, the fatwa issued against Salman Rushdie by Iranian authorities in 1989—which lead to the bombings of several bookstores in the United States and around the world—galvanized bookseller support for free expression.

Things at ABA were also changing. Longtime executive director Bernie Rath, who had joined ABA in 1985, left the organization in 1997. Rath, who had come to ABA from Canada, where he had served as the head of the Canadian Booksellers Association, was widely credited with growing the annual trade show and turning it into a very valuable asset that attracted a prominent buyer. He was succeeded by Avin Mark Domnitz, a former bookseller and lawyer from Milwaukee, Wisconsin. Domnitz's legal background would prove to be an integral part of the ABA antitrust litigation of the '90s. Domnitz retired in 2008, and I succeeded him as executive director. By then, I had worked at ABA for almost 20 years. I'll leave it to others to characterize my years as ABA's CEO, but I remain very proud of our efforts to reverse the downward slide in membership as well as our work to vastly grow ABA's educational and advocacy programs. I worked hard at developing allies both in and out of the book business to help bookstores to succeed.

I retired at the end of 2019 and was succeeded by Allison Hill, who came to ABA from Vroman's Bookstore in Pasadena, California, one of the largest and most successful indie bookstores in the country. Unfortunately for Allison, she began work at ABA just as the Covid-19 pandemic began to sweep across the country, forcing ABA to quickly switch gears and adapt to the new realities. To her enormous credit, she and her team have done just that.

Over the years, while indie stores and ABA kept fighting, there were days when all seemed lost. But sometime around 2005 things started to gradually change.

The "shop local" movement began to gain some traction with consumers; bookstores had access to less-expensive and better technology; and publishers recognized that putting all their eggs in one basket was not a good idea. Most notably, led by Penguin Random House, publishers greatly upgraded the speed with which they were able to ship books. This helped retail stores better compete with the internet. ABA invested heavily in growing its education program (the first Winter Institute was in 2005 in Long Beach, California). With the help of the regional bookseller association in Northern California, ABA expanded Book Sense, which morphed into IndieBound. And though these programs were far from perfect, they helped reestablish the importance of indie bookstores to publishers and served to remind consumers why shopping in an indie bookstore was a unique experience. Stores also put their toes into the digital space with modest e-commerce offerings and, later, with a sophisticated use of social media.

But, most important, the sense of community and common cause among indie booksellers all across the country grew and grew. While there had always been a sense of kinship between booksellers, technology allowed for far more contact and communication than ever before. There is no doubt that all that interaction helped stores become better and more profitable.

There was also a generational shift. In 2005—about halfway through my career at ABA—I could stand up before an audience of ABA members and see that 90% of us were slowly aging baby boomers. You could count the number of people under the age of 30 on two hands. Too many young people just couldn't imagine a career in bookselling. That started to change, and the energy, enthusiasm, and creativity of a growing number of younger booksellers in our ranks became infectious. In addition, though still painfully slow, indie bookselling began to become a bit more diverse with modest growth in the number of minority-owned stores.

To be sure, it was still not easy. While what was left of the chains became less threatening, Amazon's tentacles—extending into every facet of American society—seemed to have no limits. Amazon may no longer be as focused on the book business as they had been, but they continue to use books as a loss leader to expand their customer base. And their continued flouting of sales tax rules gave them a major competitive advantage. The wholesale part of our business, which had been an important factor in our growth, consolidated rapidly. Most of the regional wholesalers—Partners, Koen, Gordon's, Southern, BookPeople—all went out of business. Baker & Taylor ceased serving indie stores. Consumer-based media coverage of books diminished radically. Additionally, with the introduction of smartphones, the entire book business faced growing competition for people's time and attention; suddenly everyone was walking around with instant access to every other form of entertainment.

Then came the Covid-19 pandemic. It is the highest irony that stores that managed to survive the chains, the discounters, the mass merchandisers, the warehouse clubs, the internet, e-books, and everything else were now facing something so totally out of their control. No matter how entrepreneurial, innovative, or creative a store was, this was unprecedented. In 2020, largely as a result of the pandemic, Reed finally threw in the towel and announced the "retiring" of BookExpo.

As in the past, indie stores quickly figured out how to adapt to a new normal—their doors now closed to customers—with curbside pickup, internet sales, and virtual events. And, at least preliminarily (as of the summer of 2021) it appears that once again indie bookstores have weathered the storm. There is little doubt that the global pandemic will result in numerous longer-term changes both in the way stores operate and consumers behave.

I do believe that, eventually, when the pandemic is firmly in the rearview mirror, indie bookstores will flourish again. And while a few stores did go out of business as a result of Covid, many more opened than closed, and a trend that had already started—of existing stores selling to new owners—continued. My guess is that in the post-pandemic world consumers will crave any chance to interact in person. The importance of community will only grow. While stores in the future will need to adapt and maintain a permanent virtual connection to their customers alongside what they do in their physical space, it's hard to imagine a world without indie bookstores.

If anything, the past 40 years have demonstrated the enormous resiliency of indie bookselling. As long as stores continue to adapt and change, in my opinion, the future is assured.

*

Oren J. Teicher was ABA's CEO from 2008 to 2019. He joined ABA in 1990 and previously served as the Association's deputy executive director, chief operating officer, and president of the American Booksellers Foundation for Free Expression. Before joining ABA, Teicher was the director of corporate communications for the March of Dimes Birth Defects Foundation and a longtime staffer in the U.S. Congress.

BUYING AND SELLING FICTION
BY SESSALEE HENSLEY

Most of my job as a buyer involved meeting with sales reps and shaping each month's titles' distribution, placement, and marketing. I would put my titles into a spreadsheet and then later into Edelweiss to keep track. At the end of the month, I would review everything to see how it all fit together. I would revise as necessary depending on the strength of the title, marketing and overall place in each month's titles.

One of the first things my first boss taught me was how to think in terms of benchmarks: if a certain type of fiction sold a certain number of copies, there would need to be a compelling reason for another book of the same type to double in sales.

One of his favorite sayings was, "if you build a Mercedes, don't expect it to sell like a Ford." I bought many titles based on track record. Typically, I did not need to read authors who were bestsellers and published frequently as the track was there. For other titles—new authors with the possibility of breaking out—I took a "ready, shoot, aim" approach, more of a gut feel with knowledge behind it. And I did have "the tingle"—a feeling I would get at the back of my neck when I just knew a book was going to work. Each month, I approached new titles with another lesson from my first boss: know your backlist and you will know what you need for frontlist.

I was constantly on the lookout for trends that were developing and looking for titles that fit into those trends. Over the years there were many: chick lit, techno thrillers, home front fiction, and psych thrillers to name a few. These seemed to catch fire. But when a trend is dead, it's dead. So you have to be on the lookout for dying trends, too.

DISCOVER GREAT NEW WRITERS

The Discover Great New Writers program came about after a dinner Len Riggio had with George Plimpton. It was established as a way to bring new writers or under-appreciated writers to the forefront. I read for Discover and we usually went thru about 200 titles a season, or 600 titles a year. There was a committee of about 12 readers from all over the company, including the stores, and we would each take five or six books to read each week. There were some unanimous yes's and some easy no's. But we always had some hotly debated titles. As I buyer, I would listen to the discussion to gauge what a real reader might think.

FICTION PHILOSOPHY

I have always thought that Fiction is truer than non-fiction because it has to speak to an emotional truth rather than a factual one. It may be totally whacko, but if it can make you *believe,* then there is your truth. Though I love great writing that sings off the page, the minute I am more aware of the writing than the story, I am out of the book. What it comes down to is a good story well told. There are authors who aren't the greatest writers but who I read because of their characters and sense of place.

What makes a book great? It lets you live in someone else's shoes for a while, takes you to another place and time, and connects you to an emotional truth.

MARKETING

The number one driver of sales is placement. There is more traffic at tables and displays and I tried to think of how a book would "look" in the store. Was it a big stack on the table or a few copies in the section? There is the old adage that you can improve the sales of a title by 30% simply by putting it on a table. On the big titles, it was easy to get carried away with the numbers, but I always kept in mind that a stack of 50 copies was over five feet tall, and that was more than enough—unless it was not nearly enough!

JACKETS, TITLES, AND FLAP COPY

This is as important as placement. What is your title saying to the readers and what will make them pick it up? Chances are that if they pick it up they will buy it. What mood or place is a title evoking? Is your flap copy setting a mood but not telling too much? I always looked at jackets as the most important advertising a publisher could do. It was basically a book's billboard. There were trends in jackets, but I always thought that if a jacket was bad it was for one of two reasons:

- It accurately reflected the book, and it was a bad book.
- The publisher didn't really "get" the book and they did not know the market.

MORE UNIVERSAL TRUTHS

- Red jackets always work.
- Yellow jackets don't work in any subject, though they do seem to work online because they "pop."
- Beautiful "gifty" jackets always work.
- If a book is selling well, and the publisher can't tell you why, jump on it. It has hit the right market and will continue to sell.
- Music novels don't usually sell well until a book comes along that redefines the moment like *Daisy Jones and the Six*.
- Trends will just stop.
- Elvis novels never sell! His fans don't want a fictional Elvis.
- Men will hunt (grab and go) the new bestsellers and women will gather titles from displays.
- All the truths are true until something comes along that disproves it.

Bookselling is the most exciting business to be in whether you are in publishing or retail. Everyone is doing their best to connect an author and title with a reader! There is nothing as exciting as finding a book that you just *know* is going to work and then seeing it happen. The whole industry reinvents itself two or three times a year with new books and then there is the steady backlist that is the backbone of the business.

I would urge you to go into bookstores as a reader. What's drawing your eye? What books have been reviewed recently? Read a mega-bestseller to see why they are working—with that big of an audience, there has to be something there.

RECOMMENDED READING:

- *The Forest for the Trees* by Betsy Lerner (good common sense advice)
- *Why We Buy* by Paco Underhill (the science of retail and placement)
- *The Tipping Point* by Malcolm Gladwell (what will make a book "tip")

*

Sessalee Hensley was a fiction buyer at Barnes and Noble from 1985 to 2020. She is a lifelong fiction reader.

THROWING THE BOOK AT PUBLISHING: THE BEST BOOKS ABOUT THE BUSINESS

BY THAD MCILROY

Book publishing is uniquely situated to publish books about itself. And it has been generous: there are several hundred titles that can be crowded into your library—memoirs and histories, how-to guides, economic overviews, studies of the digital transformation of publishing, and some purely academic work.

This is a select guide to books about book publishing. It's by no means exhaustive, just the catalog of someone who loves publishing and is on a never-ending quest to understand precisely how it works. I've focused mostly on trade publishing. My criteria for inclusion is this: for someone in publishing, or soon to enter publishing, can the book increase their understanding and appreciation of how the industry functions, and what their future role could be?

I sidestep many of the academic works about the history of publishing. And so, for example, a book like the *Oxford Illustrated History of the Book* (edited by James Raven, Oxford University Press, 2000) won't be fully described here both because it covers books, not publishing per se, and much of it concerns the Renaissance and before.

Another example: rather than reading G. Thomas Tanselle's *Book-Jackets: Their History, Forms, and Use*, which covers only up to 1901, I would instead suggest Matthew Goodman's 2016 *Book Cover Designs*, where you can "browse more than 500 book cover designs and listen to more than 50 of today's top designers discuss their process for creating the perfect book cover." Or Mendelsund's and Allworth's 2020 *The Look of the Book: Jackets, Covers, and Art at the Edges of Literature*, offering "an overview of book cover trends throughout history, with insights from dozens of literary and design luminaries."

But I'm also going to sidestep the "book arts" as well as guides to typography and design. Those are specialized endeavors within the practice of publishing, and few people working in publishing are expected to know how to use Adobe InDesign or Adobe Photoshop to design a book cover.

One more thing I'm steering clear of is the even more numerous books on seeking success as a writer, though many contain insights into the publishing business. Not far from those are numerous books on self-publishing, per se, some of them excellent. I will not be considering those.

BOOK PUBLISHING DEFINED

When I tell people I work in publishing, I'm always reminded that the term "publishing" means something different to those outside the business. Sometimes they're thinking newspaper, magazine, or journal publishing; sometimes blogs; sometimes software publishing or music publishing. Book publishing is but part of a larger publishing ecosphere.

But drilling down just on book publishing, an article I recommend to everyone who is trying to see the trees within the forest is Bill Kasdorf's 2018 short post, "Clearing up Publishing Classifications," "a handy reference to the various ways publishers of books and journals are classified." (https://apexcovantage.com/blog/clearing-publishing-classifications/)

Kasdorf's big-bucket categories are trade, scholarly, educational, and reference. Some publishers, he says, are in more than one. Scholarly is then dissected. He heads on from there into the types of publishing organizations and different types of publications. This creates a road map.

THE ALL-PURPOSE GUIDES

There are at least a dozen books that distinguish themselves by offering a broad perspective on the industry. The starting point has to be Mike Shatzkin's (and Roger Riger's) *The Book Business: What Everyone Needs to Know* (Oxford University Press, 2019). It's intended to be breezy, "a succinct and insightful survey of the industry in an easy-to-read question-and-answer format." It succeeds.

Follow that with a widely read beginner's guide to the U.S. trade industry, Thomas Woll's *Publishing for Profit: Successful Bottom-Line Management for Book Publishers* (Chicago Review Press, 2014). It touches most of the bases.

Sometimes overlooked is Joe Biel's informal but comprehensive *A People's Guide to Publishing: Building a Successful, Sustainable, Meaningful Book Business from the Ground Up* (Microcosm Publishing, 2018). You'll see that its subtitle follows the advice in the book: "Your subtitle should really distinguish your book from (comparable titles) and clarify your niche." This is the sort of specific detail that some of the guides overlook. Biel is the founder and president of Microcosm Publishing, a small press guided by a strong set of principles and doing some great work.

Another cornerstone text is Giles Clark and Angus Phillips's *Inside Book Publishing*, now in its sixth edition (Routledge, 2019). It covers all publishing sectors, with something of a U.K. industry focus.

On the edge of academe is the third edition of *The Book Publishing Industry*, authored by Albert N. Greco, *PW*'s Jim Milliot, and Robert Wharton (Routledge, 2013). Its 500 pages go deep into the "consumer" book industry, including history and operations. Notably included within, a 50-page chapter on "Marketing and Selling Books," a topic that always needs more coverage.

THE MUST-READ(S)

Beyond the basics, when I'm asked which book everyone in publishing must read it's in fact two books, both by John B. Thompson, *Merchants of Culture: The Publishing Business in the Twenty-First Century* (2nd ed., Polity, 2012) and *Book Wars: The Digital Revolution in Publishing* (Polity, May, 2021).

The books are not short—between the two you'll be committing to some 800 pages of text. While most of the published reviews rave about his work, Amazon reader reviews sometimes have headlines like "Useful, though dry" or "This is a long, tedious read . . ." suggesting, not inaccurately, that Thompson's style sometimes drifts into the dense language of academe. But, push on—his books reward the effort. No one else has Thompson's ability to marshal the facts into comprehensive and illuminating accounts of publishing in all its splendor.

(Thompson has an earlier volume, covering the evolution of academic and higher education publishing from 1980 to 2005, *Books in the Digital Age: The Transformation of Academic and Higher Education Publishing in Britain and the United States* [Polity, 2005].)

If taking on Thompson's work doesn't seem too daunting, you may be ready to purchase the 480-page *Oxford Handbook of Publishing*, edited by Angus Phillips and Michael Bhaskar (Oxford University Press, 2019). Heavily foot-noted, it's a grand collection of articles on a very broad range of topics, billed as "a comprehensive overview of the different areas and sectors of the pub-lishing industry from both scholars and practitioners" (including John B. Thompson). On one hand it has chapters with subtitles like "Symbiosis in the Digital Environment" and "The Alchemy of Ideas." On the other hand, the seven chapters in the "Publishing in Practice" section include authoritative guidelines from acknowledged experts.

I sometimes test the comprehensiveness of a book about publishing on the basis of whether it discusses metadata. From where I sit, it's tough to argue that you're on top of what's going on in book publishing without an enthu-siastic embrace of the topic. The *Oxford Handbook of Publishing* fails in this regard—neither metadata nor ONIX appear in the index. A search through the text reveals that metadata for e-commerce is mentioned in passing, but not as a stand-alone topic.

When it comes to metadata for books, the must-have volume is *Metadata Essentials: Proven Techniques for Book Marketing and Discovery* by Jake Handy and Margaret Harrison (Ingram, 2018). Earlier I coauthored, with Renée Register, *The Metadata Handbook* (2nd ed., DataCurate 2015), which holds up as a reference, but *Metadata Essentials* is the book you want when you're ready to turn your metadata into a marketing advantage.

MARKETING

ONIX-based metadata *is* covered in Alison Baverstock and Susannah Bowen's magisterial 500-page *How to Market Books* (6th ed., Routledge, 2019). Multiply the number of pages by the number of editions, and you've got *the* final word about book marketing. From traditional marketing through to social media, there's really nothing like it.

A PAST STILL RELEVANT

I recently revisited a work called *The Lost World of the Craft Printer*, by Maggie Holtzberg-Call (University of Illinois Press, 1992). What is notable in the (mostly dry and academic) book is that it identifies a phenomenon I call "the Good Old Days that Never Were," an idealization, almost fetishization, of times past, when industry practices were, ostensibly, better than they are today.

I find it fascinating that books about publishing, published 40 or 50 years ago, many of them memoirs, not only describe an industry very similar to today's, but also with many of the concerns that remain top-of-mind: corporate concentration and its drive for profits, the paucity of book review media, and the challenge of selling a profitable print run's worth of literary fiction by a first-time author.

In preparation for this article, I've been most recently rereading Robert Dana's *Against the Grain: Interviews with Maverick American Publishers* (University of Iowa Press, 1986). My God, it's delightful!

Dana's extended interview with James Laughlin, the founder of New Directions publishing company, includes an account of how Ezra Pound set him on the path of publishing.

In 1935 Laughlin had been serving as a sort of secretary to Pound, then living in Rapallo, Italy, hoping that Pound would help him as a writer. After several months, Pound said to him, "Jas, let's face it, you're never going to become a writer. Why don't you go home to the States and do something useful?"

"What's useful?" Laughlin asked.

Pound's first idea was that he assassinate the editor of *Saturday Review*, who had committed the unforgivable sin of criticizing James Joyce's *Ulysses* because there was no "character development."

Laughlin thought that unrealistic, and so Pound commanded, "Well, go back and be a publisher."

Toward the end of the interview, the topic turns to the state of publishing, and the interviewer, Robert Dana, comments (this being forty years ago, in 1980), "I was talking to a friend the other day who was saying that, one day, bookstores will not stock books anymore. They will all be banked on a computer. If you want a book, you go to the store and ask for it, pay the price of the book, and it will be jet-printed overnight."

What a perfect segue to the recent publication of Keel Hunt's *The Family Business: How Ingram Transformed the World of Books* (West Margin Press, 2021). It offers both a (sanitized) history of the Ingram family and an insightful account of Ingram's rise within book publishing and its impact today, including the well-honed capacity to "jet-print" books overnight, from books "banked on a computer."

MEMOIRS

This segues nicely into the topic of book publishing memoirs. There are many. And as far as I can determine, all of them by men. Two that I can recommend are Random House founder Bennett Cerf's *At Random: The Reminiscences of Bennett Cerf* (1977) and Grove Press founder Barney Rosset's *Rosset: My Life in Publishing and How I Fought Censorship* (best read alongside the 2010 documentary film *Obscene: A Portrait of Barney Rosset and Grove Press*).

NOVELS ABOUT BOOK PUBLISHING

My editor suggested that as part of this article I visit book publishing in fiction. What a great idea. Zakiya Dalila Harris's recent bestseller *The Other Black Girl* suggested that this is fertile ground for fiction. And so I set off to find the many novels with book publishing at the center. A pretty thorough search turned up less than a dozen. Of course there are lots of novels with authors at the center. And a bunch set in the newspaper publishing industry. Novels about book publishing, no.

The search did turn up a 2012 novel that I'm looking forward to reading, *Bestseller*, by Alessandro Gallenzi, himself a publisher. One reviewer noted that Gallenzi "slips in sound insider's judgements on how this business works. Read it for the lowdown on the low trade." Sounds like fun!

SCHOLARS

I'm not paying enough attention here to scholarly publishing, which is rife with studies and reports. It's not from lack of interest, nor from a lack of appreciation of the numerous ways that scholarly publishing is different from trade publishing. It's just that I've not read as widely on the subject as I have trade publishing, and I have more personal experience on the trade side of the business.

A good starting point for anyone new to scholarly publishing is Rick Anderson's *Scholarly Communication: What Everyone Needs to Know* (Oxford University Press, 2018) (part of the same Oxford series as Shatzkin/Riger's *The Book Business: What Everyone Needs to Know*). It's an approachable overview. You can go deeper via Albert N. Greco's *The Business of Scholarly Publishing: Managing in Turbulent Times* (Oxford University Press, 2020) or Thompson's *Books in the Digital Age*, mentioned above.

Worth noting here is that Albert N. Greco, along with Thompson, is one of *the* authors to turn to for the most in-depth analyses of book publishing, including exhaustive statistics. Greco is particularly prolific: 16 scholarly books, 10 professional books, and 25 book chapters.

MAGAZINES AND JOURNALS ABOUT PUBLISHING

The publishing industry is well-served by periodicals that keep a close eye on the ever-changing industry. In the United States, *Publishers Weekly* has been going strong since 1872, primarily covering trade publishing. *The Bookseller* is the U.K. equivalent, while *Quill & Quire* covers Canadian publishing. Three scholarly journals augment the more day-to-day coverage of the magazines, including *Publishing Research Quarterly*, *The Journal of Scholarly Publishing*, and *Learned Publishing*. There are also many websites, blogs, newsletters, and podcasts, of varying quality, too many to describe in this article.

So there's a wrap-up of a range of books to inform the faithful. Now check your collection. What have I missed?

*

Thad McIlroy is an electronic publishing analyst and author based in San Francisco and Vancouver, B.C. His site, The Future of Publishing, provides in-depth coverage of the book publishing industry. He is a partner in Publishing Technology Partners and an adjunct professor in the Masters of Publishing Program at Pace University in New York.

FORGING BONDS AT THE BOOKSTORE

BY JULIE POOLE

When I first got a job as a bookseller at Malvern Books, a small independent bookstore in Austin, Tex., I thought it would be roughly akin to
working at a major chain: I'd stand behind the counter and ring people
up, but without the discomfort of having to upsell memberships. It was
through observing my gifted coworkers that I learned that bookselling
is an art. At first, I wasn't used to customers asking me for book recommendations and often felt like I was stumbling over my words. Once I
started to think of myself as a sort of matchmaker, I began to have fun.

Malvern is unique in that we sell new books, mostly fiction and
poetry, from small and independent presses exclusively. A good portion
of the store is devoted to books in translation. When I first walked in, as
a customer, I was astonished to see not just a few shelves labeled "poetry"
but an entire wall. As a poet, I was in heaven.

When I became an employee, I'd often watch people do a quick loop
around the store and leave, disappointed, I believed, because we don't
stock the latest bestsellers or books from the Big Five (or Big Four) publishers, and therefore they didn't recognize our titles. But for customers
who were open to suggestions, I had the joy of matching readers with
authors they were not aware of.

Sometimes the handselling stakes were high. Once a frazzled-looking
young woman told me that she was about to spend two weeks "trapped"
with her conservative family for the holidays. I knew just the ticket—an
engrossing feminist book about a 1950s Hollywood starlet who'd lived a
wild life and experienced an unfortunate fall from grace.

Another man announced that he'd just fallen in love and was looking
for poems. He asked for two poetry book recommendations: one to celebrate his newfound amour and another to protect him from heartbreak
if the relationship failed. "I've been hurt before," he said. I handed him
the perfect antidote (which he later told me worked like a charm).

The more I worked at the store, the more I began to notice that people
yearn for connection beyond book recommendations. Even before the

pandemic began, I'd answered phone calls that didn't have much to do with the books at all. One elderly woman wanted help looking up something on the internet, which I happily obliged. Another gentleman wanted information about how to get out of a parking ticket. A fair number of callers want to know how to get their books published, in which case I'd refer them to an organization like the Writers' League of Texas for a sense of community and support.

It can make people feel vulnerable to ask about books in subjects such as marital problems, grief, rape and incest, and substance abuse, or about books on how to deal with suicidal thoughts. Our store's collection doesn't serve these needs, but I recommend other local bookstores—BookWoman, Black Pearl Books, BookPeople—that people can turn to for personal recommendations, even if it means losing potential Bookshop.org sales.

When Malvern opened for private shopping appointments following the onset of the pandemic, customers commented on how nice it was to browse again. People connect to bookstores as physical spaces. Browsing is a meditative state that I know well. As a broke graduate student, I would often browse at Malvern, not able to buy anything but leaving feeling calm, revitalized, and better able to handle a chaotic world.

The problem with browsing online is that algorithms are based on similarities: if you liked this, you'll like this. This model prevents people from trying something new. I've recommended poetry to people who haven't read poetry for years. Some confess they're afraid of it. I'm presented with an incredible opportunity to say, "Here's something that won't remind you of the old chestnuts you read in high school."

For me, bookselling has become a second MFA degree; reading more widely has made me a better writer. I read books from all over the world translated from other languages. I read books by BIPOC and LGBTQ+ authors, which means my book recommendations have become more expansive—in short, less white. If I can connect a reader to an author— who may become, in a sense, a friend, a mentor, a bridge to other authors—that means the world to me.

Of course, as an employee at an independent bookstore, I want us to have glorious daily sales, but I know it's not just about dollar signs. Sometimes it's about recommending a Black-owned bookstore for books about anti-racism. Sometimes it's about chatting on the phone with someone who's been housebound since last March—not about books so much but about isolation, because people need to feel connected, because that's what it means to have hope.

*

A version of this article appeared in the 03/15/2021 issue of *Publishers Weekly* under the headline: Forging Bonds.

②
PEOPLE IN BOOK PUBLISHING

BECOMING A PUBLISHER
AN INTERVIEW WITH JANE FRIEDMAN

What was it like as an up-and-coming woman in publishing in the 1970s and 1980s? How has it changed?

When I graduated from NYU and walked directly into the personnel department at Random House, I said, "I want to be a publisher." I assumed this would be very easy. I assumed one did what one wanted to do. I was a strong-willed young woman. I felt I could do whatever I wanted. I didn't know what publishing was, but I thought, "I love books, so I want to be a publisher." Terry Hully was the head of personnel. She smiled and asked what my qualifications were. I said I'd wanted to be either on Wall Street or a publisher. I didn't like working for Value Line Securities, so I decided I was going to be a publisher. She said, "Well, let me see what's available, but you're not going to come in here and become a publisher. You're going to have to work your way up." And I thought to myself, of course I'm going to work my way up. I've always been a worker. I've always liked working. I *wanted* to work my way up. I was all of twenty-one years old at this point. So I hung around for a while and I interviewed with Robert Loomis, a very famous editor. He had an opening, because his assistant was on maternity leave. But she was planning on coming back and I didn't want to work part-time.

Finally, Terry said, "Well, I have an idea. There's this man called Bill Loverd—a very dapper guy who is the publicity director of Alfred Knopf." Random House had recently acquired Alfred Knopf, Inc. I had been an English major, of course, I knew Knopf. It was probably the best publishing company in America, if not the world, at that point.

I made an appointment to see this dapper Bill Loverd. He kept me waiting for a half an hour. I'll never forget this. I was good-looking. I had a matching hat to my dress. I knew exactly how to dress. I knew exactly how to wear my hair, my eye makeup. Finally after half an hour—where at this point I'm thinking, do I want to work for someone who keeps me waiting for a half an hour?—out walks this absolutely stunning guy, cigarette dangling, looking just like Albert Camus. I walked into his office and we talked and talked for about an hour. I can't tell you that I remember what we talked about, but it was probably about books and what publicity was. I didn't know what publicity was. I was going to be an editor—Rona Jaffe, *The Best of Everything*. That's what you do. You become an editor. So I said, "What is publicity?" And he said, "Well, we put authors on the *Today Show*, we do some author interviews. It's not a very important part of the business on the publishing side but on the pre-publishing side, we're the ones who send the galleys out to the reviewers. We are basically a review entity."

I told him sending galleys out for review didn't sound very exciting to me. I was fresh, but cute, and I was falling madly in love with him. He said, "We go to lunch, and we have all these fancy events, and I think you will like it." So I said, "Well, why don't you let me know if you want to hire me? I mean, you're just meeting me for the first time." He said, "I have seen twenty-one candidates. The job is yours." I said, "What is the job?" And he said, "Publicity secretary." I said, "Oh, no it's not. I didn't go to college to become a secretary." So he said, "Oh well, that's a bit of a problem." I said, "No, it's not. I'll come in as publicity secretary, but in three months you will name me a publicity associate. And if you do that, and you'll promise me that now, I'll take the job." And that's how I got hired. That's how I entered publishing.

Now, how was it different then? Well, the women were all in either publicity or the subsidiary rights area—there were some editors, but they certainly were not in the executive suites. There was no such thing as a woman in the executive suites. But nothing was going to stop me from succeeding, and it wasn't because I was going to be obnoxious about it. I was just going to learn. I felt there was nothing wrong with going to get Bill a cup of coffee in the morning, because who knew what I was going to discuss at the coffee machine? I am the true example of the woman who learned publishing from getting coffee, from answering the phone, from opening the mail, and from figuring out what was really necessary to get from that manuscript to that galley to that finished book, and to the public.

Were there other women like you at the time?
I was an anomaly. There were women in publicity. There was the Publishers

Publicity Association. Bill Loverd didn't want to belong because he was a big snob. My gut feeling was to belong to the PPA, learn from them. Everything about me, everything I've done with my life, has been with the intention of learning something new. Giving, because I'm bright and I have ideas, but learning something new from other people.

What advice would you give to young women who are entering the field?
The field of publishing today is so different than it was fifty years ago. I can't believe I'm saying fifty years ago, but I entered in 1968. My advice would be to be entrepreneurial. But not everybody wants to be. People come to publishing because they want to be editors. They want to edit good works and then help them to get them published. They are not interested in rising up the corporate ladder. The difference today is that there are women in the corporate suites. That's what's different. From the late Carolyn Reidy, who became the second global CEO, after I was the first, to Madeline McIntosh being the CEO of Random House. Now there are women in the corporate suites. They're no longer relegated to being the assistants, the associates, the rights directors. So the advice I would give to someone entering publishing today is to figure out which aspect of publishing interests you. If you want to come into publishing because you want to publish good writers, you want to bring the words of the writers to the public, come in with a sort of entrepreneurial spirit. But come in and take a job and follow the rules. There are some rules, and they're probably good rules.

What steps can publishers take to make the industry more equitable and diversified?
Diversification has been an issue from day one. I happen to have mentored Dawn Davis, who is African American and is now the publisher of *Bon Appétit* but who worked in publishing for many years. And Errol McDonald was part of my group. I also had an assistant named Lesleigh Irish-Underwood. But look at how I'm talking about—of the thousands of employees—just three I had working for me. I think that the way to diversify is, number one, pay better salaries. Even in those days we would lose some diverse candidates—some to advertising, some to TV. We certainly have a very diverse list of authors. Good writing is good writing, and that's what the goal should be: publishing the best writers, wherever they come from, whoever they are, and publishing them for reasonable sums of money so that everybody can walk away feeling good about what they've done.

Jane Friedman is a leading publishing executive, consultant, and innovator who has worked with such internationally bestselling authors and literary luminaries as Michael Crichton, Anne Rice, Dennis Lehane, and Neil Gaiman. She served as the first female global CEO of a major publishing enterprise when Rupert Murdoch named Friedman president and CEO of HarperCollins Publishers Worldwide (NewsCorp) in 1997, and she remained in that role until 2008.

In 2009 Friedman cofounded Open Road Integrated Media with Jeffrey Sharp. At Open Road, as CEO, Friedman revolutionized the digital publishing industry by creating e-books from legendary authors including William Styron, Pat Conroy, Alice Walker, James Jones, and Pearl S. Buck. For her work with Open Road, Friedman was named one of *Fortune* Magazine's most powerful women entrepreneurs.

Friedman came to HarperCollins from Random House, where she was Executive Vice President of Random House Inc., Executive Vice President of the Knopf Publishing Group, Publisher of Vintage Books, and Founder and President of Random House Audio Publishing. Friedman has been recognized by numerous organizations and publications including *Fast Company*'s Fast 50, *Publishers Weekly*'s Person of the Year and the *Wall Street Journal*'s 50 Women to Watch.

In 2018 Friedman established The Literary Studio, through which she consults in all areas of development of intellectual property.

NAT WARTELS:
THE ENTREPRENEUR AS PUBLISHER

BY NICK LYONS

Nat Wartels (1902–1990) was one of the first and surely the most unique and successful of the truly entrepreneurial book publishers. He began his long and robust career by buying large quantities of overstock and remaindered books for a few cents on the dollar and selling them at a substantial profit to bookstores across the country. These sold well, so he soon developed two related divisions: Publishers Central Bureau for direct sales to consumers and Bonanza Books, which reprinted out-of-print and remaindered books at rock-bottom prices.

Nat had gone into business in 1933 with Bob Simon, a friend from the Wharton School, and they soon extended their company vertically by founding Crown Publishers to publish original titles in 1936. Crown had the unique advantage of being able to remainder books to itself and print some with longer lives at a lower price in Bonanza. With his deft eye for profitable ways to expand further, Nat bought a number of distressed or bankrupt companies, including Covici-Friede; Howell, Soskin; Barre; Clarkson Potter; and, over lunch, the distinguished sporting-book firm Derrydale Press. He was not shy about dismantling these firms. He remaindered much or all of the stock, reprinted a few titles, kept some active, like Clarkson Potter. And he further developed his cluster of divisions and activities by starting the "Living Language" audio program, a children's list with Lothrop, Lee & Shepherd (which he had bought), and even taking "puts" (contracting to purchase a certain number of copies of a book that had not sold in a period of time, at a fixed price, *before* the books were actually printed). With his shrewd financial skills, Nat also sold off rights and properties, some of considerable value or promise, when occasions arose. Asked why he had sold all rights to such a potentially valuable backlist title as *Ideal Marriage* for a modest price, he said simply that the money was more important to him at that moment than the probable future of the book.

Crown became a freewheeling and exciting training ground for many employees who eventually took their skills elsewhere, and for future publishers. Nat always was open to fresh ideas and encouraged his staff to think of new projects or directions. One such was Harmony Books, founded by Bruce Harris, who had worked in sales; it was hugely successful, with books like *Be Here Now* and *The Hitchhiker's Guide to the Galaxy*. Bruce later became president of Workman, J.P. Leventhal started a successful firm of his own, and Michael Friedman began a variety of book-producing and marketing firms, all of which flourished. They owed much not to what Nat had taught them, but to who Nat was and what he did, and to the image of the firm—hardworking and open—that he had built.

The spirit of the place grew from Nat—the way he watched nickels and could be eminently frugal, how conscious he was of detail, and how bold he could be about new ventures and directions. He signed every check, even those for a few dollars, and he read through a folder containing the day's orders every day, even in his final years, often late at night. Key decisions for books that especially interested him—their titles and jackets, perhaps—were often made at his desk—and he once created jacket comments for one of those special books—comments like "The greatest writer about war since Hemingway," and a generous few words on how that author brought Shakespeare to mind. The heading was, "People Are Saying." When an innocent editor asked who to attribute the comments to, Nat said, "Well, I'm a people, aren't I?" His desk was a wonder to behold. Piled a foot high in places, there was correspondence dating back decades, sections of manuscripts, jacket designs, legal papers, even now and then a check. No one knew the extent for sure, but one could not miss the burns where he had placed a lit cigarette on the pile. When the company moved offices, colleagues arranged for the desk to be transported intact by an art mover.

Crown was sold to Random House in 1988. Nat remained chairman of the board and worked every day until he died, two years later. With a cherubic face, a quick wit, an openness to all ways to deal, both frugal and imaginative, Nat Wartels was one of the unique figures in modern American book world. He was also, many said, "The richest man in publishing."

*

Nick Lyons founded The Lyons Press. His latest book was *Fire in the Straw: Notes on Inventing a Life*.

PW'S 2020 PERSON OF THE YEAR: THE BOOK BUSINESS WORKER

We salute members of the industry's workforce, who faced unprecedented challenges in 2020—both in keeping the gears turning and in pushing for change.

BY JOHN MAHER, ANDREW ALBANESE, ALEX GREEN, JIM MILLIOT, AND KARINTHA PARKER | DEC 18, 2020

At 8 p.m. on March 22, the capital of the American book publishing business all but shut down. Two days earlier, Gov. Andrew Cuomo of New York had announced stay-at-home orders that would temporarily shutter all in-person businesses throughout the state that were not deemed essential—bookstores, libraries, and publishers among them—in order to combat the Covid-19 pandemic. Soon, similar orders were put in place across the country, affecting employees of book-related businesses from coast to coast.

A mere two months later, following the May 25 killing of George Floyd at the hands of Minneapolis police, bookstores in Minneapolis rushed to aid protesters and salvage what was left of their businesses following fires started during the civil unrest. For months afterward, Black booksellers at Black-owned stores across the country worked overtime to put copies of anti-racist literature and other books by Black authors into the hands of readers hungry for them and eager to patronize Black businesses. Months after that, booksellers on the West Coast scrambled to serve their communities and save their shops as massive wildfires blazed across the countryside.

All the while, workers in libraries and warehouses, like booksellers, put on their personal protective equipment and reported for duty. Publishing workers endeavored to make some sense of their new employment situation, isolated at home and making books alone together from behind screens. And authors and employees across all segments of the book business, frustrated by the lack of diversity, equity, and inclusion in publishing, made their frustrations heard, prompting the first concerted industry-wide effort to address these issues.

There's an old proverb that says, "Many hands make light work." This year, for the book business, that wasn't quite true: the work was never light. Still, without many hands, there would have been no work at all—no books made or sold or read, no milestones achieved. No individual could stand out in such a year, and no individual should be honored in it either. Instead, it is the collective of book business workers, often overworked and underpaid, that kept the industry afloat and challenged it to live up to greater standards.

The most important people in the book business in 2020 are not the powerhouse agents or the megabestselling authors or the Big Five CEOs. They are the booksellers, debut and midlist authors, editors, librarians, printers, publicists, sales representatives, and warehouse workers, to mention just a few—the workers, who have been the most important people in the business all along. What follows are some reasons why.

PUBLISHING WORKERS

This year in the book business was marked by major shifts and major actions, which often went hand in hand. Younger workers became much more active and made companies—mostly publishers at this point, but also some booksellers—take concrete steps to broaden diversity and stand on principle, all while working around the challenges presented by Covid.

The first such action came on March 5, three days after Grand Central Publishing announced that it would publish a memoir by Woody Allen, who has been accused by his adopted daughter, Dylan Farrow, of molesting her in 1992, when she was seven years old. Employees at Grand Central and Little, Brown (which published Allen's estranged son, Ronan Farrow, who severed his ties with the imprint two days earlier), as well as at other imprints at parent company Hachette Book Group, staged a walkout in protest of the acquisition—an extraordinarily rare and risky occurrence in the corporate publishing world, in which most workers are not protected by unions.

"I think all of us, especially the younger people at Hachette, feel very strongly the burden and the enormity of being gatekeepers," says an HBG employee, who spoke with *PW* on condition of anonymity. "It felt pretty amazing when people were actually standing outside, finally, in Rockefeller Center—we weren't all sure if we were going to do it—and it was pretty jubilant, to see how many people had chosen to walk. But I felt more sad than anything in the larger sense, especially for my colleagues who work at Grand Central, that it had come to this."

That walkout, however, would not be publishing's last of the year. On June 8, the day New York City began a partial reopening, more than 1,300 book business workers, from editors and publicists at major houses to literary agents and book critics, stepped off the job in protest of racist state violence and white supremacy under the banner of Pub Workers for Justice. The group says its mission is to "build a community that will protect us from the inherent exploitation and racist practices of the publishing industry." The action was taken in direct response to emails CEOs of the Big Five publishing companies sent to their employees following the killing of George Floyd—statements the workers considered inadequate.

The effort was initiated by five junior Macmillan staffers, four of whom identify as BIPOC and one of whom is white, who drafted the initial language for the action. By the time the industry was made aware of the action, however, more than 1,100 individuals had taken part in shaping the message.

Collective action was the whole point. "Together, we disinvested from the industry for a day and invested instead in our communities," the group later wrote on its website. "In doing so, we demonstrated what is possible when publishing workers come together for the common good—when we take ownership of our labor, stop outsourcing justice to CEOs, and start erecting our own systems of support and accountability."

These actions forced changes at the publishers that prompted them. On March 6, Grand Central dropped Allen's memoir, though it was published shortly thereafter by the independent house Skyhorse Publishing. And in September, Penguin Random House and Hachette Book Group each released reports on their employee demographics and pledged to take steps to diversify their workforces as well as their publishing lists.

Later in September, Macmillan announced that it will raise its entry-level salary to $42,000 on December 27. In October, Beacon Press bumped its starting salary to $44,600, Simon & Schuster increased its starting pay to $40,000, and PRH told employees that it will up its own to $45,000 in January. Then in December, Hachette announced that it will do the same "in its most expensive locations" in February. And in the six months since the June action, the Big Five launched several new imprints dedicated to diverse voices and hired a number of people of color, including former Pulitzer Prize administrator Dana Canedy (at S&S) and National Book Foundation executive director Lisa Lucas (at PRH), for positions of authority.

These are stopgap measures, not long-term solutions. Salary increases of $5,000 won't make much of a dent in the disparity between publishing pay and New York City cost of living, hiring well-established figures from outside of publishing's ranks will not solve the book business's problem with retention of workers of color, and dedicating boutique imprints to the publication of diverse books is no replacement for diversifying the flagship imprints that already exist. Still, changes were made—changes that would not have been made without worker outcry.

"It's been a wild year overall, really apocalyptic and maybe a little bit inspiring, which is probably the perfect cocktail for kicking off organizing of any kind," says editor Ben Mabie at Verso Books, which just voluntarily recognized its staff's decision to join the Washington-Baltimore News Guild. (Mabie was on the organizing committee and is now the shop steward.) "This seems like really the perfect year for organizing to happen, between the mergers happening among the Big Five—now Big Four—and Amazon's increasing grip on the industry and the more meager profits that bricks-and-mortar bookstores are able to kind of eke out and the kind of challenges and inequalities that come with working from home for extended periods of time."

Julia Judge, a senior publicist at Verso and a fellow member of its new union's organizing committee, adds that, though the industry has recently seen a move toward diverse hiring practices, "the broader structural issues that are present in publishing, such as the low pay, the precarity, the gender issues—all of these things need to be fixed before we can talk about hiring and the other steps that we can take internally to address what are really industry-wide problems. I see unionizing as one small step that we can take to fix some of those issues."

Meanwhile, the same workers who have been pushing for systemic change have also spent the year adjusting to the world of work-from-home publishing. In New York, most houses' headquarters are staffed by skeleton crews and only intermittently visited by other employees, who have been encouraged to stay home even after lockdowns were lifted in late June. This has prompted major changes in how publishing, a business that relies on interpersonal relationships, gets done.

Perhaps no employees have seen greater changes to their working methods than those in marketing and publicity departments. With physical galleys severely limited, bookstores closed to the public, and in-person events canceled until further notice, marketers and publicists have had to effectively reinvent their roles. That meant doubling down on direct-to-consumer marketing programs, increasing podcasting and video efforts, launching virtual book clubs and holding author events over Zoom, and even holding entire fan conventions digitally. It also meant, according to May-Zhee Lim, a publicist at Riverhead Books, working to find ways to make virtual events stand out in a newly saturated landscape.

"It's been a wild ride of a year for sure," Lim says. "I remember sitting in front of my computer in a dress with a homemade cocktail in one hand and a photo of Akwaeke Emezi's cat in the other. I was running the Zoom for our first ever virtual cocktail party—back in April, no less, when everything felt so new and surreal. I was all nerves!"

Despite being "deprived of our usual publicity tools," Lim says that when she looks back at the event, "I mostly remember the interesting stories that people felt like they were able to share because we had created an environment for them to do what they would do at an in-person cocktail party. That's what excites me about these new digital projects that we're rolling out at Riverhead. I love that we're making the world feel more human, one virtual cocktail party at a time."

WAREHOUSE WORKERS

Warehouse workers are pivotal in getting books from publishers to readers. Without them, the supply chain would not function. And since the pandemic hit, warehouse employees have had to cope with new protocols developed to provide protection from Covid.

Sara Point has been working at IPG since 2006, the last six years as manager of the distributor's 200,000-sq.-ft. warehouse in Chicago. She says that when the pandemic hit she was concerned about her safety and that of her staff. "Everything was happening so fast," she recalls. "Everything was so new. There was a new development every day."

To help provide the proper social distancing, IPG added a second shift. It also instituted temperature checks, a mask mandate, sanitizer stations, and protocols to ensure that those known to be exposed to the virus or presenting symptoms stayed home. As a result, the distribution center has had "minimal" positive cases, Point says.

"Things can feel relatively normal, then you may hear of a new case and you get a jolt," Point notes. Still, she feels safe coming to work and believes her staff of 100 does too. "Everyone has stuck it out," she adds. In spring, business had slowed down, but the volume is now back to what it should be for the holidays.

Like everyone, Point eagerly awaits the day when things at the warehouse can return to normal. "I miss seeing everyone's faces and their smiles," she says. With everyone wearing masks, "you forget what people really look like." The pandemic also forced the cancellation of IPG's annual holiday party. "I can't wait till 2021," she says. "It has to be better than this year."

BOOKSTORE WORKERS

As stay-at-home orders came down in states in mid-March, most of America's bookstores closed their doors to customers while taking up the challenge of online bookselling. At Cellar Door Bookstore in Riverside, Calif., online sales went from a small portion of the store's revenue to its sole source of income in a matter of weeks. But like hundreds of frontline booksellers, Cellar Door's Elisa Thomas was furloughed. She watched the store make that transition from her home, hoping to see it emerge from the swirling uncertainty of the first months of the pandemic.

When Thomas returned in May, she found a store with enormous community support. But much had shifted. Her brainchild, the store's Drag Queen Story Hour, had ceased. Cellar Door's many book clubs were just beginning to transition online. Staff picks on its website became a substitute for in-person interactions. "The entire face of the store had changed," Thomas says. "It was almost all online orders and processing phone orders."

Around the same time, Malik Thompson was returning to work at Loyalty Bookstores' Washington, D.C., location following his own furlough. Like Cellar Door, the vibrant Black-owned shop had gone from being what Thompson calls a "cultural hub" to being a digital operation. He did what many other booksellers did: he pushed ahead, meeting the needs of a customer base that grew swiftly following the killing of George Floyd.

According to Thompson, who is Black, Loyalty owner Hannah Oliver Depp prioritized employee health amid the trauma of the events in June, telling booksellers she was "not going to abuse her staff so that people can get things quicker." But they still faced the demands of new customers, many of whom were angered by shortages of key titles like *White Fragility* owing to circumstances beyond the bookstore's control.

In the worst instances, customers took out their frustration on Thompson and his colleagues in ways that repeated racist tropes about the inadequacy of Black businesses. "With half-baked practices around anti-racism," he says, "there's often this notion that 'I'm going to throw my money at Black-owned bookstores for a product. However, if they don't meet these standards that I've set for them, then it's going to fit into these preconceived narratives I subscribe to about the inferiority of Black-owned businesses. And this is just further justification for my unwillingness to support them.'"

Thompson says he often thinks about a key question, "How do I nurture and nourish the community I'm dedicated to?" Then, he adds another: "How do I also navigate being patronized by outsiders?" His answer? To give the work all the energy he can. Along with filling customer orders, he hosted two online poetry readings through the store. He also applied for a Tin House creative writing fellowship this winter, and when Depp saw on social media that he was accepted, she offered to pay the cost.

Meanwhile, at Cellar Door, the influx of orders for anti-racist titles was accompanied by community requests for the store to hold conversations about Black Lives Matter. Cellar Door met those needs, and at first, Thomas and her colleagues were gratified by the increased interest. "Those are books that we were selling before, but everything became so much more visceral," she says. "It was interesting to see all of the sales, but the change that comes with those sales was what was really important."

Still, Thomas—who is Black and Mexican—wonders whether the spike in sales was a kind of "performative allyship." For self-care, she took moments to step back. "It does become a question," she says, "of, 'Do I have the mental capacity to have this conversation right now?' and, 'Do I have the wherewithal to . . . maintain a professional presence in this moment?'"

When it came to balancing self-care with advocacy in support of their bookstores, Thomas's and Thompson's experience paid dividends. At the close of an unprecedented year, their stores are open and meeting their financial goals. Thomas and Thompson are also aware of the recognition frontline booksellers have gotten from within the publishing industry for their crucial role in keeping stores afloat.

But both booksellers want more from the industry. Thompson would like to see greater respect for the long lineage of Black-owned bookstores that, like Loyalty, serve as vibrant community, cultural, and industry leaders. He says the continued existence of these businesses requires sustained investment, not just a sales bump from liberals when tragedy strikes.

Thomas wants publishers to take steps to ensure that the books that are the lifeblood of Cellar Door are available when she needs them. "We're faced with so many difficulties with getting certain titles in, especially being at a smaller store," she says. "That in and of itself directly affects us as frontline booksellers."

Thomas says the shortages stem from a pervasive belief in the trade that sells indies short. "We eat, breathe, and sleep books," she notes. "So to underestimate us or to not give us the appreciation that we deserve is honestly disheartening sometimes. And I know that there is only so much publishers can do for us. But I feel like there is room for them to invest more in us than they do in these big monopolies."

LIBRARY WORKERS

From the start of the Covid crisis, the nation's 300,000 librarians and library workers quickly pivoted to provide new services to the reading public, including a rapid shift to digital. That shift, however, was not limited to providing more e-books and digital audiobooks. It has also meant virtual storytimes for kids, Zoom book clubs, online author events, and other digital programs and events ranging from knitting clubs to language classes. It has meant creating and marketing beefed-up resource guides, virtual reference services, online instruction sessions, and new programs for students and teachers as schools nationwide were forced to go remote. And it has meant boosting libraries' Wi-Fi signals, as library parking lots have become refuges for some of the more than 20 million Americans who still lack access to broadband.

As weather improved over the spring and summer, many libraries undertook some form of curbside service, where patrons could check out books, devices, and other physical resources online and pick them up outdoors. The Denver Public Library set up an outdoor laptop rental service, allowing those without access to technology at home to sit at properly distanced tables and use library computers. And like a number of libraries, Denver used its bookmobile to bring food and other necessities to its patrons, in addition to books.

These changes have required library workers to build the proverbial airplane as it is flying, securing their own appropriate personal protective equipment, crafting and enforcing new social distancing policies, and reconfiguring libraries with less furniture, more space between computers, hand sanitizer stations, spit guards, and plexiglass dividers. Libraries now have contactless checkouts, new cleaning procedures, and materials quarantines, and have undertaken efforts like OCLC's Project Realm, which delivered key research on how long the virus can survive on various surfaces, including wood and metal shelving, plastic CD covers, and, yes, books.

And Covid wasn't the only major challenge librarians took on in 2020. Amid the anger, outrage, and protests that followed the killing of George Floyd, the library community stood up to acknowledge systemic racism in the U.S.—including in public libraries—and then went to work. Libraries and library organizations across the country issued statements of support for the Black Lives Matter movement, provided expanded access to racial and social justice collections, and offered safe spaces for community conversations on race and equity.

More importantly, librarians have put libraries under the microscope. "Libraries as an institution are taking a stand against systemic racism, making books about anti-racism and the African American experience available to readers—and this is good," Carmi Parker, ILS administrator at the Whatcom County Library System in Washington State, told *PW* over the summer. "But libraries are also recognizing that we, like the police, are an institution embedded with systemic racism. We say that the library is for everyone, but that won't be true until our staff, patrons, and collections reflect the populations in our communities."

While library workers have stood up for their communities this year, they also stood up for themselves. As the Covid crisis hit, an idealized narrative of selfless hero librarians began to take root in the media. The reality on the ground, however, was grim: too many librarians and staff were being asked to work without proper protective equipment or safety precautions, were terrified of becoming sick, and were facing uncertainty and economic ruin as layoffs and furloughs mounted. Some public library workers were even ordered by their municipalities to redeploy from their closed library buildings to shelters, makeshift testing facilities, or other frontline, high-risk jobs.

"The flipside of all of these feel-good pieces on digital story time, backyard summer reading, and boosted Wi-Fi signals in the parking lot is library workers forced to do jobs they never signed up for [and] scolded for their attempts to fight for their well-being," wrote Massachusetts librarian Callan Bignoli in a May editorial in *Library Journal*. "It's time to say, 'Not anymore.'"

In response, library workers organized to shift the focus to issues of worker safety and well-being. It started with the #CloseTheLibraries campaign in early March, which raised critical awareness of the dangers facing library workers in the early days of the outbreak. That campaign soon expanded into two more: #ProtectLibraryWorkers, which advocated for the safety and fair treatment of library employees, and #LibraryLayoffs, which created a crowdsourced list of library layoffs and furloughs.

With a vaccine in sight, there is finally a light glinting at the end of the tunnel. But, as the rising case numbers suggest, it's going to be a long one. In 2021, as the extent of the economic damage done by the pandemic comes into focus, libraries—like bookstores and other small businesses—remain vulnerable.

"Let's be clear: when you hear there is a debate in Congress about whether to 'bail out' states and cities, that is a debate about whether your local library stays open, or closes," sociologist and bestselling author Eric Klinenberg told *PW* back in May. "And American voters are going to need to connect the dots, or we could soon find ourselves without many of the institutions that keep us stable."

THE BOOK BUSINESS WORKER OF THE FUTURE

Just as there would be no book business without words, there would be no book business without workers. This year, book business workers reminded their industry both of their import and their influence. What remains is to meet the standards they demanded and deserve: to pay them better; to hire them with a mind toward diversity, equity, and inclusion; and to provide them with more power to make a difference in the publishing process.

If this year has proven anything, it's that those who make up the backbone of the book business are more than up to the task. As long as they are adequately empowered to change the business for the better, better days for the business will always lay ahead.

*

A version of this article appeared in the 12/21/2020 issue of *Publishers Weekly* under the headline: PW's Person of the Year: The Book Business Worker.

ESO WON AND CROCKETT NAMED PW'S BOOKSTORE AND SALES REP OF THE YEAR

BY ALEX GREEN, WITH REPORTING BY EUGENE HOLLEY JR. AND CLAIRE KIRCH | MAY 25, 2021

*P*ublishers *Weekly* has named the L.A.-based indie bookstore Eso Won Books its Bookstore of the Year. Simon & Schuster sales rep Toi Crockett has been named *PW* Sales Rep of the Year. The announcement was made the afternoon of May 25 during the inaugural U.S. Book Show.

In nomination letters from their colleagues in the publishing industry, Eso Won and Crockett were hailed not only for a mastery of their respective trades but their tireless and successful work in support of the American literary scene and those who sustain it—from authors and booksellers to readers, schools, publishers, and literary organizations.

"It's truly a great honor to be named the bookstore of the year," said co-owner James Fugate who cofounded Eso Won with Tom Hamilton in 1990. The two accepted the award from their store's back office, surrounded by newly arrived books.

Crockett thanked her colleagues at S&S for their support. "It's absolutely a group effort and without them and my family and friends, I wouldn't be here," she said.

CULTIVATING READERS AND AUTHORS

Eso Won's place in the pantheon of American bookstores is difficult to over-state. The Black-owned independent bookstore has been a stop for authors including Spike Lee, Toni Morrison, and Isabel Wilkerson, and has made a practice of nurturing authors at the very beginning of their careers. In 1995, a young Barack Obama read at Eso Won from *Dreams from My Father* in front of an audience of five people. Obama never forgot Fugate's willingness to host him "back when nobody knew who I was, or could pronounce my name."

Obama has made the store a priority stop ever since, and Hamilton praised the example he has set. "The fact that he keeps reading and trying to learn, I think that's what you want to show the public," Hamilton said. "You keep learning all your life, [and] you set a great example."

The store's selection as Bookstore of the Year comes on the anniversary of the murder of George Floyd by Minneapolis police, to which Fugate referred in his remarks. "It is sort of bittersweet when you think that so many people saw what we have been talking about for years and years with the murder of George Floyd," he said. "But it made a tremendous difference at our store, and we thank you for honoring us this way."

Ellen Adler, publisher at the New Press, referred to the civil rights movement that followed Floyd's murder when she told *PW* that "Eso Won has long been one of the country's preeminent Black-owned bookstores and, of course, was indispensable this past year. But that's nothing new: it has long been indispensable—as those who are lucky enough to count it as their local bookstore or who have made the pilgrimage and had a visit well know."

Earlier this month, Fugate told *PW* how the bookstore has carved out its place at the heart of L.A.'s intellectual and literary community. "We have worked with local bookselling groups, been a part of the L.A. Times Book Fair, and done events to make sure that Eso Won was seen as not just a Black bookstore for Black people, but a Los Angeles bookstore in which everyone is welcome," Fugate said.

Fugate and Hamilton said they almost did not make it to 2021, thanking remainder dealer Powell's Books Chicago and the publishers Africa World Press, Black Classic Press, and Penguin Random House, all of which helped see the store through a challenging time 14 years ago. "We were really struggling, and those publishers really stuck by us," Fugate said.

A SALES REP TO FIGHT FOR

Simon & Schuster's reorganizations of its sales force in 2014 and 2018 sparked an outcry from bookstore accounts in the East. They did not want to lose Toi Crockett, a sales rep with 15 years of experience they said they could not bear to lose. While most of her accounts shifted west, a few stores' calls were heeded, with Crockett continuing to work with such East Coast stores as [Words] Bookstore in Maplewood, N.J.

In a *PW* profile earlier this month, the bookstore's managing principal, Jonah Zimiles, called Crockett, "consistently outstanding," and credited her honesty, integrity, and exceptional understanding of bookstores' needs in boosting the bottom line at [Words] through increased sales and savings. Barbara Peters, owner of the Poisoned Pen Bookstore in Scottsdale, Ariz., told *PW* that Crockett has "mastered the supply side," adding: "She catches my errors, she suggests opportunities, and she seems to work 18/7 days."

For Crockett, books run in the family. Her late grandfather owned a bookstore on Chicago's South Side, and she grew up in a house full of books. To this day, she said, she is "never not reading a book."

At the end of the awards presentation, there was even time for some conversation about books. Fugate said the book he was most looking forward to is Nikole Hannah-Jones's *The 1619 Project* (One World, Nov.), a book-length expansion of the *New York Times* project of the same name.

In signing off, Hamilton took a moment to thank the people who he said are most important in the ongoing success of the store, reserving his greatest praise for "all the great customers who have come in for many, many years."

③

THE BIG 5 U.S. PUBLISHERS
(SOON TO BE BIG 4)

PENGUIN RANDOM HOUSE

Penguin Random House is the international home to more than 300 editorially and creatively independent publishing imprints. Our mission is to ignite a universal passion for reading by creating books for everyone. We believe that books, and the stories and ideas they hold, have the unique capacity to connect us, change us, and carry us toward a better future for generations to come.

What We Do

Our dedicated team of publishing professionals is committed to helping authors realize their very best work and to finding innovative new ways of bringing stories and ideas to audiences worldwide. By leveraging our global reach, embracing new technologies, and collaborating with authors at every stage of the publishing process—from editorial and design, to sales and marketing, to production and distribution—we aim to provide them with the greatest platform possible. At the same time, we fiercely protect our authors' intellectual property and champion freedom of expression, ensuring that their voices carry beyond the page and into the folds of communities and societies around the globe.

Penguin Random House is the international home to nearly 275 editorially and creatively independent publishing imprints. Together, our imprints publish over 70,000 digital and 15,000 print titles annually, with more than 100,000 e-books available worldwide. Browse our divisions and imprints below to learn more about the distinct and diverse voices that make up Penguin Random House and help bring to life our authors' very best work.

PENGUIN RANDOM HOUSE AUDIO

As the premier publisher in the audiobook industry, Penguin Random House Audio is dedicated to producing top-quality fiction and nonfiction audiobooks written and read by the best in the business, including books by bestselling authors like Margaret

Atwood, Brené Brown, Ta-Nehisi Coates, Elizabeth Gilbert, John Grisham, George R. R. Martin, Toni Morrison, Celeste Ng, Delia Owens, Rick Riordan, Jacqueline Woodson, and Colson Whitehead, as well as Presidents Barack Obama, George W. Bush, and Bill Clinton, and First Lady Michelle Obama. Our audiobooks have won 17 GRAMMY Awards, 98 Audie Awards, and 23 Odyssey Awards and Honors. Random House Audio, Penguin Audio, Listening Library, and Books on Tape are imprints of the Penguin Random House Audio Publishing Group, a division of Penguin Random House LLC.

PENGUIN PUBLISHING GROUP
Avery

Avery is a mission-driven imprint dedicated to publishing groundbreaking nonfiction across a range of categories including health and wellness, accessible science and psychology, practical and inspirational self-help, and plant-based cookbooks. Our authors break news, disrupt paradigms, and help readers change and improve their lives.

Recent *New York Times* bestsellers include *Atomic Habits* by James Clear, *Unwinding Anxiety* by Jud Brewer, MD, *Nine Nasty Words* by John McWhorter, *Fiber Fueled* by Will Buscewicz, MD, *The Book of Joy* by Dalai Lama and the Archbishop Desmond Tutu, *Daring Greatly* by Brene Brown, and *Neurotribes* by Steve Silberman, and the *End of Alzheimer's* by Dale Bredesen, MD.

A longtime leader in the "food as medicine" movement, Avery has been at the fore of healthy living for decades. Our backlist features some of the bestselling health books of all time, including *Prescription for Nutritional Healing* by Phyllis Balch, *Prevent and Reverse Heart Disease* by Caldwell Esselstyn, and *The Wahls Protocol* by Terry Wahls, MD.

Berkley

An industry leader in commercial and genre fiction, Berkley has a rich tradition of discovering new talent, defining emerging trends, and building authors and series into global franchises. With Berkley's dedicated focus and guidance many bestselling authors have grown into international brand names, including Nora Roberts, William Gibson, Laurell K. Hamilton, Jim Butcher, and Charlaine Harris. We're proud to publish Jasmine Guillory, Jayne Ann Krentz, Karen White, Patricia Briggs, Christine Feehan, Mark Greaney, Susan Meissner, Kristan Higgins, and Chanel Cleeton, among others.

Our expertise in women's fiction, romance, science fiction/fantasy, and mystery/suspense makes us uniquely suited to introduce a new generation of popular novelists and to reinvigorate the publishing programs for established bestselling authors. Known for being at the forefront of trends, Berkley continues to develop authors and acquire books on the cutting edge of genre fiction.

Berkley's history of publishing in all formats and commitment to actively promoting the backlist means we remain focused on a book throughout its life . . . and on our author for an entire career.

Blue Rider Press

For more information, please visit www.penguin.com.

DAW

Founded in 1971 by veteran paperback editor Donald A. Wollheim, along with his wife, Elsie B. Wollheim, DAW Books was the first publishing company ever devoted exclusively to science fiction and fantasy. Now almost 50 years and two thousand titles later, DAW has a well-deserved reputation for discovering and publishing the hottest talents in the industry. Many stars of the science fiction and fantasy field made their debuts in the pages of a DAW book, including Patrick Rothfuss, Tad Williams, C.J. Cherryh, Mercedes Lackey, Kristen Britain, Melanie Rawn, C.S. Friedman, and Tanith Lee. Despite its high profile, DAW is still a small private company, owned exclusively by its publishers, Elizabeth R. Wollheim and Sheila E. Gilbert. Betsy and Sheila are strongly committed to discovering and nurturing new talent, and to keeping a personal "family" spirit at DAW—something they feel is all too rare in today's world of international conglomerate publishing.

DAW Books seeks to publish a wide range of voices and stories, because we believe that it is the duty of the science fiction and fantasy genres to be inclusive and representative of as many diverse viewpoints as possible.

Science fiction and fantasy have always been genres in which creators have infinite space to explore bold and inventive new ideas, while also reflecting the multiplicity of cultures, traditions, and identities of our own world. At DAW, we are proud of the work that our authors have already done to explore and celebrate diversity. We have a history of publishing feminist and LGBTQIA+ fiction, but we are always seeking to expand our own horizons, as well as those of our readers.

To this end, DAW is actively seeking new works of science fiction and fantasy written by and/or featuring people of color, Native people, disabled people, neurodiverse people, LGBTQIA+ people, and those from other underrepresented or marginalized communities.

For unagented manuscripts, please see our submission guidelines below. We encourage literary agents to reach out to our acquiring editors or email us at daw@penguinrandomhouse.com.

Submission Guidelines

DAW accepts unsolicited submissions of science fiction and fantasy novels. We cannot consider short stories, short story collections, novellas, or poetry. The average length of the novels we publish varies, but is almost never fewer than 80,000 words.

A literary agent is not required for submission. We will not consider manuscripts that are currently on submission to another publisher unless prior arrangements have been made with a literary agent. It may require three months or more for our editors to review a manuscript. If we take longer than three months to review your manuscript, we no longer require an exclusive submission.

At this time, we only accept electronic submissions through our Submittable page: submit.dawbooks.com.

Dutton

A small list with a huge audience, Dutton is a boutique imprint within the largest English-language publisher in the world. Publicity—and marketing—driven, its focused list of less than fifty books per year is half fiction and half nonfiction. Dutton's imprints include Caliber and Plume.

Dutton's roster of recent and upcoming bestselling and notable fiction authors includes Abi Daré (*The Girl with the Louding Voice*), Fiona Davis (*The Lions of Fifth Avenue* and *The Dollhouse*), Eric Jerome Dickey (*The Business of Lovers* and *Before We Were Wicked*), Joseph Finder (*House on Fire* and *Judgment*), Lisa Gardner (*When You See Me* and *Never Tell*), Hank Green (*A Beautifully Foolish Endeavor* and *An Absolutely Remarkable Thing*), Tami Hoag (*The Boy*), Jason Mott (*Hell of a Book*), Riley Sager (*Home Before Dark* and *Final Girls*), Adriana Trigiani, and Jonathan Tropper (*This Is Where I Leave You*), among others.

Recent and upcoming bestselling and notable nonfiction authors include Mark Adams (*Turn Right at Machu Picchu*), Drew Barrymore *(Wildflower)*, Sean Carroll (*Something Deeply Hidden* and *The Big Picture*), Robyn Crawford (*A Song for You*), Steven Gillon (*America's Reluctant Prince*), John Green (*The Anthropocene Reviewed),* Maria Goodavage (*Soldier Dogs* and *Top Dog*), Andre Iguodala (*The Sixth Man*), Daniel Levitin (*This Is Your Brain on Music, The Organized Mind* and *Successful Aging*), Nick Offerman (*The Greatest Love Story Ever Told, Good Clean Fun, Gumption* and *Paddle Your Own Canoe*), Mark Owen (*No Easy Day* and *No Hero*), Clinton Romesha (*Red Platoon*), and Craig Unger (*House of Trump, House of Putin*). The Caliber military history imprint includes Larry Alexander (*Bloody Ridge and Beyond*), Hugh Ambrose (*The Pacific*), Alex Kershaw (*The First Wave*), Adam Makos (*A Higher Call*), and Major Dick Winters (*Beyond Band of Brothers*).

History of Dutton

Edward Payson Dutton founded a bookselling firm in Boston in 1852, but it wasn't until 1864 that the eponymous E. P. Dutton & Co. began to publish books in earnest.

Its original focus was on religious titles, and the first bestseller was the two-volume *The Life of Christ* by Frederic W. Farrar, published in 1874.

In 1885, John Macrae began working at Dutton as an office boy; he would spend fifty-nine years with the company, rising in the ranks. He became President in 1923, and in 1928, he bought the publishing house and shared it with his two sons. During Macrae's tenure, E. P. Dutton published notable books such as *The Proper Bostonians* by Cleveland Amory, *Shakespeare of London* by Marchette Chute, *The Conquest of Everest* by Sir John Hunt, and *Bonjour Tristesse* by Françoise Sagan, as well as works by Lawrence Durrell, Milton Glaser, and Luigi Pirandello. The company went on to publish books by John Irving (*The World According to Garp*), James Beard, Peter Matthiessen, Jorge Luis Borges, Gavin Maxwell, Joyce Carol Oates, Gore Vidal, Gail Sheehy (*Passages*), Ayn Rand, and Mickey Spillane. Dutton joined the Penguin Publishing Group in 1986, and in 2015 became an imprint of the newly merged Penguin Random House.

F+W

F+W is a respected publisher of illustrated nonfiction books in art instruction, crafts, writing, genealogy, antiques and collectibles, and woodworking. It has a backlist of some 2,000 titles, which include such category leaders as *The Crystal Bible* and the *Writer's Market* series.

Putnam

For more than two decades, G.P. Putnam's Sons has led the publishing industry with more hardcover *New York Times* bestsellers than any other imprint. With its rich history of publishing established franchises and new talent, as well as award winners, with an unrivaled bestselling track record, Putnam continues to be one of the most respected and prestigious imprints in the industry.

Putnam's illustrious roster of bestselling fiction authors includes Megan Abbott, Cristina Alger, Ace Atkins, Chloe Benjamin, C.J. Box, Eleanor Brown, Tom Clancy, Robin Cook, Robert Crais, Clive Cussler, Jeffrey Deaver, Lyndsay Faye, Frederick Forsyth, Karen Joy Fowler, Sue Grafton, W.E.B. Griffin, Jan Karon, John Kenney, Philip Kerr, Frances Liardet, Delia Owens, Robert B. Parker, Nick Petrie, Kiley Reid, John Sandford, Jill Santopolo, Lisa Scottoline, M.O. Walsh, Stuart Woods, and Randy Wayne White. Among its distinguished nonfiction authors are Sophia Amoruso, Michelle Borba, Nikita Gill, Cathy Guisewite, Spencer Johnson, Hoda Kotb, Bobby Orr, Dolly Parton, and Eve Rodsky.

History of Putnam

In 1838 George Palmer Putnam, who began his career at a small New York bookstore, moved to London to establish the first American publishing branch of Wiley and Putnam in England. Ten years later, Putnam returned to the United States and the company became known as "George P. Putnam." In 1849, Putnam published the revised works of his close friend, American author and historian Washington Irving. One year later, the house published Susan Warner's *The Wide, Wide World*, which became known as America's first bestseller, selling forty thousand copies in the first few months, and eventually more than one million over its life. Over the next century and a half, Putnam published works by President Theodore Roosevelt (who worked for a year at the house before turning to politics), William Golding's *Lord of the Flies*, Norman Mailer's *Deer Park*, Vladimir Nabokov's *Lolita*, and Mario Puzo's *The Godfather*.

In 2013 G.P. Putnam's Sons celebrated its 175th year of publishing, culminating in an official "G.P. Putnam's Sons Day" declared by the New York City mayor's office on May 28, 2013. The history of Putnam is nearly as long as that of our country—and also as varied. The world is very different than it was in 1838, and the imprint is too, though many core values live on—an attendance to quality, honoring our authors, service to our readers, and of course a yen to create bestsellers. Putnam continues to hold industry dominance with an average of 30 to 35 *New York Times* bestsellers per year, applying aggressive marketing and sales acumen as it publishes established brands and new discoveries.

Penguin Books

In the early 1930s, most publishers thought the market for quality books was limited to a handful of elite readers. Allen Lane, then managing director of the Bodley Head, a British publishing company, had other ideas. While searching for something to read on his trip back to London after visiting Agatha Christie—and finding only popular magazines and reprints of Victorian novels in the railway station kiosk—he was convinced that there was a need for moderately priced editions of good-quality contemporary writing.

Setting up his business in the crypt of London's Trinity Church, he began to reprint quality fiction and nonfiction in low-cost paperback editions. In July 1935, he revolutionized publishing with the introduction of the first ten Penguin paperbacks. Within a year, more than one hundred titles were in print and one million Penguin books had been sold. In 1946, Allen Lane published classical scholar E.V. Rieu's translation of *The Odyssey* which went on to sell three million copies worldwide. That was the beginning of the Penguin Classics. Lane then asked Rieu to commission translations of other works for the new series. Little did Lane realize the impact his "paperback revolution" had on reading—today, almost 80 years later, more than 600 million paperbacks are sold annually worldwide. Now, Penguin and Penguin Classics titles carry the most recognized logo of any book publisher in the world, with a list as stimulating and diverse as readers themselves.

Penguin Classics

For more than seventy years, Penguin has been the leading publisher of classic literature in the English-speaking world. With more than 1,800 titles, Penguin Classics represents a global bookshelf of the best works throughout history and across genres and disciplines. Readers trust the series to provide authoritative texts enhanced by introductions and notes by distinguished scholars and contemporary authors, as well as quality translations by award-winning translators. Penguin Classics is proud to count among its authors John Steinbeck, Arthur Miller, Shirley Jackson, William Golding, Jorge Luis Borges, Pablo Neruda, R. K. Narayan, Ngũgĩ wa Thiong'o, Dorothy Parker, H. P. Lovecraft, Hannah Arendt, Jack Kerouac, and Graham Greene, and among its translators Robert Fagles, Lydia Davis, Edith Grossman, Royall Tyler, John Minford, and Richard Pevear and Larissa Volokhonsky.

Penguin Press

Penguin Press was founded in 2003 by Ann Godoff and launched its debut list in the Winter of 2004. Dedicated to publishing quality nonfiction and literary fiction, Penguin Press seeks to publish ideas that matter, storytelling that lasts, and books that don't just start conversations, but detonate them. Since its creation, they have published numerous *New York Times* and national bestsellers, won five National Book Critics Circle awards, one National Book Award, and five Pulitzer Prizes, most recently in 2016. Books from Penguin Press have also earned prestigious prizes and citations such as the James Beard Award, the Orange Prize, the Los Angeles Times Book Prize, the Man Asian Prize, the Mark Lynton History Prize, the Arthur Ross Book Award, the Sidney Hillman Foundation Award, and the Financial Times Goldman Sachs Business Book Award.

Penguin Press publishes a diverse list of historians, scientists, novelists, politicians, poets, artists, photographers, and some of the most respected thinkers in the world, including: Ron Chernow, Michael Pollan, Zadie Smith, Mary Oliver, Thomas Pynchon, Emily Oster, Ocean Vuong, Will Smith, Carlos Ruiz Zafon, David Axelrod, Maira Kalman, Steve Coll, Dan Barber, Daniel Yergin, Alexandra Fuller, Philip Gourevitch, Steve Inskeep, Liaquat Ahmed, Ingrid Betancourt, Roger Lowenstein, Joshua Foer, Franklin Foer, William Finnegan, Karl Ove Knausgaard, Mark Harris, John Lewis Gaddis, Tony Judt, Alan Greenspan, Al Gore, Aziz Ansari, Phil Jackson, Bryan Burrough, Errol Morris, Gordon S. Wood, Yvon Chouinard, Barton Gellman, Dave Isay, Jon Lee Anderson, Krista Tippett, Michael V. Hayden, Ottessa Moshfegh, Leon Panetta, Celeste Ng, Nate Silver, Pamela Druckerman, Alice Waters, Admiral James Stavridis, Richard Haass, Maria Konnikova, Carolyn Forche, Philip Rucker, Carol Leonnig, and Henry Louis Gates, Jr.

Plume

Founded in 1970, Plume is dedicated to finding and championing a select group of new nonfiction voices in the genres of pop culture, cultural and feminist statements, influencers in the food, wine, and lifestyle space, and humorous and whimsical gift books. Notable successes include *New York Times* bestsellers Hannah Shaw's *Tiny But Mighty*, Phoebe Robinson's *You Can't Touch My Hair*, *Trixie and Katya's Guide to Modern Womanhood*, Mamrie Hart's *You Deserve a Drink*, Louisa Thomsen Brits's *The Book of Hygge*, Anne Helen Petersen's *Too Fat, Too Slutty, Too Loud*, Marissa A. Ross's *Wine. All the Time*, Hugh Murphy's *T-Rex Trying*, and Kerby Rosanes's many coloring books, most recently *Worlds Within Worlds* and *Colormorphia*.

Plume was founded in 1970 as the trade paperback imprint of New American Library. In its early history, Plume focused primarily on nonfiction titles, publishing approximately 35 titles per year. In the early 1980s, as trade paperbacks were rapidly becoming the format of choice among a large segment of book buyers, Plume began expanding its reach, and became recognized as one of the preeminent trade paperback imprints. Today, Plume is part of the Dutton imprint, and publishes in all formats but continues a commitment to trade paperback excellence. Plume's perennial classics, many recently repackaged, include August Wilson's *Fences* and the rest of the Pittsburgh cycle, Danica McKellar's *Math Doesn't Suck*, Martin Duberman's *Stonewall*, Bernice McFadden's *Sugar*, Helena María Viramontes's *Under the Feet of Jesus*, and Brian Har and Vanessa Woods's *The Genius of Dogs*, as well as bestselling fiction from Julia Álvarez, Diane Johnson, and Joyce Carol Oates.

About Tiny Reparations Books:

Founded in 2020 by *New York Times* bestselling author, stand-up comedian, writer, actress, and producer Phoebe Robinson in partnership with her long-time publisher, Plume. Tiny Reparations Books is a highly curated imprint dedicated to publishing both literary fiction and nonfiction as well as essay collections that highlight and amplify unique and diverse voices.

Currently accepting submissions for books that will publish in 2021, 2022, and beyond, Tiny Reparations Books is committed to publishing complex, honest, and humorous work that not only reflects the current conversation but also pushes it forward.

Portfolio Penguin

Since Portfolio was founded by Adrian Zackheim in 2001, it has emerged as a major force in nonfiction publishing for ambitious people. We connect readers with powerful ideas that inform and improve their lives, within the workplace and beyond. Portfolio authors are innovators, entrepreneurs, and experts who aren't afraid to take risks and change the world, and who reflect the diversity of voices, identities, experiences, and goals we see in our community of readers. We strive to produce original books in fields such as technology, economics, entrepreneurship, biography, and investigative journalism, with a focus on educating and inspiring a new generation of innovative leaders.

Some of Portfolio's bestsellers include *Start with Why* by Simon Sinek, *#Girlboss* by Sophia Amoruso, *The Obstacle Is The Way* by Ryan Holiday, *Team of Teams* by General Stanley McChrystal, *This Is Marketing* by Seth Godin, *The Bullet Journal Method* by Ryder Carroll, *Brotopia* by Emily Chang, and *The Four* by Scott Galloway.

Riverhead Books

Founded in 1994, Riverhead Books is now well established as a publisher of bestselling literary fiction and quality nonfiction. Throughout its history, Riverhead has been dedicated to publishing extraordinary groundbreaking, unique writers. Riverhead's books and authors have won or been finalists for Pulitzer Prizes, National Book Awards, National Book Critic Circle Awards, MacArthur Genius Awards, Hurston Wright Legacy Awards, Dayton Literary Peace Prizes, and numerous other distinctions.

Sentinel

Sentinel is an imprint of Penguin Random House, the world's largest trade book publisher. Founded in 2003, we are an established publisher of critically acclaimed and bestselling nonfiction. Our mission is to provide a home for independent-minded thinkers and storytellers who challenge mainstream opinion, whether by looking to the past or reimagining the future.

TarcherPerigee

TarcherPerigee's mission is to publish books that empower readers to improve their lives. This is self-help for a new generation, encompassing mental health, creativity, mind/body/spirit, family and relationships, social justice, and gift/inspiration, along with creative journals for the inner explorer, and a few "odd ones" for the quirky teen in us all.

The TarcherPerigee list is rich with new and enduring bestsellers including *Set Boundaries, Find Peace* by Nedra Glover Tawwab, *Homecoming* by Dr. Thema Bryant, *Toxic Positivity* by Whitney Goodman, *Make Some Noise* by Andrea Owen, *Start Where You Are* by Meera Lee Patel, *The Artist's Way* by Julia Cameron, *Attached* by Amir Levine, *A Mind for Numbers* by Barbara Oakley, *Aware* by Daniel J. Siegel, *The Odd 1s Out* by James Rallison, *1 Page at a Time* by Adam J. Kurtz, and *Burn After Writing* by Sharon Jones.

We are committed to publishing fresh & diverse voices as well as new perspectives that expand and elevate the category of self-help and connect with readers where they are.

TarcherPerigee can be found online at @TarcherPerigee on Instagram, Twitter and Facebook.

Viking

Viking is a legendary imprint with a distinguished list of extraordinary writers in both fiction and nonfiction. The Viking Press was founded in New York City on March 1, 1925, by Harold K. Guinzburg and George S. Oppenheimer. When the Viking logo, a ship drawn by Rockwell Kent, was chosen as a symbol of enterprise, adventure, and exploration in publishing, the popular authors included Sherwood Anderson, James Joyce, and D.H. Lawrence. Today, Viking boasts bestselling fiction authors like Pulitzer Prize winner Geraldine Brooks, Tana French, Rebecca Makkai, Elizabeth George, Sue Monk Kidd, Jojo Moyes, National Book Award winner William Vollmann, and Nobel Prize winner J.M. Coetzee. In 1925, the Viking nonfiction writers included James Weldon Johnson and August Strindberg. Today, Viking's critically and commercially successful nonfiction authors include Nathaniel Philbrick, Daniel James Brown, Maria Shriver, Steven Pinker, Jen Sincero, Antony Beevor, and Timothy Keller. From past to present, Viking authors not only keep winning prestigious awards but also dominate bestseller lists across the world.

By the late '30s, legendary editor Pascal Coivi joined Viking, bringing John Steinbeck with him. After publishing Steinbeck's first novel, Viking brought out *The Grapes of Wrath* (1939), as well as the first American edition of James Joyce's *Finnegan's Wake* (1939) and Graham Greene's *Brighton Rock* (1938). Steinbeck and Greene would continue to publish with Viking for many years to come.

The 1950s saw Viking publish Arthur Miller's *Death of a Salesman* (1949) and *The Crucible* (1953). Saul Bellow began his long tenure at Viking with his third novel, *The Adventures of Augie March*. Jack Kerouac and Ken Kesey were at the center of a cultural shift that would occur in the 1960s and '70s. Viking also published William S. Burroughs, Hannah Arendt, Peter Matthiessen, Barbara Tuchman, Wallace Stegner, Octavio Paz, Kingsley Amis, Robert Coover, Lawrence Durrell, Frederick Forsyth, and Thomas Pynchon. In 1975, Viking was bought by Penguin Books and the company became known as Viking Penguin.

Viking Penguin's prestigious Booker Prize–winning authors include Roddy Doyle for his novel *Paddy Clarke Ha Ha Ha,* and J. M. Coetzee, who became the first author to win the prize twice, for *Life and Times of Michael K* in (1983) and *Disgrace* in (1999). Coetzee went on to win the Nobel Prize for Literature in 2003.

In recent years, Viking has been proud to publish *Eat, Pray, Love* and *The Signature of All Things* by Elizabeth Gilbert, *In the Heart of the Sea* and *Bunker Hill* by Nathaniel Philbrick, *Too Big to Fail* by Andrew Ross Sorkin, *The Rules of Civility* by Amor Towles, *Caleb's Crossing* by Geraldine Brooks, *Anticancer* by David Servan-Schreiber, *Faithful Place, The Likeness, Broken Harbor* and *The Secret Place* by Tana French, *A Delicate Truth* by John LeCarré, *Who Asked You?* by Terry McMillan, *The Boys in the Boat* by Daniel James Brown, and *A Tale for the Time Being* by Ruth Ozeki, *The Invention of Wings* by Sue Monk Kidd and *The Sense of Style* by Steven Pinker.

Viking has also had particular success in the high-end supernatural/alternate worlds category, making recent bestsellers out of novels by Deborah Harkness, Lev Grossman, Danielle Trussoni, and Jasper Fforde.

Viking currently publishes approximately 75 books a year. The Viking logotype continues to inspire its staff, its writers, and its audience. Readers, both American and international, appreciate Viking for its depth, its breadth, its uniqueness, and its originality. The adventure and spirit of Viking endure.

In January 2020, Viking, Penguin Books, and Pamela Dorman Books will debut a new publishing program that will live across all three imprints focused on inspiration, personal development, lifestyle, and healthy living—Viking Life, Penguin Life, and Pamela Dorman Books Life.

The editors in each imprint will acquire and publish the books in this program. The editorial, publicity, and marketing groups at all three imprints have been deeply involved in lifestyle and wellness books to great success, and the time has come to define these books within a program to better represent how important and success-ful these books are within Viking, Penguin, and Pamela Dorman Books. Building on our longtime success in the field—with category-defining bestsellers such as *The Body Keeps the Score* by Bessel van der Kolk, *Your Money or Your Life* by Vicki Robin, *Anticancer* by David Servan-Schreiber, *You Are a Badass Every Day* by Jen Sincero, *I've Been Thinking . . .* by Maria Shriver, and *A New Earth* by Eckhart Tolle—Viking Life and Pamela Dorman Books Life will feature authors with new theories, big ideas, and high-profile platforms, as well as practitioners and writers with credentials and first-hand experience in the areas of inspiration, self-help and personal growth, health and wellness, spirituality, home and nature, psychology, and personal finance. The program will launch with four books across three imprints and grow to fifteen books a year. Viking Life and Pamela Dorman Books Life will debut with:

- International supermodel, dietitian, and worldwide public speaker Maye Musk's *A Woman Makes a Plan*, in which Musk shares the personal stories and hard-earned lessons she's learned over the past seventy years, demonstrating that it's possible for all of us to have the life we want, at any age.

- Television and social media star Kristina Kuzmic's *Hold On, But Don't Hold Still*, an inspiring and hilarious memoir of how a single mother found the strength to transform her life and become the person—and parent—she could admire, sharing personal stories and revealing tips that empowered her.
- Japan's leading astrologer and founder of the Japanese Lunalogy Association, Keiko's *The Power Wish,* a bestselling Japanese guide to summoning the energy of the universe to make your dreams come true.
- Doctor and researcher Andreas Michalsen's *Healing Through Nutrition*, which unveils the latest extraordinary science around nutritional health and offers simple steps we can all take to change *what* and *how* we eat to reset our bodies, heal chronic illness, and live longer, healthier lives.
- Philippa Perry's *The Book You Wish Your Parents Had Read (and Your Children Will be Glad That You Did)*, a #1 international bestseller that "tells parents what it might mean to be a sane and emotionally intelligent parent" (Alain de Botton, author of *How Proust Can Change Your Life*).

PENGUIN YOUNG READERS GROUP
Dial Books for Young Readers
Heartwarming beauties, lively humor, conversation starters, much-needed mirrors: classics in the making.

Dial publishes books for two through teen that aim to entertain, enrich, and encourage our readers. We care deeply about amplifying underrepresented voices and about artistic excellence, and we're proud of the many awards that have highlighted our focus on these priorities. Recent awards include Newbery Honors for *Roller Girl* by Victoria Jamieson and *Fighting Words* and *The War that Saved My Life* by Kimberly Brubaker Bradley; the Printz Medal for *I'll Give You the Sun* by Jandy Nelson; a Geisel Honor for *The Bear in the Family* by Maya Tatsukawa; National Book Award Finalist *When Stars Are Scattered* by Victoria Jamieson and Omar Mohamed; the Morris and APALA Awards for *Darius the Great Is Not Okay* by Adib Khorram; a Caldecott Honor for *One Cool Friend* by Toni Buzzeo and David Small; a Coretta Scott King Honor for *How I Discovered Poetry* by Marilyn Nelson; a Sibert Honor for *Turning 15 on the Road to Freedom* by Lynda Blackmon Lowery; Schneider Family Book Award Honors for *Get a Grip, Vivy Cohen* by Sarah Kapit and *When Stars Are Scattered* by Victoria Jamieson and Omar Mohamed; Stonewall Honors for *Darius the Great Deserves Better* by Adib Khorram and *I'll Give You the Sun* by Jandy Nelson; the Sydney Taylor Book Award for *Dancing at the Pity Party* by Tyler Feder; and Boston Globe-Horn Book Award Honors for *Darius the Great Is Not Okay* by Adib Khorram, *The Best Man* by Richard Peck, and *It's Only Stanley* by Jon Agee.

Established in 1961, Dial Books for Young Readers was an innovator of titles for the very young, including the first quality board books published in the U.S., Rosemary Wells's Very First Books line, and some of the first wordless picture books, Mercer Mayer's *A Boy, A Dog, and a Frog* titles. More recently we continue to publish acclaimed and kid-popular picture books, such as the *New York Times* Bestsellers *Dragons Love Tacos* by Adam Rubin and Daniel Salmieri, *The Book With No Pictures* by B.J. Novak, *The Rabbit Listened* by Cori Doerrfeld, *If I Built a School* by Chris Van Dusen, and *Ordinary People Change the World* by Brad Meltzer and Christopher Eliopoulos.

Dial's history of publishing change-making books by Black, Indigenous, and creators of color includes such classic titles as Mildred D. Taylor's Newbery Medal winner *Roll of Thunder, Hear My Cry*, Julius Lester's Newbery Honor winner *To Be a Slave*, Leo and Diane Dillon's Caldecott Medal winner *Why Mosquitoes Buzz in People's Ears*, Jerry Pinkney's Caldecott Honor winner *The Talking Eggs* (written by Robert D. San Souci), and Joseph Bruchac's acclaimed *Code Talker*.

Other exemplary middle grade and young adult titles from Dial's backlist—all speaking to our "classics in the making" mission—include Richard Peck's Newbery Medal winner *A Year Down Yonder*, Ingrid Law's Newbery Honor Book *Savvy*, Holly Goldberg Sloan's *New York Times* Bestseller *Counting by 7s*, Rob Harrell's much-honored *Wink*, Jack Cheng's award-winning *See You in the Cosmos*, Nancy Werlin's National Book Award Finalist *The Rules of Survival*, Gabby Rivera's acclaimed *Juliet Takes a Breath*, and Cassie Beasley's *New York Times* Bestseller *Circus Mirandus*.

We do not accept any unsolicited submissions.

Dutton Children's Books

One of the oldest continually operating children's book publishers in the United States, Dutton Children's Books has existed for over 160 years with a mission of creating high-quality books that engage and transport young readers. Edward Payson Dutton opened the doors of his Boston bookshop in 1852 and shortly thereafter began to release "fresh and entertaining" books for young readers. Ingenuity has always marked Dutton's publishing, and in January 2011, Dutton transitioned into a boutique middle grade and YA imprint, which now publishes 10–15 hardcover titles per year.

Exceptional literary works with distinctive narrative voices and strong commercial appeal are the heart of the current Dutton list. Rich with history, Dutton is committed to the next generation of excellence with a small and highly curated list that never loses sight of audience. Our goals are to build authors for their careers and create lasting relationships with readers.

Our list is home to classic pillars of children's literature, like A.A. Milne and Ernest

H. Shepard's Winnie-the-Pooh books, Newbery medal–winning *The Westing Game* by Ellen Raskin and *My Side of the Mountain* by Jean Craighead George, and works by Paul O. Zelinsky. Continuing the tradition of literary excellence and distinctive voice, Dutton's current list includes authors such as John Green, Adam Gidwitz, E.K. Johnston, Stephanie Perkins, Ally Condie, Tahereh Mafi, Nina LaCour, and Ransom Riggs, to name a few.

Firebird

Firebird is a science fiction and fantasy imprint of Penguin Group (USA) Inc. specifically designed to appeal to both teenagers and adults. Launched in January 2002, it resulted directly from editorial director Sharyn November's ongoing work with teenagers in libraries, schools, and online; she soon discovered that some of her most avid readers were devoted to speculative fiction, and spent equal amounts of time in the teen fiction and adult genre sections.

Firebird anticipated the huge influx of genre titles into the mainstream. It's considered the premier crossover genre imprint, and November has been named a two-time World Fantasy Award Finalist in the Professional category.

Firebird titles are both paperback reprints and original hardcovers. Reprints are drawn from Penguin's children's and adult imprints; outside hardcover houses; and the backlists of the Firebird authors themselves. All have covers by adult genre artists, and feature short essays by their authors. Firebird's hardcover titles are especially unique to the imprint—short novels by some of the biggest names in the field, such as Diana Wynne Jones and Charles de Lint; and the award-winning original short story anthologies *Firebirds*, *Firebirds Rising* (a 2007 World Fantasy Award Finalist), and *Firebirds Soaring*. Overall, Firebird publishes between nine and twelve books each year. Firebird titles have won the World Fantasy Award, the Newbery Honor Medal, the National Book Award, the Locus Award, the Hugo Award, the Nebula Award, and the Philip K. Dick Award, and have been *New York Times* bestsellers.

Frederick Warne

Frederick Warne was founded in 1865 by a bookseller turned publisher who gave his own name to the firm. The new venture replaced an earlier association between Warne and George Routledge, who also went on to found his own publishing company.

During the second half of the nineteenth century, Warne's firm built a reputation based upon its children's list, publishing illustrated books by such well-known authors and artists as Edward Lea, Kate Greenaway, and Walter Crane. Toward the end of the century, Frederick Warne retired and handed the management of the business over to his three sons, Harold, Fruing, and Norman.

Warne was among the six publishers to whom Beatrix Potter submitted her first book, the story of a rabbit called Peter. As did the other five, Warne turned the proposal down. People at the company changed their minds, however, when they saw the privately printed edition of the book in 1901. They offered to publish it if Potter redid the illustrations in color. The next year, Warne published *The Tale of Peter Rabbit*, and by Christmas had sold 20,000 copies. Thus began a forty-year partnership that saw the publication of twenty-two additional Little Books and the development of a flourishing merchandising program, the first of its kind based on a children's book.

Beatrix Potter was engaged to marry Norman Warne, her editor and the youngest of the three Warne brothers. However, he died tragically in 1905, only a few weeks after their engagement. Harold, the eldest brother, took over as Potter's editor. She continued to produce one or two new Little Books each year for the next eight years until her marriage in 1913 to William Heelis. During the next few years Potter turned her attention to her farm work, but when the company fell on hard times and Harold was imprisoned for embezzlement, she came to the rescue with another new title to support "the old firm." Potter, who had no children, left the rights to her works to Warne upon her death. The company continued to publish them; it also brought out several biographical works about its most renowned author. Over the years, Warne also expanded its nonfiction publishing, issuing among others the world-famous Observer books.

In 1983, Frederick Warne was acquired by Penguin Books. As a division of Penguin, it began developing classic book-based children's character brands. Over the years Warne acquired a number of other classic book properties, including Cicely Mary Barker's Flower Fairies in 1989 and Eric Hill's Spot in 1993. The hallmarks of the publishing program are beautifully produced editions of the original works, plus lively spin-off books include treasuries, board books, novelty titles, 8x8s, and leveled readers. All of Beatrix Potter's original artwork was re-photographed in 1986, and the new editions launched in 1987 were recognized for the quality of reproduction. In 2012, the first new Peter Rabbit tale in 110 years was written by Oscar-winning actress Emma Thompson. This beautiful, critically acclaimed book, *The Further Tale of Peter Rabbit*, was followed up with *The Christmas Tale of Peter Rabbit* in 2013, also written by Emma Thompson. The Flower Fairies books were re-originated in 1990. And Eric Hill continues to create new Spot titles.

Today, Potter's characters and others appear on a host of products worldwide. They are featured in events around the globe, from the Peter Rabbit exhibitions of original artwork in such prestigious venues as the Musée D'Orsay (Paris), the Morgan Library and Museum (New York) and the Tate Gallery (London), as well as museums in Australia and Japan. Warne has commissioned an animated Peter Rabbit television show in conjunction with Nickelodeon and Silvergate Media. The episodes, which air daily on Nick Jr. in the U.S., and on the BBC in the U.K., are set in Potter's beloved

Lake District, ensuring that the real and natural worlds continue to provide a playground for the adventures of Peter Rabbit and his friends.

G.P. Putnam's Sons Books for Young Readers

G.P. Putnam's Sons Books for Young Readers publishes approximately seventy-five books a year for children, from lively, accessible picture books to some of today's strongest voices in fiction and nonfiction. We strive to publish a book for every reader (ages 0–18).

In 1838, George Palmer Putnam and John Wiley established the publishing house of Wiley & Putnam, which became known as G.P. Putnam's Sons in 1872. One of the first children's titles published by G.P. Putnam's Sons was the 1925 Newbery Honor book *Nicholas* by Anne Carroll Moore. In 1936, Putnam merged with Coward McCann, bringing *The Five Chinese Brothers* by Claire Hutchet Bishop, illustrated by Kurt Wiese, and *Millions of Cats* by Wanda Gág to the list. In 1980, Eric Hill's classic lift-the-flap *Where's Spot?* was published and became an international sensation. With the acquisition of Dodd, Mead's juvenile division in 1989, Putnam welcomed one of its brightest stars—Jan Brett, whose picture books annually climb to the top of the bestseller list. Putnam is also the proud publisher of the beloved *Goodnight, Gorilla* by Peggy Rathmann, published in 1994 and continuing to delight readers today.

Some of Putnam's recent successes include *Last Stop on Market Street* by Matt de la Peña, illustrated by Christian Robinson, winner of the Newbery Medal, the Caldecott Honor, and a Coretta Scott King Illustrator Honor book; *The Cat Man of Aleppo* by Irene Latham and Karim Shamsi-Basha, illustrated by Yuko Shimizu, winner of the Caldecott Honor; The Beautiful series by *New York Times* bestselling author Renée Ahdieh; *Frankly in Love* by *New York Times* bestselling author David Yoon; *The Queen's Assassin* by *New York Times* bestselling author Melissa de la Cruz; *The Downstairs Girl* by *New York Times* bestselling author Stacey Lee; the Iggy series by *New York Times* bestselling author Annie Barrows; The 5th Wave series by Rick Yancey, the Legend series by Marie Lu; and the E.B. White Award–winning The Apothecary series by Maile Meloy. Celebrated authors Betty G. Birney, Sherri L. Smith, Sheila O'Connor, Greg Howard, Katherine Arden, Deborah Marcero, and Kristin Levine have also garnered tremendous readership and critical praise.

We have a steady pipeline of exciting new books so please check back often to see our latest publications!

Kathy Dawson Books

Founded in 2014, Kathy Dawson Books is dedicated to middle grade and YA fiction across a variety of genres. In her more than twenty years at Penguin, Kathy Dawson has edited many bestselling award winners and her imprint will aim to continue in that tradition, publishing literary books with strong hooks and irresistible voices, with characters who live beyond the page.

She believes in celebrating the best examples of the form and strives to publish the authors who understand the craft on the deepest level, who can play with structure in unique ways, and who offer powerful voices from all walks of life—voices that have never been heard before.

That's the mission—to publish stellar novels, with unforgettable characters, for children and teens that expand their vision of the world, provide wisdom for life, celebrate the written word, and last for generations. Books that break the mold, and the heart, and still have tons of child and teen appeal.

You'll find reality-benders, survivor stories, unreliable narrators, speculative fiction, magical realism, humor, genre books with entry points for non-genre readers, all things apocalyptic, and brave authors in every sense of the word.

Kokila

Kokila (pronounced KO-ki-la) brings together an inclusive community of authors and illustrators, publishing professionals, and readers to examine and celebrate stories that reflect the richness of our world.

By centering stories from the margins and making space for storytellers to explore the full range of their experiences, we deliver books that inspire and entertain readers, and add nuance and depth to the way children and young adults see the world and their place in it.

Kokila will publish work for children and young adults across all formats and genres.

Submissions Window

We're excited to hear from new voices and accept unagented submissions that fit our mission from September 1st to December 1st of every year. Our priority will be with stories for and from marginalized communities.

Nancy Paulsen Books

Nancy Paulsen Books launched its first hardcover list in Fall 2011. The imprint publishes fifteen books a year and focuses on eye-opening, often funny picture books and fiction from diverse and distinct voices, especially stories that are inventive and emotionally satisfying. These are the kinds of books that are adopted by book clubs and that appear on state lists, generated by the votes of children.

Picture books include the *New York Times* bestsellers *The Day You Begin* by Jacqueline Woodson and Rafael López and *Miss Maple's Seeds* by Eliza Wheeler, as well as Coretta Scott King Honor winner *Each Kindness* by Jacqueline Woodson and

E.B. Lewis, *Leaves* and *Honey* by Caldecott Honor winner David Ezra Stein, and *I Hear A Pickle* by Rachel Isadora. Fiction includes National Book Award winner *Brown Girl Dreaming* by Jacqueline Woodson, Pura Belpré Award winner *Lucky Broken Girl* by Ruth Behar, and *New York Times* bestsellers *Fish in a Tree* by Lynda Mullaly Hunt and *Amal Unbound* by Aisha Saeed.

Penguin Workshop

At Penguin Workshop, we make great books for every kind of reader, from birth to age twelve. Here, you'll find unique board books, beautiful picture books, laugh-out-loud chapter books, the *New York Times* Bestselling Who HQ series, Mad Libs, and Penguin's award-winning leveled reader program.

We make readers laugh. We make readers feel accomplished. We make readers.

Penguin Young Readers

Penguin Young Readers unite the best authors, illustrators, and brands from the Penguin Young Readers Group under one umbrella. Including a comprehensive mix of esteemed authors, favorite characters, nonfiction, and licensed properties, Penguin Young Readers feature a traditional numbered leveling system, as well as the Guided Reading leveling system, to ensure quick recognition for educators, parents, and kids.

Penguin Young Readers Licenses

At Penguin Young Readers Licenses we offer the strongest collection of brands across TV, toy, online, gaming, and film. We celebrate the new and the nerdy, the retro and the reimagined; from pop culture to preschool, we're building on the best brands. We craft books that reinforce our identity, lead with innovation, and resonate with readers. Our Penguin Young Readers Licenses portfolio offers a book for every reader.

Philomel

Philomel was created in the early 1980s as part of World Publishing Books for Young People, by editor and publisher Ann Beneduce. The imprint was named after the nightingale, using a term that literally means "lover of song," which implied that these books would be lyrical, beautiful in concept and form, and fine enough to be celebrated as gifts. The early lists included such future classics as Eric Carle's *The Very Hungry Caterpillar*; Virginia Hamilton's Newbery Honor–winning *Sweet Whispers, Brother Rush*; and Ed Young's Caldecott Honor–winning *The Emperor and the Kite*.

In 1985 Patricia Lee Gauch took over as editor-in-chief of Philomel. Under her leadership, Philomel published Caldecott winners *Owl Moon* by Jane Yolen and John Schoenherr, *Lon Po Po* by Ed Young, and *So You Want to Be President?* by Judith St. George and David Small, as well as the soon-to-be iconic animal fantasy series

Redwall by Brian Jacques and the classic picture books of Patricia Polacco, including *Thank You, Mr. Falker*.

Michael Green took the helm as publisher in 2003. Under his direction, Philomel continued its tradition of producing quality picture books for the youngest of readers while simultaneously beginning to publish more commercial fiction for middle graders and young adults. The Philomel list grew to include #1 bestselling blockbuster *The Day the Crayons Quit* by Drew Daywalt and Oliver Jeffers; *Here We Are* by Oliver Jeffers; Anthony Horowitz's Alex Rider spy novels; Mike Lupica's sports-centered novels; and John Flanagan's Ranger's Apprentice epic. This quest to reach reluctant readers added to Philomel's initial mission and expanded the type of books published under the imprint's name.

In 2018, Kenneth Wright became Philomel's publisher and, working with Jill Santopolo as associate publisher, continued to expand the definition of a "Philomel book," publishing books meant to enlighten, inspire, and empower young readers. Philomel's list grew to include the #1 *New York Times* bestsellers *She Persisted* by Chelsea Clinton and Alexandra Boiger, *Just Ask* by Sonia Sotomayor and Rafael López, *Superheroes Are Everywhere* by Kamala Harris and Mechal Renee Roe, and *Girling Up: How to be Strong, Smart and Spectacular* by Mayim Bialik. These books, and many others, opened readers' eyes up to the world around them and the feelings inside them, and showed them how they could make a difference in the world.

With an editorial and design staff all working to create books that open minds and hearts and celebrate the potential in every reader, the Philomel list also includes, among others, Ruta Sepetys's award-winning and #1 *New York Times* bestselling historical fiction titles *Between Shades of Gray* and *Salt to the Sea*, and the award-winners *Mockingbird* by Kathryn Erskine, *A Tangle of Knots* by Lisa Graff, and *Audacity* by Melanie Crowder.

Whatever the genre, Philomel strives to foster a love of reading in children and young adults. It is an appreciation of story, of language, of books that can be read over and over and yet lose none of their magic that drives Philomel to make distinguished, meaningful books year after year.

Puffin Books

One of the most prestigious children's paperback publishers in the United States, Puffin Books was founded on a strong literary tradition and a commitment to publishing a successful mix of classic children's fiction and the best new literature. Over the years, Puffin has transformed from a small, yet distinguished paperback house, into one of the largest, most diverse, and successful children's publishers in business, publishing everything from picture books to groundbreaking middle grade and teen fiction.

Puffin began in England in 1941 when Allen Lane, publisher of Penguin Books, and Noel Carrington, a publisher of natural history books, teamed up to produce the first line of quality paperbacks for children. Puffin USA didn't get its start until 1978, when Penguin acquired Viking Kestrel and Viking's paperback line, Seafarer Books.

During the 1980s, Puffin Books initiated the period of remarkable growth that has become its hallmark. Puffin Books produced quality paperback editions of Viking titles, aggressively acquired titles for paperback publication from outside publishing houses, reprinted Puffin UK titles, and maintained a backlist packed with award-winning children's literature including Robert McCloskey's Caldecott Medal winner *Make Way For Ducklings*, Ludwig Bemelmans's beloved Caldecott Honor book *Madeline*, and Don Freeman's classic *Corduroy*.

In 1988, Penguin merged with New American Library and Dutton, creating a new powerhouse Puffin list. Incorporating titles from three hardcover imprints, Viking Children's Books, Dial Books for Young Readers, and Dutton Children's Books, Puffin drew on the strength of its expanded list to launch a major joint venture with Puffin UK, a newly redesigned Puffin Classics series. The 1996 merger of Penguin Books with the Putnam Berkley Group, and the subsequent incorporation of Putnam's PaperStar imprint into Puffin, cemented Puffin's longstanding position as one of the leading children's paperback publishers in the business.

With an ever-expanding list built on the winning combination of literary classics and appealing commercial fiction, Puffin Books remains a children's books innovator and perennial reader favorite. In addition to publishing the quality literary fiction that has provided such a strong foundation over the years, Puffin has started several original series with broad commercial appeal.

Publishing approximately 150 titles a year, Puffin is able to deliver the finest in every age group: picture books for young children, the best in historical and contemporary fiction for middle graders, and critically-acclaimed novels for older readers. Where else can one find beautifully bound classics like *The Wind in the Willows* and *Black Beauty* next to literary triumphs like Ruta Sepetys's *Between Shades of Gray*? Or the bestselling *Stranded* series by Jeff Probst beside moving novels such as S.E. Hinton's *The Outsiders*?

Puffin has published *New York Times* bestsellers such as *If I Stay* by Gayle Forman, the *Matched* trilogy by Ally Condie, the *Legend* trilogy by Marie Lu, and the acclaimed works of John Green. Puffin is also recognized for its award-winning fiction, which includes *Roll of Thunder, Hear My Cry* by Mildred D. Taylor (Newbery Honor Winner), *The Westing Game* by Ellen Raskin (Newbery Honor Winner), *Jerk, California* by Jonathan Friesen (Schneider Family Book Award), and *Three Times Lucky* by Sheila Turnage (Newbery Honor). This imprint is no stranger to accolades.

For the middle grade reader, Puffin splashes on to the scene with these great titles.

The classic and classically hilarious Judy Blume has landed a home for her bestselling Fudge series, including *Double Fudge*, *Superfudge*, *Otherwise Known as Sheila the Great*, and *Tales of a Fourth Grade Nothing*, in Puffin. Mike Lupica's series of middle grade sports fiction has been a long-time favorite, and Gennifer Choldenko's Newbery Honor book *Al Capone Does My Shirts* has become a lauded contemporary classic.

A highlight of Puffin's middle grade series is Puffin Modern Classics, the home to award-winning contemporary classics, including *A Long Way from Chicago*, *Summer of the Swans*, and *Sadako and the Thousand Paper Cranes*. Puffin prides itself on constantly reinventing classics to reach new generations of readers. The *Puffin Chalk* update to the Classics line, for example, combines time-honored stories with energetic, modernized artwork that echoes the whimsy of childhood.

Puffin's diverse range of nonfiction combines reliable classics that continue to engage and inform—such as Ruth Heller's range of science- and literature-savvy paperbacks, or Jean Fritz's creative approach to historical figures—with an ever-expanding list of new and noteworthy titles that are perfect for the classroom—Ilene Cooper's *Jack: The Early Years of John F. Kennedy* brings a new perspective to the young life of one of our most influential leaders. These titles fit in seamlessly with Common Core requirements while maintaining a rigorous standard of quality.

Middle graders and teen readers alike devour books by Puffin's fiction authors who include *Charlie and the Chocolate Factory* author Roald Dahl, *The Cat Ate My Gymsuit* author and Amber Brown creator Paula Danziger, award-winning historical fiction author Jean Fritz, *Travel Team*'s Mike Lupica, *Pippi Longstocking* creator Astrid Lindgren, *Lyddie*'s Katherine Paterson, Newbery Honor and Newbery Medal winner Richard Peck, *Roll of Thunder, Hear My Cry*'s author, Mildred D. Taylor, and multiple award-winning author Jacqueline Woodson.

Razorbill

Razorbill, an imprint of Penguin Random House, is committed to taking risks and exploring new ways to tell stories.

Razorbill is home to a broad-ranging young adult hardcover fiction list that includes Jay Asher's debut novel, *Thirteen Reasons Why*, a #1 and perennial *New York Times* bestseller and multiple award winner that has been published in thirty-five languages, as well as his latest novel, *What Light*, and the instant *New York Times* bestseller *An Ember in the Ashes*, an epic high-fantasy debut by Sabaa Tahir, and its #1 bestselling sequel, *A Torch Against the Night*. Razorbill's popular series titles include *Falling Kingdoms* by *New York Times* bestselling author Morgan Rhodes, *Zodiac* by Romina Russell, *The Merciless* by Danielle Vega, and Richelle Mead's #1 internationally bestselling *Vampire Academy*, *Bloodlines*, and *The Glittering Court*.

Razorbill's middle grade titles include *Ratscalibur* by *New York Times* bestselling author Josh Lieb, which the *New York Times* called "a witty mash-up of favorite fantasy motifs," *The Creature Department*, a collaboration between award-winning author Robert Paul Weston and Framestore, the Academy Award–winning visual effects company known for its groundbreaking work on *Gravity* and the Harry Potter film franchise, and the popular Shark Wars series by EJ Altbacker.

Razorbill also publishes nonfiction, including the *New York Times* bestselling *Sneakers* by Rodrigo Corral, Alex French, and Howie Khan, *Still Here*, a personal diary curated by Rowan Blanchard, the *Rookie Yearbooks*, which are anthologies featuring the best content from RookieMag.com, curated by Rookie founder and editor Tavi Gevinson, *Night Shift*, a picture book memoir by Debi Gliori, *The Teen Vogue Handbook: An Insider's Guide to Careers in Fashion*, and the *New York Times* bestselling advice book *Classy* by Derek Blasberg.

Rise X Penguin Workshop

Our mission: To engage, empower, and evolve the youngest readers (ages 0–5) with authentic, relevant, and elegant books.

Publishing books for babies, toddlers, and preschoolers is an immense responsibility. At RISE, we have the power to inspire our readers to become a generation of empowered, confident, self-loving, empathetic, and resilient people . . . all through the power of exposure. Every book we publish serves to help children feel smart, capable, important, safe, and loved.

Our authors are experts in their subjects, either lived or learned, writing in language that is age-specific. Our illustrators are artists and creators in their own right, making art infused with experience, passion, and purpose. Together, we create books with imagery and information that authentically interest our readers and grow them into people who love books and love themselves. What could be more important than this?

Follow us on Instagram @risebooks.

Submission guidelines

At RISE, we welcome any submission, text or art, that sits within our mission to empower the youngest readers, ages 0–5. We accept submissions from agents, previously published authors and illustrators, and aspiring authors and illustrators.

Established or aspiring authors, please send work that you create from a place of expertise, lived or learned.

Established or aspiring illustrators, please send samples that show your voice and feel like part of a larger idea or body of work. Concept-driven passion projects encouraged. No prior experience in the 0–5 realm is necessary, just a spark of relevancy and applicability to our mission.

For those who do not have an existing contact/relationship with someone at RISE or Penguin Workshop, please send your submission to: penguinworkshopsubmissions@PRH.com. We will do our best to get back to you, but based on volume, we unfortunately cannot guarantee a response to every submission.

Speak

Puffin Books launched Speak, a new imprint aimed at teens, in 2002. Bringing classic and cutting edge fiction to the forefront of the paperback list, Speak provides a dedicated home for older readers. With a range of the quality fiction and nonfiction Puffin is known for, Speak combines contemporary novels featuring characters with whom readers can identify, historical fiction that transports the reader to new worlds, smart, original series fiction, and a mix of award-winning authors and bright new talent. In Speak, everyone has a voice.

Everything from National Book Awards to Printz Awards to Coretta Scott King Awards and Finalists can be found on the list. The Speak list highlights these strong titles year after year. Some of our gems are Printz Medal winner *Looking for Alaska* by John Green, Printz Honor book *Fat Kid Rules the World* by K.L. Going, and Carnegie Medal Nominee *Between Shades of Gray* by Ruta Sepetys. Speak has also launched a number of original series, including the Sweep books, which are attracting fans left and right.

Speak caters to both contemporary favorites and classics that last a lifetime, ranging from poignant John Green titles—such as *Paper Towns* and *An Abundance of Katherines*—to S.E. Hinton's *The Outsiders*; the groundbreaking story that paved the way for countless young adult novels thereafter. Gripping nonfiction titles such as Christopher Award–winning *Soldier X* by Don L. Wulffson can also be found on Speak's list.

Speak also publishes books with wide commercial appeal. Authors Laurie Halse Anderson and Maureen Johnson find their names on several Speak titles, along with *Nightshade*'s Andrea Cremer, *What Happened to Goodbye*'s Sarah Dessen, and Speak original author Robin Palmer. Puffin is also the paperback home for Marie Lu's Legend series. Powerful, earnest young adult stories find great success in calling Speak—and Puffin in its entirety—a home for boundless, daring, and inspiring titles.

Viking Children's Books

Viking Children's Books was founded in 1933 as a department of the prestigious Viking Press, known for publishing such authors as Sherwood Anderson, James Joyce, John Steinbeck, and Rebecca West. The first editor of Junior Books, as it was known, was May Massee, who soon established herself as a leader in children's books. Her first list included *The Story About Ping*, and under her stewardship such classics as *Make Way for Ducklings*, *The Story of Ferdinand*, *The Twenty-one Balloons*, *Pippi Longstocking*, and the Madeline books were published.

Ms. Massee was succeeded by Annis Duff, Velma V. Varner, George Nicholson, Linda Zuckerman, Regina Hayes, and Kenneth Wright—seven publishers in seventy-five years.

Throughout Viking's history, it has been known for innovation as well as for a dedication to quality that has created the rich backlist the house enjoys. Viking has published ten Newbery Medal winners and ten Caldecott Medal winners, more than any other publishing house, as well as twenty-seven Newbery Honor books, thirty-three Caldecott Honor books, and an American Book Award winner. Sixteen Viking books have been recognized as *New York Times* Best Illustrated Books. Two Viking books have received the Coretta Scott King Award, three have been Batcheldor Honor books, five have received the Christopher Medal, and two authors, S.E. Hinton and Richard Peck, have received the Margaret A. Edwards Award for bodies of work that included Viking titles. Among the groundbreaking titles published by Viking are *The Outsiders* (1969), still the best-selling young adult book ever published; *The Snowy Day* (1963), which brought multicultural books mainstream recognition; and *The Stinky Cheese Man* (1992), widely hailed for its innovative design. Two Viking titles, *Book of the Lion* by Michael Cadnum (2000) and *This Land Was Made for You and Me* by Elizabeth Partridge (2002) were chosen as finalists for the National Book Award. In 2006, *John Lennon: All I Want is the Truth* by Elizabeth Partridge was named a Michael L. Prinz Honor Book.

In 1985, Viking won the Carey Thomas Award for creative publishing, the first children's list to receive this award. Viking has been nominated twice for the LMP Award for Best Children's list.

Viking publishes approximately sixty titles per year, ranging from books for very young children such as board and lift-the-flap books to sophisticated fiction and nonfiction for teenagers.

The current Viking list is known for such classic characters as Madeline, Corduroy, Pippi Longstocking, Roald Dahl's Matilda, Rosemary Wells's Max & Ruby, The Stinky Cheese Man, Llama Llama, Angelina Ballerina, Cam Jansen, and Froggy. Viking publishes the entire works of Ezra Jack Keats, including *The Snowy Day*, winner of the Caldecott Medal, and Robert McCloskey, author of *Make Way for Ducklings*, a Caldecott winner, and *Homer Price*. In addition, Viking is the publisher of several bestselling YA authors, including Laurie Halse Anderson and Sarah Dessen.

DK

We believe in the power of discovery. That's why we create books for everyone that explore ideas and nurture curiosity about the world we live in.

From first words to the Big Bang, from the wonders of nature to city adventures, you will find expert knowledge, hours of fun and endless inspiration in the pages of our books.

Our divisions:

Life
Gardening, food, well-being and hobbies. Advice and inspiration to give you a helping hand.

Travel
Get closer to your destination with our expert advice, beautiful photographs and detailed illustrations.

Children's
Pages to pore over for every child, from babies to starting school and beyond. We make learning fun.

Knowledge
Feed a thirst for knowledge with our popular reference books covering every topic under the sun.

Licensing
Favorite characters are brought to life from the worlds of film, TV, games and beyond.

DK around the world
With over 45 years of publishing experience, we sell to every corner of the globe and in 63 languages. We have employees worldwide with offices in London, New York, Toronto, Indianapolis, Delhi, Melbourne, Munich, Madrid, Beijing, and Jiangmen.

RANDOM HOUSE
Ballantine
Ballantine Books was established in 1952 by the legendary paperback pioneers Ian and Betty Ballantine, publishing original works of both award-winning fiction and nonfiction in both hardcover and paperback formats under one umbrella, including such bestselling novelists as Jodi Picoult, Emily Giffin, Debbie Macomber, Jonathan Kellerman, Tess Gerritsen, Justin Cronin, Jeff Shaara, Alison Weir, and Paula McLain as well as bestselling nonfiction authors including Bob Harper, David Zinczenko, and Kelly Corrigan.

Bantam

Bantam Books was established in 1945 by Walter B. Pitkin, Jr., Sidney B. Kramer, and Ian and Betty Ballantine as an exclusively mass-market paperback reprint publishing house before it began publishing other original works of fiction and nonfiction in all formats. The Bantam Books imprint boasts the entire Louis L'Amour library as well the blockbuster novelists Janet Evanovich, George R. R. Martin, and Dean Koontz; and also includes the work of Professor Stephen Hawking and recent Pulitzer Prize winner Dan Fagin.

Delacorte Press

Delacorte Press was founded in 1921 by George T. Delacorte, Jr., and first published pulp magazines, detective stories and articles about the movies before it too became a full-service house, publishing original works of fiction in all formats. The complete body of work of Danielle Steel is published under the Delacorte imprimatur. Among the many other Delacorte authors are the internationally bestselling Diana Gabaldon, Karin Slaughter, and Lee Child.

Del Rey

Del Rey Books began as an imprint of Ballantine Books in 1977. Founded by editors Judy-Lynn and Lester del Rey, Del Rey is now one of the world's foremost publishers of science fiction, fantasy, and speculative fiction, as well as media and pop culture titles.

Del Rey/LucasBooks

Del Rey/LucasBooks was the original publisher for *Star Wars* books beginning with the very first *Star Wars* novelization, which came out in 1976, the year before the classic film. In addition to the movie novelizations, Del Rey has published hundreds of original *Star Wars* novels and nonfiction titles under the LucasBooks imprint.

The Dial Press

The Dial Press was established in 1923 by Scofield Thayer, the editor and owner of *The Dial* literary magazine. Over the years, its stable of esteemed authors has included Isabel Allende, James Baldwin, Allegra Goodman, Elizabeth McCracken, Michael Paterniti, Tom Rachman, and Kurt Vonnegut. The Dial Press publishes books driven by the heart: emotionally affecting works of memoir, narrative nonfiction, and fiction that tell stories of self-revelation, help us connect with others, and offer fresh, intimate, and inspiring perspectives.

Hogarth

Drawing on its inspiration from Virginia and Leonard Woolf's original Hogarth Press founded in 1917, Hogarth re-launched in 2012 as a partnership between Chatto & Windus in the U.K. and Crown in the U.S. It is a home for a new generation of literary talent, an adventurous fiction imprint with an accent on the pleasures of storytelling and a broad awareness of the world. Its authors include NBCC award-winner Anthony Marra; *New York Times* bestselling Dutch novelist Herman Koch; Cynthia Bond, whose novel was an Oprah's Book Club 2.0 selection; Booker Prize winner Howard Jacobson; Booker International Prize winner Han Kang; Baileys Prize winner Eimear McBride; Granta's Best Young British Novelist Jenni Fagan; Whitbread nominee and international bestseller Michel Faber; and other fresh new writers both in English and in translation, whose work promises to define contemporary fiction in the years to come. In October 2015 Hogarth launched the Hogarth Shakespeare program, to coincide with the 400th anniversary of Shakespeare's death. The project sees the Bard's plays retold by acclaimed, bestselling novelists and brought to life for a contemporary readership. Hogarth Shakespeare authors include Jeanette Winterson, Anne Tyler, Gillian Flynn, Margaret Atwood, Jo Nesbø, Edward St. Aubyn, Howard Jacobson, and Tracy Chevalier.

Modern Library

The Modern Library has been an iconic publisher of American and international classics since its founding in 1917 by Boni and Liveright and subsequent purchase in 1925 by Bennett Cerf and Donald Klopfer, who two years later would found Random House. Over the years it has published works from a diverse range of writers, from St. Augustine, Plutarch, Shakespeare, Jane Austen, and Proust to Hemingway, Salinger, Didion, Peter Matthiessen, and Jane Jacobs. The Modern Library's lists of the 100 Best Novels (1998) and 100 Best Works of Non-fiction (1999) continue to guide readers and create discussion.

One World

One World is a home for authors who seek to challenge the status quo, subvert dominant narratives, and give us new language to understand our past, present, and future. One World writers represent voices from across the spectrum of humanity telling critical, universally important, and compelling stories about a changing world.

Random House

Random House was founded in 1927 when, two years after purchasing The Modern Library line of literary classics, Bennett Cerf and Donald Klopfer decided to publish other books "at random." With a distinguished history of publishing award-winning and bestselling books, Random House's list of authors includes Norman Mailer, Truman Capote, Laura Hillenbrand, Maya Angelou, Jon Meacham, William

Faulkner, David Mitchell, Anna Quindlen, Elizabeth Strout, Salman Rushdie, and George Saunders.

ADDITIONAL IMPRINTS
4 Color Books

4 Color Books collaborates with the most forward-thinking and groundbreaking BIPOC chefs, writers, artists, activists, and innovators to craft visually stunning nonfiction books that inspire readers and give rise to a more healthy, just, and sustainable world for all. 4 Color's flagship publication is *Black Food: Stories, Art, and Recipes from Across the African Diaspora* (October 2021), curated and edited by Bryant Terry, the founder and editor-in-chief of 4 Color Books.

Clarkson Potter

Clarkson Potter is the only dedicated lifestyle group within Penguin Random House. Founded in 1959, we are home to a community of award-winning and bestselling chefs, cooks, designers, artists, and writers—visionaries who seek to entertain, engage, and teach.

Convergent Books

Convergent seeks out diverse viewpoints and honest conversation that shed light on the defining challenges facing people of faith today. Our books help readers ask important questions, find paths forward in disagreement, and shape the way faith is expressed in the modern world.

Crown

Established in 1933, the Crown imprint is a leading publisher of bestselling fiction and critically acclaimed narrative nonfiction in categories that include biography and memoir, history, science, politics, and current events.

Crown Archetype

Crown Archetype is a hardcover publisher of leading voices in the pop-culture conversation. We showcase unique points of view and storytelling, from actors and comedians to athletes and coaches to musicians and performance artists.

Crown Forum

Founded in 2002, Crown Forum began as a way to inform and contribute to the national dialogue and political discourse. It is now one of the leading publishers of politically conservative authors and points of view.

Currency

Currency is an exciting new imprint dedicated to publishing thought leaders across a range of creative disciplines to help us navigate and succeed in an uncertain and rapidly evolving world. With a primary focus on business, innovation, entrepreneurship, finance, economics, organizational & societal transformation, it provides a platform for relevant, inspiring voices who challenge established boundaries and orthodoxies, encourage conversation, and offer new perspectives on building lives with meaning and purpose.

Harmony Books

Harmony Books is dedicated to inspiring and helping readers to achieve personal transformation and well-being in all facets of their lives. Publishing books that offer unique approaches to health and wellness, lifestyle, diet, self-improvement, relationships, parenting and spirituality, Harmony guides readers to become their best selves both inside and out.

Image Catholic Books

Image Books (formerly Doubleday Religion) has been dedicated to publishing solid, unswerving, admirable Catholic resources for over fifty years. Covering a multitude of topics by respected and bestselling authors, there is something for everyone. The quality of books published by Image is unparalleled and each read is sure to deepen even the most devout Catholic's faith.

Lorena Jones

Lorena Jones Books, an imprint of Ten Speed Press, was founded in 2015 and is committed to publishing the best talent in highly creative and enduring ways. We publish illustrated and non-illustrated books in the areas of cooking, work life, and health.

Multnomah

Multnomah publishes books that proclaim the Gospel, equip followers of Jesus to make disciples, and invite readers into a deeper relationship with God. We seek timeless messages from Christian voices that challenge readers to approach life from a biblical perspective.

Rodale Books

Rodale Books is the premier destination for the best in wellness content. Our mission, to help people improve their lives, is the lens through which we acquire books across the entire spectrum of wellness—from diet and fitness, to business and self-help, to cooking and lifestyle. Acquired by Penguin Random House in 2018,

Rodale Books has been publishing award-winning, bestselling books for more than 75 years.

Ten Speed Press
Based on the West Coast, Ten Speed Press spent decades as an independent publisher before becoming part of the Crown Publishing Group in 2009. Known for creating beautiful illustrated books with innovative design and award-winning content, Ten Speed actively seeks out new and established authors who are authorities and taste-makers in the world of food, drink, pop culture, graphic novels, illustration, design, reference, gardening, and health.

WaterBrook
WaterBrook publishes books that inspire readers to find rich, spiritual purpose in their daily lives. We seek creative approaches and innovative messages that draw on the Bible, experiential learning, story, and practical guidance to help readers thrive as they follow Jesus amid the complexities and opportunities of life today.

Watson-Guptill
Founded in 1937, and now an imprint of Ten Speed Press, Watson-Guptill has a storied legacy of publishing hard-working and influential illustrated art books. We seek out respected authorities who instruct and inspire artists in a wide range of art, craft, design, and photography subjects.

KNOPF DOUBLEDAY PUBLISHING GROUP
Alfred A. Knopf
Alfred A. Knopf was founded in 1915 and has long been known as a publisher of distinguished hardcover fiction and nonfiction. Its list of authors includes Toni Morrison, John Updike, Cormac McCarthy, Alice Munro, Anne Rice, Anne Tyler, Jane Smiley, Richard Ford, Julia Child, Peter Carey, Kazuo Ishiguro, and Michael Ondaatje, as well as such classic writers as Thomas Mann, Willa Cather, John Hersey, and John Cheever.

Doubleday
Doubleday was founded in 1897, when Frank Nelson Doubleday formed Doubleday & McClure Company in partnership with magazine publisher Samuel McClure. Among their first bestsellers was *The Day's Work* by Rudyard Kipling. Today, Doubleday and its Nan A. Talese imprint publish an array of commercial fiction, literary fiction and serious nonfiction titles. Among the bestselling and prize-winning authors published by Doubleday are Anne Applebaum, Pat Barker, Dan Brown, Bill Bryson, Lincoln Child, George Friedman, David Grann, John Grisham, Mark Haddon, Heidi Julavits,

Michio Kaku, Jon Krakauer, Jonathan Lethem, Candice Millard, Chuck Palahniuk, Edward Rutherfurd, Hampton Sides, Jeffrey Toobin, and Colson Whitehead. Nan A. Talese authors include Peter Ackroyd, Margaret Atwood, Thomas Cahill, Pat Conroy, Valerie Martin, and Ian McEwan.

Pantheon

Pantheon's founder, Kurt Wolff, was born in Germany in 1887 to a Catholic father and a Jewish mother. He studied German literature and in 1913, founded Kurt Wolff Verlag. Among the authors he published were Franz Kafka, Franz Werfel, and in German translation, Emile Zola, Maxim Gorky, Anton Chekhov, and Sinclair Lewis. Admiring the way young up-and- coming American publishers such as Alfred A. Knopf and Random House's Bennett Cerf employed contemporary, cutting-edge artists for text design, book jackets, and newspaper advertising, he did likewise, for which he was criticized by other German publishers.

The deteriorating German economic conditions forced Wolff to close Kurt Wolff Verlag in 1930, and the changing political climate resulted in his decision to emigrate in 1933. He spent several years in France and then in Italy, where he became publishers of Pantheon Case Editrice, which he had co-founded in 1924. Wolff and his wife, Helen, emigrated to the United States in 1941. Within a year, they founded Pantheon Books in a one-room office in lower Manhattan. Wolff specialized in publishing literature in translation by authors such as Hermann Broch, Giuseppe di Lampedusa, Boris Pasternak, Karl Jung and Gunter Grass. He also published important works on art history. In 1961, Bennett Cerf bought Pantheon and it became a part of Random House. Today, Pantheon is part of the Knopf Doubleday Publishing Group and continues to publish world-class literature. Pantheon's authors include Julia Glass, James Gleick, Ha Jin, Anne Morrow Lindbergh, Alexander McCall Smith, Marjane Satrapi, Art Spiegelman, and Studs Terkel.

Schocken

Schocken Books, founded by Salman Schocken in Germany in 1931, began publishing in the United States in 1945 and became part of Random House, Inc., in 1987. Building upon its historic commitment to publishing Judaica, Schocken's authors include S.Y. Agnon, Sholem Aleichem, Aharon Appelfeld, Martin Buber, Tikva Frymer-Kensky, Franz Kafka, Francine Klagsbrun, Harold S. Kushner, Joan Nathan, Rabbi Jonathan Sacks, Gershom Scholem, Rabbi Adin Steinsaltz, Elie Wiesel, Simon Wiesenthal, and Dr. Avivah Zornberg.

Vintage Books

Vintage Books was founded in 1954 by Alfred A. Knopf as a trade paperback home to its authors. Its publishing list includes a wide range, from the most influential works of world literature to cutting edge contemporary fiction and distinguished nonfiction. As the continuous publisher of important writers including William Faulkner, Vladimir Nabokov, Albert Camus, Ralph Ellison, Dashiell Hammett, William Styron, A.S. Byatt, Philip Roth, Toni Morrison, Ha Jin, Richard Ford, Cormac McCarthy, Alice Munro, Raymond Chandler, Orhan Pamuk, Dave Eggers, Robert Caro, Joseph Ellis, Haruki Murakami, and Gabriel Garcia Marquez it is today's foremost trade paperback publisher.

Anchor Books
Founded in 1953 Anchor Books is the oldest trade paperback publisher in America. The goal was to make inexpensive editions of modern classics widely available to college students and the adult public. Today, Anchor's list boasts award-winning history, science, women's studies, sociology, and quality fiction. Authors published by Anchor Books include Chinua Achebe, Ian McEwan, Alexander McCall Smith, Julia Glass, Karen Armstrong, Anne Rice, Jon Krakauer, Chuck Palahniuk, Mary Gordon, Dan Brown, and Margaret Atwood.

Vintage Español
A division of Random House, Inc., was founded in 1994 in an effort to publish selected works of fiction and nonfiction in Spanish. Since then, it has expanded to become one of the largest Spanish-language publishers in the United States, offering a growing list of titles across a wide variety of genres, including, in addition to fiction and nonfiction, sports, spirituality, self-help, personal finance and cooking, to name a few. Our authors include Gabriel García Márquez, Roberto Bolaño, Ken Follett, Isabel Allende, Junot Diaz, Dr. Isabel Gomez-Bassols, Jorge Amado and Cristina Garcia, among many others.

Black Lizard
Vintage Crime/Black Lizard was founded in June 1990 after Random House's acquisition of Black Lizard, the publishing company created by Donald S. Ellis and Barry Gifford. Before the acquisition Vintage Books was publishing the work of American mystery-authors such as Dashiell Hammett, James M. Cain and Raymond Chandler under Vintage Crime. As a result of the unification Random House came into the possession of the literature of Jim Thompson, and David Goodis, along with that of many other noir writers. Vintage Crime/Black Lizard is one of the preeminent publishers of crime fiction in the United States and asserts that it remains devoted to the best of "classic crime," having added Eric Ambler, Chester Himes and Ross Macdonald to their list of authors.

Nan A. Talese

Nan A. Talese is a literary imprint committed to quality publishing, both in the excellence of its authors and the quality of the production of its books.

Established in 1990, it is distinguished both by new authors of fiction and nonfiction, as well as the authors Mrs. Talese has published for many years, writers who have been staunchly supported by independent booksellers (and more recently Barnes & Noble and Borders) and reviewers. Among its writers are Peter Ackroyd, Margaret Atwood, Pinckney Benedict, Thomas Cahill, Kevin Canty, Lorene Cary, Pat Conroy, Jennifer Egan, Mia Farrow, Antonia Fraser, David Grand, Nicola Griffith, Aleksandar Hemon, Thomas Keneally, Alex Kotlowitz, Robert MacNeil, Ian McEwan, Gita Mehta, George Plimpton, Edvard Radzinsky, Mark Richard, Nicholas Shakespeare, Barry Unsworth, and Gus Van Sant.

Everyman's Library

Everyman's Library was founded on February 15, 1906, with the publication by Joseph Dent (1849–1926) of fifty titles. Dent, a master London bookbinder turned publisher, was a classic Victorian autodidact. The tenth child of a Darlington housepainter, he had left school at thirteen, and arrived in London with half-a-crown in his pocket. Dent promised to publish new and beautiful editions of the world's classics at one shilling a volume, "to appeal to every kind of reader: the worker, the student, the cultured man, the child, the man and the woman," so that "for a few shillings the reader may have a whole bookshelf of the immortals; for five pounds (which will procure him with a hundred volumes) a man may be intellectually rich for life."

(Source: www.penguinrandomhouse.com)

HACHETTE BOOK GROUP

Hachette Book Group (HBG) is a leading U.S. trade publisher and a division of the third-largest trade and educational book publisher in the world, Hachette Livre. A global publishing company based in France, Hachette Livre is a subsidiary of the French media company, Lagardère. HBG is headquartered in New York City with offices in Boston MA; Lebanon IN; Nashville TN; Boulder CO; Philadelphia PA; and Berkeley CA. HBG also owns Hachette Book Group Canada, Inc., a marketing and publicity company based in Toronto.

Our Mission: To publish great books well.

Our Vision:

- To be the #1 destination for authors, agents, customers, client publishers, and employees.
- To be a respected publisher that values diversity, nurtures talent, rewards success, and honors its responsibilities.
- To be market focused in all we do, and to lead change in popular culture.
- To anticipate change, foster creativity, and encourage risk-taking and innovation.

Our commitment to diversity

As a leading book publisher, we believe that including and representing diverse voices in all aspects of our business is fundamental to what we do. Our staff and our publishing programs must reflect the broad range of backgrounds, experiences, and ideas that shape our society. We are committed to working together and with all our partners to foster diversity and a culture of inclusion, so that HBG can provide a truly welcoming and fulfilling environment for all employees and publish books that appeal to all readers.

Grand Central Publishing

Grand Central Publishing (formerly Warner Books) came into existence in 1970. It became part of the Time Warner Book Group in 1998 and in 2006 was acquired by Hachette Livre; it is part of the Hachette Book Group USA (HBGUSA). David Baldacci, Sandra Brown, Harlan Coben, Naima Coster,

Min Jin Lee, Robin Roberts, and Nicholas Sparks are just a few of the *New York Times* bestselling authors published by Grand Central Publishing.

Forever

Forever, an imprint of Grand Central Publishing, publishes a wide array of inclusive commercial fiction and romance perfect for your next book-club pick—from uplifting contemporary stories to captivating historical fiction and delightful romantic comedies, to sweeping historical romance and small-town love stories (including western romance and Amish romance).

We're looking for stories that focus on relationships: stories about falling in love, about families and friendships, parents and children, all with an emphasis on the characters' journey and the fulfillment they find throughout the course of the novel. We're committed to publishing inclusive and diverse novels that reflect authentic experiences.

Forever books are published in various formats: hardcover, trade paperback, mass market, e-book, and audio. Our authors include *New York Times* and *USA Today* bestsellers Kristen Ashley, Carolyn Brown, Grace Burrowes, Amalie Howard, Helena Hunting, Elizabeth Hoyt, Abby Jimenez, Natasha Lester, Jodi Ellen Malpas, Emily March, Debbie Mason, Farrah Rochon, Kennedy Ryan, R.C. Ryan, and Rachel Van Dyken, as well as rising stars Christina Britton, Alexis Hall, Farah Heron, Sajni Patel, and Reese Ryan.

Twelve

Twelve strives to publish singular books, by authors who have unique perspectives, diverse, often underrepresented backgrounds, and compelling authority. Books that explain our culture; that illuminate, inspire, provoke, and entertain. Our mission is to provide a consummate publishing experience for our authors, one truly devoted to thoughtful partnership and cutting-edge promotional sophistication that reaches as many readers as possible. For readers, we aim to spark that rare reading experience—one that opens doors, transports, and possibly changes their outlook on our ever-changing world.

Hachette Audio

Hachette Audio titles earned three of the five Grammy nominations for spoken word productions in 2014, with Stephen Colbert's hilarious pop hit *America Again* winning. In 2015, *I Am Malala*, read by Neela Vaswani, was awarded the Grammy for Best Children's Album. The prestigious honor Audiobook of the Year was awarded by the Audiobook Publishers Association to Hachette Audio three years in a row this decade, for Tina Fey's *Bossypants*, *Life* by Keith

Richards, and *Nelson Mandela's Favorite African Folktales*. Since 2000, the excellence and breadth of the Hachette Audio publishing and production program has been recognized with over 200 Audie Award Nominations and 47 wins; 24 Grammy nominations and 9 wins; over 60 Listen Up! Awards from *Publishers Weekly*; and over 150 Earphones Awards from *AudioFile Magazine*. A variety of genre recognition comes from children's product award programs and prizes like Bouchercon's Anthony Award for Best Audiobook, which Robert Galbraith's *The Cuckoo's Calling*, read by Robert Glenister, won in 2014.

Hachette Nashville

Hachette Nashville is comprised of three imprints—Faithwords, a publisher of the world's best voices in the growing inspirational market; Center Street, an imprint publishing nonfiction books in such categories as Conservative Political and Military; and Worthy, an inspirational adult and children's book publisher specializing in Christian authors and bestselling nonfiction and fiction books.

Center Street

Center Street is a leading publisher in Nonfiction Conservative Politics and Military.

For media inquiries, email: CenterStreet@hbgusa.com.

FaithWords

FaithWords, a division of Hachette Book Group, is a top publisher of books and resources for the Christian inspirational market. Our bestselling authors include Joel Osteen, Joyce Meyer, Robert Morris, and T.D. Jakes. Many of our authors are pastors and Bible teachers, focusing on Christian living, spiritual growth, and devotionals. Our titles regularly appear on the *New York Times* and other national bestseller lists while inspiring millions of readers worldwide. Based near Nashville, Tennessee, FaithWords has sold over 60 million books since its founding in 2001.

For media inquiries, email: FaithWords@hbgusa.com.

Worthy Books

Worthy Books is an imprint of the Hachette Nashville division of Hachette Book Group. Worthy is an inspirational adult and children's book publisher specializing in Christian authors and bestselling nonfiction and fiction books. Worthy focuses on a boutique list of books across a broad spectrum: inspiration, fiction, Bible study, current events, devotion, leadership, biography, and personal growth. Worthy is comprised of three imprints: Worthy Books, Ellie Claire, and WorthyKids/Ideals.

Little, Brown and Company
Back Bay Books
Back Bay Books is where to find the country's best new fiction and nonfiction.
Back Bay Books is focused on the publication of the nation's best fiction and nonfiction. Back Bay's new editions of William Least Heat-Moon's *Blue Highways*, Tracy Kidder's *The Soul of a New Machine*, Evelyn Waugh's *A Handful of Dust*, and C.S. Forester's *Hornblower* novels, among many others, have given these classics fresh lives. At the same time, Back Bay paperback editions of new works by David Sedaris, Anita Shreve, Janet Fitch, and Malcolm Gladwell have been impressive bestsellers in their own right.

Little, Brown Spark
Little, Brown Spark's mission is to publish books that spark ideas, feelings, and change. Our authors are experts and thought leaders in the fields of health, lifestyle, psychology, and science. Our hope is that Little, Brown Spark readers will learn something new, improve their lives, and inspire others around them.

Mulholland Books
The goal of Little, Brown's Mulholland Books is simple: to publish books you can't stop reading. Whatever their form—crime novels, thrillers, police procedurals, spy stories, even supernatural suspense—the promise of a Mulholland Book is that you'll read it leaning forward, hungry for the next word. With a track record that includes numerous *New York Times* bestsellers, ranging across a broad spectrum of the genre, Mulholland Books has become a brand that is both critically acclaimed and fiercely embraced by the American reader. We proudly publish a wide array of authors, including J.J. Abrams, Lauren Beukes, Robert Galbraith, Joe Lansdale, David Morrell, Ben Winters, and Jim Thompson.

The history of suspense is long and storied, and Mulholland Books is proud to be part of its future. Unexpected, fresh, and with a 21st century approach to publishing, meet Mulholland: *you never know what's coming around the curve.*

Voracious Books
We are Voracious: a new imprint at Little, Brown led by Editorial Director

Michael Szczerban, launching our first list in Fall 2019. Our publishing interests are wide-ranging, but our books are driven by twin forces: appetite and curiosity.

We have an appetite for food, but more broadly for enjoyment and pleasure, for meaningful new experiences, for narrative and self-improvement and the things that tickle our brains. (What is curiosity but an appetite of the mind?)

To us, books are a matter of passion. Our mission is to connect readers with what they love most—from politics and Instant Pots to irreverent advice and pop culture. Most of our books are illustrated, and all of them are designed to make readers pick them up and immediately engage with them. Our authors are artists, entrepreneurs, cooks, photographers, tastemakers, thought leaders, scientists, storytellers, historians, humorists—and more.

Little, Brown Books for Young Readers

Little, Brown Books for Young Readers began publishing books for children in 1926. We publish a diverse, carefully curated list of the finest books for young readers of all ages and backgrounds. LBYR has the distinct honor of being the first and only publishing division to have won the Caldecott Medal, the annual award for the artist of the most distinguished American picture book for children, three years in a row. We have four imprints: Little, Brown Books for Young Readers publishes our core list of literary and commercial books, LB Kids produces novelty and licensed titles, Poppy is comprised of commercial titles for teens, and NOVL spans original digital content for teens. Our mission is to inspire a lifelong love of reading.

Orbit

Launched in 2007, Orbit has rapidly become one of the market-leading science fiction and fantasy imprints in the U.S., and the fastest growing imprint in the field.

Orbit publishes across the spectrum of science fiction and fantasy—from action-packed urban fantasy to widescreen space opera; from sweeping epic adventures to near-future thrillers. Our Redhook imprint publishes commercial fiction from a variety of genres. We publish approximately 100 titles each year from both established and debut authors.

Our authors include *New York Times* and international bestsellers Joe Abercrombie, M.R. Carey, Gail Carriger, James S.A. Corey, N.K. Jemisin, Ann Leckie, Kim Stanley Robinson, Andrzej Sapkowski, and Brent Weeks.

Visit www.orbitbooks.net for contact information and news about our publishing program.

PERSEUS

Perseus Book Group was founded by Frank Pearl in 1996 and became a part of the Hachette Book Group in 2016. Imprints at Perseus include Avalon Travel Publishing (home to Rick Steves and the Moon Guides), Basic Books, Running Press, PublicAffairs and Da Capo Press. Perseus Books is headquartered in New York City with offices in Boston, Philadelphia, Boulder and Berkeley.

Avalon Travel

For more information, please visit www.avalontravelbooks.com.

Moon Travel

Moon Travel Guides was founded in 1973 with a mission to advocate for independent, active, and conscious travel. We started out with guides to Asia printed by founder Bill Dalton on a Xerox machine (yes, really)—and nowadays, we're the #1 publisher of travel guides to the Americas and have expanded our coverage globally. We're published by Avalon Travel, a Hachette Book Group company. Our team is comprised of experienced editors, designers, cartographers, and marketers who ensure that our books are easy-to-use and reflect our brand values. Our program is simple:

Wherever we cover, we prioritize local businesses, outdoor recreation, and traveling strategically and sustainably.

We look for authentic voices: authors who share those values and are excited to share their destinations with the world. To learn more about our continued commitment to diversity and representation heard to www.moon.com/landing-page/black-lives-matter.

Rick Steves

Guidebook author and travel TV host Rick Steves is America's most respected authority on European travel. Rick took his first trip to Europe in 1969, visiting piano factories with his father, a piano importer. As an 18-year-old, Rick began traveling on his own, funding his trips by teaching piano lessons. In 1976, he started his business, Rick Steves' Europe, which has grown from a one-man operation to a company with a staff of 100 full-time, well-travelled employees at his headquarters in Washington state. There he produces more than 50 guidebooks on European travel, America's most popular travel series on public television, a weekly hour-long national public radio show, a weekly syndicated column, and free travel information available through his travel center and ricksteves.com. Rick Steves' Europe also runs a successful European tour program. Rick Steves lives and works in his hometown of Edmonds, Washington. His office window overlooks his old junior high school.

Email Rick at rick@ricksteves.com, or write to him c/o 130 4th Ave N, Edmonds, WA 98020.

Basic Books

Since its founding in 1950, Basic Books has shaped public debate by publishing award-winning books in history, science, sociology, psychology, politics, and current affairs. Basic's list of influential authors includes Stephon Alexander, Isaac Asimov, Edward Baptist, H.W. Brands, Zbigniew Brzezinski, Iris Chang, George Church, Niall Ferguson, Richard Feynman, Richard Florida, Martin Ford, Howard Gardner, Victor Davis Hanson, Jonathan Haidt, Judith Herman, Christopher Hitchens, Douglas Hofstadter, Leszek Kolakowski, Kevin Kruse, Lawrence Lessig, Claude Levi-Strauss, Alice Miller, Robert Nozick, Steven Pinker, Samantha Power, Diane Ravitch, Eugene Rogan, Thomas Sowell, Beverly Daniel Tatum, Eric Topol, Sherry Turkle, Timothy Snyder, Nicholas Stargardt, Michael Walzer, George Weigel, Bee Wilson, James Q. Wilson, Richard Wrangham, Irvin Yalom, and Shing-Tung Yau. Basic Books is an imprint of Perseus Books, a Hachette Book Group company.

Seal Press

Seal Press was founded in 1976 and stands as one of the most enduring feminist publishing houses to emerge from the women's press movement of the 1970s. What began as a letterpress in a Seattle garage has grown to an award-winning publishing house in New York and an imprint of Hachette, the third-largest publisher in the world. Seal's list is devoted to groundbreaking, boldly conceived books that inspire and challenge readers, lift up original voices, and imagine a better future. Publishing highlights include Ijeoma Oluo's *So You Want to Talk About Race*, Julia Serano's *Whipping Girl*, Michelle Tea's *Valencia*, Minda Harts's *The Memo*, and Susan Stryker's *Transgender History*.

Hachette Books

Hachette Books is a division of Perseus Books, a part of the Hachette Book Group, Inc., whose objective is to publish meaningful and provocative nonfiction. Hachette Books presents the leading writers in narrative nonfiction, business, science, history, health and wellness, pop culture, sports, and humor under two imprints: Hachette Books and Hachette Go. Hachette Book Group is a leading trade publisher based in New York and a division of Hachette Livre, the third-largest trade and educational publisher in the world.

Hachette Go

My motto has long been "books change my life every day," because no matter what my challenge, I've found a book to help. We all know that changing your life can be hard. At Hachette Go, we are inspired by that moment of breakthrough that allows change to happen and the action that follows. We are on a mission to make that change accessible to everyone. The right word, the right experience, the right book can make all the difference.

Hachette Go is a new imprint from Hachette Books with a mission to give people the best information on how to change their lives for the better. As an imprint, we'll publish the most exciting ideas for change, in both work and life, by authors ready to stand out and make a difference. Our goal is to ensure that every book finds its audience through strong campaigns and author partnership.

In all our books, you'll find a prescriptive element that seeks that positive change in health, inspiration, food, self-help, psychology, how-to, and work. We are saying that it is all about giving yourself permission to seek change, invest in yourself, and make it happen with a spirit of enterprise.

With the bold narrative voices of Hachette Books and the change-your-life prescriptive books of Hachette Go, all of your nonfiction reading is covered.

This is a space where change can happen. So let's GO!

—Mary Ann Naples | VP, Publisher

PublicAffairs

PublicAffairs is a publishing house founded in 1997. It is a tribute to the standards, values, and flair of three persons who have served as mentors to countless reporters, writers, editors, and book people of all kinds, including me.

I. F. Stone, proprietor of *I. F. Stone's Weekly*, combined a commitment to the First Amendment with entrepreneurial zeal and reporting skill and became one of the great independent journalists in American history. At the age of eighty, Izzy published *The Trial of Socrates*, which was a national bestseller. He wrote the book after he taught himself ancient Greek.

Benjamin C. Bradlee was for nearly thirty years the charismatic editorial leader of the *Washington Post*. It was Ben who gave the *Post* the range and courage to pursue such historic issues as Watergate. He supported his reporters with a tenacity that made them fearless, and it is no accident that so many became authors of influential, bestselling books.

Robert L. Bernstein, the chief executive of Random House for more than a quarter century, guided one of the nation's premier publishing houses. Bob was personally responsible for many books of political dissent and argument that challenged tyranny around the globe. He is also the founder and was the longtime chair of Human Rights Watch, one of the most respected human rights organizations in the world.

. . .

For fifty years, the banner of Public Affairs Press was carried by its owner, Morris B. Schnapper, who published Gandhi, Nasser, Toynbee, Truman, and about 1,500 other authors. In 1983 Schnapper was described by the *Washington Post* as "a redoubtable gadfly." His legacy will endure in the books to come.

—Peter Osnos, Founder

Bold Type Books

For 18 years, Nation Books, a project of The Nation Institute and Hachette Book Group, has been telling stories that inform and empower just as they inspire and move readers to action. We have been proud to publish award-winning, bestselling books by thought leaders, journalists, activists, whistleblowers, and truthtellers.

Now, The Nation Institute is announcing a new name, Type Media Center. Nation Books will become Bold Type Books.

You may be asking, "Why the name change? Why now?"

When the Nation Institute was founded fifty years ago, it was a tiny operation that worked in conjunction with *The Nation* magazine to provide internships. The name "The Nation Institute" reflected a shared history for a long time, but the scope of our work has broadened significantly over the years, and we want our name and brand to reflect that. We are now home to a half-dozen programs and a community of over one hundred journalists, authors, and writing fellows, supporting a high-impact investigative newsroom and a renowned book publisher—all with the common goal of effecting change.

The name Bold Type Books communicates our commitment to publishing books that offer necessary interventions into the conversation, challenge the narratives of the powerful, and offer visions of a more just, equitable future. Our name may change, but our mission remains the same.

We're excited and look forward to the next decade of challenging power, one book at a time.

Economist Books

For more information, please visit www.publicaffairsbooks.com.

Running Press

For more information, please visit www.runningpress.com.

Black Dog & Leventhal

For more information, please visit www.blackdogandleventhal.com.

In one year, HBG publishes approximately:
- 1,400+ adult books (including 50–100 digital-only titles)
- 300 books for young readers
- 700 audiobook titles (including print and download-only titles)

In 2018, the company had 150 books on the *New York Times* bestseller list, 31 of which reached #1.

(Source: www.hachettebook.com)

HARPERCOLLINS

arperCollins Publishers is the second-largest consumer book publisher in the world.

Headquartered in New York, HarperCollins has publishing operations in 17 countries. With two hundred years of history and more than 120 branded imprints around the world, HarperCollins publishes approximately 10,000 new books every year in 16 languages, and has a print and digital catalog of more than 200,000 titles. Writing across dozens of genres, HarperCollins authors include winners of the Nobel Prize, the Pulitzer Prize, the National Book Award, the Newbery and Caldecott Medals, and the Man Booker Prize.

The house of Mark Twain, the Brontë sisters, Thackeray, Dickens, John F. Kennedy, Martin Luther King Jr., Maurice Sendak, Shel Silverstein, and Margaret Wise Brown, HarperCollins has a long and rich history that reaches back to the early nineteenth century and offers our publishing team a depth of experience that few others can rival—from the modest print shop that James and John Harper opened in 1817 to the global house we are today.

HarperCollins was founded by brothers James and John Harper in New York City in 1817 as J. and J. Harper, later Harper & Brothers. In 1987, as Harper & Row, it was acquired by News Corporation. The worldwide book group was formed following News Corporation's 1990 acquisition of the British publisher William Collins & Sons. Founded in 1819, William Collins & Sons published a range of Bibles, atlases, dictionaries, and reissued classics, expanding over the years to include legendary authors such as H. G. Wells, Agatha Christie, J. R. R. Tolkien, and C. S. Lewis.

Today, the company consists of the HarperCollins General Books Group, HarperCollins Children's Books, HarperCollins Christian Publishing, HarperCollins UK, HarperCollins Canada, HarperCollins Australia/New Zealand, HarperCollins India, HarperCollins Germany, HarperCollins Español, HarperCollins Ibérica, HarperCollins Japan, HarperCollins Holland, HarperCollins Nordic, HarperCollins Polska, HarperCollins France, HarperCollins Italy, HarperCollins Brasil, HarperCollins Mexico and Harlequin. HarperCollins is a subsidiary of News Corp.

At HarperCollins, authors and their work are at the center of everything we do. We are proud to provide our authors with unprecedented editorial excellence, marketing reach, long-standing connections with booksellers, and industry-leading insight into reader and consumer behavior. Consistently at the forefront of innovation and technological advancement, HarperCollins also uses digital technology to create unique reading experiences and expand the reach of our authors.

GENERAL BOOKS

Amistad
The premier publisher of multicultural fiction and nonfiction, this renowned imprint showcases award-winning novelists, celebrated cultural figures, and esteemed critics and scholars.

Anthony Bourdain Books
Curated by *Kitchen Confidential* author Anthony Bourdain, a line of books by people with strong voices who are good at something and speak with authority. Books include *Vegetables Unleashed* by Jose Andres, *They Call Me Supermensch* by Shep Gordon, *WD-50* by Wylie Dufresne, *The Mission Chinese Food Cookbook* by Danny Bowien, *The Prophets of Smoked Meat* by Daniel Vaughn, and *L.A. Son: My Life, My City, My Food* by Roy Choi.

Avon
Avon Books, an imprint of HarperCollins Publishers, is one of America's preeminent romance houses and developed the careers of such bestsellers as Tessa Dare, Eloisa James, Beverly Jenkins, Lisa Kleypas, Sarah MacLean, Julia Quinn, Lynsay Sands, and Cat Sebastian. Avon is also home to some of the most important names in contemporary romance and women's fiction, such as Ilona Andrews, Alyssa Cole, Jeaniene Frost, Susan Elizabeth Phillips, Alisha Rai, Jennifer Ryan, Jill Shalvis, and Mia Sosa. In 2011, Avon introduced Avon Impulse, the industry leader in digital-first romance, highlighting authors such as Olivia Waite, Nisha Sharma, and Marie Tremayne. Avon Books has been publishing award-winning romance and women's fiction since 1941. It is widely credited with launching the historical romance genre with the publication of Kathleen Woodiwiss's *The Flame in the Flower* and remains at the forefront of romance publishing today.

Broadside Books
Conservative nonfiction, spanning the full range of right-of-center thought and opinion.

Caedmon

Caedmon began in 1952 with Dylan Thomas's milestone recording of *A Child's Christmas in Wales*, widely considered to be the world's first audiobook and launch of the spoken word industry. In the years that followed, Caedmon went on to establish itself as the preeminent publisher of spoken-word audio in the English language in the categories of literary fiction, poetry, plays, and children's titles. To this day, Caedmon is synonymous not only with distinguished poets reading their collections, but also with equally distinguished authors and readers performing classic and contemporary works.

Custom House

A curated line of thought-provoking nonfiction and distinguished literary fiction.

Dey Street Books

Dey Street Books is home to Amy Poehler, Gabrielle Union, Kate Hudson, Alan Cumming, Ilhan Omar, Jessica Simpson, Samantha Power, Jerry Rice, Debbie Harry, Dan Harris, RuPaul, Irin Carmon, Shana Knizhnik, Isha Sesay, Russell Brand, Rob Sheffield, Slash, Joseph "Rev Run" Simmons, Neil Strauss, Cass Sunstein, Mike Freeman, Jessica Valenti, Abby Wambach, Bobby Brown, Kelly Oxford, and Lindsey Vonn, just to name a few.

Ecco

In 1971 Ecco was spun off from the literary magazine *Antaeus* (founded in Tangier by Daniel Halpern with Paul Bowles), and it has been an imprint at HarperCollins since 1999. Ecco publishes distinguished fiction and nonfiction by bestselling, prize-winning authors, as well as bold debuts from promising new voices. Among the categories Ecco publishes are novels, short stories, poetry, memoir, science, politics, history, and sociology, as well as lavish contemporary cookbooks. Authors include: Rumaan Alam, Russell Banks, April Bloomfield, Anthony Bourdain, Charles Bukowski, Leonard Cohen, Richard Dawkins, Richard Ford, Louise Glück, Jennifer Haigh, Robert Hass, Dennis Lehane, Werner Herzog, Czeslaw Milosz, Joyce Carol Oates, Lisa Randall, Ron Rash, Simon Schama, Patti Smith, Cynthia d'Aprix Sweeney, and Amy Tan.

Harper Books

Best-selling, news-making, award-winning fiction and nonfiction, memoirs, biographies, narrative nonfiction, history, sports, literary fiction, thrillers, and contemporary women's fiction.

Harper Business

The gold standard in business book publishing for more than half a century, Harper Business is home to classics that form the cornerstone of every businessperson's library and to cutting-edge new releases that redefine business, management, economics, and business narrative.

Harper Design

Stunning, gorgeously produced illustrated, award-winning books in fashion, film and television, art and popular culture, music, crafts, cooking, lifestyle, and interior design.

Harper Luxe

HarperLuxe answers the demand for larger print books with stylish new packaging that will provide a luxurious reading experience.

Harper Perennial

Enduring classics, fiction and nonfiction reprints from Harper Books, and a vibrant line of paperback originals including new voices, boundary-pushing works, contemporary fiction, and intelligent nonfiction.

To Kill a Mockingbird, Brave New World, Their Eyes Were Watching God, A People's History of the United States; Barbara Kingsolver, Ann Patchett, Louise Erdrich, and Michael Chabon; John Brockman, Chad Kultgen, Yannick Murphy, Willy Vlautin, and Blake Butler.

Harper Voyager

Harper Voyager is a thriving global imprint dedicated to science fiction and fantasy. The imprint was originally founded as Eos Books in 1999 and relaunched in 2011 as a global brand, in conjunction with HarperCollins Australia and HarperCollins UK. Harper Voyager publishes some of the most notable names in science fiction, epic fantasy, and urban fantasy, including worldwide bestselling authors Raymond E. Feist, Richard Kadrey, and Brom. Harper Voyager also publishes the SFF field's fastest-growing talent, including C. Robert Cargill, S.A. Chakraborty, Becky Chambers, R.F. Kuang, and Sarah Beth Durst.

Harper Wave

Harper Wave is a list of health, wellness, and lifestyle books that offers the best thinking from top doctors, scientists, practitioners, and writers in their fields. Our objective is to empower readers with reliable, authoritative perspectives on our individual and collective well-being.

HarperAudio

HarperAudio proudly traces its roots back to 1952, when Dylan Thomas first recorded for our Caedmon label. For more than five decades, HarperAudio/Caedmon has been synonymous not only with distinguished poets reading their works, but also with equally distinguished authors and readers performing classic and contemporary texts.

HarperCollins 360

Harper 360 is our global publishing initiative, publishing books in English from HarperCollins UK, Australia, New Zealand, Canada, and India offices and books in Spanish from HarperCollins Iberica and Mexico offices. We publish in all genres of adult, children's and YA books, and in all formats—print, e-book, and digital audio.

HarperCollins Español

HarperCollins Español publishes a variety of books for the Spanish reader, from bestselling biographies, current affairs, practical guides, business, and self-help, to literary fiction, suspense, action, and book club fiction.

HarperOne

HarperOne is one of four imprints in the HarperOne Group, whose mission is to publish books for the world we want to live in. The HarperOne imprint is committed to publishing important books across the categories of religion, spirituality, health, personal growth, social change, relationships, and creativity.

HarperVia

HarperVia is an imprint dedicated to publishing extraordinary international voices, offering readers the chance to encounter other lives and other points of view via the language of the imagination.

William Morrow

One of the industry's premier fiction and nonfiction publishers, William Morrow is home to bestselling and award-winning authors such as Ted Bell, Ray Bradbury, Meg Cabot, Patricia Cornwell, Deborah Crombie, Diane Mott Davidson, Guillermo Del Toro and Chuck Hogan, Tim Dorsey, Susan Elizabeth Phillips, Dorothea Benton Frank, Neil Gaiman, Andrew Gross, Joe Hill, Greg Iles, J. A. Jance, Faye Kellerman, Christina Baker Kline, Dennis Lehane, Elmore Leonard, Laura Lippman, Gregory Maguire, Christopher

Moore, Elizabeth Peters, Peter Robinson, James Rollins, Neal Stephenson, and Charles Todd. Our bestselling nonfiction authors include Gregg Allman, Bruce Feiler, Chris Kyle, Steven Levitt and Stephen J. Dubner, Frank Warren, Ree Drummond, Guy Fieri, the Emily Post franchise, Debbie Reynolds, and Willie Nelson. Founded in 1926 by American publisher William Morrow, the house celebrated its 85th birthday in 2011.

CHILDREN'S

Amistad
Picture books through young adult works by and about people of African descent that discuss historical and cultural themes.

Balzer + Bray
Bold, creative, groundbreaking picture books and novels for kids and teens by bestselling, award-winning, and debut talent.

Greenwillow Books
Stories for children of every age created by authors and artists whose work is full of honesty, emotion, and depth.

HarperAlley
HarperAlley is a curated graphic novel imprint within a big publishing house with worldwide presence, poised to bring you some of the best creators working in the form today. It's home to many timeless treasures and bestsellers such as Neil Gaiman and P. Craig Russell's *Graveyard Book Graphic Novel*, volumes 1 and 2, and Noelle Stevenson's *Nimona*, which was nominated for a National Book Award in 2015, as well as the bestseller and Kirkus Prize–winner *New Kid* by Jerry Craft, which was also nominated for a Harvey Award. Cartoonists continue to inspire, challenge, and push the form in unexpected directions, and HarperAlley will collaborate with them to publish more graphic novels for all kinds of readers, everywhere. Everyone has a story. Find yours at HarperAlley.

HarperChildren's Audio
A stunning array of bestselling children's books and young adult favorites in audio.

HarperCollins Children's Books
Respected worldwide for publishing quality books for children and home to many classics of children's literature.

HarperFestival
Books, novelties, and merchandise for the very young—children age 0–8.

HarperTeen
Books for young adults and teens, comprising a wide range of critically acclaimed and bestselling titles.

Heartdrum
Heartdrum publishes books for children and teens by Native creators from the U.S. and Canada; it is a partnership between author Cynthia Leitich Smith (Muscogee Creek) and Rosemary Brosnan.

Katherine Tegen Books
High-quality fiction that is both literary and commercial for children and teens: thought-provoking and entertaining stories that reach a wide audience.

Quill Tree Books
Many branches, many voices. Quill Tree Books publishes literary books with wide appeal for children and teens. Our distinctive imprint is known for publishing timeless books that sell. We're passionate about what we publish, and we're proud of the excellent quality of our books. We publish picture books, fiction for middle graders and teens, chapter books, graphic novels, and nonfiction—whatever we love most. The team loves to nurture new talent such as Elizabeth Acevedo, Jerry Craft, and Noelle Stevenson, as well as publish authors whose books have become classics, such as Neil Gaiman, Gail Carson Levine, and Rita Williams-Garcia. Under the leadership of Rosemary Brosnan, the imprint has a strong focus on diverse and underrepresented voices.

Walden Pond Press
Middle grade classics—fast-paced, funny, engaging, compulsively readable stories by well-established authors and new, exciting talent.

CHRISTIAN
Bible Gateway
The world's largest Christian website with an estimated 15 million unique visitors a month. It provides free access to over 160 Bible translations in 70 languages.

Editorial Vida
The Spanish division of Zondervan. Vida maintains the largest catalog of

Christian products and resources in Hispanic culture—U.S., Latin America, and abroad.

FaithGateway
An online community that shares well-known Christian authors' content, through multi-faceted topical guides, to help people grow in their Christian faith.

Grupo Nelson
The Spanish division of Thomas Nelson providing Christian inspiration to Spanish-speaking cultures around the world.

Nelson Books
Nonfiction imprint of Thomas Nelson with focus on memoirs, political, cookbooks, biographies, spiritual growth, historical.

Olive Tree
Olive Tree offers Bible reference materials for an in-depth Bible study experience through its online store and Bible Study app, accessible across all major devices.

Thomas Nelson
A leading provider of Christian content that has been inspiring lives for more than 200 years. Its award-winning Bibles and products are distributed worldwide.

Tommy Nelson
The children's division of Thomas Nelson, dedicated to expanding imaginations and nurturing a child's faith. Its wide variety of products focus on Bible teachings.

W Publishing Group
A nonfiction imprint of Thomas Nelson with a focus on memoirs, help and hope for doing life better, and leading pastoral voices, with select practical living.

WestBow Press
A self-publishing initiative for both Thomas Nelson and Zondervan. The two publishing groups use this imprint to discover new authors and inspirational stories.

Zonderkidz
The children's division of Zondervan. Its products awaken the hearts and souls of kids under 16, and encourage the discovery of Jesus Christ.

Zondervan
A leading Bible publisher and provider of Christian communications. For over 80 years, Zondervan bestselling products have delivered a transformational experience.

Zondervan Academic
Zondervan Academic provides the scholarly community with Christ-honoring resources and biblical-theological studies in service of the academy and the church worldwide.

Harlequin
Carina Press
Carina Press is Harlequin's digital-first adult fiction imprint, publishing first in digital, with releases also becoming available in audio and print. Carina Press publishes a variety of genres, including romance of all heat levels, mysteries, historical fiction, fantasy, and more. Also under Carina Press is Carina Adores, the new trope-driven LGBTQ+ contemporary romance line, which launched June 2020.

Graydon House Books
Graydon House Books is a select hardcover and trade paperback imprint dedicated to publishing book club–worthy women's fiction with strong commercial appeal. Graydon House novels range in tone from lighthearted relationship fiction to emotional tearjerkers, domestic suspense to historical dramas, and is home to an exciting mix of debut voices and established bestsellers such as Tarryn Fisher, Kelly Rimmer, Michelle Gable, and Viola Shipman.

Hanover Square Press
Hanover Square Press publishes compelling fiction and nonfiction encompassing a broad range of genres—from crime, thrillers, literary and high-concept fiction to narrative history, journalism, science, biography and memoir, including *New York Times* bestsellers from Dan Abrams and David Fisher, and Rick Ross.

Harlequin Books
Harlequin is one of the world's leading publishers of books for women. A

pioneer of the category romance series novel, Harlequin continues to publish over 66+ new series novels under 11 unique romance lines each month. Many well-known authors have written for Harlequin series, including Nora Roberts, Brenda Jackson, Debbie Macomber, Robyn Carr, Heather Graham, Susan Mallery, RaeAnne Thayne, and many more! Harlequin has been publishing romance novels since 1949 and is a globally recognized brand.

HQN Books

HQN has redefined the romance genre by publishing the best in mainstream romance and women's fiction by the finest authors in the field. Originally a mass market paperback imprint, HQN still dominates in that format with a mix of romance royalty and diverse new voices, but also publishes a wide array of romantic women's fiction in Trade Paperback and Hardcover by the likes of Sarah Morgan, Susan Mallery, Gena Showalter, Adriana Herrera, and Audrey Carlan. Since 2004, HQN has helped build the careers of such romance luminaries as RaeAnne Thayne, Julia London, Maisey Yates, Linda Lael Miller, Lori Foster, Brenda Jackson, and Diana Palmer. And, in 2019, HQN placed 42 titles on major industry bestseller lists, and continues to offer the most entertaining reading experience for readers across all romance sub-genres.

Inkyard Press

Bestselling. Award-winning. Critically acclaimed. Inkyard Press offers smart, engaging YA fiction across a variety of genres, from realistic contemporary to epic fantasy. We are passionate about publishing diverse voices and relevant stories that appeal to older teens and an adult crossover audience. We are looking for compelling commercial YA fiction stories across genres—including horror, fantasy, mystery, romance and thriller—and want to work with a diverse group of creators so that readers see themselves reflected in the stories we publish. Harlequin TEEN was rebranded and relaunched as Inkyard Press in 2019.

Love Inspired

Love Inspired offers a wide range of uplifting and inspiring stories about love and friendship, family and community for readers to enjoy and share with their own family and friends. Building on the success of Love Inspired's long-established romance lines, Love Inspired has expanded with a trade paperback program featuring a broad range of longer faith-based novels with deeper, more emotional character explorations and multi-layered story lines. Discover the full range of books from Love Inspired.

MIRA Books

Launched in 1994, MIRA Books is known for publishing buzzworthy and blockbuster commercial fiction across all genres and formats, including contemporary and historical fiction, romance, suspense and psychological thrillers. MIRA is home to numerous *New York Times* and *USA TODAY* bestselling authors such as Robyn Carr, Jude Deveraux, J.T. Ellison, and Alka Joshi—as well as industry-anticipated debut authors.

Park Row Books

A boutique line of thought-provoking fiction and nonfiction, Park Row Books publishes a variety of genres with a special focus on fresh voices, original stories, and books that celebrate authenticity and empowerment. Home to award-winning and bestselling authors such as Pam Jenoff, Mary Kubica, and Nancy Jooyoun Kim, Park Row aims for the highest standard of books that speak to a broad audience.

(Source: www.harpercollins.com)

MACMILLAN

INDEPENDENT. FORWARD-THINKING.
AUTHOR-FOCUSED. GLOBAL.

Macmillan Publishers is a global trade publishing company operating in over 70 countries, with imprints in the United States, Germany, the United Kingdom, Australia, South Africa, and India. Macmillan is a division of the Holtzbrinck Publishing Group, a large family-owned media company headquartered in Stuttgart, Germany.

Macmillan operates eight divisions in the U.S.: Celadon Books; Farrar, Straus and Giroux; Flatiron Books; Henry Holt and Company; Macmillan Audio; Macmillan Children's Publishing Group; St. Martin's Press and Tor/Forge. Our writers come from a vast array of literary backgrounds and have won awards including the Nobel Prize, the Man Booker Prize, the Pulitzer Prize, the National Book Award, and the Printz Award. In the U.K., Australia, India, and South Africa, Macmillan publishes under the Pan Macmillan name. The German company, Holtzbrinck Deutsche Buchverlage, includes among its imprints S. Fischer, Kiepenheuer and Witsch, Rowohlt, and Droemer Knaur.

ADULT TRADE
Celadon Books

Celadon Books publishes a mix of fiction and nonfiction, a highly curated list of twenty to twenty-five new titles a year. The list strives to publish books that have range, depth, and impact. Reflecting the eclectic taste of founders Jamie Raab and Deb Futter, Celadon Books draws on their unique ability to publish commercial and literary books and discover and nurture talent.

Farrar, Straus and Giroux

Farrar, Straus and Giroux was founded in 1946. Farrar, Straus and Giroux authors have won extraordinary acclaim over the years, including numerous National Book Awards, Pulitzer Prizes, and twenty-one Nobel Prizes in Literature. Prize winners include Pablo Neruda, Joseph Brodsky, Shirley Hazzard, Susan Sontag, Alice McDermott, Seamus Heaney, Nadine Gordimer, Richard Powers, Marilynne Robinson, Isaac Bashevis Singer, C. K. Williams, Tom Wolfe, John McPhee, Thomas Friedman, Jonathan Franzen, Jeffrey Eugenides, and Richard Powers.

North Point Press

North Point Press specializes in hard and softcover literary nonfiction, with an emphasis on natural history, travel, ecology, music, food, and cultural criticism. Authors past and present include Peter Matthiessen, Evan Connell, Beryl Markham, A. J. Liebling, and M.F.K. Fisher.

Hill and Wang

Hill and Wang focuses on hard and softcover books of nonfiction written for the educated reader. The list is strong in American history, world history, and politics; among its authors are Roland Barthes, John Allen Paulos, William Cronon, Thomas Bender, William Poundstone, and Elie Wiesel.

Sarah Crichton Books

Sarah Crichton Books, an imprint of Farrar, Straus and Giroux, publishes a wide variety of literary and commercial fiction and nonfiction. From *A Long Way Gone*, Ishmael Beah's bestselling memoir of his time as a boy soldier, to Roy Blount's witty celebration of words, *Alphabet Juice*, to Jason Goodwin's mystery series set in 1830s Istanbul and featuring a eunuch detective, Sarah Crichton Books offers books to engage and delight all readers.

FSG Originals

FSG Originals are driven by voices that insist on being heard, stories that demand to be told, writers who are compelled to show us something new. They defy categorization and expectation. They are, in a word, original.

For more about FSG Originals, visit www.fsgoriginals.com.

Scientific American / Farrar, Straus and Giroux

Scientific American / Farrar, Straus and Giroux publishes nonfiction science books for the general reader. The marriage of two internationally renowned, award-winning publishers, the imprint publishes a select number of titles that extend *Scientific American* magazine's 165-year tradition of bringing the insights and developments in science and technology to the widest possible readership.

For more about Scientific American / Farrar, Straus and Giroux books, visit www.ScientificAmerican.com.

Farrar, Straus and Giroux Books for Younger Readers

Books for Young Readers, established in 1953, is an imprint of Macmillan Children's Publishing Group. We are committed to publishing books of the highest literary quality for children and teenagers. FSG BYR is known for its award-winning list of fiction, nonfiction, and picture books. Our goal is to help create books that positively impact the lives of young people; books that make them laugh and think and wonder and question and dream. We care deeply about building long-term partnerships with our authors and illustrators and helping them tell the stories they are passionate about telling. Our imprints include Frances Foster Books (founded in 1996) and Margaret Ferguson Books (founded in 2011).

We do not accept unsolicited submissions.

Flatiron

A division of Macmillan, founded in 2014 with a simple philosophy: publish a relatively small number of titles so that each book could be supported by an extraordinary amount of editorial attention, marketing, and publicity. Founded by publishing veteran Bob Miller, President and Publisher, known for starting and running Hyperion Books for Disney for 18 years, Flatiron has published forty *New York Times* bestsellers in its first four years, including ten #1 bestsellers. Flatiron has published nonfiction by such authors as Oprah Winfrey, Vice President Joe Biden, Jenny Lawson, James Comey, Dr. Michael Greger, Nigella Lawson, Jamie Oliver and Brad Meltzer, and fiction by such authors as Liane Moriarty, Laurie Frankel, Leigh Bardugo, Shobha Rao, Jane Harper, Stephanie Garber and Melissa Albert.

Henry Holt

From the poetry of Robert Frost to classic works by Robert Louis Stevenson, Erich Fromm, and Norman Mailer, Henry Holt and Company has, for almost a century and a half, published writers that define their era and endure far beyond it. Founded in 1866 by Henry Holt and Frederick Leypoldt, Henry Holt is one of the oldest trade publishers in the United States. Today the company continues to build upon its illustrious history by publishing bestselling, award-winning books in the areas of literary fiction, mysteries and thrillers, history, biography, politics, current events, science, psychology, and books for children and young adults. In addition to the Henry Holt imprint, the company also publishes books under the Metropolitan Books, Times Books, Holt Paperbacks, Picador, Books For Young Readers, Square Fish, and Audio Renaissance imprints. Each imprint offers a distinctive list of books that contributes to the spectrum of views and voices that Henry Holt brings to readers of all ages each day.

Henry Holt

The flagship imprint of Henry Holt and Company continues to carry on the house's long history of publishing books of high quality that appeal to a diverse and substantial readership. Under the Henry Holt imprint, the company publishes fiction and nonfiction with a focus on the following categories: literary fiction, mysteries and thrillers, history, current events, social science, adventure, biography, and psychology. Maintaining the award-winning tradition of the imprint, Henry Holt titles have in recent years won the Pulitzer Prize and the National Book Award. The Henry Holt list features such acclaimed authors as Paul Auster, Rick Atkinson, John Banville, Phil Caputo, Robert Frost, Tony Horwitz, Hilary Mantel and Bill O'Reilly.

Metropolitan Books

Metropolitan Books, established in 1995, publishes American and international fiction and nonfiction. With a mission to introduce unconventional, uncompromising and sometimes controversial voices, Metropolitan publishes titles in categories ranging from world history to American politics, foreign fiction to graphic novels, social science to current affairs. In 2003 Metropolitan launched The American Empire Project, a collection of books dedicated to bringing progressive voices on U.S. politics and policy to mainstream audiences. Writers such as Barbara Ehrenreich, Atul Gawande, Susan Faludi, Orlando Figes, Tom Segev, Noam Chomsky, and Thomas Frank are featured on the Metropolitan list. Regardless of the writer or topic, Metropolitan always upholds its commitment to diversity, distinction, and surprise.

Times Books

Times Books is a publishing partnership between The New York Times and Henry Holt and Company. Times Books publishes quality nonfiction books in the fields of politics, current events, international relations, history, science, and American society and culture. Approximately half of the imprint's books are written by *New York Times* reporters, and the rest are written by some of America's leading intellectuals, journalists, and public figures; all of these works are informed by their authors' unparalleled expertise on the most important issues of our day. Times Books is also the home of the American Presidents Series of brief biographies of the presidents of the United States, for which Arthur M. Schlesinger, Jr., serves as general editor. The Times Books list includes works by Jim Dwyer and Kevin Flynn, Linda Greenhouse, Gary Hart, Stephen Kinzer, Bill McKibben, Jeffrey Rosen, Michael Shermer, and David Weinberger.

Holt Paperbacks

Holt Paperbacks publishes reprints from all the company's adult imprints including Henry Holt, Metropolitan Books, and Times Books. Holt Paperbacks also publishes original trade paperbacks across all the categories that Henry Holt focuses on, including literary fiction, mysteries and thrillers, history, current events, social science, adventure, biography and memoir, personal development, and psychology. Whether as an original or reprint, every book on the Holt Paperbacks list strives to deliver to the paperback reader the same high caliber of information and entertainment that is the hallmark of all Henry Holt publications. Acclaimed and bestselling authors published under the Holt Paperbacks imprint include Rick Atkinson, Noam Chomsky, Barbara Ehrenreich, Harville Hendrix, Julie Morgenstern, and Stacy Schiff.

Henry Holt Books for Younger Readers

Henry Holt Books for Young Readers is known for publishing quality picture books, chapter books, and novels for preschoolers through young adults. Covering a wide variety of genres, our books feature imaginative authors and illustrators who inspire young readers. Our list includes the classic picture books *Tikki Tikki Tembo* and *Brown Bear, Brown Bear, What Do You See?*; Caldecott Honor Winners *In the Small, Small Pond* and *Hondo and Fabian*; and National Book Award Winner *When Zachary Beaver Came to Town*. Our award-winning authors and illustrators include Melvin Burgess, Eric Carle, Bryan Collier, Denise Fleming, Nikki Giovanni, Kimberly Willis Holt, Laurie Keller, Betsy Lewin, Bill Martin Jr., and Peter McCarty.

Macmillan Audio

Macmillan Audio was founded in 1987 as Audio Renaissance and published its first programs in 1988. Audio Renaissance was acquired by Holtzbrinck in 2001 and changed its name to Macmillan Audio in 2007. Macmillan Audio records the best fiction and nonfiction available for both adults and children from Macmillan's publishers, in addition to publishing original productions and titles from other publishers. The company's line of products also includes the language-learning series Behind the Wheel. Macmillan Audio narrators include Meryl Streep, Lorelei King, Stanley Tucci, Simon Vance, Gwyneth Paltrow, Katherine Kellgren, Holter Graham, and Cynthia Nixon, as well as President Jimmy Carter, Billy Crystal, Rob Lowe, and Bill O'Reilly, who have read their own audiobooks. Macmillan Audio productions have been nominated for six Grammy Awards and have won numerous Audie Awards and

Earphones Awards. Macmillan audio titles are available digitally as well as on CD.

St. Martin's Press

St. Martin's Press has a long and respected history of publishing a solid and varied list. We are dedicated to publishing emerging new authors, and offering a fresh perspective on classic genres, while maintaining a diverse and interesting range of books. Our strength is derived from a dedication to solid publishing of many books, while consistently producing the occasional blockbuster. The vast majority of our hardcovers are published in paperback through our internal paperback lines.

Griffin

The Griffin list features a wide range of contemporary paperbacks (some original publications, others published in conjunction with the St. Martin's Press hardcover list), and includes hundreds of bestselling works of fiction— from commercial, literary, and graphic (illustrated) novels to titles of African American and young-adult interest. The hallmarks of Griffin's varied nonfiction publishing program extends to such categories as: biography and memoir, pop-culture and politics, business and self-help, humor and reference, gay and lesbian, health and fitness, home and travel (including the Let's Go guides), crafts and hobbies, nature and medicine, *New York Times* crossword puzzles and Will Shortz's sudoku, and much more.

Minotaur

Established in 1999, Minotaur is a premier publisher in the bestselling category of crime fiction. Garnering domestic and international awards from the Edgar to the Gold Dagger, the list encompasses the entire genre from cozies to historicals to thrillers. Minotaur is dedicated to nurturing rising new talent as well as cultivating the fullest potential of its popular genre mainstays.

St. Martin's Paperbacks

St. Martin's Paperbacks continually produces a strong list of bestselling mass-market books—from already established to up-and-coming authors—in both original and reprint form. The scope of the SMP list is extensive and inclusive—from contemporary fiction and historical romance to paranormal suspense, mysteries (under the Minotaur imprint) and thrillers to the True Crime library, military nonfiction to movie tie-ins, and many other subcategories in each genre.

Thomas Dunne Books
From 1986 until 2020, Thomas Dunne Books published popular trade fiction and nonfiction. With an output of approximately 175 titles each year, this group covered a range of genres including commercial and literary fiction, thrillers, biography, politics, sports, popular science, and more. The list was intentionally eclectic and included a wide range of fiction and nonfiction, from first books to international bestsellers.

Castle Point Books
Castle Point Books specializes in necessary nonfiction that is quick-to-market and trend-responsive. CPB creates and develops books that are value-driven, practical, timely, and with mass appeal. Started in July 2015, Castle Point's list includes coloring books (under the St. Martin's Griffin imprint), cookbooks, journals, humor, and children's activity books. Castle Point Books is a development deal between Castle Point Publishing, LLP and St. Martin's Press.

Wednesday Books
Wednesday Books serves the insatiable reader every day of the week.

St. Martin's Essentials
St. Martin's Essentials is one of the premier lifestyle imprints in the publishing industry. From bestselling authors to tomorrow's leaders, Essentials is dedicated to publishing the books that will create positive change in lives, and in the world.

TOM DOHERTY ASSOCIATES
Tor/Forge
Tor Books is the most successful science fiction and fantasy publisher in the world. Winner of the Locus Award for best SF publisher 20 years in a row, Tor regularly puts books like Robert Jordan's *Knife of Dreams* and Terry Goodkind's *Chainfire* atop national bestseller lists. Tor's Orb imprint offers trade paperback editions of outstanding, award-winning SF and fantasy backlist titles. Additionally, the Tor Kids program includes Starscape, Tor Teen, and one of the largest classics lines in North America.

The Forge imprint publishes a wide range of fiction, including a strong line of historical novels and thrillers, plus mysteries, women's fiction, and a variety of nonfiction titles. Tor/Forge has also become the leading modern publisher of American westerns.

Well-known authors recently published by Tor and Forge include Andrew

M. Greeley, Douglas Preston, Orson Scott Card, Michael & Kathleen O'Neal Gear, Harold Robbins, Susan Kearney, Jonathan Carroll, Brian Herbert, Kevin J. Anderson, Andre Norton, Terry Goodkind, Robert Jordan, former Secretary of Defense William B. Cohen, Susanna Clarke, Allan Folsom, Eric Lustbader, Elizabeth Haydon, Gene Wolfe, Morgan Llewelyn, David Lubar, David Weber, Christopher Pike, and Philip K. Dick.

About Starscape and Tor Teen Books
The richly imagined worlds of science fiction and fantasy novels encourage readers to hold a mirror up to their own realities, exploring them in a way that is secure yet challenging and demanding. Whether surviving in a complex alternate universe or navigating life on Earth in the presence of a strange new discovery, the characters in these works help readers realize what it truly means to be a human being. Starscape and Tor Teen strives to encourage such critical discoveries by making the very best science fiction and fantasy literature available to young readers, providing numerous unique universes through which young readers can travel on the critical journey to the center of their own identities.

Starscape
Award-winning science fiction and fantasy for middle grade readers ages 10 and up (grades 5 and up), published in hardcover and paperback. All titles are age- and theme-appropriate. Some editions include reader's guides and other supplemental materials.

Tor Teen
Critically-acclaimed science fiction and fantasy for young adult readers ages 13 and up (grades 8 and up), published in hardcover and paperback. All titles are age- and theme-appropriate. Some editions include reader's guides and other supplemental materials.

CHILDREN'S
Farrar, Straus and Giroux Books for Younger Readers
Books for Young Readers, established in 1953, is an imprint of Macmillan Children's Publishing Group. We are committed to publishing books of the highest literary quality for children and teenagers. FSG BYR is known for its award-winning list of fiction, nonfiction, and picture books. Our goal is to help create books that positively impact the lives of young people; books that make them laugh and think and wonder and question and dream. We

care deeply about building long-term partnerships with our authors and illustrators and helping them tell the stories they are passionate about telling. Our imprints include Frances Foster Books (founded in 1996) and Margaret Ferguson Books (founded in 2011).

We do not accept unsolicited submissions.

Feiwel & Friends

Feiwel and Friends is a publisher of innovative children's fiction and nonfiction literature, including hardcover, paperback series, and individual titles. The list is eclectic and combines quality and commercial appeal for readers ages 0–16. The imprint is dedicated to "book by book" publishing, bringing the work of distinctive and outstanding authors, illustrators, and ideas to the marketplace. Feiwel and Friends is defined and guided by our principle: Our books are friends for life.

First Second Books

First Second Books publishes graphic novels for children, adults, and everyone in between. Our graphic novels continually break new ground for the comics medium: Gene Luen Yang's *American Born Chinese* was both the first graphic novel to win the American Library Association's Michael L. Printz Award and the first graphic novel to be a National Book Award finalist. First Second is committed to the highest quality in every aspect of book-making—literary, artistic, and production.

Henry Holt Books for Younger Readers

Henry Holt Books for Young Readers is known for publishing quality picture books, chapter books, and novels for preschoolers through young adults. Covering a wide variety of genres, our books feature imaginative authors and illustrators who inspire young readers. Our list includes the classic picture books *Tikki Tikki Tembo* and *Brown Bear, Brown Bear, What Do You See?*; Caldecott Honor Winners *In the Small, Small Pond* and *Hondo and Fabian*; and National Book Award Winner *When Zachary Beaver Came to Town*. Our award-winning authors and illustrators include Melvin Burgess, Eric Carle, Bryan Collier, Denise Fleming, Nikki Giovanni, Kimberly Willis Holt, Laurie Keller, Betsy Lewin, Bill Martin Jr., and Peter McCarty.

Odd Dot

Odd Dot is a publisher of nonfiction books with innovative formats for kids of all ages, with lists that range from STEM-oriented workbooks, to board books with wheels, and beyond. Combining fun and delightful artists with expert, knowledgeable, and creative authors allows Odd Dot to make joyful books for curious minds. You can learn more about the imprint's lists on www.odddot.com or by following along on social media @odddotbooks.

Priddy Books

Priddy Books publishes innovative, photographic books for children. Using simple, attractive elements, our books are specially designed to stimulate your child's imagination and encourage their development and awareness of the world around them. We have taken great care to use the highest-quality materials in the production of our children's books—all of which are rigorously tested. Our range is aimed at three key age groups: Happy Baby 0–2 years, Preschool 2–5 years and Smart Kids for children aged 5 and over. We produce books for a worldwide market, with translations into 30 different languages.

Roaring Brook Press

Roaring Brook Press is a publisher of high-quality literature for young readers of all ages, from toddler to teen, and in all categories: picture books, fiction, and nonfiction. Our authors and artists are the focus of our list; their talents define us. Since our first list was published in 2002, our books have received numerous awards, including the 2014 Michael L. Printz Award, the 2011, 2004 and 2003 Caldecott Medals, three Caldecott Honor awards and a Newbery Honor award, among many others.

Square Fish Books

Square Fish is the paperback imprint of Macmillan Children's Publishing Group, representing the best of Farrar, Straus and Giroux, Feiwel & Friends, Henry Holt, Imprint and Roaring Brook Press. Founded in 2007, the list contains a multitude of awards and honors and is one of the most impressive rosters of titles in the children's book world. The list of outstanding authors and artists include: Madeleine L'Engle, William Steig, Marissa Meyer, Leigh Bardugo, Natalie Babbitt, Katherine Applegate, Marie Lu, Steve Sheinkin, Hafsah Faizal, Kimberly Willis Holt, Remy Lai, Barbara O'Connor, Christian McKay Heidicker, Shane Evans, and many others.

Neon Squid

Neon Squid creates beautiful nonfiction books for inquisitive kids (and kids at heart). We believe the most amazing stories are real ones, so our books are for children who want to decipher ancient scrolls, orbit distant stars, and dive into the deepest oceans. Our books are a labor of love—written by experts, illustrated by the best artists around, and produced using the finest materials, including sustainably sourced paper. We hope that by reading them kids are encouraged to further explore the world around them.

(Source: us.macmillan.com)

BERTELSMANN TO BUY S&S FOR $2.2 BILLION

BY JIM MILLIOT | NOV 25, 2020

Bertelsmann has emerged as the winning bidder for Simon & Schuster. In an announcement this morning, the parent company of Penguin Random House said it had reached an agreement to buy S&S from ViacomCBS for $2.175 billion.

Following regulatory approvals, the deal is expected to be completed sometime in 2021. Until the purchase is completed, S&S will continue to operate independently under the direction of Jonathan Karp, president & CEO of S&S, and Dennis Eulau, COO and CFO.

In his letter to employees, PRH worldwide CEO Markus Dohle wrote: "Simon & Schuster aligns completely with the creative and entrepreneurial culture that we nurture by providing editorial autonomy to our publishers, funding their pursuit of new stories, ideas, and voices, and maximizing reach for our authors. We recognize—and our success has demonstrated—that collaboration makes us all stronger, and by bringing Simon & Schuster onto our global platform, we will be able to connect their authors and books with even more readers."

The purchase combines the country's largest and third-largest trade publishers, and it will have revenues of close to $3 billion. In bringing the two companies together, Dohle wrote, "we will apply the same thoughtfulness and respect to the process with Simon & Schuster that we did with the Penguin and Random House merger in 2013, and we will communicate and share with you directly and regularly throughout this time."

In a statement, Bertelsmann chairman and CEO Thomas Rabe said following Bertelsmann's acquisition of the final stake Pearson had owned in PRH earlier this year, the S&S purchase "marks another strategic milestone in strengthening our global content businesses," adding: "the book business has been part of Bertelsmann's identity since the founding of C. Bertelsmann Verlag more than 185 years ago and has lost none of its appeal to this day."

In acquiring S&S, Bertelsmann beat out several competitors, most notably HarperCollins, the country's second-largest trade publisher. Last week, the *New York Times* reported that Bertelsmann and HarperCollins were the top contenders for S&S, with the purchase price put over $1.7 billion. The nearly $2.2 billion price tag for S&S is likely the reflection of the fact that a publisher its size will not be on the market in the foreseeable future. If HC had acquired S&S, it would have closed the gap between PRH and itself considerably; HC's U.S. sales are estimated at about $1.1 billion, compared to PRH's current sales of about $2.2 billion.

A very happy Dohle told *PW* today was a "good day for books, book publishing, and reading." He said the S&S purchase reflects Bertelsmann's "firm belief in the future of book publishing."

The merger of Penguin and Random House met with little regulatory resistance, and the deal was closed in about eight months. Dohle would not put a timetable on when the S&S deal would be completed, but said he does not expect any antitrust issues to arise. He said the U.S. book market remains highly fragmented and that even since the Penguin Random House merger eight years ago, new publishing companies have been formed and continue to grow. He said looking at the entire book market including self-publishing, PRH's market share is about 14.2%, and S&S's 4.2%.

SIMON & SCHUSTER

Simon & Schuster, Inc. is a global leader in the field of general interest publishing, providing consumers worldwide with a diverse range of quality books across a wide variety of genres and formats. It is the publishing operation of CBS Corporation, one of the world's premier media companies.

Simon & Schuster was founded in 1924 by Richard L. (Dick) Simon and M. Lincoln (Max) Schuster. Their initial project was a crossword puzzle book, the first ever produced, which was a runaway bestseller. From that, the company has grown to become a multifaceted publishing house that publishes approximately 2000 titles annually. Its publishing groups and divisions—the Simon & Schuster Publishing Group, The Scribner Publishing Group, the Atria Publishing Group, the Gallery Publishing Group, Simon & Schuster Children's Publishing, Simon & Schuster Audio, and Simon & Schuster Digital, and international companies in Australia, Canada, India and the United Kingdom—are home to some of the most distinguished imprints and recognizable authors in the world of publishing. Simon & Schuster and its imprints have won 56 Pulitzer Prizes, and been the recipient of numerous National Book Awards, National Book Critics Circle Awards, Grammy Awards, and Newbery and Caldecott Medals.

From the beginning, the two founding entrepreneurs approached the business in a much different manner than their more buttoned-down colleagues along Publishers Row. The history of S&S is marked by numerous significant industry "firsts." Dick Simon and Max Schuster were aggressive marketers, often spending five to ten times more for advertising and promotion than their competitors: they were the first publisher to offer booksellers the privilege of returning unsold copies for credit; they were the first to apply mass market production and distribution techniques to books, and in 1939, with Robert Fair de Graff, launched the paperback revolution with the founding of Pocket Books, America's first paperback publisher. In 1945, they published the first "instant book." And in 2000, Simon & Schuster became the first publisher to offer an original work by a major author exclusively in electronic form with the publication of Stephen King's e-book *Riding the Bullet*, a worldwide publishing and media phenomenon.

In 1944, Simon & Schuster and Pocket Books were sold to department store magnate Marshall Field. Upon Field's death in 1957, the company was repurchased by Simon, Schuster, Leon Shimkin and James M. Jacobson, who among them held it in various combinations of ownership until 1975, when Shimkin sold it to international conglomerate Gulf + Western.

In 1984, the company began a period of intense expansion through acquisition, acquiring more than 60 companies, including Prentice Hall and Silver, Burdett, and culminating with the 1994 acquisition of Macmillan Publishing Company. With the addition of these educational, professional, and reference businesses, by 1997 Simon & Schuster revenues were more than $2 billion. Along the way, in 1989 Gulf + Western restructured to become Paramount Communications, and in 1994, shortly after the Macmillan acquisition, Viacom Inc. acquired Paramount.

In 1998, Viacom sold the S&S educational, professional, and reference units to Pearson PLC. In 2002, Simon & Schuster was integrated with the Paramount motion picture and television studios as part of the Viacom Entertainment Group, and in 2004 direct oversight of the company returned to Viacom corporate headquarters.

In 2006, with the separation of Viacom and CBS into separate publicly traded companies, Simon & Schuster became a part of the CBS Corporation.

As a major international publishing company, many Simon & Schuster titles are published globally, and its products—hardcovers, trade and mass market paperbacks, children's books of every format, electronic books, audiobooks (in compact disk and digital download) of bestselling and critically acclaimed fiction and nonfiction for readers of all ages and every conceivable taste—are distributed in more than 200 countries around the world.

SIMON & SCHUSTER ADULT PUBLISHING

The Simon & Schuster Adult Publishing Group includes a number of publishing units that offer books in several formats. Each unit has its own publisher, editorial group and publicity department. Common sales and business departments support all the units. The managing editorial, art, production, marketing, and subsidiary rights departments have staff members dedicated to the individual imprints.

Adams Media

Adams Media, an imprint of Simon & Schuster, informs, instructs, and inspires readers across a variety of lifestyle categories by providing the content they're looking for, from the experts they follow and trust. From Parenting to DIY, Personal Finance to Self-Help, Adams Media researches, identifies, creates, and distributes accessible content with implicit discoverability. Embodying a uniquely flexible "ground-up" publishing model, Adams Media navigates within or between consumer categories as market opportunity dictates. These are the books people are searching for.

Atria

Atria, defined as "central living spaces open to the air and sky," perfectly describes the mission of this innovative publisher. Founded in 2002, Atria was from the start intended to be an environment where new ideas could flourish, the best writers of fiction and nonfiction could thrive and connect with an ever-widening readership, and the best practices of traditional publishing could be integrated with cutting-edge developments in the digital world. In short, a place where great books could come to light.

In the years that have followed, the Atria Publishing Group has realized this vision with its creative and motivated staff acquiring, publishing, and marketing a list of successful and highly acclaimed books, many of them award-winners and bestsellers. At Atria, brand-name authors soar to new heights while the finest new voices—the bestsellers of tomorrow—are discovered and nurtured with an eye toward a limitless future. Among the many successful authors Atria is proud to publish are Fredrik Backman, Jack Carr, Common, Armando Lucas Correa, Janet Evanovich, Vince Flynn & Kyle Mills, Philippa Gregory, Maria Hinojosa, Lisa Jewell, Thomas Keneally, Karen Kingsbury, William Kent Krueger, Shirley MacLaine, Signe Pike, Rebecca Serle, Diane Setterfield, Dr. David Sinclair, Brian Stelter, Brad Thor, Tina Turner, Cleo Wade, Jennifer Weiner, and Zane.

The Atria Publishing Group publishes books for readers of all tastes and interests under these imprints: Atria Books, Atria Trade Paperbacks, Atria Books Espanol, Washington Square Press, Emily Bestler Books, Atria/Beyond Words, Howard Books, and One Signal.

Avid Reader Press

Avid Reader Press, a new division of Simon & Schuster, is built on the idea that the most rewarding publishing has three common denominators: great books, published with intense focus, in true partnership. The staff at Avid Reader Press, a small band of cheerful literary warriors, strives to publish every book with avidity.

Emily Bestler Books

For more information, please visit www.emilybestlerbooks.com.

Enliven

For more information, please visit www.simonandschuster.com.

Folger Shakespeare Library

Home to the world's largest Shakespeare collection, the Folger Shakespeare Library is a world-class center for scholarship, learning, culture, and the arts. Along with Simon & Schuster, it also publishes the Folger Editions, the leading Shakespeare texts used in secondary schools in the United States.

Free Press

For more information, please visit www.simonandschuster.com.

Gallery

For more information, please visit www.simonandschuster.com.

Howard

For more information, please visit www.simonandschuster.com.

Jeter

For more information, please visit www.simonandschuster.com.

One Signal

We are a new imprint at a 100-year-old publisher.
We believe nonfiction storytelling is having a moment.
We believe in opening gates, not keeping them closed.
We believe in discovering untold stories, elevating unique voices, and celebrating hidden figures.
We believe in publishing people, not just writers.
We believe new ideas are important.
We believe old ideas are important, too.
We believe the noise can't block the signal.

Scout Press

Scout Press is a literary imprint dedicated to being on the lookout for modern storytellers. A scout is always on the front line—the first to see what is on the horizon; what is coming next. We publish ambitious, conversation-starting novelists who are pushing the boundaries of contemporary fiction while also creating books that will stand the test of time.

Scribner

Founded in 1846 by Charles Scribner, Scribner was originally a publisher of religious books. By 1870, the company had turned to literature and begun publishing, in addition to books, *Scribner's Monthly*, "an illustrated magazine for the people." The magazine and its successor, *Scribner's Magazine*, attracted fresh young writers, many of whom became Scribner authors.

Charles Scribner II took over in 1879 after the deaths of his father and older brother, and under this guidance, the company became identified with the giants of twentieth-century American literature, such as Henry James and Edith Wharton. In short succession, Charles Scribner's Sons published Ring Lardner, Ernest Hemingway, Thomas Wolfe, and Marjorie Kinnan Rawlings. Famed editors Maxwell Perkins and John Hall Wheelock realized that a new era in American literature was dawning, and in 1920 F. Scott Fitzgerald's first novel, *This Side of Paradise*, proclaimed the Jazz Age.

In 1978, Scribner acquired Atheneum, and in 1984 merged with Macmillan. Today, under president Susan Moldow and publisher Nan Graham, Scribner has a distinguished list of writers that includes Annie Proulx, author of *Brokeback Mountain* and *The Shipping News*, winner of the Pulitzer Prize and the National Book Award; Frank McCourt, whose memoir *Angela's Ashes* won the Pulitzer Prize and the National Book Critics Circle Award; Don DeLillo, whose novel *Underworld* won the Howell Award from the Academy of Arts and Letters. Scribner also publishes #1 bestselling author Stephen King, awarded the National Medal of Arts in 2015; Anthony Doerr, author of Pulitzer-winner *All The Light We Cannot See*; and a host of other luminary authors including Jeannette Walls, Andrew Solomon, S. C. Gwynne, Colm Toibin, Siddhartha Mukherjee, and Miranda July.

Simon & Schuster

Simon & Schuster was founded in April 1924 when Richard L. Simon and M. Lincoln Schuster pooled their resources and published Simon & Schuster's first book, *The Crossword Puzzle Book*, packaged with a pencil. What was a revolutionary idea at the time went on to become a runaway bestseller and a modern publishing company was launched.

In its early years, Simon & Schuster achieved commercial success from such groundbreaking mega-sellers as Will and Ariel Durant's *The Story of Philosophy* and Dale Carnegie's *How to Win Friends and Influence People*. Simon & Schuster, Inc. has since grown into a large publishing house with many divisions, but the Simon & Schuster trade imprint has remained as a cornerstone of the company and one of the most venerated brand names in the world of publishing. Among its award-winning works are *The Rise and Fall of the Third Reich* by William L. Shirer; *Walt Whitman* by Justin Kaplan; *Lonesome Dove* by Larry McMurtry; *The Making of the Atomic Bomb* by Richard Rhodes; *Parting the Waters* by Taylor Branch; *A Frolic of His Own* by William Gaddis; *The Prize* by Daniel Yergin; *Lincoln at Gettysburg* by Garry Wills; *No Ordinary Time* by Doris Kearns Goodwin; *Carry Me Home* by Diane McWhorter; *A Beautiful Mind* by Sylvia Nasar; and numerous books by David McCullough—*Truman, John Adams, Mornings on Horseback*, and *The Path Between the Seas.*

Many Simon & Schuster books have had pervasive cultural influence over decades: *Gentleman's Agreement* by Laura Z. Hobson; *How to Succeed in Business Without Really Trying* by E.S. Mead, *Zorba the Greek* by Nikos Kazantzakis, *The Man in the Gray Flannel Suit* by Sloan Wilson; *Eloise* by Kay Thompson; *Gypsy by Gypsy* Rose Lee; *The Organization Man* by William H. Whyte, *The Carpetbaggers* by Harold Robbins; *The American Way of Death* by Jessica Mitford; *The Chosen* by Chaim Potok; *Once Is Not Enough* by Jacqueline Susann; *Catch-22* by Joseph Heller; *Nice Guys Finish Last* by Leo Durocher; *Pumping Iron* by Charles Gaines and George Butler; *Looking for Mr. Goodbar* by Judith Rossner; *A Book of Common Prayer* by Joan Didion; *The Human Factor* by Graham Greene; *Arnold: The Education of a Bodybuilder* by Arnold Schwarzenegger; *Jane Fonda's Workout Book* by Jane Fonda; *Hollywood Wives* by Jackie Collins; *Knock Wood* by Candice Bergen; *Less Than Zero* by Bret Easton Ellis; *Wiseguy* by Nicholas Pileggi; *Postcards from the Edge* by Carrie Fisher; *The 7 Habits of Highly Effective People* by Stephen R. Covey; *Den of Thieves* by James Stewart; *The Road Less Traveled* by M. Scott Peck; *Diplomacy* by Henry Kissinger; *Undaunted Courage* by Stephen E. Ambrose; *Bobos in Paradise* by David Brooks; *When Pride Still Mattered* by David Maraniss; *A Heartbreaking Work of Staggering Genius* by Dave Eggers; *Living History* by Hillary Rodham Clinton; *Benjamin Franklin* by Walter Isaacson; *Chronicles* by Bob Dylan; *The Year of Living Biblically* by A.J. Jacobs, *Team of Rivals* by Doris Kearns Goodwin.

In 1974, Simon & Schuster published the landmark bestseller *All the President's Men* by Bob Woodward and Carl Bernstein, and has continued to publish Bob Woodward's books to this day. It has long maintained its reputation as a premier publisher of nonfiction, with books by Jonathan Alter, Mark Bittman, Steven Brill, Susan Cheever, Jennet Conant, Richard Ben Cramer, E.J. Dionne, David Herbert Donald, Timothy Ferris, Frances FitzGerald, Betty Friedan, George McGovern, Robert Putnam, Richard Reeves, William Shawcross, Ron Suskind, Evan Thomas, and Amy Wilentz. Simon & Schuster also publishes scores of bestselling and critically acclaimed fiction writers, including Nicholson Baker, Sandra Brown, James Lee Burke, Mary Higgins Clark, Richard Paul Evans, Stephen Hunter, Stephen McCauley, Martin Cruz Smith, Jean Thompson, and Marianne Wiggins.

SIMON & SCHUSTER CHILDREN'S PUBLISHING

Simon & Schuster Children's Publishing, one of the leading children's book publishers in the world, is comprised of the following imprints: Aladdin Paperbacks, Atheneum Books for Young Readers, Little Simon, Margaret K. McElderry Books, Salaam Reads, Simon & Schuster Books for Young Readers, and Simon Spotlight. While maintaining an extensive award-winning backlist, the division continues to publish acclaimed and bestselling books in a variety of formats for children ages preschool through teen, including such high-profile characters as Eloise, Raggedy Ann & Andy, Olivia, Henry & Mudge, The Hardy Boys, Nancy Drew, Buffy the Vampire Slayer, and Shiloh. Simon Spotlight, an imprint wholly devoted to media tie-ins, has become one of the fastest growing imprints in the children's book industry, with bestselling series based on Nickelodeon's Rugrats, Blue's Clues, The Wild Thornberrys, and Little Bill, HIT Entertainment's Bob the Builder, Fox Family's Angela Anaconda, and Jim Henson's Bear in the Big Blue House properties.

Aladdin

Aladdin publishes for a diverse community of readers with books that are enduring and culturally relevant. From picture books to chapter books to middle grade, both fiction and nonfiction, we create books that provide readers with mirrors in which to see themselves and windows into understanding others.

Atheneum

Founded in 1961 by Jean Karl, Atheneum Books for Young Readers is known for publishing enduring literary middle grade, teen, picture book, and graphic novel titles. The imprint has garnered more than forty Newbery and Caldecott Medals and Honors throughout its celebrated history. It has also published a list of books that have won innumerable other awards and accolades, including Coretta Scott King medals, National Book Award medals and nominations, Printz medals and honors, PEN USA Literary Awards, *New York Times* bestsellers, and being named to countless state reading lists. Our commitment to publishing commercial books with outstanding literary merit is evident in every title we acquire as well as in our extensive backlist.

Simon & Schuster Books for Young Readers

Simon & Schuster Books for Young Readers is the flagship imprint of the S&S Children's Division. We are committed to publishing a wide range of contemporary, commercial, award-winning fiction and nonfiction that spans every age of children's publishing. BFYR is constantly looking to the future, supporting our foundation authors and franchises, but always with an eye for breaking new ground with every publication. We are also deeply invested in developing new talent, new formats, and new avenues of publication. S&S BFYR's publishing program's eclecticism, elasticity, and sensibility to the ever-changing marketplace makes it the home for a vast array of blockbuster children's titles.

Beach Lane Books

Beach Lane Books, founded in 2008 and located on a flower-filled lane in San Diego, publishes books for all ages and across all genres, with a primary focus on lyrical, emotionally engaging, highly visual picture books for young children—and the adults who love them. Our list features established authors and illustrators in the field as well as brand-new talent, and our overarching goal is to publish books that are truly for children, books that connect with readers on a deep level and that become beloved childhood treasures people will return to throughout their lives.

Denene Millner Books

I've always loved children's books—the illustrations, the color, the whimsy, the beauty of the stories. I'm particularly drawn to books that speak to the human experience of African American children, beyond the typical subjects saddled on them, like the Civil Rights Movement, slavery, and the lives of sports and music icons. Don't get me wrong: I appreciate that those books give our history an airing for our babies. But I'm infinitely more interested in stories that celebrate the everyday beauty of being a little human of color. Black children believe in the tooth fairy, get scared when they contemplate their first ride on the school bus, look for dragons in their closets, have best friends who get into mischief with them. In other words, Black children have the same universal childhood experiences that any other human revels in as a kid, and they should be able to see that part of their lives reflected in the stories on their bookshelves. My goal is to have my imprint add to that small but important canon. Denene Millner Books, then, is a love letter to children of color who deserve to see their beauty and humanity in the most remarkable form of entertainment on the planet: books.

—Denene Millner, Vice President and Publisher

Little Simon

Little Simon publishes innovative books for young children. Among our award-winning and bestselling titles are Sandra Boynton's *The Going to Bed Book*, Karen Katz's *Where Is Baby's Belly Button?*, Robert Sabuda's *The Wizard of Oz* pop-up, and David Carter's *The Happy Little Yellow Box*. Little Simon's Classic Board Book collection features timeless favorites perfectly designed for the youngest of readers, such as *Cloudy with a Chance of Meatballs, We're Going on a Bear Hunt*, and *Little Quack*. Our original chapter book line includes homegrown series such as *Heidi Heckelbeck, Captain Awesome, Galaxy Zack,* and *The Critter Club*.

Margaret K. McElderry

Founded by legendary editor Margaret K. McElderry in 1972, Margaret K. McElderry Books is a boutique imprint of Simon & Schuster's Children's Division, recognized internationally as a publisher of literary author-driven fiction and nonfiction for the teen, middle grade, picture book, and poetry markets. We specialize in high quality literary fantasy, contemporary, and historical fiction, as well as character-driven picture books and poetry for all ages. McElderry Books is proud of our global identity. We are a leader in acquiring properties from foreign publishers as well as being known for attracting and nurturing talent from other countries.

Paula Wiseman Books

Paula Wiseman Books is an imprint of Simon & Schuster Children's Publishing that, since 2003, has published many award-winning and bestselling books, including picture books, novelty books, and fiction and nonfiction. The imprint focuses on stories and art that are childlike, timeless, innovative, and represent many cultures and varied voices.

We publish thirty to forty books per year created by many of the most beloved talents working in children's books today, including Matthew Van Fleet, Patricia Polacco, Lesa Cline-Ransome, James E. Ransome, Raúl Colón, Susan Vaught, Rosemary Wells, Lisa Mantchev, Stephen T. Johnson, Taeeun Yoo, Bryan Collier, Sandra Neil Wallace, Melissa Castrillon, Anita Lobel, Alexandra Diaz, and Matthew Forsythe.

Our mission is to publish books for children that enlarge their world and we strive to find books that will endure, especially stories told by underrepresented voices. We are committed to publishing new talent in both picture books and novels. We are actively seeking submissions from new and published authors and artists through agents and from SCBWI conferences.

Saga Press

Saga Press, an imprint of Gallery Books and Simon & Schuster, is a publisher of award-winning speculative fiction. Dedicated to curating a bespoke list of powerful and diverse voices, Saga is proud to publish acclaimed authors like Amal El-Mohtar, Charlaine Harris, Stephen Graham Jones, Ursula K. Le Guin, Ken Liu, and Rebecca Roanhorse.

Salaam Reads

Founded in 2016, Salaam Reads is an imprint that aims to introduce readers of all faiths and backgrounds to a wide variety of Muslim children and families and offer Muslim kids an opportunity to see themselves reflected positively in published works. The imprint, which takes its name from the Arabic word for "peace," plans to publish books for young readers of all ages, including picture books, chapter books, middle grade, and young adult.

In addition to publishing works acquired through literary agents, Salaam Reads will also consider for publication unagented and/or unsolicited manuscripts. Submissions can be sent to SalaamReads@SimonandSchuster.com.

Simon Spotlight

Simon Spotlight is an imprint devoted to licensed properties, brands, and original paperback series, publishing across a wide array of formats and age ranges. From board books to storybooks, unique novelty books to chapter books, and every format in between, Simon Spotlight is dedicated to creating innovative publishing programs that are specially tailored to each brand and its identity.

For media tie-ins, Simon Spotlight has a proven track record with television properties such as Olivia, Daniel Tiger's Neighborhood, Batman, and PJ Masks and blockbuster movies such as *The Peanuts Movie*, *Kung Fu Panda 3*, and *Hotel Transylvania 2*. The tie-ins capture the spirit of the brand and provide young fans with great stories featuring their favorite characters. The various formats also appeal to children with different reading levels and interests.

Spotlight also houses Simon & Schuster's Ready-to-Read program, a line specifically dedicated to emerging readers, which includes the popular series Robin Hill School, Henry and Mudge, Annie and Snowball, and many others. Spotlight's leveled nonfiction readers such as History of Fun Stuff, Science of Fun Stuff, and Living In . . . bring fun to learning.

In addition to licensed tie-ins, Spotlight also publishes original paperback series for readers of all ages, with a focus on middle grade. These titles include the successful Cupcake Diaries, Sew Zoey, and Billy Sure Kid Entrepreneur series.

Simon Spotlight is one of the leading mass-market imprints in the children's book industry.

SIMON & SCHUSTER AUDIO PUBLISHING

Simon & Schuster Audio is a leading publisher of general interest audiobooks including bestselling fiction, nonfiction, business/finance, self-improvement, inspiration, language learning programs, and original audiobook productions. Simon & Schuster Audio has produced audiobooks that have won five Grammy awards and twenty-six Grammy nominations since 1989.

Simon & Schuster Audio
(Source: www.simonandschuster.com)

④

THE NEXT 15 PUBLISHERS

(Ranking based on data obtained from NPD BookScan.)

SCHOLASTIC

As the largest children's book publisher in the world, Scholastic is entrusted with the promotion of literacy through books for millions of kids of all ages and reading levels.

Our mission is built on helping children learn to read and love to read. We believe that independent reading is a critical part of children's learning and growth. With support from teachers, parents, and schools, children choose from Scholastic the books they want to read, and discover the pleasure and power of reading. Finding the right book at the right time can light an emotional spark within children that motivates them to read more, understand more, and read joyfully.

When that happens, the world opens. Everything becomes possible.

(Source: www.scholastic.com)

DISNEY

For more information, please visit www.books.disney.com.

WORKMAN

Workman Publishing Co., Inc., is an independently owned family of publishers, including Workman Publishing, Algonquin Books of Chapel Hill, Algonquin Young Readers, Artisan, Storey Publishing, and Timber Press. We are also partners with The Experiment, duopress, Erewhon Books, and Familius.

We are publishers of award-winning cookbooks, parenting/pregnancy guides, books on gardening, country living, and humor, as well as children's books, gift books, fiction, and the bestselling calendar line in the business. Located in the heart of New York's Greenwich Village, in a converted printers' building, our offices are high-energy and creative, filled with people who are passionate about what they do. We also have offices in Chapel Hill, North Carolina; North Adams, Massachusetts; and Portland, Oregon.

(Source: www.workman.com)

SOURCEBOOKS

Sourcebooks' mission is to reach as many people as possible through books that will enlighten their lives.

We are a company bound together by the idea that Books. Change. Lives.

Sourcebooks—an independent vision

For us, it means a passion for books and a dedication to the belief that books change lives. It means innovative publishing, where every book is personal and every author's voice has a place. And it means not being afraid to say "I don't know" and forging a new path when we have to.

We are a group of passionate, energetic and enthusiastic book lovers, and we are committed to helping readers experience each book.

Thank you for being a part of our story.

So much has changed since we started this journey twenty+ years ago in a spare bedroom—the industry, the technology, the world. And at Sourcebooks, things are no different. The conversations we get to have now are different from those we had even just five short years ago. We've launched new imprints to great success and built the careers of authors whose voices have a vital place in today's community.

But what hasn't changed for us is our passion for books and our dedication to the belief that books change lives. All voices matter. So while our current list may be different than those first few books, you can bet that our mission hasn't and won't change one bit. If anything we find ourselves even more committed to that conviction than ever before.

So take a fresh look at Sourcebooks. The Sourcebooks you thought you knew has grown up a bit—we just might surprise you.

(Source: www.sourcebooks.com)

ABRAMS

Founded in 1949, ABRAMS was the first company in the United States to specialize in publishing art and illustrated books. The company continues to publish critically acclaimed and bestselling works in the areas of art, photography, cooking, craft, comics, interior and garden design, entertainment, fashion, and popular culture; children's books ranging from middle grade to young adult fiction to picture books to board books. ABRAMS creates and distributes brilliantly designed books with the highest production values under the following imprints: Abrams; Abrams ComicArts; Abrams Image; Abrams Press; The Overlook Press; Abrams Books for Young Readers; Amulet Books; Abrams Appleseed; and a gift and stationery line, Abrams Noterie. ABRAMS also distributes books for Blackwell & Ruth, Booth-Clibborn Editions, Cameron + Company, Alain Ducasse Édition, Getty Publications, Lucky Spool,

The Museum of Modern Art, Obvious State, SelfMadeHero, Tate Publishing, V&A Publishing, and The Vendome Press.

(Source: www.abramsbooks.com)

JOHN WILEY

Wiley empowers researchers, learners, universities, and corporations to achieve their goals in an ever-changing world.

For over 200 years we have been helping people and organizations develop the skills and knowledge they need to succeed. We develop digital education, learning, assessment, and certification solutions to help universities, businesses, and individuals move between education and employment and achieve their ambitions. By partnering with learned societies, we support researchers to communicate discoveries that make a difference. Our online scientific, technical, medical, and scholarly journals, books, and other digital content build on a 200-year heritage of quality publishing.

Who We Are

Our mission has always focused on helping our customers succeed, wherever they are in their education and professional careers.

We are bridging the higher education gap by delivering content solutions in new and innovative ways to enrich the learning experience. We are a proven leader in strategic higher education consulting and partnering with educators and institutions globally to achieve success, and our print and digital solutions enable students and instructors worldwide. We encourage learning to be a continuous, lifelong experience—an integral, essential part of every stage of building a career.

We are closing the talent deficit by supporting employers, helping them find and retain top talent, assess their employees' skill sets, and implement training in order to transform company cultures. For decades we've helped people learn; today we're showing them new ways to achieve, get certified and advance their careers.

We are strengthening the research community by partnering with learned societies and supporting researchers to communicate discoveries that make a difference. We collaborate with authors, societies, libraries, and other members of the research community to generate, communicate, and enable access to the scientific and scholarly insights that are helping to solve some of the world's biggest challenges.

Our commitment to partnership helps us advance innovation and connect researchers, learners, and professionals with the content, platforms, and tools they need to be successful.

(Source: www.wiley.com)

CHRONICLE BOOKS
Who We Are
Chronicle Books is an independent publisher based in San Francisco that has been making things since the Summer of Love. We are inspired by the enduring magic of books, and by sparking the passions of others. We believe in partnering with artists, writers, and organizations that represent the diversity of our world, and we are committed to an inclusive company culture that respects and uplifts people of diverse backgrounds and points of view.

What We Do
As soon as you pick up our publishing, we want you to be able to tell that what you're holding comes from us. We consider every detail, and ask questions like these: does the design support and enhance the content? How does it feel in your hands? What special touches can we add to make it an object you'll treasure? We apply this approach to everything we make, whether it's a book, journal, game, e-book, or our newest invention.

Where We Do It
Based in San Francisco, our headquarters are in an old maritime machine shop and warehouse. There are four floors: one for sales, marketing, and operations, one for editorial and contracts, another for design and production, and meeting space where we all come together. There's even a storefront you can visit. Stop by the next time you're in town and bring your favorite tote, or take home one of ours.

How You Can Find Us
We've often been told "I see your books everywhere" and that's just how we like it— you'll find our telltale spectacles on store shelves of all kinds, all over the world. Once you start looking, you can't miss us. Wherever you are, we invite you to see things differently too.

You can find your nearest bookstore using IndieBounds' Bookstore Finder tool. (Source: www.chroniclebooks.com)

W.W. NORTON
Whether you are a reader in search of enduring fiction, nonfiction, and poetry, a student or instructor seeking outstanding course books and digital materials, an enthusiast eager for food and lifestyle inspiration, or a professional looking for authoritative new works, you have come to the right place. Independent since 1923, employee-owned, and proud to publish "books that live," Norton is here for you.

Norton Professional Books

For over 30 years, Norton Professional Books has published leading works in mental health, well-being, architecture and design, and education.

Countryman Press

Founded in 1973, Countryman Press publishes beautiful lifestyle books—from healthy-living cookbooks to hiking guides—that entertain and teach.

Liveright

With progressive literary sensibilities in both fiction and nonfiction, Liveright publishes 20th-century classics and new works that provoke thought and discourse.

Norton Young Readers

Norton Young Readers is growing readers for life, from preschoolers to young adults.

(Source: www.wwnorton.com)

ANDREWS MCMEEL PUBLISHING

We aspire to bring joy to people's lives through the work of our talented creators. Since 1970, AMU has honed an uncanny ability to tap into the zeitgeist of popular culture to nurture and share the fresh, new voices that resonate with their generation and remain relevant for years to come. While other companies try to mitigate surprises, we anticipate disruption and embrace change. Our growth and forward momentum come from taking creative risks and finding new ways to share the unique and powerful messages of our creators with the world.

Our Genesis

Our story begins with the dynamic partnership of Jim Andrews and John McMeel, two charismatic innovators who challenged convention to give voice to the groundbreaking comic storytellers and cultural commentators of their day.

Jim and John joined forces in 1970 with a bold vision, a progressive business philosophy and a steadfast commitment to the artistic goals of each creator. Their enterprising vision and values continue to serve as the foundation of our corporate culture today.

(Source: www.publishing.andrewsmcmeel.com)

KENSINGTON PUBLISHING CORP.

Founded in 1974, Kensington Publishing Corp. is located in New York City and is known as "America's Independent Publisher." It remains a multi-generational family business, with Steven Zacharius succeeding his father as Chairman, President and

CEO, and Adam Zacharius as Vice-President and General Manager. As the foremost independent commercial publishing house in the United States providing hardcover, trade paperback, mass market, and digital releases, Kensington publishes the books that America wants to read.

The house of *New York Times* bestselling authors, including Fern Michaels, Lisa Jackson, Joanne Fluke, William W. Johnstone, and many others, Kensington publishes over 500 fiction and nonfiction titles each year. Its diverse imprints—Kensington Books, Zebra, Pinnacle, Dafina, Citadel Press and Lyrical Press—are well known for providing readers with a range of popular genres such as thrillers, romance, historical fiction, cozy mysteries and nonfiction, as well as true-crime, western, and commercial fiction titles.

Our History
2020 marks Kensington Publishing Corp.'s 46th year in business, and it is one of the last remaining independent U.S. publishers of hardcover, trade and mass market paperback books. From the time our very first book (*Appointment in Dallas* by Hugh McDonald) became a bestseller, Kensington has been known as an astute and determined David-vs.-Goliath publisher of titles in the full spectrum of categories, from fiction and romance to health and nonfiction. In addition to the close-to-500 new books the company releases through its diverse imprints per year, it has a backlist of more than 5,000 titles. Kensington is considered a leader and innovator in such areas of publishing as African American, cozy mysteries, westerns, and of course, romance.

Since its founding in 1974, Kensington has introduced the world to dozens of bestselling writers and developed countless marketing innovations while remaining steadfastly independent. The staff totals over 80 employees, many of whom have been with us for over 30 years. Kensington boasts both a dedicated on-staff sales team as well as the full strength of Penguin Random House Publisher Services' global sales force. The company can respond quickly to trends, to put books into the hands of readers faster than larger publishers can, and we support them with targeted promotional and marketing programs to generate reader excitement.

Kensington continues to be a full-range publisher large enough to command respect in the market, yet small enough to maintain author, reader, and retailer loyalty.

(Source: www.kensingtonbooks.com)

TYNDALE HOUSE PUBLISHERS
For more than 60 years, Tyndale has helped readers discover the life-giving truths of God's Word. We publish Bibles in English and Spanish along with a broad spectrum of books from trusted authors, also in English and Spanish, to equip and encourage readers in their Christian faith. Our nonfiction books provide insight to renew

the spirit while tackling life at street level, and our fiction from new and celebrated authors alike captures the imaginations of millions of fans. We also engage and enrich the next generation through children's books and Bibles.

Today we're one of the largest independently owned Christian publishers in the world. Though our business has grown, our mission remains the same: to open God's Word to as many as possible in language they can relate to and understand.

Yet our vision reaches beyond publishing and extends to transforming the hearts and minds of people across the globe. We pursue this vision by channeling the profits of Tyndale House Publishers directly to Tyndale House Foundation. The Foundation uses these funds to support ministries involved with Bible translation, literature distribution, leadership training, and humanitarian aid.

With every book you purchase, you help to meet the physical and spiritual needs of people around the world.

(Source: www.tyndale.com)

B&H PUBLISHING GROUP

B&H Publishing Group, an imprint of Lifeway Christian Resources, is a team that believes Every Word Matters. We seek to provide intentional, biblical content that positively impacts the hearts and minds of people, cultivating lifelong relationships with Jesus Christ. We publish (print and digital) in the trade, church, and academic markets, as well as the CSB translation.

(Source: www.bhpublishinggroup.com)

BAKER PUBLISHING GROUP

Baker Publishing Group publishes high-quality writings that represent historic Christianity and serve the diverse interests and concerns of evangelical readers.

Bethany House has been publishing high-quality books for more than 60 years. From humble beginnings as the publishing arm of a missions organization, we are now a division of Baker Publishing Group, the industry's largest independent Christian book publisher.

Revell began over 125 years ago when D. L. Moody and his brother-in-law Fleming H. Revell saw the need for practical books that would help bring the Christian faith to everyday life. From there, Fleming H. Revell Publishing developed consistently solid lists that included many notable Christian writers over the years. This same vision for books that are both inspirational and practical continues to motivate the Revell publishing group today. Whether publishing fiction, Christian living, self-help, marriage, family, or youth books, each Revell publication reflects relevance, integrity, and excellence.

Baker Books has a vision for building up the body of Christ through books that are relevant, intelligent, and engaging. We publish titles for lay Christians on topics such as discipleship, spirituality, encouragement, relationships, marriage, parenting, and the intersection of Christianity and culture. We also publish books and ministry resources for pastors and church leaders, concentrating on topics such as preaching, worship, pastoral ministries, counseling, and leadership.

Baker Academic serves the academy and the church by publishing works that further the pursuit of knowledge and understanding within the context of Christian faith. Building on our Reformed and evangelical heritage, we connect authors and readers across the broader academic community by publishing books that reflect historic Christianity and its contemporary expressions. Our authors are scholars who are leaders in their fields, write irenically, and display a healthy respect for other perspectives and traditions. Our goal is to publish books that are notable for their inherent quality and deemed essential reading by students and scholars.

Ever since the 1971 publication of *The Hiding Place* by Corrie ten Boom, **Chosen** Books has been publishing powerful books that help millions to live the Spirit-filled life. Attracting evangelicals and charismatics, professionals and laypersons, books published by Chosen help believers to better know and love the Lord Jesus Christ, to pray about the concerns that are on God's heart, to be empowered by his Spirit for ministry, to fulfill the Great Commission, and to transform their communities and their world. Several hundred titles over more than thirty years, from Charles Colson's *Born Again* to Cindy Jacobs' *Possessing the Gates of the Enemy*, reflect the publishing goal of Chosen Books: to publish well-crafted books that recognize the gifts and ministry of the Holy Spirit and help readers live more empowered and effective lives for Jesus Christ. Challenged by the written word, these hungry readers are joining the incredible adventure of what God is doing in the world.

Brazos Press fosters the renewal of classical, orthodox Christianity by publishing thoughtful, theologically grounded books on subjects of importance to the church and the world. We serve authors and readers from all major streams of the historic Christian tradition, recognizing that the renewal of Christian orthodoxy transcends many traditional boundary lines and polarities.

(Source: www.bakerpublishinggroup.com)

MCGRAW-HILL

Our vision is to unlock the full potential of each learner.

Our mission is to accelerate learning.

We accomplish this by creating intuitive, engaging, efficient, and effective learning experiences—grounded in research. We're helping create a brighter future for students worldwide by applying our deep understanding of how learning happens and how the mind develops. Learning science is the key.

(Source: www.mheducation.com)

OXFORD UNIVERSITY PRESS

At OUP we have a clear mission which informs everything we do—to create the highest-quality academic and educational resources and services and to make them available across the world. We share the University's uncompromising standards, defining qualities, and belief in the transformative power of education to inspire progress and realize human potential.

We have an incredibly diverse publishing programme, which often surprises people who are expecting a traditional university press offering.

We publish in many countries, in more than 40 languages, and in a variety of formats—print and digital.

Our products cover an extremely broad academic and educational spectrum, and we aim to make our content available to our users in whichever format suits them best.

We publish for all audiences—from pre-school to secondary level schoolchildren; students to academics; general readers to researchers; individuals to institutions.

As a department of the University of Oxford our worldwide publishing furthers the University's objectives of excellence in scholarship, research, and education. Our main criteria when evaluating a new title for publication are its quality and whether it supports those aims of furthering education and disseminating knowledge.

We publish more than 6,000 titles a year worldwide, in a variety of formats.

Our range includes dictionaries, English language teaching materials, children's books, journals, scholarly monographs, printed music, higher education textbooks, and schoolbooks.

Many of these titles are created specifically for local markets and are published by our regional publishing branches. We sell more than 110 million units each year, and most of those sales are outside the U.K.

Our publications regularly win prizes and awards at national and international level.

We also look beyond traditional publishing to develop new ways of supporting our customers. A few examples of this include:

- offering support to teachers
- delivering digital learning and assessment platforms, such as Oxfordenglishtesting.com
- creating online research tools, such as Oxford Bibliographies Online, that enable students and researchers to find relevant content quickly and easily
- providing digital language data via Oxford Languages

(Source: www.global.oup.com)

WHO ARE THE BIG 25?

BY JED LYONS

We all know who the Big Five publishers are. When Simon & Schuster is sold, there will be the Big Four. But who are the other large publishers operating in the U.S.? It depends on whether you count just trade houses or add in academic, educational, technical, and STM companies.

In the trade alone, there aren't many sizeable houses left after the Big Five. The rapid consolidation of trade publishers has left few Independents of any significant size. Workman, with revenue of $134 million, was just snatched up by Hachette. A list of the top 25 publishers of *all kinds* operating in America today would have to include all of the following publishers.

Chronicle Books is still independent and quite large. Globe Pequot and its numerous trade imprints is a subsidiary of Rowman & Littlefield, another large independent house. Kensington, Skyhorse, Andrews McMeel, W.W. Norton and Scholastic are substantial players in the trade with the two latter firms also publishing in the educational space. Who else? History Press and Arcadia in Charleston are growing. Quarto on Boston's north shore is a large U.K.-owned trade company. SourceBooks is now half-owned by Random so it's no longer an indie house. There are hundreds of independent publishers, but few are generating sales of more than $10 million a year.

Among academic publishers, the U.K.'s Taylor & Francis is a behemoth and is certainly the largest in the U.S. They are followed by two more Brits: Oxford University Press and Cambridge University Press. Germany's Springer is next. Fiercely independent SAGE is over a half-billion in sales. Rowman & Littlefield is one of the few remaining U.S.-owned companies with a large academic publishing program.

Wiley and McGraw-Hill are still major players, albeit smaller in the academic and educational publishing realm than they used to be. U.K.-owned Pearson is a huge education publisher. Cengage is more of an online player than a traditional book publisher, but they are quite large.

Elsevier, with over $5 billion in annual worldwide sales, is a huge player in the journals space. It retains a large presence in the U.S., as do several other international companies with Asian and European ownership.

*

Jed Lyons is the president and CEO of Rowman & Littlefield.

THE GLOBAL 50 WORLD PUBLISHING RANKING: A PREVIEW

BREAKS, BUT NO BREAKDOWNS: THE PANDEMIC AND ITS IMPACT ON THE INTERNATIONAL BOOK BUSINESS

A Preview of the Global 50 World Publishing Ranking 2021

BY RÜDIGER WISCHENBART

"Why Books and Publishing are Flourishing" ran the headline of Markus Dohle, Penguin Random House's international CEO, for a recent conversation organized by *Publishers Weekly*, in which he promised to "rethink" the publishing business with a view to the pandemic.

Of course, 2020 was "a tough year for everyone," he said, but in the end "business went through the roof last year," with great growth, especially for printed books in the USA, and this development continued in the first half of 2021.

2020—A Good, Albeit Complex Year for the Largest Trade Publishing Groups

In fact, the annual reports of many of the largest international book companies make people sit up and take notice with positive to extraordinary results.

France's leading publishing group, Hachette Livres, got away with a red zero despite massive bookstore closings in France due to the lockdown, and thus helped considerably in stabilizing the results of parent group Lagardère, whose second mainstay in the tourism business brought it a decline of -38 % in overall turnover.

The strong deviations according to submarkets are remarkable. While the book business in Hachette's home market of France fell by 4.3%, owed, among other things, to a weak schoolbook sector, the company's sales in Great Britain grew by a whopping 9.9% in the crisis year, and in the USA by 3.9%, thanks to strong bestsellers such as J.K. Rowling's *The Ickabog* and Stephenie Meyer's *Midnight Sun*.

It looked even better in terms of profitability. Over the year the yield grew by 12%, whereby similar to a roller coaster, the second half of the year saw an increase of 19%, after a considerable lockdown-related decrease of 25%.

Despite the impressive results, spring 2021 brought the end of long-term CEO Arnaud Nourry, who had led, and expanded, the second-largest trade publishing group since 2003. The rift in spring 2021 came due to a fundamentally strategic difference of opinion with majority owner Arnaud Lagardère.

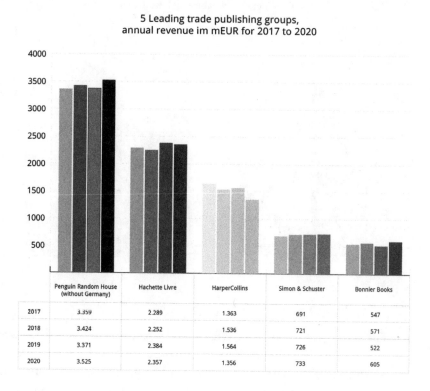

5 Leading trade publishing groups, annual revenue im mEUR for 2017 to 2020

	Penguin Random House (without Germany)	Hachette Livre	HarperCollins	Simon & Schuster	Bonnier Books
2017	3.359	2.289	1.363	691	547
2018	3.424	2.252	1.536	721	571
2019	3.371	2.384	1.564	726	522
2020	3.525	2.357	1.356	733	605

Since joining Hachette, Nourry has stood for an exclusive focus on the book sector in all its facets. Lagardère, meanwhile, spoke of possible synergies with the mixed media group Vivendi, which also includes the second-largest French publishing group Editis.

Many of the large publishing corporations experienced wild ups and downs, albeit in different periods. Bloomsbury in Great Britain, with a strong output also in the USA, and the publishing home not only of J.K. Rowling, but a broadly differentiated portfolio extending into the academic sector, saw its best first fiscal half-year since the economic crisis of 2008 between March and August 2020, and expected a stronger full year than originally expected in terms of sales and earnings.

A recurring refrain in the annual reports are statements about massively pessimistic expectations when the pandemic began to emerge more clearly in the first half of the year, followed, however, by much more positive actual results at the end of 2020, and with a strongly positive trend that continued in 2021.

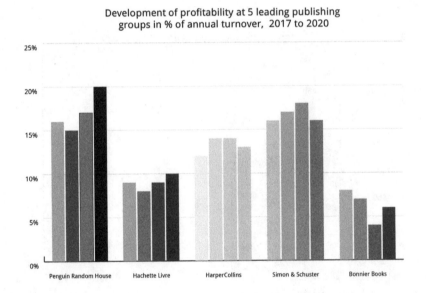

Development of profitability at 5 leading publishing groups in % of annual turnover, 2017 to 2020

Håkan Rudels, CEO of Bonnier Books, and thus responsible not only for the result in Sweden, but also in Germany and Great Britain, expected a slump in sales of around one billion Swedish kronor (almost 100 million euros) in spring 2020. But at the end of 2020 Bonnier had even increased significantly with total sales from the national and international publishing business of 6,112 million kroner (around 600 million euros), 6% more than in 2019.

Adlibris, Bonnier's Swedish bookstore chain, increased 19% in sales in 2020 (at 2705 million SEK, or 268 million euros). (Bonnier Annual Review 2020)

Note: As companies report profitability at diverse standards, the above graphic is to highlight the evolution just within each company. Comparisons between companies are misleading, due to that diversity in accounting practices.

Various Drivers Behind the Positive Performances

The positive performance at many of the strongly performing enterprises could build on a bundle of factors that each had instigated well before the Covid-19 crisis struck.

These programs for innovation included various initiatives for optimizing in-house processes, from IT all the way to logistics, strategic key accounting across all sales channels, direct-to-consumer marketing, a carefully targeted international expansion, and not the least substantial investments for operating and exploiting creative properties across territories, through physical as well as digital channels and platforms.

Reaching out beyond the old ways in the book business often included the creation of strategic partnerships far beyond the sector, for tapping into talent recruitment from self-publishing, as much as cross media content development.

At Bonnier for instance, the strongest positive driver of sales and earnings was the digital distribution platform BookBeat, which is already active in more than two dozen countries, including Germany since 2017. (Bonnier Annual Review 2020)

2020 marked a special milestone for digital offerings, and in particular for audiobook subscriptions. Not only the achieved total volume with sales of 500 million crowns (almost 50 million euros) mark a significant growth curve. With 500,000 paying customers around the world who consume BookBeat's offers on average 25 hours a month, they make a big difference.

New usage patterns are emerging, which will probably continue after the pandemic, with a young target group on the one hand, under 25 years of age, and on the other hand with older digital users over 65 years of age who have now been recruited.

This tipping point is highlighted by a number: in 2020, for the first time in Sweden, more digital books were consumed than printed ones, and the lion's share was not due to digital downloads, but to subscriptions. (SVB 15FEB2021)

But even at the comparatively traditionalist book company Hachette, the digital share—mainly from e-books—increased markedly to 9.5% of all group income in 2020 (compared to 7.8% in 2019). The revenue from audio books grew from 3.4% in 2019 to 4.3% in the Covid-19 year 2020.

An even greater factor of the total volume was, of course, the growth in favor of online sales for printed books. In Sweden, this helped Bonnier's book chain Adlibris to turn around and return to profitability after several difficult years.

In the major international markets, this also boosted the role of Amazon. For the USA, Markus Dohle reports that four out of ten books that Penguin Random House sells are now delivered by Amazon.

Overall, Dohle sees six decisive trends for his optimism: Continuous growth in the world market for books, not least due to increasing literacy worldwide, the now well-established mix of physical and digital delivery with a stable ratio of 80% printed and 20% digital income, growth in children's and young adult's books as well as the boom in audiobooks.

A Push to Further Innovation

The transformative push for innovation does not stop with the re-opening of bookstores and an easing of restrictions as seen in many countries by summer 2021.

Announcements by several of the transnational publishing groups are clear in the assumption that home office and remote work for individuals and for teams is expected to become a permanent feature. For many companies, hybrid formulas between time in the office and remote work are being considered or have been introduced already.

At Hachette UK for instance, staff are about to work three days per week in the office, while Bloomsbury opted for two days per week. (BS 21APR2021, https://bit.ly/Office-HachetteUK, and BS 23APR2021, https://bit.ly/office -Bloomesbury)

These changes result ultimately in companies reconsidering the role and functionality of central facilities of their organizations altogether, or as Madeleine McIntosh, U.S. CEO of Penguin Random House has stated in a message to employees: "At some point, it's possible that we will want to undertake a significant redesign of 1745 Broadway [PRH's iconic New York headquarters], but we're not there yet." (PW 28APR2021, https://bit.ly/Office-PRH)

A Trend Favoring the Largest and Strongest Players

This confidence is of course also nourished by the strong starting position in which around a dozen leading groups in consumer book publishing from around the world were able to get themselves, each with good access to the English-speaking book markets, as well as thanks to strong rationalization efforts started years before the pandemic, and their ability to leverage ever more complex value creation and supply chains.

In many parts of fragmented Europe, the upheavals were sharper. For Germany, the buchreport ranking of publishers shows a slight minus of -4.1% even for the Random House publishing group, and significantly more substantial, often double-digit percentage losses in turnover for the Holtzbrinck Group's trade publishers.

Only Bonnier's German holdings, with imprints Carlsen, Ullstein, or Piper the third corporate group in the market, as well as a few mid-sized publishing houses saw gains—notably Bastei Lübbe, C. Hanser or children's and YA houses Ravensburger and Oetinger. (BR 100 Verlage)

A similar drifting apart of strong market leaders, and a few specialists who succeed in outperforming many other players, is likely to emerge in many places and industry sectors around the world. (Details on this will be provided in the updated edition of the Global 50 World Ranking of Publishers, available at www.wischenbart.com/ranking)

In the first survey of the pandemic impact on publishing for Europe, based on national markets, the European Publishers Association (FEP) recently presented its analysis of "winners, losers and the middle ground" under the catchphrase "uneven."

The winners include Norway (+ 10% growth in the overall book market), Sweden (+8.7%), Finland (+12% for trade), but also the Netherlands (+6% for trade) and Great Britain (+5, 5%), with e-commerce, digital formats and subscriptions being identified as main growth drivers.

Italy (+2.4%), Spain (-1% for Trade) and Germany (-2.3% in total) are in the middle of the field. Austria (-4.4%) and Poland (-5.5%) recorded somewhat larger losses. There were significantly more drastic slumps in Bulgaria (-10% to -15%), Hungary and Slovenia (around -20% each).

Competition, Consolidation, and New Alliances Beyond the Core of the Book Industry

A comparison between strong market leaders and the market as a whole indicates that the competitive situation at the lower end of the scale is likely to intensify significantly.

Even among the international market leaders, there are many signs of upheaval, not necessarily as a direct result of the crisis triggered by the pandemic, but rather reflecting the acceleration of centrifugal forces on the market that had already started.

Two major acquisitions in the USA are in the spotlight. Penguin Random House, already the world's largest general-interest publisher, is taking over Simon and Schuster for $2.2 billion (approx. EUR 1.85 billion), and HarperCollins

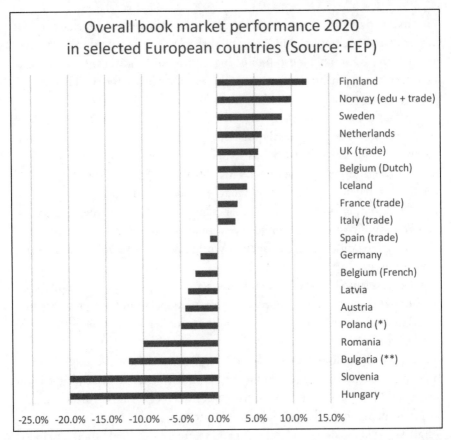

Publishing market developments in 2020 across Europe. Courtesy of Federation of European Publishers 2021, chart for this report.
Notes:
(*) Resulting more from price wars than market contraction;
(**) Est. Between -10 to 15%.

secured the consumer book division of Houghton Mifflin Harcourt for $349 million (almost $300 million), expecting significant savings from streamlining combined operations. (BS 25NOV2020 and PW 10May2021)

As a side note, and to put that into perspective: In 1998, German Bertelsmann had acquired Random House, that "shiny crown jewel of American publishing" (*The New York Times*) for just US$1.4 bn (roughly US$2.3 bn in today's money). What a bargain, which in hindsight kickstarted globalization in the book industry for the following quarter century! (NYT 24MAR1998)

The current re-structuring which, again, was not started, but given additional momentum by the pandemic, includes several lines of action:

- Mergers and acquisitions in consumer books, which are not at all limited to the globally leading players;
- Mergers and acquisitions especially in educational publishing, a sector hit much more strongly, and deeply, than trade, often spearheaded rather by private equity than by genuine publishing enterprises, in reaction to the surge of distance learning as schools were closed;
- Mergers and acquisitions in the service and distribution sector supporting the book industry, including alliances reaching into secondary markets;
- Re-positioning and globalization of new entrants such as self-publishing and cross-media platforms.

The following highlights are, by no standard, not a complete list of recent transactions, but rather exemplary cases to illustrate a freshly emerging pattern.

Already in early 2020, Paris-headquartered Vivendi bought into Spanish Prisa group, the parent of educational publisher Santillana, to broaden its portfolio in the ambition to become a "global leader in content, media and communications, while extending its access to the Spanish-speaking markets in Europe, Latin America and US Hispanics." (PW 25JAN2020) A few months later, in April 2020, Vivendi also entered the capital of Lagardère, expanding its share to 29% by mid-2021, which ultimately had also led to the ousting of Arnaud Nourry as CEO of Hachette in fall 2020, as has been mentioned above in this report. In a general assembly in June 2021, the influence of Vivendi at Lagardère was further cemented by transforming the group into a Société Anonyme. (Capital.fr 21APR2021, Reuters 2OCT2021, LH 30JUN2021)

In Scandinavia, Danish Egmont announced plans to gain full ownership from Swedish Bonnier over Norwegian Cappelen Damm, while Håkan Rudels, Bonnier's CEO, announced plans of his own to expand his group's position in Norway.

Digital, and in particular digital audio, will certainly be a central factor in the group's strategy. Bonnier had made several investments, notably into Norwegian Strawberry Publishing, throughout 2020 to expand its hold on audiobook operations across the Nordic countries, and well beyond. (SVB 30JUN2021)

In France, the founding family with Irène Lindon of the iconic literary Editions du Minuit, which had published Samuel Beckett, secured a long-term perspective for the publisher under the corporate roof of Gallimard. (LH 23JUN2021)

In Germany, the book retail group Weltbild acquired the insolvent coffee-table and art book publisher teNeues in fall 2020. (BR 30SEP2021)

Less flashy, but not less relevant, are the transformations occurring in the service sectors that are the prerequisite for smooth operations throughout the book industry.

A publishing portfolio of multiple formats in print and digital, catering to ever more segmented target audiences through an increasing number of channels, again for both physical and digital products, need ever more complex operations for a satisfactory fulfillment. Books are not the only, but a particularly granular, sector where the competition for meeting consumers' expectations has been rising for years. And in this critical field, Amazon, in many regards an overwhelming player of singular scope and scale, competes with everybody else.

In this context, book distributors operate under difficult conditions, as has been highlighted in Germany by the insolvency of distributor KNV in 2019, and its subsequent takeover by general logistics operator Zeitfracht, or in France by restructuring processes and tensions at Interforum, the distribution arm of Editis in the Vivendi group, to emphasize just two recent cases. (BR, and LH)

In digital distribution, German Bookwire, a sponsor of the Global 50 reports, accelerated its expansion over the past years by gaining a new investor, VR Equitypartner, taking over local competitor Readbox, and opening new offices in both the U.S. and in France, after expanding already successfully to Spain, Brazil and Mexico. (www.bookwire.de/en/press/ and https://bit.ly/VC-Bookwire)

Also on a global level, the book marketing platform NetGalley of U.S.-based Firebrand Technologies was acquired by the leading Japanese e-book distributor Media Do. (BS 21FEB2021)

Unsurprisingly, opportunities for book retail outside of traditional channels have been explored in several directions. In the U.S. and in Great Britain, the launch of a collaborative online book retail platform, Bookshop.org, in early 2020 occurred just in time as the series of temporary bookshop closures due to lockdowns in the pandemic threatened the survival of numerous independent brick-and-mortar bookstores. (uk.bookshop.org/pages/about)

In Germany, Dirk Rossmann, the founder of a chain of drugstores, and an author of successful crime novels, invested in general consumer publisher Bastei Lübbe (whose authors include Dan Brown and Ken Follett), in order to expand book distribution in secondary market sectors. (BR 13APR2021)

In a global push, Disney also remembers its publishing division, which was barely present for a long time, to develop spin-off books from its huge film and TV library and the subscription service Disney+. "We are 100 percent prepared for takeovers," said the $22 billion media giant. (PW 16APR2021)

In educational publishing, McGraw-Hill, after calling off its intended merger with Cengage in spring 2020, has now announced it will be acquired by private equity firm Appollo in a deal worth $4.5 bn, emphasizing "the increase in digital sales over the last eight years, which have risen from about 25% of total revenue to approximately 60% now." (PW16JUN2021)

In scientific publishing, Clarivate—formerly the science and business division of Thomson Reuters, acquired and further developed by Asian private equity group Onex—is taking over the science data base and academic library service company ProQuest in a deal worth $5.3 bn. (Clarivate, 17May2021)

All these moves are clearly made with an agenda of speeding up the digital transformation across all sectors of the publishing industry.

An Old Strategic Debate Reframed

The dynamics behind these various mergers, acquisitions and restructuring initiatives are not at all limited to what is traditionally summarized under publishing, in the Global 50 ranking or elsewhere.

When German media corporation Bertelsmann acquired U.S. publisher Random House in 1998, then CEO Thomas Middelhoff explained his strategic concept in an interview: "Our music company BMG has staged the opera *Turandot* in Beijing's Forbidden City. That production was turned into a CD, and our TV company CLT-Ufa made a movie out of it, while our magazine *Stern* wrote an article. Now we can distribute that CD through our book clubs and on the Internet." (Der Spiegel 15NOV1998)

Reality turned out to be more complicated. Such a paramount exploitation of creative content across all media and territories worked out only in exceptional events, instead of becoming the "magic sauce" for an integrated global content market. But in his statement of 23 years ago, Middelhoff introduced his *Turandot* anecdote with a reference that very much governs boardroom debates today: "In our struggle for the end-consumer," Middelhoff said, "we have worldwide 44 million subscribers—I see lots of underexplored opportunities."

By today's standards, a global reach of 44 million subscribers is a modest goal. Streaming TV operator Netflix passed this threshold by the end of 2014 and has currently over 200 million paying subscribers. (Statista 2021)

But the notion of measuring reach and audiences for evaluating a business strategy, rather than products and turnover, was a bold anticipation in 1998.

In a way, the dichotomy in today's big media debate can be drawn along a line separating enterprises betting on their products (as in "content is king"), and those others who, first of all, look at audiences and how to continuously feed their services to these audiences (as in a "network and platform" or "eco-system" economy). The first model is about "sales," the latter is about "access" and "subscription."

(Note: On the evolution of "subscription models" in book and audiobook publishing, see our Digital Consumer Book Barometer, www.global-ebook.com, and the "subscriptions pro and contra" debate at www.rebootbooks.org)

One of the fastest expanding players, the Swedish audiobook and subscription pioneer Storytel, has engaged in talks with the music streaming platform Spotify, which already had ventured into publishing territory in the field of podcasts. In November 2020, Spotify took over Megaphone, an advertising and publishing platform, for $235m. (Deadline 10NOV2020) It is everyone's guess how the cooperation between Storytel and Spotify will further evolve.

Another example is Canadian Wattpad, initially a fanfiction writing community turned into a global self-publishing platform which subsequently expanded into moving images and entertainment with the creation of a Wattpad Studio division. Wattpad has announced it will be acquired by Korean Naver through its Webtoon Studios division, at reportedly over US$600 m. Upon closing of the deal in May 2021, Wattpad was said to grow its teams by nearly 50%, bringing together global audiences of a combined 166 million monthly users for an "audience-based storytelling," combining moving images and reading, to compete with the likes of "Amazon's new Kindle Vella and Seoul's Kakao." (PP 11MAY2021)

To be clear, no media company, and no publishing venture of any sensible scope, would operate today without having established numerous interfaces with platforms, or without broadly addressing directly the end consumers. Also, it is not foreseen whether the "books first" approach will prevail as the winning option in the long run, or if the changing game is favoring bookish enterprises embedded with other media and formats in one fully integrated ecosystem.

But the race is open and in full swing, all over again, and the book industry will not escape its dynamics.

List of abbreviations:
BR buchreport (www.buchreport.de)
BS The Bookseller (www.thebookseller.com)
LH Livres Hebdo (www.livreshebdo.fr)
PP Publishing Perspectives (www.publishingperspectives.com)

PW Publishers Weekly (www.publishersweekly.com)
SVB Svensk Bokhandel (www.svb.se)
YA young adult

This White Paper and the *Global 50 World Publishing Ranking* are available for download at
www.wischenbart.com/ranking
Contact: office@wischenbart.com
Find out more about our work at
www.rebootbooks.org
www.global-ebook.com
www.sidt-books.eu

⑥

INDEPENDENT PUBLISHING

INDEPENDENT PUBLISHING: A PLACE FOR EVERYONE

BY ANGELA BOLE

How does one get a sense of the current independent publishing landscape? Exhibiting rapid changes amid exponential growth, there's no one-size-fits-all definition of "independent publishing." Instead, there are small presses, indie presses, hybrid publishers, association presses, regional publishers, publishing service providers, and the ubiquitous, not-to-be-ignored "self-published author."

That all these varied and sometimes competing business models are lumped together under the single umbrella of "independent publishing" is one of the many ways traditional publishing tries to minimize and gloss over this powerful and diversified market. "Oh, that? That's just independent publishing. Nothing to see there." But there is something to see. A lot to see, actually. As the CEO of the Independent Book Publishers Association (IBPA), I know this because we've been looking for a long time.

In 1983, a group of 15 Southern California independent publishers who couldn't afford to attend the American Booksellers Association's (ABA's) annual conference decided to pool their funds and send Jan Nathan to represent them and their books. Jan returned excited about possibilities, and the Publishers Association of Southern California (PASCAL) was born.

Very quickly, the leaders within PASCAL realized that national marketing was one of the greatest challenges facing independent publishing, so the concept of cooperative marketing became the backbone of the association. As the group grew, the name changed to reflect this focus. PASCAL became the Publishers Marketing Association (PMA), and new programs were developed.

As more time passed, the PMA Board of Directors came to understand they needed another name change, this time to reflect the concerns of independent publishers beyond cooperative marketing. In 2008, PMA became the Independent Book Publishers Association (IBPA). Now, in addition to cooperative marketing programs, IBPA works hard to support its over 3,700 members through advocacy, education, and tools for success.

DEFINING "INDEPENDENT PUBLISHER"

In the United States, the standard definition for "independent publisher" is any publisher not part of a large conglomerate or multinational corporation. In most cases, this definition includes an expectation of annual sales below $50 million or an average of 10 or fewer new titles per year.[1] IBPA membership doesn't require a certain annual sales revenue or number of new titles published per year. Instead, IBPA bases its membership ranks on three business models:

- **Independent Publisher:** Persons or organizations involved in publishing other people's work using a traditional, royalty-based publishing model and/or an author-subsidized (hybrid) publishing model. (An Independent Publisher might also publish their own work.) An Independent Publisher is defined as one not operated by a major publishing house (e.g. one of the "Big Five") and its imprints.
- **Author Publisher (aka Self-Published Author):** Persons who exclusively publish their own work.
- **Publisher Partner:** Persons or organizations involved with supplying services or products to the field of independent publishing, including publishing service providers, printers, book designers, consultants, booksellers, distributors, wholesalers, and other industry vendors.

Within the ranks above, size varies greatly. A July 2021 survey of IBPA's 3,700 members found that 12% had one active title in circulation, 28% two to five titles, 29% six to 20 titles, 16% 21 to 100 titles, and 11% more than 100 titles. Couple this with the fact that, in the context of their own businesses, 41% said a book only needed to sell between 1 and 999 copies to be considered successful (only 5% said 20,000+ copies needed to be sold to be successful) and you begin to understand the niche nature of independent publishing in all its forms.

Of course, "niche" doesn't mean independent publishers aren't making money. The success of independent publishing is often apparent from company

---

1   https://www.tckpublishing.com/complete-guide-to-small-press-publishing-for-writers/

by company, as illustrated by *Publishers Weekly*'s annual list of the fast-growing independent publishers, but where it's particularly clear is in the aggregate. Let's go way back to begin illustrating this point.

In 1997, IBPA, then known as the PMA, and the Book Industry Study Group (BISG) jointly surveyed America's 53,000 independent, smaller book publishers (those publishers with between one and ten active ISBNs). The survey was conducted to gain a better understanding of the characteristics of these publishers and to quantify the sales they made. As the final report stated in its preface, "because the smaller and independent firms are scattered across the country, it's hard for either industry watchers or industry insiders to form a clear picture of them in the aggregate."

The key statistic that emerged from this report was startling; over $14.3 billion dollars of sales were being generated by this publisher segment. At the time, this was equal to about two thirds of the total sales generated by the industry as reported in BISG's *Book Industry Trends 1998*, a figure that reflected almost entirely the sales of larger publishers.[2]

The $14.3 billion sales figure gave credence to the claim that independent publishers' books were more widely available and more influential than they were perceived to be. These sales also suggested that the smaller, independent publishers were (or certainly should have been) important vendors the publishing industry ought to heed.

A repeat of the 1997 survey conducted in 2002 produced similar results. Although roughly 70% of the respondents to the 2002 survey reported annual sales of less than $100,000, respondents in the aggregate registered annual sales of between $29.4 billion and $34.3 billion—approximately 15% to 27% greater than the reported base for the entire publishing industry.[3]

But what does this look like today?

THE RISE OF SELF-PUBLISHING

If the authors of IBPA's 1997 and 2002 *The Rest of Us* thought it was hard for industry watchers to form a clear picture of the 53,000 small press publishers surveyed for these groundbreaking reports, what would they make of the 1.6 million self-published print and e-books with registered ISBNs documented by Bowker in 2018, the last time it published its once-annual study entitled *Self-Publishing in the United States?*[4]

---

2   *The Rest of Us*, © 2003 the Publishers Marketing Association, page 6
3   *The Rest of Us*, © 2003 the Publishers Marketing Association, page 22
4   https://pq-static-content.proquest.com/collateral/media2/documents/bowker-selfpublishing-report2019.pdf

Without a doubt, the rise of self-publishing has fundamentally altered the independent publishing landscape. Once seen as vanity publishing by those who couldn't secure a traditional deal, self-publishing is now a sought-after choice so pervasive that publishing insiders such as Mike Shatzkin have determined to "discover" it for those east of New Jersey.[5]

Fueled largely by self-publishing platforms CreateSpace, now Kindle Direct Publishing, and Lulu (both founded in 2000), and necessarily enabled by print-on-demand technology, the quality of self-published books continues to improve. All signs point to even more self-publishing in the future as traditional publishing continues to consolidate and close doors to stories from the margins. Having put its *Self-Publishing in the United States* report on hold in 2019, Bowker says it is in the process of designing a new, more meaningful one with an expected release of late 2021. We should all look forward to the findings in this report if we're expected to understand the true state of book publishing in the United States.

A PLACE FOR EVERYONE

At the beginning of this chapter the question was posed: How does one get a sense of the current independent publishing landscape? To close, I'm reminded of the F. Scott Fitzgerald quote: "The test of a first-rate intelligence is the ability to hold two opposed ideas in mind at the same time and still retain the ability to function." This is how I think of independent publishing. It's this . . . and it's that.

Sometimes independent publishing is traditional in its business model, sometimes author subsidized; sometimes DYI, sometimes highly collaborative; sometimes it relies on distribution, sometimes it shuns it; sometimes it is mission based, sometimes solely finance driven.

It's magnificent to be all these things at once. It's malleable and open and ready to make space for the next new idea. All this considered, heterogenous nature of independent publishing is unquestionably a force for good in our industry, giving diverse voices the chance to make a way for themselves alongside what are mostly monochromatic traditional publishing spaces. This is absolutely something to celebrate: a place for everyone.

*

Angela Bole is chief executive officer of the Independent Book Publishers Association (IBPA). IBPA's mission is to lead and serve the independent publishing community through advocacy, education, and tools for success. IBPA's vision is a world where every

5 https://www.idealog.com/blog/enterprise-self-publishing-is-coming-the-third-great-disruption-of-book-publishing-since-the-1990s/

independent publisher has the tools and knowledge needed to professionally engage in all aspects of the publishing industry.

Prior to joining IBPA, Angela served two years as deputy executive director of the Book Industry Study Group (BISG), an organization that fosters conversation and consensus across all sectors of the book business. Before that, she served two years as BISG's associate director and two years as its marketing and communications manager.

Angela holds a master of science degree in book publishing from New York University and a bachelor of arts degree in English with a minor in gender studies from Indiana University Bloomington. In 2018, she was awarded the Book Industry Study Group's Community Builder Award, given to an individual in recognition of significant work done to engage a representative set of book industry stakeholders. In 2019, she was named a *Publishers Weekly* notable person of the year.

SMALL AND LARGE PUBLISHERS: SYMBIOSIS

BY HUGH L. LEVIN

From *Poor Richard's Almanack* to *Fifty Shades of Grey*, small publishers have always been a vital part of America, but perhaps no more so than in the last three decades of the twentieth century. These were the years of Workman, Running Press, Joshua Morris, and a small publishing company called Hugh Lauter Levin Associates. These were also the years of large publishing conglomerates. RCA owned Random House. The *Los Angeles Times* owned trade and professional book publishing companies and in the reverse, Harcourt Brace Jovanovich purchased SeaWorld!

The image of a small publishing company might be of someone with a printing press in his basement, taking his books to bookstores in a Volkswagen bus, but this is hardly the case. The small publishers of the twentieth century were often successful through the help of large companies—they were independent but hardly isolated. The success of these companies was due to being able to leverage their success with large printing companies, book distributors, and large retailers.

I launched Hugh Lauter Levin Associates in 1973 with the publication of a facsimile edition of *The Boston Cooking-School Cook Book* by Fannie Merritt Farmer, originally published in 1896. The book became a great success, selling hundreds of thousands of copies. From the beginning, the success was made possible by large companies.

I was raised in a publishing family. My father, Martin P. Levin, worked at Grosset & Dunlap for 17 years before becoming president of the Times Mirror book publishing group. My mother, Marcia O. Levin, was a writer of children's books, including the Donna Parker series for young girls. My brother, Jeremy Leven, is a novelist and screenwriter. Even though I studied art and architecture at the University of Pennsylvania, it was probably inevitable that I would work in publishing.

It was at Penn that I had first used the Fannie Farmer cookbook—to make my student meals. I noticed that the book, first published in 1896, was the first cookbook to use standard measurements. The mid-1970s was an era of "back-to-basics"—from macramé to the first days of organic food—and I thought there might be interest in the Fannie Farmer 1896 back-to-basics recipes. From family dinner-table conversations, I had a basic knowledge of copyright law and understood that the book could be republished without needing to clear any rights. I was able to track down a copy of the book at a university library right in Philadelphia. Now what?

My father referred me to several book printers, and I selected Book Press, one of the largest printers of trade books. I then met with Nat Wartels at Crown Publishing, who had been extremely successful with a facsimile edition of an old Sears, Roebuck catalog. He liked the idea of the cookbook and agreed to have Crown distribute the book.

Crown was one of the largest independent publishing companies at that time, but they did their own distribution as well as the distribution for other publishers. By distributing for other publishers, they were able to use their sales and distribution facilities at minimal additional cost and with no investment in project development or inventory. For this work, Crown would keep a percentage of the sales. This model was used and continues to be used by many large publishing companies.

Crown may have been the most dynamic publishing company of the 1970s. The company was the country's largest remainder book company, buying overstocks from other publishers and selling them at reduced prices. Crown was also a trade publishing company with bestsellers ranging from *The Joy of Sex* to novels by Judith Krantz and Jean M. Auel. Nat Wartels, famous for the piles of ledgers, manuscripts, and correspondence on his desk, was the force behind the company. He was aided by his nephew Alan Mirken and by Joe Reiner. Crown became a great school for future independent publishers including J.P. Leventhal, Michael Friedman, and Bruce Harris.

While Book Press was printing the book and Crown was doing the distribution, other large companies were vital for the success of *The Original Boston Cooking-School Cook Book*. New American Library, a paperback company, purchased both mass market and trade paperback rights from Levin. Both Book of the Month Club and Doubleday Book Clubs licensed rights for the title.

Crown sold out the first printing of the book prior to publication and there were numerous reprints for the book trade market. In these years, the book trade was booming in part due to vitality of bookstore chains such as Waldenbooks, B. Dalton Books, Crown Bookstores (unrelated to Crown Publishing), Pickwick Books, and Doubleday Book Shops as well as the national wholesalers Ingram and Baker & Taylor along with regional wholesalers.

This model for successful publishing by independent publishers through the efficiency of large companies was vital to the success of not just the publishers but of the distributors, retailers, and wholesalers as well.

After the success in 1973 of *The Original Boston Cooking-School Cook Book*, I successfully published two other titles. Having grown up around publishing, I was aware of how rare it was for books to be successful and that I had been very lucky with these three publications. I was offered a job as assistant to the president at Harry N. Abrams, Inc., the art book publisher, and I decided that Abrams would be a great and much-needed educational experience. I worked at Abrams from 1974 through 1983 at various positions including director of production and publisher of Abrams Original Editions. I developed projects including *Television: The First Fifty Years* by Jeff Greenfield and *100 Years of National Geographic*, both of which became Abrams bestsellers. I also developed the Abradale imprint of promotional reprints of Abrams backlist titles.

One of the jobs that I had at Abrams was arranging for U.S. production of some of the books. One of the bestselling Abrams titles, *The Art of Walt Disney*, had to be printed in the United States for copyright reasons. After publishing the large $45 edition of the book, Abrams published a 160-page, magazine-sized, concise edition of the book. The first printing was set at 500,000 copies. This was my turn to have a large company help a small one. I was introduced to a Wisconsin printer with one printing press and fewer than 20 employees. The owner of the company had been the head of a large book manufacturing company, and the printing samples shown to me of the magazines and advertising work the small printer had done were of a very high quality. Even though this company had never printed a book before, I tried them with one title to begin with. Everything worked out perfectly, and the company received the order of the *Disney Concise Edition*. Abrams was the first book company to use this printer and one of the first ten customers. The company was Quad/Graphics, started by Harry "Larry" Quadracci Jr. It's now a $4 billion company. An example of big helping the small.

In 1984, while completing the Executive MBA program at the Wharton School at the University of Pennsylvania, I restarted Hugh Lauter Levin Associates. While at Abrams, I realized that Abrams was aware of their most successful titles when the projects were being initiated. Abrams was publishing approximately one hundred titles a year, but they knew which titles had the greatest chance of success from the beginning. They knew this based upon the success of prior similar titles and input from major customers such as bookstore chains and book clubs.

Between 1984 and 2007, when it was purchased by Rizzoli, Levin Associates published approximately 250 titles ranging from its annual Jewish Calendar to *The Complete Works of Michelangelo*. Its business grew to over $10 million in annual sales with a staff of no greater than six. As in the beginning, the success of the company was due to large companies. While the greater the unit sales, the greater the profits of a company, this is especially true in book publishing. It is the first copy of the book that has the highest costs due to the costs of the author, editor, designer, photo research and rights, typesetting, color separations, etc. After the first copy, the run-on costs are essentially paper, printing and binding, shipping, and royalties. With the assistance of large companies, Levin Associates was able to create titles with significant print runs and backlist sales.

The "editorial committee" for Levin Associates was its large customers. These included Advanced Marketing Services (the wholesaler for Price Club, Costco, Sam's, and BJ's), Borders, Book of the Month Club, Doubleday Book Clubs, and others. I would develop presentation dummies of possible future titles, show them to these customers, and then select the titles with the most positive input for publication.

For production, Levin was able to use some of the largest printing companies in the world, including Toppan Printing, Dai Nippon Printing, Mandarin Offset, Leefung Printers, and C&C Offset Printing.

Crown Publishing and Outlet Books were extremely helpful in the creation of art books with high development costs, often $100,000 or more. J. P. Leventhal of Outlet created a way for Outlet to partially fund the initial costs of creating some books in exchange for the future reprint rights of bargain editions of the titles. Outlet would pay Levin a royalty on these reprints, which Outlet would produce. More than ten titles were initially created in this fashion. While the initial trade sales by Levin of these books were less than five thousand, over the years, Outlet sold over a million copies of the books.

For large retailers, one advantage to working with Levin Associates was the company's ability to act quickly and to change directions quickly. Examples of this are *Great Paintings of the Impressionists*, *Images of Nature*, and *The Great Scrapbooking Kit*.

In 1983, I had attended the Moscow International Book Fair on behalf of the Association of Jewish Publishers, an ad hoc group of publishers of books of Jewish interest that wanted to make their books accessible, if only for a few days, to Jews in the Soviet Union. At that time, Soviet Jewry was severely repressed. It was actually illegal to own a book in Hebrew. At the 1983 Moscow Book Fair, I met the staff of Aurora Publishing, a Soviet publisher that specialized in art books.

Serendipitously, it was two years later, during the 1985 Moscow Book Fair, that a cultural exchange agreement (the first in many years) was negotiated by Armand Hammer on the part of the United States. As part of the first exchange, Impressionist paintings from the National Gallery in Washington, D.C., would tour the Soviet Union, and Impressionist paintings in Soviet museum collections would tour the United States. The exchange would take place in less than six months.

Levin and Aurora agreed to publish a book combining Impressionist paintings from the National Gallery and the Soviet museums. The book would be created by the two companies working together and simultaneously published in the United States in English and in the Soviet Union in Russian with both companies' imprints. There were also simultaneous French, Spanish, and German editions.

With commitments from the Metropolitan Museum of Art, the Museum of Fine Arts, Boston, the Los Angeles County Museum of Art, and Book of the Month Club, Levin and Aurora proceeded to create the book in record time. With freelance designer Philip Grushkin, I traveled to Leningrad and worked together with the Aurora team to design the book. I then flew from Leningrad to Tokyo to give the production material to the printer, Toppan Printing Company. Toppan produced the first proofs in record time and even sent their production manager to Moscow and Leningrad to correct the color proofs alongside the original paintings. The book was produced within 90 days from concept to bound books, perhaps a record for a large-format art book at that time, prior to the advent of digital files.

Images of Nature, which featured photographs by the great nature photographer Tom Mangelsen, was started by Ron Palmer at Advanced Marketing Services. Ron had seen an exhibition of Mangelsen's work while changing planes at the Denver Airport and thought Advanced Marketing could sell a book featuring Mangelsen's photos. Mangelsen was a well-established nature photographer with several gallery shows and assignments from *National Geographic*, but there had not been a book on his work. Within a few days, Palmer and I met with Mangelsen in Wyoming and put together a team including an author and a book designer to create a book. One of the reasons Mangelsen and I made a good team was that I gave Mangelsen great freedom to make sure the book that he wanted was the book that we created. Mangelsen even went to Hong Kong with me to approve every printed sheet. *Images of Nature* is still in print in 2019.

One advantage of Levin Associates was that there were no in-house editors. Obviously a different editor would be better for *Images of Nature* than the same editor for *Great Impressionist Paintings*. All of the employees at Levin Associates were project managers rather than editors or designers.

Levin Associates also published craft books that were very successful with book clubs. Andy Arbuckle of Borders came to me wanting a scrapbooking book and kit that would outdo all the others. I was able to put together a book with various scrapbooking accouterments including a binder, colored paper, scissors, stickers, glue, color markers, and on and on. It is doubtful that large publishers would be able to source all of the materials and create a kit for such a reasonable price. Borders would order 10,000 copies several times a year for many years.

The Impressionist book *Images of Nature*, and *The Great Scrapbooking Kit* are just a few examples of how the agility of Levin Associates provided great incentives for large companies to support and even help create Levin's publishing program.

In addition to its art books, Judaica, and crafts books, Levin Associates is known for its various large-format illustrated books on the military. Serendipity played a major part in Levin starting to publish in this category as well.

Levin had published two books with the Smithsonian National Air and Space Museum. The museum's publishing director was Trish Graboske. Trish's husband, Fred, is an archivist. He had been the archivist of the Nixon tapes and in 1996 was the archivist for the U.S. Marine Corps. At a casual meeting, Fred and I discussed publishing a large-format illustrated book on the Marines. *The Marines* was published in 1998. It was not only distinctive in that its authors were generals, great military historians, and even a Marine Corps commandant, but it was printed with a unique enamel and gold-plated medallion on the cover. *The Marines* was an outstanding success and led to the development of two series of military books on all of the armed forces. Through publication of these books, well over $1,000,000 in royalties were paid to military and veterans associations.

Foreign co-editions are often one way for publishers to increase the print runs for their publications to cover some of the development costs. At the Jerusalem Book Fair in 1996, I met Ludwig Koenemann. Koenemann had been one of the founders of the publisher Taschen in Germany and had recently created his own company. The philosophy of Taschen and Koenemann was to publish illustrated books in multiple languages at the same time and distribute the books themselves. Levin had up to this time sold very few foreign rights to its publications. Co-editions could be quite difficult regarding scheduling, requested changes by the copublishers and even payment. Working with Koenemann solved these problems for Levin. Levin licensed multiple language rights to Koenemann in exchange for royalties, and Koenemann used Levin's printing films and did all of their own production. In a period of several years, more than 25 titles were licensed to Koenemann and published in languages including German, French, Spanish, Italian, and Dutch, as well as others.

Selling to the large customers had great advantages over selling only to the book trade. Companies like Advanced Marketing and Book of the Month Club bought books under very different terms than bookstores. They would give firm, nonreturnable large orders prior to printing. They paid the shipping costs from Asia and the customs clearance costs. They received no co-op advertising. They paid quickly and reliably. By buying under different terms than booksellers, Levin was able to offer the special sales customers lower prices and in turn, the special sales customers offered lower prices to the retail customers. This was a very good and efficient model, but the American Booksellers Association members were not pleased with the fact that books were being sold at lower prices than the bookstores could sell them.

In 1994, the American Booksellers Association sued five publishing companies regarding different prices to different customers. The publishing companies were Penguin, Houghton Mifflin, St. Martin's Press, Rutledge Hill, and Hugh Lauter Levin Associates. Levin and the ABA settled the suit by Levin agreeing to sell to the ABA members at the same prices and terms as the special sales customers. The ABA aggregated advance orders from their member bookstores and the books were purchased nonreturnable, FOB Asia, with no advertising allowance and payable within 90 days. While the news of the 1994 ABA convention was the suit, at the 1995 ABA convention, Levin titles were on display at the ABA booth for sale to members! The system worked for two years, but after that, the stores preferred to order books returnable, with an advertising allowance, from Levin's distributor.

In 1984, when Levin Associates restarted, their books were distributed by Scribner's. Scribner's was bought by Macmillan, which was later bought by Simon & Schuster. Levin Associates was like plankton on the food chain and later moved distribution to Publishers Group West, a company that specialized in distributing independent publishers.

Levin's largest special sales customer was Advanced Marketing, representing over 25% of the business. Publishers Group West was another 25% of the business. In 2002, Advanced Marketing purchased PGW, resulting in more than 50% of the Levin business with one customer. All was fine until 2007 when Advanced Marketing filed for bankruptcy at the time of year that they owed the most to Levin Associates. Partially because of this and for personal reasons, in 2007, Levin Associates was sold to Rizzoli International, the book division of the Italian company RCS which since then has been bought by an even larger company, Mondadori.

Rizzoli continues to reprint the Levin Associates backlist and publish new titles with James Muschett, the former vice president at Levin Associates, overseeing the publishing program. From the beginning Hugh Lauter Levin Associates always had "Associates" as part of the name of the company. I understood the importance of a team and was fortunate to have longtime employees Ellin Yasky, Leslie Carola, and Jim Muschett as part of the team.

Since 2007, I have developed nearly 100 books for other publishing companies, as well as establishing Artepublishing, a publisher of enhanced electronic books. I have consulted for the Ingram Content Group and was publisher of Thunder Bay Press, a division of Baker & Taylor, creating the Canterbury Press series of elegantly produced and bound classics that is currently one of the top series of classics in the world.

FOUNDING AND RUNNING AN INDEPENDENT PUBLISHING COMPANY

BY NICK LYONS

F ounding an independent book-publishing firm is a seductive gamble. The great joy and challenge of running such a company is that you can be fiercely independent and publish exactly what you deem worthwhile, profitable, important. The biggest danger is that you can lose all your own, a rich relative's, or your investors' money by going flat bust; you can accomplish this sooner or later.

Not everyone wants to own an independent publishing firm—for financial or psychological reasons: worry about one's set of skills, fear of leaving the comfort of a job where others have built a safe haven and have experts in the dozens of tasks needed for a fully staffed book firm. Many editors at larger, corporate publishing houses either fear the complexity of, say, production or sales, or simply prefer only to edit. But independent book-publishing firms are flourishing. Some have only one or two owner-workers. And others are fully staffed with hundreds of employees. This is terrifically healthy. As more and more of the large corporate publishers gather in clusters, the smaller independents are surely preserving a part of the book world otherwise lost. In fact, independents can and often do publish books the large corporations, with many people pressuring them, either cannot or will not bring to print. Technological advances have of course facilitated both the ability to produce and sell books, and a small publisher is restricted only by his or her own sweet conscience.

How to get started? This of course depends upon the size firm one envisions—and the necessary vision one has for the firm's focus. A very small firm, planning only to publish a few books each year, can be funded with some modest amount of one's own capital, as little as, say five to ten thousand dollars, and working from a room in one's home. Even that small, it is wise to incorporate, with the help of a lawyer, to limit financial vulnerability. You will need to prepare a contract, according to your needs but comparable to the standard contracts used by other firms, to be used with authors; it should lay out the obligations and responsibilities of each party, including (but not limited to) due dates, royalties on various kinds of sales, legal responsibilities, and eventually reversion of rights. You will need to plan the approximate number of books you expect to publish in your first few years and how many employees, at what salary level, you will need. Expert outside help may be needed to provide editorial, production, promotional, and sales advice. You must know how much of these tasks you can perform yourself and how much it will cost to hire those needed to do other work that must be done. You can go bankrupt with too many employees but also with too few, or too inexperienced a crew. Be sure the total salary budget determines how many people you can afford when held against the revenue you can depend upon. Outside contractors can be expensive. And the more you can learn yourself will earn dividends as you grow: you become less dependent upon outside help, and you're mostly cheaper.

For a more ambitious program, you will need to raise capital. Some of this, depending upon your needs, can be acquired from places and people that fund start-ups, such as can be found on Kickstarter. A firmer, long-distance source can be independent investors, who can lend you the money for a specified time and interest or buy shares in your company. Raising money privately, through the latter methods, makes the most sense but you should retain at least 51% of such shares. It's as important for you to know your investors as it is for them to know you. Private investment often requires the investor to sign a document affirming that he or she has more than a certain net worth and can afford to lose the entire investment. You will want to have among your stockholders some or all who will stay with you for the long haul and who might help in a variety of ways, such as by providing financial advice, general business suggestions, or contacts with others who can help in some seminal way. You should be prepared to meet with your stockholders once or twice a year. A strong business plan is needed for most investments. A good accountant is essential.

A small independent publisher should start with a core specialty: poetry or fiction; current affairs; country life; cooking; outdoor leisure sport; books on or by celebrities; books for some segment of college life or needs; children's books; and a vast "and so forth." Niches and specialties. The more knowledge you have of a specific field, area, or niche, the better able you will be to choose, edit, produce, and sell your books. The world probably does not need many small general publishers who must compete for authors and sales with big corporate firms.

You will need to choose wisely to ensure the quality and salability of the books you publish, and to balance a list at least at a level capable of sustaining your firm. You can choose "the important books you think the world needs" and those that will satisfy your aesthetic values, but you will always be a business that needs to generate enough sales to remain solvent and profitable. You must, above all, survive. Many do not. Dozens that publish excellent, even bestselling, titles, do not: one had two major bestsellers in less than two years, generating millions of dollars of revenue and soon afterward went bankrupt when they thought they were a three-million-dollar company rather than one much smaller; they expanded, forgot to calculate that their bestsellers could not be duplicated, found no new ones, and suffered further when tens of thousands of their old ones were returned. A large percentage of most very successful books will be returned and remaindered.

You must study the cost of producing books, reliably estimate the number of copies to print, print neither too few or too many, judge how much revenue will come from sales, how much you will be required to pay in royalties, the cost of sales (publicity and commissions, for instance), and you must add some portion of the general office expenses (rent, salaries, insurance, utilities), taxes, and the amount you have offered to authors as advances against royalties and thus a form of loan, only a portion of which will be recoverable. Expensive parties and expensive lunches don't help.

You will need to determine how many copies should be sent to generate prepublication comments and reviews, and how many should be sent to post-publication reviewers, and which. Keeping every name for these purposes is essential; such lists are a true asset and should be compiled with rigor and care.

The great pleasure of independent publishing is funding and then helping books that you hope will be taken to heart by enough people. You are absolutely free to choose what you will.

It is possible to lose your savings and your investors' money through poor choice of books, careless management, incorrect print runs, profligate spending, taking too many risks, or avoiding risk. But it can be exhilarating and profitable to make books that go bravely into the world—and even might change that world.

*

Nick Lyons founded The Lyons Press. His latest book was *Fire in the Straw: Notes on Inventing a Life*.

WHAT IT MEANS TO BE INDEPENDENT

BY JEANNETTE SEAVER

B y definition, an independent publisher is one which operates free of corporate accountability.

When my husband, Dick Seaver, and I started Arcade Publishing some thirty years ago, being independent meant that we could take risks—financially and otherwise—to follow our taste, to make mistakes without suffering punishment, to seek out literary voices from different cultures, and to introduce new authors to American readers. In 2008, as we began our twenty-first year as independent publishers, Dick noted that "we have kept fairly close to our original commitment to publish quality to the best of our ability, eschewing the facile for the challenging, and ranging far afield as we discovered and introduced new literary voices."

Along with our list of American authors, we have published more than 300 writers from 34 countries, and today our growing backlist generates a substantial portion of our annual volume. To name but a few: Jacques Attali, Jurek Becker, Ingmar Bergman, Bertold Brecht, Melvyn Bragg, William Burroughs, Octavio Paz, E.M. Cioran, Eugene Ionesco, Alistair Cooke, Nuruddin Farah, Gerald Durrell, Lawrence Durrell, Ismail Kadare, Leslie Marmon Silko, Natalia Ginzburg, Amin Maalouf, Andrei Makine, Tahir Shah, Shashi Tharoor, Sir Peter Ustinov, Tim Parks, Marquis de Sade, and countless others, including the 2012 Nobel Prize for Literature recipient Mo Yan. Most recently, Arcade rescued and published Woody Allen's autobiography after it had been dropped by the corporate Hachette.

Had we stayed the course within corporate publishing, many of these important literary voices would no doubt have been viewed as not "lucrative," and publication would have been vetoed.

Yes, our endeavor was perhaps more romantic than realistic. But for all of us—and our glorious staff of talented and dedicated editors, designers, publicity—it was worth the journey.

*

Jeannette Seaver is the cofounder of Arcade Publishing and a contributing editor to Arcade and Skyhorse Publishing.

FAST-GROWING INDEPENDENT PUBLISHERS, 2021

BY JIM MILLIOT AND CLAIRE KIRCH

aunched in 2013 to publish digital editions of out-of-print genre fiction from the 1960s and '70s, Las Vegas's **Wolfpack Publishing** reports that while revenue growth was steady in its first five years, its strongest growth was between 2018 and 2020. In this period, 90% of Wolfpack's sales were books in digital formats. The company does things its own way, releasing titles weekly, president and CEO Mike Bray says, rather than seasonally. "We publish four to eight titles a week, both fresh stuff and reissues."

Though Wolfpack's list focuses on westerns, it has been supplementing its offerings with adventure, mystery, and historical fiction releases. And series are an essential component in its business model, publisher Rachel Del Grosso says, explaining, "When we are approached by any author or agent, the first thing we're looking at is how many titles the author is bringing to the table. We invest in an author, not a single book."

Bray, whose background is in digital marketing, says his marketing focus has been on consumers rather than on the trade. Besides running targeted advertisements on Amazon and social media, Wolfpack has a mailing list of 45,000.

Wolfpack does offer a print-on-demand option for authors interested in print books, but Bray says he's not interested in pursuing a distribution deal in which he would need to surrender distribution of e-books to another company. Still, he isn't ruling out some sort of print distribution in the future. "We have original titles from some well-known authors in our pipeline," he says. "Authors like Max Allan Collins, W. Michael Gear, and Kat Martin would do well in the traditional channels, so we are looking for a print-only distribution deal on select titles."

Blue Star Press, based in Bend, Ore., turned five in 2020 and has developed enough of a backlist to take advantage of some of the trends that developed during the pandemic. According to COO Peter Licalzi, the publisher worked with one of its house authors to release a series of children's drawing books to meet the increased demand for activity books for kids, and *How to Draw All the Animals* by Alli Koch was its bestselling title of 2020. Blue Star's Our Little Adventures box set of children's books, written by speech pathologist Tabitha Paige, also performed well at a time when parents were looking for educational and entertaining titles for their children. And its Beautifully Organized books, produced by its Paige Tate & Co. imprint, had a good year, too. Overall, the company's backlist in such areas as arts, crafts, home organization, and journaling sold well, Licalzi says.

Last year was Blue Star's first full year as a client of Penguin Random House Publisher Services, and Licalzi credits PRHPS with expanding the press's reach into bricks-and-mortar retailers, especially independent booksellers, as well as getting it into international markets for the first time.

After posting a 60% sales increase last year, Licalzi says he is confident about Blue Star's future. To help expand its list, the company added a new designer and publishing operations lead last year.

The Innovation Press, a four-year-old children's publisher in Seattle, is making its first appearance on *PW*'s list of fast-growing independent publishers this year, fueled by a 83% jump in revenue in 2020 compared to 2019. Founding publisher Asia Citro, Innovation's sole employee, thinks switching distribution in 2018 to Baker & Taylor Publisher Services had a significant impact on the company's financial performance, but she attributes its success primarily to a strong list that emphasizes quality over quantity. Innovation titles have received plaudits from the New York City Public Library and the Chicago Public Library, as well as many organizations dedicated to children's education and literacy.

Citro launched Innovation to publish her own chapter book series, Zoey and Sassafras. That eight-volume series has sold more than 1.5 million copies to date. Also in 2017, Innovation began publishing the Amazing Scientists series of rhyming picture books featuring famous female scientists. With five volumes published, Amazing Scientists, written by Julia Finley Mosca and illustrated by Daniel Rieley, has sold approximately 400,000 copies to date. And last year, two frontlist titles had a good start: the picture book *Your Name Is a Song* has sold 50,000 copies to date, and *Busy Toddler's Guide to Actual Parenting* has sold 25,000 copies.

Mango Publishing Group, based in Miami, has found different ways to grow in its six-year history—and 2020 was no exception, with the publisher seeing big gains in international markets. According to the company, it sold books in more than 200 countries last year, with "significant" growth in India, Malaysia, Mexico, Singapore, and South Africa. Mango CEO Chris McKenney says one reason for the growth was more global SEO and social media reach. "It's really gratifying to see our five-year-old analytics team innovating book discovery and reader conversion to the point that we can generate eye-popping sales increases in all sorts of different countries," he notes.

Mango is also working to develop global authors, and the company has high international hopes in 2021 for Australian baker and food scientist Ann Reardon, whose YouTube series *How to Cook That* has been viewed more than 63 million times worldwide since 2019. In June, Mango will publish *How to Cook That*, Reardon's book of extravagant cakes, chocolates, and desserts, in the U.S., Canada, Australia, and New Zealand.

Back in the U.S., Mango's lifestyle line had another good year, led by Bobbi and Dessi Parrish's FlavCity cookbook series. Special markets were another source of growth. Becca Anderson's *Badass Affirmations* was a hit at Costco and other special markets, and *Your Work from Home Life* did very well at Target, as did the first two books in Dino Dana's Field Guides series, which are also seeing strong sales at the warehouse clubs and discovery museums.

A book acquired by associate publisher Brenda Knight before the pandemic hit and released in March was another big seller: *Mindfulness for Warriors*, a meditation book for first responders, has benefitted from bulk buys by different organizations to give to first-responder teams. *Find the Helpers* by Fred Guttenberg, father of Parkland victim Jaime Guttenberg, was another title that resonated with different organizations last year, with group orders coming from the American Federation of Teachers and also by congressional leaders and staff.

Though the pandemic forced **Media Lab Books** in New York City to alter some of its plans last year, 2020 sales were up 41% over 2019. MLB v-p and publisher Phil Sexton attributes the gain to a range of factors, including an increased focus on specialty sales, custom sales, and foreign-language rights sales.

Another important move was to lessen MLB's dependence on licensed titles—it has worked with such partners as Disney, Nickelodeon, and Smithsonian—by adding more author-driven books. As a result, 2020 sales were split evenly between author-led titles and licensed properties, and in early 2021 author-driven titles were accounting for 70% of sales, Sexton says. Among MLB's top sellers last year were *The Game Master's Book of Random Encounters*, *The Unofficial Harry Potter Character Compendium*, and *Sweatpants & Coffee: The Anxiety Blob Comfort & Encouragement Journal*.

In 2018, MLB began trimming the number of new titles it releases annually to create better books with more backlist potential. Sexton says it had hoped to begin expanding the list again in 2020 but pushed those plans back to 2021 and 2022. The publisher will add a few more new titles this year, among them *Cooking for Wizards, Warriors and Dragons* by Hugo Award–winner Thea James and *The Official John Wayne Handy Book of Bushcraft* by Billy Jensen, a retired Green Beret.

Sexton sees the MLB list rising to 20 titles in 2022, and to more than 30 in 2023. Even as the list expands, he notes, MLB will look for projects from authors that have "highly engaged followers" or information to share that will stand out in a crowded market. "We try to maintain a very high bar for what we're willing to publish, with a clear vision for the channels we expect each book to sell in," he adds.

Entangled Publishing launched on Valentine's Day 10 years ago in Denver as a publisher of romance fiction for YA and adult readers. In 2012 it had a national bestseller, *The Marriage Bargain*, CEO and publisher Liz Pelletier says. The company has evolved over the years, moving beyond contemporary romance into subgenres such as erotic and historicals, cutting its annual title output, and trimming its number of full-time employees (though it recently made four new hires). But perhaps its biggest change was to lessen its dependence on e-book sales and shift to emphasizing mass market paperback romances under its Amara single-title adult imprint.

"We published fewer books, but bigger books," Pelletier says of 2020. "And there was a more substantial marketing budget. We're not looking to sell paperbacks that sell 200,000 copies—we don't need to in order to make a profit." Initial print runs average 50,000 copies, and company sales are now evenly divided between print and digital.

Another factor in Entangled's success, Pelletier notes, is that half the list is "collaboration publishing." The company develops the concepts for certain novels and their packaging based on its own market research. The publisher and author draft a synopsis, and then the author writes the book. Macmillan, which is Entangled's distributor, also provides feedback on concepts and packaging.

Entangled publishes some of the biggest names in romance for adult readers, such as Amalie Howard, but the company's current bestsellers are the first three volumes in the Crave series, a YA quartet by Tracy Wolff, which has sold 400,000 copies in the U.S. since its launch in hardcover last April.

Familius cofounder and president Christopher Robbins considered 2020 a success not only because the company increased sales by 12% over 2019 but because it also began several initiatives he is convinced will position the family-oriented children's and adult publisher for the future. One of its most important pivots last year was improving the discoverability of its books online, as more sales migrated there because of bricks-and-mortar lockdowns. "We realize how important book discoverability is," Robbins says. "We've continued to invest in that initiative as readers explore more online." In addition, Familius, which is based in Sanger, Calif., increased its consumer-oriented marketing efforts.

Those changes gave a big boost to Familius's backlist sales, which accounted for 66% of total revenue last year, up from 48% in 2019. Backlist titles that performed well include *Made for Me, But First We Nap, Good Moms Have Scary Thoughts, Alphatrain*, and *The Big Book of Family Games*. Another important factor in the company's growth in 2020, Robbins says, was the shift in late 2019 to Workman for distribution. (Prior to that, Familius had been doing its own distribution since 2015.)

During 2020, Familius launched the *Helping Families Be Happy* podcast, which was reaching a global audience by the end of the year. The company also completely reengineered its website to provide free family-focused content from Familius's authors and illustrators, launched a storytime video program to help families discover the company's children's content, and began the Familius Helping Families Be Happy virtual conferences, in which Familius authors provide ideas and solutions to help families deal with a range of issues.

Those new efforts notwithstanding, Robbins says all Familius programs begin with the book. "Our responsibility as stewards of our authors and illustrators' intellectual property is to ensure it is as discoverable as possible," he notes. "All activities surrounding the book are to execute on that objective."

Magination Press, the children's book publishing imprint that has been affiliated since 1997 with the American Psychological Association in Washington, D.C., reports that sales growth was steady before 2018 but then leapt between 2018 and 2020. Editorial director Kristine Enderle attributes the success to the APA's strategic focus on reconfiguring and rebranding the press, first implemented three years ago. Changes made include a greater commitment to digital and innovative marketing, the hiring of more editors, and bringing production and design in-house. More attention was also placed on subsidiary rights sales.

Magination has also made its titles more trade friendly, with an emphasis on titles about mental health and wellness topics that can appeal to a range of readers. "We shifted away from publishing books that you would find in therapists' offices," Enderle explains. "These are books that kids can go to that are accessible—though still authoritative."

The press's bestselling series, What to Do Guides for Kids, launched in 2005 and "showcases the best that we do," Enderle notes. There are 12 volumes, all written by child psychologists, with a 13th, *What to Do When the News Scares You*, scheduled for release in 2022. The titles are huge backlist bestsellers, each typically selling tens of thousands of copies annually, and the book that introduced the series 16 years ago, *What to Do When You Worry Too Much*, sells 70,000 copies per year.

A 2018 Magination title was also pushed onto the bestseller lists after George Floyd's murder last spring, with 100,000 copies sold to date: *Something Happened in Our Town: A Child's Book About Racial Injustice* has just gone back to print for another 30,000 copies.

Unlike many publishers last year, **Chelsea Green**'s sales gain in 2020 was led not by backlist sales (up 34%) but by frontlist (up 66%). That was due in part, publisher Margo Baldwin says, to several drop-in titles, including two books tied to the pandemic: *The Invisible Rainbow* by Arthur Firstenberg and *Corona False Alarm?* by Karina Reiss and Sucharit Bhakdi.

According to Baldwin, frontlist sales were helped by Chelsea's ability to work with niche partners to quickly create online events to support new book launches. Its entire list benefited from people being stuck at home and thinking about "growing their own food and becoming more self-sufficient," she notes. As a result, Chelsea, which is based in White River Junction, Vt., saw an "incredible surge of interest in our how-to books, especially food, farming, gardening, and alternative economics."

Investments made in several areas also contributed to big sales gains in 2020 over 2019 at Chelsea. Baldwin says investments in its direct-to-consumer website sales and marketing allowed the house to handle the higher demand and volume "pretty easily." The company had the largest gain in its direct-to-consumer channel, with revenue jumping 130%. Sales through Amazon rose 41%, while business with Ingram increased 76%. Digital sales rose 34%, aided in part by Chelsea's investment in digital audiobooks.

A final piece to 2020's growth came from investment in Chelsea's new U.K. operation, and Baldwin says that division had "huge" gains driven by new releases of U.K. titles and backlist.

Las Vegas–based **LMBPN Publishing Worldwide** has ridden steady digital sales gains to post a 35% revenue increase in 2020 compared to 2018. Over that same period, the company has increased its number of employees to keep pace with its rapid expansion of annual title output. Its operating model calls for publishing lots of digital content for voracious readers of urban fantasy and science fiction, and though that strategy has paid off, it is looking to add print formats. To date, e-books and digital audio have accounted for nearly 99% of the company's revenue.

To help LMBPN expand, late last year it appointed a new president, Robin Cutler, who had headed up IngramSpark, with LMBPN founder Michael Anderle focusing on creative direction. Cutler says that in addition to broadening its reach into bookstores and libraries by offering print editions, other initiatives involve promoting its titles directly to readers and fans, and growing overseas by increasing sales of translation rights and expanding distribution in foreign markets.

Bicoastal publisher **Ulysses Press**, which has 13 employees divided between offices in Berkeley, Calif., and Brooklyn, publishes books on emerging trends in a range of categories, including pop culture, travel, lifestyle, and cookbooks. It had a 20% increase in sales in 2020 over 2018, and publisher Keith Riegert attributes the improvement to a combination of factors, including the move to Simon & Schuster on Jan. 1, 2020, for distribution.

After sales dipped last spring when the pandemic first struck, Ulysses rebounded by expanding its frontlist. A record 65 titles were released last year. Recent bestsellers include sleeper hit *The Unofficial Hogwarts for the Holidays Cookbook*, which sold 20,000 copies in 2020. The company, which Riegert describes as a "very research and market-driven enterprise," is also placing even more of an emphasis on digital marketing and consumer analytics to develop its list. And with backlist accounting for 70% of Ulysses's revenue last year, he notes that the publisher will add resources to promote those titles.

Looking ahead, Riegert says he intends to launch a children's imprint this summer focusing on hot topics in pop culture, such as diversity and the #MeToo and Black Lives Matter movements.

Founded in 2006, **Rocky Nook**, now located in San Rafael, Calif., specializes in educational photography books. Its mission is to "help photographers of all levels improve their skills in capturing those moments that matter." The company has seven full-time employees, but a growing number of freelancers perform a variety of tasks ranging from website development and hosting to database development.

Though sales remained stable throughout Rocky Nook's early years, a new management team put in place in 2014 built up its web presence, grew its marketing outreach, and enhanced its authors' visibility. Those changes put the company on a general upward track, and though sales dipped in 2018, they rose the past two years, closing at a record high in 2020. New title output also hit a high last year.

Rocky Nook publisher and CEO Scott Cowlin regards 2020's strong finish as the culmination of a new business strategy that it implemented in 2019, through which the publisher strengthened its list while adding new topic areas, new authors, new sales channels, and new markets.

Those actions led Rocky Nook to publish more photography books with appeal to the indie bookstore market last year and to hire commission sales reps to call upon both bricks-and-mortar and online camera stores. The company expanded its list by adding a spiral-bound pocket guide series for popular cameras, as well as a deck of posing cards.

Rocky Nook's efforts succeeded, and Cowlin describes himself as being "blown away with sales across the board, of both our traditional photography titles as well as our diversification titles." Bestsellers included Scott Kelby's

FAST-GROWING INDEPENDENT PUBLISHERS 2018–2020

PUBLISHER	SALES GROWTH 2018 v. 2020	EMPLOYEES 2018	2020	NEW TITLES 2018	2020
Wolfpack Publishing Las Vegas	309%	4	12	160	256
Blue Star Press Bend, Ore.	176%	5	7	9	18
The Innovation Press Seattle	140%	1	1	7	5
Mango Publishing Miami	119%	23	33	99	97
Media Lab Books New York City	100%	22	19	14	12
Entangled Publishing Denver	80%	20	14	225	131
Familius Sanger, Calif.	66%	8	9	61	70
Magination Press Washington, D.C.	55%	6	9	22	33
Chelsea Green White River Junction, Vt.	41%	26	25	23	25
LMBPN Las Vegas	35%	13	29	211	359
Ulysses Press Berkeley, Calif./New York City	22%	12	13	52	65
Rocky Nook San Rafael, Calif.	17%	7	7	22	32

SOURCE: PUBLISHERS WEEKLY

The Digital Photography Book (17,000-plus copies) and Lindsey Adler's *The Photographer Guide to Posing* (9,000-plus copies).

*

A version of this article appeared in the 04/26/2021 issue of *Publishers Weekly* under the headline: Fast-Growing Independent Publishers.

FAST-GROWING
INDEPENDENT PUBLISHERS,
2017–2020

FAST-GROWING INDEPENDENT PUBLISHERS, 2017

Almost half of the companies on this year's list posted triple-digit gains between 2014 and 2016

BY JIM MILLIOT AND CLAIRE KIRCH

In the more than 20 years *PW* has been doing its fast-growing independent publishers feature, it is hard to find another year when publishers on the list reported such impressive growth rates. Five of the 11 publishers on this year's list posted triple-digit revenue gains in 2016 compared to 2014, and two publishers saw their revenue shoot over the $10 million mark in the past year.

The company that had the biggest gain on this year's list was founded in 2014, but it didn't sell its first book until 2015. **Cottage Door Press**, which publishes children's books, released 18 titles in 2015 and another 82 titles last year. It plans to publish 50 in 2017. Between 2014 and 2016, the press also doubled in personnel, from nine to 19 employees, and it is preparing to move from Barrington, Ill., to a larger facility in the Chicago suburb of Deerpark.

Cottage Door's 2016 revenue skyrocketed 558% from the previous year's figure. The publisher's debut list in 2015 focused on titles for babies and toddlers up to age three, but the publisher intends to expand its target audience to include four- and five-year-olds, beginning with a line of titles published in partnership with the Smithsonian Institution.

Though Cottage Door is a young company, its apparent overnight success might be due to the fact that most of its staff are children's publishing industry veterans—most notably its founder, Richard Maddrell, who served until his retirement as president of Publications International. Cottage Door's creative team conceives, designs, and produces the press's list with the assistance of freelance illustrators. The emphasis, says marketing manager Melissa Tigges, is on high-quality books that are "on top of current trends"—such as STEM and STEAM—and "hot formats," including padded board books, lift-a-flap, touch-and-feel, books that make sounds, and books made with engineered paper.

Every Cottage Door book has a removable sticker it calls the Early Bird Learning Guide: the sticker informs the buyer of the book's appropriate age range and which skills the child is developing when that particular book is read. "We believe in educating and entertaining both children and their grown-ups," Tigges said. "We choose artwork and language that interests, informs, and stretches their growing minds."

Fast-Growing Independent Publishers 2014–2016

Publisher	Sales Growth 2016 v. 2014	Employees		Titles	
		2014	2016	2014	2016
Cottage Door Press Barrington, Ill.	558%*	9	19	0	82
Callisto Media Berkeley, Calif.	286%	24	34	36	122
Europa Editions New York, N.Y.	277%	3	4	29	29
Greystone Books Vancouver, Canada	253%	11	14	20	20
Page Street Publishing Salem, Mass.	117%	6	12	21	54
Diversion Books New York, N.Y.	84%	2	11	336	426
Haymarket Books Chicago, Ill.	67%	11	14	60	79
Sasquatch Books Seattle, Wash.	55%	16	19	36	27
Graywolf Press Minneapolis, Minn.	49%	11	13	34	34
Nimbus Publishing Halifax, Canada	31%	14	16	32	48
Shambhala Boulder, Colo.	8%	33	36	78	86

*Sales growth is for 2016 v. 2015

Ever since it released its first list in 2012, **Callisto Media** has relied on the same formula for success: increasing title production, selling more copies per title, and broadening distribution. Those goals were achieved in 2016, according to v-p for marketing Holly Smith, and revenue jumped by 111% compared to 2015. Last year's revenue soared 286% above the 2014 figure, and the company surpassed the $10 million sales level last year.

Smith says that in 2016, Callisto had some "extremely successful" frontlist releases, including *Instant Pot Electric Pressure Cooker Cookbook, Kid Chef*, and *The Whole 9 Months*. And, she adds, the publisher's backlist, now at 383 titles, has become a "very strong component of our success as well." New areas for Callisto, which continues to use data analytics to spot consumer trends, include parenting and kids, fitness, and self-help.

At **Europa Editions**, the popularity of Elena Ferrante's Neapolitan Quartet has increased steadily over the past few years, propelling a sales gain of 156% in 2015 over 2014 and another 47% revenue rise in 2016. Editor-in-chief Michael Reynolds acknowledges the importance of Ferrante to the 12-year-old company's success, but he notes that the balance of its list, focused on publishing authors from all over the world in the British and North American markets, has also contributed to its growth.

The company's backlist has performed solidly, with two titles that Europa released in 2015, *The Distant Marvels* and *The Pope's Daughter*, continuing to sell well into 2016. Frontlist books that did well last year included *The Natural Way of Things*, *Shelter in Place*, and *The Life of Elves* by Muriel Barbery, whose *The Elegance of the Hedgehog* was one of Europa's first hits.

Reynolds thinks the success of Ferrante's series has helped Europa's entire list gain more visibility in the market, but he also believes the company is doing a more effective job marketing its books. Title output has remained around 29 per year, and its four-person American office shares staff (designer, financial officer, production manager, and typesetter) with Edizioni E/O, its sister company in Rome.

Canada's **Greystone Books** has flourished since it was relaunched as an indie press in 2013, when former publisher Rob Sanders led a consortium that bought the imprint from its bankrupt parent company. With Sanders as publisher, the press, which is best known for its books on nature and the environment by authors from Canada and elsewhere, has grown its revenue. Its 2016 sales were more than double the 2015 figure, and were up 253% compared to 2014.

Greystone, which counts among its 14 employees a U.K.-based publicist to promote books and authors there, attributes its success to a focus on international sales. According to sales and marketing manager Jen Gauthier, "Publishing worldwide is a key strategy."

A glance at Greystone's top sellers also reveals a savviness about making acquisitions that appeal to a broad market. Almost every year, the publisher has released a best-seller, beginning with 2013's pictorial chronicle of devastating floods in Alberta in partnership with the *Calgary Herald*. *The Flood of 2013* has sold 55,000 copies to date. In 2015 Greystone acquired North American English-language rights to the German bestseller *Gut: The Inside Story of Our Body's Most Underrated Organ* by Giulia Enders, which has sold 90,000 print copies and 24,000 e-books to date.

But it was a 2016 release that caused Greystone's sales to skyrocket this past year: *The Hidden Life of Trees* by Peter Wohlleben, originally published in Germany, was translated into English and released simultaneously in North America and in the U.K. The Greystone edition has sold 240,000 copies worldwide (150,000 in the U.S.). The press hopes to keep up the momentum by releasing another book by Wohlleben, *The Inner Life of Animals*, in November.

Page Street Publishing has continued its rapid sales growth since it was launched in 2013 by Will Kiester. The press's revenue was 31% higher in 2016 than in 2015 and up 117% from 2014. Page Street's early success has helped to propel more success, as Kiester says he feels confident reinvesting in the company by continuing to add new employees and titles.

In fact, Page Street expects more increases in the next few years and is upping its title count to around 70 for 2017. Earlier this year, the company hired Kristen Nobles to head its effort to establish a new children's book list. Kiester hopes the list "will serve as a significant growth engine starting in late 2018 and hitting its stride in 2019."

In 2016, Page Street expanded beyond cookbooks, its core focus, to other lifestyle subjects. Kiester says *A Touch of Farmhouse: Easy DIY Projects to Add a Warm and Rustic Feel to Any Room* was a good example of a book "outside of our comfort area" that performed very well, even selling out shortly after its release in December. He notes that he is prepared to slow Page Street's growth if he believes the quality of its products is starting to decline, but adds that "that hasn't been the case to date."

Diversion Books has undergone quite a metamorphosis since Scott Waxman launched the company as the e-book publishing arm of his literary agency in 2010. Diversion was spun off as its own company several years ago and signed with Ingram Publisher Services in late 2014, and the addition of print publishing and distribution components sparked a 84% increase in revenue in 2016 compared to 2014.

The lack of quality backlist e-book rights to acquire, combined with the resurgence in print sales and the decline in digital sales, convinced Waxman that more changes were needed. So in late 2015 he hired Jaime Levine as Diversion's publishing director, and Levine began a program to put out 50–60 frontlist books annually in both print and digital formats. Waxman says the change in strategy yielded immediate dividends last year, with a doubling of print sales compared to 2015 offsetting a 30% decline in e-book sales.

Last year also saw the launch of two new divisions of Diversion: EverAfter Romance and Radius Book Group. EA is a print distribution service that offers bestselling indie authors the chance to reach more bookstores, Waxman explains. It works on a roy-alty-split model and requires authors to deliver ready-to-print book files and handle their own marketing.

According to Waxman, authors are joining EA due to "its flexible model—authors can retain digital rights—as well as the potential for significant bookstore distribu-tion through IPS." EA distributed close to 500 titles in 2016 (both new and backlist books) and plans to release roughly the same number in 2017. It accounted for about 40% of Diversion's revenue last year, and Waxman is looking for a 50% increase in revenue in 2017.

Waxman describes RBG as a "high-end custom imprint serving entrepreneurial authors who want to self-publish by partnering with a top-tier publisher." It offers full-service publishing but not à la carte services. He hired Mark Fretz in February as editorial director and is looking to increase sales in the unit more than 300% in 2017 over last year.

Haymarket Books is a nonprofit publisher of political and social justice titles that celebrated its 15th anniversary last year. In an October *PW* profile, marketing man-ager Jim Plank attributed Haymarket's recent success to its commitment to "put-ting out books that speak to the current moment." These include one of its all-time top-sellers, 2014's *Men Explain Things to Me* by Rebecca Solnit.

Since the election of Donald Trump as president in November, Haymarket's sales have, Plank says, "shot through the stratosphere," with such frontlist releases as Solnit's *The Mother of All Questions*, which has already sold almost 20,000 copies in paper since its March release. Solnit's earlier work, *Hope in the Dark*, which was originally published after the 2004 election, has sold 32,000 copies in paperback and 5,000 digital copies since November. (In addition, Haymarket gave away more than 31,000 *Hope* e-books as part of a promotion.)

The press finished 2016 with a 21% revenue increase over the previous year and a 67% gain compared to 2014. And Haymarket is off to a good start in 2017, with net revenue to date of almost $700,000.

Seattle-based **Sasquatch Books** followed up a 20% increase in sales in 2015 over 2014 with another solid year in 2016, when revenue was up 55% compared to 2014. Little Bigfoot, the company's children's imprint started in 2014, had another year of gains helped by its growing backlist.

The biggest sales driver last year, however, was Sasquatch's 52 Lists journal series by Moorea Seal, who refers to herself as a creative entrepreneur. The series, which features *The 52 Lists Project* and *52 Lists for Happiness* has more than 375,000 copies in print, according to senior publicity and marketing manager Corinna Scott. Other standout titles in 2016 included *Dead Feminists* and *The Hidden Lives of Owls*. The company has another Seal title coming this September, *Make Yourself at Home: Design Your Space to Discover Your True Self.*

For the second year in a row, **Graywolf Press** has been named one of *PW*'s fast-growing indie presses, as it held on to the large year-over-year revenue gain it posted in 2015 and finished 2016 up 49% from 2014. Its focus continues to be on literary fiction, nonfiction, and poetry.

Citizen by Claudia Rankine, which was published in October 2014 and accounted for a significant portion of Graywolf's huge spike in revenues in 2015, is still the literary nonprofit's bestselling release, with 200,000 print copies sold to date. In September, *Citizen* even popped back onto the *New York Times*' bestsellers list when Rankine received a $625,000 MacArthur "genius" grant and announced she is using the money to study whiteness. Two newer titles have also made important contributions: David Szalay's novel *All That Man Is* was a Booker Prize finalist, and Somaz Sharif's collection *Look* was a finalist for the National Book Award in poetry—and the critical acclaim for these books translated into strong sales.

"We're not really doing anything different," notes sales and marketing manager Casey O'Neil, pointing out that Graywolf released 34 new titles and reissues in 2016, up from 30 in 2015. "Rankine's out there in the media often, and our books across the board are simply performing at a stronger level than in previous years," due in large part to academic course adoptions and support from indie bookstores.

Nine Graywolf books were named Indie Next titles in 2016, and six Graywolf releases are Indie Next titles this year through May. "Indies are doing better, and we've benefited from that," O'Neil says. "Plus, more people seem to be reading poetry these days. We're seeing an amazing surge in our poetry list."

Canada's **Nimbus Publishing** realized the benefits of stepping up its international marketing and promotion in the fiscal year that ended March 31, 2017, which included a 31% increase in revenue compared to fiscal 2015. The press, which is based in Halifax and is approaching its 40th anniversary next year, releases adult and children's books primarily about the Atlantic Canadian provinces.

General manager Terrilee Bulger attributes much of Nimbus's growth to a tenfold increase in funding from the Nova Scotia provincial government, which allowed the company to invest in production, marketing, and innovation, and to grow its staff. The press has added new editors to increase output and, for the first time, hired an international rights editor, a publicist who focuses on export, and a digital marketing specialist. Nimbus is also expanding its marketing reach to the rest of Canada by hiring freelance publicists in major cities to better promote its titles to their local contacts.

Although exports to the U.S. have accounted for 5% of the company's business and international rights 2%, Nimbus expects, with the added resources, to grow these areas to each account for 10% of its revenue. "Increased investment from our provincial government has allowed us to take our marketing initiatives to a higher level, which in turn, drives sales and profit," Bulger explains. "Increased investment has also allowed for increased production. The more books we sell, the higher the sales and the higher our capacity to do more."

Shambhala Publications may have only posted an 8% growth in sales in 2016 compared to 2014, but after seven years of steady gains, the company will not be eligible for next year's list of fast-growing indie publishers, since participation is capped at annual sales of $10 million. Shambhala president Nikko Odiseos says the company's growth is due to "a multiplicity of causes": new imprints, acquisitions, readership building, and export editions.

Shambhala started its lifestyle imprint, Roost Books, in 2012, and the unit has become a bigger part of its business. Roost sales were boosted by the fact that its books won James Beard awards in each of the past two years. Snow Lion Publications was acquired in 2012, which cemented Shambhala's position as the largest publisher of Buddhist books in English in the U.S. And in May 2015, Shambhala acquired Rodmell Press, which not only buttressed its Buddhist list but doubled its line of yoga books.

Shambhala has also increased its overseas business by partnering with several publishers and distributors in Asia to print books in English that are priced for the Asian market. To better market its growing list (it will release 100 books this year), Shambhala sends out between 1.5 million and two million targeted emails per month to specific segments on its email list.

FAST-GROWING INDEPENDENT PUBLISHERS, 2018

To be successful, presses forge a unique path

BY JIM MILLIOT & CLAIRE KIRCH

Filling underserved niches and meeting the needs of consumers looking to understand changes in the country's political and cultural environments helped several independent publishers make this year's fast-growing indie publishers list. A number of these presses are relatively new, having barely been operating for longer than the three-year minimum required in order to qualify for the *PW* list.

Cottage Door Press has had extraordinary growth ever since it released its first titles in 2015, a year after it was founded by former Publications International president Richard Maddrell. The company's focus continues to be on producing a range of products for babies and toddlers that align with its mission of "promoting reading aloud from birth."

According to marketing manager Melissa Tigges, much of Cottage Door's growth last year, when sales grew 107% over 2016, was driven by increased distribution and an expanded list. In addition to other new initiatives in 2017, Cottage Door published its first licensed books with Baby Einstein and the Smithsonian, expanded its bestselling Early Book Song Book series, and added to its Love You Always series, which is done in a padded board book format. The company also took advantage of the gift market, expanding its seasonal offerings with line extensions in its lift-a-flap, padded board, and peek-a-flap formats for Valentine's Day, Easter, Halloween, and Christmas. The company's top-selling title continues to be the board book *Grandma Wishes*, which has more than 850,000 copies in print.

In addition to expanding its title count, Cottage Door has significantly broadened its distribution reach. Though its initial success was fueled by selling titles in targeted mass merchandisers, its recent growth, Tigges says, "is being driven by a diversity of titles and customers, including e-commerce, independent toy and bookstores, and international markets." The publisher will continue to expand its reach in 2018 with the launch of a trade line that will feature four titles, including Cottage Door's first picture book, *Nothing Is Scary with Harry*, by first-time author Katie McElligott. To accommodate its growth, Cottage Door plans to move to new offices this summer.

Milli Brown, founder and CEO of Brown Books, says the hybrid publisher has been able to grow its sales over the past three years by "staying focused on a select number of authors and frontlist titles each season." That approach, she says, has enabled the company to significantly boost placement at independent and national bricks-and-mortar stores, as well as in school, classroom, and public libraries.

"Our authors create our success and feed their own," says Brown, who notes that Brown Books authors retain full rights and control over their own books. Among last year's bestsellers were *Sage Alexander and the Hall of Nightmares*, *10 Pillars of Wealth*, *Wounded Tiger*, and *Magnet Max*. Brown Books authors also have access to an integrated public relations and marketing firm that produces, on average, exposure to more than 5,000 media outlets per book launch, says Tom Reale, Brown's COO.

The publisher's distribution agreements reach both the trade and education markets. In 2016 its licensing practice began maturing, with rights sales for multiple titles made across Asia and Europe. Now with a backlist of 150 titles, Brown Books' list has expanded beyond nonfiction to include YA fantasy, juvenile, mystery, and coffee-table books.

Wisdom Publications in Somerville, Mass., specializes in books about Buddhism, mindfulness, and meditation, and publisher Daniel Aitken says some of the company's growth last year was due to increasing numbers of people searching for tools to better deal with the change and uncertainty in their worlds. But he points to actions taken by the publisher that contributed to the gains as well. Specifically, he notes that the 30-year-old company implemented a more aggressive strategy regarding its frontlist last year.

"We set a goal of growing frontlist revenues for 2017 by more than 100%," Aitken explains. "We achieved this goal by increasing the number and quality of our frontlist titles. We also tested and refined a number of pricing strategies to help maximize revenue." He adds that the company also streamlined the publishing process and communication among its production, editorial, and marketing teams.

Though he declines to disclose sales, Aitken says that the press's top three sellers in 2017—*The Suttanipata: An Ancient Collection of the Buddha's Discourses Together with Its Commentaries*, *Mindfulness in Plain English*, and *Bearing the Unbearable*—grossed a total of more than $350,000. Several new marketing initiatives also fueled the company's growth, including a podcast featuring interviews conducted every other week with leading Buddhist thinkers; the *Wisdom Journal*, a biannual publication with illustrations that highlights new releases and bestsellers; and Wisdom Academy, an online course platform accompanying the books that has provided the press with a separate stream of nonbook revenue.

Last year, marketing manager Jim Plank described Haymarket Books' sales as shooting up "through the stratosphere" since Donald Trump's election a few months earlier, putting the Chicago-based publisher of left-wing political and social justice titles on our list of fast-growing indie presses. Haymarket's rapid upward trajectory has continued, with sales jumping 187% in fiscal 2017 from fiscal 2015. The sales increase came despite cuts to the number of titles released between 2015 and 2017.

According to Plank, Haymarket's strategy is to "put out books that speak to the current moment." Shortly after Trump's inauguration, Haymarket partnered with Random House Canada and Allen Lane in the U.K. to release a paperback edition of Naomi Klein's *No Is Not Enough: Resisting Trump's Shock Politics and Winning the World We Need*. Knopf Canada took the lead in editing and production, and Haymarket and Allen Lane tweaked the cover design and tailored title pages to their own specifications to drop the book simultaneously in the three countries. It was Haymarket's top title this past year, having sold 60,052 copies.

Rebecca Solnit's three books on politics and feminism also continue to sell well in this era of women pushing back against sexual discrimination and harassment. *Men Explain Things to Me*, published in 2014 and updated in 2015, sold 53,763 copies last year, followed by Solnit's *Hope in the Dark*, originally published in 2004 when George W. Bush was reelected. Updated in 2016, it sold 40,773 copies in 2017. Solnit's most recent work, *The Mother of All Questions* (2016), last year sold 24,804 copies. Another strong seller was Angela Davis's 2016 collection of essays, *Freedom Is a Constant Struggle*, which sold 35,036 copies in 2017.

Plank notes that Haymarket has always focused on publishing books about people's histories and their struggles. "Since the election in 2016, the audience for these ideas has grown exponentially, as many more people are interested in connecting with those ideas," he says.

Since Familius was first started in 2013 by former Gibbs Smith executive Christopher Robbins, the company has focused on publishing family-friendly books. "We create and sell titles that appeal to diverse families and encourage communication and focus on values that make families happy," says Kate Farrell, the new marketing and public relations director. The publisher sells its list across a wide range of channels and last year saw gains in all markets—including chains, independent bookstores, gift stores, libraries, international, club, and specialty outlets.

Among Familius's bestsellers last year were *Beauty and the Beast Book and Puzzle Box Set*, *101 Amazing Uses for Apple Cider Vinegar*, *101 Amazing Uses for Coconut Oil*, *101 Amazing Uses for Essential Oils*, and *Lit for Little Hands: Alice's Adventures in Wonderland*. Last year the publisher slightly broadened it offerings with increased investment in children's and regional children's programs.

Since its launch, Familius has built a backlist of more than 250 titles. Using that as a resource, it recently created the Happy Family Box, which combines books with crafts and other family-bonding activities. The package is subscription based and priced at $29.99 per month, though consumers receive 35% off their first boxes.

Looking for new talent, Robbins was at the recent Bologna Children's Book Fair, where he was selling translation rights and scouting for new international illustrators. "The children's illustrator market has exploded globally, and our ability to work with these artists regardless of geographic boundary has been a tremendous benefit for Familius, as these artists have very unique and fresh approaches," Robbins says. "The majority of Familius illustration now comes from international partners."

Page Street Publishing president Will Kiester cites a number of factors for the independent publisher's consistent growth between 2015 and 2017. The first is the quality of Page Street's content. When Kiester first launched Page Street in 2011, he said that if he ever saw the quality of the books decline, he would cut back title output. But that has not happened. "As we do more books, the books are coming out better," he says.

A second factor has been Page Street's ability to better promote and merchandise its books as sales increase. "I think more accounts are finding us and are stocking our books, so when we have a hit, it has more merchandising opportunities," Kiester says.

Certainly, the quickened sales rate has justified Kiester's approach. He notes that in the fourth quarter of 2017, Page Street's bestselling books were selling at three times the rate they were in the fourth quarter of 2016. That growth led Page Street to ship $2 million worth of books in a single month twice in a row for the first time, this past November and December. Among Page Street's bestsellers in 2017 were *101 Asian Dishes You Need to Cook Before You Die*, *Hand Lettering for Relaxation*, *The Simple Kitchen*, and a number of Instant Pot titles.

On the kids side, *Epic Lego Adventures with Bricks You Already Have* and *The Superkids Activity Guide to Conquering Every Day* "are paying the bills," Kiester says, as the company pushes deeper into the children's market. This fall its first children's picture books will land, and they follow the recent release of the publisher's first young adult titles, *Beneath the Haunting Sea* and *It Should Have Been You*. Sales have been slow, Kiester acknowledges, but he says the books have been getting "rave reviews," and he will continue to provide marketing support to give them an opportunity to get attention and traction.

Kiester also notes that as Page Street's title count increases, he is seeing more opportunities—and stronger sales—in different areas and subjects: "It's nice to see the heavy hitters spread out nicely from our cooking list, with surprising strong sellers like *American Duchess Guide to 18th Century Dressmaking*, and the year before, *A Touch of Farmhouse Charm*, which in turn is creating new opportunities. The goal is to continue to create quality content in every category into which we venture."

Seven Stories Press posted double-digit gains in both 2016 and 2017, leading to a 62% increase in 2017 over 2015. Publisher Dan Simon says there were a number of factors that have led to consistent gains over the past three years.

The company started its children's list in 2012, and sales began to show solid growth in the fall of 2013 with the release of *A Is for Activist*. In a relatively short period of time, Seven Stories has built a strong children's backlist, and titles including Howard Zinn's *A Young People's History of the United States* and Cory Silverberg's *Sex Is a Funny Word* sold well last year.

On the adult side, last year Seven Stories had two big books: *Requiem for the American Dream*, Noam Chomsky's bestseller on income inequality, sold more than 40,000 copies, and sales of Kurt Vonnegut's *Complete Stories* topped 20,000 copies.

Simon points to two other factors that had a positive impact on sales in 2017. The company relaunched its website, which he says has made it "far more effective than it had been in building our community online." Last year also marked Seven Stories' fifth year as client of Penguin Random House Distribution Services. "The better you get to know your distributor, and the better they get to know you and your books, the more effective the partnership becomes," Simon notes.

Jump is living up to its name: net revenue in 2017 leapt 40% from 2016, with 2016's revenues up 14% from the previous year. "We have achieved fast growth over the past three years by staying laser focused on meeting a major need in the education and library market; there's a shortage of high-quality low-level books for emerging and struggling readers," president Gabe Kaufman says of the company he founded in Minneapolis in 2012 to serve the library market.

In 2016, Jump entered the education market by publishing books in paperback for classroom usage, as well as in a hardcover format with reinforced binding for libraries. The various series, published under three imprints—Tadpole Books for children beginning to read, Bullfrog Books for high-interest low-level readers, and Pogo for readers in grades two to five interested in STEM topics—are made "easily recognizable" to teachers and librarians, as well as young readers themselves, Kaufman says, with "clean white covers and bright, warm interior spreads" that feature vibrant photos and simple text.

Two series that especially pushed up sales in 2017 were STEM Careers, a series (under the Pogo imprint) of eight volumes that has sold 1,200 collections, and Celebrating Differences, a series (under the Bullfrog imprint) with five volumes that has sold 1,300 collections. "With everything that's going on in this country, it's probably not surprising such a series as Celebrating Differences would do so well," Kaufman says.

Compendium, which is better known in the gift market than in the publishing industry, has landed for the first time on *PW*'s list of fast-growing publishers after 2017 sales jumped 38% from 2015. Its title output went up 21% in the past three years, with 35 frontlist releases in 2017, up from 29 in 2015. The Seattle-based company specializes in publishing children's books, gift books, guest books, notebooks, and journals, as well as greeting cards, boxed note cards, stationery, and pop-up cards, although trade books do account for a portion of its overall sales.

Founded in 1985, Compendium attributes its recent sales increase of books to the fact that librarians and educators have finally discovered the company's products, due in part to the somewhat unexpected success of company president Kobi Yamada's What Do You Do series of three picture books: *What Do You Do with an Idea?* (2014), *What Do You Do with a Problem?* (2016), and *What Do You Do with a Chance?* (2018). "We're a small company, and we do almost no marketing and advertising," says marketing manager Angeline Candido. "Yamada's first book hit the *New York Times* bestseller lists a year after it published. It was all word of mouth." The three books together now have a million copies in print.

Compendium's sales are also being driven by backlist titles, particularly adult activity books such as *The 5 Book: Where Will You Be Five Years from Today?* by Dan Zadra, which, almost a decade after its release, continues to appeal to the lucrative gift market for graduations, job promotions, and retirements.

After a soft 2016, Morgan James came roaring back in 2017, posting a 35% increase from last year, giving the company a 32% sales gain in 2017 over 2015. According to president David Hancock, the rebound was led by titles from its core business—entrepreneurial business nonfiction. But he adds that the publisher did have its first fiction bestseller last year: *On the Clock* by Tim Enochs and Bruce Tollner hit #1 on the *Los Angeles Times* and landed spots on the *New York Times* and *USA Today* lists. The novel was one of two frontlist books to be among Morgan James's top five sellers last year; the other was *Expert Secrets* by Russell Brunson, whose *DotCom Secrets*, released in 2015, was the company's top seller in 2017.

Overall, Hancock says, Morgan James is seeing continued solid sales from its growing backlist, mostly in trade paperback. Unlike most larger trade houses, Morgan James has seen an increase in e-book sales, and growth has been strong enough that the company is preparing to launch an e-book subscription service through which subscribers will have unlimited access to all Morgan James titles for a $10 monthly fee.

The company also expanded its international efforts last year, opening an office in Vancouver, which lifted sales to Canada. It also now has an office in Melbourne and just opened in London. As part of Morgan James's international expansion, Hancock says he expects to soon sign an enhanced distribution deal for global print sales with Ingram Publisher Services that he hopes "will help our international sales significantly."

Finally, Hancock says he is "strategically" releasing more hardcover titles, and the publisher is joining with the rest of the industry in taking advantage of the boom in audiobook sales through the recent hire of an audio publisher "to lead the charge."

Charlesbridge director of marketing Donna Spurlock says the Boston-based publisher's double-digit sale growth in 2017 over 2016 was due to gains across all of its markets, with increases in sales of both its frontlist and backlist titles. Among the publisher's bestselling 2017 frontlist titles were *Malala: Activist for Girls' Education*; *Lola Gets a Cat*, the latest in Charlesbridge's popular Lola Reads! series; and *Baby Loves Thermodynamics* and *Baby Loves Quantum Physics*, the newest books in Ruth Spiro's Baby Loves Science series, which launched in October of 2016. A couple of titles that were released in 2016—the picture book *Whoosh! Lonnie Johnson's Super-Soaking Stream of Inventions* and *Samurai Rising*—enjoyed higher sales in 2017 due to award recognition.

Spurlock also says that Charlesbridge's STEM/STEAM titles had sales gains last year, as did its general backlist, led by *Baby Animals Black & White* (1998) and *I'm New Here* (2015). Sales also remained strong for the perennial back-to-school favorite *First Day Jitters*, originally released in 2000, while its companion book, *Last Day Blues*, remains popular.

Last fall saw the publisher launch a new young adult imprint, Charlesbridge Teen. The inaugural list included titles covering paranormal, contemporary fiction, and political issues, with Spurlock noting Charlesbridge has plans to further diversify the list. To help market its growing list, Charlesbridge has increased its overall advertising and promotional efforts, and it has also adopted a more aggressive direct-to-consumer approach through social media and boosted posts.

Agate Publishing bounced back in 2017, from a down year in 2016, to post a 7% gain over 2015. Besides a boom in sales of books and other educational content in its Agate Development unit (its digital content development service business), Agate founder Doug Seibold says last year's improvement was spearheaded by *Crown: An Ode to the Fresh Cut*, written by Derrick Barnes and illustrated by Gordon C. James. The children's picture book, released as part of Agate's new multicultural children's book line, Denene Millner Books, was published in October 2017 to critical acclaim. The book was a runner-up for some of the most prestigious awards in U.S. children's book publishing: it was named a Newbery Honor book for content, a Caldecott Honor book for illustrations, and a Coretta Scott King Honor book for both text and illustrations.

Crown also appeared on several year-end best-of lists for 2017, and it is now in its fifth printing, bringing the number in print to 65,000 copies. It's the fastest-selling book Agate has published since 2012, which was the first year Agate appeared on our fast-growing list.

Seibold also notes that *Crown* was only the third title in the Denene Millner line, as the imprint debuted in spring 2017 with *My Brown Baby* by Millner. One new Denene Millner book will be released this year, *What is Light?*, with three of four books planned for 2019. Seibold also has high hopes for *Ruth Bader Ginsberg: In Her Own Words*, set for release later this month.

After only minor growth in 2016 over 2015, Berrett-Koehler had a stronger 2017, leading to a 7% sales increase from 2015. Though print book revenues were flat between 2015 and 2017 and e-book sales had a small decline, other B-K initiatives drove up total revenue.

Audio sales doubled in 2017 over 2016, in large part because B-K now releases nearly all of its new books in digital and CD formats, says Katie Sheehan, senior communications manager. Subsidiary rights income also had a nice increase, rising 15% in 2017 over 2015. B-K has long conducted various types of conferences, and its Servant Leadership Online Training Summit held in October attracted nearly 20,000 participants from 146 countries.

A move that B-K hopes will set it up for future growth came last July, when it acquired Management Concepts Press. The purchase added 127 titles on project management, federal acquisition and contracting, federal financial management, leadership, and public administration. Sheehan says B-K is using those titles as a beachhead to establish a professional publishing program, which will expand into other professional subject areas over time.

AUSTIN MACAULEY TAKES ROOT IN N.Y.C.

Austin Macauley Publishers, a hybrid press founded in the U.K. in 2006, opened a New York City office last year. The American office has enjoyed rapid growth since it was launched, signing more than 200 authors. One of Macauley's big releases last year was entertainment attorney Lloyd Zane Remick's *Two Times Platinum*, a legal mystery that looks "behind the scenes of the sports and entertainment industries," the company says.

International director Jade Robertson is expecting a huge increase in title output in 2018, and to accommodate the growth, more staff has been added to the New York office; the press is now being distributed by Baker & Taylor Publishing Services. "It's been truly rewarding to see how the New York office has grown since opening its doors in 2017, and we are committed to continuing to broaden our presence both at home and abroad to support our expanding list of talented authors," Robertson says.

In addition to the London and New York offices, Austin Macauley has an office in Sharjah and plans to expand into Australia, Canada, and South Africa in the next few years. Overall, Austin Macauley reports that worldwide sales between 2015 and 2017 rose 330%. —John Maher

Fast-Growing Indie Publishers

Publisher	Sales Growth	Employees		Titles	
	2017 v. 2015	2015	2017	2015	2017
Cottage Door Press Barrington, Ill.	1,222%	13	24	18	158
Brown Books Publishing Group Dallas, Tex.	287%	15	15	25	31
Haymarket Books Chicago, Ill.	187%	11	16	67	59
Familius Sanger, Calif.	104%	4	5	40	56
Page Street Publishing Salem, Mass.	94%	8	22	34	67
Seven Stories Press New York, N.Y.	62%	8	9	29	36
Jump Minneapolis, Minn.	59%	4	9	85	125
Compendium Seattle, Wash.	38%	57	64	28	24
Morgan James New York, N.Y.	32%	38	49	141	188
Charlesbridge Watertown, Mass.	28%	21	22	46	50
Wisdom Publications Somerville, Mass.	22%	14	14	28	44
Agate Publishing Evanston, Ill.	7%	17	17	24	24
Berrett-Koehler Oakland, Calif.	7%	26	28	40	40

*

A version of this article appeared in the 04/09/2018 issue of *Publishers Weekly* under the headline: Fast-Growing Independent Publishers, 2018.

Capitalizing on trends spurs growth

BY JIM MILLIOT AND CLAIRE KIRCH

I t is not uncommon for new companies to top *PW*'s list of fast-growing independent publishers, and that is the case this year. (A publisher is eligible for inclusion in the list if its net sales were between $2 million and $10 million in 2018.) Mango Publishing was started in 2014 by Chris McKenney, whose background includes serving as chief operating officer of PGW and who was also the cofounder of Mobifusion, a digital startup seeking to make content compatible across different mobile platforms. In forming Mango, McKenney assembled a team that includes such publishing veterans as Michelle Lewy, who worked with McKenney at Mobifusion, and Brenda Knight, former publisher of Cleis Press, as well as newcomers to the industry. Some of Mango's 23 employees work at the company's Miami headquarters, while others work remotely, including several who live outside the U.S.

From the outset, McKenney structured Mango to publish a diverse list. "Our secret sauce is our diversity—new voices, different backgrounds, and exceptional talents all publishing for a rapidly growing and diverse audience of readers," McKenney says. That mix of staff has led to an eclectic list in subjects that includes cooking, crafts, feminism, health, LGBTQ issues, self-help, spirituality, and mindfulness, as well as fiction, poetry, and children's and young adult books.

Knight, who is editorial director, says her criteria for building a list is simple: "Acquiring distinctive books we can sell. Period."

To help organize its wide-ranging list, Mango has created several imprints, including Books & Books Press, Dreams-on-Paper-Entertainment (DOPE), FranklinCovey, and the Tiny Press (founded by author Alexandra Franzen). Mitchell Kaplan, founder of the independent bookstore chain Books & Books, is an acquiring editor for the Books & Books imprint, which had success within its first year with Patrick Alexander's *The Book Lover's Guide to Wine* and the memoir *A Dedicated Life* by David Lawrence Jr., editor and former publisher of the *Miami Herald*. Another important book for Mango last year was *Essential Retirement Planning for Solo Agers* by Sarah Zeff Geber, which was named one of the best books of 2018 by the *Wall Street Journal*.

To help drive sales, Mango has an analytics team looking for patterns relating to book discoverability. The company also has two statisticians on staff who focus on understanding online book-buying behavior. Mango has grown rapidly since its launch and has no intention of slowing down. It plans to publish 150 titles in 2019—books on space exploration, spirituality, creativity, feminism, and the civil rights movement, as well as mystery anthologies, self-help titles, and YA histories geared toward children of color.

Similar to many bigger publishers, Dallas-based Brown Books did well in 2018 with some political books, led by *Hold Texas, Hold the Nation: Victory or Death* by Allen B. West, a former U.S. congressman and Iraq War veteran. Another political strong seller was *Licensed to Lie* by Sidney Powell, which hit the *Wall Street Journal* bestseller list, says Tom Reale, who added the title of president to his COO role during the year. Staying in nonfiction, Reale says, from Brown's Christian list, *The Right Fight: How to Live a Loving Life* by John Kennedy Vaughan "far outstripped expectations as a drop-in fall title." Another way Brown Books, which is a hybrid publisher, took advantage of industry trends last year was by moving into the audiobook market, producing some titles in-house and licensing others.

Brown also expanded its children's list last year, moving further into the classroom and school library markets. Leading the way here, Reale says, were the Finding My Way readers and *Lucas the Lion Loves the Tiny Talker* by Brittani and Ryan Rollen, which moved the publisher into the special needs and inclusive education markets. Young adult remained an important area for Brown, as Steve Copling followed up on the Sage Alexander series with *Sage Alexander and the Blood of Seth* and veteran YA author Devri Walls made her print debut with *Venators: Magic Unleashed*.

Higher foreign subrights income contributed to the overall sales gain at Brown last year as well, Reale says. For instance, he notes, the company sold rights to *The 10 Pillars of Wealth: Mindsets of the World's Richest People* by Alex Becker to publishers in China, Hungary, Portugal, Romania, South Korea, and Vietnam. Further expansion into international markets is being implemented this year with an English export agreement covering 32 countries across the Asia Pacific region, Europe, and South America.

Founded in 2012 by Christopher Robbins, Familius, which is based in Sanger, Calif., has seen accelerating sales in recent years as it begins to scale its publishing program. Last year was the company's best year to date, with revenue up 48% over 2017. Familius continues to focus on publishing regional and interactive children's books, as well as family-oriented adult nonfiction in the categories of parenting, relationships, self-help, education, and cooking.

In 2018, Familius had strong growth domestically and internationally in its adult and children's programs. In particular, Robbins, who is also the owner of American West Books, attributes the rapid gains to aggressive distribution in the gift and chains channels. "It's a product-driven business," he notes. "Fortunately, our growing program found additional traction, and we were well positioned to take advantage of some current trends in multiple markets."

Familius's top-selling title last year was the *PW* bestseller *Made for Me* by Zack Bush and Gregorio De Lauretis. But Robbins says the company's sales were spread across its 300-plus titles, including *Let Me Tell You My Story*, a book that gives voice to the current global refugee crisis, which Robbins says is the most important work he's ever published.

Page Street Publishing saw steady—and rapid—growth between 2016 and 2018, with new titles jumping from 50 in 2016 to 89 last year. Publisher and founder Will Kiester attributes the growth to an increase in sales per title, as well as low return rates, which enabled the Salem, Mass.–based company to invest in new editors and titles.

Cookbooks was Page Street's first major category, and though sales in that area rose about 10% last year, the big sales drivers were crafts, YA, and children's picture books. Page Street has a young staff, and Kiester says its new editors have created "standout books" from their personal experience, such as *Hand Lettering for Relaxation* by Amy Latta and *Seamless Knit Sweaters in Two Weeks* by Marie Greene.

Page Street had nearly 300 titles on its backlist at the end of 2018, and backlist accounted for 49% of its sales last year. In the last week of 2018, Page Street's gross sales for the year crossed a milestone, topping $10 million, with the growth aided by expanded business in the mass merchandiser channel and "a surge of sales growth in Canada," Kiester says.

Another key to Page Street's success has been its location near Boston, which allows it to recruit from the city's many publishing programs. Kiester is confident that Page Street's investment in new talent will continue to bear fruit in 2019, and he is projecting revenue to grow by more than 30% this year. Among the drivers will be the publisher's children's picture book list, which will have 19 titles this year.

Kiester also expects the YA list to hit its stride in 2019, after earning critical praise but slow sales in its first year. "The program has stuck to its guns, kept producing original story lines, and engaging characters with surprising and satisfying transformative personality development," he says. Page Street has been rewarded with its first YA strong seller, *Echo North* by Joanna Ruth Meyer, which is now in its third printing.

Another promising YA title is *An Affair of Poisons* by Addie Thorley, which Kiester says is getting a lot of prepub attention, including from the Discover program at B&N. "We aren't looking for bestsellers, but rather strong titles from debut authors we can invest in and that earn an honest living," Kiester says.

Jump!, founded seven years ago, has obviously found its niche: this is the second year in a row that the Minneapolis-based children's publisher has landed on *PW's* annual listing of fast-growing indie publishers. Launched in 2012 by Gabe Kaufman to publish hardcover nonfiction books for emerging and reluctant readers, with reinforced bindings to accommodate the library market, Jump has seen its sales explode with 70% sales growth since it expanded into the educational market in 2016. For the past three years, the company has published books in paper as well for classroom usage—pre-K through third grade, although the books are appropriate for high-interest, low-level fifth graders.

Jump's Tadpole Books imprint targets beginning readers, and Bullfrog Books focuses on high-interest, low-level readers. The company increased its output from 110 titles in 2016 to 125 in 2017 and 187 titles in 2018. It has also doubled in size, from five employees in 2016 to 10 in 2018.

Kaufman notes that Jump has added social studies titles to its third imprint, Pogo, which publishes books for early fluent readers; it previously focused solely on STEM topics (Pogo STEM). Pogo Social Studies titles emphasizing civic engagement played a major role in the company's continuing growth this past year. "It's a definite hot topic in these times," Kaufman notes. "It's in such great demand by educators, especially those teaching second and third graders."

Pogo's five-volume Being an Active Citizen series sold 2,500 sets last year, while Building Character, its eight-volume series under the Bulldog Books imprint, sold 3,000 sets.

Jump continues to expand its reach into the school market: Kaufman says that the company will launch a fourth imprint in January 2020: Blue Owl Books, which will focus on social and emotional learning for elementary school students.

Barefoot Books in Cambridge, Mass., had phenomenal growth between 2016 and 2018: revenue jumped by nearly 45% after the company almost doubled its output from 16 frontlist titles and reissues in 2016 to 31 last year. Domestic sales (including the trade, gift, and educational markets) were up 25% in the period, while international sales rose 50%, and the company is seeing a triple-digit increase in subrights revenue.

Elaine Stone, Barefoot's product marketing and publicity manager, notes that a 72% increase in frontlist titles (currently 20–25 releases each year) fueled the growth, as did company initiatives such as an aggressive outreach into new foreign markets, notably Asia. Barefoot is also seeing results pertaining to an aggressive campaign to revitalize its engagement with its core market—librarians, booksellers, and consumers. Barefoot's Ambassadors program encourages direct sales to entrepreneurs, in person and online.

Approximately 65% of Barefoot's business comes from the trade, and the remaining 35% comes from the web and from ambassador direct sellers. Barefoot reports that trade sales growth in North America and the U.K. especially has been driven by two activity decks: Mindful Kids, with 100,000 sold, and Yoga Pretzels, with 50,000 sold. Barefoot's third deck, Global Kids, will be released in September.

Serendipity and an emphasis on a multicultural list has also been a major factor in Barefoot's success. Last year's *La Frontera: El viaje con papá/My Journey with Papa* by Deborah Mills, Alfredo Alva, and Claudia Navarro, an immigration tale inspired by the true story of a boy and his father making their way by foot from Mexico to the U.S., touched on a hot-button issue and, Stone says, brought attention to Barefoot's "diverse and inclusive backlist," which resulted in an upswing in sales across the board. Though Barefoot declined to provide sales figures, it disclosed that *La Frontera* is in its fourth print run.

Charlesbridge Publishing in Watertown, Mass., is celebrating its 30th year of publishing primarily nonfiction children's and young adult titles, though its publisher, Mary Ann Sabia, notes that the company has expanded its fiction offerings in recent years. In 2018, Charlesbridge had "the best frontlist sales in the history of the company," she says, adding that trade book net sales were up 15% over 2017.

Explaining that "a lot of our books fit holes in the market, while others are highly topical," Sabia attributes the company's 43% growth in revenue between 2016 and 2018 to an increase in sales across the board: chains and indies, the school and library market, the gift and toy market. E-book sales, she notes, "are strong and continue to grow," while a relatively new revenue stream, sales to subscription box vendors, spiked this past year.

Notable successes among the press's 49 frontlist releases in 2018 are such bestsellers as *We Are Grateful: Otsaliheliga* by Traci Sorell, which was just named a Robert F. Sibert Award Honor book by the ALA; *Like Vanessa* by Tami Charles, a winter/spring 2018 Indies Introduce title; and the latest entries in Ruth Spiro's Baby Loves Science series of board books, *Baby Loves Coding* and *Baby Loves Structural Engineering*. But, as always with Charlesbridge, it's not just about frontlist: the company's robust backlist is also pumping up sales. The nine titles in the Lola Reads series, of which five are available in Spanish as well as English, continue to drive sales. Anticipation is high for *Lola Goes to School* (June) by Anna McQuinn, illustrated by Rosalind Beardshaw, as the company hopes to replicate the success of such bestsellers as 2000's *First Day Jitters* by Julie Danneberg, illustrated by Judy Love, sales of which were up 22% in 2018 over 2017; *Beaks!* by Sneed B. Collard III, illustrated by Robin Brickman, a 2002 picture book illustrating the importance of beaks to birds; and *Global Babies* by the Global Fund for Children, a 2007 board book celebrating the diversity of the world's population through photos of babies from 16 different countries.

Evanston, Ill.–based Agate Publishing had a strong 2018, with sales up 32% over 2017. Founder and publisher Doug Seibold attributes the solid year to the success of a children's book it published in late 2017: *Crown: An Ode to the Fresh Cut* by Derrick Barnes, illustrated by Gordon C. James. Part of the Denene Millner Books children's imprint, the title will soon have 115,000 copies in print. In early 2019, Denene Millner took her imprint to Simon & Schuster, but the five-book backlist remains at Agate. There has been some discussion about selling the backlist to S&S, but no deal has been reached as yet.

Seibold says there are no hard feelings about Millner's departure. "We set up the imprint in such a way that it would be easy for Denene to leave if she wished," he explains.

Though *Crown* was a major driver of 2018 sales, Agate had other books that contributed to the gain. Seibold continues to seek out titles that are typically overlooked by larger publishers. He points to two in the cooking area that did well last year: *The New Fillipino Kitchen* by Jacqueline Chio-Lauri, now in its second printing, and *Craft Coffee* by Jessica Easto and Andrea Willhoff, which has had four printings.

In 2011, Seibold started the In His Own Words series with a book that contains quotes from Steve Jobs, and, since that time, the line has proved to be a steady seller. Last year, Agate released separate In His Own Words books using quotes from Jeff Bezos and Mark Zuckerberg, and Seibold says he is considering broadening the line beyond successful businesspeople.

Seibold was an early proponent of publishing a diverse list, a belief that led to the creation of the Bolden Books imprint, which focuses on African American writers. He says that the line continues to sell but that, as larger publishers have taken a greater interest in books from people of color, he is not seeing the same influx of projects he had in the past.

Agate's strong sales gain resulted in 2018 being one of the publisher's most profitable years to date. Rather than using the proceeds to push for fast expansion, Seibold is using them to bide his time and think about the future. "You have to be disciplined," he says. "I won't compete for pricey projects. We will be doing fewer projects in 2019." He adds that he will analyze Agate's businesses in an attempt to find the sweet spot where it has the best chance to be consistently profitable.

In 2018, founder Steve Piersanti's last full year as CEO and publisher of Oakland, Calif.–based Berrett-Koehler, the company posted a 16% sales increase over 2017, giving it a 30% growth rate between 2016 and 2018. Beginning May 1, David Marshall will take over as CEO/CFO, and Johanna Vondeling will become president/publisher, with Piersanti transitioning to acquiring editor.

The 2018 revenue gain was led by several bestsellers, including *On the Brink of Everything: Grace, Gravity & Growing Old* by Parker Palmer, and the release of the third edition of one of B-K's all-time bestsellers: *Leadership and Self-Deception* by the Arbinger Institute, which has sold more than two million copies since it was published in 2000 and sells more copies each year than the year prior. Complementing those big titles were six new books that sold well: *The Age of Overwhelm* by Laura van Dernoot Lipsky; *The Body Is Not an Apology* by Sonya Renee Taylor; *Decolonizing Wealth* by Edgar Villanueva; *A Great Place to Work for All* by Michael C. Bush and the Great Place to Work Research Team; *Servant Leadership in Action*, edited by Ken Blanchard and Renee Broadwell; and *Talent Magnet* by Mark Miller. Sales of all print titles were helped by B-K's Jan. 1, 2018, move of its trade distribution to Penguin Random House Publisher Services. As a result of the switch, according to a B-K spokesperson, "Our international print sales approximately doubled while our domestic print sales also increased."

In addition to moving to PRH, B-K continued to build out its digital marketing systems, which increased the publisher's direct and trade sales. The upgraded marketing system also supported B-K's new online training business, which featured a Women's Leadership Online Summit that brought in more than 20,000 participants from 150 countries. B-K also launched a Dare to Serve Online Training Master Course.

A couple of other nonprint initiatives also contributed to B-K's sales gains last year. The company began publishing audio editions of nearly all new titles in 2016, and it saw large audio sales growth in 2017 and 2018. And e-book sales, which had been flat in 2017, began growing again in 2018.

Even though it cut its output from 67 titles to 55 between 2016–1018, Westminster John Knox, part of the Presbyterian Publishing Corporation, the

U.S. publishing arm of the Presbyterian Church, had a 22% sales gain in the same period. WJK's achievement is even more noteworthy, because, less than 20 years ago, WJK had to cut 20% of its staff in its Louisville, Ky., offices as a cost-saving move. In the past two years, however, it has grown its staff from 28 to 40. WJK attributes its growth to two new initiatives: it has begun publishing children's books, and, in 2018, it acquired a curriculum publishing unit from the Presbyterian Church.

In the fall 2017, WJK published three children's books and was encouraged enough by the results that it formed the Flyaway Books imprint in 2018. One of the eight 2018 releases under that imprint, Barbara Brown Taylor's first children's book, *Home by Another Way: A Christmas Story*, became a bestseller for the press, selling 8,000 copies. There will be eight Flyaway Books frontlist titles in 2019, including *The Night of His Birth*, a Christmas picture book written by Katherine Patterson, the 2010–2011 U.S. national ambassador for young people's literature, and illustrated by Lisa Aisato.

"While half of our children's titles are religious in nature, half go beyond any denominational religious tradition; they're for the average family with children," notes WJK publisher David Dobson, explaining that Flyaway Books' list emphasizes diversity. "There is a real hunger for such books, and we're trying to meet that need."

Though WJK's new children's imprint and curriculum publishing program are adding to the company's revenue, its 2018 adult releases for the trade contributed to its success as well: *Interrupting Silence: God's Command to Speak Out* by Walter Brueggemann sold 5,000 copies; *Advent for Everyone: Luke* by N.T. Wright sold 4,200 copies; and *Transforming: The Bible and the Lives of Transgender Christians* by Austen Hartke sold more than 4,100 copies. Its top two sellers in 2018 were Brueggemann's *A Way Other Than Our Own: Devotions for Lent*, which sold more than 8,100 copies, and *A Bigger Table* by John Pavlovitz, which sold 7,200 copies.

Tim McKee, the publisher of Berkeley, Calif.–based North Atlantic Books, says that the 45-year-old company's 11% growth between 2017 and 2018 comes from its continuing focus on its core market. Like several others of this year's group of fast-growing publishers, North Atlantic benefited greatly from publishing books about topics that are no longer considered marginal or alternative but have entered the mainstream, such as books about the therapeutic use of psychedelic drugs, somatic psychology and trauma, homeopathic medicine, natural foods, deep ecology, and sustainability.

North Atlantic's top three bestsellers in 2018 were *Come of Age: The Case for Elderhood in a Time of Trouble* by Stephen Jenkinson, with more than 9,100 copies sold to date in all formats; *Nurturing Resilience: Helping Clients Move Forward from Developmental Trauma—An Integrative Somatic Approach* by Kathy Kain and Stephen Terrell, with nearly 9,000 copies sold to date in all formats; and *Climate: A New Story* by Charles Eisenstein, with more than 8,600 copies sold to date in all formats. North Atlantic's investment in audio over the past five years is also having a huge impact: it has seen a 50% growth in audio sales year over year.

North Atlantic attributes its success to having a list that is increasingly relevant to readers, and McKee also notes that the press, which became a nonprofit in 1980, has been "working on our own health as an organization." It aspires to fulfill its mission of publishing books that transform lives and heal people, he says, and to do so on a more solid financial footing.

Thus, for the past year or two, North Atlantic has been engaged in such activities as updating and fine-tuning workplace policies, conducting racial equity trainings, and diversifying its board. "We're asking ourselves if we are acting in a way that empowers staff and yields the strongest outcomes," McKee says. "We've been working to become as actualized of an entity as we can be. This takes a lot of time and collective effort, but it undoubtedly impacts the books we do and how they fare in the world."

Founded in 1994, San Francisco–based No Starch Press is celebrating its 25th anniversary of publishing technical books infused with popular culture—or, as it describes its catalogue on its website, "the finest in geek entertainment." Having released 28 titles in 2018, No Starch reports that sales were up 8% in the year over 2016. And there's even more cause for celebration: the company says that there will be a 50% increase in 2019 frontlist releases over 2018's number, and 2019 sales to date are up 50% over the similar period in 2018.

Sales and marketing analyst David Bugden explains that No Starch's success in the marketplace is primarily due to the company's commitment to quality over quantity, noting that its titles are released only when there is a consensus that "they are ready" for the marketplace. "This focus has built a fan base of tens of thousands of readers who trust that any No Starch Press title will deliver the information they desire, whether that is to learn a new programming language, improve their skills as a security researcher, teach children to program, build stunning Lego models and cool robots, play with electronics, or simply exercise their brain."

Bugden also notes that moving No Starch's distribution to Penguin Random House Publisher Services in 2017 expanded its niche and opened new sales channels. For instance, the company has begun to work more closely with

Barnes & Noble and other bricks-and-mortar retailers to promote its professional, STEM, and Lego titles in stores. At the same time, it is upping its presence on social media and elsewhere online with digital advertising that has been creating awareness and sales of No Starch titles.

One particularly lucrative digital sales channel since 2015 has been the Humble Bundle online storefront, where consumers set prices for bundled products, with a portion going to charity. "No Starch Press was one of the very first publishers to work with Humble Bundle and has brought in millions from their bundles over the years," Bugden notes, adding that No Starch has raised more than $1.5 million for charitable causes through the service.

Feature Fast-Growing Independent Publishers 2016–2018

Publisher	Sales Growth	Employees		Titles	
	2018 v. 2016	2016	2018	2016	2018
Mango Publishing, Miami	400%	11	23	41	99
Brown Books Publishing Group, Dallas	220%	15	15	35	48
Familius, Sanger, Calif.	77%	6	6	52	61
Page Street Publishing, Salem, Mass.	73%	12	32	50	89
Jump!, Minneapolis	70%	5	10	110	187
Barefoot Books, Cambridge, Mass.	45%	20	20	16	31
Charlesbridge, Watertown, Mass.	43%	23	26	40	49
Agate Publishing, Evanston, Ill.	35%	20	20	26	20
Berrett-Koehler Publishers, Oakland, Calif.	30%	26	31	38	42
Westminster John Knox Press, Louisville, Ky.	22%	28	40	67	55
North Atlantic Books, Berkeley, Calif.	11%	24	22	41	44
No Starch Press, San Francisco	8%	17	23	22	28

*

A version of this article appeared in the 04/08/2019 issue of *Publishers Weekly* under the headline: Fast-Growing Independent Publishers, 2019.

Presses find their own paths to move ahead

BY JIM MILLIOT

For the second year in a row, **Mango Publishing** topped *PW*'s fast-growing small publisher list. Mango's sales growth rate between 2017 and 2019 was less than half its rate in the previous three-year span, but that is to be expected from a maturing company: Mango celebrated its fifth anniversary last year.

Mango attributes its success in 2019 to its diverse list of authors. The publisher discovered artist Kate Allan and her animal drawings on Tumblr, and her *You Can Do All Things* sold well in the trade market as well as in the gift and special markets, Mango says. Women's studies scholar Becca Anderson has been another important Mango author. Her bestselling *The Book of Awesome Women* led to a new series, which includes *The Book of Awesome Women Writers* and *The Book of Awesome Black Americans*.

Your Next Level Life by Karen Arrington, founder of the Miss Black USA pageant and a goodwill ambassador to Sierra Leone, was another strong seller in 2019. "Karen Arrington is an exemplar of the kind of author Mango is proud to publish," says Mango associate publisher Brenda Knight. "She is not only inspiring young women of color but working hard to make a difference in the world."

Mango is continuing to expand its partnership with Franklin Covey, publishing the 7 Habits of Highly Effective People card deck. And Franklin Covey executive v-p Scott Jeffrey Miller's *Management Mess to Leadership Success* hit bestseller lists in the management science category in 2019 as well.

International sales were another strong spot for Mango, quadrupling over the past two years, the company says, and it now expects 30% of its English-language sales to be from outside of the U.S.

Mango also benefitted last year from the October purchase of Conari Press, and it expects to see Conari make a more meaningful contribution in 2020 when it relaunches the imprint under the direction of Knight (who is Conari's former associate publisher). Mango followed the Conari purchase by acquiring lifestyle and regional title publisher Yellow Pear Press in early 2020.

Mango founder and publisher Chris McKenney notes that "while 2019 was full of many wonderful things," what he is most proud of about the year was Mango's ability to win six auctions when competing with representatives from the Big Five publishers. He attributes those victories to Mango's revenue-sharing model, which offers authors up to 50% of net sales for each book sold, as well as its "modern marketing techniques."

Media Lab Books, a unit of Topix Media, began life as a bookazine publisher before launching a book division in 2015. MLB's initial focus was on licensed publishing done in collaboration with companies like Disney, Jack Hanna, and Nickelodeon, explains MLB v-p and publisher Phil Sexton. After publishing 25 titles in 2017, the company changed tactics to concentrate on acquiring better titles that will have longer backlist lives, he says.

That decision delivered almost immediate results. In 2018, sales rose 60% over 2017—and they increased another 42% in 2019, even as the number of titles steadily declined. MLB's bestsellers last year included *Smithsonian 10-Minute Science Experiments*, *Everything I Need to Know I Learned from John Wayne*, and *The Unofficial Ultimate Harry Potter Spellbook*.

Sexton, who joined MLB from F + W Media, says the company's strategy now is to work with authors and licensors "who have the platform and desire to support their titles with us over time." This approach, he says, has created a "far more efficient and profitable publishing model for everyone involved."

MLB's publishing model varies depending on the kind of book it is doing and the kind of author or licensor it is working with, Sexton says. For some projects, the agreement is the traditional advance/royalty model. For others, where a brand or content is licensed but MLB is doing all of the creative in-house, it may be royalty only. And in other cases, books are original works being written by in-house staff. "We try not to limit the kind of deals we're willing to come up with in order to create the book we want, so long as we're doing so in a financially responsible way," Sexton adds.

Despite cutting the list in recent years, Sexton says that, moving forward, MLB is planning "a thoughtful, measured expansion of the list." It will release 12 books this year, going up to 24 in 2022. "We intend to limit ourselves to 24 titles from 2022 onward to help ensure we're focusing on the best projects we can," Sexton notes. MLB's titles are distributed by Macmillan.

"We had another banner year," says **Familius** founder and president Christopher Robbins. Among the metrics Robbins follows, sales per employee and sales per title had large gains between 2017 and 2019. The company's growth drivers last year included its Lit for Little Hands series, interactive board books, and regional titles, says marketing and public relations director Kate Farrell. A top-selling individual title was *Good Moms Have Scary Thoughts* by Karen Kleiman, founder of the Postpartum Stress Center, illustrated by Molly McIntyre.

The Road Not Taken, based on the poem by Robert Frost and illustrated by Vivan Mineker, got a boost last year when it received a mention in the *New York Times Book Review*—the first time a Familius title made it into the *NYTBR.* Another solid seller was a padded board book version of Familius's *PW*-bestselling picture book *Made for Me. Big Book of Family Games*—which "provides tech-free fun and games to families," Farrell says—was also a hit in 2019. And *The Munchy Munchy Cookbook for Kids* by Pierre Lamielle, winner of the reality cooking show *Chopped Canada*, was a good performer last year, too.

Familius is now distributed by Workman, after previously doing its own distribution. Robbins hopes the move will expand its visibility to the trade.

Blue Star Press had immediate success when it launched in 2015, taking advantage of the surge in interest in adult coloring books. Originally known as Blue Star Coloring, the publisher's two top-selling books in the adult coloring category hit the *New York Times* bestseller list, combining to sell more than 500,000 copies. That success "motivated us to charge ahead and expand into other genres," says Blue Star chief operating officer Peter Licalzi, who started the company with Camden Hendricks.

Blue Star's first move was to expand in the creative art and wellness categories in 2016, followed by games and other gift products in 2019, Licalzi says. The company's Paige Tate & Co. imprint publishes how-tos, lifestyle titles, devotionals, and coloring books.

Among Blue Star's bestsellers last year were *Hand Lettering 101, Millennial Lotería,* and *Mind Your Business.* Early on, Licalzi says, the company worked to build relationships with independent booksellers and other bricks-and-mortar retailers such as Hobby Lobby, Joann Fabric, and Magnolia. Blue Star's quick success drew the attention of Penguin Random House, which added it as a distribution client in September 2019.

Based in Bend, Ore., Blue Star's core staff of five employees are all 35 years old and under and work from Los Angeles and Austin. Licalzi attributes a large part of the company's early success to its relationship with its authors, whom it considers creative business partners and friends. "We are very selective about who we collaborate with," he says, "and have worked hard to carefully nurture these relationships and get our authors excited about releasing a series of new titles with us year after year."

Founded in 1964 by aerial photographer Robert Cameron, **Cameron + Company** was acquired in 2009 by his granddaughter Nina Gruener and her husband Chris Gruener following Robert's death. The couple moved the boutique publisher of photography, art, food and wine, children's, and regional interest books from San Francisco to Petaluma, Calif. The company has seen its strongest sales period over the past few years, growing 25% between 2017 and 2019, led by a particularly good 2019. Chris, who is the publisher, attributes its recent success to a number of factors.

Cameron's most important initiatives include the 2016 launch of the Cameron Kids imprint, which was formed to complement its line of children's picture books and is headed by Nina, who is also a children's author. Cameron Kids publishes picture and chapter books, and though it began by releasing two books per season, it will release 12 in 2020, Chris says.

A second growth area has been Cameron Studios, which offers custom book, packaging, and design services for movie studios, video game studios, artists, photographers, and other publishers. Cameron has also seen solid gains in its Roundtree Press imprint for general nonfiction. Roundtree is distributed by PGW, and in 2018 Cameron signed with Abrams for sales and distribution of its Cameron list.

A final contributor to its strong sales last year was the fall release of what Chris says were two of the biggest books in the publisher's history: *Rick Baker: Metamorphosis*, a $250, slipcased, two-volume set on the Hollywood legend, and the children's picture book *The President Sang Amazing Grace*, which Chris describes as "a lyrical account of the day President Obama sang with a grieving nation following the 2015 shooting in a Black church in Charleston, S.C."

Brown Books Publishing Group president and chief operating officer Tom Reale says the company was able to overcome sluggish sales to Barnes & Noble to post its fifth consecutive year of gains and make *PW*'s fast-growing list for the third consecutive year. He adds that offsetting slower sales to B&N were a strong backlist performance, a refocus on online and independent store sales, the addition of direct sales, and an increase in export sales.

One of Brown Books' big titles of 2019 was Ed Curtis's *Why Texas: How Business Discovered the Lone Star State*, which features interviews with business leaders describing why they moved their operations to Texas. "As a Dallas-based publisher, Brown Books' leadership felt a strong affinity towards publishing this title," Reale says.

Another Texas-themed book also performed well last year: *Hold Texas, Hold the Nation: Victory or Death*, by former congressman and retired Army officer

Allen B. West, saw a bump in sales following West's announcement that he would enter the race for the chair of the Texas Republican Party. His follow-up, *We Can Overcome: An American Black Conservative Manifesto*, had strong early sales following its publication in February 2020, Reale says. Brown Books has been adding more titles from military veterans, he explains, noting that *Baghdaddy: How Saddam Hussein Taught Me to Be a Better Father* sold well last year.

Brown Books' children's list had a solid 2019, as well. *Sweet Child Born in California,* the newest volume in Whitney Strauss's Sweet Child series, sold well, Reale says, adding that *Sweet Child Born in New York* will come out this year. Brown Books also continued to focus on the K–12 classroom library market—and books that discuss special needs and inclusion in particular, led by Jo Mach's Finding My Way series.

Brown Books has capitalized on the boom in audiobook sales following its entrance into the market in 2018. According to Reale, the company expanded its in-house production and its relationship with Recorded Books, whose Tantor division produced the first two audiobooks in Devri Walls's Venators series last year.

North Atlantic Books is another publisher that benefitted from growth in the audiobook market. According to Tim McKee, publisher of the nonprofit, North Atlantic's investment in its audiobook infrastructure contributed to a doubling of sales of the format in 2019 over 2018.

Last year was another year during which North Atlantic benefited from growing interest in its core areas of trauma, plant medicine, grief, racial justice, the liminal, self-healing, and indigenous cosmologies. The increased interest, McKee notes, led to strong backlist sales. Top backlist sellers in 2019 included the ever-popular *Walter the Farting Dog* which sold more than 38,000 units across all formats, followed by *Accessing the Healing Power of the Vagus Nerve*, *Waking the Tiger*, *In the Realm of Hungry Ghosts*, and *The Wild Edge of Sorrow*. Backlist accounts for about 75% of North Atlantic annual sales. The publisher's two bestselling new releases in 2019 were *Teaching Yoga Beyond the Poses* and *Evolutionary Herbalism*.

Another long-term aspect of North Atlantic's publishing program—putting a priority on the diversity of its authors, particularly with regard to race, age, sexual orientation, and gender—also contributed to a better financial performance, McKee says, as did the increased impact of diverse voices within North Atlantic's organization.

Working with its distributor, Penguin Random House, North Atlantic had a strong performance in special markets last year, McKee notes. PRH also helped North Atlantic reduce the number of returns to the point where the return rate is now about half of what it was several years ago, he adds.

Charlesbridge Publishing executive v-p and publisher Mary Ann Sabia says the company's sales gain last year was spread across a number of channels, including "very strong growth" in the school and library market. Other solid increases came in sales of subscription boxes and e-books, while Charlesbridge also had a "nice bump" in sales in the U.K.

The breadth of Charlesbridge's sales is reflected in its bestselling frontlist titles from last year. *SumoKitty* was a Kids Indie Next List pick, and *Woodstock: 50 Years of Peace and Music* was released by its Imagine adult imprint. Other bestsellers were a new paperback edition of *Whoosh!* and *Lola Goes to School*, the latest release in its Lola Readers series, written by Anna McQuinn and illustrated by Rosalind Beardshaw.

Key backlist titles last year, Sabia says, were *Baby Loves Science Board Box Set, Boo-Boos That Changed the World, Feathers: Not Just for Flying, Last Day Blues, Rickshaw Girl,* and *We Are Grateful: Otsaliheliga* (a Sibert Honor book).

Charlesbridge was founded in 1989 and has regularly appeared on the *PW* fast-growing small publishers list in recent years. "2019 marked our 30th anniversary, and it's been so rewarding to see our continued growth," Sabia says. "It was the enthusiasm of independent booksellers back in 1989 that gave us our start, and over the years that support spread across many and varied marketplaces."

Morgan James founder and president David Hancock says contributions from a number of areas helped to drive sales gains in 2019. Bestsellers came from the publisher's business, faith, and fiction imprints, and Hancock called out *Becoming Us* by Jeff and Beth McCord as exceeding his expectations. One of the company's business books, *The Bezos Letter*, was a steady seller in the U.S. last year and garnered more than $200,000 in foreign rights sales. In general, Hancock says, Morgan James had a strong performance from its growing backlist, particularly in nonfiction.

Morgan James supported its entire list last year with expanded marketing efforts to both consumers and the trade. "For example," Hancock says, "we placed significantly more ads in *PW* and in *Foreword* magazine during 2019 and had very positive reactions."

Digital initiatives also added to the publisher's growth. Sales in the audio division rose 31% over 2018, due in part to additional distribution channels opened up for Morgan James by its distributor, Ingram Publisher Services, Hancock says. A new strategy of promoting e-books before pub date grew sales of that format last year, and Morgan James's partnership with Open Road Media led to a 900% jump in backlist e-book sales.

Hancock is planning more digital initiatives for 2020, including rolling out its free e-book bundle to all print titles, driven by FlexPub. In addition, Morgan James has partnered with Bookshop to drive more online sales through independent booksellers.

Strong backlist sales drove growth at **Greystone Books**, which returns to *PW*'s fast-growing list after initially appearing in 2017. In that year, the company was riding high following the release in 2016 of two hits, *The Hidden Life of Trees* by Peter Wohlleben and *The Obesity Code* by Jason Fung. Those two titles remain extremely popular, says associate publisher Jen Gauthier. To date, *Trees* has sold 600,000 hardcover copies, while *Obesity Code* has sold more than 425,000 print copies and 200,000 e-book copies.

FAST-GROWING INDEPENDENT PUBLISHERS 2017-2019

PUBLISHER	SALES GROWTH 2017–2019	EMPLOYEES 2017	EMPLOYEES 2019	TITLES 2017	TITLES 2019
Mango Publishing Miami	162%	15	27	68	130
Media Lab Books New York City	128%	21	19	25	12
Familius Sanger, Calif.	117%	5	8	57	58
Blue Star Press Bend, Ore.	105%	6	5	13	20
Brown Books Publishing Group Dallas	75%	15	15	31	33
North Atlantic Books Berkeley, Calif.	27%	24	24	36	39
Cameron + Company Petaluma, Calif.	25%	8	12	15	26
Charlesbridge Watertown, Mass.	25%	23	30	50	54
Morgan James New York City	20%	49	50	188	190
Greystone Books Vancouver	17%	15	23	24	31

SOURCE: PUBLISHERS WEEKLY

Both authors remain important contributors to Greystone. The company published Wohlleben's *The Inner Life of Animals* in 2017 and *The Secret Network of Nature* last year, along with an illustrated edition of *The Hidden Life of Trees*; in 2018, Greystone released Fung's *The Diabetes Code*, followed by *The Obesity Code Cookbook* in 2019. "We have more books coming from both authors," Gauthier says.

Last year's sales received a lift from the fall launch of a children's imprint focused on books in Greystone's core areas of nature, science, environment, health, and social issues. Greystone Kids started with five books, including a middle grade nonfiction adaptation of *The Hidden Life of Trees*, titled *Can You Hear the Trees Talking?*, and *Birdsong*, a picture book by Cree-Metis author Julie Flett, which received multiple starred reviews and was an ALA American Indian Youth Literature honoree. "We will continue to build the children's list, publishing a mix of picture books and middle grade nonfiction and growing the list to 12–16 titles per year," Gauthier promises.

*

A version of this article appeared in the 04/06/2020 issue of *Publishers Weekly* under the headline: Fast-Growing Independent Publishers, 2020.

WANT A HEALTHY PUBLISHING ECOSYSTEM? SUPPORT THE INDIES

A leading indie publisher warns against taking independents of all stripes for granted

BY DAN SIMON

Consolidation in our industry suddenly seems to have reached a tipping point. We begin the new year with just one main wholesaler for the book trade and another for libraries, as Baker & Taylor departs from the retail sector; not just new ownership but a new guiding philosophy at our nation's largest bookstore chain; and Amazon's near-monopoly dominance of the online bookselling arena—well, that's probably past the tipping point. The largest publishing houses are seeking higher profits based on new efficiencies. And high-speed delivery is the new black, ushering in lower returns and quicker replenishment (along with higher printing, transportation, and fulfillment costs), in a marketplace that's smaller than it was but holding its own.

With all this going on, we can count our blessings that there's a powerful independent streak in our profession that serves as a counterweight to the corporate side. It spans independent book publishers, independent booksellers, librarians, and the organizations and independent media that protect and cover our industry—AAP, AAUP, Above the Treeline/Edelweiss, BINC, CLMP, IBPA, IPC, PubWest, SPD, *Booklist, Choice, Foreword, Kirkus, Library Journal, Publisher's Lunch, Shelf Awareness*—keeping us informed by the week, by the day, by the hour. Most are small, independently run outfits. And the redwoods at the heart of this thriving forest—*PW*, the ABA, and the ALA—are all independent and, in the case of the ALA and the ABA, are membership driven.

The dynamic shifts we're living through aren't easy to interpret. Let's be optimists and say they aren't definitively bad for books or book culture. Kurt Vonnegut used to say, "We can never tell what is the good news and what is the bad news!"

But let's remember also the words of Kurt Wolff, founder of Pantheon, who brought us Kafka and others: "The books of great writers have not been published as a rule by giant companies," and, "Important literary movements were supported and developed by small firms."

Right now there's a dangerous trend in our industry toward bigger, faster, more opportunistic—the hallmarks of a smooth-running capitalist machine. That course definitely risks pulling us off course, away from craft, from ideas and the soulfulness that is at the heart of books.

But as long as we can keep alive publishing's complex ecosystem, things can still be balanced, and our exuberance and optimism—the true mainstays of our industry and our professions—are still warranted. Along with the five corporate publisher groups, this ecosystem's vitality stems from the hundreds of independent publishers and university presses that act analogously to the Amazon rainforest by protecting species (including the clearly endangered one of working writers at the start of their careers!), and that are incubators for teeming DNA pools—translation from far-flung cultures and countries, radical politics, environmentalism.

Tens of millions of copies of these independent publishers' books are sold every year, generating hundreds of millions of dollars in revenue and keeping our nation's creative cutting edge sharp. A major publisher might bring out a book by a bestselling journalist on an environmental threat or a Nobel Prize–winning novelist in translation. But a small publisher will be the one to publish a distant literary voice in translation year after year, decade after decade, until she wins that Nobel. And a university press will publish the environmental scientist that inspires the bestselling journalist's bestseller.

If this were an industry solely dominated by our biggest players, my New Year's forecast—anybody's forecast—for its future good health would be dire. The leadership in the corporate sector itself is very cognizant of the fact that they are a part of a complex ecosystem, and in order for any parts to thrive, the whole organism must do so.

The Big Five account for the lion's share of book sales, and the majority go through a small number of outlets—Amazon, Barnes & Noble, Follet, and Ingram. We're grateful for all that they do. But in terms of influence, in terms of literary prizes, and in terms of leadership and the courage it takes to commit to new voices and new kinds of voices, you could say it's about an even split between the handful of bigs and the army of small-to-medium, often quirky independent outfits.

What keeps our industry alive and well, and able to serve writers and readers as well today as we ever have, is the mix of large and small, commercial and literary, smart and smarter. Let's make sure we support our librarians, independent booksellers, independent publishers, and the independent media and service providers that underpin all our efforts. Let's not take our independents for granted.

⑦

CHILDREN'S PUBLISHING

NOTABLE PW CHILDREN'S PUBLISHING STORIES OF 2021

Keller, Goade, Nayeri Win Newbery, Caldecott, Printz Awards

By Diane Roback and Emma Kantor | Jan 25, 2021

Tae Keller has won the 2021 John Newbery Medal for *When You Trap a Tiger* (Random House), edited by Chelsea Eberly. Michaela Goade has won the 2021 Randolph Caldecott Medal for *We Are Water Protectors*, written by Carole Lindstrom (Roaring Brook), edited by Mekisha Telfer. And Daniel Nayeri has won the 2021 Michael L. Printz Award for *Everything Sad Is Untrue (a true story)* (Levine Querido), edited by Arthur A. Levine. It is a first-time win for all three recipients. The Youth Media Awards were announced Monday morning during the American Library Association's midwinter conference, which is being held virtually this year due to the pandemic.

Five Newbery Honor Books were named: *All Thirteen: The Incredible Cave Rescue of the Thai Boys' Soccer Team*, written by Christina Soontornvat (Candlewick); *BOX: Henry Brown Mails Himself to Freedom*, written by Carole Boston Weatherford, illustrated by Michele Wood (Candlewick); *Fighting Words*, written by Kimberly Brubaker Bradley (Dial); *We Dream of Space*, written by Erin Entrada Kelly (Greenwillow); and *A Wish in the Dark*, written by Christina Soontornvat (Candlewick).

There were four Caldecott Honor Books: *A Place Inside of Me: A Poem to Heal the Heart*, illustrated by Noa Denmon, written by Zetta Elliott (FSG); *The Cat Man of Aleppo*, illustrated by Yuko Shimizu, written by Irene Latham and Karim Shamsi-Basha (Putnam); *Me & Mama*, illustrated and written by Cozbi A. Cabrera (S&S/Denene Millner); and *Outside In*, illustrated by Cindy Derby, written by Deborah Underwood (HMH).

Four Printz Honor Books were named: *Apple (Skin to the Core)* by Eric Gansworth (Levine Querido); *Dragon Hoops* by Gene Luen Yang, color by Lark Pien (First Second); *Every Body Looking* by Candice Iloh (Dutton); and *We Are Not Free* by Traci Chee (HMH).

217

The 2021 Margaret A. Edwards Award for lifetime achievement in writing for young adults went to Kekla Magoon, whose books include *X: A Novel*, co-written by Ilyasah Shabazz; *How It Went Down*; *The Rock and the River*; and *Fire in the Streets*.

The Children's Literature Legacy Award, which honors an author or illustrator whose books have made a substantial and lasting contribution to literature for children, was given to Mildred D. Taylor, whose award-winning works include *Roll of Thunder, Hear My Cry*, which earned the 1977 Newbery Medal and a Coretta Scott King Author honor; *The Land*, the 2002 Coretta Scott King Author Award winner; *The Road to Memphis*, recipient of the 1991 CSK Author Award; *All the Days Past, All the Days to Come*; and *The Gold Cadillac*, among others.

The Robert F. Sibert Award for the most distinguished informational book for children went to *Honeybee: The Busy Life of Apis Mellifera*, written by Candace Fleming and illustrated by Eric Rohmann (Holiday House/Neal Porter Books). There were three Sibert Honors: *How We Got to the Moon: The People, Technology, and Daring Feats of Science Behind Humanity's Greatest Adventure*, written and illustrated by John Rocco (Crown); *Exquisite: The Poetry and Life of Gwendolyn Brooks*, written by Suzanne Slade, illustrated by Cozbi A. Cabrera (Abrams); and *All Thirteen: The Incredible Cave Rescue of the Thai Boys' Soccer Team* by Christina Soontornvat (Candlewick).

The Mildred L. Batchelder Award for best work of translation went to *Telephone Tales*, originally published in Italian as *Favole al telefono*, by Gianni Rodari, illustrated by Valerio Vidali, and translated by Antony Shugaar (Enchanted Lion). One Batchelder Honor Book was selected: *Catherine's War* by Julia Billet, illustrated by Claire Fauvel, and translated from the French by Ivanka Hahnenberger (HarperAlley).

This year's Coretta Scott King–Virginia Hamilton Award for Lifetime Achievement was given to Dorothy L. Guthrie, in recognition of her work as a children's literature advocate. A retired librarian, district administrator, author, and school board member, Guthrie also founded the first African American museum in her home of Gaston County, N.C.

Before the Ever After by Jacqueline Woodson (Penguin/Paulsen) won the Coretta Scott King Author Award, and the Coretta Scott King Illustrator Award went to Frank Morrison for *R-E-S-P-E-C-T: Aretha Franklin, the Queen of Soul*, written by Carole Boston Weatherford (Atheneum).

Three King Author Honor Books were selected: *All the Days Past, All the Days to Come* by Mildred D. Taylor (Viking); *King and the Dragonflies* by Kacen Callender (Scholastic Press), winner of the 2020 National Book Award for Young People's Literature; and *Lifting as We Climb: Black Women's Battle for the Ballot Box* by Evette Dionne (Viking).

Three King Illustrator Honor Books were chosen: *Magnificent Homespun Brown: A Celebration*, illustrated by Kaylani Juanita, written by Samara Cole Doyon (Tilbury

House); *Exquisite: The Poetry and Life of Gwendolyn Brooks*, illustrated by Cozbi A. Cabrera, written by Suzanne Slade (Abrams); and *Me & Mama*, illustrated and written by Cozbi A. Cabrera (S&S/Denene Millner Books).

The Coretta Scott King/John Steptoe New Talent Author Award went to *Legendborn* by Tracy Deonn (McElderry).

The William C. Morris Award, for a debut book published by a first-time author writing for teens, was given to *If These Wings Could Fly*, written by Kyrie McCauley (HarperCollins/Katherine Tegen Books). Four finalists were announced in December: *Black Girl Unlimited: The Remarkable Story of a Teenage Wizard* by Echo Brown (Henry Holt/Christy Ottaviano Books); *The Black Kids* by Christina Hammonds Reed (Simon & Schuster); *It Sounded Better in My Head* by Nina Kenwood (Flatiron); and *Woven in Moonlight* by Isabel Ibañez (Page Street).

The Stonewall Book Award–Mike Morgan & Larry Romans Children's and Young Adult Literature Award, given to children's and YA books of exceptional merit relating to the gay, lesbian, bisexual, and transgender experience, went to *We Are Little Feminists: Families*, written by Archaa Shrivastav, designed by Lindsey Blakely (Little Feminist). Four Honor Books were named: *Beetle & the Hollowbones*, written and illustrated by Aliza Layne (S&S/Atheneum); *Darius the Great Deserves Better* by Adib Khorram (Dial); *Felix Ever After* by Kacen Callender (HarperCollins/Balzer + Bray); and *You Should See Me in a Crown* by Leah Johnson (Scholastic Press).

The Theodor Seuss Geisel Award for the most distinguished beginning reader book went to *See the Cat: Three Stories About a Dog*, written by David LaRochelle, illustrated by Mike Wohnoutka (Candlewick). Four Geisel Honor Books were named: *The Bear in My Family*, written and illustrated by Maya Tatsukawa (Dial); *Ty's Travels: Zip, Zoom!* written by Kelly Starling Lyons, illustrated by Nina Mata (HarperCollins); *What About Worms!?* written and illustrated by Ryan T. Higgins (Disney-Hyperion); and *Where's Baby?* written and illustrated by Anne Hunter (Tundra).

The YALSA Award for Excellence in Nonfiction for Young Adults went to *The Rise and Fall of Charles Lindbergh* by Candace Fleming (Random House/Schwartz and Wade). There were four finalists: *All Thirteen: The Incredible Cave Rescue of the Thai Boys' Soccer Team* by Christina Soontornvat (Candlewick); *The Cat I Never Named: A True Story of Love, War, and Survival* by Amra Sabic-El-Rayess with Laura L. Sullivan (Bloomsbury); *How We Got to the Moon: The People, Technology, and Daring Feats of Science Behind Humanity's Greatest Adventure*, written and illustrated by John Rocco (Crown); and *You Call This Democracy?: How to Fix Our Democracy and Deliver Power to the People* by Elizabeth Rusch (HMH).

The Pura Belpré Awards, honoring a Latinx writer and illustrator whose children's books best portray, affirm, and celebrate the Latino cultural experience, went to *¡Vamos! Let's Go Eat*, illustrated and written by Raúl Gonzalez (HMH/Versify) for the

Illustrator Award; *Efrén Divided* by Ernesto Cisneros (Harper) for the Author Award; and *Furia* by Yamile Saied Méndez (Algonquin), for the Young Adult Author Award.

One Belpré Illustrator Honor Book was named: *Sharuko: El Arqueólogo Peruano/ Peruvian Archaeologist Julio C. Tello*, illustrated by Elisa Chavarri, written by Monica Brown (Children's Book Press). Two Belpré Children's Author Honor Books were named: *The Total Eclipse of Nestor Lopez* by Adrianna Cuevas (FSG), and *Lupe Wong Won't Dance* by Donna Barba Higuera (Levine Querido). And two Belpré Young Adult Author Honor Books were named: *Never Look Back* by Lilliam Rivera (Bloomsbury) and *We Are Not from Here* by Jenny Torres Sanchez (Philomel).

The Sydney Taylor Book Award for outstanding books for young readers that authentically portray the Jewish experience are presented by the Association of Jewish Libraries. This year's Gold Medalists are: in the Picture Book category, *Welcoming Elijah: A Passover Tale with a Tail* by Lesléa Newman, illustrated by Susan Gal (Charlesbridge); in the Middle Grade category, *Turtle Boy* by M. Evan Wolkenstein (Delacorte); and in the Young Adult category, *Dancing at the Pity Party*, written and illustrated by Tyler Feder (Dial).

Sydney Taylor Book Award Silver Medalists include: in the Picture Book category, *I Am the Tree of Life: My Jewish Yoga Book* by Mychal Copeland, illustrated by André Ceolin (Apples and Honey) and *Miriam at the River* by Jane Yolen, illustrated by Khoa Le (Kar-Ben); in the Middle Grade category, *No Vacancy* by Tziporah Cohen (Groundwood), *Anya and the Nightingale* by Sofiya Pasternack (HMH/Versify), and *The Blackbird Girls* by Anne Blankman (Viking); and in the Young Adult category, *They Went Left* by Monica Hesse (Little, Brown).

The Schneider Family Book Awards, for books that embody an artistic expression of the disability experience, went to *I Talk Like a River*, written by Jordan Scott, illustrated by Sydney Smith (Holiday House/Neal Porter Books) in the young children category; *Show Me a Sign* by Ann Clare LeZotte (Scholastic Press) in the middle grade category; and *This Is My Brain in Love* by I.W. Gregorio (Little, Brown) in the teen category.

Two Schneider honor books for young children were selected: *All the Way to the Top: How One Girl's Fight for Americans with Disabilities Changed Everything*, written by Annette Bay Pimentel, illustrated by Nabi H. Ali (Sourcebooks eXplore), and *Itzhak: A Boy who Loved the Violin*, written by Tracy Newman, illustrated by Abigail Halpin (Abrams). Two middle grade honor books for middle grade were selected: *Get a Grip, Vivy Cohen!* by Sarah Kapit (Dial), and *When Stars Are Scattered*, written by Victoria Jamieson and Omar Mohamed, illustrated by Jamieson, color by Iman Geddy (Dial). No honor books for teens were selected.

The Asian/Pacific American Award for Literature, which promotes Asian/Pacific American culture and heritage, announced three winners in three categories: picture book, children's literature and youth literature. The picture book winner is *Paper Son: The Inspiring Story of Tyrus Wong, Immigrant and Artist*, written by Julie Leung, illustrated by Chris Sasaki (Random House/Schwartz & Wade), and there was one honor title: *Danbi Leads the School Parade*, written and illustrated by Anna Kim (Viking). The children's literature winner is *When You Trap a Tiger* by Tae Keller (Random House), and there was one honor title: *Prairie Lotus* by Linda Sue Park (Clarion). The youth literature winner is *This Light Between Us* by Andrew Fukuda (Tor Teen), and there was one honor title: *Displacement* by Kiku Hughes (First Second).

The Odyssey Award for best audiobook produced for children and/or young adults went to *Kent State* (Scholastic Audio), produced by Paul R. Gagne, written by Deborah Wiles, narrated by Christopher Gebauer, Lauren Ezzo, Christina DeLaine, Johnny Heller, Roger Wayne, Korey Jackson, and David de Vries. Four Odyssey Honor audiobooks were selected: *Clap When You Land* (HarperAudio), produced by Caitlin Garing, written by Elizabeth Acevedo, narrated by Elizabeth Acevedo and Melania-Luisa Marte; *Fighting Words* (Listening Library), produced by Karen Dziekonski, written by Kimberly Brubaker Bradley, narrated by Bahni Turpin; *Stamped: Racism, Antiracism, and You* (Hachette Audio), produced by Robert Van Kolken, written by Jason Reynolds and Ibram X. Kendi, narrated by Jason Reynolds; and *When Stars Are Scattered* (Listening Library), produced by Kelly Gildea and Julie Wilson, written by Victoria Jamieson and Omar Mohamed, narrated by Faysal Ahmed, Barkhad Abdi and a full cast.

The Excellence in Early Learning Digital Media Awards, given to a digital media producer that has created distinguished digital media for an early learning audience, went to *The Imagine Neighborhood*, produced by Committee for Children. The committee selected one honor title: *Sesame Street Family Play: Caring for Each Other*, produced by Sesame Workshop.

'Remarkable Adaptability': Children's Publishing in the Time of Covid

Children's publishers on the industry in the time of Covid

By Clare Swanson | Feb 12, 2021

With 2021 well underway, *Publishers Weekly* spoke with the heads of several children's publishing divisions to see how the industry weathered the onset of the pandemic and the months that followed, and to discuss what comes next in the midst of persistent uncertainty. Among the chief concerns related to new Covid practices were frontlist sales and launching debut authors, the reinvention of office culture with the advent of near-universal remote working, and the health of bricks-and-mortar stores. Yet for all the disruption the pandemic wrought, the unprecedented year also, in equally unanticipated ways, paved the way for opportunities that may set the standard for how the industry functions in a post-Covid world.

During the course of our survey on how Covid has affected all facets of the industry, the need for greater diversity, in both acquisition and staffing, was repeatedly cited as a top priority for children's publishers. While there are issues of equity and diversity entangled in pandemic publishing—such as marketing BIPOC creators at a time when traditional tools are no longer available—it became clear that documenting how the industry responded to last summer's Black Lives Matter protests, and the work that must be done going forward, merited a dedicated, meaningful story—one *PW* will publish in a future issue.

The new virtual reality

Nearly every publisher *PW* spoke with said the pivot from in-person events was among the biggest hurdles of the last year, and that it came with a steep learning curve. The shift, though, was not without its silver linings.

Ellie Berger, president of Scholastic Trade, says that when it comes to virtual tours, the team has learned over the last 10 months that "quality prevails over quantity," noting, "A 20-city, in-person tour where the author could repeat their presentation does not resonate as well in the virtual world, where each stop needs to offer something different to keep readers coming back for more." Instead, Scholastic often opts for three to five "robust" and varied events to combat "Zoom fatigue," as Berger puts it. Tami Charles's virtual tour for her new YA novel, *Muted*, for example, featured a discussion with *The Fresh Prince of Bel-Air* actor Karyn Parsons on the exploitation of Black women in the entertainment industry, as well as a conversation about the #MeToo movement with CNN senior legal analyst Laura Coates, among other events.

Suzanne Murphy, president and publisher of HarperCollins Children's Books, says that the organization has thus far seen "great success" with its virtual tours. Among what they've discovered works in the digital space: ticketed events, unique pairings of conversational partners, and special incentives. HarperCollins implemented the latter for the launch of Angie Thomas's *Concrete Rose*, sending shoelaces themed on the book to the first 100 people to RSVP to each of the author's tour events. "We're embracing both the live views for author events and the audience who watches later," Murphy says. "It's a long tail."

At a time when so much of personal and professional life feels curtailed and isolated, the forced pivot has, for all of its challenges, in fact opened up the world of publishing to new readers—especially those who may not be able to afford or have access to travel. HarperCollins Children's Books will continue to rely on virtual events and digital promotions for at least the next six months, according to Murphy. "They have become so much more accessible for our authors to participate in and for readers to join," she says. "I hope that as we transition back into in-person events, we keep the expansion of access as a top priority."

Jen Loja, president and publisher at Penguin Young Readers, agrees, noting that "one of the huge positives is that readers who live in remote parts of the country, or who have mobility constraints, can now attend virtual book readings with their favorite authors." She adds that Penguin has seen more virtual teacher engagement, and it has been able to connect authors with students across the country through large-scale literacy events with digital education platforms like Microsoft Education and Flipgrid. Loja believes even when the pandemic is in the rear-view mirror, book tours will continue to include a combination of in-person and virtual programming.

"The pivot to virtual consumer-facing events has allowed us to connect authors with readers in exciting ways that we weren't previously able to in the past," says Jon Anderson, president and publisher at Simon & Schuster Children's Publishing. "While the experience of physically meeting an author in person can't be replicated, virtual events have allowed us to pair two or more authors who aren't in the same geographic area, for an engaging conversation, and have authors who live outside of the U.S. connect with a U.S. audience virtually. We've had debut authors connect with readers across the country, rather than in just their local regions. Readers seem to really enjoy the opportunity to visit with their favorite authors from the comfort of their own living rooms."

The buzz factor

The cancellation of in-person events redirected the typical word-of-mouth channels to the virtual space. And, according to many publishers we spoke with, the obliteration of the traditional ecosystem for prepublication buzz—industry conferences and book fairs alongside the distribution of physical galleys—is most problematic when it comes to launching new authors without existing platforms or readerships.

"That word-of-mouth buzz is particularly important for our debut authors," Scholastic's Berger says. "We are acquiring new, exciting talent and have made great strides to diversify our list. These new authors and illustrators don't have the opportunity to meet tastemakers in person, so we want to shine a spotlight wherever we can. It's so important to launch debuts with gusto, despite publishing in a moment when discoverability is challenged."

Galley strategies—continuing with physical copies or opting for digital—differ between publishers. "Like our colleagues, we have had to pivot when it comes to the largely digital distribution of advance copies," Berger says. "Many media outlets, for example, had a very physical and visual method of cataloging what galleys came in the mail to plan their coverage, and have had to overhaul that system. Likewise, we can't distribute galleys at events, seeding buzz at conferences the way we used to."

At Peachtree Publishers in Atlanta, president and publisher Margaret Quinlin and her team had completed galley printing for the full year before the shutdown struck last March, which proved fortuitous. "Because we had our galleys in, we offered them at our virtual booths," she says. "We went into the office and shipped them out to the educators and librarians. People requested them, and were really pleased that we could send them, especially picture books."

Like Berger, Quinlin is concerned about discoverability in the age of Covid-restricted buzz making. "With the well-known authors, the word is going to get out," she says. "For those debut authors, or authors without quite the platform, it's harder to get attention."

And while Quinlin predicts that the publisher will not attend this year's Bologna Book Fair (which has moved from April to June), she says that attending conferences virtually has been effective, and sometimes advantageous. "Zoom meetings have actually been really, really good," she notes. "We've had a number of wonderful meetings with our overseas partners, especially in the U.K., where we do a lot of work. You're seeing more people than you would at Bologna, and you can have longer conversations."

Jen Besser, who was named president of the Macmillan Children's Publishing Group at the end of January, saw the benefits of the company's pandemic galley strategy. "As with virtual events, many of the changes to our review copy distribution practices were born of necessity, but they've also offered advantages and opportunities," she says. "The change to digital galleys has freed up resources, both time and budget, for other marketing efforts, and it's far better for the environment. We've also discovered that the vast majority of gatekeepers we work with have been more receptive to digital review copies than expected, including many who, pre-pandemic, would never have read a book on a screen." Macmillan saw a year-over-year increase in national media hits for its titles, Besser notes.

Most of the larger children's houses that ceased printing physical galleys in 2020 have since resumed. "Throughout the pandemic, we have continued to print galleys and advance reading materials for our titles, and will continue to do so," Anderson says. "Though we may be printing fewer because of the lack of physical shows, we are still mailing galleys to accounts, influencers, reviewers, media, and even virtual show attendees, both trade and consumer, via online submission forms."

The decision to carry on with distributing physical copies was an important one, according to Anderson. "We saw a significant year-over-year increase in the social media coverage and buzz for our titles, and our ability to provide physical advance copies of our titles was crucial to this outcome," he says.

Holiday House plans to provide print galleys on select titles going forward, says Derek Stordhal, executive v-p and general manager. "But we're also watching how expectations change in terms of reviewers and show attendance," he adds. "We have seen the reviewer, bookseller, and librarian communities adapt to receiving materials in a digital format. At the same time, we're making sure we provide galleys that do help with buzz, word of mouth, and review coverage."

Abrams is predominantly using e-galleys across its list and finds that its media coverage is as "robust as ever," says Andrew Smith, senior v-p and publisher of children's books.

Barbara Marcus, president and publisher at Random House Children's Books, says the publisher's pandemic galley strategy has not negatively impacted overall buzz or reviews. "We have seen remarkable adaptability," she says, "and we know that while there isn't a substitute for the experience of reading from a physical copy, reviewers and retailers are adjusting to using digital."

There is one demographic, according to Marcus, more affected by the cancellation of large industry events than others. "I do think that word of mouth with teens picking up books at shows and festivals is impacted, and we have to be more patient for teens to learn about new books, as we know that was one way that they did," she says.

In order to reach young readers, Loja says that digital influencer campaigns have emerged as "an invaluable tool for building word of mouth in the Covid era." She notes, "Building relationships with influential bookstagrammers, YouTubers, and BookTokers of all sizes and backgrounds has allowed us to authentically introduce our books to readers across digital communities and generate significant word of mouth."

Buoying bookstores

With shutdowns, capacity limitations, and decreased foot traffic, many publishers expressed concern about the well-being of bricks-and-mortar stores. "We continue to keep them front of mind across marketing and sales channels as we navigate this new retail landscape," Anderson says. The publisher has "marshaled all of the tools in its arsenal"—including its authors and illustrators, social media and other digital channels, and sales reps—to "shine a spotlight on its bookseller partners, drive traffic their way, and provide them with resources."

Strategies to help stores rebound range from traditional fund-raising to creative social media efforts to direct digital traffic. Abrams partnered with the Book Industry Charitable Foundation on a fund-raising challenge to assist booksellers, resulting in a $200,000 donation, which was double the goal. "Our own authors, artists, partners, employees, and friends of the house contributed with us," Smith says.

Last October, Penguin Random House launched VESPER (the Virtual Events Support Program), a corporate initiative that offers financial assistance to independent booksellers who are hosting virtual events with its authors. "In addition, we are providing physical and digital merchandising materials to help booksellers capture customer attention," Penguin's Loja says, "including upcoming cover blow-ups and window displays."

Similarly, Scholastic created a Welcome Back kit for independents that included curbside pickup window signs, a safety guidelines poster, and Clifford paw floor decals to help customers stay six feet apart. "We continue to focus on engaging window displays, hoping to bring customers in and increase that foot traffic in the safest way possible, as well as merchandising vehicles that help create an engaging in-store environment," says Berger. She adds that the publisher is, in particular, working toward building closer relationships with Black-owned bookstores, "from highlighting specific titles for them to partnering with them on virtual events."

Each week, HarperCollins features five to six independent bookstores via social media, and communicates with booksellers about titles hitting shelves the following week, sharing marketing assets, directly with links to preorder graphics, video book trailers, and social media graphics, in order "to help booksellers be nimble in promoting the books they're most excited about and to have the tools at their fingertips to do so," Murphy says. "I think we're all poised for a renaissance of in-person interaction when we come out of this," she adds, "including the kind of shopping and event experience only bricks-and-mortar stores can provide."

Bridging the divide

With many schools operating under limited to zero in-person learning, equitable access to books, especially for children in low-income families, is more problematic than ever. In response, many publishers made certain titles free of charge, and worked with nonprofits to get books to kids in need.

"There are many 'book deserts' in this country, and they will unfortunately grow in the aftermath of this pandemic," Loja says, referring to areas, most often those with high poverty rates, with limited access to printed reading materials. Penguin donated more than half a million physical books in 2020, Loja says, and they will continue those efforts in 2021. Additionally, the publisher, along with many others, extended online storytime permissions for educators and librarians.

"This is such a crisis for our country's children," says Karen Lotz, president and publisher of Candlewick Press. "And the gap between wealthy families and those who are less well off, which was far too wide even before the pandemic, has been growing exponentially." Like many publishers, Candlewick donated books through nonprofits like First Book, the National Book Foundation's Book Rich Environments Program, and United Through Reading.

"We also found it important to recognize caregivers', educators', and librarians' needs for engaging, shareable content," Lotz adds. To do so, the publisher created new initiatives such as a virtual summer camp called Camp Candlewick, and the Stay

Home with Candlewick Press portal on the company's website, which offers videos and activities for home learning.

Simon & Schuster has "always been aggressive" with its book donation initiatives to organizations like First Book and the National Book Foundation, and "actively stepped them up in 2020," according to Anderson, expanding to new charities in the last year, such as the Toys for Tots Literacy Program.

S&S author Jason Reynolds, the current National Ambassador for Young People's Literature, has a platform built on engaging with "children in underserved, rural communities, many of which were hit hard by the pandemic," Anderson says. Though the author's scheduled tour for the October release of his new book, *Look Both Ways*, was reimagined as a virtual one, Reynolds visited seven school districts through the course of the tour, with 5,000 students receiving a copy of the book.

The Scholastic Education group has been "on the ground" working with districts and foundations to get books in the hands of kids, Berger says. "Scholastic is also uniquely committed to book access for all kids through our clubs and fairs channels, so we partner closely with them on their efforts to pivot during this time."

Working together, apart

According to a survey conducted by *PW* at the end of 2020, the majority of publishing houses have not yet set firm dates for employees to return to offices. But even when Covid restrictions ease, some publishers believe the integration of remote working, to varying degrees, may be the new norm.

"People are pretty happy working from home," Quinlin says. "Unless they have four kids that they have to help educate. I think there are going to be significant changes there. In thinking that through, how do we keep our culture together, keep communicating with each other internally, even though we may be dispersed?"

Lotz, too, predicts that work culture will settle into a new normal. "Sometimes we find ourselves pulling off feats of gathering, and sometimes we frankly fall into the abyss of isolation," she says. "We definitely will not be returning, post-pandemic, to exactly what was. We hope to engage with our staff and, through the wisdom of our collective experience, come to a new working experience that is even better suited to the needs of the company, of individuals, and their families."

Marcus believes that in the future, Random House will be working in a hybrid way. "Not that the beginning wasn't truly difficult," she says. "But we have figured out how to work using technology, and I think it has made us more focused on certain areas."

Marcus says that she and her Random House colleagues now "operate more in real time," and aim to respond more quickly to the feedback they receive. As it became clear that parents are, more than ever, an integral component of their children's education, she pushed her editors to publish more general nonfiction to aid in at-home learning efforts. "Children's books remain ever important to families—from education, to entertainment, to emotional balancing, to diversity. In some ways, we are more important than we knew."

*

A version of this article appeared in the 02/15/2021 issue of *Publishers Weekly* under the headline: "Remarkable Adaptability".

Keeping Connections with Young Readers: Bookselling in the Pandemic
By Alex Green | Feb 12, 2021

There's a 10-year-old boy in Upstate New York who never sees anyone these days other than his parents and the booksellers at Oblong Books & Music in Rhinebeck. "He's discovered a love of reading during the pandemic that has absolutely blossomed," says Oblong manager Nicole Brinkley. "He can't get enough of funny or sweet animal chapter books."

Despite Covid-19 restrictions and countless other hurdles, a handful of dedicated children and teens come into the store for recommendations each week. But, as Brinkley says, "They're being tugged in even more directions than usual, always at the whims of adults who want them to sit in front of a screen for however many hours a day. The things they read aren't only an escape. It can be something that's completely in their control."

Brinkley isn't the only bookseller thinking about children and reading during these challenging times. Nearly one year into the pandemic, life has not returned to normal, and across the country booksellers are finding their own ways to forge, maintain, and deepen their connections with the kids who turn to them for books. Some of their approaches are temporary and some may last well into the future, but all are geared toward ensuring that children continue to know that bookstores are there for them.

Clear the shelves

Chicago bookseller DL Mullen lost a major lifeline to readers when the Chicago Public Schools shuttered due to the pandemic last year. With three elementary schools in walking distance of her Semicolon Bookstore & Gallery, she had delighted in setting up "Semicolon Corners" in the school hallways as a first connection to kids that would get them to enjoy reading and come to the store.

"The books were a representation that a lot of the students didn't see otherwise—characters who may be Black or disabled, or from a nontraditional home," Mullen says. It was an important give-back from the store, aligned with her mission to foster reading in the community and her personal joy in meeting young readers. When she got the news that schools were closing on March 13, she was filled with despair.

"We recognized that children wouldn't have access to the schools, children wouldn't have access to books, and the educational gap that exists in communities of color is only going to grow larger," Mullen says. "And that's problematic for me."

In response, Mullen did something radical. "While we're closed, we have an entire room of children's books that are just sitting there," she notes. "So we packed up every book, hit up the Chicago Public Schools teachers and principals we knew, and said, 'Come get these books for free.' "

Only then did Mullen try to figure out how to pay for what became the #ClearTheShelves program, and customers joined in support. To date, the program has raised more than $165,000, and it has also maintained Mullen's connection to her readers. At #ClearTheShelves events, families often receive food and other supplies, and children get to pick a book of their choice.

The events allow Mullen and her employees to see readers face-to-face, albeit from behind masks, and they have been fascinated to observe which books readers are choosing during the pandemic. Younger readers continue to love board books. Middle schoolers are gravitating toward books by Kwame Alexander, Brittney Morris, and Trevor Noah but are also beginning to read titles for older readers, like *The Autobiography of Malcom X*. High school students have been seeking out a mix of speculative fiction by writers such as Octavia Butler and practical books on entrepreneurship and life skills.

Those choices are a source of hope for Mullen, and a sign that young people are not passively accepting the worst of the pandemic but are instead finding ways to grapple with its meaning and think about their own futures. With Semicolon now reopened to limited foot traffic, the #ClearTheShelves events are also a chance for children and young adults to make a first connection with the store's booksellers that encourages them to come back in again.

"I happen to have a really cool staff," Mullen says with a laugh. But she also knows that it is a helpful draw, because children and young adults begin to associate reading with people whom they admire.

It's a boost for Mullen, too, at a time when she had feared losing ties to the readers who give her purpose. "It works very well," she says. "These teenagers normally walk in with their heads down, like they don't want to be here, and their parents told them to come. By the time they're leaving, they're laughing, joking, and dancing, and it's comfortable for them."

300 storytime books and counting
Stephanie Heinz, children's buyer and events coordinator at Print: A Bookstore in

Portland, Maine, was standing six feet from a boy who could not find a book he wanted to read. A few questions and answers later, she produced a book that she promised would be funny. "I couldn't see his mouth, but his eyes lit up. He said, 'Yeah, that looks really cool,'" she recalls. "That moment was so great. It added years to my life."

Shopping by appointment has been among the many ways that Heinz has kept a relationship with her customers alive. When readers come to the door she slips bookmarks, stickers, and dinosaur tattoos to them. "There's this element of surprise, when everything feels so controlled," she says. "Just going out requires so much deliberate action, that to have something surprising is really nice."

Since the beginning of the pandemic, Heinz has done everything she can to reach young readers. As soon as Print was forced to close to in-person shopping last spring, she began doing storytime picture book readings on Instagram TV and Facebook Live, via her home webcam. Nearly one year later, she still does them twice a week. By her count, she has read more than 300 picture books in that time.

But Heinz says there are limits to her ability to serve children online or in the store. The best way remains by deepening connections through Portland's schools, which have many students who qualify for free and reduced-cost lunches and who are more economically insecure than they were before the pandemic.

Last summer, Heinz worked with local teachers on a project called My Book Forever. Collectively they raised $5,000 to mail books directly to students. Instead of mailing the same book to everyone, Heinz put her handselling skills to work, tailoring book choices to each student. The success of the program encouraged her to take on a similar project, called the Portland Readers Program, that is currently underway with a local teacher and library.

Heinz says the store has helped boost efforts like the Portland Readers Program. On a recent phone call, a customer offhandedly said, "I just really want to do something to help kids right now." Heinz told her about the program, and when the customer came to pick up her order, she also left a check for $1,000 to support the effort.

Heinz does not foresee the outreach programs she has created with educators going away after the pandemic, though she's less sure about the storytimes, which have been possible only because publishers have relaxed their rules about sharing content online. But the book appointments might stick around longer, and for now, they provide her with the connection to keep going.

Just before Christmas, Heinz says a parent gave their child—a regular customer—a shopping spree at the store. They played hooky from remote learning and came in to browse. Every few minutes, the child hemmed over one book or another, and the mother kept saying, "It's whatever you want. This is your birthday present. Get whatever you want."

Heinz says, "Especially after dealing with so many months of these limitations and regulations, it was just so sweet and endearing."

Stepping back from the screen

Eight Cousins Bookstore co-owner Sara Hines notices how families move around her Cape Cod store in packs since it reopened, carving out sections for themselves. In-person shopping is still far from normal.

"I suspect that it is partially intentional, and partially just that we're changing the way that we move these days," Hines says.

In response to those changes, Eight Cousins has made a few alterations of its own, some of which Hines and her fellow co-owners plan to keep in the future. Given the traffic in downtown Falmouth each summer, she says curbside pickup is there to stay.

But for a bookstore known as a hub of children's literature, Eight Cousins is an outlier. As many indies moved to enhance digital offerings for children during the pandemic, Hines chose to take a very deliberate step back, even though it comes at the cost of engagement with the readers she loves.

"Everyone's interacting with technology, and kids are interacting with technology a lot more through school," Hines says. Though that may reduce isolation, she is concerned about the amount of time children are spending looking at screens.

"They need the real world around them," Hines says, "but that's a hard conversation to have right now, because we're all doing so many things virtually, and that's needed. Technology has come to mean something very different in the last year."

For now, Eight Cousins is sustained by foot traffic and online orders, while much of the outreach Hines does is through established groups that are already working with children. But even for her, there have been two cases where the rules about screens have fallen to the side.

Years ago, Eight Cousins' previous owner, Carol Chittenden, formed a relationship with a local health group to share children's books and literacy tips with expectant and new mothers. Hines has continued that relationship and has been meeting virtually with the group. At first, she says, it was difficult, but then she remembered that the screen was less important than the sound. "It was about language enrichment, so it was really more about hearing the story," she realized. After two sessions, she committed to doing two more this coming spring.

Hines also couldn't resist an opportunity to do a virtual visit with local elementary students about advance reader's copies and book publishing. She sent ARCs to the class, and then during her visit she explained how books are published. The experience was invigorating for her, with students asking questions about every aspect of the writing and publishing process. Next, the students will write reviews of the ARCs they were sent.

Meanwhile, Hines walked away from the class happy to have reengaged with young readers for a time. "It was fun," she says, "and it was great to hear their questions. They had very, very detailed questions."

Hines plans to return to the class to talk about writing the reviews and has a couple of other class visits planned for the spring. Until the virus abates, she says it is enough to sustain her in the absence of having kids running freely through the store.

The keys to the bookstore

When the pandemic began, well-to-do families started fleeing the coasts for less populated places, including the resort communities of Ketchum and Sun Valley, Idaho. A few miles south, in Hailey, Sarah Hedrick quickly adapted to the needs of the new visitors as well as the residents who live year-round in the small community. She put her cell phone number on the website for her bookstore, Iconoclast Books, and told people to reach out anytime.

A customer from New York did just that, asking if she could send her teenage son down to pick up some books. Since Hedrick was heading out to make deliveries, she did the first thing that came to mind and offered to leave the keys for him.

"She said, 'What?'" Hedrick recalls. "And I said, 'I'll just hide a key and he can help himself.'"

An hour later, Hedrick returned to a darkened store to find the teen sitting in a chair, mask on, reading a book, with stacks of puzzle books, cookbooks, and novels on the counter. She jokingly asked if his parents had ever told him what a light switch was, and he replied, "I'm just having so much fun being in the moment."

Hedrick's nonchalance belies a passion to make sure that kids see her store as a potent balancing force in such a challenging and uncertain time. An ad-hoc book giveaway started up in front of Iconoclast, and children often stop by to leave books they have already read so that others can take them.

The road to Hailey was not an easy one for Hedrick, a mother of four who raised her children after her husband died. She downsized and moved her store from Sun Valley, and as she did, she also gave up employees. Through the pandemic, she has run Iconoclast entirely herself, with an occasional volunteer (a 12-year-old who has grown up shopping at the store), a cat, and a dog named Barkley, after former basketball star Charles Barkley.

Despite the challenges, Hedrick says, "I wake up every day so grateful because moving into the smaller space, not having other employees, and having 100% contact with every customer has made my life so unbelievably rich in friendships and kindness and acts of love."

Hedrick points to a local father who moved to town with his family and signed his nine-year-old up for basketball. A few weeks ago, the father called on a Monday night and said, "Hey, I've got a car full of boys chanting 'Barkley.' Is he at the store with you?" When she said yes, he replied, "Great. We're on our way in."

Soon, four boys in basketball uniforms and masks barreled into the bookstore, and now it has become a routine. Every Monday and Wednesday after basketball practice, they come to the store and the father buys a book for each kid. "He doesn't put any limits," Hedrick says. "One kid got a hardcover *Guinness Book of World Records* and another got a $4.99 DC comic."

After their first visit, Hedrick burst into tears. "I get to see something like that almost every day in the store now," she says.

*

A version of this article appeared in the 02/15/2021 issue of *Publishers Weekly* under the headline: Keeping Connections with Young Readers.

Kid Lit Community Rallies Against Anti-Asian Racism
By Sarah Yung | Mar 04, 2021

Outraged by the exponential increase in hate crimes targeting Asian Americans since the onset of the Covid-19 pandemic, a group of Asian American children's authors has sought to make change—literally.

For Asian/Pacific American Award for Literature winner Stacey Lee, "The last straw was when my cousin told me she was spit on in public as she was taking a walk on her birthday." Lee, a co-founder of the nonprofit organization We Need Diverse Books, immediately contacted her friend Kat Cho, founder of the Asian Author Alliance—"a group of Asian kid lit authors of which I'm a member"—to brainstorm if there was anything to be done. "Within a day," Lee said, "[Kat] was already putting a plan into action."

The duo decided upon an auction because of successful precedents, such as Kid Lit Says No Kids in Cages. "Auctions are brilliant," Lee explained, "because they can raise funds quickly, and also bring together communities—in this case, the book community, writers, readers, publishers, illustrators." After announcing the call for donations on the Asian Author Alliance Twitter page on February 21, Lee and Cho, along with National Book Award finalist Traci Chee, Debbi Michiko Florence, and Van Hoang, got to work bringing the auction to life.

The group took to Wordpress, creating individual posts for 450 items ranging from calls with authors, editors, or agents, critiques, copyedits, advance readers copies, framed illustrations, signed books, and more. Interested parties could bid on the items between February 26 and February 28 by commenting under the appropriate post. Winners received their prizes after sending proof of their donated bid amount to either Stop AAPI Hate or Hate Is a Virus.

Lee had been following Stop AAPI Hate "ever since its inception in 2020," as "they provided one of the first reporting systems to monitor" the increasingly common crimes against Asian Americans and Pacific Islanders, she said, as well as offering multilingual resources and supporting "community-based safety measures and restorative justice efforts." Cho brought to Lee's attention #HateIsAVirus, another movement founded to combat xenophobia and racism against Asian Americans and raise funds for BIPOC community organizations, and so they decided to benefit both.

Lee said she was "astounded" by the results of the auction, during which people bid "down to the wire." She added, "I figured we would raise $4,000 to maybe $12,000. I was pretty overcome when Kat told me we had made over $50,000."

The top three items, Lee revealed, were a picture book mentorship with Chronicle editor Melissa Manlove ($2,010), an advance readers copy of Lee's forthcoming novel *Luck of the Titanic* ($1,000), and a manuscript critique by Anne Ursu ($910).

But the authors' efforts became even more efficacious when people began matching donations. "I felt so grateful [when Cho told me]," Lee said. "People were showing that they cared."

"The kid lit community is an intricate network of diverse opinions and perspectives, but one thing we can agree on is that there is never a place for racism," Lee concluded. "As an Asian American who writes about Asian Americans, the issue hits close to home, and I'm so thankful for all the people who came together to support this cause."

Comics Formats Go Younger
By Brigid Alverson | Feb 26, 2021

As sales of middle grade graphic novels continue to grow, publishers are bringing the format to a younger audience, with a new wave of graphic novels for early readers, ages four to eight. Within the past year, the number of graphic novels aimed at the youngest readers has increased sharply, including titles such as *My Pencil and Me* by Sara Varon (First Second); *Donut Feed the Squirrels* by Mika Song (RH Graphic); *Pea, Bee & Jay* by Brian "Smitty" Smith (HarperAlley); *Baloney and Friends* by Greg Pizzoli (Little, Brown); and *Dewdrop* by Katie O'Neill (Oni)—with more on the way.

Established authors are getting into the act as well: Jonathan Stutzman and Heather Fox, creators of *Llama Destroys the World*, are launching a new series, Fitz and Cleo, this May at Henry Holt. Beak & Ally, which debuted from HarperAlley in January, is by Norm Feuti, author of *The King of Kazoo*. And the Baby-Sitters Little Sister graphic novels, launched last year by Scholastic Graphix, are already bestsellers.

Though many publishers prefer standalone graphic novels for early readers, others are bringing the graphic format to existing brands: HarperCollins's I Can Read

Comics, Simon & Schuster's Little Simon Graphics and Ready-to-Read Graphics, and Holiday House's I Like to Read Comics will all launch in 2021. The educational publisher Capstone, which has published My First Graphic Novel books for more than a decade, added a second early readers line, Discover Graphics, earlier this year.

The first graphic novels specifically designed for early readers were Françoise Mouly's Toon Books, which launched in 2007 and whose titles have won numerous library and industry awards over the years. More recently, the success of Ben Clanton's Narwhal and Jelly series (Tundra), which are pitched at readers ages six and up, has caught editors' attention.

"Just as [Raina Telgemeier's] *Smile* turned us on to an entire category, the popularity of Narwhal and Jelly is something publishers are clearly hoping to emulate," says Andrea Colvin, editorial director of graphic novels at Little, Brown Books for Young Readers. "There are three or four times more early reader graphic novels that have been announced but not yet published than those in the market right now."

The Narwhal and Jelly books led Michelle Nagler, v-p and associate publishing director of Random House Children's Books, to start thinking about extending graphic novels down to younger readers. "The graphic novel moment had begun," she says, "but we were starting to see it in that younger chapter book space." Random House launched two early reader graphic novel series in 2020: Stephen Shaskan's Pizza and Taco in May and Brian Yanish's Shark and Bot in September. Two more will debut in 2021: Mélanie Watt's Scaredy Squirrel in May and Vikram Madan and Nicola Slater's Bobo and Pup-Pup in September.

"All the parents I know tell me there's tremendous interest in graphic novels from their younger readers," says David Saylor, editorial director of Scholastic's Graphix graphic novel imprint. "But not all younger readers are ready to dive into a book by Raina Telgemeier, Kazu Kibuishi, or Jeff Smith. We feel there's a real need, and room on the shelves, for graphic novels more directly tailored for emerging readers." Graphix recently launched its own young readers line, for "newly independent readers" ages six and up, with Jess Keating's *Bunbun & Bonbon*, Kevin Sherry's *Squidding Around,* and James Kochalka's *Banana Fox.*

Some of these books overlap with Graphix's middle grade titles, such as the Dog Man series, which is targeted for ages seven to nine. "Categorizing kid readers is always a bit tricky, because I think all children read things that are below their age level, at their age level, and above their age level, often all at the same time," Saylor says. "At the end of the day, these distinctions end up being a general guide so that parents can make buying decisions and retailers can figure out where to shelve the books. These new books are kid friendly and kid focused, and absolutely appeal to fans of Dog Man. So in short, I do feel it's an overlapping audience."

Colvin sees the category as encompassing several different age levels. "I think there

Children's Publishing | **235**

are actually a few types of early reader graphic novels," she says, "ranging from the very young—maybe the book you read right after *Elephant and Piggie*—to the just pre-middle grade—the book you read right before *Dog Man*. And these represent rungs on the ladder from pre-reader to reader."

The increased acceptance of graphic novels led Capstone to create Discover Graphics, which associate publisher Beth Brezenoff describes as a bit more sophisticated than its My First Graphic Novels line, which launched in 2009. "Discover Graphics still assume you are not quite at the point where you can read the big kid graphic novels," she says, "but because it's been 10 years, we think there is a little more general knowledge of graphic novels, so we have elevated the art style a bit. We want them to look a bit more like the big siblings' graphic novels."

Formats with kid appeal

Though publishers are using several different approaches for early readers, all agree on some basics. "Simply, simplify, simplify," says Sarah Gaydos, editor-in-chief of Oni Press. "Really think about how this book is going to be enjoyed: likely with an adult reading to the kid at first, and then hopefully they are able to enjoy it themselves. Keep vocabulary on the younger edge of things; [use] fewer panels and super-clear storytelling."

Format is also important. The Random House titles are paper-over-board hardcovers with a 6 1/2" × 8 1/2" trim size that makes them feel more like graphic novels than picture books. All are chapter books. "Chapters lend a sense of accomplishment," Nagler says. "They lend a structure to the story." The early reader books are shorter than middle grade graphic novels, and they have fewer panels and simpler vocabulary.

While Random House Graphic publishing director Gina Gagliano doesn't have strict guidelines for authors of books for early readers, she does discuss reading levels and storytelling with them. "One of the things we think about is how many characters are talking in a panel," she says, "because we want to get that one comprehensible moment at a time, so kids are able to easily follow the story without people having a back and forth conversational exchange within a single panel."

Andrew Arnold, editorial director of HarperAlley, also emphasizes clarity in storytelling. "The reader should always know who's speaking/thinking/narrating, how to move from one panel to the next, and how to decipher a particular character's pose and/or expression," he says. "And even though these books are for beginning readers, I also think it's important to avoid exposition as much as possible. The beauty of comics storytelling is its ability to communicate through both illustrations and text, so while the two should reinforce each other, they should enhance each other as well."

This interdependence between text and art makes graphic novels particularly appropriate for early readers, says Karen MacPherson, children's and teen services coordinator at the Takoma Park (Md.) Library. "One of the frustrations of a beginning reader is that when you are sounding out the words, you are losing the thread of the story," she notes. "In the traditional beginning reader, words are paramount, and pictures provide detail. Toon Books made the pictures paramount and words provide the detail. For many young readers who are struggling, that makes a big difference. They can keep track of the story and are eager to learn the words."

Indeed, Mouly says she got the idea to create comics for early readers when her son was learning to read. In the early readers she saw, the text simply repeated what was in the pictures. Comics, on the other hand, use text, pictures, onomatopoeia, gestures and facial expressions, even the way the panels are arranged.

"All of these together tell a story," Mouly says, "and if a kid is not understanding one word, it's one word in a symphony, so you start understanding the story through the context, which is exactly what reading is. It's creating that context and putting the pieces together. All the early readers were doing the opposite—they were isolating the words."

When she first tested Toon Books in classrooms, Mouly observed that students would quickly understand the story and even read the dialogue with the correct intonations. "At the end," she says, "the teacher often asked, 'What was your favorite part?'—and the kids knew exactly their favorite parts. They were uncannily perceptive about coming to the turning points and climaxes of the story."

In terms of content, there's a strong trend in early reader graphic novels toward humor, often involving animals, food, or animals named after foods. Most are structured as series because, as Nagler says, "we know when a kid loves a character at this level, they really want to stay with them."

Though some of the publishers who are extending their leveled-reader lines to include graphic novels are building on existing series, Holiday House is taking a different approach with its I Like to Read Comics, says v-p and editor-in-chief Mary Cash. "Our I Like to Read Comics are originals," she notes. "We view the format of picture book and graphic novel readers as quite distinct. These formats are telling stories in different ways. Although the art strongly supports the texts in our I Like to Read series and in many cases is essential to the plots, character development, and settings of those picture books, pictures in graphic novels play an even more integral role. Graphic Readers provide a more cinematic experience that requires and helps develop more kinds of visual skills such as sequencing, imaging, and reading facial and body cues."

Regardless of publishers' approaches, it's clear that young readers are not only ready but eager to dive into graphic novels. MacPherson sees preschoolers pulling middle grade graphic novels off the shelves, attracted by the colorful artwork, and deciphering the story through the pictures. And as the field has evolved, so have the gatekeepers.

"Parents and gift givers are much less likely to show aversion to comics and are handily using the term 'graphic novel,'" says bookseller Griffin Mauser of BookPeople in Austin, Tex. "While they continue to encourage chapter book reading, they are slowly becoming aware of the value and depth of quality graphic work, and increasingly recognizing its bridging effects [to other books]. For the youngest, these are serving as alternative readers and first chapter books."

What's next? While young readers are snapping up stories about animals and snack foods doing silly things, Gagliano sees more variety on the horizon. "The next step is you're going to get all sorts of different stories, from mysteries to stories about people to the sweet, quiet, thoughtful stories that you find in so many picture books," she says. "There's definitely something in the category that is working, and now it's time to branch out and try more things."

*

Brigid Alverson is a comics journalist and the editor of the *Good Comics for Kids* blog.

A version of this article appeared in the 03/01/2021 issue of *Publishers Weekly* under the headline: Comics Formats Go Younger.

2020 Children's Bestsellers: Graphic Novel Powerhouses, Beloved Picture Books, and More

Compiled by Gilcy Aquino and Emma Kantor | Mar 23, 2021

Our 2020 Facts and Figures compilation of children's bestsellers includes a wide variety of titles, dominated by contemporary graphic novel series and their spinoffs, illustrated middle grade novels, and classic picture books. Our lists are based on print unit sales at outlets that report to NPD Bookscan, which tracks approximately 85% of the print market. Here we compile the books that sold more than 100,000 copies in four categories: Hardcover Frontlist, Paperback Frontlist, Hardcover Backlist, and Paperback Backlist.

Last year's overall top-selling book was *Grime and Punishment*, book nine in Dav Pilkey's hugely popular Dog Man series, which sold more than 1 million copies in hardcover. The middle grade series had a strong showing across multiple categories (see below).

In addition to *Grime and Punishment*, the hardcover frontlist category features Pilkey's *Cat Kid Comic Club*, which kicked off a graphic novel series starring Dog Man character Li'l Petey. Jeff Kinney's mega-selling Diary of a Wimpy Kid series also made a splash: *The Deep End* and spinoff title *Rowley Jefferson's Awesome Friendly Adventure* hold the second and fourth slots, respectively. And Katherine Applegate brought big sales with *The One and Only Bob*, sequel to her 2013 Newbery winner *The One and Only Ivan*.

The Baby-Sitters Club graphic novel adaptations rule the paperback frontlist: *Logan Likes Mary Anne!* (Baby-Sitters Club Graphic Novel #8) by Ann M. Martin, illustrated by Gale Galligan; and *Karen's Roller Skates*, book two in the Baby-Sitters Little Sister Graphic Novel series that launched in 2019, illustrated by Katy Farina, earned high rankings. And rounding out the list is holiday staple *The Elf on the Shelf.*

For hardcover backlist, Eric Carle took the cake with sales for *The Very Hungry Caterpillar* totaling more than 600,000 copies. Pilkey's eighth Dog Man title, *Fetch-22*, also sold like hotcakes. Meanwhile, a pair of cookbooks for young readers—one inspired by America's Test Kitchen and the other by Harry Potter—held steady, suggesting that kids may be hungry for activity titles during the pandemic.

Finally, paperback backlist reveals the enduring popularity of *The Wonky Donkey* by Craig Smith, illustrated by Katz Cowley. Sales for the 2009 picture book, which originated in New Zealand, skyrocketed after a read-aloud by "the Scottish Granny" went viral in summer 2018.

Hardcover Frontlist
500,000+
1. Grime and Punishment (Dog Man #9). Dav Pilkey. Scholastic/Graphix (1,240,277)
2. The Deep End (Diary of a Wimpy Kid #15). Jeff Kinney. Abrams/Amulet (920,709)

200,000+
3. Cat Kid Comic Club. Dav Pilkey. Scholastic/Graphix (412,894)
4. Rowley Jefferson's Awesome Friendly Adventure. Jeff Kinney. Abrams/Amulet (398,133)
5. The Ickabog. J.K. Rowling. Scholastic (300,742)
6. The One and Only Bob. Katherine Applegate. HarperCollins (262,408)

100,000+
7. FGTeeV Presents: Into the Game! FGTeeV, illus. by Miguel Díaz Rivas. HarperAlley (175,899)
8. The Tower of Nero (Trials of Apollo #5). Rick Riordan. Disney–Hyperion (170,604)
9. The World Needs More Purple People. Kristen Bell and Benjamin Hart, illus. by Daniel Wiseman. Random House (166,148)
10. 5 More Sleeps 'Til Christmas. Jimmy Fallon, illus by Rich Deas. Feiwel and Friends (157,342)

11. The Office: A Day at Dunder Mifflin Elementary. Robb Pearlman, illus. by Melanie Demmer. Little, Brown (152,863)
12. The World Needs Who You Were Made to Be. Joanna Gaines, illus. by Julianna Swaney. Tommy Nelson (144,610)
13. The Last Kids on Earth: June's Wild Flight. Max Brallier. Viking (144,588)
14. I Promise. Lebron James, illus. by Nina Mata. HarperCollins (143,536)
15. Harry Potter and the Sorcerer's Stone. J.K. Rowling, illus. by MinaLima. Scholastic (142,243)
16. The Last Kids on Earth and the Skeleton Road (The Last Kids on Earth #6). Max Brallier. Viking (129,006)
17. The Bad Guys in Dawn of the Underlord! (The Bad Guys #11). Aaron Blabey. Scholastic (122,924)
18. Dragonslayer (Wings of Fire: Legend #2). Tui T. Sutherland. Scholastic Press (116,584)
19. The Elf on the Shelf. Carol V. Aebersold and Chanda A. Bell, illus. by Coe Steinwart. CCA&B (113,733)
20. Antiracist Baby (board book). Ibram X. Kendi, illus. by Ashley Lukashevsky. Kokila (110,329)
21. Marvel Storybook Collection. Disney/Marvel (104,743)

Paperback Frontlist
100,000+
1. Logan Likes Mary Anne! (Baby-Sitters Club Graphic Novel #8). Ann M. Martin, illus. by Gale Galligan. Scholastic/Graphix (208,413)
2. Karen's Roller Skates (The Baby-Sitters Little Sister Graphic Novel #2). Ann M. Martin, illus. by Katy Farina. Scholastic/Graphix (102,331)
3. The Elf on the Shelf. Carol V. Aebersold and Chanda A. Bell, illus. by Coe Steinwart. CCA&B (100,285)

Hardcover Backlist
400,000+
1. The Very Hungry Caterpillar (board book). Eric Carle. Philomel (610,032)
2. Fetch-22 (Dog Man #8). Dav Pilkey. Scholastic/Graphix (601,337)
3. If Animals Kissed Good Night (board book). Ann Whitford Paul, illus. by David Walker. FSG (532,454)
4. Oh, The Places You'll Go! Dr. Seuss. Random House (513,516)
5. Brown Bear, Brown Bear, What Do You See? (50th-anniversary edition board book). Bill Martin Jr., illus. by Eric Carle. Holt (472,186)

6. Chicka Chicka Boom Boom (board book). Bill Martin Jr. and John Archambault, illus. by Lois Ehlert. Little Simon (435,647)
7. Wrecking Ball (Diary of a Wimpy Kid #14). Jeff Kinney. Abrams/Amulet (429,070)
8. I Love You to the Moon and Back (board book). Amelia Hepworth, illus. by Tim Warnes. Tiger Tales (407,899)

300,000+

9. Goodnight Moon (board book). Margaret Wise Brown, illus. by Clement Hurd. HarperFestival (377,485)
10. Giraffes Can't Dance (board book). Giles Andreae, illus. by Guy Parker-Rees. Cartwheel (376,397)
11. For Whom the Ball Rolls (Dog Man #7). Dav Pilkey. Scholastic/Graphix (346,017)
12. Green Eggs and Ham. Dr. Seuss. Random House (338,391)
13. First 100 Words (board book). Roger Priddy. Priddy (326,886)
14. How to Catch a Unicorn. Adam Wallace, illus. by Andy Elkerton. Sourcebooks Wonderland (320,509)
15. One Fish, Two Fish, Red Fish, Blue Fish. Dr. Seuss. Random House (311,661)

200,000+

16. How to Catch a Mermaid. Adam Wallace, illus. by Andy Elkerton. Sourcebooks Wonderland (289,393)
17. The Polar Express (30th anniversary edition). Chris Van Allsburg. HMH (288,309)
18. Moo, Baa, La La La! (board book). Sandra Boynton. Little Simon (283,281)
19. The Going to Bed Book (board book). Sandra Boynton. Little Simon (272,477)
20. How the Grinch Stole Christmas! Dr. Seuss. Random House (262,745)
21. Where's Spot? (board book). Eric Hill. Frederick Warne (259,636)
22. There's No Place Like Space: All About Our Solar System. Tish Rabe, illus. by Aristides Ruiz. Random House (255,936)
23. Brawl of the Wild (Dog Man #6). Dav Pilkey. Scholastic/Graphix (785,328)
24. The Pout-Pout Fish (board book). Deborah Diesen, illus. by Dan Hanna. FSG (252,371)

25. Dr. Seuss's ABC: An Amazing Alphabet Book! (board book) Dr. Seuss. Random House (245,902)

26. What Should Danny Do? Ganit and Adir Levy, illus. by Mat Sadler. Elon (244,947)

27. Little Blue Truck's Christmas (board book). Alice Schertle, illus. by Jill McElmurry. HMH (233,213)

28. The Wonderful Things You Will Be. Emily Winfield Martin. Random House (230,691)

29. The Complete Cookbook for Young Chefs: 100+ Recipes That You'll Love to Cook and Eat. America's Test Kitchen Kids. Sourcebooks Explore (230,635)

30. The Unofficial Harry Potter Cookbook: From Cauldron Cakes to Knickerbocker Glory—More Than 150 Magical Recipes for Wizards and Non-Wizards Alike. Dinah Bucholz. Adams Media (230,616)

31. Grumpy Monkey. Suzanne Lang, illus. by Max Lang. Random House (226,329)

32. Baby Touch and Feel: Animals (board book). DK (223,652)

33. Dog Man (Dog Man #1). Dav Pilkey. Scholastic/Graphix (221,801)

34. The Giving Tree. Shel Silverstein. HarperCollins (219,888)

35. Little Blue Truck (board book). Alice Schertle, illus. by Jill McElmurry. HMH (217,928)

36. Lord of the Fleas (Dog Man #5). Dav Pilkey. Scholastic/Graphix (217,365)

37. The Cat in the Hat. Dr. Seuss. Random House (216,587)

38. Harry Potter and the Goblet of Fire: The Illustrated Edition (Harry Potter #4). J.K. Rowling, illus. by Jim Kay. Scholastic (207,572)

39. Dog Man Unleashed (Dog Man #2). Dav Pilkey. Scholastic/Graphix (201,976)

100,000+

40. I've Loved You Since Forever. Hoda Kotb, illus. by Suzie Mason. HarperCollins (198,630)

41. Wonder. R.J. Palacio. Knopf (197,131)

42. Little Blue Truck's Springtime (board book). Alice Schertle, illus. by Jill McElmurry. HMH (195,712)

43. The Monster at the End of This Book. Jon Stone. Random House/Golden (195,644)

44. Dog Man and Cat Kid (Dog Man #4). Dav Pilkey. Scholastic/Graphix (192,643)

45. Waiting Is Not Easy! Mo Willems. Hyperion (189,039)

46. P Is for Potty! (board book). Naomi Kleinberg, illus. by Christopher Moroney. Random House (185,222)

47. A Tale of Two Kitties (Dog Man #3). Dav Pilkey. Scholastic/Graphix (184,976)

48. Good Night, Little Blue Truck. Alice Schertle, illus. by Jill McElmurry. HMH (181,599)

49. 5-Minute Princess Stories. Disney Press (178,822)

50. 5-Minute Marvel Stories. Disney Press (174,778)

51. Goodnight, Goodnight Construction Site (board book). Sherri Duskey Rinker, illus. by Tom Lichtenheld. Chronicle (174,328)

52. Diary of an Awesome Friendly Kid: Rowley Jefferson's Journal. Jeff Kinney. Abrams/Amulet (172,312)

53. Guess How Much I Love You (board book). Sam McBratney, illus. by Anita Jeram. Candlewick (172,190)

54. Harry Potter and the Sorcerer's Stone: The Illustrated Edition (Harry Potter #1). J.K. Rowling, illus. by Jim Kay. Scholastic/Levine (171,602)

55. The Night Before Christmas. Clement C. Moore, illus. by Christian Birmingham. Running Press (171,340)

56. Are You My Mother? (board book). P.D. Eastman. Random House (166,148)

57. Your Baby's First Word Will Be Dada (board book). Jimmy Fallon, illus. by Miguel Ordóñez. Feiwel and Friends (162,813)

58. Dragons Love Tacos. Adam Rubin, illus. by Daniel Salmieri. Dial (162,813)

59. Hair Love. Matthew A. Cherry, illus. by Vashti Harrison. Kokila (162,067)

60. Tales from a Not-So-Best Friend Forever (Dork Diaries #14). Rachel Renée Russell. Aladdin (161,243)

61. The Last Kids on Earth (The Last Kids on Earth #1). Max Brallier. Viking (161,120)

62. Corduroy (board book). Don Freeman. Viking (160,938)

63. I Am Enough. Grace Byers, illus. by Keturah A. Bobo. HarperCollins/ Balzer + Bray (160,662)

64. On the Night You Were Born (board book). Nancy Tillman. Feiwel and Friends (159,169)

65. Welcome Little One (board book). Sandra Magsamen. Sourcebooks Wonderland (157,819)

66. 5-Minute Frozen Stories. Disney Press (156,546)

67. Mr. Brown Can Moo! Can You? (board book). Dr. Seuss. Random House (156,137)

68. Love You Forever (board book). Robert Munsch, illus. by Sheila McGraw. Firefly (155,706)

69. Are You My Mother? (board book). P.D. Eastman. Random House (152,459)

70. Dear Girl. Amy Krouse Rosenthal and Paris Rosenthal, illus. by Holly Hatam. HarperCollins (151,342)

71. Touch and Feel: Never Touch a Dinosaur (board book). Make Believe Ideas (151,078)

72. The Meltdown (Diary of a Wimpy Kid #13). Jeff Kinney. Abrams/Amulet (150,634)

73. Dear Zoo (board book). Rod Campbell. Little Simon (149,520)

74. You're My Little Cuddle Bug (board book). Nicola Edwards. Silver Dolphin (149,186)

75. Fox in Socks. Dr. Seuss. Random House (144,033)

76. The Day the Crayons Quit. Drew Daywalt, illus. by Oliver Jeffers. Philomel (143,696)

77. Peek-a-Who? (board book). Nina Laden. Chronicle (141,574)

78. If You Give a Mouse a Cookie. Laura Numeroff, illus. by Felicia Bond. HarperCollins (141,547)

79. An Elephant & Piggie Biggie! Mo Willems. Hyperion (140,915)

80. A Is for Apple (board book). Georgia Birkett. Tiger Tales (140,314)

81. Little Blue Truck's Halloween (board book). Alice Schertle, illus. by Jill McElmurry. HMH (139,610)

82. It's Not Easy Being a Bunny. Marilyn Sadler, illus. by Roger Bollen. Random House (138,738)

83. Gravity Falls: Journal 3. Alex Hirsch et al. Disney Press (138,283)

84. When God Made You. Matthew Paul Turner, illus. by David Catrow. Convergent (137,418)

85. God Gave Us You. Lisa Tawn Bergren, illus. by Laura J. Bryant. WaterBrook (136,976)

86. Eric Carle: Hear Bear Roar. Veronica Wagner. P I Kids (135,781)

87. Frozen 2 Little Golden Book. Nancy Cote. Random House/Disney (135,776)

88. I've Loved You Since Forever (board book). Hoda Kotb, illus. by Suzie Mason. HarperFestival (135,653)

89. Everything Is Mama (board book). Jimmy Fallon, illus. by Miguel Ordóñez. Feiwel and Friends (135,627)

90. Oh Say Can You Say Di-no-saur? Bonnie Worth, illus. by Steve Haefele. Random House (135,586)

91. Refugee. Alan Gratz. Scholastic Press (135,305)
92. I Wish You More. Amy Krouse Rosenthal, illus. by Tom Lichtenheld. Chronicle (134,220)
93. See, Touch, Feel (board book). Roger Priddy. Priddy (131,472)
94. The Book with No Pictures. B.J. Novak. Dial (129,788)
95. 5,000 Awesome Facts (About Everything!). National Geographic (128,953)
96. The Rainbow Fish (board book). Marcus Pfister. NorthSouth (128,703)
97. Disney 5-Minute Snuggle Stories. Disney Press (128,592)
98. Press Here. Hervé Tullet. Chronicle (128,155)
99. The Day You Begin. Jacqueline Woodson, illus. by Rafael López. Penguin/Paulsen (127,766)
100. Eric Carle: Around the Farm. Mark Rader. PI (127,127)
101. The Complete Baking Book for Young Chefs. Sourcebooks Explore (126,311)
102. Where Is Baby's Belly Button? (board book). Karen Katz. Little Simon (126,117)
103. Bedtime Favorites. Disney (124,191)
104. Go, Dog. Go! P.D. Eastman. Random House (123,653)
105. Trucks (board book). Roger Priddy. Priddy (122,008)
106. Construction Site on Christmas Night. Sherri Duskey Rinker, illus. by A.G. Ford. Chronicle (121,569)
107. Room on the Broom (board book). Julia Donaldson, illus. by Axel Scheffler. Dial (120,316)
108. The Pigeon HAS to Go to School! Mo Willems. Hyperion (119,838)
109. Dr. Seuss's ABC. Dr. Seuss. Random House (115,774)
110. You're My Little Pumpkin Pie (board book). Natalie Marshall. Silver Dolphin (114,924)
111. An Elephant & Piggie Biggie-Biggie! (#2). Mo Willems. Hyperion (112,753)
112. Hop on Pop. Dr. Seuss. Random House (112,656)
113. My First I See You (board book). Eric Carle. Little Simon (112,537)
114. Pete the Cat: Big Easter Adventure. James Dean. HarperFestival (112,256)
115. Letters ABC (board book). Priddy (111,464)
116. Llama Llama I Love You (board book). Anna Dewdney. Viking (110,152)
117. What Should Darla Do? Ganit and Adir Levy, illus. by Doro Kaiser. Elon (109,295)
118. Seuss-Isms! Dr. Seuss. Random House (109,077)
119. National Geographic Little Kids First Big Book of Why. Amy Shields. National Geographic (108,997)

120. Barnyard Dance! (board book). Sandra Boynton. Workman (108,610)
121. A Is for Awesome!: 23 Iconic Women Who Changed the World (board book). Eva Chen, illus. by Derek Desierto. Feiwel and Friends (108,160)
122. I Am a Big Brother. Caroline Jayne Church. Cartwheel (108,066)
123. Llama Llama Red Pajama (board book). Anna Dewdney. Viking (107,997)
124. I Am a Big Sister. Caroline Jayne Church. Cartwheel (107,128)
125. The Getaway (Diary of a Wimpy Kid #12). Jeff Kinney. Abrams/Amulet (105,586)
126. The Tyrant's Tomb (Trials of Apollo #4). Rick Riordan. Disney-Hyperion (105,549)
127. The Cool Bean. Jory John, illus. by Pete Oswald. HarperCollins (105,157)
128. Where the Wild Things Are. Maurice Sendak. HarperCollins (101,974)
129. When I Pray for You. Matthew Paul Turner, illus. by Kimberley Barnes. Convergent (101,833)
130. Disney 5-Minute Christmas Stories. Disney (101,673)
131. The Crayons' Christmas. Drew Daywalt, illus. by Oliver Jeffers. Penguin Workshop (101,482)
132. Noisy Farm (board book). Tiger Tales (101,427)
133. The Lorax. Dr Seuss. Random House (101,281)
134. Where the Sidewalk Ends. Shel Silverstein. HarperCollins (101,206)
135. Charlotte's Web. E.B. White, illus. by Garth Williams. HarperCollins (100,242)
136. The Last Kids on Earth and the Midnight Blade (Last Kids on Earth #5). Max Brallier. Viking (100,052)

Paperback Backlist

200,000+
1. The Wonky Donkey. Craig Smith, illus. by Katz Cowley. Scholastic (411,032)
2. The One and Only Ivan. Katherine Applegate. HarperCollins (320,378)
3. Love You Forever. Robert Munsch, illus. by Sheila McGraw. Firefly (301,329)
4. Guts. Raina Telgemeier. Scholastic/Graphix (299,299)
5. Harry Potter and the Sorcerer's Stone (Harry Potter #1). J.K. Rowling, illus. by Mary GrandPré. Scholastic (279,936)
6. Where the Wild Things Are. Maurice Sendak. HarperCollins (277,397)
7. I Need a New Butt! Dawn McMillan, illus. by Ross Kinnaird. Dover (273,203)

8. Kindergarten, Here I Come! D.J. Steinberg, illus. by Mark Chambers. Grosset & Dunlap (251,151)
9. The Big Book of Silly Jokes for Kids. Carole Roman. Rockridge (243,245)
10. Room on the Broom. Julia Donaldson, illus. by Axel Scheffler. Puffin (222,998)
11. New Kid. Jerry Craft. Quill Tree (221,718)
12. A Long Walk to Water. Linda Sue Park. Clarion (211,874)

100,000+

13. The Care and Keeping of You: The Body Book for Younger Girls (revised edition). Valorie Schaefer, illus. by Josée Masse. American Girl (196,086)
14. Llama Llama Loves Camping. Anna Dewdney. Penguin (189,955)
15. Hatchet. Gary Paulsen. Simon & Schuster (185,983)
16. The Lightning Thief (Percy Jackson and the Olympians #1). Rick Riordan. Disney-Hyperion (184,737)
17. The Girl Who Drank the Moon. Kelly Barnhill. Algonquin (178,541)
18. Harry Potter and the Chamber of Secrets (Harry Potter #2). J.K. Rowling. Scholastic (175,238)
19. The Bad Guys in the Baddest Day Ever (The Bad Guys #10). Aaron Blabey. Scholastic (153,906)
20. Pax. Sara Pennypacker. HarperCollins/Balzer + Bray (150,034)
21. We're Different, We're the Same. Bobbi Kates, illus. by Joe Mathieu. Random House (149,866)
22. The Dinky Donkey. Craig Smith, illus. by Katz Cowley. Scholastic (144,901)
23. Because of Winn-Dixie. Kate DiCamillo. Candlewick (144,644)
24. The Backyard Bug Book for Kids. Rockridge (140,380)
25. Drama. Raina Telgemeier. Scholastic/Graphix (138,776)
26. Karen's Witch (The Baby-Sitters Little Sister Graphic Novel #2). Ann M. Martin, illus. by Katy Farina. Scholastic/Graphix (138,610)
27. Harry Potter and the Prisoner of Azkaban (Harry Potter #3). J.K. Rowling. Scholastic (138,399)
28. The Invisible String. Patrice Karst, illus. by Geoff Stevenson. Little, Brown (137,545)
29. Holes. Louis Sachar. Random/Yearling (137,354)
30. Number the Stars. Lois Lowry. HMH (135,792)
31. Sisters. Raina Telgemeier. Scholastic/Graphix (132,733)
32. Wish. Barbara O'Connor. Square Fish (131,352)
33. Pete the Cat Goes Camping. James Dean. HarperCollins (129,376)

34. The Bad Guys (The Bad Guys #1). Aaron Blabey. Scholastic (126,412)
35. Uni's First Sleepover. Amy Krouse Rosenthal, illus. by Brigette Barrager. Random House (125,020)
36. Dinosaurs Before Dark (Magic Tree House #1). Mary Pope Osborne, illus. by Sal Murdocca. Random House (124,039)
37. Best Friends. Shannon Hale, illus. by LeUyen Pham. First Second (122,625)
38. Pete the Cat: Trick or Pete. James Dean. HarperFestival (118,199)
39. Esperanza Rising. Pam Muñoz Ryan. Scholastic Press (117,322)
40. Ghosts. Raina Telgemeier. Scholastic/Graphix (116,517)
41. Trapped in a Video Game. Dustin Brady. Andrews McMeel (112,682)
42. Harry Potter and the Order of the Phoenix (Harry Potter #5). J.K. Rowling. Scholastic (111,743)
43. Boy-Crazy Stacey (The Baby-Sitters Club Graphix #7). Ann M. Martin, illus. by Gale Galligan. Scholastic/Graphix (111,288)
44. Harry Potter and the Goblet of Fire (Harry Potter #4). J.K. Rowling. Scholastic (110,021)
45. The Gruffalo. Julia Donaldson, illus. by Axel Scheffler. Puffin (109,870)
46. The Dragonet Prophecy (Wings of Fire #1). Tui T. Sutherland. Scholastic/Graphix (109,130)
47. The 7 Habits of Highly Effective Teens. Sean Covey. Simon & Schuster (108,998)
48. Smile. Raina Telgemeier. Scholastic/Graphix (108,192)
49. Restart. Gordon Korman. Scholastic Press (103,177)
50. Harry Potter and the Half-Blood Prince (Harry Potter #6). J.K. Rowling. Scholastic (101,625)
51. Tales of a Fourth Grade Nothing. Judy Blume. Puffin (101,251)
52. The Care and Keeping of You: The Body Book for Older Girls (#2). Cara Natterson. American Girl (101,006)
53. Kristy's Great Idea (The Baby-Sitters Club Graphix #1). Ann M. Martin, illus. by Raina Telgemeier. Scholastic/Graphix (100,364)

2020 YA Bestsellers: Familiar Franchises, Young Readers' Editions, and More

Compiled by Gilcy Aquino and Emma Kantor | Mar 30, 2021

Last week, we ran our compilation of 2020 children's bestsellers, and this week we're following up with our 2020 Facts and Figures roundup of young adult bestsellers, which include a wide variety of titles dominated by mega-selling franchises and their sequels and prequels, as well as time-tested classics for teens. Our lists are based on print unit sales at outlets that report to NPD Bookscan, which tracks approximately 85% of the print market. Here we compile the books that sold more than 100,000 copies in three categories: Hardcover Frontlist, Hardcover Backlist, and Paperback Backlist. (No paperback frontlist YA novels met these sales criteria.)

Last year's overall top-selling YA book was *Midnight Sun* by Stephenie Meyer, with more than 1 million copies sold in hardcover. The novel retells Meyer's franchise-launching book, *Twilight*, from Edward Cullen's point of view. Her Twilight Saga, comprised of four core novels and three companion volumes, has sold nearly 160 million copies worldwide since its debut in 2005.

In addition to *Midnight Sun*, the hardcover frontlist category features almost equally strong sales by Suzanne Collins's Hunger Games prequel *The Ballad of Songbirds and Snakes* and another new fantasy novel by a high-profile author, *Chain of Gold* by Cassandra Clare. On the nonfiction front, *Stamped: Racism, Antiracism, and You* by Jason Reynolds, the young readers' adaptation of Ibram X. Kendi's National Book Award–winning title, has a strong showing, revealing the demand for books grappling with urgent national issues for a young audience.

The Hate U Give by Angie Thomas holds the top slot for hardcover backlist. The Black Lives Matter-inspired novel has been a steady seller since its debut in 2017 and subsequent film adaptation in 2018; and this past January, Thomas released a prequel, *Concrete Rose*. Karen M. McManus's breakout debut *One of Us Is Lying*, a teen thriller, also ranks high on the list. (Her 2020 sequel, *One of Us Is Next*, sold more than 120,000 copies in hardcover frontlist.)

Finally, paperback backlist is topped by two classic novels: *The Outsiders* by S.E. Hinton and *The Giver* by Lois Lowry. Rounding out the list are contemporary titles by Suzanne Collins, E. Lockhart, Nic Stone, and Markus Zusak, among others.

Hardcover Frontlist
500,000+
1. Midnight Sun. Stephenie Meyer. Little, Brown (1,311,147)
2. The Ballad of Songbirds and Snakes. Suzanne Collins. Scholastic Press (1,235,099)

200,000+
3. Stamped: Racism, Antiracism, and You: A Remix of the National Book Award-Winning Stamped from the Beginning. Jason Reynolds and Ibram X. Kendi. Little, Brown (317,011)

100,000+

4. Chain of Gold. Cassandra Clare. S&S/McElderry (161,591)
5. Live: Remain Alive, Be Alive at a Specified Time, Have an Exciting or Fulfilling Life. Sadie Robertson Huff. Thomas Nelson (128,609)
6. One of Us Is Next. Karen M. McManus. Delacorte (122,696)

Hardcover Backlist
200,000+

1. The Hate U Give. Angie Thomas. HarperTeen/Balzer + Bray (224,392)

100,000+

2. One of Us Is Lying. Karen M. McManus. Delacorte (189,854)

Paperback Backlist
200,000+

1. The Outsiders. S.E. Hinton. Speak (308,996)
2. The Giver. Lois Lowry. Houghton Mifflin Harcourt (247,736)

100,000+

3. The Silver Eyes (Five Nights at Freddy's #1). Scott Cawthon. Scholastic (171,680)
4. The Hunger Games. Suzanne Collins. Scholastic Press (160,072)
5. We Were Liars. E. Lockhart. Ember (156,695)
6. The Book Thief. Markus Zusak. Knopf (137,861)
7. Into the Pit (Five Nights at Freddy's: Fazbear Frights #1). Scholastic (137,806)
8. Dear Martin. Nic Stone. Ember (124,303)
9. The Boy in the Striped Pajamas. John Boyne. Ember (115,898)

Middle Grade Snapshot: Spring 2021
Editors in the field share their latest observations
By Shannon Maughan | Apr 09, 2021

As we roll into a second year affected by the ripples of uncertainty caused by the pandemic, one of the consistent bright spots in the children's book arena has been the performance of titles in the middle grade category. Award winners, works by favorite authors like Rick Riordan and Tui T. Sutherland, and, of course, a slew of popular graphic novel properties (Dav Pilkey's Dog Man, Jeff Kinney's Diary of a Wimpy Kid) filled most of the top slots in *PW*'s "Facts and Figures" accounting of 2020's bestselling children's books.

While such analyses provide a snapshot of what has stayed the same in middle grade over the past year, we wanted to learn what's new and what might be changing in the world of books for readers ages eight to 12. We asked a number of editors to tell us more about the kinds of middle grade projects they are seeing and to share their insights on any shifts they perceive in the category.

More storytellers, more stories

The editors we spoke with unanimously mentioned a distinct uptick in the number of diverse and #OwnVoices manuscripts they are receiving. "So many different voices are telling stories," says Alvina Ling, v-p and editor-in-chief at Little, Brown Books for Young Readers. "It's been wonderful to see more underrepresented characters and stories in middle grade, especially with LGBTQIA+ characters." She mentions *Ana on the Edge* by A.J. Sass as a recent example.

Margaret Raymo, v-p and senior editorial director at HMH Books for Young Readers and Versify, agrees, noting that in her view, "submissions from BIPOC creators are continuing to rise."

Trisha de Guzman, an editor at Farrar, Straus and Giroux Books for Young Readers, points to a welcome shift in storytelling that is taking place alongside the arrival of more diverse authors and book projects. "I'm seeing a lot of more nuanced and thoughtful representation in middle grade, which is wonderful," she says. "The success of titles like *Merci Suárez Changes Gears* and *Aru Shah and the End of Time* have paved the way for more BIPOC voices across the spectrum of stories, from light-hearted adventure to more introspective, emotional stories. Characters of color aren't limited to single-issue story lines anymore; they can go on magical adventures while dealing with complicated immigrant family issues and eating their grandma's pastelitos, like in *The Total Eclipse of Nestor Lopez*."

For Donna Bray, v-p and copublisher of the Balzer + Bray imprint at HarperCollins, the picture is similar. "It's been exciting to see more and more diversity and intersectionality in middle grade, with stories that center BIPOC, neurodiverse, and LGBTQIA+ characters in all genres," she says, highlighting such examples as *Amari and the Night Brothers* by B.B. Alston, *Ophie's Ghosts* by Justina Ireland, Elana Arnold's Bat books, and *The Best at It* by Maulik Pancholy.

At G.P. Putnam's Sons, executive editor Stacey Barney also welcomes this development. "I note a diversity of writers coming to the table, and their narratives center on joy and adventure where kids are becoming their own superheroes," she says.

Caitlyn Dlouhy, v-p and editorial director of her eponymous imprint at Atheneum, says, "I've noticed more LGBTQ characters in novels, and not because the novels are driven by some type of torment or sexually related issue. This representation is increasingly just part of the fabric of a story or of a friendship, and that's incredibly pleasing to see."

De Guzman says that she has received "more middle grade stories that are comfortable with the exploration of gender and sexuality," adding, "I love seeing books like *King and the Dragonflies* and *Ivy Aberdeen's Letter to the World* succeed." She draws an important distinction in terms of the content presented within the typical parameters of the middle grade category: "One thing I constantly want to reiterate is that orientation does not automatically equal sex," she says. "An 11-year-old can know that they are queer without necessarily having it be linked to physical attraction. The fact that middle grade readers can now read about gender expansive and queer characters is awesome. It just further encourages the empathy that we strive to foster in young readers."

This broadening of perspectives under the middle grade tent has most certainly been influenced by highly regarded grassroots movements like We Need Diverse Books, #DVPit Twitter pitch parties, and other efforts created to address the long-standing lack of diversity in book publishing. And the editors we spoke with are excited to see this work bearing fruit.

"There have been many, many more #OwnVoices manuscripts coming in," Dlouhy says. "I think with the shift in the past year in how everybody's looking at literature for kids—and at everything going on in America—more people are recognizing not only the need for more #OwnVoices manuscripts but also the feasibility of them. Agents who are getting the manuscripts to editors are realizing, 'Wait, yes, we can really do great things with these projects that we have perhaps loved but had worried wouldn't find the market and now the market is arms wide open.' I have goosebumps up and down my arms just even saying that. Now we need to just publish faster and get these books out there!"

Graphic novels still booming

Not surprisingly—especially based on many of the top-selling middle grade titles of 2020—the graphic novel format continues to be an area of enormous growth within the middle grade category. "In the past six months, I've seen more MG graphic novels come in to acquisition than in my whole career," Dlouhy says.

That's largely been the case across the board, with Ling reporting "a huge graphic novel boom in middle grade especially."

Raymo at HMH also sees middle grade graphic novels "exploding, as are hybrid illustrated novels."

And Bray notes the same phenomenon. "There's been an explosion in the graphic novel space, driven by reader tastes but definitely boosted by the groundbreaking Newbery Award winner, Jerry Craft's *New Kid*," she says. In this area, she notes that her list represents a wide variety of titles within the format, including the nonfiction book *Unsolved Cases Files* by Tom Sullivan; an LGBTQ debut, *The Real Riley Mayes* by Rachel Elliott; and the bestselling Emmie & Friends series by Terri Libenson.

Responding to the current moment

The editors we spoke with did not report an influx of middle grade manuscripts that incorporate aspects of the pandemic. "I haven't seen a shift or response to the pandemic yet, aside from authors having to decide what year to set their novels, and whether or not to include any references to the pandemic," Ling says. "We've seen many picture books in response, and a few YA novels with 'love in the time of the pandemic' themes, but not so much in MG." The exceptions, she notes, are "a few nonfiction projects that might include a section on pandemics or coronaviruses."

It may well be that any flurry of middle grade books about the pandemic just aren't finished yet. "The pandemic is obviously in the zeitgeist as a very high level, and I think, while we're in it, people are trying to figure out what that looks like on a page," Dlouhy says. "I had been wondering if the pandemic will lead to more dystopian in middle grade, but I've not seen anything that's come across my desk. Then again, it takes a long time to write a novel."

Citing another aspect of the pandemic's ripple effect, Dlouhy adds, "I've had authors put aside things they were working on before the pandemic because psychologically they didn't want to be in that place at this time. And they also wanted kids to be in a different space, hopefully through their work, so they shifted gears."

In what may be an additional ripple, Raymo says that though she hasn't received books that specifically address the pandemic, she has "seen increased submissions about kids with anxiety, which might be related."

On a broader level, Barney says, "I am certainly seeing a lot of middle grade that is responding to the current state of the world. Particularly narratives that center activism, featuring characters getting involved in their communities and understanding how the sociopolitical landscape affects their lives and those of the people they love, and what effect they can in turn have both locally and globally. Middle grade readers are generally very aware of the world and their place in it, and many of the submissions crossing my desk and much of what's being published reflects that as middle grade readers also parse difficult current events."

Bray concurs, saying she is seeing "more novels that respond directly to our cultural and political moment." Titles on her list that fall under that umbrella include *A Good Kind of Trouble* by Lisa Moore Ramée, about a girl who takes a stand to support the Black Lives Matter movement; *The Shape of Thunder* by Jasmine Warga, which follows friends coping with the aftermath of a school shooting; and *Pax* by Sara Pennypacker, which explores a friendship, loss, and grief during wartime. "Kids are grappling with these realities every day," Bray says. "And writers are responding with stories that honor their ability to process the complexities of difficult topics that in the past might have been considered too tough for this age group."

Ling has observed a bump in books addressing current events such as wildfires and climate change, and social justice issues, such as *Paradise on Fire* by Jewell Parker Rhodes, as well as contemporary realistic stories involving student activism, such as *Margie Kelly Breaks the Dress Code* by Bridget Farr.

In terms of books navigating issues of racial justice and social justice, Dlouhy says, "What's been interesting is there's more nonfiction coming out in this regard: more biographies of people who have been overlooked who should never have been, and collections bringing attention to women or barrier breakers. I've been getting a number of those types of projects and so have colleagues."

And Raymo notes that in addition to nonfiction titles focused on current events, middle grade nonfiction in general has been an area of growth.

Other developments

Fantasies for middle grade readers are ticking up, too, according to Ling. "We've been seeing and acquiring more MG fantasies in the vein of Rick Riordan Presents, including *Amira & Hamza: The War to Save the Worlds* by Samira Ahmed, which is coming out this fall," she says.

At Atheneum, Dlouhy says, "I've been getting more MG fantasy submissions that are really strong. Their plotlines are very unique, their plot twists are things you don't see coming. There's a different sophistication to the MG fantasy that's been coming in, which I'm welcoming."

Another development Dlouhy has observed is in how writers are approaching their content. "I see a little bit more experimenting with form, things that aren't traditionally told," she says. "I've been having things come in that aren't typically set up, that are playing around with perspective and voice, trusting that a younger reader is capable of more than just a traditionally told narrative." She believes this is a sign of the times. "Many kids, because of the influence of being on their smartphones and devices, have shifted the amount of attention they will give to things," she says. "I think narratives that play around a bit hold their attention."

De Guzman, too, points to innovative forms and formats as part of a new wave in middle grade. "Now more than ever, there is an emphasis on bridging distances through creative means," she says. "Letters, postcards, video calls, text messages, and more are all a major part of our lives, and I'm seeing the integration of these means of communication play an increasingly important role in the submissions I receive. It's an indication of how intertwined technology and storytelling has become."

On the horizon

When asked to consult the proverbial crystal ball for predictions about the future middle grade landscape, the editors we spoke with indicated that the areas of growth they have spotlighted will still be moving in an upward direction. One reason for that, Bray says, is that "we still have so far to go in making our middle grade offerings truly reflect the incredible diversity of the children reading them."

Dlouhy's view picks up that thread with a hopeful note. "Knowing what's coming up and going to be published in the next two years, there is so much more diversity in every direction, flat out," she says. "There's more for all sorts of readers and interests than there ever used to be."

Middle grade expansion will roll on because "the books have a much longer tail, especially once they get established in the institutional market," Raymo says. "I love the increase in the number of #OwnVoices authors and the stories they are telling, which will only continue apace." But she raises one potential change in the middle grade lists to come: "I wonder about the middle grade graphic novel space becoming oversaturated," she says.

Barney says she believes "there will be a greater diversity of stories and authors, courting many new readers with a true respect for how smart and engaged the middle school readership is. And you'll start to see more narratives where themes important to the middle grade readership like body positivity, gender, privilege, and more will play out organically in unexpected places—i.e., not stories that are issue-oriented but stories that are really about magicians in outer space."

When de Guzman envisions the middle grade space of tomorrow, she says, "I think that it will only continue to be more nuanced and intersectional, especially as young readers continue to increase their appetite for books with progressive values. I also think that with the internet's role in globalization, there will be a greater influx of middle grade books with international settings." She adds, "This generation is so much more aware, and as time passes, I don't believe they'll be satisfied with one-dimensional, single-issue books anymore. They're smarter, savvier, and have a ton of information at their fingertips. And their books will reflect that!"

*

A version of this article appeared in the 04/12/2021 issue of *Publishers Weekly* under the headline: Middle Grade Selfie

YA Anthologies Bring Diverse Voices Together
By Sara Grochowski | Apr 30, 2021

In recent years, a rising number of both fiction and nonfiction anthologies have been published for the young adult audience, capitalizing on the format's accessibility and its unique capacity to allow for a variety of voices and perspectives to be featured within one volume. We spoke with the editors of five recently published and forthcoming anthologies for teens about the origin of their collections, how they built their lists of contributors, and their hopes for these volumes as they reach readers.

A spark of an idea

For anthology editors Laura Silverman and Dahlia Adler, previous experience collaborating with their YA author peers led to their respective projects. Silverman, who had collaborated with Katherine Locke on *It's a Whole Spiel: Love, Latkes, and Other Jewish Stories*, was eager to embark on another cooperative endeavor after realizing she "could get paid to work with talented people and just read their stories" while creating an anthology. The concept for *Up All Night: 13 Stories Between Sunrise and Sunset* (Algonquin, July) was inspired by the magic of the hours after parents and other adults are tucked in bed but teens are still awake.

"Every single teenager has had something important happen during those midnight hours," Silverman says. "The world gets quiet, and things that would never happen in the daytime are suddenly possible. You can be someone else and explore new things."

Adler, the editor of the recently published *That Way Madness Lies: 15 of Shakespeare's Most Notable Works Reimagined* (Flatiron), had previously edited an anthology focused on Edgar Allan Poe. After seeing the success of *His Hideous Heart: 13 Stories of Edgar Allan Poe's Most Unsettling Tales Reimagined*, including its use in classrooms and libraries, she sensed an opportunity to create another anthology highlighting a widely read and studied author. She landed on Shakespeare, whom she dubbed an "obvious choice."

For others, a drive to subvert the stereotyping, misunderstanding, and vilification of their cultures and bodies was the genesis of their collections. Both *PW* StarWatch honoree Saraciea J. Fennell, editor of *Wild Tongues Can't Be Tamed: 15 Voices from the Latinx Diaspora* (Flatiron, Sept.), and Margarita Longoria, editor of *Living Beyond Borders: Growing Up Mexican in America* (Philomel, Aug.), say the rhetoric and actions of the previous administration moved them to push back.

"I was an English teacher for years and I'm a librarian now," Longoria notes. "So I've always loved books and feel books can change things, and provide an opportunity to learn about other people and cultures." She aimed to create an anthology for teens that highlighted the beauty of Mexican and Mexican American culture, showing that Mexican people are not violent and ignorant, as many anti-immigrant politicians suggest, but are a "good, strong, and proud people with much to offer." For Longoria, creating this collection was a way for "one little person to fight back through something she knows: books."

Similarly, Fennell was disheartened and disturbed by the previous administration's denigration. "I thought, how can we, the Latinx community, combat this and show that we aren't this way?" she says. "How can we share our truths while subverting stereotypes?" At the same time, she realized that there is not a lot of nonfiction in the YA space that features Latinx writers from the diaspora, particularly Black Latinx writers, which she found important to address.

Cassandra Newbould, editor of *Every Body Shines: Sixteen Stories About Living Fabulously Fat* (Bloomsbury, June), had just finished writing her middle grade novel, *Fat Like Me*, and was considering starting a podcast when the idea of an anthology occurred to her. "When I was a teenager, the only books I found that featured a relatable fat character treated that character horribly," she says, recalling the Sweet Valley High books. "The poor girl was running across the track most of the book, just so she would be accepted by people." She realized that she wanted to create an intersectional anthology because "fat is not a monolith and, all too often, the stories that are published focus on straight, cis, white main characters." Instead she wanted to show "all the ways fat bodies thrive while fighting against the world," where "none of the characters change themselves to fit the narrative, but rather change the narrative to fit them."

Building an A-team

Newbould was nervous when she began reaching out to potential contributors for *Every Body Shines*, unsure whether anyone would want to participate or have a story to tell. "Too often the world is telling [fat people] to keep our stories to ourselves, but to break out of that mindset is a freeing thing," she says. "Sometimes it can be intimidating and scary, but the moment you start putting the words down, the dam breaks and you realize these are the stories you've been wanting to tell your whole life."

Newbould approached Rebecca Sky first, whose response was overwhelmingly positive. She continued from there, asking for stories that came from the contributors' hearts to create a collection that shows how distinct individual experiences can be, while making a concerted effort to be inclusive of people who live or have lived the fat experience—from the contributors to the editor to the cover illustrator. The other thing that ties the stories together, she says, is that "every protagonist finds their shine in the end. Some have it from the beginning, and others don't find it until the last page, but it's there."

To build her contributor list for *Up All Night*, Silverman decided to, appropriately, "shoot for the stars," asking authors whose writing she knew and admired while being mindful to include writers from a variety of backgrounds and experiences. "You want to be sure you consider representation while being aware that, to sell an anthology, you need names that pack a bit of a punch," Silverman says. "And those authors are highly in demand, of course." She kept the submission guidelines open-ended but asked contributors to send pitches so as to avoid any direct overlap of plot or trope and to ensure a balance in tone.

Similarly, Fennell says she put a lot of thought and care into choosing the contributors, to be certain that young readers would be able to see themselves in the stories. "There is a lack of diverse Latinx voices out there," she says. "I was very conscious of that as I curated *Wild Tongues Can't Be Tamed* and, though it was hard not to include some people, it all came down to presenting a list of contributors who could address various stereotypes while writing about identity, racism, queerness, belonging, anti-Blackness, and finding oneself within the Latinx community."

Adler says that for her, selecting contributors was a bit of a "mixed bag," with some authors, like Lily Anderson and Anna-Marie McLemore, being "clear choices because they had already done Shakespeare reimaginings," but other picks were more unexpected. Striving to balance comedies and tragedies, Adler asked each contributor which original Shakespeare work they would like to retell, then recalibrated which writer she would ask next to deliver what she felt was lacking. "If someone surprised me by saying they were going to do a comedy when I assumed they would choose a tragedy, I would then reach out to someone I thought would do a comedy," she recalls. "In some cases, I had to give authors very few choices to ensure the stories I felt were most important to have in the collection, based on what is commonly read in schools, were represented."

Reaching readers

"I think collections are a great way to get to know new authors," Adler says. "High school kids have so much reading to do, so, if you're going to read for pleasure or a teacher is going to pair a young adult text with a classic text, it feels much more accessible and realistic for that to be short-form." She also notes that a short story anthology is a great way to see different ways of interpreting and approaching a classic text. Anthologies allow for the exploration of various genres, and they also provide an opportunity to look through a variety of lenses.

"Most of Poe's stories, for example, feature white, male narrators, but there are no white, male narrators in *His Hideous Heart*," Adler says. "An anthology works well to update these stories and make them feel more relevant to a modern audience while showing how you can work creatively with text." She hopes that educators embrace this new collection, "because there are some kids who are always going to struggle with Shakespeare because it isn't accessible and relevant to everyone." She believes these retellings can help change that and allow readers of all experiences to feel seen.

Adler has been thrilled to hear readers say *This Way Madness Lies* is ideal for readers who have a tumultuous relationship with Shakespeare, and she hopes the book continues to find exactly those readers. "If you love Shakespeare, it's fascinating to see the ways these stories build on the original," she says. "If you don't like Shakespeare, this collection gives inroads to appreciate the original text in a different way. And, if you have a love-hate relationship with his work, you'll find that many of the stories reimagine things you may have taken issue with in the original and show it through a different lens that allows you to appreciate the work more fully."

Newbould, Longoria, and Fennell hope to change hearts and minds by tapping into the accessibility of the anthology form and its ability to expose readers to voices and perspectives traditionally underrepresented and unheard.

"From the beginning, I created *For Every Body* for the kids that danced in the shadows because they were taught to hide themselves," Newbould says. "I want this book to tell every reader that it is okay to take up space, now, today. You don't have to wait, regardless of your journey in the future." In this collection about finding one's strength and power, the stories feature fully realized fat characters on journeys of "self-discovery, self-reflection, and self-recognition" of the internalized and external fatphobia they experience and that magical moment when they find "their true selves."

With contributions that elicit joy and pieces that prompt readers to reckon with their own beliefs and perspectives, *Wild Tongues Can't Be Tamed* "will be an eye-opener," Fennell says, for anyone who has "ever wondered about Latinx cultures you don't often hear about, or how the Latinx community is navigating whiteness, Blackness, and racism within our own community."

Longoria hopes that *Growing Up Beyond Borders* will have a similar impact, validating those who identify as Mexican and Mexican American while allowing all readers to see her Mexican and Mexican American community as individuals with families and friends, good days and bad days, and triumphs and losses, just like everyone else. "We love just like everyone else. We love our own culture and other cultures, too; we are not the ugly people others make us out to be," she says. "I am humbled and grateful that we are able to give this book to the world at this time."

*

Sara Grochowski is a youth librarian and writer in Michigan.

A version of this article appeared in the 05/03/2021 issue of *Publishers Weekly* under the headline: One Book, Many Stories.

Setting Sights on Summer Learning
By Shannon Maughan | Jun 11, 2021

Typically, as the school year comes to a close, many educators' and parents' thoughts turn to how they can stem summer slide, or the learning loss associated with students' being away from school—a key access point for books—during summer vacation. But in the wake of all the disruptions that school districts nationwide have experienced during the Covid-19 crisis, concerns about students' pandemic learning loss and students' and educators' social-emotional well-being have also mounted. As educators, students, and parents gear up to meet these challenges, many publishers, ed tech companies, libraries, and nonprofits are expanding their traditional summer reading offerings and/or creating new tools to help.

The companies *PW* spoke with unanimously named two key elements of effective summer reading programs: access to books—in print and/or digital formats—and the opportunity for students to choose their own reading materials. Research has long supported the importance of these two factors. According to the *Kids & Family Reading Report 7th Edition* from Scholastic, conducted in 2019, for example, 53% of kids access books they read for fun from school, and 50% of kids get them from the public library. And for most kids, schools are the least-available access point for books during the summer.

The same report finds that parents also focus on book access and choice when they encourage summer reading at home. Fifty-four percent of parents said that taking trips to public libraries was one of the top strategies to bolster their kids' efforts. That was closely followed by ordering from school book clubs or book fairs (42%) and taking books on road trips for vacations (42%). And 70% of kids ages six to 17 participating in the survey noted that they like summer reading because, "I get to read whenever/whatever I want." A companion study titled *Teacher & Principal Report*, conducted in 2020, highlighted the significance of book access, as well, revealing that 96% of teachers, principals, and school librarians believe that providing year-round access to books in the home is important to enhancing student achievement.

On the publishing front, Scholastic, which has offered a free summer reading program for kids since 2008, rolled out this year's version in late April, with some tweaks that reflect the current climate. "Our 2021 program continues to keep reading motivation at the core, while addressing new challenges presented by the Covid-19 pandemic, including book access and providing kids with a safe digital community to interact with their peers," says Lizette Serrano, v-p of educational marketing at Scholastic. From now until September 3, kids can participate in the program by creating accounts on Scholastic Home Base, which Serrano describes as "a safe, 24/7 moderated digital destination."

Home Base allows kids to join a community of readers, as well as meet some of their favorite authors via virtual events, read e-books, and watch author readaloud videos. Participants can track their reading progress by keeping Reading Streaks, during which they mark milestones and can earn virtual rewards. The volume of reading tracked through participants' Reading Streaks, Serrano says, will help to unlock "a donation of 100,000 print books from Scholastic, which will be distributed to kids in rural areas with limited or no access to books by Save the Children, a nonprofit organization that has transformed the lives of more than one billion children since its founding more than 100 years ago."

Serrano believes that this summer presents an opportunity for "learning acceleration." She adds, "We know that districts and families nationwide are working to ensure their summer learning plans include social-emotional support, online experiences, and holistic learning opportunities for all students." The Scholastic Home Base online community provides options for social-emotional learning and connection.

As an example, Serrano points to the format of this summer's programming. "Every Thursday from May 6 to August 26 at 3 p.m. ET, award-winning authors including summer reading ambassadors Sayantani DasGupta, Varian Johnson, Ann M. Martin, and Kelly Yang will host virtual events for kids to interact via a moderated chat function, ask questions, and learn behind-the-scenes information about the authors' books," she says. "And for budding writers, there will be opportunities to write a short piece with the authors."

In addition to the summer reading program, Scholastic is offering a number of resources for students and families, including a Family Help Desk staffed by experts in trauma, anxiety, early childhood, and reading development from the Yale Child Study Center + Scholastic Collaborative. Among the other available tools are a resiliency workbook for kids, the opportunity to host/participate in summer reading virtual Book Fairs, and themed grab-and-go take-home student book packs for purchase.

Ed tech on board

Other companies are making available curated packs of books for home use this year, as well. "We created the take-home/summer reading book packs because distance learning has further highlighted the longstanding inequities that our students face," says Deidra Purvis, director of classroom services at ed tech company Mackin. "Not all students have reliable access to the internet or to books at home. This has always been a challenge for schools, but even more so when students are spending less time in school and more time at home. The number of books in a student's home has been found to correlate with their level of academic achievement. We also know, based on the science of reading engagement, that when provided with books that they find personally relevant, students are more likely to engage in reading, and thus become better readers. That is why we have designed an easy solution for schools to pick and choose inclusive book packs to be sent home to build ownership over reading for their students. It was most important to us that these books are of high interest and personally relevant to the lives of students."

The grab-and-go model has become an essential element of Follett's work with nonprofits and with school districts this summer. Last year, for the first time, it teamed up with two early literacy organizations—Page Ahead in Seattle and Start Reading Now in Minneapolis—to provide low-income families with books to read over the summer. The partnership idea was born when the pandemic forced the closure of schools, and thus the cancellation of the large in-school book fairs that the nonprofits had traditionally used to get summer reading materials to their participating students. Follett stepped in and offered an online ordering and shipping solution on a tight turnaround, using its book eFair template. All parties chose to continue the arrangement in 2021.

"We've made some improvements this year, to make it easier for students to be able to order the books that they want and have them bagged and packed and shipped," says Britten Follett, executive v-p of Follett School Solutions. "Last year books went to a central location and the organization worked on the distribution. We're doing the same this year, but we also have the ability to ship to homes as well."

The summer reading pillars of access and choice are in play here, too. "Both organizations have a goal that allows for student choice," Follett says. "There are a lot of organizations out there trying to get books in the hands of kids, but if it's not a book the kid is interested in reading, they're probably just going to put it on the shelf and not remember it. If the student has the opportunity to pick from popular titles, the idea is that they're going to be far more engaged and potentially remember the book and develop their literacy skills further. That's why they like the eFair platform, because it essentially allows kids to go shopping virtually."

Follett's relationship with Page Ahead has expanded this summer. The number of eFair events has increased from 32 to 45, and in a new twist, Follett will additionally be working with the school districts that participate in Page Ahead's Book Up Summer program, which focuses on grades K–2. "The school districts that Page Ahead serves were so pleased with the events that they decided to use their own funds to also provide books to students in grades 3–5," Britten Follett says. "It's an interesting public-private partnership where the nonprofit [organization] funds K–2, the school district funds 3–5, and Follett is able to provide the platform for the distribution of the books."

Beyond Washington State, Follett notes that, "from a school district perspective, we are seeing a huge demand in books-to-home [shipping]. School districts across the country are funding what we're calling a grab-and go model—basically books in a bag for a student to keep at home to build their home library—because they're concerned about the Covid slide combined with having an additional two-and-a-half months off over the summer."

Districts are also looking at potential programming for high-needs students over the summer, according to Follett. "It's not a requirement from the federal government, but some states are strongly encouraging school districts to offer summer programming for high-needs students due to the Covid slide," she says. "I think it has just elevated the discussion, associated with the fact that many families don't have books at home for students to read. So, if we know that that's a gap, how can we use the large amount of federal funding that's descending on K–12 schools to help fill it? That's how some districts are thinking about it: What if we could help every student build their home library so that, when they're not in the school building, they can have print books that are at their age and grade level and access them throughout the year?"

Follett says her company sees expanding on this nonprofit concept as a positive new business strategy. "If we can tap into third parties that are looking to get books into the hands of students, that's additional revenue into the funnel," she notes. "The idea of giving publishers a virtual fair option to test new authors, new genres, new concepts, new characters—those are things we're interested in talking to our publishing partners about because, again, by selling directly to students and allowing them to select books without the financial limitations of a book fair, I think it's an interesting potential test market." As Follett explains, "In a book fair you can only buy what you can afford; in this case we set it up so the nonprofit is actually funding the selection of the books, which gives students an opportunity to choose more books than they might have previously shopped for."

At OverDrive, educational general manager Angela Arnold reports that summer reading is among the top-of-mind concerns for the school districts and partners that use the company's Sora reading app. In this unprecedented era when "every month, every quarter, every unit of time creates a different challenge for our school partners," she says. "The way we can help is by really listening to their needs. Right now, they're saying that they need to be able to deliver summer reading. They are looking for low-cost summer reading options like our Sweet Reads program, which is very popular and will help them provide some books right away." She notes that OverDrive has "really turned on the gas on that program this year," pointing out that it includes more titles (38) and more types of content (audiobooks, graphic novels).

Sweet Reads addresses such overarching questions as, "What kinds of materials are going to entice kids?" and, "What do they need right now and what do they want?" Arnold says. "Whereas in the past it was strictly a pleasure reading program to keep kids engaged over the summer, now it's a little more prescriptive."

Arnold pointed to the impressive success of last year's program and noted that 2021 is already off to a strong start. In 2020, nearly 25,000 schools around the world took part in Sweet Reads, a 90% increase from the number of schools that participated in 2019. Student participation grew more than five times from 2019, resulting in a 500% increase in checkouts year over year. In total, more than 250,000 students joined in, reading at least one of the program's 31 simultaneous-use titles. So far more than 48,000 schools are enrolled in the current Sweet Reads program, which runs May 5–August 20.

Apart from the Sweet Reads program, OverDrive's school partners "are looking for additional free content and that's something else that we're bolstering in our Sora offering," Arnold says. "Our publishers have very generously agreed to go back and make sure that they participate in the free content models we offer. School partners are also looking for us to help them provide structured programming or support the school's structured programming."

Arnold points to the example of ongoing discussions with one school district that does a community outreach program working with parents and families for whom English is a second language. "They're providing reading materials, webinars, and weekly touch bases for those families," she says. "And they're talking to us because they are interested in how we can support that with digital books."

Ann Arbor Public Schools in Michigan is one of the district partners taking advantage of OverDrive's offerings to support its summer school programs. Jennifer Colby, library services department chair for AAPS, shared information on what her students will be able to access in the coming months. AAPS is offering summer school for students in kindergarten through 12th grade via online platform Schoology, which integrates access to Sora. To help make that connection, she says that all students will retain or be provided with district-issued devices (iPads for lower elementary and Chromebooks for upper elementary through high school). In all the programs, school librarians will showcase how to access and use the Sora e-book library and simultaneous use collections like Sora Sweet Reads and AudioSync Audiobook programs as well as a social and emotional learning lineup of titles.

"Access to these free, simultaneous use collections affords our teachers and students the opportunity to discuss choice book literature circles," Colby says. "These discussions help students to share their understanding of a text and make connections with the text to their own lives and the lives of their fellow students. A major focus of our summer school curricula is community. These connections to the people within and outside of our communities are especially important as we have lived a socially distanced life over the past year and our students have not been able to personally interact with each other to the extent that they normally do."

AAPS summer school students will have access to the district's Sora curated e-book library collection, too. "Providing choice books to our students allows them to read and enjoy books of interest to them," Colby says. "Without the opportunity to check out print books from our library collections since March 2020, access to books for pleasure reading has been limited. Our Sora e-book library, available to our students since November 2020, is growing in popularity every day. With continued promotion and use throughout the summer we hope to start the 2021–2022 school year with a robust and engaging e-book library."

Colby adds that continued use and instruction in the Sora e-book library this summer will help students "develop their digital decoding and comprehension skills," which will serve them well in the future. "As our AAPS curriculum and instruction will continue to incorporate digital resources, access to digital texts and knowing how to use the Sora interactive features strengthens student comprehension of texts and prepares our students for engagement with digital texts provided in other platforms as they move through our program and into college," she says.

Programs and materials abound

In another partnership geared toward keeping students engaged and reading during the summer break, large-print publisher Thorndike Press has teamed up with the Beanstack reading tracking app and entrepreneur Mark Cuban to deliver Level Up, a national K–12 summer reading challenge for schools. Between June 1 and July 15, participating students will log the books they read on the Beanstack app, where they can earn virtual achievement badges and engage with friends in addition to discovering new books. Level Up participants can choose any genre or format of book to read, and large print books—a proven literacy intervention tool—will be one of the formats featured during the program.

Schools whose students log the most reading time will win cash prizes provided by Cuban, and prize packs of middle grade and YA large-print books. The grand-prize-winning school will receive $5,000 cash and a $1,000 collection of large print books, as well as a virtual chat with one of four authors: Kimberly Brubaker Bradley, Meg Medina, Kwame Mbalia, and Jewell Parker Rhodes. There will also be a second-place prize awarded, and four runners-up will earn cash and books, too.

Digital reading platform Epic plans to keep kids' attention when school's out with the launch of its first-ever summer program, Camp Epic. Under the Camp Epic umbrella, the app will release a 10-page comic each week for five consecutive weeks beginning July 5. The comics mark a crossover event and star characters from the Epic Originals line of titles joining together for fun and adventure with a summer camp backdrop. Each of the weekly comic installments will also include a hands-on activity for campers, including classics like making a friendship bracelet or tie-dye shirt.

While not every publisher runs a distinct summer reading program, many of the companies that created online resources for students, educators, and families to access during the pandemic continue to support those offerings, keeping them available during the summer break. Others may expand their marketing efforts behind books whose appeal may spike during the summer, from award-winning titles that often appear on schools' summer reading lists, to workbooks and skills-boosting tools. At

Penguin Young Readers, Mad Libs is offering such print supplemental educational materials as its Mad Libs Workbook series. New titles include *Mad Libs Workbook: Grade 1 Reading* and run through *Mad Libs Workbook: Grade 4 Reading.*

The library story

Public libraries have always been at the forefront of offering summer reading programs, book clubs, and other special resources and programming for students during the summer. Though many librarians have found creative ways to bring these opportunities to their local kids over the years, the nonprofit Collaborative Summer Library Program has been helping libraries across the country plan and implement themed summer reading programs since 1987, when, according to the organization's timeline, 10 regional library systems in Minnesota teamed up to develop a reproducible summer reading program for kids that had a theme and dedicated artwork, as well as incentives for libraries to purchase and use. These days the group collaborates with libraries to create an annual "inclusive literacy-based program that is enjoyable for all ages," according to its mission statement. The reproducible programs and materials are available to babies through adults. This year's theme is Tails & Tales and features artwork by Salina Yoon.

Luke Kralik, organizational coordinator for CSLP, says that the group has weathered the pandemic stresses and disruptions fairly well and looks forward to regaining some footing as summer reading programs kick off this time around. "Last summer was quite a wild ride for us," he recalls. "March and April are huge shipping months for CSLP, and sudden library closures caused hundreds and hundreds of orders to become undeliverable. There were days when over 60 boxes were showing back up at the warehouse."

As a result, Kralik says, CSLP had to temporarily halt shipping. "But at the time, there was still tremendous optimism that things would be back to normal in the summer." He adds that fellow coordinator Melissa Hooke "was contacted by, or personally reached out to, thousands of libraries, and had their delivery addresses changed from their closed libraries, to their own personal addresses."

CSLP scrambled to pivot in other ways, as well. "We also put together a small committee of volunteers to find and repackage worksheets, handouts, and reproducibles from previous CSLP manuals," Kralik says. "This was to help folks with their new curbside grab-and-go programming." As 2021 summer programs launch, "things have not quite returned to normal, but have been much more manageable," he adds. "We have had a lot of libraries put off ordering until the last minute, and it does seem like we are seeing a lot of people new to their position placing orders. This, compounded by some manufacturing and sourcing issues, has caused us to run out of products a bit prematurely, but nothing too bad."

Processing learning loss

Many educators and schools have been working hard to create summer learning support for their students, but Morgan McCullough, OverDrive librarian, believes they may not be thinking too much about learning loss—yet. She works directly with schools, brainstorming with them about their needs and how OverDrive can provide the best solutions for them.

Most often these days, McCullough says, schools want "supportive materials, things they can access when they're not in school, on weekends, and, of course, in our current circumstances, in blending learning environments." In terms of how schools are addressing learning loss concerns, "I'd say they're not quite there yet," she adds. "The past year it's been like putting out fire after fire. We all know learning loss is on the horizon, but we're still triaging moment by moment what their needs are. SEL [social and emotional learning] is coming to the fore, because educators know there are going to be traumatized kids. The expectation is a sharp increase. You can't really do anything practical until you manage your kids' emotions to the point where they can regulate themselves and take in what you're giving them."

To that end, McCullough says that OverDrive is offering a free SEL collection for partners "that our publishers helped us create. We have professional development that is key for SEL, because teachers have to be able to regulate themselves. They've had tough years, as well. They need to figure that out before they can help their students."

Arnold agrees, offering that she has seen a shift in the types of professional development that schools are seeking. "One of the key differentiators between this year and last year is that the professional development gap that schools were looking to address last summer revolved around how to teach in a remote or hybrid model—how do you 'do digital'?" she says. "Now the need seems to be more about, how do you care for the kids who are not necessarily in a good place?"

Referring to the aforementioned Family Help Desk and other SEL resources Scholastic is offering this summer, Serrano says, "As a parent myself, I see firsthand how critically important these elements are, and the research confirms it—according to the *Scholastic Teacher & Principal School Report*, 99% of educators agree that for students to reach their highest academic potential, their social-emotional needs must be met, and nearly all educators, 98%, agree that literacy is critical to students' health and emotional wellness."

Beyond the summer

Arnold believes that school administrators continue to face tremendous challenges this summer and further down the line. "They have to now think about how to preserve learning and address unfinished learning as they wind down this school year," she says. "They need to think about how to enter the fall and what will happen. If that weren't enough, they are also going to be presented with opportunities to participate in education stabilization funding—and it's a lot of money. They're going to be asked to start preparing proposals, to start thinking about which are the most worthy projects for this funding, and how this money could best be applied in their districts for what their kids need. In any other time that would be its own full-time job."

Ultimately, Arnold says, "I think there's hope; it's going to be okay. We really have to home in on that message and convey that to parents and everybody, that we will get through this together." She believes that message has never been more important in the context of K–12 education.

"Of course, the downside," Arnold says, "is that, due to many inequities in the educational system, not everyone had the same kind of experiences during the pandemic, and some kids were impacted way more than others. But it's important to reinforce and recognize that it's okay and that students are probably commensurate with their peers. One thing I've learned from our school partners is to eschew the terms 'learning loss' and 'summer slide' and I'm starting to adopt the term 'unfinished learning.' It's a subtle distinction, but I think it's one of many ways we can help reduce anxiety, especially among kids and parents. It's not done yet; we'll get there. Your teacher will know where you left off and where you are."

McCullough concurs. "We all know our students might have some gaps and might need extra help or commitment to make sure they're meeting some of those benchmarks," she says. "We all understand, and we're all there walking in lockstep together. There is learning loss, but there's not a loss of support."

*

A version of this article appeared in the 06/14/2021 issue of *Publishers Weekly* under the headline: Setting Sights on Summer Learning.

NPD Webinar Details Big Changes in Children's and Licensed Publishing
By Karen Raugust | Jun 29, 2021

The mature and typically stable book publishing industry has experienced a period of volatility since the start of the pandemic, accompanied by some big changes to segments such as young adult titles, comics and graphic novels, educational workbooks, and licensed publishing. "Understanding Trends in the U.S. Kids' Book and Licensing Market," a June 23 webinar presented by Kristen McLean, executive director and U.S. book industry analyst for the NPD Group, covered several key developments.

As of June 5, 2021, total unit sales of books (for all ages) have grown 21.4% year-to-date, compared to the same period in 2020, with signs pointing to a strong finish for the year as a whole. Typically, sales of books are very stable, with an increase of about 3% considered a very good year. "This speaks to how volatile 2021 has been," McLean said, pointing out that the growth in the first six months comes after an out-of-the-ordinary year in 2020.

Adult fiction and nonfiction are driving the growth in 2021, followed by juvenile fiction. The last segment has seen unit sales up 13% through the week of June 5, driven by holiday bursts for Valentine's Day, Easter, and the Dr. Seuss-driven Read Across America week in March. McLean describes the Seuss event as "very impactful" and noted that the controversy surrounding the discontinuation of certain Seuss titles also contributed to a doubling of franchise sales in March.

Total Market Print Book Sales up 21% YTD
This is unprecedented performance for the US market

McLean highlighted the young adult "super-category" a normally small and stable segment, as one that is seeing some notable changes. Unit sales grew 50% in 2021 to date, following a fairly strong 2019. "But what was driving 2020 is not the same as what's driving sales in 2021," McLean explained. In 2020, YA was driven by best-sellers, including major frontlist releases like Stephenie Meyer's *Midnight Sun* and Suzanne Collins's *Ballad of Songbirds and Snakes*. In 2021, however, there have been no major releases.

"There's a really, really engaged community that has emerged this year called #BookTok," McLean said, noting that the group's advocacy has pushed certain titles, especially backlist books, to the bestseller lists and kept them there. Several of the top YA books this year fall into this category, including *They Both Die at the End* by Adam Silvera, *We Were Liars* by E. Lockhart, and S.E. Hinton's *The Outsiders*. "It's really shifting the whole dynamic of YA," McLean said. "This is the first time we're seeing a meaningful impact from organized social media to put backlist titles back on the bestseller lists." She noted that retailers are watching this trend too, which increases the community's influence on sales.

Juvenile nonfiction has been the only super-category to show a decline in 2021 so far, with units down 1% year-to-date. But that is due to the strength of that category last year, as home schooling drove unprecedented sales of workbooks and coloring and activity titles from the likes of Rockridge Press, Workman, School Zone, Spectrum, and Scholastic. "It's down a little this year but still strong," McLean said of the category. She expects educational nonfiction to remain robust into the fall, saying, "Parents are worried about their kids falling behind."

The comics and graphic novel space is also an interesting one. The category has seen unit sales grow from 14 million units in 2006 to 30 million in 2020, representing an 8% compound annual growth rate. In 2020, unit sales were up 17%. But the drivers have changed in the past year.

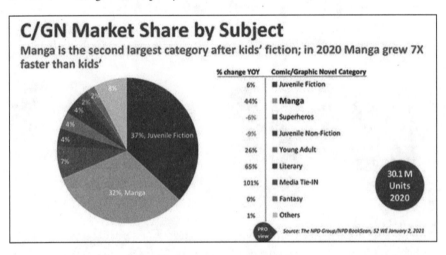

C/GN Market Share by Subject
Manga is the second largest category after kids' fiction; in 2020 Manga grew 7X faster than kids'

% change YOY	Comic/Graphic Novel Category
6%	Juvenile Fiction
44%	Manga
-6%	Superheros
-9%	Juvenile Non-Fiction
26%	Young Adult
65%	Literary
101%	Media Tie-IN
0%	Fantasy
1%	Others

30.1 M Units 2020

Source: The NPD Group/NPD BookScan, 52 WE January 2, 2021

Growth through 2019 was propelled by juvenile titles, notably Dav Pilkey's Dog Man franchise, which remains "an absolute juggernaut," McLean said. But in 2020, the market for kids' titles plateaued due to store closures, and adult manga, particularly titles associated with anime programs on Netflix, Hulu, and Crunchyroll, started to push the market forward. "Manga went from a passionate niche category to something mainstream," McLean said. "This in my opinion is one of the few true white spaces in publishing," as manga is expanding the comics audience by bringing in brand-new readers. So far in 2021, the total comics and graphic novel market has seen an increase of 112%, with manga up 284%, YA titles up 123%, and kids' titles up 33%.

McLean also noted the current strength of board books. The format has seen unit sales rise 19% year to date in 2021, a pace of growth that is one and a half times the rest of the kids' print market, which is up 11% collectively. "There's lots of competition from new and small presses with well-priced lookalikes taking share," McLean cautioned. "It's a supercompetitive part of the market. There are a lot of quick and nimble publishers muscling in on the space."

In kids' books (as in publishing overall), there has been a trend away from frontlist and toward backlist sales. The children's space has witnessed a 13-point shift toward backlist between 2004 and 2020. In 2004, frontlist titles accounted for 35% of unit sales, declining slightly to a 33% share in 2016. In just three years after that, however, in 2019, frontlist sales had shrunk to 28%. And, with stores closed in 2020, making it more difficult to discover new titles, frontlist books accounted for just 22% of unit sales.

Despite the fact that stores are open again, the trend continues into this year, with frontlist titles commanding a 21% share at the year's halfway point. McLean noted that the business is structured around frontlist, which generates less and less return on investment as its share vs. backlist shrinks. "If you ask me what's the number one risk for the book market, it's in the discovery of new frontlist books, especially for children," she said. "How will brand-new authors or children's books find an audience right now?"

The growing challenge of discovering new frontlist titles is one reason for the current strength of series books in the children's space. "Series offer parents an easy buy and keep kids engaged at home," McLean said. In 2021, two of every three kids' books sold have been series titles—led by Beginner Books, Dog Man, Little Golden Books, Dr. Seuss, Step into Reading, and Harry Potter—and series saw a huge bump in unit sales in 2020, to 174 million units from 154 million in 2019.

Challenges on the Licensing Front

The strength of backlist and series publishing is one of several factors impacting the licensed portion of the kids' book market. This is one area that has faced challenges in recent years, accelerated by the pandemic. It remains an important segment of publishing, with 15% of all books and 31% of all kids' books sold in the U.S. featuring a licensed IP. NPD defines licensed properties as including both book-native properties that are licensed to other companies, as well as non-book properties that come into the industry through what it terms a "pure licensing" arrangement.

"Like series books, [licensed titles] make their case at a glance at retail or online," McLean said. But she pointed out that licensed books are underperforming the rest of the market, with unit sales rising just 5% in 2020. The challenges facing this segment are not just pandemic-related; licensed publishing has seen a decline of 11% in units since 2016.

Backlist dominance is even greater in licensed publishing than in kids' books as a whole, with frontlist titles representing just 16% of the total. The licensed portion of the market has become dominated by literary licenses, which represent 73% of total volume of licensed titles, at the expense of "pure licenses."

"Mass retailers have played a very strong role in this," McLean said. "[Literary licenses] sell like hot cakes in the mass category, and they're starting to push pure licenses off the shelf." Literary licenses include Dr. Seuss, which NPD pegs as the top licensed property in the book industry, accounting for 14% of sales of licensed books and driving more than 50% of the growth in licensed titles for young readers ages four to eight this year.

Another factor impacting licensing is the fragmentation of the licensed IP landscape, as the business moves away from tentpole properties such as movies and toward alternatives such as streaming video on demand (VOD), video games, and the like. The number of properties has been proliferating, but fewer are the mainstream hits that formerly characterized the licensing market.

"More and more licenses are asking for our attention," McLean said. "There are more of them and they're smaller. Traditional pure licenses are at a disadvantage in the current marketplace." This evolution in media consumption makes it difficult for consumers to discover a new favorite license, for retailers to decide which licenses to support, and for publishers to figure out a rollout strategy for tie-in books.

As a result, the business model for licensed publishing is changing to more of an evergreen strategy. "We're just not seeing these large tentpole releases perform the way they did just a few years ago," McLean said. "There is evidence that streaming VOD paired with a movie and a retail play does have the ability to keep IP on the shelf longer than in the past. But it's early days." Video game-based book franchises like Five Nights at Freddy's and Minecraft, on the other hand, tend to see sales remain steady or even increase over time, unlike film licenses where sales plummet shortly after the movie release without a successful streaming VOD window.

Furthermore, an evergreen property can perform as well as a high-profile tentpole film these days. Disney's Frozen franchise drove sales of three million books over 294 titles, with a total value of $38 million, from 2017 to 2019 leading up to the release of *Frozen 2*, NPD estimates, with the top title, a Little Golden Book, selling 131,000 units. At the same time, Sesame Street drove 3.1 million unit sales across 373 titles, for a value of $31 million, with the top title, *The Monster at the End of This Book*, selling 274,000 units, a comparable performance to Frozen over that period.

As McLean said, "An evergreen strategy is essentially investing in backlist that will keep selling."

Children's Booksellers on Which Pandemic-Era Changes Are Here to Stay
By Alex Green | Jul 16, 2021

Even as parts of the United States emerge from the Covid-19 pandemic, the retail outlook for children's booksellers remains unclear. Store browsing protocols are complicated by the fact that children under 12 are unvaccinated. Varied and inconsistent school reopening plans make fall planning a challenge. Author tours will likely remain digital through Christmas. But children's booksellers know that something extraordinary has happened, too.

Despite predictions of a pandemic-induced retail apocalypse, booksellers swiftly incorporated new tools, learned novel skills, deepened their engagement with readers, and survived, and in some cases thrived. Having adapted their businesses to the most extreme retail challenges in generations, many are now taking stock of which pandemic-era changes are here to stay.

PW caught up with four children's booksellers to see what postpandemic bookselling looks like to them. Some see their businesses being transformed by a few major shifts in how they work. Others see changes that affect every aspect of their businesses, from the back office to the front door. But all are certain that the ways they buy and sell children's books are not what they were a year and a half ago, and never will be again.

Shifting patterns, new insights

When in-store events came to a halt at 4 Kids Books & Toys in Zionsville, Ind., owner Cynthia Compton filled the event space with books for teen readers—a decision that reflects the strong sales to individual readers that made up for lost event sales. She says that the effective decisions she has made since the pandemic began come down to one major shift, brought on by the store's success with e-commerce.

"Data is king," Compton says. "We're in communication with our customers way more. We know much more about their buying habits. We're crunching the numbers on who our top 200 customers are, what they buy, and what the categories are that turn. We're just much more aware of what our sales look like and how to buy for it and how to sell to it."

The data led to major changes in the way Compton runs her store, which then led to new data that has helped her deepen her understanding of customer buying habits even more. Among the biggest changes she has made is the way she orders books from publishers. Prior to the pandemic, she placed orders seasonally, as almost all other booksellers do. But the uncertainty of the pandemic meant that seasonal ordering was risky.

"We needed to dial back and be more immediate about things, and be able to respond to openings and closings," Compton recalls. "We weren't sure if we were going to stay open or stay closed, or if it was going to go back and forth. So we felt strongly that we needed to get away from the large seasonal order."

Compton began placing monthly orders instead. As the store's social media sales channels developed to market new releases that customers once learned about in-store, she found that thinking in terms of months created opportunities to develop marketing that was more responsive to readers' preferences in a given moment than seasonal orders would allow.

In the process of shifting orders and marketing, Compton saw two changes in customer buying habits. Preorders dropped off, which she believes is a reflection of competing digitally with other e-tailers. At the same time, midlist sales grew substantially.

Looking back, Compton says the midlist boost that came from shifting her ordering is entirely understandable. "When you cut down your ordering to a monthly basis and you're really only looking at the frontlist that's coming out in the next six weeks, you're paying attention to a much smaller number of books, and you're marketing differently. Rather than pitching a book ahead to your customers that's coming out three months from now, you have the opportunity to talk about each and every title, which likely is going to be midlist. If it's not on one of the eight big days of the year, when everybody has to publish their books all at the same time, you have a chance to really focus on all of those different titles."

Increased midlist sales reflect a growing readership, especially among middle graders. "The pandemic was like fertilizer for middle grade sales," Compton says. For her summer reading program alone—a program with a substantial middle grade readership—she saw a 30% rise in participation in 2020 compared with the previous year. This year, 1,800 readers are participating, which is a rise of another 18%.

The slow return to something that resembles pre-pandemic business does not mean that Compton is prepared to drop the methods that have given her so much new insight into her customers' reading interests. For the foreseeable future, she is planning a hybrid approach of the new and the old. She will continue to buy on a monthly basis, except for the holiday season, when advance ordering is crucial for having stock on hand. Her only exceptions will be for major releases and books from smaller publishers, to ensure they know she is committed to them in the long-term, since she knows that the advance notice is helpful for their sales projections. "I am writing to them for the full season just to say, you're important, we're going to keep buying from you, and you can know to have this many copies in your pending list," she says.

Gaining new (e-)space

In 2017, Peter Glassman opened a second location of Books of Wonder, his children's bookstore near Union Square in Manhattan, on the Upper West Side. "Having a second store gave us a little more clout with publishers, and more options for events," Glassman says. "It gave publishers just a little more reach for events throughout the city."

But unlike his store's flagship location, which draws a loyal and longtime clientele, the West 84th Street store was vulnerable during the pandemic. The store shuttered from March to July 2020. When it did reopen, it was the only retail store on the block to do so. GameStop closed on the corner nearby. The AMC movie theater across the street remained closed. Then the building changed hands, and at the end of June, Glassman closed the store permanently while he sought out new locations.

Yet despite the loss of a major events venue, Glassman is sanguine about his experience—in part because the pandemic also created conditions where he could solve a preexisting problem for the store. For years, he has scrambled to find large venues for hosting author events that draw sizable crowds. In New York City, cost and space availability both posed significant challenges.

While some stores struggled to move their events online, Glassman realized that virtual events could eliminate the need for large venues while engaging the large base of customers around the world who have visited the store on trips to New York City. At the same time, authors who might visit the city infrequently but want to support the store could join from anywhere.

Over the past year, Glassman has tested the idea. The store had just completed a website overhaul prior to the pandemic, which helped optimize the sale of signed editions. While it was closed to in-person traffic, Glassman added the online events platform Crowdcast for hosting readings, and began scheduling events.

In the past year he has hosted virtual author events with audiences of more than 1,000 attendees and equally high book sales. Among them were events for Rick Riordan and Kwame Mbalia, who appeared together in conversation for the launch of Riordan's *The Trials of Apollo* last October, and Tui T. Sutherland, who had the launch for her 14th Wings of Fire title, *The Dangerous Gift*, this March.

Along with reducing the cost of hosting events and reaching a broader audience, Glassman has also been able to feature authors who otherwise might not have made their way to New York. For the launch of *The Other Side of the Sky* in September 2020, coauthors Amie Kaufman and Meagan Spooner joined the event from Australia and Washington, D.C., respectively.

Events for fall 2021 will almost certainly continue to be virtual to some degree, and Glassman says he is excited to keep using the system he's established, while incorporating some aspects of pre-pandemic, in-person events. Multi-author events are more successful than single-author ones, he says, and weekend events are easier for parents to watch with their kids than those on weekdays.

In September, Glassman will host a large event for the release of Brian Selznick's *Kaleidoscope* (Scholastic), and he is fully prepared to host it online. But he is already looking past the pandemic and envisioning hybrid events hosted in the bookstore with a live audience, and streaming to viewers through Crowdcast. Having sold books for 45 years, he says he is always thinking about ways to reach more readers while ensuring the long-term stability of his store. "The fact of the matter is, no matter how long we do this for," he says, "we're never going to reach as many of the kids as we want to." But with a new way to host events, he is able to reach more than ever before.

Burnout and breakthroughs

With the pandemic, the protests, and a presidential election last year, the Washington, D.C., area was a study in burnout. At Barston's Child's Play, book buyer Molly Gilroy Olivo saw firsthand how these overwhelming events led to positive change, but also felt that a postpandemic world could not come soon enough. Much of what she encountered involved the store's close working relationship with public schools for summer reading list orders and school book fairs.

The rise in e-commerce at the beginning of the pandemic put the store's reliance on Shopify to the test. Uploading title information was labor intensive, and creating lists was difficult, especially for virtual book fairs. "The front-end labor was high," Olivo says, and the payoff was questionable.

Out of five virtual book fairs, only one went well. Olivo quickly learned that the digital format fundamentally changed what the fairs were for kids and their parents. "A book fair is an exciting event," she says. "Everyone gets to go, you get to shop around, and you get to tell your friends which books you're reading. But when the events were solely online, they felt more like an obligatory ask for money to support the school, at a time when people were already under pressure."

Barston's will return to in-school book fairs when it can, but Olivo says the virtual experience was not a loss in the long run. When fairs resume, the store plans to offer a digital component even when in-school options are available, too. Barston's ability to provide e-commerce sales and support is the result of two new hires, who are off-site digital marketing and online sales support staff. The new positions reflect the store's streamlining of systems and operations overall.

Prior to the pandemic, Olivo says each of the store's three locations had varied approaches to the workflow issues in a given day. "In a multi-location business that operates with really strong managers, we end up in situations where we're all kind of operating very independently most of the time," she notes. Throughout the year, the staff steadily abandoned different approaches in favor of universal ones. Group chats are used for broad communication while shared documents guide universal processes. "It's something we've gotten significantly more efficient about," she adds.

By the end of this school year, the increased bandwidth created by the new systems and hires allowed Olivo to take a more active role in developing orders for school accounts, at a moment when teachers and librarians were running out of energy. Many schools turned to Barston's to place orders for the end of the fiscal year, and to support summer reading. But school personnel were also less able to develop the reading lists themselves. For the first time, they asked Olivo to do much of the work, and she was able to. With one school, she developed a list of 127 children's books that reflected the diversity of the region's student body. Only four titles were authored by white men.

"I was really excited," Olivo says. "From a bookseller perspective, being able to say that I'm getting to influence the amazing potential diversity that these kids are going to read all summer? That part is really great." She is uncertain whether she'll continue to play that role after the pandemic, but she hopes she will. "It was a Covid-19 byproduct. The school gave us a little more leeway and said, 'We trust you.' "

Cementing social media

Within weeks of the emergence of Covid-19 in the U.S., the booksellers at the Novel Neighbor in St. Louis, Mo., knew they would need to improve the store's social media if they wanted to reach readers. "We had been talking about trying to get into TikTok, but no one here knew anything about how to do it," says children's buyer and event coordinator Melissa Posten. Then a résumé arrived in her inbox.

At first, Posten was confused by it. Kassie King had moved home to St. Louis after working in Los Angeles and on Capitol Hill. But she did not seem to have bookselling experience. Then Posten learned that, as a kid, King had been a BookTuber. "She's obsessed with books," Posten says.

During her first month as social media and marketing manager at the store, King made a BookTok for a novel titled *Honey Girl* and it went viral, garnering half a million views; boosting the store's followers to 20,000; and resulting in nearly 100 copies sold. That was just the beginning.

In the year since, the Novel Neighbor has come together in support of King's social media work, learning which platforms are best for certain titles and tailoring content to each. When the bookstore staff accidentally told BookTok viewers that the trade edition jacket of Rachel Griffin's YA novel *The Nature of Witches* was a special edition cover, King followed up with a video joking about their mistake. The humorous approach paid off, and the store sold 80 copies.

Posten says she and King have learned that YA sells well on TikTok, Instagram is good for parents of young children, Facebook adds on grandparents, and Twitter is the place for reaching educators. She is seeing the same trends that Compton observed at 4 Kids Books & Toys, including the rise of interest in midlist titles on social media. For the posts, she says, "We use new releases that are not the big splashy titles. Taylor Jenkins Reid does not need any more publicity. Everybody knows the new Wimpy Kid book is coming. We want to try to get people excited about other new titles, and I think at least it's helping us sell midlist."

In addition, Posten has seen a boost in paperback backlist sales, with readers sometimes coming into the store and buying entire series at once. "Someone will just come in and say, 'I saw this Stuart Gibbs book on your social media. I'll just take the whole series,' " she notes.

"It's very low tech," Posten says of social media marketing. "You don't have to have video editing software. You don't have to learn how to use iMovie or anything like that, as long as you can figure out how to use TikTok—and frankly, there are a billion videos out there showing you how, if you don't have a Kassie like we do."

Instead of the past 16 months leading to bookstore closings, stores like the Novel Neighbor have expanded their reach while improving the services they offer customers. All of it means a more stable business that can weather the uncertainty of the current stage of the pandemic and last well into the future.

"Now we're everywhere," Posten says. "We're on Twitter, we're on Instagram, we're on Facebook. Especially during the last four to five months, when stuff was opening a little bit, and people were unsure about coming in, it was a way to keep our at-home customers engaged with the bookstore. And now that we've sent these orders out all across the country, we have a slightly more national audience that we're also reaching out to."

*

A version of this article appeared in the 07/19/2021 issue of *Publishers Weekly* under the headline: The New Children's Bookselling.

A Hybrid Future for Children's Sales Reps
By Alex Green | Jul 16, 2021

Sales reps took on an unprecedented workload during the past 16 months, adapting to the needs of booksellers amid pressing demand for children's and YA titles—all while working remotely. The question of which pandemic-era innovations are effective, and which should go by the wayside, is one that many are considering as they return to in-person appointments, in an industry that has undergone substantial change in a short period of time.

"Every single account is doing something just a little bit differently in terms of how they are buying, how they are ordering, and how they are paying attention to books," says Scholastic senior manager for field brand marketing Nikki Mutch. In many ways, Mutch adds, the diversity of approaches taken by booksellers has created opportunities for her to develop deeper relationships with stores.

For instance, with buyers, managers, and owners pressed for time during the pandemic, they have had to rely more on frontline booksellers, Mutch says. For the first time, those booksellers—with approval from managers—have been calling to talk about forthcoming titles, which provides her with a better sense of what the employees who deal most frequently with customers are seeing and hearing.

"They're the gatekeepers to the customer," Mutch notes. "They're the ones who recommend books to them. They're the ones who stock the shelves. And it is also coming from younger booksellers, who I love to hear. They have new ideas, and their owners and booksellers are letting them run with those ideas. It's been a very exciting thing to see."

With increased digital communication, Chronicle sales representative Emily Cervone says that remote sales calls are also here to stay. "I love my stores that are far away," Cervone says. "But sometimes I spend four hours in the car, and the way that everything is on Edelweiss now, it's hard to want to drive for hours when you're going to talk to them for 40 minutes."

Cervone believes that a generational divide among sales reps will have a lot to do with which publisher accounts go back to all in-person meetings and which take a more hybrid approach. "There are a lot of old-school, traditional reps," she says, "who are going to say, 'I still need to go see this teeny tiny account in Vermont.'"

But instead of driving, Cervone says she has been able to take the time she saves to prepare digital tools that enhance her conversations with booksellers. For example, French publisher Twirl, which is distributed by Chronicle, has highly interactive books that children's booksellers need to see, but the cost of creating advance reader's copies is prohibitive. Instead, Twirl has created videos for its titles that Cervone's customers can watch.

Since Cervone also handles much of the Edelweiss catalog information for Chronicle and its affiliates, she embeds the videos in the Edelweiss listings and goes through them with booksellers, using the digital catalog as a guide for their meetings. Going forward, she says, "I feel like you're going to see a lot more of that kind of marketing."

Chesapeake & Hudson sales rep Keith Arsenault says social media has also been a new space for conversations with booksellers who post about books they're interested in. He notes that it has been exciting to engage booksellers in what feels like a sustained and ongoing dialogue about books during a time when he could not see them face-to-face. But, he adds, publishers will need to make print material available for in-person sales calls, especially for children's books, and he worries that many publishers are moving away from providing them.

For children's books, some of Arsenault's biggest accounts still rely heavily on blads and f&g's. Prior to the pandemic, he would occasionally even leave his entire sales kit with a store in advance of a meeting so its buyers had time to review everything closely. He worries that publishers will try to find short-term cost savings by ceasing the production of advance print material, but warns that it poses "a real problem."

"There's a lot of screen fatigue out there," Arsenault says, "and a lot of the buyers whom I've talked to, old and young, are saying, 'Okay, if I have to, I will use the digital format. But I am tired of staring at the screen, and I really want to hold a book, especially a picture book. I want to be immersed in the text and see the interplay of the texts and the images. And I don't get that from flipping through them on my laptop or my iPad.'"

As with Mutch and Cervone, Arsenault sees the coexistence of traditional and digital approaches as the way forward, with careful consideration about how to balance them in the interest of getting new children's books into the hands of booksellers and, ultimately, young readers. As he navigates the uncertainties that are likely to continue in the trade for some time, Arsenault's decisions are focused on using both approaches. "These kids are going to become the next generation of adults who are going to have kids," he says. "You want to nurture their love of reading."

*

A version of this article appeared in the 07/19/2021 issue of *Publishers Weekly* under the headline: A Hybrid Future for Children's Sales Reps.

Reaching Readers at the Dollar Store
By Karen Raugust | Jul 16, 2021

One of the fastest-growing sectors in retail over the past decade has been the value channel. This includes dollar stores and dollar sections, such as Target's Bullseye's Playground, as well as other low-price retail formats, such as off-price chains like Burlington and TJ Maxx. Books in dollar stores typically represent a small percentage of each chain's sales, and the category tends to be remainder driven. But there are opportunities for sales of new books, especially for children, if publishers can make the economics work.

"It's a very important channel for consumers to access incredible value, and that's important," said George Papp, CEO at Papp International, whose business was founded to sell books to dollar stores in the U.S., Canada, and Latin America. "It's a service to the communities these stores are based in. But it's a tricky market."

The top player among dollar retailers, Dollar General, has boasted same-store sales increases for 31 straight years and, with sales of more than $33 billion in 2020, ranks among the top 20 U.S. retailers, according to the National Retail Federation. In the pandemic-impacted year of 2020, its sales were up more than 20% over 2019. Not far behind are Dollar Tree and its Family Dollar division, which together brought in sales of more than $25 billion in 2020. Collectively, dollar stores saw sales rise 12% year-over-year in 2020, versus a 7% gain in 2019, according to Bloomberg Second Measure.

Meanwhile, as many retail stores have closed in recent years, dollar chains have taken the opposite path, even during the pandemic. Dollar General maintains 17,000 stores in 46 states (compared to 3,570 Walmart Supercenters in the U.S.) and is expected to add more than 1,000 stores in 2021. Dollar Tree and Family Dollar, which have 15,000 locations across the two chains, plan 591 new outlets this year.

"Dollar stores are looking for high-quality books at insane value, especially in the U.S.," Papp explained. That results in very low margins for publishers.

Beth Peters, cofounder of Dreamtivity—which was purchased by Readerlink Distribution Services in May, in part because of its strength in the value channel—pointed out that high volumes help compensate for those thin margins. A title might sell 10,000–30,000 units into a mass retailer, she said, but 100,000–150,000 units into a dollar store.

"The best thing about the value channel is it helps us get the proper balance between returnable vs. nonreturnable," Peters noted. Unlike most other retailers of books, dollar and similar stores purchase almost everything on a nonreturnable basis. "It guarantees a really good mix. If you can get to 70/30 or 60/40 returnable versus nonreturnable, that's good for the health of the overall business."

Wayne Bell, publisher and founder of Really Big Coloring Book Co., does business in the value channel primarily for competitive reasons. "If we were not there, there's someone else who would be there," he noted. He said he has to sell 14–18 books in a dollar store to earn a net profit equal to the average he normally gets from the sale of one book at most other retailers. "We own two high-end, high-speed printers, and we can be competitive as long as we get the paper at a reasonable price. But it's a very tough market."

Ben Ferguson, CEO of Bendon Publishing, which was built with the value channel in mind and is the dominant publishing player, said, "We constantly tweak our infrastructure, overhead, and costs to make sure we're competitive."

The fact that books command a tiny share of dollar retailers' total sales can also be a challenge. "Books are pretty much the lowest on the list of what they're buying," Papp said. "There's a lot of turnover in book buyers and not a lot of continuity. We have the most success when the buyer is involved and gives us feedback so we can change the product based on their suggestions."

What sells in the book aisle?

Coloring and activity books dominate the kids' assortment, but picture and story books, board books, and leveled readers can be found, especially in chains with higher value-channel price points of $5 or so. (Bibles, puzzle books, and cookbooks, as well as remaindered novels, are some of the key formats on the adult side.) And when selling into these stores, "the seasonal business is really important," Papp noted. In that regard, dollar store buyers are looking for good value for the price, which typically takes the form of books with large trim sizes and/or a large number of pages, as well as bells and whistles like glitter or foil on the covers.

Licensing also sells. "It's a good marriage of bringing the perceived value to the customer and making the best quality product you can within the overall margins," Peters said. "It's about big value and low price," Ferguson agreed. "The retailers are looking for as much margin as they can possibly get."

Peachtree Playthings recently signed a license with Disney to publish comic books and magazines to be sold through the value channel, where it also offers licensed products including stationery, night lights, coin banks, and the like.

Licensors have been increasing their focus on the value channel across all consumer products categories. "We have to reach parents and kids wherever they are," said Gabriela Arenas, v-p, global licensing at Sesame Workshop. "When you have 15,000 doors or 16,000 doors, often in places where there are no big-footprint stores for the neighborhood to access, we have to be there."

"The economics challenge us, but with that challenge comes innovation," said Lourdes Arocho, senior v-p, Paramount Pictures Licensing, Global Games, and Publishing at ViacomCBS Consumer Products, which handles licensing for Nickelodeon and other corporate divisions. "There are definitely opportunities to cross-promote product in this space. We have built some exciting cross-category programs this fall for the Paw Patrol movie."

Several chains are opening new, slightly higher-priced concepts that will give publishers some breathing room on margins, especially as costs for transportation and materials rise. "It opens up a whole new world," said Peters of Dreamtivity, which offers a range of formats at $1, $3, and $5.

Dollar General opened its $5-and-below Popshelf department in 2020 and has plans to expand to 50 locations by the end of 2021. Similarly, the 1,000-store chain Five Below, which already focuses on goods priced at $5 or less, hopes to expand its higher-priced Five Beyond section to 280 stores by year-end 2021. Dollar Tree expects to open combined Dollar Tree/Family Dollar locations in rural areas; these would carry both Family Dollar's range of household goods at various price points and Dollar Tree's $1-or-less product array.

"You can give more value at $3.99 or $5.99 than at $1.99," said Ferguson, who estimated that about 80% of Bendon's overall business to mass and value retailers involves products priced at $3.99 or higher.

No matter the price point, publishers need to commit to dollar stores and other value retailers to succeed in this market. "You have to develop programs for these low-price-point, high-volume stores," said Mark Tasman, president of Peachtree Playthings. "You can't sell one item. It's about how important you can be to them and how important they can be to you."

*

A version of this article appeared in the 07/19/2021 issue of *Publishers Weekly* under the headline: Reaching Readers Through Dollar Stores.

Veteran Editors on Their New Children's Imprints

By Claire Kirch | Aug 10, 2021

Despite the disruptions due to the pandemic, publishers are launching children's imprints at a record pace. Some companies, such as Peachtree Publishing Group and Sterling Publishing, want to expand into the lucrative teen market, with Peachtree Teen and Sterling Teen respectively. Another, Welbeck Children's Publishing in the U.K., is extending its reach into the global marketplace by launching its first two fiction imprints, Welbeck Flame and Orange Mosquito. Then there's Neon Squid, a Macmillan Children's Book Group imprint: it is focused on a smaller slice of the market with nonfiction intended to make complex subjects more accessible to young readers.

A number of new children's imprints are emerging from a confluence of factors: a publisher wants to fill a void in the marketplace, primarily with more diverse offerings, while an editor seeks to realize their vision. Several editors have even moved from one house to another in pursuit of their passion. Most recently, industry veteran Jill Davis joined Astra Publishing earlier this summer to launch a yet-to-be-named imprint dedicated to illustrated children's books.

Nine editors launching nine imprints during the pandemic recently reflected upon what drove them, what they hope to accomplish, and how the books they intend to publish will stand out in an already crowded marketplace. While most of these imprints will debut in fall 2022, a few editors already have introduced their lists.

Flamingo Books

Shortly before the pandemic erupted, Margaret Anastas moved from HarperCollins Children's Books, where she had served as editorial director, to Penguin Young Readers, to launch Flamingo Books, a picture book imprint under Viking Children's Books.

Anastas, a seasoned editor who worked at HarperCollins for 17 years, noted that her biggest challenge in launching an imprint at another house was doing so during a pandemic. "I was laser-focused on establishing Flamingo's place among all the other impressive imprints and divisions within PYR, and in getting to know the team," Anastas recalled. "Establishing a new work rhythm is tricky when you can't connect in person."

As for what Anastas hopes to accomplish with Flamingo, her goal is simple: she wants to create lifelong readers. "I never underestimate the impact a picture book can have on a child," she said. "Introducing children to their new favorite character, the unexpected page turn, or a catchy refrain that gets stuck in their head for days—that's what I hope to accomplish."

Christy Ottaviano Books

Last fall, Christy Ottaviano moved her eponymous 13-year-old imprint from Macmillan Children's Publishing Group to Little, Brown Books for Young Readers. The imprint will feature a mix of literary and commercial fiction and nonfiction for preschool through teen readers.

"We're fortunate to be able to work off two foundational pillars," Ottaviano told *PW*—"award-winning and author-focused publishing, which has always been the cornerstone of the imprint." Disclosing that her imprint will feature a mix of debut authors and house authors who followed her from Macmillan to LBYR, Ottaviano referred to the imprint's rebranded logo as symbolizing what she hopes to accomplish.

"Butterflies are symbolic of many important themes in life," she said, "Hope, renewal, change, fragility, strength, beauty, growth, and freedom. These are all themes that I feel represent the types of ideas we aim to capture in the books we publish."

The books, Ottaviano explained, will remain similar to those published under her previous imprint: "Books for children and teens that explore milestones, intersections, transitions and that foster emotional and educational growth in equal measure."

Little, Brown Books for Young Readers publisher Megan Tingley described Christy Ottaviano Books as an imprint designed to grow LBYR's list. "I've always felt that Christy is a kindred spirit," she said. "We share the same mission of publishing works that speak directly to young readers and that reflect the diversity of our world. Her books win the hearts and minds of readers, along with plenty of awards—and they backlist brilliantly."

Labyrinth Road

Liesa Abrams also switched houses last fall to launch a new imprint at Random House, Labyrinth Road, which will focus on middle grade and YA novels that, Abrams said, "marry commercial, high-concept hooks with character-driven stories." Unlike Ottaviano, though, this is the former Simon & Schuster editor's first imprint.

"It's a very different experience from having a full existing list of authors and titles going back years," Abrams admitted, adding that launching an imprint in 2020 created even more challenges, as she had to meet new colleagues and learn new systems and "office culture" remotely.

"I'm sure that one challenge of launching an imprint can often be the introduction of added demands on the time of various departments," Abrams said, "but so far I've been met only with excitement and enthusiasm. I was stunned and moved by the extensive imprint logo design options the design group created for me. I'm also aware that the titles on our first few seasons will carry extra weight of communicating clearly exactly what to expect from Labyrinth Road."

Labyrinth Road's YA offerings will contain such themes as sexuality and grief "that present inner labyrinths for characters to explore," Abrams explained, adding, "Representation in many forms is a key goal for the imprint, especially expanding the scope of readers who can see themselves within genres like fantasy—particularly queer and intersectional representation."

The middle grade series she will curate will be characterized "by the intersection of epic world-saving stakes with deeply emotional character journeys." Projects range from a medieval fantasy series featuring a non-binary protagonist fighting both dragons and a patriarchal society to a contemporary series about a queer Black boy who must defeat the Horsemen of the Apocalypse.

"I've long been an advocate for the notion that it's not only permissible but essential to tackle more complex, mature experiences and ideas about identity within middle grade series," Abrams said. "This is how we offer readers windows and mirrors to lives that are less than smooth, that contain twists and turns, and yes, sometimes jagged, painful edges."

Random House Books for Young Readers Group publisher Mallory Loehr, who persuaded Abrams to move from S&S and launch Labyrinth Road, disclosed that the two had discussed whether or not Abrams should take the helm of an existing imprint or launch a new one. "Her taste and strategy is very clear, both creatively and from a business perspective," Loehr said. "Pairing that with her success rate at building beloved, sustainable middle grade series, as well as strong YA, it ultimately felt right for Liesa to have her own imprint."

Joy Revolution

In addition, Random House is launching a children's imprint by a duo who may not have professional editorial experience, but certainly have expertise regarding teen romances: David and Nicola Yoon. The authors will—with the assistance of Delacorte Press editor Bria Ragin—acquire titles and shape Joy Revolution, a teen romance imprint by and about people of color.

In a joint statement, the Yoons wrote that they have long been frustrated with the "almost complete lack of POC representation in our beloved genre of romantic comedies" and have wanted "to carve out a safe space for love stories that star POC and allow the full breadth of their humanity."

The primary challenge, they noted, comes from the fact that they are, first and foremost, writers. "It's really important to keep our publisher and writer personae as separate as possible, in order to protect both," they wrote. "We don't want our specific writer aesthetic to get in the way of seeing the real potential of a manuscript," yet "we don't want to let buzzy market trends cloud our own artistic visions."

The Yoons told *PW* that they primarily hope to dispel stereotypes with Joy Revolution. "Black girls were always cartoonishly sassy sidekicks, never the hero, and

Asian men were always horribly emasculated foreigners or lab techs," they recalled of popular culture during their youth. "It sounds silly to say, but POC fall in love all the time and are heroes of their own epic romances. It's critically important to show that side to a broader audience, because if you don't counter bad stereotypes, bad stereotypes will simply persist."

The Yoons envision Joy Revolution books as "a safe place" where POC readers "can simply be swept away by a great story, free from the dread of running into some horribly typecast POC character. That's why the logo is a little heart just chillin' under a sturdy stone shelter—our imprint is a place to relax and just be yourself."

As for competition, they welcome it. "There's plenty of room for POC love stories, which is a nice way of saying there's a huge void to fill," they wrote. "In fact, we look forward to the day when the market is so rich with leading POC characters that we don't even have to make an obvious statement like 'POC fall in love'—because that's when the revolution will finally have been fulfilled."

As for the strategy behind enlisting authors to head an imprint, Delacorte executive editor Wendy Loggia expresses the rationale succinctly: "Romance readers are clamoring for stories about people of color and these two authors have star power. This imprint is dedicated to what [the Yoons] do best."

Anne Schwartz Books and Random House Studio

Besides recruiting a top editor from another company as well as two popular authors to launch new children's imprints, Random House has launched two imprints led by two veteran editors—Anne Schwartz and Lee Wade—who for 15 years had co-piloted Schwartz and Wade Books. Schwartz has transitioned to Anne Schwartz Books under the Knopf Books for Young Readers imprint, and Wade to Random House Studio.

"With Anne Schwartz Books, I'm launching an imprint for the fourth time, so it's almost old hat," Schwartz told *PW* of the new imprint, which will focus on picture books, with "a smattering" of middle grade and YA reads.

Schwartz hopes to acquire and create books "that will resonate deeply with young readers—that will comfort them, excite them, move them, motivate them, make them think, shape the way they see and interact with the world, and that they'll remember for years to come."

For her part, Wade promised "a broad and diverse list of titles that are each thoughtfully and respectively edited and art directed, gorgeously designed and produced, and that become reliable backlist titles that live on for a long time."

RISE x Penguin Workshop

Another PYR imprint, RISE x Penguin Workshop, which launched in fall 2020, is meant to "create literature that empowers babies, toddlers, and preschoolers,"

Publishing director Cecily Kaiser hopes that the board book and early picture book imprint inspires others to "create, stock, sell, lend, teach, and read aloud such books for the youngest audience."

Kaiser compares launching an imprint to childbirth, explaining, "The long build-up to the moment in which the imprint meets the world is arduous: the preparations are endless, with waves of anxiety balanced by waves of giddy anticipation. You are growing something very quietly, very internally, that might change the world! You know its books are special, but that it's entering a world with many other special books. You know you'll have to work special hard to advocate for it to be seen and heard, whether it's one of several children's imprints in a house, or the only children's imprint in an otherwise adult house. And the naming! Having named two human children of my own, I can unequivocally say that naming an imprint is more difficult. But when you find the name, it sings!"

Kaiser, a children's industry veteran who joined Penguin Workshop in 2019 after overseeing the launch of the Abrams Appleseed imprint for preschool books and the re-launch of Phaidon's children's imprint, noted, "Children ages 0–5 deserve authentic and powerful books that transcend basic concepts, fuzzy animals, and superficial love. I hope that the existence of RISE draws attention to the fact that publishing for this age group demands the same level of consideration and grace as goes into the creation of award-winning books."

When asked how RISE releases can stand out in a crowded marketplace, Kaiser explained that the books will do so by virtue of their subject matter, "written authentically by authors with first-hand knowledge, lived or learned," and their aesthetic, "often involving artists working in their 'adult' style, in which their passion shines through and speaks to young children." But, she added, she actually hopes RISE books will not stand out. "I'd prefer the 0–5 shelves to be full of books like these," she said. "I'd prefer that anyone in a bookstore or library be able to approach the youngest bookshelves, close their eyes, spin around, and point to a book that makes the reader feel smart, safe, capable, and important."

Heartdrum and Quill Tree Books

Finally, at HarperCollins Children's Books, editorial director Rosemary Brosnan recently launched not one but two imprints: Heartdrum, in partnership with author Cynthia Leitich Smith, a member of the Muscogee Creek Nation, and Quill Tree Books.

With Heartdrum, Brosnan said, HarperCollins hopes to "create a welcoming space for Native and First Nations authors and illustrators," with picture books, chapter books, middle grade and YA fiction, graphic novels, and nonfiction.

"We're working with debut writers and illustrators as well as previously published ones," she explained. "We want Native children and teens to recognize themselves in the books we publish, and we are focusing on Native young people as the heroes of their own stories. We also want non-Native kids and teens to have a chance to read about contemporary Native people."

Brosnan pointed out that Heartdrum is the first Indigenous-focused imprint from a major publisher. "Small, Native-owned presses have been doing the work for years," Brosnan noted. "And so have some university presses. But with Heartdrum, we are doing something new and very exciting, focusing only on Native and First Nations creatives. We have published five books under the Heartdrum imprint so far, and together they have garnered 19 starred reviews."

As for Quill Tree, Brosnan described it as a general imprint that publishes picture books, chapter books, middle grade and YA fiction, graphic novels and nonfiction by authors from underrepresented communities with strong points of view. "The imprint is really a continuation of what my wonderful team and I have been publishing for a number of years," she said, "with the addition of an imprint name."

Brosnan believes that because so many authors are writing essential books for increasingly diverse audiences, a new imprint like Quill Tree is not so much competing with other imprints as "complementing one another, making sure that great authors and illustrators will find a good home, and that readers have plenty of wonderful books.

WORKING IN PUBLISHING

THE PW PUBLISHING INDUSTRY SALARY SURVEY, 2019

More small strides were made in 2018 in addressing issues of pay disparity and diversification of the workforce

BY JIM MILLIOT | NOV 15, 2019

The publishing industry made more incremental improvements in 2018 in several areas that have been long-standing trouble spots, according to *PW*'s annual salary and job survey. The industry's racial makeup became slightly more diverse last year—though, with whites comprising 84% of the workforce, publishing remains an overwhelmingly white business. In 2017, whites comprised 86% of publishing employees. (This year's survey was sent out to employees at publishing houses in September and we received 699 responses, the majority of which, 66%, came from trade houses.)

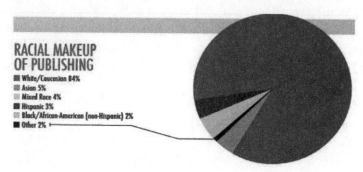

RACIAL MAKEUP
OF PUBLISHING
White/Caucasian 84%
Asian 5%
Mixed Race 4%
Hispanic 3%
Black/African-American (non-Hispanic) 2%
Other 2%

The pay gap between men and women closed by $7,000 in 2018 compared to 2017, but that reduction was due to a decline in the median compensation for men in 2018 compared to 2017 (compensation fell from $87,000 to $80,000), while median pay for women held even at $60,000. A major reason women maintained their pay levels is that, in the area of operation and production—where women have long held a greater share of the jobs than men—they outearned men in 2018 by $13,000; in 2017, men earned more than women.

2017 was the first time women held a greater share of management jobs than men, and in 2018 they once again had a majority of jobs in that area, though their share fell to 52% (from 59% in 2017). Still, the median compensation for a woman in management was $126,000 last year, up from $110,000 in 2017. Male managers also had an increase, with their median pay rising to $139,000 (from $118,000 in 2017).

A key factor in the overall gap between the pay of men and women is that men have more experience than women. The median number of years of men in the industry who responded to the survey was 17.5, compared to 10 years for women. Far more men have been in the industry for more than 20 years than women—38% compared to 17%—while women, as has long been the case, dominated the ranks of workers with three years or less experience by a count of 12% to 5%. Moreover, 29% of women who reported to the survey had three to seven years of experience, compared to 17% of men.

THE NONWHITE EXPERIENCE

Nonwhite survey respondents were much more likely to be new to the industry than whites. Nineteen percent of nonwhites said they have been in publishing for three years or less, compared to 10% of whites. Employees with three to seven years of time in the industry accounted for 38% of nonwhite respondents, compared to 25% of whites. Only 10% of nonwhite respondents said they have been in the industry for more than 20 years, compared to 23% for white workers.

Editorial is the department that has attracted the highest percentage of nonwhite employees, with 44% of nonwhite respondents working in that department. Thirty-five percent of non-whites said they were in sales and marketing, while only 5% of nonwhites were in management, compared to 10% of whites.

In terms of job satisfaction, 42% of nonwhite respondents said they were either extremely or very satisfied with their jobs, compared to 50% of white employees. Forty-two percent of nonwhites were somewhat satisfied with their jobs (36% for whites), while 17% were unsatisfied with their jobs (14% for

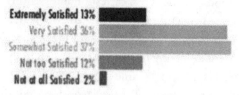

JOB SATISFACTION

- Extremely Satisfied 13%
- Very Satisfied 36%
- Somewhat Satisfied 37%
- Not too Satisfied 12%
- Not at all Satisfied 2%

HAS DIVERSITY IMPROVED IN THE WORKFORCE?

	White/Caucasian	Non-White
YES	50%	44%
NO	25%	38%
Don't Know	24%	18%
Total Respondents:	577	108

whites). Of those who were somewhat or not satisfied with their jobs, low salary was the top problem for both whites (62%) and nonwhites (68%). For the most part, there wasn't much discrepancy between the complaints of whites and nonwhites about the causes for dissatisfaction with their job, with one exception: 30% of nonwhites said their work was unfulfilling, compared to 17% of whites.

FUTURE EXPECTATIONS

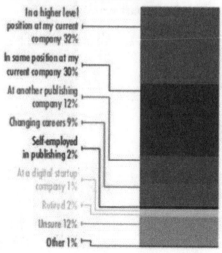

- In a higher level position at my current company 32%
- In same position at my current company 30%
- At another publishing company 12%
- Changing careers 9%
- Self-employed in publishing 2%
- At a digital startup company 1%
- Retired 2%
- Unsure 12%
- Other 1%

Perhaps because a high percentage of nonwhites have been in publishing for a relatively short period of time, 43% of respondents said they expected to be at a higher position at their current company in two years, compared to only 29% for whites. Conversely, 33% of whites said they expect to be in the same position at their current company in two years—much higher than the 15% of nonwhites who expect to be in the same position.

Progress made in diversifying publishing's workforce continues to be viewed differently by whites and nonwhites. Fifty percent of whites believe strides have been made in diversifying publishing, compared to 44% of nonwhites. Nonwhites also have a stronger belief that little progress has been made in adding more people of color to publishing, with 38% saying no strides have been made, while only 25% of whites believe not much progress has been made.

Both whites and nonwhites have a more positive view of the industry's success in diversifying the types of titles published: 80% of whites said progress has been made, as did 74% of nonwhites. But a still-significant percentage of people of color, 19%, believe no progress has been made in diversifying title output, compared to only 9% of whites.

WOMEN STILL DOMINATE THE WORKFORCE

The gender composition of publishing did not change in 2018—80% of respondents said they were women, 19% were men, and 1% were nonbinary.

For the 2017 survey, we asked for the first time if companies had sexual harassment policies in place, and 77% of respondents said their companies did. That percentage rose slightly in 2018, to 80%. However, a higher percentage of respondents this year, 62%, said they don't know if complaints are followed up on, compared to 50% last year.

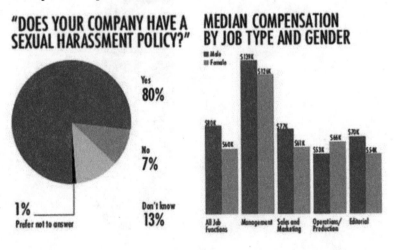

"DOES YOUR COMPANY HAVE A SEXUAL HARASSMENT POLICY?"

Yes 80%
No 7%
Don't know 13%
1% Prefer not to answer

MEDIAN COMPENSATION BY JOB TYPE AND GENDER

For the third year in a row, the median pay raise in 2018 was 2.7%. Forty percent of respondents who received a raise in 2018 said it was a merit increase, while 32% said it was a cost of living increase. Twenty percent of respondents said they received no raise in 2018.

*

A version of this article appeared in the 11/18/2019 issue of *Publishers Weekly* under the headline: Inching Forward.

WORKING FROM HOME TOOK HOLD IN 2020

BY JIM MILLIOT | DEC 18, 2020

(Editor's note: The Covid-19 pandemic forced PW to cancel its annual salary and jobs survey this year. Instead, we sent out a smaller survey to assess the impact of Covid-19 and the Black Lives Matter movement on the publishing industry in 2020. The questionnaire was emailed to 7,023 PW subscribers who work at publishing companies.)

In response to a *PW* survey assessing the impact of Covid-19 on work policies, 93% of publishing employees said they have worked remotely at some point this year—and of those who have, 96% said they continue to do so. The survey was conducted online between November 10 and December 1 and drew 404 responses. (Responses were from individual employees and were not grouped by company.)

More than 97% of respondents in the New England and mid-Atlantic regions reported having worked from home at some point this year, and nearly all of those who have are still not back at their offices. In the southern and western U.S., 85% of respondents have worked from home, and more than 92% of those still are.

Employees at bigger publishers were more likely to work from home than those at smaller presses. Only 77% of respondents at publishers with annual revenue under $1 million said their companies had work-from-home options (and all respondents who worked from home at some point this year still are).

Among the large number of employees still working from home, 76% said their companies had not yet set firm return-to-the-office dates. New England publishers seemed to have a better idea of when employees will return—35% of respondents in the region said they have been given a return date—than those in the west, where only 11% of respondents said a date was fixed. By a wide margin, July 2021 was the month targeted for returns to offices, particularly for respondents in the mid-Atlantic.

Commuting on mass transit and proper social distancing protocols are the two biggest concerns employees expressed about returning to the office. Those concerns were cited by about 70% of all respondents. In the mid-Atlantic, which includes New York City and other major metropolitan areas, where subways and buses are key, 89% of respondents said traveling on mass transit is their biggest concern. In all other regions, office safety protocols are the number-one concern. Several respondents listed other reasons for a reluctance to return to the office, among them, losing a better work-life balance, the cost of commuting, and having moved to less expensive locations. Others noted that their offices have been permanently closed.

OTHER NEW MEASURES

Working remotely was not the only way publishers reacted to Covid-19. Forty-five percent of respondents said their companies had instituted a hiring freeze, and 26% said their companies had laid people off. Salary cuts, furloughs, and reductions in hours were some of the other ways publishers looked to save money.

Publishers have partially restored some of the temporary cost-saving measures they took this spring. Sixty-one percent of employees whose companies instituted furloughs said those furloughs had ended, while 25% said furloughs were still intact (14% didn't respond or weren't sure). Salary cuts had been restored at companies where 72% of respondents work.

A hiring freeze is the tool most companies are still using to control costs, with 47% of respondents saying freezes are still in place at their companies. Only 29% said freezes have been lifted (24% didn't respond or weren't sure). Publishers seem to be split on restoring hours: 46% of respondents said hours are back to pre-pandemic levels, and an equal number said hours are still reduced.

TITLE COUNTS AND TRADE SHOWS

Moving the launch of titles out of the spring in hopes that the effects of the pandemic would soon ease was a strategy used by many trade houses. Some publishers also ended up cutting titles: 30% of respondents said their companies had reduced their 2020 title counts, while another 30% said no cuts were made (the remaining 40% said their companies' title counts stayed the same, or they weren't sure). Publishers appear to be optimistic about 2021: 70% of respondents said their companies' title counts in 2021 will remain the same or increase over those of 2020.

One of the industry staples disrupted by Covid-19 is conventions and trade shows, most of which have moved online or been canceled. Sixty-one percent of employees said they don't know whether their companies planned to attend in-person trade shows in 2021, but 30% said their companies had no plans to do so. In addition, 56% of employees said they would feel uncomfortable attending in-person shows next year. Only 8% said they would have no worries about attending live events.

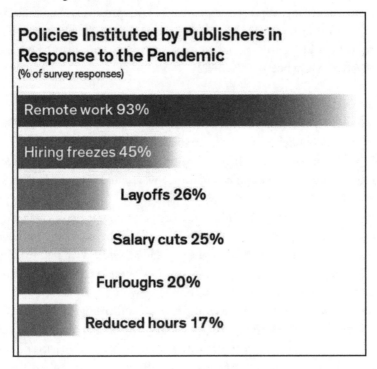

Policies Instituted by Publishers in Response to the Pandemic
(% of survey responses)

Remote work 93%

Hiring freezes 45%

Layoffs 26%

Salary cuts 25%

Furloughs 20%

Reduced hours 17%

*

A version of this article appeared in the 12/21/2020 issue of *Publishers Weekly* under the headline: No Place Like Home.

ARE BOOK BIZ DIVERSITY EFFORTS STARTING TO KICK IN?

BY JIM MILLIOT | DEC 31, 2020

Publishers appear to have responded to calls last year to increase their diversity efforts as part of a national outcry for social justice reforms. Seventy-five percent of the 404 employees at publishing companies who responded to a *PW* survey on workplace and diversity changes said their company had increased their diversity programs in the last 12 months. (Survey results on workplace policies ran in the December 21 issue of *PW*.) In general, the larger the publisher, the more likely the company had made a change to its diversity, equity, and inclusion programs. Fifty percent of employees who work at companies with sales of under $1 million said their company had instituted some form of greater DEI efforts, while more than 90% of staffers at companies with revenue of more than $100 million said their company had broadened the scope of their DEI programs. The survey was conducted online between November 10 and December 1. (Responses were from individual employees and were not grouped by company.)

Just under half (49%) of respondents who work at publishers that have added DEI initiatives think those programs will help bring change to the industry, while 38% said they didn't know. Only 13% said they thought the new actions would lead to no real change.

Asked to give examples of new or greater DEI efforts begun by their company, the most frequently cited actions fell into a number of general categories.

Broadening recruitment efforts to attract more BIPOC employee candidates

- Expanding outreach at HBCUs
- Offering more remote internships and work opportunities

- Hiring more BIPOC freelancers and contractors
- Changing wording on job descriptions to eliminate bias
- Establishing dedicated BIPOC internships and fellowships

Raising awareness of the importance of DEI
- Hiring executive to oversee companywide DEI initiatives
- Forming DEI committees within different departments
- Holding companywide training and educational workshops and town hall meetings
- Adding a retail manager to work with BIPOC-owned stores

Adding diverse authors
- Auditing author demographics
- Starting BIPOC imprints
- Increasing marketing support for BIPOC titles
- Partnering with new organizations to find new voices

Raising entry-level salaries

Sample comments from respondents:

"We've hired a v-p of diversity, equity, and inclusion, as well as a sales and marketing specialist focused on diversity. We've offered anti-racism training. We've allocated extra budget for marketing campaigns for BIPOC titles."

"We've had a huge uptick in activity after hiring a manager of inclusion and diversity. There are many employee resource groups for race, disability, sexual identity. Our CEO is a champion of inclusion and diversity, and there is a growing inclusive culture in our company."

"We are examining the backlist to identify and address titles with content that is offensive or noninclusive; we have created employee resource groups for various cultural groups."

"We've analyzed our title lists across imprints and pinpointed our weaknesses in terms of gender and race demographics."

"We've instituted companywide anti-racist reading and group discussions, as well as new anti-discrimination and harassment training programs required for all employees."

"I am on newly formed Diversity Councils and Diverse Employee Resource Groups that are doing *fantastic* work!"

"Hired a DEI officer. Not much else, alas."

Publishers' Response to Diversity in 2020					
(based on employee responses)					
Size of Company	Under $1M	$1M–$9.9M	$10M–$99.9M	$100M–$499.9M	$500M+
Increased diversity programs	50%	70%	75%	94%	97%
Did not increase diversity programs	35%	18%	13%	0%	2%
Don't know	15%	12%	12%	6%	1%

*

A version of this article appeared in the 01/04/2021 issue of *Publishers Weekly* under the headline: Diversity Efforts Start to Kick In.

SURVEY REVEALS A NEED FOR GREATER WORKPLACE INCLUSIVITY

BY CALVIN REID | JUN 25, 2021

People of Color in Publishing and Latinx in Publishing collaborated on an online survey in summer and fall 2018, reaching out to current and former BIPOC industry members about the extent to which they've experienced racism on the job. The results of the survey are now being released in a report, "Workplace Racism Survey," that documents the ways racism manifests itself at publishing houses. (Organizers delayed the release of the findings because of the pandemic and the uncertainty it created about the future of the industry.)

Of those who responded, 72.9% reported experiencing microaggressions—brief, commonplace encounters that communicate racial prejudice or cultural diminishment. And the survey chronicles numerous instances in which junior and midlevel BIPOC professionals encountered half-hearted or poorly managed efforts at diversity where they work. Of the people of color who responded, 86% cited unfair or extra workloads placed on them in order to educate their colleagues about racism, while 47.4% said they had been asked to act as ad hoc sensitivity readers without compensation.

"The burden on BIPOC to educate white colleagues is an onerous task that contributes to burnout," according to the report. "Not only does this unpaid labor take time away from BIPOC employees' own pursuits and career advancement, but it sometimes results in repercussions."

The report also offers specific guidelines to white colleagues, encouraging them to support their BIPOC colleagues and avoid "bystander racism"—witnessing and recognizing a microaggression but not challenging it or providing support to the BIPOC staff forced to deal with it.

The "Workplace Racism Survey" is the latest in a series of strategic efforts by People of Color in Publishing and Latinx in Publishing—along with similar efforts aimed at children's publishing organized by We Need Diverse Books—to expose and decry racism and microaggressions in publishing and offer pathways to foster diversity, equity, and inclusion.

Survey participants responded anonymously and work at Big Five houses as well as small independent publishers, though no publishers are cited by name. There were 211 submissions (190 current and 21 former book workers), with answers to yes-or-no questions supported by written responses that describe respondents' experiences. The report breaks down respondents by race or ethnic background, as well as job type: editorial (103), marketing/publicity (85), production (31), sales (24), and design (21).

Despite actions taken in the past year to bring more diversity into publishing, the survey's findings remain relevant, those associated with the report said. The goal of the survey, according to Kait Feldmann, the director of special projects for People of Color in Publishing and a senior editor at HarperCollins, is to "start the conversation again." She added, "Things have not improved in the workplace as much as we hoped: the issue of microaggressions goes unresolved, and we need to shake our white colleagues awake. We worried about the survey being three years old, that maybe things are different now—but no, they are not."

Saraciea Fennell, who is a publicist and the founder of the Bronx Is Reading book festival, and also the board chair and communications director of Latinx in Publishing and the director of public relations and an advisory board member for People of Color in Publishing, said, "We've had conversations about how racist the publishing industry is, but the conversation has been about the books and not about the industry's professionals. This takes the conversation to another, deeper level."

Nancy Mercado, the board secretary and special events director at Latinx in Publishing and the associate publisher and editorial director at Dial Books for Young Readers, said, "Every institution in the U.S. is built on white supremacy, and book publishing is no different." She added that the industry hasn't changed much since 2018. "Liberals and left people in the industry may be congratulating themselves, but if you work at a toxic place, these are the answers you get from the people most affected."

The report also offers specific information and comments on the ways microaggressions function in the workplace—from "showcasing" POC staff inappropriately to mistaking individuals of the same race for one another and making blanket statements about a given culture or race. The report also looks at the issues surrounding both staff- and company-led diversity committees, as well as problems with human resources departments (76% of respondents did not report racist behavior to HR, and of the 24% who did, most said it was ineffective).

And though the survey did not ask participants to discuss the content of the books their companies publish or their marketing efforts, most respondents brought the topic up. They offered numerous examples of ill-informed comments from coworkers—from claims that Black people don't read, to an expressed assumption that every book must appeal to a white readership, or that racist historical figures in works should be tolerated.

Feldman said the tumultuous nationwide protests in 2020 in response to the murder of George Floyd were a "wake-up call" for the book industry. But she also emphasized that the protests may have led to even more microaggressions, as publishers lean on their BIPOC staff to address the reality of racial inequity in the workplace.

The survey organizers interviewed acknowledged the strategic nature of the report and their organizations' tactical approach to addressing the issue of racism in the workplace. "We wanted data to be accompanied by action points," Feldman said. "When people talk about microaggressions and our white colleagues ask, 'What can we do?' we didn't want BIPOC staff to have to come up with the solutions."

Mercado described the survey as "data plus storytelling, words of direct experience that were painful to read through."

The report provides a detailed plan for "dismantling racism in publishing" that includes actions designed specifically for entry-level employees, management, and leaders. Talking about the issues outlined in the report, Feldman said, is a start. "Amplify the dialogue, share this up the corporate ladder, even though it will make people uncomfortable," she added. "If you see a POC addressing an issue around racism and it's dismissed, jump in and talk about it. White allies want to help but don't back their POC colleagues up."

This dialogue, survey organizers emphasized, will encompass issues like how to improve retention rates. Among the factors prompting BIPOC employees to leave publishing, respondents said, are a lack of recognition, preferential treatment of white colleagues, and the struggle to live on entry-level salaries in one of the most expensive cities in the country. The report also noted the need for mentoring, especially given the lack of senior BIPOC staff. Thirty-one percent of BIPOC respondents who've been working in the industry for less than five years are already acting as mentors, "to support others despite not having that same support themselves," the authors of the report noted.

And as publishing begins to emerge from the pandemic, the survey organizers see an opportunity for the industry to change its practices in a manner that will address racism and a range of issues related to staff equity, job satisfaction, and retention. "The pandemic has shown that the business of publishing is more flexible than the industry thought," Feldman said. "There are other ways to do our business. You don't have to be in New York."

She added, "The pandemic has also made publishers of every size evaluate where they spend money. How will we reevaluate how things are done, spending on buildings and real estate, the need for salary increases, finding out what employees need and investing in them, and reaching out to find diverse voices to publish?"

Mercado said, "All of this must come from the top down. Racial justice needs to be emphasized from the top and not be lip service or dumped on POC staff."

The report will be available on the websites of People of Color in Publishing and Latinx in Publishing.

Sample Findings from the Workplace Racism Survey

92% of respondents reported attending meetings where they were the only people of color present

61% of respondents said that they modify their behavior to fit in to their workplace culture

40% of respondents believe they have been overlooked for advancement opportunities because of their race

*

A version of this article appeared in the 06/28/2021 issue of *Publishers Weekly* under the headline: Amplify the Dialogue.

TIME FOR PUBLISHERS TO BROADEN THEIR VIEW

A multicultural marketing expert says publishers need a better understanding of people of color's interests

BY LEYLHA AHUILE | MAR 13, 2020

The publication of *American Dirt* raised a host of issues that the publishing industry is likely to be dealing with for some time. The release of the novel forced the industry to ask who should write certain books, reignited the conversation over the lack of diversity within the industry, and also exposed the continued lack of understanding of the Hispanic/Latino consumer by most all publishers.

On January 29, a statement by Bob Miller, president of *American Dirt* publisher Flatiron Books, noted that the publishing house was "surprised by the anger that has emerged [in response to the book] from members of the Latinx and publishing communities." The anger was the result of Flatiron's demonstrated lack of understanding of Latino readers. This lack of understanding is by no means unique to the imprint but is a reflection of a prevalent problem within the book publishing industry. It is clear that the gatekeepers in publishing do not reflect, nor do they appreciate, the complexities of Latinos. Latinos are not a homogenous group; they are as vastly different as the general population, but with the added intricacy of acculturation.

The vast majority of adult trade books are written and published with the white, non-Hispanic reader in mind, at the exclusion of multicultural readers. Can the publishing industry afford to continue on this path? The consumer landscape has greatly changed in the last 20 years. The country has become much more diverse: almost 40% of the U.S. population is nonwhite, and almost 50% of Gen Zers are from communities of color.

This is a shift the industry must recognize and address, as most other industries are already devoting greater resources to capture revenue from diverse communities. Publishers can't afford to continue publishing for 60% of Americans while excluding the rest. It just doesn't make business sense.

Some publishers think they have solved the problem by having an imprint or two dedicated to books by authors of color, but diverse voices should be part of all publishing plans and not relegated to a single or limited number of imprints. Creating an imprint for these titles often leaves their authors pigeonholed and without the possibility of reaching wider audiences.

Marketers and publishers also need to go beyond the thinking that Latino readers will only read books written by Latinos or that Black readers will only read Black authors. That is a simplistic formula publishers often use to reach nonwhite audiences, but it will never deliver on the true potential of reaching multicultural readers. This signals a problem with an industry that lacks understanding of the multicultural consumers and seldom markets to them.

According to the U.S. Census Bureau, in 2019 there were 58 million Latinos in the U.S., making up 18% of the total U.S. population. Based on 2019 data from research firm MRI-Simmons, 13% of non-Hispanic white consumers had purchased a book (print or digital) within the three months prior to the survey, but only 7% of Hispanics had done so. Some will see this data and say Latinos don't buy books, yet some books have been wildly successful among Latinos. For example, *Unbreakable*, the autobiography of singer Jenni Rivera, also published in Spanish as *Inquebrantable*, went on to sell a total of more than 300,000 copies, according to Simon & Schuster.

A diversified workforce will only take a company so far. If people of color don't have seats at the table when editorial and marketing decisions are being made, then publishers shouldn't be surprised if the problem of engaging multicultural consumers persists. Increasing the number of employees of color is important, but publishers need to ensure they have staff in positions of influence with true expertise and knowledge of multicultural consumers.

American Dirt might have kicked up a storm, but it has also served as a wake-up call for the publishing industry. Some have answered the call. The nonprofit group Latinx in Publishing, a network of book professionals, has launched a new initiative called the Writers Mentorship Program. The program is aimed at offering unpublished and/or unagented writers who identify as Latino to partner with an experienced published Latino author in order to "strengthen their craft, gain industry knowledge, and expand their professional connections."

Though this is a small but significant step, a seismic shift is needed. Publishers cannot continue to look at the books they publish through the same set of outdated lenses. They need a new perspective that allows them to see the entirety of the consumer landscape. Solving the problem should not be treated as a public relations tactic but rather as a way to grow one's business.

*

Leylha Ahuile is the editor of *PW*'s Books in Spanish department and has led multicultural marketing for various organizations, including eBay.

A version of this article appeared in the 03/16/2020 issue of *Publishers Weekly* under the headline: Time for Publishers to Broaden Their View.

HOW THE BOOK BUSINESS CAN, AND MUST, BUILD A NEW FUTURE

A Black author challenges publishing to be more daring in creating space for all writers

BY MYCHAL DENZEL SMITH | JUN 5, 2020

Books have, for so many of us, been a lifeline. The clichés and platitudes about them being a portal to other worlds, that books can change and save lives, that they help connect us to something bigger than ourselves, are all true. I know that from my own experience and because in moments like the one we are in now, where thousands of protestors have taken to the streets in response to the continued police violence against Black people, thousands more people are online sharing resources to help people understand the importance of this movement and how we got here. They are sharing books.

Because of the nature of the issue, people are largely sharing books by and about Black people, though there are plenty of others that have become key to forming an antiracist worldview. There are the old stand-bys, of course, like *The Fire Next Time* by James Baldwin and *The Souls of Black Folks* by W.E.B. Du Bois, new classics such as *The New Jim Crow* by Michelle Alexander and *The Warmth of Other Suns* by Isabel Wilkerson, and new books that probe old questions of the American racial divide, such as *Minor Feelings* by Cathy Park Hong, *Heavy* by Kiese Laymon, and *Eloquent Rage* by Brittney Cooper. These are only examples. There are hundreds more.

Books afford us the opportunity to read about our past and present while engaging with ideas that will help us to imagine our future. We are reminded that it is our duty to create a new antiracist paradigm. And while we're thankful for the existence of these books, the path that many of them took to get here reflects the very racist structure that these books are meant to challenge. It is not only that the world of books is as white as every other major institution in America; it is that it makes nonwhite writers perform their deservingness in a way that is discouraging at best and prohibitive at worst.

The book business is a business, and the constraints that come from needing to sell a product are certainly understood. The book-buying public is also fickle, and it's not clear where the winds will move from moment to moment. But that is all the more reason for the book industry to not tether itself to the shifting tastes and desires of the public, which has a way of hemming in authors, so concerned with our future publishing potential, that we are asked to produce books solely because they have the potential to sell quickly. For writers of color, this more often than not means that we are called upon to produce work that responds to a particular moment of social unrest related to our racial group and that mines our personal stories for sympathetic or tragic narratives that are easily consumed by white audiences. Or we are called upon to write inspirational stories, ones in which we've directly confronted the racism that overdetermines our lives and won. We are asked to perform either our sadness, our triumph, or both, because these kinds of stories soothe the guilt of the imagined white audience, who believe themselves to be engaged in some kind of righteous act by way of learning about someone who does not look like them or share their life experience.

The problem here feels as though it should be obvious, but in case it is not: these stories, as consumed by white readers, do little to nothing to change institutional racism. At best, they expose white people to stories about nonwhite people, but exposure has its limitations, especially when what these narratives can reinforce is the distance white people can put between themselves and the systems that are responsible for creating these stories. For writers of color, it limits the imagination, artistically and politically, to constantly be responding to white readers' voyeurism, and it is exhausting to know that they will do precisely nothing even after they have read the last page.

What white readers do or do not do as a result of reading is not the responsibility of the book industry, but what the book world must recognize is that it has potential to do so much more. Each arm of the industry must do more to be more inclusive, of course, but it cannot stop at bringing in nonwhite faces to fill existing roles. Everyone in the book industry must grant themselves permission to be a bit more daring, to create space for every writer to produce the most challenging work possible, even when that does not fit the established narratives of minority trauma and/or success. It can stop demanding that nonwhite writers perform their stories for white audiences, wrapping them in neat packages that are digestible and ultimately meaningless. The industry cannot be so precious about its own standing; it must be willing to take its lumps and face the prospect of its own reckoning.

An antiracist future requires a self-reflective present. Books taught me that.

*

Mychal Denzel Smith is the author of the forthcoming book *Stakes Is High: Life After the American Dream* and the bestselling *Invisible Man, Got the Whole World Watching*. His work has appeared in *Artforum*, Harper's, the *Nation*, the *New Republic*, the *New York Times*, *Oxford American*, the *Washington Post*, and more.

A version of this article appeared in the 06/08/2020 issue of *Publishers Weekly* under the headline: Building a New Future.

HOW TO GET INTO THE
PUBLISHING INDUSTRY

BY DARA KUSHNER AND SUSAN GORDON

The publishing industry is evolving, and as with many other industries, getting your foot in the door can be challenging. But by using a strategy of research, networking, and effort, you will find that there are endless opportunities available. A lot of different types of talented people are needed in publishing for various roles, including publicity and promotion, editing, marketing, finance, sales, art and design, production, information technology, audio, and more. So where do you start?

Research. Research is an essential first step for getting into the publishing industry. Publishing careers typically encompass a wide variety of skills such as editing, copywriting, and media relations. Explore all areas of publishing to understand the requirements of various positions and be flexible about what department might suit you. With the digital nature of publishing changing by the day, it is imperative to do your research to become familiar with all of the different publishers to determine which companies fit best with your goals and interests, and to decide what area or areas you are most passionate about. Take it a step further and research what is on the *New York Times* bestseller lists and familiarize yourself with industry trends.

Networking. Just like with the entertainment industry, publishing is all about who you know. Networking is key to getting a job in the publishing industry and will greatly increase your chances of success. This would include connecting via LinkedIn or Twitter and targeting what types of professionals you want to connect with, where you want to make contacts, and knowing what questions you want to ask them. In addition to LinkedIn, look at sites that cater to the publishing industry such as Publishers Lunch, Mediabistro, and Bookjobs. com to check out ideas on jobs and companies that might be expanding. Try to connect with the right people in your desired roles to get informational interviews—these will provide you with real-life experience and information to find out more about the job and if it suits your personality and interests. Consider joining organizations such as Women's National Book Association (www.wnba-books.org) and the Young to Publishing Group (www.youngto-publishing.com), just to name a few, as well as online groups. And networking in person as much as you can (as Covid-19 restrictions lift).

Internships and Education. Consider internships if you are still in college or early in your career. Internships allow you to network, get hands-on experience in the industry, and add more achievements and real-life experience to your résumé. Bookjobs.com lists internships, general industry information, and additional publishing programs. Additionally, it might be helpful to consider taking advanced courses within the area of publishing you are interested in pursuing. Massive open online classes (MOOCs) offered by Coursera and Udacity are another option for learning some new skills or polishing already acquired ones. There are also major summer publishing programs such as New York University's Summer Publishing Institute, Columbia University's Publishing Course, and the Denver Publishing Institute. All of these offer intensive programs to acquire training for the publishing industry.

Skills/Résumé. Freelancing and temp work are also good options for both networking and gaining experience. Keep honing your skills and be able to demonstrate your excellent verbal and written communication skills as well as computer and social networking skills. Having relevant transferable skills is golden and is the best way to figure out what those are is to try out several areas and see what suits you best. Additionally, don't forget that every role in publishing requires excellent editing skills and keen attention to detail, so make sure that your résumé is completely error-free.

Keeping an open mind. Be flexible and keep an open mind about other areas of publishing. While editorial might be the most sought-after area, there are vast opportunities within design, marketing, audio, rights, and sales as well. Digital technology is changing the publishing landscape. Be open to relocation, because publishing hubs such as New York City might offer more in-person openings, but be aware that many roles that might not have been previously available to someone outside New York City can now be done remotely or hybrid due to the post-Covid-19 landscape.

Be flexible and embrace your passion for publishing. With the right research, networking, skills, and résumé building, along with the vast array of publishing roles that exist for entry-level job seekers, the opportunities are endless.

*

Dara Kushner is a research assistant at Lynne Palmer Executive Recruitment, Inc. Dara is a media professional who started off as a freelance writer for magazines before pivoting to celebrity photography, a field in which she ran her own company for close to 20 years. Her images are syndicated through many of the top photo agencies and are published daily across all entertainment and news platforms, both digital and print, throughout the world. Her work has also been featured in gallery shows, books, and advertising.

Susan Gordon is the president and owner of Lynne Palmer Executive Recruitment, Inc. Susan joined Lynne Palmer Executive Recruitment as a recruiter in 1983. Before joining the company, Susan was on staff in the human resources department at Random House. She purchased the company in 1989, and from that time on has endeavored to expand the company's success, creating new departments to keep pace with the publishing/media industry's ever-expanding demand for qualified personnel at all levels. As an active member of the publishing community, Susan is a speaker at University of Denver Publishing annual publishing seminar. Previous engagements have also included NYU Publishing Institute, Society for Scholarly Publishing, Pace University, Bookbuilders, Women's National Book Group, Manhattan Publishing Group, and other various publishing associations across the country.

14 PUBLISHING ASSOCIATIONS AND ORGANIZATIONS

Association of American Literary Agents
The Association of Authors' Representatives (AAR), the national organization of literary agents that has been a leading force in furthering the interests of agents, authors and the publishing industry at large since 1991 has been renamed the Association of American Literary Agents.
302A West 12th Street, #122, New York, NY 10014
Website: www.aalitagents.org

American Book Producers Association (ABPA)
The American Book Producers Association was founded in 1980 as the trade association for independent book producers, also called packagers, in the United States and Canada. Members of this rapidly growing profession produce, from concept through bound books, a wide variety of titles for trade and other publishers.
23 Waverly Place, 6B, New York, NY 10003
212-620-9440
Email: office@abpaonline.org
Website: www.abpaonline.org

American Booksellers Association (ABA)
The American Booksellers Association, a national not-for-profit trade organization, works with booksellers and industry partners to ensure the success and profitability of independently owned book retailers, and to assist in expanding the community of the book.
333 Westchester Avenue, Suite S202, White Plains, NY 10604
800-637-0037
Email: info@bookweb.org
Website: www.bookweb.org

American Library Association (ALA)
The American Library Association is the oldest and largest library association in the world.

Founded on October 6, 1876, during the Centennial Exposition in Philadelphia, the mission of ALA is "to provide leadership for the development, promotion and improvement of library and information services and the profession of librarianship in order to enhance learning and ensure access to information for all."

225 N Michigan Avenue, Suite 1300, Chicago, IL 60601

312-944-6780

Email: ala@ala.org

Website: www.ala.org

Association of American Publishers (AAP)

The Association of American Publishers (AAP) represents the leading book, journal, and education publishers in the United States on matters of law and policy, advocating for outcomes that incentivize the publication of creative expression, professional content, and learning solutions. As essential participants in local markets and the global economy, our members invest in and inspire the exchange of ideas, transforming the world we live in one word at a time.

455 Massachusetts Avenue NW, Suite 700, Washington, DC 20001

202-347-3375

Website: www.publishers.org

Association of American University Presses

AUPresses advances the essential role of a global community of publishers whose mission is to ensure academic excellence and cultivate knowledge. The Association envisions a world that values the many ways that scholarship enriches societies, institutions, and individuals. Together, we are a community of publishing professionals and institutions committed to the highest caliber of research-based scholarship. Together, we advocate for the fundamental role of scholarly publishing in achieving academic excellence and in cultivating and disseminating knowledge.

1412 Broadway, Suite 2135, New York, NY 10018

1775 Massachusetts Avenue NW, Washington, DC 20036

212-989-1010

Email: info@aupresses.org

Website: www.aaupresses.org

Association of Writers & Writing Programs (AWP)

AWP provides support, advocacy, resources, and community to nearly 50,000 writers, 550 college and university creative writing programs, and 150 writers' conferences and centers. Our mission is to amplify the voices of writers and the academic programs and organizations that serve them while championing diversity and excellence in creative writing.

5700 Rivertech Court, Suite 225, Riverdale Park, MD 20737

Email: awp@awpwriter.org

Website: www.awpwriter.org

The Authors Guild

Founded in 1912, The Authors Guild is the nation's oldest and largest nonprofit professional organization for writers. We empower working writers by providing them with the resources necessary to succeed in the business of writing and by advocating for their rights as published authors. We protect free speech and intellectual property rights, particularly advocating for more rigorous copyright laws and enforcement given the explosion of e-book piracy; fight for fair publishing contracts and a livable income; and represent authors' concerns in Washington, DC, including educating and advising Congress and regulatory agencies on legislation that would help—or harm—authors.

With the philanthropic support of our sister organization, the Authors Guild Foundation, we also develop free educational programming to help authors at all stages in their careers, including our popular Money Matters, Writers Business Bootcamps, and Manuscript to Marketplace series. More members than ever take advantage of our free legal services, including contract reviews, legal advice, and assistance getting paid or getting their rights reverted. Recently, we launched a Writers Marketplace where members can list and seek out writing services, such as proofreading, editing, book coaching, and more. With nearly 10,000 members, which include literary, mainstream, and genre fiction writers; general, academic, business, and creative nonfiction writers; journalists; poets; and translators, the Authors Guild offers an engaged and welcoming community for both traditionally published and self-published authors. Finally, we consistently advocate for the importance of a rich, diverse, and vibrant body of American literature to help build a culture of ideas essential to an effective democracy. To learn about all the benefits of membership, visit www. authorsguild.org.

31 East 32nd Street, Suite 901, New York, NY 10016

212-563-5904

Email: staff@authorsguild.org

Website: www.authorsguild.org

Book Industry Study Group (BISG)

The Book Industry Study Group (BISG) works to create a more informed, empowered and efficient book industry. Our broad membership includes trade, education, professional and scholarly publishers, as well as distributors, wholesalers, retailers, manufacturers, service providers and libraries.

232 Madison Avenue, Suite 1200, New York, NY 10016
646-336-7141
Email: info@bisg.org
Website: www.bisg.org

Book Manufacturers Institute (BMI)

BMI supports book manufacturing leaders in their work to drive the promotion, efficiency, and growth of book markets for readers and educators in North America.
7282 55th Avenue East #147, Bradenton, Florida 34203
386-986-4552
Website: www.bmibook.com

Evangelical Christian Publishers Association (ECPA)

ECPA is the association of Christian publishers, who work together to strengthen and lead the industry through connection, education, and resources. ECPA programs provide tools and opportunities for networking, collaboration, professional development, business solutions, market intelligence, and discoverability. Participate in an industry on a mission.
Website: www.ecpa.org

Independent Book Publishers Association (IBPA)

IBPA is an association of independent book publishers dedicated to professionalism and excellence. IBPA makes it easier for independent publishers to navigate the sometimes intimidating publishing process with over 60 unique member benefits.
1020 Manhattan Beach Blvd., Suite 204, Manhattan Beach, CA 90266
310-546-1818
Email: info@IBPA-online.org
Website: www.ibpa-online.org

Independent Publishers Caucus (IPC)

We've formed the Independent Publishers Caucus to foster a sense of community among those dedicated companies helping to keep the written word alive. Now more than ever, independent media is crucial to keeping discussion moving in the public square.
The Independent Publishers Caucus
c/o Seven Stories Press
140 Watts Street, New York, NY 10013
Email: info@indiepubs.org.
Website: www.indiepubs.org

PubWest

The Publishers Association of the West (PubWest) is a national trade organization of publishers and of associated publishing-related members. PubWest is dedicated to offering professional education, providing publishing-related benefits, creating opportunities for our members and associate members to do business, speaking as an advocate for members, recognizing outstanding achievement in publishing, and providing a forum for networking to our publishing and associate members from across the United States and Canada.

Email: executivedirector@pubwest.org

Website: www.pubwest.org

PUBLISHING SUMMER PROGRAMS: TRAINING NEW TALENT FOR THE INDUSTRY

BY JILL SMITH

In publishing, personal connections can often lead to a career. But how do people enter the industry without connections? Intensive summer publishing courses offer opportunities to learn about the field and build a network from the ground up. The three oldest programs in the country are the Denver Publishing Institute (DPI), Columbia Publishing Course, and NYU's Summer Publishing Institute. More recently, the LA Review of Books Publishing Workshop (LARB) launched in 2016. These publishing certificate programs are distinct from master's in publishing programs, which are longer and involve a steady commitment over time. The certificate programs are intensive "one-and-done" options for those who want to jumpstart their careers in publishing. They vary in length: four weeks for DPI, five weeks for LARB, and six weeks for NYU and Columbia. DPI focuses exclusively on book publishing, while Columbia, NYU, and LARB split their time between books and magazine publishing.

Publishing certificate programs prepare students to enter the publishing world through a short, focused curriculum that covers the process of publishing. They are designed to enable graduates to step into publishing careers with a fundamental understanding of how the business works. Hiring managers know that when they interview a candidate that has been to one of the certificate programs, they are looking at an individual who can hit the ground running. This means that they will need to do less on-the-job training and can quickly fold the individual into the department.

Each summer, the Denver Publishing Institute brings together a community of devoted book people. Ninety-five students interact with and learn from over 50 visiting speakers from all areas of publishing. Through the broad curriculum, students learn about the entire publishing ecosystem and, through that breadth, they begin to see what career paths fit their unique talents and passions. Hands-on workshops teach students about various aspects of editing and marketing while also providing practical experience making acquisitions decisions in adult trade, children's books and scholarly publishing. A highlight of the DPI program is an Independent Publishers workshop, where students learn what makes independent publishing unique and special. The curriculum continues to evolve as it tackles issues such as diversity, equity, and inclusion in companies and the books they publish.

Visiting speakers for the certificate programs come from top publishing companies around the country. By employing real-life case studies, speakers bring the process of publishing to life for the students. The active and loyal engagement of the publishing community demonstrates a wonderful partnership. The students benefit by having an up-to-date curriculum that covers current practices and trends in the industry, while the publishing community benefits by helping nurture the next generation of publishing professionals.

Differences in geographic locations lend a distinctive feel to each program. In their off-hours, DPI students are encouraged to explore the vibrant literary communities in Denver and Boulder, and take time to enjoy the access to Colorado's beautiful Rocky Mountains. In 2020, when the program shifted to a fully virtual format, students got together for virtual happy hours. Lindsey Vargas (editorial assistant, HarperCollins) and Elysse Villalobos (marketing coordinator, Macmillan Children's) would get together in the evening on Zoom to do homework and talk about the day's lectures. The DPI 2020 students were able to form such strong bonds that a group of them gathered in Denver after the program finished to go hiking and connect in person.

The alumni networks formed by the publishing certificate programs are robust. Students make lifelong friendships through their shared experience and they are eager to share their experiences with others. Through the DPI program, alumni provide job tips and networking assistance long after the summer course is complete. Carter Moran used his experience to springboard into a career at Rowman & Littlefield. He said that "I was able to speak fluently about academic publishing in the interview, and I gained a connection from DPI who pointed me toward her company as a great place to work. The skills and habits I learned at DPI gave me the edge I needed to get hired."

Publishing certificate programs open doors to the industry for those who do not have connections. Almost 50 years ago, the founders of the Denver Publishing Institute wished to pilot a program that could bring new life to an industry that was led by family legacy companies. Promoting access is just as important now: Maxx Zenisek, marketing director for Apogeo Spatial, said that his favorite part of DPI was "feeling empowered to enter the publishing industry and seeing a clear way forward to do so that had not been available to me earlier."

In 2021, publishing certificate programs are engaged in a new transformation as they double down on their efforts to recruit BIPOC applicants and ultimately help publishing to recruit a more diverse workforce. Alternative programs such as Inkluded Academy have launched to provide similar training specifically geared toward typically underrepresented groups. Emerging from this cultural moment are numerous partnerships with the publishing community to offer financial assistance to encourage minoritized applicants to consider publishing as a career. Simon & Schuster, Park & Fine Literary and Media, Shambhala Publishing, Ecco/HarperCollins, Macmillan Publishers, Penguin Random House, and Hachette among others have generously offered financial assistance for attendees of the publishing institutes. Dozens of alumni of the Denver Publishing Institute have come together to fund the DPI Community Scholarship, which will also fund scholarships for BIPOC individuals.

With the support of the book community, through scholarships, visiting speakers, and networking events, the publishing certificate programs will continue their mission to educate students and develop strong talent for the publishing world for many years to come.

*

Jill Smith is the director of the Denver Publishing Institute. She joined DPI in 2003 and brings to the program her deep knowledge of the curriculum and love of books. During her time at the University of Denver, Ms. Smith has completed her MBA through the University of Denver Daniels College of Business. She also earned an MFA from the University of Kansas, and her undergraduate degree in English Literature from Skidmore College in Saratoga Springs, New York.

FOUR SUMMER PUBLISHING CERTIFICATE PROGRAMS

Denver Publishing Institute, University of Denver

The Denver Publishing Institute is the ideal launching pad for your career in book publishing. During four weeks, it will introduce you to the exciting and ever-changing world of book publishing. The course will provide a solid educational foundation and an excellent network for your subsequent job search. The Institute is taught by industry professionals who work at trade, university, textbook, and small independent publishers throughout the country as well as in New York. Our graduates go on to publishing careers around the country and the world. You'll find some of our recent graduates at HarperCollins, Penguin

Group, Oxford University Press, Chicago Review Press, Sourcebooks, Inc., Pearson, McGraw-Hill, and many more.

Summer Publishing Institute, New York University

The Summer Publishing Institute (SPI) is an intensive study of books and digital/magazine media in the heart of the publishing world—New York City. The program combines workshops, strategy sessions, and presentations by some of the leading figures in publishing. Students hear from more than 200 guest speakers on the content creation, editing, marketing, sales, and digital aspects of the industry. Hands-on projects and dynamic networking events ensure that students gain real-world experience.

LA Review of Books Publishing Workshop

During an intensive five-week summer program, workshop fellows work with industry professionals who are at the top of their fields and leading transformations in traditional and digital publishing. Through lectures, seminars, and practical instruction, fellows learn the foundations of book, magazine, and online editing and production, digital and print publishing, and the financial and business aspects of the industry. The Publishing Workshop also offers skills-based workshops with editors, art directors, web designers, marketing professionals, and specialized tracks for hands-on experience with book and magazine production.

Inkluded Academy

Inkluded Academy is a tuition-free publishing course taught by industry professionals to college graduates from typically underrepresented groups. Held over the course of seven Saturdays in the summer, the program includes a rigorous curriculum, invested mentoring, and a commitment to job placement. The curriculum covers the foundational aspects of agenting, editorial, publicity, marketing, sales, scouting, production, and subsidiary rights. Each participant receives career counseling, one-on-one sessions, and guidance from a mentor. Inkluded Academy aims to be a much-needed pipeline between the book business and aspiring professionals from diverse backgrounds.

GRADUATE PUBLISHING PROGRAM UPDATE, 2020

BY JUDITH ROSEN | DEC 18, 2020

I n a year marked by a global pandemic and renewed social justice protests, it's not just publishers that have been forced to pivot. So too have the graduate programs that serve as feeders for trade houses and scholarly presses. To find out how graduate publishing programs have maintained their educational missions and reacted to calls for more diversity in publishing, *PW* spoke with directors and faculty at five of the largest programs: Emerson College, NYU School of Professional Studies, Pace University/Dyson School of Arts and Sciences, and Rosemont College in the U.S., as well as Simon Fraser University in Vancouver, Canada.

GOING VIRTUAL

In March, when it became clear that the U.S. and Canada were heading to a public health crisis, colleges and universities moved classes online almost overnight. That was true even for programs like SFU's, which didn't offer virtual classes before. "Part of the attractiveness of our program is in-person," says Suzanne Norman, lecturer and industry liaison at SFU Publishing Workshops. This year's first-year class has 11 Master in Publishing (MPub) students, who are from Canada, India, Iran, Ireland, and Mexico.

"Overall the academic rigor has not faded or been diminished in any way," Norman says, adding that in fall 2019 the program graduated its first PhD in publishing student, a first in Canada and likely North America. SFU is also heading to another milestone with the transition of MPub from a program to a separate School of Publishing in the coming year.

As for how the measures that SFU has taken during the pandemic have affected the program, Norman says the biggest impact has been on community. Quoting student comments, she notes that one of the biggest challenges has been connecting with classmates, since there is no time to talk before class on Zoom.

Another student says they find time zone differences particularly hard to bridge: "The group activities usually started after the morning class, that is, after 11 a.m.—which is 10:30 p.m. for me. I could only stay up two or three hours—until around 2 a.m.—to work with the other team members simultaneously. And it was even tougher since I couldn't be more flexible to change my lifestyle based on that, with having a little child."

An unexpected positive that one SFU student points to is learning how to work together as a team online. Norman cites the student as saying, "The pandemic has shown that people can work online, and there is a possibility that publishing may decrease physical spaces to cut overhead costs and better pay their staff members. If this is the case, our skills with Zoom meetings and working together remotely will be extremely important."

Other publishing programs also were able to quickly create transitions at the beginning of the first Covid-19 wave. "Moving online in the spring of 2020 was a surprise, but it wasn't a shock," says Marshall Warfield, director of graduate publishing programs at Rosemont in suburban Philadelphia. That's because he was already in the midst of planning to shift the Master's in Publishing program to online only this fall, he says. Part of the reason for moving to asynchronous online classes, he explains, is to accommodate double-degree students, who may have scheduling conflicts with their MFA in Creative Writing classes.

"The MFA program is still on-ground," Warfield says. "There is something special about being gathered around a writing workshop table."

In Boston, Emerson, which has long offered online classes, held flex classes (online and in-person) this fall and will continue them again in the spring. As for moving fully online like Rosemont, assistant professor of digital publishing John Rodzvilla—who stepped down as graduate program director when William Beuttler took over the position in the fall—says the college is committed to offering both online and in-person classes whenever possible. That said, the college plans to expand online offerings.

To try to keep Covid in check, Emerson rented extra space at a nearby hotel to enable social distancing and provided weekly Covid tests for students and faculty to administer to themselves. "I felt safe and the students felt safe," Rodzvilla says. "All our numbers stayed very low until right before Thanksgiving."

But it wasn't just Emerson. Numbers began to climb throughout the state and the rest of the country in mid-November.

FLEXING OPTIONS

One of the positive things to emerge from the pandemic, Rodzvilla says, is that it has given Emerson faculty and students a chance to experiment. Though most of the school's online classes, as well as nonacademic meetings like book clubs and movie nights, have moved to Zoom, he has been using Discord in his e-publishing courses, which lets users talk over voice, video, and text. It's made him ask, "What does it mean to have classes? Everything's changing all the time. Why not have boot camp and hackathons instead of 14-week classes?"

Manuela Soares, director of Pace's MS in Publishing program and of Pace University Press in New York City, also sees some silver linings, including the graduation of the program's thousandth student in January. The Pace program, which began nearly two decades ago, has long held classes online and in-person. "I think the pandemic is really going to revolutionize that," she says, referring to the university's installation of Zoom stations in the classroom that allow teachers to offer classes simultaneously in-person and online.

In fall 2021, Soares looks forward to seeing Covid recede and getting back to "a semblance of normality," she says. That's also when she anticipates that the publishing program will be in its new space in Pace's downtown campus on William Street. Over the summer, she oversaw the program's move from Midtown Manhattan into temporary quarters. Other changes in the works include adding more combined BA/MS in publishing degrees: one with a BA in commerce and another in writing and rhetoric. Currently, the university offers a combined MS and a BA in English or a BA in modern languages and cultures (Spanish).

That's not to say that there haven't been issues along the way. Like her colleagues, Soares notes that students and faculty have experienced some mental health issues. For some students, it's been exacerbated by being trapped with family and the lack of casual conversations with teachers before or after class. Her observations dovetail with a Gallup poll released earlier this month indicating that only 34% of Americans say their mental health is excellent, down from 43% in 2019.

NYU in Manhattan also offers online-only classes as well as hybrid classes that allow for in-person teaching in classrooms equipped with cameras and microphones that enable simultaneous participation online. Despite the pandemic and some students choosing to defer acceptance, the program has seen a slight uptick in the number of students, according to Andrea Chambers, executive director of both the Center for Publishing and the MS in Publishing: Digital and Print program. While the total number of graduate students hovers at 80, in fall 2020 the school admitted 32 students, up from 30 in 2019.

REACHING OUT GLOBALLY

With a number of international book fairs canceled due to Covid, including BookExpo in New York as well as shows in London and Bologna, schools have had to find other ways to connect their students with the larger book world. "We have worked very hard this semester to keep our students engaged with the book industry through a roster of virtual events," Chambers says. "We felt it was highly important to continue our tradition of industry visits, a hallmark of our program."

Among the highlights has been a chance to take a virtual look at the launch of HarperAlley, a graphic novel imprint, with Rich Thomas, VP and publishing director of HarperCollins Children's Books. Last month, NYU partnered with *PW* to cohost its annual PubTechConnect series. This year's program was titled, "Marketing Inside and Out: How Publishers and Retailers Are Moving Books Now."

SFU took advantage of Zoom to enable students to meet industry leaders from around the world, including OR Books cofounder John Oakes and Picador U.K. publisher Philip Gwyn Jones. In 2021, the school's annual Emerging Leaders in Publishing Summit will go virtual as representatives from the book business meet to discuss the topic of "change."

Next spring, Pace has an ambitious set of virtual appearances lined up. Among them are a lecture by Wade and Cheryl Hudson, the school's Distinguished Professors for the Year; a panel titled "Diversity in Publishing and the Life Cycle of a Book" with Atria Books; and a conversation about graphic novels with former DC president Paul Levitz. It has also moved its speed mentoring program to Zoom.

INTERNING AND OTHER OFFERINGS

The decision to cancel international book fairs spurred Rosemont's Warfield to give the school's students a different type of publishing experience by focusing on internships. "As a small school, finding the resources to make internships a required part of the program has been difficult," he says. Upcoming changes to the program include creating more robust internships that place students with companies and work experiences that match their career objectives.

Other schools, like Pace, have dedicated faculty members who line up internship opportunities. This semester, 12 Pace students interned remotely with publishers.

At NYU, Chambers says that interning remotely "opened new doors" for students to gain experience outside the tristate area. One student interested in academic publishing worked with Louisiana State University Press.

SFU offers its students professional placements in lieu of internships. Their projects have to benefit the host, and the students have to be paid. Moving some placements online has worked well for projects that don't require a physical presence, like one researching accessibility issues with Orca Book Publishers, which is based in Victoria, British Columbia.

For the past few years Emerson has been working with the *Boston Globe* and having students pitch ideas for a special section. Now students are working on the spring relaunch of the *Independent*, a nonprofit online magazine about independent film, which has transferred ownership to the college. Rodzvilla, who serves as lead editor, says that students have had to figure out how to create a style guide and how to write about film.

Though some students have complained that they don't know anything about the subject, Rodzvilla doesn't see that as an issue. "This is how publishing works," he says. "You don't know anything about the subject, and you're going to have to learn it."

PROMOTING DIVERSITY

Progress in creating a diverse student body has been mixed to date. Many colleges have a diverse student body through their international outreach. They have also sought out minority students in North America. "[Diversity] is something we have to be aware of, and we've been aware of it for a long time," says Soares, noting that Pace was the number-one private college for intergenerational upward opportunity in a list published in 2017 by the *Chronicle of Higher Education*. "We've provided a lot of the diversity you see in the industry. Our motto is 'opportunitas.'"

Soares adds that Pace was the only graduate publishing program to receive a Carolyn Kroll Reidy Memorial Scholarship for historically underrepresented groups in publishing. NYU's SPS Summer Publishing Institute also received a grant.

"Emerson has done a big push to attract a diverse student population," says Rodzvilla, adding that the school has not seen big numbers of Black or Native American students. Those who do attend, he adds, "are not finding the publishing industry that welcoming. It's overwhelmingly white, straight, and female."

Warfield acknowledges that Rosemont could do better and is working to make the program more diverse. "While some of our faculty and students during my time here may have self-identified as people of color, having numbers is not enough," he says. "I know I have a thing or two to learn from operations here in Philadelphia like Harriett's Bookshop [a Black bookshop named for Harriet Tubman]."

As for fall 2021, the educators contacted by *PW* say it won't be possible to predict what school will look like until a vaccine is rolled out widely and the health crisis begins to wane. Like her colleagues, NYU's Chambers says, "We try very hard to maintain a sense of community with students and faculty via virtual events. It's so important that they feel they are part of a vibrant virtual environment until they can again gather in person."

For now, schools are trying to make virtual life as full as it can be and incorporate in-person classes whenever possible.

*

A version of this article appeared in the 12/21/2020 issue of *Publishers Weekly* under the headline: Graduate Publishing Programs Update

9

ISSUES IMPACTING THE AUTHOR COMMUNITY, RESPONSES, AND DEVELOPMENTS

BY THE AUTHORS GUILD

2020 was a noteworthy year in publishing. Despite bookstore closures, lockdowns, and event cancellations, book sales grew by as much as 8.2% over the previous year according to NPD Bookscan estimates, and publisher revenues by 10.2% according to the American Association of Publishers. Even though much of this growth was driven by backlist and children's and young adult books,[1] as well as popular celebrity memoirs, political nonfiction,[2] and bestsellers, the figures signify how books held their ground in the increasingly crowded field of content choices, underscoring the close relationship between reading communities and their favorite authors. As industry insider Michael Cader put it during a panel hosted by the Authors Guild, "The pandemic both cemented the relationship that core readers have for books as being primary in their lives, in times of need and not, and may also have brought in some of the occasional customers—those who came for educational materials but saw what a boon it was, saw what it did for their kids—and have gotten them hooked on a new series or a new outlet and awakened them to books."

Strong revenues and book sales, however, did not translate to a bump in author incomes overall as the community, already entrenched in economic precarity, faced new and more serious challenges from the pandemic. During the pandemic, the Authors Guild conducted periodic surveys of its members and nonmembers, which found that 71.4% of the respondents[3] had on average lost

---

1   https://www.publishersweekly.com/pw/by-topic/industry-news/bookselling/article/85453-a-year-for-the-record-books.html.

2   https://www.nytimes.com/2020/12/29/books/book-publishing-2020.html.

3   https://www.authorsguild.org/industry-advocacy/authors-guild-covid-19-survey-3-summary-of-responses/.

49% of their pre-pandemic income from all sources. Cancellation of speaking engagements and loss of freelance journalism work were most frequently cited as the leading causes of income decline, followed by lack of teaching opportunities, falling book sales and self-published income, contract cancellations, and payment delays as the other contributing factors.

The negative impact of the lockdowns and loss of supplementary income opportunities on author incomes was compounded by the lack of relief opportunities available to authors. Early on in the pandemic, authors widely reported experiencing significant challenges in qualifying for unemployment benefits due to their classification as 1099 "independent contractors" rather than traditional W-2 workers. The CARES Act, which was enacted on March 27, 2020, to forestall the economic fallout as a result of the pandemic, authorized independent contractors to receive unemployment benefits under the Pandemic Unemployment Assistance program; however, confusion about eligibility criteria, in particular the requirement that PUA applicants must not be able to "telework for pay," as well as the reluctance of many state unemployment agencies to fund benefits for nontraditional workers, forestalled assistance to most authors.

The Authors Guild wrote letters to the labor secretary and congressional leadership[4] asking for clarification of the "telework" requirement, leading up to the Department of Labor's creation of a new regulation that allows independent contractors to receive PUA benefits if they had suffered diminution in income due to the pandemic—regardless of whether they could work from home. While this change enabled some authors to get unemployment benefits, it came after some had already been rejected. In addition, a significant number of those who had earnings from both W-2- and 1099-based sources were given reduced benefits based only on their W-2 income from sources such as adjunct teaching, which often is only a small portion of their total income. This "mixed-income" benefits gap[5] affected thousands of creative workers who had part-time traditional jobs in addition to their freelance careers, leading a coalition of 102 groups organized by the Authors Guild, Freelancers Union, SAG-AFTRA, the Record Academy, RIAA, the Music Artists Coalition, and the Songwriters Guild to lobby for benefits for mixed-income earners, which were finally enacted in December 2020 as part of Congress's second Covid-19 relief package.

---

4 https://www.authorsguild.org/industry-advocacy/authors-guild-asks-congress -to-expand-freelance-worker-unemployment-benefits/
5 https://www.authorsguild.org/industry-advocacy/letters-sent-to-congress-and-white -house-to-address-mixed-earner-gap/

In addition to heightened advocacy efforts by professional organizations to meet the unprecedented and urgent needs of authors during the pandemic, the author community itself showed a strong trend toward grassroots organizing and self-advocacy, with social media playing an important role in allowing authors to share resources, voice objections, build coalitions, and mobilize. In a few noteworthy cases, this grassroots organizing complemented advocacy by professional organizations to achieve significant outcomes in a relatively short period of time that might not have been possible through a disconnected approach.

Aside from the effects of the pandemic, the most salient issues that the author community confronted in 2020 and 2021 include: fair treatment and transparency in payments, unequal bargaining power in the market, lack of affordable health insurance, piracy, and morals clauses and book cancellations.

FAIR TREATMENT AND TRANSPARENCY

A number of high-profile campaigns in 2020 featured demands of greater transparency in royalty reporting and payments to authors. These included the #DisneyMustPay campaign, the AudibleGate call to action, and the response to McGraw Hill's imposition of an arbitrary commission for payments of freelancer invoices.

Audiblegate

The Audiblegate campaign started when a technical glitch in the ACX dashboard revealed that Audible was deducting so-called "returns" from ACX rights holder accounts, including independently published authors and most smaller audiobook publishers, without reporting the number of returns or the amounts deducted. While it was known that Audible had an easy return or exchange policy, authors had not known that Audible actually deducted royalties paid for books purchased if the reader at any point within 365 days "returned" the book, whether read or not. With this policy, Audible actually provided a subscription program for its listeners—meaning they can listen to as many books as they want by paying the subscription fee. But Audible was providing this benefit at authors' expense, since the author would lose their royalties when a book was returned. Following the discovery of this practice, a group of independent ACX authors formed a Facebook group, Fair Dealing for Authors and Narrators, to raise awareness about Audible's accounting policies and to demand transparency and restitution. The Authors Guild, the U.K.-based Society of Authors (SOA), and the Alliance for Independent Authors (ALLi) led an international coalition of author organizations in conveying the demands made by ACX authors through a public letter[6]—which was signed by 13,000 authors, narrators, and supporters—to the company's CEO and general counsel. That letter called on Audible to:

- Provide full and complete accounting of returns made pursuant to this policy since it was first implemented.
- Limit the time period of returns and exchanges that could be deducted from royalty counts from 365 days to a reasonable period, such as 48 hours, and allow only "true returns" (i.e., where less than 25% of the book has been read) to be deducted from royalty accounts.
- Show the total number of unit purchases and returns on author dashboards, not just the "net sales" already adjusted for any returns.
- Take action against abuse of the "return and exchange" terms by listeners.

The Authors Guild and the SOA also held meetings with Audible's CEO and general counsel to discuss the company's unfair returns policy and to seek transparency on Audible's accounting methods—in particular the Audible Listener Allocation Factor (ALAF) it uses to calculate the rights holder's royalty rate on membership plan sales. As a result of those conversations, Audible agreed to only deduct returns made within seven days of purchase from authors' ACX accounts (as opposed to 365 days) and to retool its dashboard to provide returns data and not just the net sales (after deducting returns). After further complaints from the Fair Dealing for Authors and Narrators group and ALLi about the ACX contract's terms around exclusivity as well as conversations with the Authors Guild and SOA, Audible agreed to shorten its mandatory distribution period from one year to 90 days as well as its mandatory term for exclusive licenses from seven years to 90 days, allowing ACX rights holders to switch from exclusive to non-exclusive distribution much sooner than previously allowed.

Notably, however, despite multiple requests, Audible has never shared information about all of the figures used to calculate what it refers to as the "ALAF," a multiplier that it uses to calculate royalties. The Authors Guild, SOA, and ALLi continue to seek information about this. At the same time, a group of independent authors, with support from ALLi, have initiated an "Equitable Rights Movement" to increase the pressure on Audible. These ongoing efforts

---

6   https://www.authorsguild.org/industry-advocacy/sign-our-letter-and-tell-audible
    -to-stop-charging-authors-for-returns/

together mark one of the most significant mobilizations of authors, author organizations, and their supporters against an industry giant.

#Disneymustpay

In 2020, veteran sci-fi and fantasy author Alan Dean Foster initiated a complaint with the Science Fiction and Fantasy Writers Association Grievance Committee for not receiving royalties that were contractually due to him for book rights acquired by Disney when it bought Lucasfilm and 20th Century Fox. Disney argued that it had purchased the rights but not the obligations of the contract. SFWA was forced to take the matter public[7] to get a resolution, and soon other authors (or their agents) reported that they were also affected by Disney's refusal to honor the contractual obligations of companies it had acquired. To advocate on behalf of the authors, SFWA formed the #DisneyMustPay Joint Task Force[8] with the Authors Guild, Horror Writers Association, National Writers Union, Novelists, Inc., Romance Writers of America, and Sisters in Crime, and high-profile writers such as Neil Gaiman, Tess Gerritsen, Mary Robinette Kowal, and Chuck Wendig. The task force is demanding that Disney:

1. Honor contracts now held by Disney and its subsidiaries.
2. Provide royalty payments and statements to all affected authors.
3. Update their licensing page with an FAQ for writers about how to handle missing royalties.
4. Create a clear, easy-to-find contact person or point for affected authors.
5. Cooperate with author organizations who are providing support to authors and agents.

In response to the campaign, Disney assigned staff to liaise with the task force and to individually settle unpaid royalty claims.

McGraw Hill

In March 2021, McGraw Hill's freelance contractors received a notification from the textbook giant that it would apply a 2.2% fee for processing their invoices, claiming that this so-called Small Supplier Fee would support the company's compliance costs, including expenditures on minimizing the

---

7   https://www.sfwa.org/disney-must-pay/
8   https://www.writersmustbepaid.org/about

company's risks from misclassifying independent contractors. McGraw Hill unilaterally imposed this fee during a pandemic, when freelance creators were already losing work opportunities and unable to access the full scope of unemployment benefits due to their independent contractor status. In response to McGraw Hill's unfair processing fee, the Authors Guild led a coalition of 15 organizations representing freelance authors and photographers to demand the immediate removal of the invoicing fee. In a letter to its CEO and general counsel,[9] the organizations chastised McGraw Hill for "pursuing a deliberate strategy to cut payments to independent contractors even as it continues to generate hundreds of millions of dollars in revenue through its growing digital business, which has benefited from the shift to online learning as a result of the pandemic." McGraw Hill, despite these widespread calls and social media pressure, refused the demands, and the campaign continues. McGraw Hill claimed that its independent contractors had not objected to their pay cuts—which is not only inaccurate but indicative of the disparities in bargaining power between large companies and their freelance workers who are unable to fight back against adverse terms.

Authors Guild Model Contract—Transparency

The Authors Guild has included a set of new provisions in its revised model contract[10] that require publishers to provide detailed information about sales, sublicenses, remainders, and discounts. These new provisions:

- Require publishers to provide detailed information in their accounting statements, including number of copies sold, returned, and given away as well as gross prices.
- Provide for de-escalating royalties, rather than a sudden jump for deeply discounted sales, given the increasing use and amounts of discounts provided to retailers.
- Allow authors to receive copies of sub-licenses executed by the publisher.
- Require publishers to clearly mark copies for export, remainder, overstock, and review to prevent resellers from selling them as "new" in online marketplaces like Amazon.

9   https://www.authorsguild.org/industry-advocacy/tell-mcgraw-hill-to-stop-charging
    -freelancers-for-processing-invoices/
10 https://www.authorsguild.org/member-services/legal-services/model-book-contract/

BARGAINING POWER

Led by the Authors Guild, writer organizations have increased their calls for changes to labor and antitrust laws that would enable authors to engage in collective bargaining with publishers and others in the marketplace. According to the Authors Guild, authors' lack of bargaining power in the marketplace is a major factor underlying the decline in earnings from writing. The main reason authors, freelance writers, and other independent content creators (unlike TV and screenwriters and full-time journalists) do not have a union is that under current law, only employees are permitted to unionize and collectively bargain with their employers. Antitrust laws prohibit authors from sharing information about advances, fees, or other financial matters, as well as from collective bargaining. Antitrust laws treat individual authors as independent, competing businesses capable of negotiating with publications and book publishers. From an author's perspective, however, especially given the limited number of players in the publishing market, walking away from onerous contract terms is very rarely a realistic option.

The Authors Guild—which has tracked standard publishing contract terms for decades and has a legal department that reviews hundreds of contracts per year from all types of publishers—reports that publishers have found a number of ways to cut authors' actual royalties through standard contract terms and norms that have devolved over the last decade. Many publishers are also increasing their discounts to retailers and selling large quantities of books through special sales that reduce or, in many cases, entirely eliminate the author's royalty; paying royalties on "net receipts"; paying authors a percentage of a book's list price; "bundling" books into subscription programs that pay royalties not as individual sales but on a pro rata basis; and making other cuts to author incomes.

HEALTH INSURANCE

Health insurance remained one of the biggest concerns for the author community in 2020, gaining urgency due to part-time job and income losses suffered by authors during the pandemic. As the industry continues to find durable solutions for affordable insurance, a coalition of 10 organizations, including the Authors Guild, working together as the Book Industry Health Insurance Partnership (BIHIP)[11] partnered with Lighthouse Insurance Group (LIG) Solutions to provide their members with concierge assistance in finding the

---

11 https://www.authorsguild.org/industry-advocacy/coalition-of-eleven-book-industry-associations-launch-official-book-industry-health-insurance-partnership-bihip/

right ACA-compliant major medical insurance and providing supplemental insurances such as Medicare, short-term, vision, dental, and critical care, as well as small group/Health Reimbursement Arrangements (HRAs).

BIHIP's partnership with LIG simplifies the process for authors to buy insurance through ACA-compliant exchanges. LIG's concierge service helps authors identify and obtain the best ACA health-care options based on their needs in their state.

Because the ACA options remain so expensive, writer and other professional creator organizations continue to advocate for association health care, as well as collective bargaining for professional creators, so that they can offer a health insurance option to their members.

COPYRIGHT

Authors have become increasingly active at the grassroots level in copyright enforcement and fighting piracy. Concerned by the growing amount of digital piracy, some authors have formed social media communities to share resources and take action. Authors are calling out pirate sites and their facilitators on social media and reporting pirate sites to search engines and other platforms, as well as their professional organizations. There has also been a growth in individual author engagement on legislative issues, including through communications and meetings with their local representatives.

The amount of e-book piracy, the number of services devoted to e-book or audiobook piracy, and the wiliness of the pirates has grown exponentially in recent years. The Authors Guild is leading or supporting litigation against some of the most notorious infringing sites. Last year, the Authors Guild helped to organize a lawsuit against the Ukraine-based pirate site KISS Library, which was illegally selling pirated e-books at discounted prices to unsuspecting U.S. readers until it was shut down as a result of an injunction. The plaintiffs in the lawsuit are bestselling authors Lee Child, Sylvia Day, John Grisham, Scott Turow, members of the Authors Guild, including the Guild's board president, Doug Preston; Amazon Publishing; and Penguin Random House. The litigation is also notable because it not only took KISS Library offline, but also forced third parties, including search engines, ad services, domain registrars, payment processors, and privacy proxies to suspend services, locate and freeze the pirates' assets, and turn over documents and records related to the piracy scheme.

The Authors Guild is also supporting the publishers' ongoing litigation against Internet Archive for the mass scanning of more than 1.4 million books and distributing copyrighted literary works to the public through its branded Open Library and National Emergency Library. The suit was filed in the U.S.

District Court for the Southern District of New York, on June 1, 2020. A trial date has been set for November 2021.

Copyright Alternative in Small Claims Enforcement (CASE) Act of 2021

The enactment of the Copyright Alternative in Small Claims Enforcement (CASE) Act[12] on December 27, 2020, marked the end of a decade-long campaign by the Authors Guild and other creator groups, thanks to intense lobbying by authors and other creators who attended meetings with and wrote countless letters to members of Congress, as well as op-eds and blogs, and also took to social media to express their support for the bill.

The CASE Act directs the Copyright Office to establish a dedicated forum—called the Copyright Claims Board (CCB)—for the resolution of disputes involving small copyright claims with awards of up to $15,000 per claim and $30,000 total. Because the average copyright case in federal court costs almost $400,000, and can be much higher, suing for copyright infringement, no matter how blatant the infringement, is out of reach for most individual creators and small businesses, leaving them without the ability to enforce their rights and resolve disputes. Starting in 2022, authors, publishers, and other creators and copyright owners will be able to bring claims in the CCB for a modest fee and without the need for an attorney. The statute lays out the broad parameters for the structure and processes of the CCB and leaves the task of implementing the legislation to the Copyright Office. The Copyright Office has 12 months (with a possible extension of another six months) to conduct all of the rulemaking necessary to launch the Copyright Claims Board and make it operational. Rulemaking commenced in early 2021 and is expected to continue through 2021.

DMCA Reform

The Authors Guild has for several years been very active in discussions about the responsibility online platforms have to protect their works from being pirated, taking part in congressional initiatives to reform the Digital Millennium Copyright Act—the provisions of copyright law that provide safe harbors to online platforms for the copyright infringement of their users under certain conditions. Those safe harbors have been interpreted by courts extremely broadly and allow online platforms to host the piracy and even benefit from it as long as they take down single items of infringing content upon receipt of an official DMCA notice from the copyright owner identifying the

---

12 https://www.authorsguild.org/industry-advocacy/congress-passes-case-act/

specific copy and URL where it resides. This has led to an absurd game of Whac-a-Mole where infringing copies get put right back up, often in multiple copies. Authors have lobbied Congress to clarify the law so that infringing content stays down, and Douglas Preston, president of the Authors Guild, testified before members of the Senate Judiciary Committee[13] in June 2020 about the severe impact of digital piracy on author incomes. The Authors Guild also submitted a written statement to both Senate and House lawmakers using testimonials of authors hurt by piracy and recommending changes to the law that would compel online platforms to assume greater responsibility for keeping piracy off their sites.

MORALS CLAUSES

The #MeToo movement and other high-profile controversies have led to morals clauses becoming a standard feature of most publishers' form contracts in just the last few years. Publishers insist they need the clauses to protect themselves in the event an author's reputation becomes so tarnished after the book contract is signed that it will damage sales. But often these clauses are drafted in an overly broad manner and allow a publisher to terminate a book deal based on individual accusations or the vague notion of "public condemnation," leaving authors vulnerable to arbitrary decisions.

The Authors Guild objects to the use of these clauses because they can be used unfairly to cancel book contracts[14] and they let publishers police an author's behavior unrelated to the book. They can also be asserted as a form of censorship, and the public should not be denied books because the author behaved badly.

In order to contain their effects and discourage their use without clear and compelling reasons, the Authors Guild's latest model contract includes recommendations to limit the scope of morals clause so that they apply only to:

- Proven or admitted conduct, and not merely allegations.
- Conduct that is illegal or objectively morally condemnable behavior.
- Conduct that has become public.
- Conduct that is likely to adversely affect the sale of the book.
- Conduct that the publisher did not know about when it signed the agreement.

---

13 https://www.authorsguild.org/industry-advocacy/ag-president-doug-preston-testifies -before-senate-committee/
14 https://www.authorsguild.org/industry-advocacy/why-we-oppose-morals-clauses -in-book-contracts/

The Authors Guild also recommends that these clauses should stipulate that:

- The publisher may only terminate the contract; it should agree not to pursue any damages.
- The rights revert to the author upon termination, and the author does not have to repay any part of the advance previously received.

PART II.
PATHS TO
PUBLICATION

GETTING PUBLISHED

LITERARY AGENTS IN BOOK PUBLISHING

BY MARK GOTTLIEB

L iterary agents are often referred to as the gatekeepers within the book publishing industry, especially since most major trade book publishers will not accept unsolicited submissions, unless they come by way of a literary agency. The reason for this is that literary agents serve as the on-ramp to the superhighway of book publishing: a competent literary agent will know how to gear up their client for a highly successful publishing experience—not to mention that publishers would much rather work with an author who is ready to merge into the traffic of the publishing process.

FINDING A LITERARY AGENCY

Finding a literary agent is the easy part—it's getting signed with a literary agency and going on to get published successfully that's difficult. But here's a start: most literary agencies within book publishing are ranked online, via the publishing newsletter site *Publishers Marketplace* (*PM*), which had humble beginnings as a publishing blog. On *PM*, literary agents and literary agencies are ranked, according to volume of deals (last six months, 12 months, all-time) and six-figure+ deals (as well as other individual categories of fiction, nonfiction, children's books and graphic novels). For instance, the literary agency where I work, Trident Media Group, has ranked #1 across the book publishing industry in overall lifetime volume of deals and six-figure+ deals, consecutively, year after year, since 2004—when *PM* first began ranking deals. In exploring the deal rankings and drilling down into the information contained within those deals, an author can click into a literary agent's contact details, thereby making *PM* something of a publishing rolodex. That is the extent of the value of *PM*, as the rest of the news on the site is largely recycled from other news sources. Much like the *New York Times*, *Publishers Weekly* magazine is the gold standard in the book publishing industry for highly credible and original news.

PM's deal-maker rankings lists these literary agencies as leaders in overall volume of deals as of July 2021:

1. Trident Media Group (2001 deals)
2. Writers House (1821 deals)
3. Andrea Brown Literary Agency (1326 deals)
4. Marsal Lyon Literary Agency (1195 deals)
5. ICM (1081 deals)
6. William Morris Endeavor (999 deals)
7. Folio Literary Management (972 deals)
8. Inkwell Management (957 deals)
9. Duran Kim Agency (889 deals)
10. Janklow & Nesbit (834 deals)

PM's deal-maker rankings lists these literary agencies as leaders in six-figure+ deals as of July 2021:

1. Trident Media Group (296 deals)
2. Writers House (211 deals)
3. Folio Literary Management (153 deals)
4. The Bent Agency (151 deals)
5. Sterling Lord Literistic (125 deals)
6. Foundry Literary + Media (97 deals)
7. Pippin Properties (89 deals)
8. Marsal Lyon Literary Agency (88 deals)
9. William Morris Endeavor (83 deals)
10. Andrea Brown Literary Agency (79 deals)

After an author homes in on a number of literary agents they would like to work with, they should visit the websites of the individual literary agencies. This will give authors a better understanding of both the literary agent and the literary agency where they work. An author should not only read the company descriptions and employee bio(s), but also look at the client list of the company to be even more informed. Above all, an author should follow the submission guidelines as set out by each of the literary agencies on their websites, as particular terms and conditions are often set out there.

DEVELOPMENTS AMONG LITERARY AGENCIES

There are new developments on the literary agent side of the book publishing industry over the last few years, some of which are a result of the Covid-19 pandemic. Most notably, mergers and acquisitions among the big five trade publishing companies have led to fewer places where literary agencies can submit manuscripts for consideration. One of the first significant turns of events occurred when Penguin Books and Random House merged into Penguin Random House (PRH) and began consolidating their publishing imprints and office spaces. Following that merger, the publishing industry has seen more consolidation, in the recent acquisition of Houghton Mifflin Harcourt by HarperCollins. Additionally, PRH's move to acquire Simon & Schuster (S&S), after S&S CEO Carolyn Reidy's passing and CBS putting the company up for sale, has led to a Department of Justice investigation into the merger as a potential antitrust issue.

Amid the challenges of an industry facing consolidation, book publishers have become aggressive about keeping audiobook rights, in order to help make their numbers work on new acquisitions in a challenging marketplace. For literary agents and authors, this means one less additional right to be able to hold on to in negotiations and later exploit with an independent audiobook publisher, for an additional advance and royalties. There are very few exceptions where literary agents are able to hold on to audiobook rights in new negotiations for clients, and the case is usually where there is a big-name author with an existing relationship with an audiobook publisher.

As previously mentioned, Covid-19 brought with it new developments and challenges for the literary agency side of the book publishing industry. Work from home changed things for everyone, and literary agencies and book publishers were no exception. This made editors very difficult to reach as they were seldom at their desks or office numbers. Interestingly enough, there was a boom in book buying among customers early on at the start of the pandemic, most notably of paperback classics. Many readers realized they finally had time to read classic novels and massive tomes, such as *Moby-Dick* and *War and Peace*. Customers would later have to turn to buying instantaneous content, such as e-books and digital audiobooks.

The real challenges arose when Amazon began struggling to meet many of these book orders, as publishers were facing limited operations at printing plants and printing plant closures, as well as the fact that Amazon decided to prioritize the delivery of essential items (food, water, medicine, etc.) to customers, over printed books. Bookstores also began struggling to stay open and many closed, resulting in further shortages, thereby putting pressure on publishers, literary agencies, and authors to operate at limited capacity. In order to address cashflow issues, many publishers resolved to break out payments on their contracts into thirds, quarters and fifths, whereas typically publishers had paid in halves (signing and delivery and acceptance of manuscript). Luckily, publishers were still buying books from literary agencies, as most books are published 12 to 18 months from the date of a signed contract, so publishers were able to envision a day beyond the pandemic when the industry would stabilize.

The next big challenge facing literary agencies and authors will come from subscription pricing models from publishers and retailers. Similar to Netflix, Disney+, and HBO, many book publishers have moved into the subscription space for books. The financial terms under subscriptions—in favoring the subscription companies—are usually unfavorable to authors. Most subscription models will tend to benefit big-name authors, rather than midlist or debut authors, making it even more of a challenge for newer books to stand out and thrive. Furthermore, many book publishing contracts never contemplated subscription models, making it a challenge to discern with whom the subscription rights reside on backlist titles. If mishandled by publishers, in the same way they mishandled agency e-book pricing between Amazon and Apple, subscription pricing could end up further damaging the print, audiobook, and e-book business for authors and literary agents. It can therefore only be the hope of authors and literary agents that subscription models will be properly managed and bolster the publishing industry, rather than serving as another technological disruptor.

*

Mark Gottlieb is a prominent literary agent working at book publishing's leading literary agency, Trident Media Group in New York City. He has ranked highly among literary agents across the industry for overall number of deals and other individual categories. While at Trident Media Group, Mark has represented *New York Times* bestselling authors as well as major award-winning authors. He has optioned and sold numerous books to production companies and studios for film and TV adaptation. Mark greatly enjoys working with authors to help manage and grow their careers with the resources available at Trident Media Group. In addition to having worked at the company's foreign rights department, he also ran the company's audiobook department. Utilizing his drive and intuition for discovering talented writers, he is currently expanding his client list of authors. As a literary agent, he looks forward to bringing authors to the largest possible audience.

HOW TO WRITE A QUERY LETTER

BY MARK MALATESTA

Authors are often confused about how to write a query letter. That's because most query letter "experts" have limited experience—or the wrong *type* of experience.

One source of "how to write a query" information is literary agents, but their advice is based on reading queries rather than writing them. In addition, agents usually give advice based on their personal opinions and preferences. In other words, they say to write queries a certain way because that's what they like. With more than one thousand agents, it's no wonder there's a lot of conflicting information out there.

Another source of "how to query" info is published authors, who sometimes share the queries that landed them agents. But these aren't reliable models either. One reason is that they represent just one author's experience, which is limited. And another reason is that some of the letters aren't great. (Yes, sometimes authors get agents despite mediocre queries. And yes, a bit of luck is occasionally involved in publishing.)

Instead of relying on luck—or modeling what one agent recommended or one author has written—write your query using principles that have helped *hundreds* of authors get literary representation and/or book deals, with traditional publishers such as Random House, HarperCollins, Simon & Schuster, Harcourt, and Thomas Nelson. Some authors who've used this method have gotten *multiple* offers for representation from agents and multiple offers from publishers.

THE FUNDAMENTALS OF A SUCCESSFUL QUERY

Literary agents and authors explain how to write a query letter on a basic, or "micro," level. In other words, they mainly share what they believe should be the main parts of a query. I'm going to do that too, but I'm also going to share four "big picture" fundamentals. Understanding them will help you make you and your book look as appealing as possible.

1. **Include items likely to help.** Sounds obvious, but what's most important? Only include information showing: a) what your target market is, b) what your book is about, c) what it's similar to and how it's unique, and d) that you're professional, pleasant to work with, uniquely qualified to write a book like yours, and both willing and able to get exposure for your book. With this information, agents can make an informed decision instead of incorrect assumptions.

2. **Arrange everything in the best order.** Most authors assume agents are going to read their entire query. Instead, assume they're only going to read the first sentence. And, if that sentence pulls them in—or doesn't trip them up—they'll read the next sentence. And so on. That's why it's critical, if you have something you must share in your query that might be an agent turnoff, that you put it near the end of the query. And that's why you should start the query with your *best* thing. What that "best thing" is varies for each book and author.

   Examples of your best thing are a highly unusual book premise; you being one of the only people on the planet with access to some of the information in your book; an article you've written having been published in a major print or online media outlet; or that you have 50,000 social media followers. Examples of things you might want to put at the end of your query include that your word count is excessively low or high (each genre has different expectations); or that your book has already been published (something most agents don't like).

   The idea is to get some traction and momentum in your query before you address something difficult. Start your query with the most impressive item, followed by your book title, word count, and genre, along with a one- or two-sentence description. And, for the small number of agents for whom you can do so, tell them why you believe—based on what you've seen in their bios and/or on their websites—they might like a book like the one you are pitching.

   If the above information "hooks" the agent, they'll then want to know more about your book. So, the next part of your query should be a paragraph or two about that. Think six to 12 lines of text, like the copy you'd find on a book's back cover. Though most agents don't ask for it or require it, you should follow the above with another six to 12 lines of text comparing/contrasting your book with other, similar titles. Doing so will help agents get a better feel for what your work is like, it will give them the impression that you're knowledgeable about your competition, and it will give them the sense that you might be doing something special.

Finally, include another six to 12 lines of text telling the agent about yourself. They should be things that show any of the following: you're educated, professional, coachable, have had leadership positions, or that you understand success, business, advertising, marketing, or media; you're a good writer and/or uniquely qualified to write a book like yours; and you have the time, connections, resources, skill, and desire to get exposure and sell books. You don't need all those things, but any of them will make you more attractive to agents.

3. **Omit items that don't matter or could hurt your odds with agents.** Many authors unwittingly volunteer information they should, for the moment, keep to themselves. For example, the number of queries the author has sent out unsuccessfully or any information that isn't relevant to the book. If it's not going to make agents believe you're the best person to write and/or promote your book, leave it out.

4. **Make your query concise.** In most cases, your query shouldn't be more than one single-spaced page. Include everything you believe should be included. Then put everything in the best order. After that, do one last edit to make the query tight. As you likely know, successful people—including literary agents and publishing house executives—move fast. They must, to survive. Top agents get 10,000 to 15,000 queries a year, so you can lose them if you ramble or if you're redundant. Instead, present everything as outlined above. Give agents exactly what they want and need to sell your book, and they'll trust you more because of it.

In a perfect world, authors would not need to write query letters. Instead, agents would just read every author's manuscript. But that's not how it is. We all must work within the system we're in. For example, I could write a book about how to write a query (and one day I will), but when I was invited to write this chapter, I was told it should be no more than 1,250 words. So, guess what? It's 1,250 words. Make every word count.

*

Mark Malatesta is a former literary agent who's helped hundreds of authors (fiction, nonfiction, and children's books) get literary agents and/or traditional publishers as a coach. He is president and founder of The Bestselling Author and Literary Agent Undercover, and he is the creator and curator of the Directory of Literary Agents. Authors Mark has worked with have gotten six-figure book deals and been on the *New York Times* bestseller list. They've had their work optioned for TV, stage, and feature film with companies such as Paramount Pictures, DreamWorks, Lionsgate, and HBO Max. They've won countless awards. And they've had their work licensed in more than 40 countries, resulting in millions of books sold.

HOW AUTHORS CAN INVENT THEIR OWN ADVANCES

An author offers up sources writers can tap into to help finance their next books

BY VANESSA BLAKESLEE

Funding a book-length project, whether it's a first book or a fourth, can be challenging—even more so without an advance, or with a nominal one. However, with some research, organization, entrepreneurial spirit, and persistence, a writer at any career stage can find resources to "invent" an advance and obtain the support to complete a manuscript. Below are some options writers can look to.

If you're working on a first book, the Elizabeth George Foundation provides one-time yearlong grants. Funds may be used for living expenses, travel for research, artistic residencies, writers conferences, necessary enrichment or related coursework, or tuition in accredited MFA programs in the U.S. Short story writers, poets, unpublished novelists, emerging playwrights, and unpublished creative nonfiction writers who are U.S. residents may apply.

The Sustainable Arts Foundation supports writers who are parents by giving unrestricted cash awards to individuals as well as by funding family-friendly artist residencies. Recent individual awardees received $5,000 each.

For creative writing projects with an international focus, the Fulbright Awards considers and funds both teaching/research and research awards. If you have a BA or are a recent graduate, you'll likely want to apply under the Fulbright Student Program; graduate-degree holders who have been published will likely apply under the Fulbright Scholar Program for midcareer and established professionals. Many countries do not have a foreign language requirement, so you may undertake your book project research in English. For some awards, the Fulbright now offers a "flex option," which means if you are granted that award (either for a semester or full academic year abroad), you may allocate the research over shorter time periods.

If you're the adventurous type, perhaps consider volunteering for the Peace Corps. While this experience isn't for everyone, I've met several writers who have mined their experience as Peace Corps volunteers for both fiction and nonfiction books upon their return. Though many perceive the Peace Corps as a venture undertaken in youth, that simply isn't true—many have volunteered later in life, postretirement, or as a "gap year" after a divorce, loss, or similar reboot. You'll have to embrace learning a new language and culture for the months you're deployed, but you won't have to worry about living expenses or student loan payments for that time—and you might just encounter a gripping story that demands to be told.

If you're a historical writer working on a subject in America pre-1830, the Hodson Trust-John Carter Brown Library Fellowship supports two months of research and two months of writing. The stipend is $5,000 per month for a total of $20,000, plus housing and university privileges. The research is conducted at the John Carter Brown Library on the campus of Brown University in Providence, R.I. The two-month writing period of the fellowship will be at the Starr Center at Washington College in Chestertown, Md., during the summer following the research term.

If you're able to work remotely or get away, seek out writing residencies that offer a stipend. The Jack Kerouac Writers-in-Residence Project of Orlando offers a three-month stay in the Florida bungalow where Kerouac wrote *The Dharma Bums* and includes $1,000. Other residencies offer similar fellowship awards and stipends, such as the Mastheads ($900 stipend), Soaring Gardens/Ora Lerman Trust ($500 stipend), Headlands ($500), Newnan ArtRez (varies), and others. Check the Alliance of Artist Communities database, prioritize your list, and apply.

Crowdfund, crowdfund, crowdfund. Whether one likes it or not, we now live in a Kickstarter, GoFundMe, and Indiegogo world. The great news is that crowdfunding provides a great tool to match funds as you invent your advance. Asking backers to support you for a year to pen your novel would truly be a tough sell, even for a well-respected and popular writer—but if you've already secured some funding elsewhere, your crowdfunding "ask" to match funds should be much easier. Since many residencies are unable to provide travel expenses or child care, you might use a crowdfunding platform to fill in the gaps on your invented advance.

No two writers' circumstances are exactly alike, and some of these avenues may appeal more than others. But by increasing your awareness of the funding options available, the inventiveness you bring to your book project can be applied to raising financial support for its completion, no matter where you are in your literary career. Hopefully you'll meet your project goals sooner than later—with the focus on your creative vision, independent of a publisher's advance.

*

Vanessa Blakeslee's most recent book, *Perfect Conditions,* was named the 2018 gold Forward Indies winner for short stories by *Foreword Reviews.*

A version of this article appeared in the 03/30/2020 issue of *Publishers Weekly* under the headline: Inventing Your Advance.

THE EMOTIONAL COST
OF THE BOOK DEAL

BY ANJALI ENJETI

For years, at writers conferences, I kept hearing the same well-meaning pieces of advice: keep writing, keep submitting, your book(s) will eventually find a home.

Though it's meant to encourage writers to push through rejection, the advice doubles as a toxic literary theory of bootstrapping (bookstrapping?), which suggests that hard work and persistence will yield the reward of a book deal. That isn't necessarily true. Through my 11 years of submitting multiple books, I wish one person had taken me aside and said, "Look, it's a brutal business that oftentimes has nothing to do with talent. If it doesn't work out for you, know you are not alone." It might have saved me from years of self-blame for what I deemed my own shortcomings as a writer.

"The right agent is out there for you" was another common refrain. What isn't as commonly known is how many agents some authors go through before they find one who is the right fit. Over 11 years, I signed with two agents from two top agencies. The first worked her tail off to sell one of my books but didn't succeed. We parted ways, amicably, when she wasn't interested in representing my third book. The second agent represented two of my friends. We hit it off. A few months after signing me, he disappeared. I fired him two years later, though he didn't know it for a while because he rarely ever opened my emails.

I had been querying agents for more than three years for one of my seven books—my novel, *The Parted Earth*—when I received yet another racist rejection from a Big Agent at a Big Agency. "This book isn't as strong as other books coming out of India," I was told—as if "India" is some kind of genre and there is a quota for books set there. I had also received a string of rejections from agents explaining that they couldn't "connect with the voice"—a painful reminder that so much about getting published depends on an agent's familiarity with the protagonist's experiences, not necessarily the quality of the writing or the significance of the story.

These rejections were the last straw. Aside from replying to the occasional random request from an agent to see my work—a few months after publishing an essay in the *Atlantic* detailing a decade's worth of rejections—I quit looking for an agent. But then, the following summer, my nearly nonexistent publishing journey had an unexpected twist. A book contract appeared in my mailbox, in response to a proposal (unagented) that I submitted a year earlier to the University of Georgia Press for an essay collection. *Southbound: Essays on Identity, Inheritance, and Social Change* would eventually make its way out into the world. My confidence returned full force, which led me to submit *The Parted Earth* (unagented) during Hub City Press's open-reading period. Seven months later, I had my second book contract. Both books will be out this spring.

But let me be transparent. My advances from both books total less than what some writers earn from writing a single article. Subtract my out-of-pocket expenses for authenticity editing, line editing, page proofing, and hiring an independent publicist, and I'm considerably in the hole (though the sale of the audiobook for *The Parted Earth* has helped me dig part of the way out). My ability to go into this kind of debt is a privilege—one that most writers can't afford. I only hope that both books sell well enough that my nonprofit presses can continue to publish minority authors like me, because if I'd had to rely on the Big Five houses, these books would never have seen the light of day.

I am currently in the throes of rewriting my first novel. I'm trying to focus on the experience of writing, on the soulful energy that comes from creation, the adrenaline rush when I uncover a fascinating detail during my research— all of the parts of writing I can control. But now that I have two books under my belt, I'd be lying if I said I didn't crave a third ISBN. Slaying the publishing dragon twice has made me greedy for more, but it hasn't made me invincible. I can't submit books for another 11 years. I no longer have the steely stamina I once did.

Now that I'm on the other side, writer friends often ask me whether it was worth it. Did the book deals make up for the tears and the trauma? Of course it was worth it. I still can't believe how lucky I am. But I wish I didn't have to lose so much of myself to get here. Don't we all deserve a way to engage in this process while also remaining whole?

*

Anjali Enjeti is an organizer, teacher, and the author of *Southbound: Essays on Indentity, Inheritance, and Social Change* (Univ. of Georgia, Apr. 15) and the novel *The Parted Earth* (Hub City, May 4).

A version of this article appeared in the 04/05/2021 issue of *Publishers Weekly* under the headline: The Cost of the Deal.

FAIR USE

BY ALEX GIGANTE

air use is a doctrine of U.S. copyright law[15] that permits limited quotation from another work without the author's permission. A denial of permission does *not* affect the fair-use analysis, i.e., fair use can still be claimed after a permission request has been refused. As there is no harm in first asking for permission, it is the better practice to ask and to fall back on fair use when permission cannot be obtained.

Section 107 of the Copyright Act sets out the factors for determining whether a use is "fair": (1) the purpose and character of the use, including whether it is for profit; (2) the character of the copyrighted work; (3) how much of the total work is used; and (4) what effect the use will have on the market for or value of the copyrighted work. The analysis under these criteria can be complicated and typically rests on the particular facts of the case, but an essential element is that the quoted material be used either for comment or criticism, or in a "transformative" way, i.e., that it be reworked by the quoting author into something new and original (Factor #1). It is not fair use to use material simply for itself, where it could serve as a substitute or replacement for the original source (Factor #4).

There is a popular misconception that any quotation of fewer than 300 words (or 350, or 400, etc., depending on the alleged source) qualifies as fair use. Quantity is just one factor (Factor #3). Also important is the quality of the quoted material, i.e., whether it is the heart of the original work (Factors #1 and #4). Thus, while it generally would be fair use to quote just a few hundred words from a 400-page book, in one famous case involving an as-yet-unpublished presidential memoir, a quotation of just a few hundred words was held to be an infringement because it usurped the market for one of the book's most spectacular—and most salable—revelations (Factor #4).

Another consideration is the nature of the work using the quotation (Factor

---

15 Fair use is unique to U.S. law. Other jurisdictions, like Canada and the U.K., are much more restrictive in allowing quotation by a subsequent author.

#1). Nonfiction works have more fair-use latitude than fiction simply because it is easier to show a "transformative" aspect in a nonfiction work. For the same reason, it is easier to establish fair use of nonfiction content because nonfiction material generally invites discussion and commentary and sometimes reformulation (Factor #2).

There is very little fair use allowed for unpublished works, as the presidential-memoir case established (Factor #4). Quotations from unpublished sources should be sparing in both length and total quantity and should have a clear commentary/criticism purpose or a strong "transformative" character.

*

Alex Gigante is a leading publishing attorney with over forty years of experience who advises individual and corporate clients in a wide range of litigation, publishing, media, online and intellectual property matters.

COPYRIGHT IS A QUESTION OF CONTROL

An author says calls to limit copyright are misguided

BY LINCOLN MICHEL

Writing is a strange career. You spend countless hours pouring your soul on the page for no promise of pay, no benefits, and no guarantee anyone will even publish you. Then you go online and find out people think you have it too damn good. That was the recent situation when—as part of the controversy over the Dr. Seuss estate's decision to cease publication of six largely obscure titles with offensive content—former *Vox* writer Matthew Yglesias tweeted that "books that are 30 years old should be in the public domain."

Many agreed with Yglesias and wanted to go further. The top reply suggested "even 15 or 20" years would be sufficient, while others said maybe that was too much. After all, they argued, it's not like you pay dentists or bakers for work they did years ago!

The debate was a perfect internet storm, in that it made everyone mad, was filled with bad faith arguments, and was entirely pointless. Copyright is not about to drop to 30 years, much less five. Thanks to the 1886 Berne Convention and the author advocacy of Victor Hugo, the global standard is a minimum of life plus 50. (Contrary to popular belief, this standard was set long before Mickey Mouse, though Disney did successfully lobby for an extension in the '90s.) Still, the kerfuffle highlighted some common misunderstandings about both how authors' careers and copyright work.

Being a novelist or poet is not like being a baker, dentist, lawyer, or any job that pays wages for services rendered. We give up wages and security in order to get copyright: the right to control the art we create and—if we are very lucky—parlay that intellectual property into some (typically modest amount of) money.

If we must think in business terms, being an author is like being an entrepreneur. Writers have ideas and work for themselves to make those ideas a reality. We build a brand. We do countless hours of unpaid work in the hopes that one day, down the road, it will pay off . . . or at least get us on a few panels at AWP. It doesn't work out for most of us, as internet commentators were happy to point out—but that's true of many industries. The vast majority of restaurants fail within a few years, yet no one claims anyone should be able to walk into a successful restaurant and use the kitchen for free.

When it does work out, it takes time—lots of time: years to write, years to establish a readership, and often years to catch a lucky break. Success tends to come late for authors. If you don't believe me, go turn on Netflix and watch its recent hits *Bridgerton* and *The Queen's Gambit*, based on decades-old novels by Julia Quinn and the late Walter Tevis, respectively.

Let's say an author doesn't ever succeed and spends their life crying over their MacBook. Well, so what? Why shouldn't they still control their creations? This is what copyright is really about: who gets control. It's a question that goes beyond money. Almost every author of color has a story about Hollywood wanting to adapt their work but whitewash the characters. Without copyright, Hollywood could do so freely. The editor who wants to rewrite a book's ending or change the author's vision? Without copyright, they could.

It's worth emphasizing that copyright only gives authors the right to their specific works, not to general ideas. If you want to write about a magical boy in wizard school, you can do so today as long as you don't call him Harry Potter. No one can copyright a concept like "boy at wizard school"—and good thing for Rowling, since Ursula K. Le Guin got there first with 1968's *A Wizard of Earthsea*.

Every year, countless copycats, homages, and parodies are published—to say nothing of the fan fictions and fan adaptations that populate the web for free. In addition, plenty of authors come up with similar ideas independently of one another. Unlike physical property, intellectual property can be unlimited. There are many, many more books published each year than anyone could ever read. Copyrighting books doesn't "stifle creativity" or lock away ideas, it merely offers authors (and a generation or two of descendants) some measure of control and perhaps a little cash.

Are there legitimate problems that copyright critics bring up? Yes, but most of them can be better solved another way than shrinking copyright protections. Want more public access to free books? Advocate for library funding. Worried about school budgets? Advocate for better education funding. Want to sell Superman and Mickey Mouse products? Fight for trademark reform (which is stricter than copyright and indefinite) or changes to corporate ownership.

But don't ask individual authors to give up copyright. It's really the only thing we have.

*

Lincoln Michel is the author of *The Body Scout* and can be found online at lincolnmichel.com and @thelincoln.

A version of this article appeared in the 03/22/2021 issue of *Publishers Weekly* under the headline: Copyright Is a Question of Control.

PUBLISHING SERVICES PROVIDERS

BY DAVID ZEOLLA

When considering the publication of a book, a strong analogy can be made to the construction of a house.

If a prospective homeowner is knowledgeable about home construction, that person might just set out to "self-construct."

It is unlikely that our self-constructor would have the knowledge and skills to complete every task needed to build a house from scratch. Most likely, he would subcontract some work to others who had superior knowledge and skills. Or, he would hire a general contractor to oversee the entire construction process.

The author who wants to have total control over the publication of a book can act as the contractor, subcontracting the many tasks involved in bringing a book into print to others. Or, the author could choose to hire a contractor to do all of the work.

That is when they hire a publishing services firm like Dorrance Publishing Company. The publishing services provider charges the author a flat fee to manage and complete all of the many tasks needed to bring a book into print. The author hands the manuscript and payment to the services provider and it is the provider's job to create and market the book, while keeping the author informed along the way.

The author is a client of the publishing services provider and has input and the final say on all aspects of book production (editing, page design, cover design) and develops a very specific promotion and distribution plan in conjunction with the services provider.

Just like the blueprint of a house, the author and services provider agree upon the basic details before work begins (trim size of the book, binding type, color or black and white, etc.), the scope and cost of marketing, book sales and accounting services, the time it will take to have the book on the market, and the earnings paid to the author for each book sold by each book sales channel.

Then, a fee to accomplish the agreed-upon goals is set and a publishing services agreement signed.

Like when the contractor finishes building the house, the contractor doesn't own it. The same holds true in this business relationship. The author continues to own the rights to the work and the work is copyrighted in the author's name.

When shopping for publishing services providers, keep these important points in mind:

Make sure that all the necessary services are detailed and included in the publishing services agreement that you sign. Some firms entice authors to begin work with them for an unrealistically low fee, and then relentlessly try to sell the author additional expensive, unnecessary services and products. Or, you find out that you need to pay additional for basic publishing necessities at an inflated cost.

- Will you be required to pay extra for an e-book?
- Will you be required to pay extra to have your books returnable by a bookstore (an absolute necessity)?
- Will you be required to pay extra to have your book promoted to the media and on-line?
- Will you have to pay extra to make your work available at retailers such as Barnes & Noble?

Consider how long has the firm been in existence. With the advent of the internet it seems that a new firm opens daily and some fail. Unfortunately, authors paid fees to these companies and never became published authors. Dorrance Publishing was the first publishing services provider in the United States, founded in 1920.

Be clear on what will you get paid on book sales. Some providers present confusing earnings schedules that pay earnings for some books based on wholesale, some on retail, and some on the wholesale minus the cost of printing. Some firms claim you will earn 100% of sales. How could that possibly be?

If it sounds too good to be true, it probably is. Some firms will exaggerate book sales abilities to encourage an author's participation. Publishing services firms have equal access to the same book distribution channels. No firms have special access to bookstores or the media, and no firm can guarantee a level of bookstore participation or media attention for any given title.

Be clear on how your book will be promoted before signing any publishing services agreement. Make sure all aspects of the proposed promotion are detailed. *Publishing* means to deliver and promote a book to the marketplace and fulfill orders for the book. Without a promotion campaign and fulfillment plan, you just have a printed book.

More and more authors are turning to publishing services providers, and at Dorrance we continue to serve more authors each year. With the arrival of the pandemic of 2020–2021 we experienced a surge in interest for our services. We are optimistic that interest in our full-service, turnkey publishing services will continue into 2022.

*

David Zeolla is the President of Dorrance Publishing Company, the oldest publishing services provider in the United States, founded in 1920. As a 30-year veteran of the company, he arguably has more experience than anyone currently in the publishing services industry. He and his team of publishing professionals take great pride in making "publishing dreams come true" every day.

FROM SENSITIVITY TO AUTHENTICITY TO ACCURACY: THE EVOLVING ROLE OF THE CULTURAL ACCURACY READER

BY SARAH HANNAH GÓMEZ

When a crime novelist consults a detective to verify that they've correctly depicted the investigative process, no one bats an eye. We would all generally agree that the author of a biology textbook should not be someone whose last foray into biology was in ninth grade. But somehow, as soon as socially marginalized people ask to be consulted before books presuming to tell their stories hit bookshelves, people from all points on the political spectrum complain about "censorship" and "political correctness"—when what they really mean is "someone is challenging our privilege."

"Marginalized" is a term used to describe members of the nondominant social classes within identities and demographics such as race, ethnicity, gender, sexual orientation, (dis)ability, socioeconomic status, or religion—individuals also referred to as diverse, disadvantaged, or oppressed. These are individuals who have been routinely, casually, and systematically antagonized, silenced, or barred from entry into places of power, like policy making, corporate governance, education, and creative industries like publishing—that are predominantly populated by people who are white, cisgender, nondisabled, and middle to upper class.

The call for more diverse lists and equity in publishing, rooted in children's literature studies and libraries, goes back to at least 1965. However, over the last decade the word has begun to spread more widely thanks to the internet and social media–based movements such as #BlackLivesMatter, #MeToo, #OscarsSoWhite, and #WeNeedDiverseBooks, as well as other grassroots movements. These have been catalysts for publishers to begin to take real action. Measures taken as a result include grant programs for otherwise unpaid interns, mentorships for unpublished writers and illustrators, special events for unagented writers to pitch editors directly, and what was first called "sensitivity reading."

The last of these initiatives, more appropriately described as "cultural accuracy reading," is a service typically provided by freelancers from marginalized backgrounds hired to critically examine manuscripts and write editorial reports, with an eye toward a minority or marginalized experience represented in the text. The role of a cultural accuracy reader is to educate the writer and give them the opportunity for growth—both as a person and as a writer—so they can better serve their readers. The cultural accuracy reader may correct items like outdated terms in the marked-up manuscript, accompanied by an editorial letter explaining why certain changes were made and providing additional context. In a sense, a cultural accuracy reader should reduce (but not eliminate) the author's need for a reader in the same areas in the future.

The provenance of the term "sensitivity reading" cannot be definitively pinpointed, but it is typically attributed to YA author Justina Ireland, who first built a database of people willing to do this work in 2016. Publishing professionals could consult her list to identify and hire potential editors whose backgrounds and interests aligned with their manuscript's content.

Unfortunately, freelance sensitivity readers found themselves in the same position of disenfranchisement the service was ostensibly designed to fix: the fees were too low and often nonnegotiable; vulnerable and sensitive information offered in confidence by readers was shared by authors in public forums such as Twitter; and authors and publishers invoked freelancers' names as insurance policies or endorsements if other readers criticized their books.

In addition, the commentariat outside publishing declared this process a form of censorship, characterized sensitivity readers as random people with no credentials, and jumped on the word "sensitivity" to call the freelancers "snowflakes," "the PC police," or "social justice warriors."

As a result, the marginalized people who provide these services have begun to describe themselves and their work in new terms, the most common of which are authenticity reader, targeted expert reader, and cultural accuracy reader. While some readers have distinguished themselves in the book world independently as authors or illustrators, book bloggers or vloggers, or trade reviewers, what qualifies them for the job is who they are—passionate and critical readers with culturally specific knowledge. Remember, powerful systems keep marginalized people out, so demanding specific items on a résumé is discriminatory and perpetuates the same inequalities their work is supposed to break down and repair.

It is imperative that publishers and authors recognize that a cultural accuracy read is a privilege, not a favor. It is high-quality professional (nearly academic) work akin to an editor's, and it is emotionally taxing for the cultural accuracy reader, who must share and explain experiences or concepts that can be traumatic or fatiguing. The ad hoc nature of the work, however, coupled with the industry's inability to pay contractors in a timely fashion, has made it financially untenable for many freelancers. The flat rates typically offered simply do not amount to a fair wage by hourly or professional standards.

Publishers have financial incentives to engage these freelancers, too. Manuscripts that have undergone revisions as the result of cultural accuracy reads enter the marketplace stronger and potentially perform better. Notable critical backlash to books not reviewed for cultural accuracy, such as *The Continent* by Keira Drake, published by Harlequin Teen in 2018, *The Bad Mood and the Stick* written by Lemony Snicket and illustrated by Matthew Forsythe, published by Little, Brown Young Readers in 2017, and *When We Was Fierce* by e.E. Charlton-Trujillo, released for review by Candlewick in 2016, resulted in books being delayed, recalled, or canceled altogether. The wasted costs of print galley mailings, ads, and author tours, as well as the added costs of resetting interiors after major edits, eclipse any fee that might have been paid to a cultural accuracy reader. Moreover, the cultural accuracy reader can play a pivotal role in reshaping the manuscript so that it is stronger and better received by reviewers and book buyers.

Cultural accuracy reading should be a regular part of the editorial process, no different from developmental edits, line edits, and copyediting. While cultural accuracy readers are most often engaged for reading non-#ownvoices fiction, these readers can provide detailed insight and advice in all genres, including illustration and cover art. Because they usually come from social demographics under- or unrepresented in the publishing industry, they can identify outdated language, tired tropes, foreign language errors, and microaggressions—not just in a fictional character or fantasy world but in a recipe, textbook, travelogue, or self-help book.

This process matters, not because books should be sanitized, simplified, censored, or bowdlerized, but because inaccuracy is lazy, and lazy writers produce bad books. Misrepresentation harms readers who assume stereotypes are true and internalize them, and it victimizes readers from groups that are already routinely victimized in everyday life.

*

Sarah Hannah Gómez is the Senior Editor of Cultural Accuracy Reading Services at Kevin Anderson & Associates, the first in-house position of its kind in the publishing industry. Before joining KAA, she led multiple initiatives to promote diversity in books, performed cultural accuracy readings for major publishers, and played various roles in and around the book world, including library services, trade reviewing, audiobook proofing, podcasting, and ghostwriting. She is a PhD candidate (2022) in social, cultural, and critical theory of children's and young adult literature at the University of Arizona and holds MA and MS degrees from Simmons University. Find her on various social media platforms @ shgmclicious.

GETTING THE MOST
FROM YOUR PUBLISHER

BY BART DAVIS

Let's face it. Most of us are so grateful to be published the first time, we wouldn't care if the actual "publisher" was the devil himself. We are so emotionally indebted it leaves us at a disadvantage, because the difference between a writer and a bum is a published book. It is also the difference between proud parents and those who avoid conversations about what their kids do, the difference between being a mate with validation and one still desperately seeking it, and—disregarding the truth that the vast majority of novels and nonfiction books don't sell enough copies to warrant their being published in the first place, and don't change your life, and don't make you rich and famous—nonetheless, it is our publisher who carries us over that very fine line between success and failure. We are published authors. We belong to a literary tradition stretching back into the mists. We are the storytellers. We get paid for our work.

So, if this is true, how come we rarely know anything about the house that publishes us? Why do we enter that house so shyly? Why don't most authors know how a manuscript physically becomes a real book or have a clue about the components of the publishing process? And how is it that no one tells us how to get the most from the houses to which we belong? Part of the answer is simple. Most often, the power you have in your house is in direct proportion to the sales of your book. Yet, not everybody is a bestselling author, so for those who aren't—and even for those of us who are—I offer some advice.

First rule. You may dream of fame and fortune, but your star can fall quickly, so be reasonable in your working relationships, especially with your editor. Do not be afraid of your editor. A good editor will make your book better. They believed in you sufficiently to champion your book and now have the same vested interest. They want your book to be as literarily perfect and commercially marketable as possible. Their life is their work, same as you, so weigh their advice carefully. Test it. Not always, but quite often, their objectivity will add depth and insight to your work.

Second rule. Let your agent handle big negatives. In situations where you and your editor or art director or the sales force are in direct and irrevocable conflict, let your agent handle the problem. Agents see things from a different angle—the business angle. They are used to pouring oil on troubled waters. I was told this by my own remarkable agent (from whom I learned much of what I suggest here) almost 40 years ago. It has proved great wisdom. Agents are best at conflict resolution, so let them do their job—leaving you free to make artistic decisions and allowing the first rule to, well, rule.

Third rule. And here's a tough one: make the phone call, it's *your* book. Writers can lessen a great deal of frustration if we allow ourselves not to be straitjacketed by what we perceive as—or are told is—protocol. Confused by editorial decisions, book design, cover art, publicity, jacket copy, social media, and so on? Whether or not you have contractual control of any of these, you must approach them all as if you do. Assuming the first and second rules are in operation, you're in for a surprise. The art director is a person. So are the head publicist and the VP of sales and the editorial director. Shockingly, so is your publisher. You have a problem? You want things a certain way? You have something to add? It's your book—make the phone call. My experience has been that these valuable people will listen and take what you want into consideration and try to execute most ideas within reason.

Finally, should all that be taking place: rule four. Be publicly appreciative. Recognize those who have welcomed your ideas and worked for you. Send that email to the publisher thanking them. Acknowledge your editor and others who shared your creative journey. Forget the old adage about catching flies, do it because they are dedicated professionals who care deeply about what they do, and they have gone out of their way to give you their very best.

The balance of power that is a publishing relationship is not unique. Here's the truth. You can decide what's in your book, but they can decide not to publish it. We're all invested as to how that goes.

My editors and publishers over the years have made me a better writer, a more sensitive collaborator, and a wiser man. I thank them for helping me be part of the unique partnership that gives so much to so many—the world of books.

*

Bart Davis is the international bestselling author of 10 novels and nine nonfiction books. He has also written two feature films and, with coauthor Julian Lennon, the *New York Times* bestselling children's book series *Touch the Earth*, *Heal the Earth*, and *Love the Earth*. Davis lives in New York.

PW

THE END OF EDITING

An author argues that editors have become too hands-off

BY SADIE HOAGLAND

We have so many fantasies of what the writer's life is like: jotting down notes at a café, time to dream, and a certain ease of getting published. While many of these, particularly the last, quickly fade, either because of early rejections or the need for a steady paycheck, there is one fantasy that I held on to until my first book was published: that of the overly involved, tough-love editor who would take my work to some next level—the Gordon Lish to my Raymond Carver—and care about it as much as I did.

My first book, a story collection, was published by a university press. The peer reviewers each gave a few careful comments. One reviewer wanted one story cut, the other thought it could be reworked. A second story was recommended for "fine-tuning."

I agreed to address these small issues, and I waited for the editor to whom I had originally submitted the work to give me her edits. They never came. She told me to make the changes the reviewers had suggested, and then I was whisked right on to copy editing. I know she cared about the book. She just wasn't going to edit it in the way I thought she would.

Rewind a year, to when I found an agent for my debut novel. He and I spent months going back and forth with my revisions, his comments, and more revisions. Here was the editing process I expected: where sentences are debated, scenes deleted, problems large and small addressed. Throughout this process, he kept telling me editors these days like really clean copy, and I started to realize that editors don't really edit anymore.

"My agent used to be an editor," says author Keith Lee Morris, whom I contacted after hearing him discuss the editing process at a book event, "and she quit to become an agent so that she could work more closely with authors on their manuscripts."

My own agent, Madison Smartt Bell, agrees that editing has shifted:

"Editors now can expect manuscripts submitted to them to be in an extremely finished state, perfected whether by writers teaching in the academy, or by agents drawing on their past experience as editors, or a combination of those two."

Morris adds that editors are now expected to promote their books, and I know this was true of my university press editor, who not only acquired the book but was its marketing department, as well.

So, what have we lost with these changes in the industry? Is it just romantic ideals, or has some real care and attention to detail been lost? My debut novel, *Strange Children*, comes out with an independent press this month, and while the editor was certainly not a line-by-line editor, she did give me several helpful notes and talked me through ideas at length. I appreciated both her insight and her trust in me to take her comments and change the book how I saw fit. I know the time she spent made it a better book.

Morris did eventually seek out an "old-school" editor for one novel, but the experience was challenging: as writers, we may not be used to hands-on editing anymore, either. However, he admits, "There's absolutely no doubt in my mind that, ultimately, he made it a much better book. He pushed me beyond my comfort zone in a couple of crucial scenes, for which I'll always be grateful, even though it was painful at the time."

Another writer, Lauren Kate, requires an extensive three-pass editing process. "I need the agonizing, visionary collaboration with my editor to end up anywhere near the story I'm trying to tell," she says.

When we don't have that, what's lost isn't just the quality or the not-quite-reached potential of a book, but also a sense of collaboration and mentorship. And though teachers, agents, and other writers are stepping up to fill the gap, there's no guarantee that will always happen. As a writer, I regret not knowing that publication acceptance meant that the more rigorous editing process was behind me, not ahead of me.

The university press that published my book recently asked me to peer review a new book, and when I voted yes on the manuscript, I also handed in several pages of editorial notes, knowing I may be the only reader to do so. The editor and writer both responded with gratitude. And yet there were many small edits I would have suggested if I had been the actual editor, many places I thought a talented writer could be pushed more. As it stands, it doesn't seem likely that push will happen. And that push, to me, seems like something we should seek out as writers, and make time for as publishers.

*

Sadie Hoagland is an associate professor of English at the University of Louisiana at Lafayette and directs the creative writing program there. She is the author of the novel *Strange Children* (Red Hen, May) and the 2019 story collection *American Grief in Four Stages*.

A version of this article appeared in the 05/17/2021 issue of *Publishers Weekly* under the headline: The End of Editing.

⑪

GHOSTWRITING

EVERYONE HAS A BOOK INSIDE THEM . . . JUST WAITING TO BE WRITTEN

BY GLENN PLASKIN

In fact, 81% of all Americans say they want to write a book, with an ever-increasing number of them striking out to do so.

From motivational speakers to corporate executives, from entrepreneurs to entertainment personalities (not to mention anyone with a story to tell), would-be authors are appearing in droves, the market flooded with new titles.

In the United States alone, there are approximately 300,000 books commercially published annually. Additionally, 1.7 million books are *self*-published, a 264% increase in five years thanks to the phenomena of Amazon and other self-publishing entities. Some of these self-published books are so-called legacy projects, intended for only a private audience of family and friends, while the vast majority of new authors aspire to the public spotlight.

The appeal of a book is indisputable: It's an author's billboard—a portable calling card that lends instant credibility, a "halo" effect from the boost in prestige. This in turn leads to potential media appearances, speaking engagements, business leads, and higher fees.

But first you have to write the book—or have it written.

In this rapidly expanding book market, ghostwriting (or simply "ghosting) has become a thriving industry, a sought-after service for thousands of would-be authors who do not have the skill set or the time to write a book.

The ghostwriter is a literary professional who captures the voice of the subject, creates a viable structure for a book, interviews the author, conducts needed research, fleshes out the content, and writes a compelling narrative.

The result is a book created within the space of 3–10 months, ready for submission to a publisher.

Some ghostwriters (particularly the most established ones) will have their bylines listed on the cover of the book ("with" or "as told to"). Others will only be recognized in the acknowledgments. But many ghosts, by definition, are unattributed. In such cases, there is usually a confidentiality clause in the publishing contract that obligates the ghostwriter to remain anonymous. In any case, most typically, all copyrights of hardcover, softcover, audio, e-book, foreign and motion picture rights are obtained in the name of the author and are usually owned solely and exclusively by the author.

Whether it's a how-to book or a motivational guide, a memoir, a religious-based work, a financial self-help book, a political biography, a family story, a cookbook, or a company history, there is a specialized ghostwriter out there for *every* genre.

To find a high-quality ghostwriter: Publishers and individual clients can: (1) Search for individual ghosts or ghostwriting agencies online, which is a hit-and-miss process, as there are over 17 million listings. (2) Acquire a ghost through a literary agent with an established selection of experienced writers, usually at a premium price, though many agents are on the hunt for viable ghosts themselves. (3) Hunt in safe spaces like LinkedIn. (Stay away from Craigslist and Upwork, primarily populated by less-credentialed writers who may offer to write your book for a bargain price.) (4) Pay special attention to the paid ads on Google from ghostwriters who may be better established vis-à-vis their websites and client testimonials. (5) Reach out to ghostwriting agencies, such as the U.K.'s United Ghostwriters or New York City–based Gotham Ghostwriters, a one-stop matchmaking agency with a stable of more than 1,000 ghosts of varying experience levels and price points. (6) Check out Independent Editors Group, Book Editors Alliance, The American Society of Journalists and Authors (ASJA), Writers Guild of America, and the Association of Ghostwriters. (7) You can also post ads to the Association of Journalists and Authors and sector-specific groups such as Financial Writers Society and the Education Writers Association. **The search:** When looking for a match, it is recommended to play the field and audition prospective ghosts. Provide the ghost with a short sample of notes or text and have the ghost rewrite it in the author's voice. Authors should also request multiple referrals and study the past work of the ghost to establish credibility. And beyond a ghost's track record, published work, style, and reputation, *chemistry* between the author and ghostwriter is paramount. The personalities must click. And one size does not fit all. That's why interviewing a panel of potential ghostwriters is highly recommended.

The process for ghostwriting includes first defining an author's vision and purpose. What does the client most want to convey to readers? What are the main themes? What will the book accomplish? How long will it be? What will the book look like? How will it benefit both the author and the reader?

Next, the ghostwriter assembles all the research materials and details the book's structure, often created in storyboard format with chapter-by-chapter titles and a sequential, detailed outline of the topics for each chapter.

Then the ghostwriter interviews the subject over a period of weeks or months, using the storyboard as the guide. Interviews with other people key to the story or close to the author can also be conducted, including key professional colleagues, family members, and friends.

The interviews are transcribed, the first draft is established, revisions are exchanged at length, and the book is edited, copyedited, and proofread.

WHAT DOES THIS ALL COST?

The fees for ghostwriters are highly variable commensurate with the ghostwriter's background, experience, and track record. The cost also depends upon the scope of the work—the length of the book, the amount of time involved, the number of interviews, research required, and even travel, should it be required.

The majority of ghostwriters are compensated with a flat fee (a "work for hire") while others charge a fee plus a percentage of the royalties (typical only in large-advance projects with celebrity authors, such as presidents and First Ladies, film stars, major newsmakers, etc.)

In general terms, for a typical nonfiction book of 250–350 pages, ghostwriters in the United States fall into three ranges (as cited by Gotham Ghostwriters):

Basic: The average price for a straightforward memoir, a business book, a how-to guide, or a family legacy book will fall in the $30,000 to $60,000 range. (However: With a click on Google, it is easy to find ghosts of varying quality who will offer to write a book for as little as $5,000 to $15,000, but these are not credible prices for the amount of work involved, and may result in an unacceptable product.)

Intermediate: This group of experienced ghostwriters have typically written books for major publishers, and have a documented list of former clients, full-fledged websites, sample books, and multiple testimonials. Their price ranges from $65,000 to $150,000.

Elite: This tier of ghostwriters are typically celebrity journalists or established authors who have written *New York Times* bestsellers for celebrities, national figures, or high-net-worth individuals. Their credibility is well-established via book reviews, media appearances, and book sales. Again, they have complete websites that present credible client testimonials. Their prices range from $150,000 to $300,000 (though the ghostwriter for Hillary Clinton's 2002 memoir is believed to have been paid $500,000, as Clinton received an $8 million advance.)

Fees to ghostwriters are typically paid in halves or thirds. Any potential ghostwriter who requires the *full* amount up front is not credible and should not be hired.

Sometimes the fee is paid to the ghostwriter directly from the client; less often, the publisher will pay the ghostwriter, especially in multimillion-dollar-advance projects where everything is riding on a stellar product.

*

Glenn Plaskin, a *New York Times* bestselling author and celebrity journalist, is one of the nation's premier ghostwriters (www.ghostwriteyourbook.com). His more than 25 books include collaborations with CEOs, entertainment personalities, motivational experts, media figures, performing artists, and public speakers. His own books include: *Horowitz: The Biography of Vladimir Horowitz, Turning Point: Pivotal Moments in the Lives of America's Celebrities,* and *Katie Up and Down The Hall: The True Story of How One Dog Turned Four Neighbors into a Family.*

His profiles and syndicated columns have appeared in the *New York Times,* the *Daily News, San Francisco Chronicle, Los Angeles Times, Chicago Tribune, Family Circle, US Weekly, Ladies Home Journal, Cosmopolitan, W,* and *Playboy.* His interview subjects have included such figures as Meryl Streep, Al Pacino, Robert De Niro, Katharine Hepburn, Nancy Reagan, Bill Gates, Calvin Klein, Edward Kennedy, Audrey Hepburn, Elizabeth Taylor, Michael Jackson, Paul Newman, Dolly Parton, Leona Helmsley, Barbara Walters, Diane Sawyer, Peter Jennings, Yoko Ono, Sylvester Stallone, Donald Trump, Cher, Diana Ross, Bette Midler, Harrison Ford, Lionel Richie, Carol Burnett, Shirley MacLaine, Judge Judy, Betty White, and hundreds of others. His TV appearances include *The Today Show, Oprah, Larry King, Joan Rivers, Sally Jessy Raphael, Geraldo,* and *Good Day New York.* He lives in New York City.

10 GHOSTWRITERS

The following is a short list of reputable ghostwriters. There are thousands of ghosts out there, many of whom can be found through literary agents and full-service ghostwriting agencies.

Glenn Plaskin
Website: www.ghostwriteryourbook.com
Email: gplaskin@ghostwriteyourbook.com

Bill Blankschaen
Website: www.faithwalkers.com
Email: blankschaenbill@gmail.com

Mark Davis
Email: texdavis@aol.com

Joscelyn Duffy
Website: www.joscelynduffy.com
Email: joscelyn@joscelynduffy.com

Barry Fox
Website: www.barryfox.us
Email: barry@barryfox.us

Wynton Hall
Website: www.wyntonhallco.com
Email: wynton@wyntonhallco.com

Michael Levin
Website: www.michaellevinwrites.com
Email: MichaelLevinWrites@gmail.com

Marji Ross
Website: www.marjirossconsulting.com
Email: mross@marjirossconsulting.com

Leon Wagener
Email: leonwagener@yahoo.com

Robert Bruce Woodcox
Website: www.theghostwriter.net
Email: ighostwrite@icloud.com

MATCHMAKER, FREELANCER, OR FIRM?: UNDERSTANDING THE EVOLVING GHOSTWRITING MARKET

BY KEVIN ANDERSON

Ghostwriters have long been the secret force behind many big-name authors. Speechwriter Ted Sorensen, for example, penned John F. Kennedy's Pulitzer Prize–winning *Profiles in Courage*. Harry Houdini published a story in *Weird Tales* that was actually written by H.P. Lovecraft. Even bestselling authors James Patterson and Tom Clancy are known to have hired writers to flesh out their artistic vision. It's common knowledge among industry insiders that a significant portion of bestselling nonfiction, and even fiction, is written by a ghost or with a close collaborator.

While ghostwriters often used to work in the shadows, the stigma and secrecy surrounding the practice has dissipated significantly in recent years. In fact, the open use of ghostwriters has become widely accepted and even respected within the publishing industry. It seems most people have come to accept that aspiring authors with powerful stories and messages shouldn't be blocked from sharing them with the masses just because they lack writing skills.

The trend toward acceptance has led to a proliferation of ghostwriters and platforms through which authors can locate and collaborate with them. In some ways, it's never been easier to find a ghostwriter, but the sheer number of options can be daunting, and many authors lack the professional experience to adequately judge a writer's qualifications and reputation. A poor choice of ghostwriter can mean more than just a bad investment, but also lost time, production dates missed, and in some cases publishing contracts canceled. Choosing the right writer is of paramount importance.

Traditionally, authors find a ghostwriter in one of two ways: by independently searching for writers and then contacting them directly (or via their agent), or by using a matchmaker service that pairs the author with a writer and then steps aside. In recent years, however, a new model has emerged: the ghostwriting firm. In this option, the author's contract is with the firm, which pairs an author with a writer and then oversees and supports the process.

There are benefits and drawbacks to each of these approaches.

The advantages of connecting with a freelance writer directly are typically cost and simplicity. The author and ghost can negotiate a fee directly, and they each have immediate access to the other. Changes to the contract or working arrangement can also be made quickly and on the fly.

These advantages, though, also make this option the most risky. By trusting the entire project to one person, the author has no recourse should anything go wrong nor does the author have anyone to advocate for their interests. It's also not uncommon for writers to overpromise; a freelancer's workload is often uncertain, so it shouldn't come as a surprise that the answer to any new contract offer is often "yes," leading to potential scheduling bottlenecks down the road.

Matchmaking services mitigate some of these risks. Companies like Gotham Ghostwriters and Reedsy allow an author to pitch their project to a large number of potential ghostwriters, who then bid on the contract, with the matchmaker taking a percentage of the freelancer's fee. While matchmakers typically don't oversee any part of the writing process, they do serve as a loose vetting tool, highlighting writers with a more established track record and publishing history. Reedsy even offers a "Project Protection" program, which serves as a financial insurance policy against breach of contract. One of the biggest advantages to the matchmaker approach is the sheer volume of collaborator options (and associated ranges in cost) that it presents to an author.

The third and newest option, the ghostwriting firm, offers additional layers of protection and quality control. A ghostwriting firm is composed of a team of in-house editors, writers, project managers, and other staff who collectively ensure the success of the collaboration. As a result, the ghostwriter becomes just one part of a larger team geared toward a project's success and not the deciding factor in whether it fails or flourishes.

In the case of an unfortunate writer/author mismatch, the author doesn't have to go through the whole solicitation process again. The ghostwriting firm replaces the writer without kill fees or renegotiations, ensuring that momentum continues, deadlines are safeguarded, and the project is completed.

The ghostwriting firm can also provide an author, especially an unagented one, with many other beneficial book-related service options that a freelance writer isn't in a position to offer. A single package may include book-planning sessions as a team; layers of editorial review and direction from former acquisitions editors; beta reader testing; cultural accuracy readings; book proposals and pitch materials; publisher and agent solicitation; marketing, publicity, and bestseller sales strategies; and general industry guidance throughout the process.

While the ghostwriting firm would seem to favor the author, some ghostwriters actually prefer this option. Eric Spitznagel, who's collaborated on dozens of books with celebrities, chefs, and CEOs, says, "I've had substantially better experiences working with a firm than doing it alone or with matchmakers. There's a freedom in knowing everything doesn't rest on your shoulders. The extra layers aren't just there to protect the author; the ghostwriter also benefits, whether it's help with scheduling or an objective set of eyes on first drafts."

The ghostwriting firm is also well-suited to serving publishers and agents with multiple ghostwriting needs. Rather than hiring individual writers for every project, a firm can operate as their one-stop shop with each book falling under the same boilerplate contract and editorial management. "It streamlines everything when you're not having to micromanage each writer," says Tim Burgard, a senior acquisitions editor at HarperCollins Leadership. "You know the firm is going to get the books done on schedule even if a writer replacement needs to be made."

Of course, the ghostwriting firm may not be right for every author or project. While costs can be comparable to freelancers—as some writers are willing to accept lower fees in exchange for the firm's advocacy and author handling, steady workflow, and editorial assistance—the additional oversight and management comes at an additional cost to the firm and, ultimately, the client. If an author wants to work one-on-one with a writer and isn't concerned about the writer's dependability, then the direct and matchmaking options can be less expensive. And some authors, as well as some ghosts, simply prefer a one-on-one relationship, especially when the material is highly personal or sensitive.

In the end, choosing a ghostwriter is a personal and professional choice that depends on the author's comfort level, priorities, and goals. As the publishing landscape continues to change—with publishing staffs being trimmed, but not lists, thereby leaving editors overloaded and with less time than ever to work with authors on their manuscripts—ghostwriting firms and freelance editorial options are likely to play an ever-increasing role in the process of bringing books to publication.

*

Kevin Anderson is the CEO and editor-in-chief of Kevin Anderson & Associates, a Manhattan-based editorial firm that provides a range of ghostwriting, editing, and consultation services to literary agents, publishers, and authors. Kevin began freelance editing and tutoring in 2005 while completing his graduate studies at Harvard University.

Since then, he's launched multiple consulting and editorial services businesses both in the United States and the U.K. Learn more about Kevin and his firm of former acquisitions editors and editorial directors, who have overseen the development of thousands of books, including multiple #1 *New York Times* bestsellers, at kawriting.com.

HOW TO BE A GHOSTWRITER

The ghostwriter of V.C. Andrews's titles for 32 years shares some secrets

BY ANDREW NEIDERMAN

There is so much more ghostwriting being done since I began writing V.C. Andrews over 32 years ago. Recently *PW* reviewed *The Silhouette Girl*, and the review ended with "Andrews fans should be satisfied." What greater compliment could a ghostwriter receive? He or she is keeping the style, treatment, characters, and plot concepts authentic enough for the fan base to support the title.

But what is ghostwriting? What is required? When my agent, Anita Diamant, who represented Andrews, proposed I try to keep the books alive, I studied every published Andrews novel to capture her essence, syntax, vocabulary, and unique approach to character. I picked up on how she used dialogue, setting, and surprise.

When I first began the assignment, I was writing far more graphic novels under my own name, the highlight being *The Devil's Advocate*, which became a major motion picture. At one point, I actually wrote on two different computers to embed the differences in writing for Andrews and my other writing work and in a sense became multipersonality.

Writing from the POV of a young girl wasn't alien to me. My first published novel, *Sisters*, released by Stein and Day, was from the point of view of a young woman. I love using the line from *Shakespeare in Love* when asked how I can do that: "It's a mystery." In a sense it is, but there really isn't a big mystery to successful ghostwriting.

You literally need to absorb everything the writer wrote and become a good mimic. You have to be able to subordinate your instinct to change it, and when you arrive at a story line, you have to question whether it is something the writer would have thought of or found intriguing. You also have to imagine, based on what you know, what would intrigue the writer if he or she had gone on. For that you might very well have to get into the writer's life, learn as much as you can about what forces developed his or her talent and respect them.

After a while, if you're successful, you won't feel you're mimicking. You'll feel it's you, especially if, like me, you've done it for over 32 years. And then the pride will sink in and the ambition will double. You now have an obligation to keep the writer alive. You will try harder to get film adaptations. And that is just what I did.

I wrote a script to adapt *Rain*, and it was produced with Faye Dunaway, Robert Loggia, and Brooklyn Sudano (Donna Summers's daughter) in the featured roles. I pounded the pavement with producer Dan Angel in Hollywood, and we generated what became 10 straight Andrews films at the Lifetime Network, with potential for more in the works. And I've revived *Flowers in the Attic* with more novel sequels, the current one being *Beneath the Attic*, branching out among the secondary characters and family history—the family being the notorious Foxworths. Because I was a director of dramatics and had published plays, I considered *Flowers in the Attic* for the stage, and now a stage play is in development.

There are a few personal factors that have made this possible and successful. I taught film studies for more than 20 years and had a deep understanding of film adaptations of novels. Getting *The Devil's Advocate* and eight additional titles adapted familiarized me with the Hollywood machine. Pitching an Andrews story was more complicated because it was ghostwritten, but now that there are more than 146 million copies of books in the series in circulation (print copies plus e-book sales) and at least one title has been published in just about every country that has a publisher, including China, I had more opportunity and motivation to find film opportunities.

It's very exciting when it works, and to make it work, you have to have had the cooperation and support of your publisher. The Andrews novels have outlasted a few publishers, but everyone who assumed the mantle joined in the effort until we are where we are today, still successfully publishing 40 years after *Flowers in the Attic* was released and took the world market by storm.

Ghostwriting is definitely an art form; it has its own rules and methods. After a while, you'll look at your work and yourself and think, I'm a ghost who gives life to history.

*

Andrew Neiderman's next two V.C. Andrews novels, *Out of the Attic* (Feb.) and *Shadows of Foxworth* (June), will continue the history of the Foxworth family.

A version of this article appeared in the 01/13/2020 issue of *Publishers Weekly* under the headline: How to Be a Ghost.

THE BOOKLIFE GUIDE TO SELF-PUBLISHING

I. SELF-PUBLISHING I0I

DIY: How to Self-Publish an E-book
By Alex Palmer

Here is a roundup of the major e-book platforms that are available, and what they have to offer.

A self-publisher has a growing number of options for how to get his or her book out to the public, but that can present its own challenges. With so many e-book platforms—old, new, and updated—to choose from, which is the right fit? Here is a roundup of the major e-book platforms that are available, and what they have to offer self-publishers.

Amazon Kindle Direct Publishing (KDP)—Amazon's e-book publishing platform offers a royalty rate of 70% of list price minus delivery costs, with a few exceptions. One of the chief advantages of working with Amazon is the incentives it offers to authors through its KDP Select program. Authors who offer their books exclusively through KDP can have them included in the Kindle Owners' Lending Library (earning money every time their book is borrowed), and get access to promotional tools such as free copies for readers during specific periods. The disadvantage of this is that the author is limiting his or her discoverability by only offering the book through one platform.

Smashwords—The largest distributor of indie e-books in the world now carries more than 180,000 titles in its catalog. Through the company's free "Meatgrinder" program, authors can convert their Word document into any of nine e-book formats to transfer into any of the major e-bookstores. Authors receive 85% of net sales made directly through Smashwords, and 70.5% through affiliate sales to retailers like Apple iBookstore, Barnes

& Noble, Sony, and Kobo (full distribution details at www.smashwords.com). It also offers authors a helpful, free book-marketing guide that is worth a read.

NOOK Press—The recently rebranded version of PubIt!, this platform from Barnes & Noble distributes books through the NOOK Bookstore, so it is more limited in distribution than platforms like KDP or Smashwords. It varies its royalty rates by the price of the book, offering 65% royalty for titles priced between $2.99 and $10, but just 40% for those priced below $2.99 or above $10. The new interface makes it simple for authors to convert, upload, and edit their work, plus it has now added the ability to collaborate with other writers, sharing their work through a new Web-based authoring tool.

Vook—This platform emphasizes its design offerings for both digital and print books, in addition to marketing and distribution. Authors can enhance e-books with video and audio features, or get "bookstore-worthy copies" of their print book on demand. The company puts great importance on the personal touch it offers, and urges every prospective author to sign up for a free consultation before it provides a quote. Vook distributes through all the major online book retailers, with royalties ranging from 45% to 85% of the list price (its wholesale relationship with Amazon ensures that regardless of the e-retail giant's discounts, the author is still paid by the price he or she sets). Its dashboard also provides daily reports on e-book sales.

iBooks Author—Available as a free download for Mac users, this platform is geared toward those looking to create graphic-heavy projects, whether children's books or interactive novels. The design process is similar to laying out a PowerPoint presentation, beginning with template choices like "craft" or "cookbook" and adding in text and images, as well as animation and 3D objects. It can then be distributed for free through Apple's iBookstore, though unlike other distributors, it does not provide authors with an ISBN for their books, instead directing them to Bowker's Identifier Services page (which charges $125 for one ISBN and $250 for 10).

BookBaby—This platform allows authors to distribute their e-book through Amazon, Apple iBookstore, and other major e-bookstores. BookBaby's unusual payment model makes it a better fit for authors expecting strong sales of their books: it does not take a cent from royalties, but charges a $99 initial sign-up fee and $19 for every year afterwards. Special offers are available for authors seeking more hands-on assistance, including the Standard Package for $199, which includes e-pub conversion and e-book proofs; or the Premium Package for $349, which provides lifetime membership and a free author website among other offerings.

Lulu—This platform offers a free e-book conversion as well as a number of for-pay premium services covering everything from editing a manuscript to creating a promotional author video. According to its revenue calculator, Lulu takes about 10% commission on books sold through retailers like Apple's iBookstore, in addition to the 30% that Apple itself takes.

Booktango—This e-book platform from self-publishing giant Author Solutions allows authors to convert, upload, and edit their manuscript, distributing through Nook, Amazon, and others. Booktango advertises that it offers the "best royalties in the book industry," with 100% of royalties from its own online bookstore going to the author, as well as 100% of net royalties from other online retailers (after Amazon and others have taken their 30% or so).

DIY: Print-on-Demand 101
By Daniel Lefferts & Alex Daniel

Here's a breakdown of some of the major POD players and the attributes that make each service unique.
E-books may be the future of publishing, but print editions continue to make up a large portion of book sales, and, for many indie authors, printing remains a crucial aspect of the self-publishing process.

One of the most popular ways indie authors print physical books is through POD—or print-on-demand—services. The clearest benefit of using a POD service is that authors don't have to spend money printing large quantities of physical books that customers may or may not end up buying; with POD, authors only have to print as many books as they sell.

Most services also ship to customers directly, which cuts down on delivery time and allows authors to attend to the many other tasks and responsibilities that come with self-publishing. And, because books are always ready to be printed (assuming the contract with the service remains active), titles are never out of stock. Finally, many POD providers offer ancillary services, such as cover design and copy editing, which can be of tremendous help to indie authors who lack the contacts or expertise to manage these aspects of the process on their own.

Beyond these features, which are common to most services, POD providers vary widely in the benefits they provide, the business models they follow, and the fees they charge. Here's a breakdown of some of the major POD players and the attributes that make each service unique.

(Note: This article was originally published in June 2014 and was updated on April 10, 2020 and March 4, 2021.)

KINDLE DIRECT PUBLISHING

Amazon's Kindle Direct Publishing program (formerly CreateSpace) is one of the few POD providers that doesn't charge a set-up fee, and its roster of additional services—which includes copy editing, cover design, interior design, and marketing—is one of the more robust. The service lets authors set the price of books and also offers two distribution plans: Standard Distribution, through which authors can make books available on Amazon and Kindle Direct; and Expanded Distribution, through which authors can make books available to libraries, bookstores, and academic institutions. (Be aware that the Expanded Distribution plan involves a significantly higher "sales channel" deduction, and thus lower royalties.) KDP's main selling point—its sheer abundance of options—can also prove somewhat bewildering. Fortunately, the service provides some guidance in the form of community message boards, customer service, and instructional videos.

INGRAMSPARK

IngramSpark, a POD service operated by the book wholesaler Ingram, offers an impressively streamlined process for publishing, producing, and distributing both electronic and physical indie books. Though printing with the service requires some setup expenses and legwork—authors will need to secure an ISBN as well as compile metadata and stipulate territory rights—the benefits of publishing with Ingram are clear. As the site states, it has "Access to over 39,000 retailers, libraries, schools and universities—online and in stores." This also includes "E-book distribution from more than 70 online partners serving readers across the globe." In addition, the service boasts that it offers a wide range of paper options, trim sizes, and bindings, making it a potentially good choice for authors with particular printing needs.

LULU

According to its website, Lulu has printed more than 2 million books in more than 225 countries and territories since its inception in 2002. The service charges no set-up fee, and provides a book cost calculator that lets authors estimate per-book printing fee, which is dependent upon factors such as trim size, binding type, and page count. Assuming a book meets the distribution requirements, Lulu will make authors' titles available on Amazon.com and BN.com, among other retailers, at no cost. The site also offers estimates of royalties from each sales channel. Volume discounts kick in starting at 15 copies, and increase up to 20% off for orders of over 1,200 copies. Lulu also offers add-on services, such as copy editing and book video production, but these tend to be significantly more expensive than those offered by other POD services. Lulu is an especially good option for authors printing books for personal use that they don't plan to sell via retail, in which case an ISBN is not required.

iUNIVERSE

iUniverse offers five packages for indie authors, ranging in price from $999 to $7,499. Features of the most basic option include ISBN assignment, custom cover, author copy discounts, e-publication, and up to 25 black-and-white inserts. The offerings included in the more expensive packages consist largely of eligibility for iUniverse author programs and upgraded versions of the more basic services, such as an "elite" custom cover. In addition to offering a range of binding sizes and paper types for both soft- and hardcover books, the site also allows authors to create their own audiobooks. The cost of that service is $999.

AUTHORHOUSE

AuthorHouse caters to authors who'd like help with all aspects of the self-publishing process. For a fee of $899, authors can get the basic Discovery package, which includes ISBN assignment, custom cover and interior design, digital proofs of books, availability in print and e-book format, marketing consultation, and distribution to online retailers including Barnes & Noble and Amazon. Other packages include the Book to Network package ($1,799), which includes a radio interview, and the Book to Hollywood package ($1,599), which includes a free "industry-standard synopsis" (presumably intended for the eyes of producers). Be aware that AuthorHouse charges separate fees for many other important, even crucial, services, such as post-production revisions. While the site's one-stop-shop model will certainly appeal to some indie authors, others—especially those who are taking care of editing and marketing on their own—may find the prices a bit steep.

DOG EAR

(Note: As of the March 2021 article update, Dog Ear Publishing's services are no longer available.)

Dog Ear Publishing's services start at $1,498 (for the Basic Package), and run up to $7,999 (for the Ultimate Package). All packages include an ISBN assignment, a Library of Congress number, paperback and hardcover formats, custom cover and interior design options, free author copies, and inclusion in Google Book search. The more expensive packages include copy editing services, extensive marketing materials, and the creation of an author website with a domain of the author's choosing. Dog Ear's retail partners include Barnes & Noble, Amazon, and Books-A-Million; the site also allows authors to set their own prices and offer competitive printing costs.

Perhaps what really sets Dog Ear apart, though, is that they provide an extensive—not to mention refreshingly honest—comparison between their services and those of other POD providers.

The Indie Authors Guide to DIY Audiobooks
By Ryan Joe and Alex Daniel

So you want to produce an audio edition of your self-published book? Here's what you need to know.

(Note: This article was originally published in June 2015 and was updated on Nov. 4, 2016 and on March 4, 2021.)

So you want to enliven your self-published book with a rousing audio edition? To hear your work performed is an exciting prospect, but, before you get too deep into the weeds, understand that creating, marketing, and distributing an audiobook on your own will require a considerable commitment. In other words: it can get really expensive really quickly, and the return on investment isn't guaranteed because audio editions can be difficult to sell. If you're like most authors, you need serious support for every facet—from narration through production, all the way to marketing and distribution.

"It's a big endeavor," says Tyson Cornell, the founder of the small press Rare Bird Books and the boutique marketing and promotions shop Rare Bird Lit. Cornell's background in the music and literary industries gives him familiarity with the worlds of publishing and audio production. "It's more than setting up a mike and doing a podcast," he says. "People get into their own heads really quickly. They think: I don't need expertise, and if I have someone helping me, I'm getting scammed."

SEEK OUT SERVICES

There are many companies and individuals that offer some or all the services needed to self-publish an audiobook. Whatever you decide to do—whether to let a single company produce and distribute your audiobook or to enlist the talent and expertise à la carte—depends on your needs, your budget, and sometimes even the genre of your book. Certainly the Audiobook Creation Exchange (ACX), hosted by Amazon-owned Audible, is the go-to marketplace for finding talent to help narrate, produce, and distribute self-published audiobooks.

"Of course, the ACX site is the prevailing way for a self-published author to hire a narrator," says Debra Deyan, cofounder of the Deyan Institute, a school to train audiobook narrators, and head of the production company Deyan Audio Services.

ACX connects authors to three tremendous buying platforms: Amazon, Audible, and Apple's iTunes. And while it's true that ACX is still the go-to for indie authors interested in creating audiobooks, many e-book publishers have developed audio production services. Here's a look at some notable providers.

Deyan Audio Services

The name Deyan is legendary in audiobook circles. Deyan Audio—which was cofounded by Debra Deyan and her late husband, Bob Deyan—offers complete audiobook production at $500 per finished hour (i.e., an hour of fully produced audio) and offers over 1,800 actors.

For authors who simply need help with editing and mastering, Deyan Audio charges $100 per finished hour for editing and $25 per finished hour for mastering.

Dog Ear Publishing

(Note: As of the March 2021 article update, Dog Ear Publishing's services are no longer available.)

"Dog Ear is a small business," says Miles Nelson, cofounder of the Indianapolis-based company. "We take the approach that we're the high-end boutique guys."

The same can be said for the company's audiobook production arm, which Nelson concedes is still a small part of Dog Ear's overall business. For $1,600, the author can read her own work. Dog Ear provides a recorder and direction over the telephone. It also provides the editing and mastering services in-house as well as the ISBN and distribution services.

It gets a bit pricier if the author wants to use one of the professional narrators Dog Ear sources from the Indianapolis area: the rate can be north of $4,600 depending on the length of the book.

eBookIt

eBookIt's initial foray into audiobook production simply meant running a book through a text-to-speech offering. Clients—mostly nonfiction authors—liked it. But the company changed its model after founder Bo Bennett had his book professionally narrated. "Once we heard that, we couldn't listen to the computer-generated ones," says company president Ryan Levesque. "We scrapped that and went with the human narration."

The company now maintains a stable of eight voice actors, whose prices range between $150 and $350 per finished hour. For a $149 services fee and 15% of net sales, eBookIt manages the entire project, which includes providing an ISBN, developing the actual audiobook files, and creating an audiobook cover image from the e-book.

Because the final price varies based on options the author chooses, eBookIt has an online calculator to help authors figure out the services they want and the associated costs in advance.

Infinity Publishers

When Arthur Gutch started at Infinity Publishers, its AudioBrite arm did production work for large publishing houses such as Hachette. Gutch, now the chairman, wanted to focus more on indie authors, and Infinity offers two services catering to that smaller group. The first is unabridged audio production through Infinity's Audio Books Publishing unit, which releases both CDs and digital files via Audible and iTunes.

The basic services include script preparation and contact with the narrator, plus recording, editing, proofing, mastering, publishing, and distribution. Depending on word count, the cost can run $4,000 to $5,000 or more. Additional services include abridgment ($599 per 10,000 words), sending audio copies to reviewers ($25), and hour-long phone consultations ($250).

For $779, Infinity's One-Hour Audio option will abridge a book, distilling it into an hour-long listening experience. "It's more attuned to nonfiction work, but, for shorter novels, it also applies," Gutch says.

(*Note: As of the March 2021 article update, pricing for these services no longer appear on Infinity Publishers' website.*)

FINDING YOUR NARRATOR

These high-touch services naturally aren't for everybody. Many authors would prefer to handpick their own talent. ACX remains the most comprehensive tool for this, allowing authors to listen to recorded samples of prospective narrators and request auditions.

"Choose the audition selection from your book wisely," narrator P.J. Ochlan says. For instance, it shouldn't be longer than five to seven minutes or 1,000 words. "And it may be good to pick something that features dialogue between key characters," he adds. "And if your book requires special skills such as accents, make certain they're in the narrator's wheelhouse." Additionally, as both Ochlan and award-winning narrator Johnny Heller point out, narrators on ACX double as audiobook producers—which is why authors need to assess production quality as well as performance.

This leads to another important consideration: payment. That is, deciding whether to offer a royalty share or a flat per-finished-hour fee. And it's up to the narrator to decide whether to accept. "If your book is already out there in an e-book or something, you should be able to tell the narrator what your sales are like," Heller says. "Not free downloads: sales. Is there profit potential for the narrator?"

If sales aren't great—or if an e-book hasn't been released—it might be difficult to convince a professional narrator to agree on a royalty-share model. Narrator Jeffrey Kafer says there is no solid cutoff: "If the author is selling a thousand a month on

Kindle, yup, I'll do a royalty share. But is 500 a month a good number? Probably. Two hundred? It depends how much risk a narrator wants to take." Other considerations, Kafer says, are an author's social media presence, promotion efforts, and prolificacy. New releases, after all, can spur sales of the back catalogue.

Of course, paying on a per-finished-hour basis is a different story. "Get a realistic estimate of the total running time," veteran narrator Robert Fass says. "That's critical." Running time should be based on word count because the variability of margins and font sizes makes page count unreliable. "It you've got 100,000 words, you can count on a 10-hour finished audio product," Fass says, adding that it often takes a professional two hours to create one finished hour.

Another thing to keep in mind is that there's a pricing floor for hiring members of SAG-AFTRA as readers. The minimum rates are negotiable but typically begin at $200 per finished hour, according to a union spokesperson, plus a 13% contribution to the guild's health and retirement fund. "That said, narrators are free to set their own, higher rates," the spokesperson says.

Additionally, Kafer urges indie authors to relax and let the professionals do their jobs. "One of the big things that authors do is they feel they need to direct or micro-manage," Kafer says. "I've heard horror stories where the narrator submits the book and gets a spreadsheet of a thousand things the author didn't like. That's the worst thing an author can do. I understand this is your baby, but you hired the narrator for a reason. You have to let go of your baby and let the professional you hired do their job."

Grow Your Writing Inspiration
By Shelli Chosak

I wanted to write this article because I know how important inspiration is and I have found something missing in the materials I've read previously on the topic. I finished writing my own article, then went for a walk in my neighborhood, a village-like setting with modest homes scattered on sloping grassy areas amid walking paths and a variety of very mature trees that dominate the landscape.

The trees give off an energy that fills me with peace and erases the daily trivia. Being in nature has always opened up something in me, and I found myself flooded with positive feelings, sensations, and new perspectives.

The article I had just finished came from a place of discipline, determination, and thoughtfulness, and is probably good enough. How many times have you written from that place? To move from good enough to inspiring requires you to expand your self-imposed boundaries. If you aren't writing from true inspiration, your readers will likely pick this up—and they won't be inspired.

How many books have you read that you thought were well-written and were solidly informative, but were soon forgotten? When we remember books, it's usually because we picked up on the writer's inspiration, which touched our hearts and souls or challenged our curiosity and intellect.

A clear understanding of the elements of inspiration will not only help you recognize it—it will also help you create pathways to allow it in.

In his essay "Why Inspiration Matters," published in the *Harvard Business Review* in 2011, Scott Barry Kaufman explores how inspiration impacts levels of productivity and satisfaction. He writes that people who are inspired report "higher levels of important psychological resources, including belief in their own abilities, self-esteem, and optimism. Mastery of work, absorption, creativity, perceived competence, self-esteem, and optimism were all consequences of inspiration, suggesting that inspiration facilitates these important psychological resources."

It's important to notice where your motivation is coming from. If you are mainly writing to seek praise, financial gain, or fame, these motivations, while understandable, can interfere with the authenticity of your work.

When I started writing, someone asked me what my goal was. My response: I just want to share what I have learned.

So how do you create space and allow inspiration in? Consider some big questions. I strongly suggest that you write your responses down. Start with:

- What excites you about writing?
- When did you first realize you wanted to be a writer?
- What stimulated your interest?
- Whom are you really writing your book for?
- What are your hopes and dreams about what will happen once your book is finished?
- What goals or dreams might possibly interfere with your inspiration?

The substantial energy required to write, edit, and market your book will be sustained when your inspiration is based on a burning curiosity about or true love for your subject and a desire for honesty, quality, and clarity.

The following activities will help you grow inspiration. These activities are not about developing and improving your specific writing skills. They are designed to help you develop and maintain the inspiration that will make it all work.

Increase your self-awareness. This is the most important and significant thing you can do to awaken your inspiration. Even if you think you know yourself well, there's always more to learn. Self-awareness is key to developing and maintaining inspiration and will also provide additional insights into your writing.

Keep a journal. Write something in it every day. Usually, the end of the day is the best time. If something comes up that throws you off balance, take a few minutes to write down the event, what you are feeling, and what you do with your feelings. Or just start writing, stream of consciousness—writing whatever comes into your mind, even if it's writing about not wanting to write, or feeling like this is a worthless exercise.

Pay attention to your thoughts. Notice what thoughts you have, and how you react to them. For example, do worry, fear, and judgment of others or yourself dominate your thoughts? These are automatic negative thoughts. "Don't believe everything you think," as the author Allan Lokos has said. How do your thoughts affect your inspiration to write and the quality of your writing?

Regularly pay attention to your feelings. See if you can identify them, even if you think they are unimportant. What do you do with a feeling? Brush it off or bury it, rationalize it, blame it on someone or something else, get upset that it exists, or just let it all out? The healthiest way is to acknowledge the feeling and then ask yourself what you want or need to do with that feeling. (This is the first step in emotional intelligence.)

Seek experiences that will allow inspiration in. This can mean listening to music, being in nature, or embracing solitude in other ways.

Get comfortable with vulnerability. Vulnerability is inevitable in writing: you are exposing yourself and allowing yourself to be judged. It is a great asset in your writing. In her 2010 TED talk "The Power of Vulnerability," author Brené Brown calls vulnerability "the birthplace of joy, of creativity, of belonging, of love."

Invite regular and honest feedback from people you trust. This is much easier to do when you allow your vulnerability to surface. Listen to the feedback, but avoid dismissing or accepting it too quickly. Give yourself time to think about and evaluate the feedback—both negative and positive.

Best wishes for continued inspiration!

*

Shelli Chosak is a psychotherapist and the author of *Your Living Legacy: How Your Parenting Style Shapes the Future for You and Your Child*, which was a finalist for the 2019 BookLife Prize Nonfiction Contest.

A version of this article appeared in the 06/14/2021 issue of *Publishers Weekly* under the headline: Grow Your Writing Inspiration.

The Trouble with Big Deals

By Brooke Warner

Why huge advances aren't always huge wins for budding authors.

Many indie authors dream of landing a traditional book deal with a seven-figure advance to match. Big book deals make publishing news every month, but rarely have we witnessed the blowback and ire that have followed the recent release of *American Dirt*, which has plenty of people questioning the inequities at play when it comes to what kind of authors get such advances. Americans are culturally conditioned to celebrate anyone who makes bucketloads of money for anything, never mind whether it's merited. Like beauty, merit is in the eye of the beholder—especially when it comes to fiction, a genre that's subjective by its very nature. Indie authors are uniquely positioned to recognize this truth, and when it comes to their careers, they would be well served to keep in mind that big money doesn't necessarily equate to meaningful success.

So far in 2020, Publishers Marketplace has reported 14 "major deals," meaning advances of $500,000 and up. *Publishers Weekly* has run stories about the known seven-figure deals among those, including *The Other Black Girl*, the debut novel by former Knopf assistant editor Zakiya Dalila Harris, and a memoir by Marie Yovanovitch, the former U.S. ambassador to Ukraine.

How publishing houses dole out advances is complicated, insofar as editors insist that they'll only pay for books they believe can earn out. But P&Ls exist to be manipulated, and there are countless factors at play when it comes to earn-out potential, including foreign, derivative, and serial rights, all of which are difficult—sometimes impossible—to estimate at the point of acquisition. Then there's the fact that taking a huge gamble on a debut or unproven author puts the author's entire career at risk since a "successful" book is one that earns out its advance. This means that a book that sells 10,000 copies and earns out its $10,000 advance is successful, whereas a book that sells 25,000 copies and fails to earn out its $100,000 advance is not. The publisher either drops authors who fail to earn out their advances or offers far less money for their follow-up efforts.

In the 1990s, there were few seven-figure advances, and they were certainly not for debut novelists. The first debut novel to hit the *New York Times* bestseller list in its first week may well have created a new formula for success that involved the seven-figure advance. In 2005, Little, Brown published *The Historian*, Elizabeth Kostova's Dracula story, for which it had paid $2 million. The publisher spent $500,000 promoting the book, sent out thousands of ARCs, and sent Kostova on extensive author tours leading up to publication. In the 15 years since, we've seen publishers attempt to create success stories borrowing from this playbook with Cynthia D'Aprix Sweeney's

The Nest, Kristen Roupenian's *You Know You Want This,* and Jeanine Cummins's *American Dirt,* to name a few of the better known.

During my nine-year tenure as an acquiring editor at Seal Press, which at the time was an independent press that seldom offered advances greater than $10,000, I heard lots of stories from former six-figure-deal authors who'd been cast aside by their publishers for failing to earn out.

The author Marion Winik came to Seal Press in 2005 after a three-book run with Random House. Seal was able to acquire her fourth book specifically because Random House had cut her loose.

Winik was complimentary of Random House when I called her up to confirm my memory of the events surrounding her move to Seal. She told me it had done everything it could, and her take was that the success of any book is as much about luck as it is about how much the publisher gets behind it.

Maybe this is so. But publishers have many titles on a given list, with unbalanced amounts of resources and attention going to certain books over others. These days, publishers' attempts to break out particular books are inextricable from enormous advances, accompanied by the frenzy of auctions and bidding wars that result in seven-figure advances. I've only participated in two auctions, but, from the perspective of the underdog in the bidding, it was clear that my competitors' willingness and capacity to come to the table with giant offers was the way they threw their weight around. It's also how top editors maintain their relationships with top agents, and how the industry itself maintains the status quo.

In 1997, Stephen King made news when his reported asking price for *Bag of Bones* was a jaw-dropping $17 million. He ultimately sold the book to Simon & Schuster as part of a three-book deal for $2 million that included 50% profit sharing. This was King's entrepreneurial solution to an issue that already-famous authors sometimes face, which is the flip side of the imbalance of publishing: when a book does really well, the publisher's gains are disproportionate to the author's. That the advance is meant to offset this issue is a flaw in the system.

Authors have no choice but to say yes to huge advances even if they understand the inherent gamble the publisher is making with their careers. I asked Winik if, knowing what she knows now, she would have accepted the six-figure advance that she got back in the early 1990s. "Absolutely," she said. "You have to take every chance you have in this industry."

That authors' careers have been ruined or cut short because publishers offered too much money for projects is a travesty. Setting some authors up for failure is the natural outcome of a system in which some bets win and others lose. For that reason alone, authors looking for a book deal would do well to remember that a modest advance can be a blessing and an opportunity.

While I can't imagine a world in which every aspiring author has an equal shot, I do dream of a future where the measure of a book's worth lies in readers' experience of it rather than the money that's thrown at it.

*

Brooke Warner is publisher of She Writes Press and SparkPress, a TEDx speaker, writing coach, and author of *Write On, Sisters!* and *Green-Light Your Book.*

A version of this article appeared in the 03/30/2020 issue of *Publishers Weekly* under the headline: The Trouble with Big Deals.

DIY: Crowdfunding 101
By Jennifer McCartney

How to use Kickstarter and other services to fund your book.
While crowdfunding isn't for every author, it can be an essential tool for the right project.
Without an advance or the support of a publisher's art, publicity, and marketing departments, securing funding to publish and publicize a book can be an uphill battle. Because of this, many enterprising indie authors have turned to crowdfunding platforms—which pair artists and projects with donors—to support their publishing efforts. Crowdfunding can be a fun and creative way to raise money to support a new book.

There are book-specific crowdfunding sites well worth checking out such as Pubslush, which calls itself a "global book club with a cause" and Authr.com. Though these have a smaller audience, the advantage is that funders are specifically looking to support publishing projects. The two largest and most popular sites, however, are the more established Kickstarter and Indiegogo.

(Note: As of March 2021 Pubslush and Authr's services are no longer available.)

Kickstarter
Kickstarter is the most popular crowdfunding platform. Via Kickstarter's user-friendly interface, an author creates a profile for her proposed book that includes a short description, how much she wants to raise, and what exactly she plans to do with the funds. This can cover everything from printing and shipping costs, layout and design fees, ISBN registration, photography expenses, the hiring of an illustrator, or editing and proofreading expenditures. Authors can upload images and post a personal video to add interest to their listing. The site offers helpful tips for creating the best page possible to showcase your idea. Authors should follow these guidelines to ensure that their pages are as engaging as possible.

If the project is fully funded by Kickstarter's deadline (30 days is the recommended length of time for a project) the author receives the money minus the company's 5% fee, as well as a 3%–5% processing fee that goes to Amazon Payments. Contributors can receive rewards from the author based on their level of funding. Authors should think of creative rewards to offer potential funders—such as a Skype chat for a book club, a bookmark, or signed copies of the finished book.

To begin, authors should check out the Kickstarter guidelines and note that the self-help genre (including business, health, and relationship advice) is not eligible as a Kickstarter project. Authors must also be a U.S. resident with a Social Security Number, U.S. bank account, and credit or debit card, and they must be 18 or older.

Ariane Roberts is using Kickstarter to fund her illustrated children's book *Jamie Loves Her Natural Hair*. Her advice to authors is: "plan, plan, and plan!"

"Before you even start your campaign, have your contact list ready to notify everyone about your project once it has launched," says Roberts. "Make sure you are building a list of contacts that you feel will be genuinely interested in sharing your project with their audience."

Kate Agnew, who is hoping to fund her *Donuts: A Photo Book* project through Kickstarter, says her desire to have total ownership over her project led her to the crowdfunding site. She advises potential authors to do their research before setting up their campaign, citing the two to five day waiting period before the project goes live as an example of something for which authors need to plan.

Both Agnew and Roberts cite getting word out about their campaigns to be the hardest challenge. Roberts cautions, "You may need to do some foot work by getting out and speaking to people or groups that could potentially become supporters of your project."

Crowdfunding also gives an author a sense of how popular her book might be. "It is kind of like testing the water before jumping in, which made it a good fit for me," Agnew says. "While safe in some ways, I'm still putting myself out there—still taking the risk. That's what writing is all about."

Indiegogo

Indiegogo is a popular crowdfunding site that's available to anyone in the world with a bank account, making it an option for authors based outside the U.S. Unlike Kickstarter, Indiegogo allows users to keep the funds they raise even if they don't make their funding goal with a program called Flexible Funding. The site takes a fee which is 4% of the money raised if an author's funding goal is met or 9% if it's not met. Authors are also charged 3% for credit card processing, plus a $25 wire fee for campaigns outside the U.S.

Indiegogo also offers something called the Gogofactor, which measures the activity of an author's campaign with an algorithm, rewarding active authors with newsletter or blog mentions and better search rankings.

Linnie von Sky successfully crowdfunded her first children's book, *Our Canadian Love Story*, with Indiegogo and is following that success with another campaign for an anti-bullying children's book.

"Running a campaign is a full-time job," von Sky says. Most funders are people in her extended social circles, but she notes that, given the broad appeal of the anti-bullying message of her second project, she was able to attract funding from people she doesn't know. She says the key to making a campaign successful is to be fully engaged on all social platforms. "Defending your idea and its place in the crowded crowdfunding universe is an excruciatingly exhausting effort," von Sky says.

While crowdfunding isn't for every author, it can be an essential tool for the right project—if an author is willing to work hard to promote her book.

*

Jennifer McCartney is a freelance writer, editor, and author of the novel *Afloat*. Follow her at *@jennemem*.

Are Self-Published Authors Still Indie Authors?
By Mark Coker

Amazon is replacing traditional publishers and agents as a publishing gatekeeper.

Twelve years ago, on the eve of the modern-day indie author revolution, few writers aspired to self-publish. Self-publishing was seen as a fool's errand. At the time, many writers embraced the false narrative that only publishers and literary agents possessed the divine wisdom to decide which writers are worthy of publication.

It was a different era back then: e-books accounted for less than 1% of the book market; self-publishing was all about print. Without an agent, it was difficult to get the backing of a publisher, and without a publisher it was nearly impossible to get books into physical bookstores, where most readers discovered and purchased books. So of course early self-published authors failed.

Retail distribution has always been critical to a book's success. The more stores that carry a book, and the more prominent the placement within each store, the greater the sales. Once a print book lost retail distribution, or lost prime shelf space, sales plummeted. Physical shelf space has always been precious to the author and expensive for the retailer.

When booksellers moved their stores online and opened e-book stores, it created new opportunities for self-published authors. For the retailer, virtual shelf space is cheap and unlimited.

Around 2007, the major booksellers began opening their virtual shelves to self-published e-books, making self-published e-books discoverable to readers alongside the e-books from traditional publishers. This new opportunity was nothing short of revolutionary. Self-published e-book authors began hitting national and international bestseller lists. The industry—to the mutual surprise of writers and publishers everywhere—learned that readers care more about great writing than they care about the name of the publisher.

Self-published authors celebrated their newfound freedom to publish and distribute. They celebrated their vanquishing of the gatekeepers: the agents and publishers whom they perceived as having wrongly denied them opportunities to reach readers.

Authors learned to do the hard work of publishers—and often they did it better. In the absence of large marketing budgets, they pioneered new best practices for e-book publishing, pricing, and marketing. Each time a self-published author hit a bestseller list, it inspired other writers to take a second look at e-book self-publishing. The stigma of self-publishing faded with each success.

By 2011, self-published authors began to self-identify as "indie" authors. They wore this identity as a badge of pride. Indies became the cool kids.

With the retail distribution problem solved, indie authors turned their attention to promotion. The virtual store shelves were growing more cluttered by the day with e-books from both indie and traditional publishers. Smart indies set to work breaking the code for discoverability. This code was the retailer algorithm. Algorithms are computer programs that retailers use to automatically determine when, where, and how one book is made more discoverable to readers than another.

Authors began shifting their marketing focus to please the algorithms, especially those of Amazon. Amazon's ever-changing algorithms quickly became the subject of lore. A sudden tweak could decimate an author's sales overnight—or it could catapult an unknown author to bestsellerdom. Amazon kept moving the cheese in an algorithm and policy maze.

In December 2011, Amazon introduced KDP Select, which promised greater discoverability and more e-book promotion tools for indie authors who made their books exclusive to Amazon. Thousands of indie authors embraced this new option with gusto. Soon, over one million indie e-books could only be purchased at Amazon. In other words, Amazon convinced indie authors to abandon all other retail distribution.

It is no coincidence that, following the introduction of KDP Select, other competing e-book stores saw their sales plateau or begin precipitous declines. These retailers began losing the millions of customers who wanted e-books that could only be purchased at Amazon.

Even authors who resist the siren call of KDP Select and distribute to all retailers do 70% or more of sales through Amazon. If a self-published author is earning 70% or more of their income from a single retailer, can they honestly call themselves an indie author?

Self-published authors have traded one gatekeeper for another. Unlike the traditional publishing gatekeepers of yesteryear that sought to preserve the value of books, the business model for the new gatekeeping overlord is all about stripping suppliers of pricing power, profits, and independence.

It's not too late for self-published authors to take back their independence, but time is running out. Authors should reject KDP Select exclusivity as antithetical to author independence and embrace broad distribution to all retailers. Retailers cannot survive long-term without access to the full depth, breadth, and diversity of self-published e-books. And if other retailers fail, authors will have fewer options to reach readers and greater dependence upon Amazon.

*

Mark Coker is the founder of Smashwords and the host of the *Smart Author* podcast.

A version of this article appeared in the 04/13/2020 issue of *Publishers Weekly* under the headline: Are Indie Authors Still Independent?

Slouching Toward Equity
By Brooke Warner

Like people across many industries, I braced myself for the worst when Covid-19 first started ripping into our communities in March. The first impacts on the publishing industry were event cancellations. The shuttering of indie bookstores was alarming; Powell's Books in Portland, Ore., laid off nearly 400 employees in late March, for example. Countless publishers I know, myself included, furloughed staff. The outlook was dire, and I worried about the survival of my imprints. But soon enough, the coronavirus pandemic started to exacerbate more insidious, systemic issues of inequity—within the nation, yes, but also within our industry.

Before the pandemic hit the U.S., 2020 had already ushered in some fraught stories. In January, the much-anticipated novel *American Dirt* was lambasted for stereotyping and appropriating. In February, Barnes & Noble took serious heat for its Black History Month initiative, which rolled out new covers for 12 classic books—including *Frankenstein* and *Moby Dick*—that reimagined their protagonists as people of color. The feedback was consistent and clear: honor and respect writers of color enough to let them tell their own stories, then work toward making those stories part of the literary canon. In March, Grand Central Publishing dropped Woody Allen's memoir after its employees, as well as those at several fellow Hachette Book Group imprints, staged a walkout in solidarity with Ronan Farrow (who's published by HBG's Little, Brown imprint) and victims of sexual abuse, showing the power of staff to hold a publisher accountable for the books it publishes.

By the time the protests erupted in the aftermath of the killing of George Floyd by police in late May, publishing was already teeming with agitation. This is an industry whose racial inequities run deep—an industry that has been called out for decades for its lack of diversity. Since 2015, Lee & Low Books has issued a Diversity Baseline Survey detailing how systemically unequal the industry is. The national protests brought on a surge of anger and awareness, forcing the publishing industry to contend with the fact that, while it pays a lot of lip service to issues of diversity, its actions have not aligned with its professed values.

A pandemic alone would be disrupting, but the added social unrest has posed an existential question for the industry about how it perceives itself and what it wants to be going forward. As the United States faces similar questions about who we are as a nation, it has been heartening to see publishing take some important steps to meet the moment.

One force for positive change was the response to #PublishingPaidMe, which went viral in June and resulted in countless authors sharing their advances, shining even more light on publishing's inequities. The compiled responses showed that writers of color are paid far less than their white counterparts, and that they're less likely to be accordingly compensated when their books reach high levels of success or when they achieve accolades in the form of awards and prizes.

In July, two of the Big Five publishers announced unprecedented changes in leadership in the hiring of two Black publishers: Dana Canedy at Simon & Schuster and Lisa Lucas at Penguin Random House's Pantheon and Schocken Books. "Ten years from now, I don't think anything will look the same," said Reagan Arthur, the publisher of Knopf since January, speaking with the *New York Times* in July for an article titled "In Publishing, 'Everything Is Up for Change.'" That change is welcome and long overdue.

As the publisher of two hybrid imprints, I know how resistant the industry is to change. This resistance stems from people in power benefiting from the way things have always been done. There's little incentive to change models, or paradigms, or payment structures, or the makeup of publishers' lists—until there's agitation. In a June *Atlantic* article, Zeynep Tufekci wrote that protests work because "they can scare authorities into changing their behavior."

In publishing, the outrage sparked by all of the incidents mentioned above—by no means an exhaustive list of all that has happened this year—is pushing the industry to change its behavior. Publishing cannot continue to benefit from the experiences of the "other" without ensuring that marginalized peoples are fairly represented; it cannot cash in on the trauma of marginalized peoples without consequence; it cannot reward accused abusers without examining more deeply how doing so emboldens a culture of enabling and silencing; and it cannot continue to pledge to be more inclusive only to be disproved year after year. This industry is part of the problem, but it can also stand up to be part of the solution.

*

Brooke Warner is publisher of She Writes Press and SparkPress, a TEDx speaker, a writing coach, and the author of *Green-Light Your Book* and *What's Your Book?*

A version of this article appeared in the 08/17/2020 issue of *Publishers Weekly* under the headline: Slouching Toward Equity.

Cosmic Shifts
By Matia Madrona Query

The founder of Gatekeeper Press weighs in on the state of indie publishing.

Indie author Rob Price had a clear vision when he launched Gatekeeper Press in 2015: "to open the gates of the book publishing world." Price, who has served a term as chairperson of the Independent Book Publishers Association since the press's founding, says he has since observed a noticeable shift in how self-publishing is perceived, both within the industry and by readers in general.

"As more and more self-published titles hit major bestsellers lists," Price says, "we've seen a thawing in the book industry's attitude toward self-published books as a whole." There are clear signs of this—including self-published titles increasingly appearing on the shelves at bricks-and-mortar stores and libraries, as well as recognition of the value and viability of indie books from professional review channels.

Price says freedom and autonomy for authors is central to Gatekeeper Press's approach, and that writers are seeing the advantage of the increased control over the publishing and promotional process. Having navigated self-publishing himself, Price says he recognizes the need for new models that will guarantee writers "100% royalties and rights, 100% control, global distribution, one-on-one attention, and a single, trusted location to have their books professionally edited, designed, formatted, and made available for sale all over the world."

For many authors, self-publishing is becoming a preference rather than the default option following rejection from agents or traditional publishers. Tony Chellini, director of sales and business development for Gatekeeper Press, says self-publishing is having its moment. "I genuinely believe self-publishing is the way of the future—and, in fact, it's really the way of the present," Chellini says. "Traditional publishing is great for those that can make millions in book advance fees, but for the 99% of the rest of us, self-publishing has risen to the challenge and surpassed traditional publishing."

Price points to one of Gatekeeper Press's earliest authors, Elise Kova, whose indie success led her to turn down subsequent offers from multiple traditional publishing houses, as an example of self-publishing's growing favorability among authors. "We've worked with many authors who had done the same thing," he says, "and countless others who chose to self-publish with us after having been published traditionally."

Price is aware that, despite how far self-publishing has come, predatory companies still exist in the space. A number of writers have come to Gatekeeper Press after negative experiences, Price says. "We hear horror stories from our authors about terrible service, poor quality, price gouging, complete unresponsiveness, and theft of royalties," he says. "This is why we think looking to independent reviews and getting referrals is so important in the self-publishing space."

Publishing in isolation

Price says there has been a steep uptick in the number of people who have contacted Gatekeeper Press for consultations over the past several months. "With more people home from work, they have more time to write," Price says. He sees another reason for the increase in consultations during these peculiar times: "This massive global event has altered the course of history and caused us all to reexamine life in general," he says. "The pandemic is wreaking incalculable suffering and heartache; it is tearing some families apart and bringing others together. It is a cosmic shift for everyone alive today—and cosmic shifts lead to new ideas, thoughts, and stories."

Price has also observed thematic trends since the pandemic began. Numerous authors have sought consultations for children's books that aim to help young readers cope with the changes brought on by social distancing. There have also been pandemic-related medical books, and even dating books with chapters on "dating during quarantine," he says. And since the killing of George Floyd in late May, Price says he has observed an increase in submissions of books about racial inequality. "We've seen an influx of African American authors telling all kinds of stories," he says, "from those that directly address the tragedies of systemic racism, to those intended for traditionally underserved audiences, like young African American readers."

Chellini says he is accustomed to meeting authors "who have been working on their books for so long—sometimes years, even decades." In many cases, he notes, recent circumstances have stirred in these authors a desire to finish their manuscripts and finally publish their work. "They are ready and excited to take the leap and to share their creativity with the world." Another recent trend he's noticed is that a number of Gatekeeper Press authors have chosen to include last-minute prologues that address the paradigm-shifting events of the moment—a perk of indie publishing's flexibility.

More than ever before, Price finds himself in a position to give urgently needed writing and publishing advice to authors who may be facing uncertainty in their own lives. That being said, his advice has remained consistent since before the pandemic. He tells authors to "ask questions and research, research, research." Specifically, he says, authors need to determine how much attention their book will receive from a publishing service, where their book will be listed for sale, and what percentage of royalties and ownership rights they will be allowed to retain. "The physical world is a scary enough place right now as it is," Price says. "The world of self-publishing doesn't have to be if you're armed with the right information and have the helping hand of a trusted partner."

*

A version of this article appeared in the 08/31/2020 issue of *Publishers Weekly* under the headline: Cosmic Shifts.

The Best First Option
By Sassafras Lowrey

Too often, I hear writers discuss self-publishing as what they would do if they couldn't get a traditional publisher to buy their books. This is true for some authors: they try to get published, and, after a series of rejections, decide that there's nothing left to do but self-publish. However, there are many reasons why self-publishing might be the best first option.

My biggest wish is that self-published authors could stop apologizing directly or indirectly for the ways in which their books came to be in the world. As an author who has been self-published and traditionally published with multiple books, I believe that there are significant pros and cons of both paths. Contrary to popular belief, traditional publishing isn't better for every author or for every book. The most important thing for the success of a book is that the author has confidence in whatever publishing decisions are being made—especially if the decision is to self-publish.

Although traditional publishing has made a lot of progress in prioritizing and uplifting #OwnVoices work, many marginalized writers, including LGBTQ writers and writers of color, are still locked out of lucrative book deals. Even if traditional publishers buy books, they may not pour resources into them, leaving the labor of promoting and marketing to the authors. At that point, are authors better off doing all the work themselves and receiving the full sales revenue instead of a small royalty? Sometimes!

Self-publishing can also mean not having to adjust a story or voice to fit with a publisher's vision. If authors are writing stories for their communities, there are very valid reasons for taking publication into their own hands. Especially for marginalized writers, self-publishing can be the best way to reach readers who need them most, and to maintain artistic control over their projects.

Traditional publishing can open some doors, but it doesn't mean that those doors are closed to those who decide to self-publish. If authors consider self-publishing to be a less legitimate publishing experience, then they've already set themselves up for their books to fail. A book's success depends on its author's confidence and commitment.

For me, the most important part of being an author is the joy in knowing that a book I wrote touched someone, made them laugh, made them think, made them cry, changed their life in some small way. That is what brings me to the keyboard day after day. My readers don't care how my book got into their hands, whether a publisher signed off on it, or if I clicked the publish button on a print-on-demand website.

I urge fellow authors not to let people tell them that something isn't possible for a self-published book. Instead, I want them to believe their goals are possible—and to work hard to make them happen. My self-published books have been just as success-ful as my traditionally published titles in terms of awards and recognition, getting shelved by libraries, and sales numbers. I have made more money from some of my self-published titles than I will likely make from some of my traditionally published books.

That said, there are some areas in which self-publishing can be a disadvantage. Getting an indie book onto bookstore or library shelves and into book awards is all going to fall on the author. Sure, there will be some places where a book will auto-matically be excluded by virtue of being self-published, but those are becoming fewer and farther between. The success of my self-published books comes down to the work I put in to promoting them; the networking I do with booksellers, librarians, and readers; and my commitment to bringing them to broader audiences. To get a book on the shelf, the writer has to build a literary community.

No matter how a book is published, its author should feel empowered. Authors must be the cheerleaders for their books, and this responsibility is even greater when self-publishing. In traditional publishing, authors can falter or let others trust the inherent value of their works. With self-publishing, authors must always be their book's biggest advocates. Their role is to make people fall in love with their books enough that they will want to buy them. In order to do that, writers have to believe in their books more than anyone else does—and that includes believing in the chosen path to publication.

*

Sassafras Lowrey writes fiction and nonfiction and was the recipient of the 2013 Lambda Literary Award for emerging LGBTQ writers.

A version of this article appeared in the 10/12/2020 issue of *Publishers Weekly* under the headline: The Best First Option.

How to Make Your Indie Book Project Grammatically Flawless
By Curtis Honeycutt

Pretty much all authors have the same goal: to write a perfect book that makes *To Kill a Mockingbird* look like it was written in crayon by a kindergartner. If you're an author, you imagine publishing your groundbreaking work. Once it releases, people will line up at your doorstep to hand you huge bags of cash in exchange for your once-in-a-generation work of award-winning literature. Is that too much to ask?

I can guarantee you that you will not achieve your noble, Pulitzer-worthy goal unless your grammar is on point. If you leave modifiers dangling or misspell obvious words, your books aren't likely to land on any bestseller lists.

A part of me dies a little whenever I find an error or typo in a book. After a certain number of syntactic strikes, I begin to question if the author accidentally sent the file of the book's rough draft to the printer. Although internally I am incredibly judgmental, I don't think I'm alone in this harsh manner of reading a new book.

The fact is, a book riddled with grammatical gaffes usually indicates an overall lower-quality final product. Because I know you want your books to be the best they can possibly be, I'd like to share five ways to help ensure that your book gets an A+ for grammar.

Let the robots take the first pass

I write a weekly column called "Grammar Guy" that appears in newspapers across the U.S. Most of my editors make changes here and there, and occasionally I'll receive a report of an error in one of my articles. This is fine when it comes from an editor and prior to the newspaper's printing; it's embarrassing when a reader informs me of an error in my writing. I'm the Grammar Guy, for goodness' sake!

After a few readers found alleged mistakes in my articles, I decided that it was time to turn to the robots. I ran my columns through a free version of Grammarly before I sent them out, but the algorithms at Grammarly weren't catching some of the more nuanced grammar transgressions. I upgraded to the paid annual version and noticed a major improvement.

Using an error catcher such as Grammarly is like having the option of buying a filter for your home's air conditioner that catches 80% of the germs in the air or one that catches 99.5% of them. You're going to go with the filter that catches more germs. While there are other competing products out there, I prefer Grammarly; it integrates into Google Docs, Microsoft Word, and even text messages on my iPhone.

Find an editor and pay well

There are dozens of ways to approach finding the right editor for your project; the bottom line is that you need to do it. And, once you do, you need to pay your editor well.

For my book, *Good Grammar Is the Life of the Party: Tips for a Wildly Successful Life*, I contracted my retired AP English teacher in Oklahoma to make my manuscript bleed. I printed the pages of my manuscript and secured them with a fat binder clip and stuffed them into a large manila envelope before mailing my project to my teacher. I also included a Starbucks gift card and a pack of red pens in the package. For the record, she used both to their greatest potential.

Sure, it was awkward to discuss payment with someone whose first name you're uncomfortable using 20 years after high school, but I wanted to pay her in a way that made editing my book worth her valuable time. This rate will differ based on the length of your project and the extent to which you want your editor to dig into your book (proofreading, copyediting, line editing, or developmental editing).

Use beta readers to catch the rest

While writers use beta readers in various capacities, I found that the most valuable way my beta reader team helped me was by sending me errors that fell through the cracks. I had a prepublication version of my book printed through IngramSpark and mailed or delivered the copies to a team of around 25 early readers.

Just as with my editor, I treated my local beta reading team to coffee treats and asked them to send me any mistakes that they noticed. I found that giving out my phone number and having my readers text me photos of the errors they found was the most efficient way for them to communicate with me. This group found a few dozen mistakes that I'm grateful never made it into publication.

Read the book aloud

You may find it uncomfortable to read your own "stuff" aloud, but the biggest things you'll catch with this method are awkward sentences and phrases. After all, you've been staring at your document to the point where the letters no longer resemble recognizable words.

When you read your book out loud, you'll find the kind of wonky word woes that you didn't catch before. For instance, you'll realize if you're using a certain word over and over. You'll highlight entire pages that may have survived several rounds of edits that now sound like word barf. If you're feeling particularly brave, I dare you to ask a partner or friend to read your manuscript aloud to you.

Look at your book in a different format

Have you been staring at your project in a Word window? Print it out. Is your book printed out from your home printer in blue ink because you ran out of black ink? Convert the file to an e-book format and send it to your e-reader. For details on how to do this, consult Dr. Google.

By looking at your book in a different format, you'll notice even more ways in which your text can be improved. While this may seem over the top, ask yourself this: Have you actually read your book? Have you sat down to experience your book from beginning to end?

Perfection?

At this point, have you achieved novel nirvana? Is your copy clean enough to eat off of? I'll make a confession: after my book was out in the world, I noticed two or three typos that ate my breakfast, lunch, and dinner. I couldn't believe that I had gone through all of these book purification steps only to find flaws in my final version.

The good news is, you can always fix your mistakes and upload a new version. Because you are an indie author, you have control over your book files. Make your edits and then upload your "final final" files.

If you take typos seriously, you're much more apt to have flawless grammar in your book projects. And that means you'll need a sturdy golden rake to gather up the piles of royalty money that come rolling in.

*

Curtis Honeycutt is a syndicated humor columnist and the author of *Good Grammar Is the Life of the Party: Tips for a Wildly Successful Life*, which was a semifinalist for the 2020 BookLife Prize Nonfiction Contest.

A version of this article appeared in the 04/26/2021 issue of *Publishers Weekly* under the headline: Tips from the Grammar Guy.

2. DESIGN

DIY: Book Jacket and Cover Design
By Jennifer McCartney

Indie authors may be tempted to go it alone, but hiring a professional designer can be a great investment.

Finding the right cover and jacket design for a book can be one of the most exciting parts of the publishing process—and one of the most challenging.

Indie authors will want to give some serious thought to the jacket design of their print editions, including the front cover, spine, back cover, and flaps. If done right, a smart design can have a big impact on book sales; almost nothing will turn off a reader more than a jacket that looks amateurish. Many authors may be tempted to go it alone—and there are lots of tools available for those who choose to do so—but hiring a professional designer who has experience creating book jackets can be a great investment.

(Note: This article was originally published in June 2014 and was updated on February 25, 2021.)

CONDUCT RESEARCH

Before hiring a designer, an author should conduct some research so she can communicate her needs and expectations to the designer. Natalie Olsen, the founder of Kisscut Design, suggests that authors begin by browsing the shelves at their local bookstore and noting which titles catch their eye. Next, Olsen advises checking out some online resources like The Book Cover Archive, The Casual Optimist, FaceOut Books, and Design Observer's 50 Books/50 Covers for more ideas. "Your cover should look like it belongs alongside these creative, polished, professional examples—but it should also stand apart, commanding attention," she says.

Once an author has an idea of what she wants her jacket to look like, she can start searching for a designer.

CHOOSE A DESIGNER

"It's important to not only hire an experienced designer, but an experienced book cover designer," says Sophia Feddersen of the Scarlett Rutgers Book Design Agency. She notes that first time authors "may not know about cover genre conventions, design specifications, and other best-practices." Authors should start by looking at a few designers' websites in search of a good match. There are many excellent options out there, so it's worth it for an author to take the time to find the right person for the project. Questions an author should consider:

- Does the designer have experience creating book covers? Are the designs appealing?
- Are the prices reasonable and in line with what other designers are charging? Keep in mind a full jacket design will be more expensive than just a front cover.
- Has the designer designed books in a similar category? A science fiction book cover specialist may not be the best choice for a romance novel.
- Does the designer respond quickly to inquiries and seem enthusiastic and professional?
- Is it clear who will be doing the design work, and is the author able to communicate directly with them?

MAXIMIZE THE DESIGN

Some important factors to carefully consider when designing a book are:

- **Blurbs:** A book jacket usually includes a number of blurbs from other authors or reviewers. Pick the best blurb from the most prominent author or outlet and include it on the front cover. Additional blurbs can go on the back cover.
- **Image Size:** Look at a thumbnail-sized image of the potential cover. Is the title readable and the image clear? Most readers browsing online won't take the time to click on the image to see it full size, so make sure the design looks sharp and clear for someone browsing on a mobile phone.
- **Updates:** Jackets should be updated accordingly. If an author's work wins an award or hits a bestseller list, that should be added to the front cover. Additional blurbs and reviews can be added to the back.

"Remember that the cover of your book isn't for you; it's for your audience," Olsen says. She cautions that while feedback from friends and family is important, authors should work to get more objective input from outsiders who are not as familiar with the project. "[Your audience] includes a lot of people you've never met, but who you are about to influence with your work. So make it for them."

DIY: Art and Illustrations
By Daniel Lefferts

When it comes to art and illustrations, consulting with a professional is almost always ideal.
In addition to cover art and interior layout, there are additional image- and design-related issues that every indie author will encounter when self-publishing a book.

Among these are interior visual elements, namely art or illustrations. Both of these elements are important and the process of securing them—and the challenges they can present—are similar. Here are a few things indie authors should keep in mind when obtaining, creating, or preparing art for their books.

(Note: this article was originally published in October 2014 and was updated on February 18, 2021.)

ART AND ILLUSTRATIONS: WORKING WITH A PROFESSIONAL AND DIY

When it comes to art and illustrations, consulting with a professional is almost always ideal.

Jeff Feuerstein and his sister Dayna Brandoff self-published their children's book, *Half Popped*, which includes several cartoon-style illustrations of food. They initially tried to illustrate the book on their own, but "felt something was missing." "The cartoon food didn't have any emotion," Feuerstein says. "And that's when we sought another artist to complement my sister's photography style." The designer they ended up working with, Alex Miller, "brought the characters to life," Feuerstein says.

Though Feuerstein and Brandoff found Miller (along with other designers they originally auditioned) through word-of-mouth, there are a number of resources and databases that authors can use to find artists. Indie authors writing children's books should look to The Society of Children's Book Writers and Illustrators, which offers an Illustrator Gallery that's searchable by illustration type and region. Another site, ChildrensIllustrators.com, offers a portfolio directory, as well as a listing of illustrator agents.

If an indie author happens to have some design savvy and feels confident creating her own artwork or illustrations, there are several popular design programs she can use. Adobe InDesign and Adobe Photoshop are among the most popular, but can be pricey. GIMP, a free design program, offers features similar to those found on Photoshop. Another free program, Inkscape, offers a number of design tools and purports to be a free alternative to Adobe InDesign.

WORKING WITH SELF-PUBLISHING AND POD SERVICES

Whether an indie author is working with a designer to create images or producing her own artwork, it's best to know which self-publishing service she'll be using, and, thus, what limitations she'll be working with. Many self-publishing services have specific formatting requirements for illustrations or other images. While these specifications can be limiting, they can also act as useful parameters.

Feuerstein and Brandoff used CreateSpace to publish *Half Popped*. By the time they entered the design phase, Feuerstein says, they had all the information about dimensions and specs that they needed. "We knew where we were going to get cut off based on how the book was going to be put together; we knew the ratio of everything that had to be submitted," says Feuerstein.

In addition to providing guidelines for artwork, many self-publishing services also offer design services. Outskirts Press, for example, offers custom full-color illustrations. Though prices are established by quote, they generally range from $479 (for one illustration) to $4,119 (for 15). Outskirts provides examples of illustrations they've done in the past, and authors do not need to publish with Outskirts in order to purchase the service. Other self-publishing companies that provide design and artwork services include CreateSpace, Lulu, and AuthorHouse.

DIY: How to Design an Indie Book Cover
By Alex Palmer

The first step for any author looking for a great cover is to get some outside help.
For a self-published book to sell, the cover is key. Regardless of how eloquent or entertaining its text may be, a book will have trouble catching a buyer's eye or being taken seriously by reviewers if it looks homemade. Thankfully, authors have more ways than ever to give their books polished, good-looking covers.
(Note: This article was originally published in February 2014 and was updated on February 25, 2021.)

Hire a Professional
The first step for any author looking for a great cover is to get some outside help. While self-publishers tend to be confident and capable do-it-yourselfers, unless they are also highly skilled artists, it's best to hire someone who does graphic design for a living.

"A novice will spend way too much time working on the cover, and in the end it will just look handmade," says Ron Pramschufer, owner of author consulting service Self Publishing Inc. "You will wrestle with a design all afternoon, while a professional designer will take the idea and send something beautiful back in ten minutes."

Instead, the author should look for a skilled designer with experience. These designers can be tracked down through a number of ways:

- Seek out layouts similar to what you want for your book and track down the designer through his or her agent or personal website. Try to stay genre specific in making these design decisions.
- Use online cover services such as KillerCovers or Okay Creations.
- Use design-bidding sites such as crowdSPRING, 99designs, or Elance,

which allow visitors to post the job they are looking to assign and choose from the submissions.

Pramschufer advises that authors should expect to pay a few hundred dollars for a quality cover, but no more than $1,000.

"You should never pay more than that, no matter how many awards the designer's won," he says. "Your text is the value added, the designer is there to keep you from getting embarrassed."

Doing It Yourself

If an author is determined to do the cover on his or her own, there are plenty of services available. While Adobe Illustrator is a standard software used by professional designers, an author can also use online services such as Gimp, a free alternative to Adobe; Amazon's Cover Creator through CreateSpace; or Cover Design Studio, among many others.

But more likely than not, the author would be better served focusing his or her energy on just providing the designer with plenty of graphic elements, from fonts to images, to give a clear sense of the look he or she is seeking.

To help generate ideas, a few good sources to consult are:
- Design Observer's annual 50 Books/50 Covers list.
- The Book Cover Archive, a website of hundreds of artistic covers.
- *Huffington Post*'s "Under the Cover" series.

Other Considerations

When appropriate, short selections of critical praise of the book should be included on the cover. The single best line of praise or the one from the most prominent source should appear on the cover itself, with additional comments on the back cover.

Think of the cover blurb as something of an extra subtitle, clarifying what readers can expect from the book, with the added benefit of a personal endorsement. This makes it important for the author to reach out early to bloggers and reviewers in the book's genre, as well as get advanced reading copies to any prominent connections that may be open to providing a blurb.

One of the advantages of e-book covers is that they can be updated. So, if a good blurb comes in even after the book has been out, it is a simple enough process to update the cover to include it. Similarly, if the work is nominated for some kind of award or hits a bestseller list, this should be added to the cover as well to help catch the eye of readers. Of course, choose what is placed on the cover carefully—clutter should be avoided.

*

Alex Palmer is a freelance journalist and the author of *Weird-o-Pedia*.

Top Five DIY Book Layout Mistakes

By Joel Friedlander

How indie authors can avoid book design pitfalls

Book designer and author Joel Friedlander takes a look at pitfalls self-publishers face when doing their own book formatting, and explains how to avoid these mistakes in the first place.

With more and more authors taking the production of their books into their own hands, more and more of those books look . . . strange. That's not a good thing for either authors or their readers.

Book design used to be a pretty arcane branch of graphic design, pursued by a handful of practitioners, many of whom were employed by typesetters and publishing houses. Like many other specialties, only the insiders knew or cared about the intricacies of long-form typography and all the small nuances that go into creating beautiful books.

Along with editors, these professionals made sure that the books they produced conformed to long-established publishing industry standards. That's important when you're sending your book to store or chain buyers, to media bookers, to reviewers, or to anyone who is used to looking at traditionally published books as part of her job.

So, it really behooves authors who decide to become DIY publishers to educate themselves as to how books are supposed to look, how they are constructed, and what book professionals expect to see. As my father used to say, it doesn't cost any more to print a book that's properly designed and laid out than it does to print one that's a typographic train wreck, so why not do it right the first time?

Let's take a look at the mistakes that seem to occur most frequently when self-published authors decide to do their own book formatting and how to save yourself the embarrassment of making these mistakes in the first place:

1. **Blank right-hand pages:** It's very common, especially in nonfiction books, to have blank left-hand pages, and there's nothing wrong with that. This occurs naturally if your chapters always open on right-hand pages. But if you've designed your book to use a two-page spread as your chapter opening (for instance, with an illustration on the left-hand page and text on the right-hand page), you run the risk of having a blank right-hand page immediately preceding the spread (since there's no guarantee that the preceding chapter will end on a right-hand page). This is a no-no in book layout. We never want to have a blank right-hand page. To solve it, either adjust the typography, or have quotations or artwork on hand that will augment the message of your book, and put those on the otherwise-blank right-hand page.

2. **Folios running rampant:** We need folios (that's what book designers call page numbers) on most of the pages in our book, but not all. Remember to turn off page numbering for the title page, the copyright page, any blank pages, any "display" pages like part-openers, and any advertising pages at the end of the book.

3. **Running heads misbehaving:** This seems to be a challenge for a lot of amateur book formatters. If a page is blank—and there are usually going to be a number of blank pages in your book—technically it's not part of the text. After all, there's no text on the page, is there? A blank page should be just that: blank, with nothing on it at all. By the same token, those "display" pages mentioned above shouldn't have running heads—text at the top of the page that lists title, author, chapter, etc.—on them either. Yet many books I've seen from self-publishers show that the author just didn't know that, or didn't know how to turn the running heads off—and nothing looks worse to me than a chapter-opening page with a running head on it.

4. **Ragged composition:** Here's another oddity you may never have seen before. Of course, there are books that can be typeset in a rag-right style to good effect. (This means the type is unjustified, so the right-hand margin is uneven, unlike most books, the margins of which are perfectly squared away on both sides of the type column.) Examples include art, architecture, poetry, photo books, and similar illustrated works—but not memoirs, novels, histories, or other standard trade books. Whatever the merit of rag-right composition, these books aren't a good place for it. Stick with justified copy.

5. **Odd-numbered pages on the left:** Okay, I saved the best for last. Or is that the worst? Just think about this for a moment. When you open a book, the very first page you see is p. 1. There is no logical way that p. 1 can be on the left, because then it wouldn't be the first page. This is an ironclad rule in book layout: all odd-numbered pages in your book should be right-hand pages. Make sure you get this right.

There are a lot of other ways your book might inadvertently signal that you're a design "amateur," but these five errors, once you know about them, are easy to avoid. You want your book to stand out for your great writing, thoughtful arguments, or the tremendous value it brings to readers, not because it looks unprofessional.

Remember, if you want your book to be taken seriously, it's important that you take book design and layout just as seriously. And, if this seems disturbingly detailed, you can always hire a professional book designer—and make sure that everyone who holds a copy of your book in their hands will recognize, consciously or unconsciously, that it has been properly constructed, providing a comfortable experience for your readers.

*

Joel Friedlander was a book designer and author; he blogged about book design, marketing, and the future of the book at thebookdesigner.com.

3. MARKETING

DIY: How to Build Buzz for Self-Published Books
By Alex Palmer

Creating buzz starts earlier than you think.

Building a bestselling self-published book is all in the timing. That is, it's best to start marketing early and roll out promotions in deliberate, timed waves to maximize interest ahead of the book's publication date. A useful way for an author to approach this is as a calendar counting down to the book's launch—starting at least a year before the book's ready to read.

A Year Before Publication

Creating buzz starts earlier than you think.

"Typically I tell my clients that they need to think about publicity at least 12 months in advance," says Crystal Patriarche, founder of BookSparks PR, which helps self-published authors manage their marketing and PR.

Among the things writers should be taking care of in this early stage of the book are:

Establish a web presence. Set up an author Facebook page, Twitter account, and blog if you don't already have one.

Build an email list. Gather email addresses of fans and potential book buyers. Whether using a basic service like Gmail's Contact Manager or something more sophisticated like Constant Contact, your online and social media efforts during this early stage should be geared toward gathering these addresses.

"An email list lets you directly communicate with readers," says Bob Baker, author of *55 Ways to Promote & Sell Your Book on the Internet*. "It's one of the most potent marketing actions you can take." For more details on email lists and early marketing, see *PW*'s piece on How to Market Your Self-Published Book.

Six Months Before Publication

Build awareness. Get the word out about your book and your plans for it, connecting with other authors and readers in your genre.

Keep readers in the loop. "Rather than talking about the book every day, think about the big moments of the book that you want to share," says Patriarche.

That means promoting milestones like the cover reveal, new blurbs it receives, and any other announcements to remind readers of the project and its imminent publication.

Also update readers on the progress of the book itself, through your email list as well as social media outlets. This can include anything from tweets about research you are doing, to blog posts that connect your book's subject matter with a topic of the day.

Release excerpts and other content. Besides social media updates, authors might also want to help build buzz by releasing excerpts of their book or other related material.

For example, as Baker ramps up for the release of his new book, *The DIY Career Manifesto*, he launched an interview series on YouTube with one-on-one chats with many of his sources for the book, and releases them as podcasts. All of these encourage viewers and listeners to sign up for his "VIP List" to get emailed excerpts of the new book.

There are several strategies an author can use in posting book excerpts, depending on where you expect the strongest following:

- Post excerpts on your social media outlets (blog, Facebook, etc.).
- Post just a few paragraphs on social media, and make a full sample chapter available only through your mailing list.
- Release the sample chapter on Wattpad, FictionPress, or other free book sites.

Three Months Before Publication

Contact book bloggers. By this time, the book should be all but complete, and now advanced reading copies should be sent out to book bloggers and reviewers. Make sure they have plenty of time to read and review the work, and to schedule it for posting.

"A lot of people don't realize that even smaller blogs have a lead time," says Patriarche. "A lot of them work 60 to 90 days in advance."

Promote the positive reviews and coverage the book gets through social media and post the strongest review excerpts on the book's Amazon page to drive up interest.

Set up a blog tour. At the same time you are reaching out to reviewers, seek other ways to get your book in these outlets. Depending on your book's subject matter, this can mean writing a guest post, doing an interview, or offering some other content that can post a week or two prior to the book's release.

Three Weeks Before Publication

Run a book giveaway. This is a good time to promote the book with a Goodreads giveaway. Give 5 to 25 copies (whatever you can afford) out to readers on the site. This has the dual benefit of alerting Goodreads' many members that the book is coming out and increasing the likelihood they will review it on Amazon and elsewhere.

Rally the troops. Directly email friends and family to ask for their help in promoting the book. This includes letting their friends know about it and any special promotions you are running for it.

Day of Publication

Celebrate. Toast your book's launch on social media and through thank-you emails to those who have helped it along the way. There's plenty of work to do post-publication, but enjoy the moment and the hard work you have put in building buzz for your book.

DIY: How to Market Your Self-Published Book
By Alex Palmer

Probably the most effective way to reach readers is by building a strong web presence.

For a self-published author, marketing the book can be more important than writing it. With a few key steps, an author can build a loyal following, get the word out about his or her work, and get people to buy it.

1. Build a Web Presence

Probably the most effective and least expensive way to reach readers is by building a strong web presence, including an author website with an up-to-date blog, as well as active profiles on social media sites including Twitter, Goodreads, and Facebook.

The website should be simple to navigate, and make it easy for visitors to learn about and buy your book. In building a website, authors can go through free hosting services such as Wordpress or Blogspot, but better yet is for authors to host their own websites.

"I'd have real concerns about authors who don't want to invest in their own hosting," says Lori Culwell, author of *How to Market a Book* and founder of BookPromotion. com.

Regular updates on the social media platforms, along with a steady stream of blog posts on topics and keywords that interest readers will advance an author's search engine optimization. Culwell says a good target for authors is to take up the entire first page of Google results when their name is searched for.

2. Build a Mailing List

All of these platforms should make it easy for visitors to sign up for the author's mailing list—one of the best ways to get a well-timed message in front of interested readers. This can simply inform readers of a new blog post, to add attendees for a live event, or to boost early book sales.

"Develop an audience of people who like your writing so you can sell enough copies on the first day to get your book up to the top of Amazon, where it will then get more attention," suggests Culwell.

A few services to help build a mailing list and track its performance are:

- MailChimp (free and good for basic email list)
- aWeber (costs $1 to sign up)
- iContact (works well for both beginners and more advanced lists)
- Benchmark Email (can add video and image customization)
- Constant Contact (allows for XHTML and other design elements)

Once they have built a strong list, authors should also try to segment it, based on interests and geographic regions, so messages promoting specific projects or book appearances can go to recipients who will find it most relevant.

3. Target Your Messaging

Reach out to prominent blogs and publications that cover books or topics discussed in your book. Tell them about your book and volunteer to write a guest post on something related to it.

There are also numerous sites where an author can promote his or her e-book, often through targeted giveaways, including Addicted to eBooks, Free eBooks Daily, or FreeBooksy. Worthwhile outlets for hosting giveaways for print books are Goodreads and LibraryThing.

For authors willing to spend a little more money, a number of services are available to help promote the book to readers and add them to your mailing list. These include:

- Google Adwords
- Goodreads ads
- Facebook ads

But these kind of expenditures should only be made once the many free (and often more effective) avenues have been tried.

4. Keep Up the Maintenance

Just as authors are urged to write every day, self-published authors should also be marketing every day. Culwell suggests setting aside just 15 minutes each day to take some kind of marketing action, whether reaching out to an organization that might want to promote a Skype chat, or commenting on message boards like www.boardtracker. com where members are discussing topics relevant to the book.

Perhaps more important than anything else: Keep working at it. Authors should remember that marketing involves plenty of trial and error and if one channel is not getting a strong response, it may be time to try something else.

"You have to be willing to try things and have them fail," says Culwell. "Marketing is not something that you will ever really finish."

Ten Tips for Autopilot E-book Marketing
By Mark Coker

These set-and-forget marketing tricks help make books more discoverable.

Marketing is critically important to a book's success, yet time spent on marketing means less time for writing. Here, I share 10 set-and-forget tips to put an e-book's most important marketing on autopilot. These tricks work 24 hours a day to make an author's books more discoverable to readers.

1. ADD THESE THREE SECTIONS TO YOUR BACK MATTER

These sections drive sales and build an author's social media following:

About the Author: A short two- or three-sentence bio to humanize the author.

Connect with the Author: Listing social media hyperlinks will make it easier for new fans to start following authors and subscribe to their mailing lists.

Other Books by This Author: The reader just discovered a new favorite author, so help them find their next read!

2. ADD A DISCUSSION GUIDE

It's great to sell one book to one reader, but if the reader's a member of a reading group, that could mean even bigger sales. If they see a reading group discussion guide at the end of the book, they're more likely to recommend the book for the group's next read.

3. ADD SAMPLE CHAPTERS FROM OTHER BOOKS

The reader just finished the book, they loved it, and now they're ready to read more. Let them jump into other e-books by offering generous samples of other titles.

4. DO A SAMPLE-CHAPTER SWAP WITH ANOTHER AUTHOR

Many indie authors have friends who also write in their genres or categories. Offer to swap sample chapters. Each author places the other author's sample chapter in the back matter of their books. Be selective. Only swap with quality writers who target the same readership.

5. ADD ENHANCED NAVIGATION TO E-BOOKS

E-books support a hyperlinked table of contents. If the author adds the enhanced back matter recommended above, they can advertise and link to those sections in the table of contents.

6. MAKE AT LEAST ONE BOOK FREE

Free e-books get about 30 times more downloads on average than books that cost money, which means that more readers are exposed to the enhanced back matter. Nothing hooks a reader like a free first book, especially for series. Authors who write standalone books should consider running free promotions of priced titles to help introduce first-time readers to their bodies of work.

7. EDITING TURBOCHARGES WORD OF MOUTH

Good books aren't good enough anymore. An author only gets one chance to wow a new reader with a five-star reading experience. It's the five-star read that leads to the ultimate form of autopilot marketing: reader word-of-mouth. To maximize reader satisfaction, hire a professional editor, preferably one with experience editing other books that became bestsellers in the same genre or category. There are multiple types of editing: developmental editing, copy editing, and proofing. Each is critically important, and none can be skipped. Developmental editing is the most expensive but will have the biggest impact on reader satisfaction.

8. WORK WITH BETA READERS

Beta readers are test readers. They read the author's book prior to publication and provide feedback to help guide the final revision. A properly managed beta round could provide feedback similar to that offered by a developmental editor. To learn how to run a beta reader round, check out my December 2016 column, "Making the Most of Beta Readers," or listen to Episode 5 of the Smart Author Podcast.

9. OCCUPY MULTIPLE PRICE POINTS

Readers harbor pricing bias. One reader's bias will be different from another's. Some readers will only try a new author if the book is free, while others will only try the author if the book is priced under $3.99. Other readers will avoid low-cost e-books altogether for fear that lower prices indicate poor quality. By occupying multiple price points, the author can accommodate a wider range of pricing biases so that more readers will give the work a chance. Once the author earns the reader's trust with one book, price is less of a factor.

10. ALWAYS RELEASE WITH A PREORDER

Books released as preorders sell more copies because preorders enable more effective book marketing. Much of this benefit is on autopilot. Indie authors can get their books listed for preorder up to 12 months in advance of release. During this entire preorder period, these upcoming titles are merchandised alongside the author's other books at retailers. It means more months of selling time.

Mark Coker is founder of Smashwords and the host of the new podcast *Smart Author.*

Helping Authors Find Their Readers
By Savannah Cordova

In 2014, Reedsy was founded as a marketplace and resource hub for authors, helping them write and publish professional-grade books. Over the next five years, however, our founders realized that something was missing. For many indie authors, no matter how they marketed, readers just weren't finding their books: they were being drowned in a sea of titles with powerhouse publishers behind them or passed over by Amazon's algorithms in favor of authors who'd gamed the system.

To address this problem head-on, we launched Reedsy Discovery, a platform that connects indie authors with real readers and reviewers—who, as authors can attest, are usually the key to *more* exposure. Just over two years later, we've published more than 3,000 editorial reviews on Discovery and built a user base of nearly 200,000 readers. And, as part of the team that's made this possible, I've been thrilled to watch Discovery grow, and am constantly amazed by our commitment to human curation and experience.

For a flat fee of $50, you can submit an advance reader's copy of your book to our general pool of reviewers *or* to a specific reviewer whose work you admire. Your book will then be "picked up" for review in time for your release, so you can launch with a thoughtful assessment—giving you a major advantage over most new releases. Then, when your launch date arrives, your book will appear on our Discovery feed to be upvoted and commented on by readers. You'll even get a chance to be featured in our weekly newsletter sent to hundreds of thousands of subscribers.

The best part about Discovery is how much of it is driven by people rather than machines. Reviewers can sift through their options to find exactly the sort of books that they want to read. Readers follow specific genres and other users to cultivate their feeds. Every book that gets featured on the main Discovery page and in our newsletter is handpicked. Critically, if a book is ever in danger of *not* being reviewed on time, it's pitched by our Discovery team to reviewers—rather than being crushed by a deluge of new books and dismissed by Amazon's algorithms.

This is the nuance and care that most mainstream book promotion platforms simply don't offer. Yet it's precisely what indie books require to succeed: an actual person taking notice of your book and saying to an audience, "*This* one is worth your time." And that's what sets Discovery apart from Amazon and even Goodreads— our reviewers make indie titles a priority, and their endorsements can make a real difference, even in our algorithm-driven world. (Just ask the authors whose reviewers have cross-posted their praise to other platforms.)

Of course, not every book will receive praise. It's the nature of any review platform—at least any legitimate one—and can also be exacerbated by human error. If you feel you've received an unfair review on Discovery, you can report it under your submissions and our team will look into it. Alternatively, if your book hasn't been picked up yet and you change your mind, you can cancel your review from that same page (within 60 days of your submission).

With all that in mind, there are a few other actions I'd strongly recommend to any author submitting their book to Discovery—or aiming for good reviews on any platform, for that matter. The first and most important thing you can do is refine your book's presentation. Your cover and your description are particularly vital; they immediately convey whether your book is worth reading in the first place. Think seriously about investing in a professional cover design, and spend a few hours tweaking your book description until it's snappy, distinctive, and intriguing.

That said, another key point here is not to *misrepresent* your book. Having a flashy cover that barely relates to your subject, a blurb that promises more than you have to offer, or several tangential genres attached to your book might seem like great ways to attract more readers, but the resulting reviews can ruin your book's reputation. This is a big issue we see on Discovery, and understandably so! Indie authors are often told to go all-out to get readers' attention—and, for the most part, this is fine advice. I'd only temper it with caution: don't take your marketing tactics so far that your book starts to sound like a stranger's.

Finally, if you like the review you receive, make sure to comment on it and tip the reviewer (a feature available on Discovery). This is the most concrete way to let them know you appreciate their work, to encourage them to cross-post their review if they haven't already, and to potentially lay the groundwork for them to review *another* one of your books. Let them know if they can look forward to a sequel, or if you have any similar titles they can read right now.

It's certainly true that, as an indie author, publishing success can itself feel almost fictitious—and I'll be the first to admit that it takes a great deal of work. But Reedsy Discovery makes it that much easier, leveling the playing field so that *every* author has a shot at a quality review, and helping readers find hidden gems they might otherwise never unearth. It's the platform that indie authors need and intrepid readers deserve, and that I look forward to evolving in the years to come.

*

Savannah Cordova is a content marketer with Reedsy, a marketplace that connects self-publishing authors with the world's best editors, designers, and marketers.

A version of this article appeared in the 05/17/2021 issue of *Publishers Weekly* under the headline: Helping Authors Find Their Readers.

People Don't Have to Read Your Book to Support It
By Jane Friedman

Indie authors need to refine their approaches when seeking support from influencers.

If you're an indie author, I suggest you start your book marketing plans by making three separate lists:

Owned media: Existing resources and assets you control that can help spread the word about your book. These can include your website or blog, email newsletter, social media presence, or anything that reaches readers directly, whether digital or analog.

Paid media: Where you pay for attention or exposure. This includes advertising and paid reviews.

Earned media: Media coverage or attention that you secure for free—what publicists typically help with.

Everyone wants earned media, but, though it comes without cost, it does require effort. Because outlets that cover books are shrinking or disappearing, there is more competition than ever for reviews and attention. Still, traditional book publishers' marketing plans tend to focus on securing earned media that they know and have experience approaching. These include recognized review publications, as well as TV, radio, print, and online outlets.

As a self-published author, you should seek alternative options to gain momentum. These include local and regional media, influencers in your target market, and any person who is likely to answer your emails or pick up the phone when you call.

How thoughtfully you make your approach will determine your success rate, and it's essential to suggest a specific method of support—and a single action step is ideal. You have to figure out the right ask and then make it as easy as possible for your contact to say yes.

First, here are two things that do not have to happen for people to support your book:

They don't have to read the book or have a copy of it. Consider that reading a book takes hours of time that someone might not have. Though it may seem counterintuitive (and some authors are hurt by the implication that not everyone is eager to read their books), if your targets already know you or your work very well, don't put them on the spot to read the book. They may already be prepared to support you. Of course, you should always offer to send a copy. Just don't make that central to your ask (e.g., "May I send you the book?"). Instead, think about what you'd like to see happen if they agree to support the book. Do you want them to tweet about it? Post on Instagram? Have you on a podcast?

They don't have to review the book to help spread the word. Authors are commanded to secure as many customer reviews as possible in the first weeks after release; as a result, "Would you write a review at Amazon?" tends to be the default ask. Once again, reading the book and then writing a review is time intensive—that may be hard to agree to. It also leads to a low success rate, even when people initially say yes.

Now, here are some things to help you get to yes:

Respect the person's time. I don't know anyone who isn't pressed for time. Just about all of us have too much work, too much to read, and too much we owe others. Though people you reach out to will likely want to help, if it requires too much time—especially if you ask for a conversation or meeting—you've just decreased your chances.

Figure out the method of support that best fits the situation. If you don't know already, you should find out how, where, and when your targets share or discuss books. Is it on social media? Do they run book clubs? Do they have blogs, email newsletters, or podcasts? Figure out their standard communication or publishing channels and make your ask specific to their existing behavior. Don't ask them to do something they've never done before.

Don't make your request complicated or broad. Your initial ask shouldn't require research, intensive deliberation, or a multifaceted response addressing several different issues. "I'd love to collaborate with you!" could strike fear in the heart of your contact, especially if collaboration is not strictly defined. Make it easy for targets to agree to something specific—something they can envision themselves doing or adding as an item on their to-do lists.

As someone with an active blog, newsletter, and social media account, I receive frequent requests for coverage, but only a tiny percentage of pitches express awareness that I don't review books and I rarely interview authors. However, I do run excerpts, so that's what I offer instead of a review. But not all people you reach out to will offer an alternative method of support. They'll simply say no.

That's why, if someone does say no, keep that person on your list for the future. As the author James Clear has said, *no* often means "not right now" or "not in that way." Your timing might be better next time—as well as your ask.

*

Jane Friedman teaches digital media and publishing at the University of Virginia and is the former publisher of *Writer's Digest*.

A version of this article appeared in the 01/27/2020 issue of *Publishers Weekly* under the headline: Finding the Right Ask.

4. SALES

Smooth Sales
By Janine Kovac

An indie author offers tips for promoting and selling books.

If you're an indie author, bricks-and-mortar sales in your own backyard can lead to a range of opportunities—from finding venues for author events to building stronger ties within your neighborhood. Three ways to sell your book offline are consignment sales, outright sales, and hand-selling.

Consignment sales

For consignment sales, you provide a store with copies of your book for a designated period of time. If the books sell, the store gives you a cut. If they don't, you go back and get the remaining copies. Indie bookstores are the most likely to sell on consignment, but sometimes other sellers, such as lit-friendly coffee shops and boutiques, will, too.

Guidelines vary, but here are the industry norms:

Inventory is three to five copies.

Books are stocked for three months.

Stores take 40%–50% of revenue.

Authors are responsible for collecting payment and unsold books at the end of the term.

If you have an indie bookstore that you frequent (and you should), start there. It's easier to funnel all sales through one store than it is to direct friends and family to several locations. It's also easier to keep track of inventory and sales.

Signs that your local bookstore is a good fit:

It has a local author section.

It hosts readings and events.

It participates in events such as Independent Bookstore Day.

You have an established relationship.

Indie bookstores are often happy to support local authors, but they also want to sell books. You can help by letting the store know that you will list it as an official bookseller on your website and elsewhere.

The more you sell, the more likely it is that your bookstore will carry your book past the three-month mark. If staff members know that your promotion brings in traffic, they'll find ways to support you. Never underestimate the power of an indie bookstore recommendation!

Outright sales

Some gift stores and boutiques buy books from indie authors outright. This means that they'll pay you 50%–60% of the cover price at the outset and then it's up to them to sell your book to make a profit. Stores willing to take this risk know their inventory and their customers well. Paying for inventory up front is less of a hassle than keeping unpaid stock on the books.

Here's how you can appeal to small businesses:

Go in person with signed copies as gifts for them to keep or sell.

Let them know why you think your book is a good fit for their stores.

Be respectful of their time and resources.

Let them know that you would list them as partners on your website and in promotional materials.

Let the stores know if there is a holiday or month that pertains to your subject matter. For example, my memoir centers around my career as a ballet dancer and life as the mother of micro-preemie twins. My "seasons" are National Dance Week in April, Mother's Day in May, and National Prematurity Awareness Month in November.

Hand-selling

In addition to allowing you to keep 100% of the profit, hand-selling means that you can adjust your price to make a sale. You're completely in charge.

But here are some aspects to consider:

Carrying copies of books can cause them to be damaged.

You need to have change on hand if you are collecting cash.

If you collect payment through PayPal, Square, or Venmo, know what hardware and connectivity are required.

Know ahead of time whether you need to collect sales tax or whether you need a seller's permit.

For many authors, hand-selling feels pushy. If this is beyond your comfort level, don't do it. Concentrate on bookstores and boutiques. When people ask how they can get copies of your book, direct them to your local bookstore.

Even if you aren't actively hand-selling, it's a good idea to keep half a dozen books in a shoebox under your desk or in your car. Be prepared to strike while the iron is hot.

*

Janine Kovac is a producer and curator with the San Francisco literary festival Litquake. Her memoir, *Spinning: Choreography for Coming Home*, was a semifinalist for the BookLife Prize.

A version of this article appeared in the 02/24/2020 issue of *Publishers Weekly* under the headline: Smooth Sales.

DIY: How to Price a Self-Published E-Book
By Alex Palmer

Setting a book's price requires some creativity on the part of the author. Once the e-book is written, the marketing plan in place, and the work ready to release to the public, self-published authors find themselves with an unexpected challenge: assigning a value to their work. Setting an e-book's price requires some creativity on the part of the author, a careful consideration of the book's potential audience, and an assessment of what the author hopes to accomplish with the book.

By following a few basic steps, an author will be able to make an informed choice in naming her price, and not feel like a losing contestant on *The Price Is Right*.

SET GOALS
By the time indie authors get to the point where they are naming a book's price, they should have a clear idea of what they would like their book to do. There are two main goals that will determine how much an author should charge, according to Miral Sattar, CEO and founder of Bibliocrunch, a company that helps self-published authors market and promote their books.

"You have to ask yourself, 'Am I looking to get more readers or more sales?'" says Sattar.

While most authors would probably say they want both, when it comes to pricing strategy, it's best to focus on one and let the other follow. Either approach can be successful, so indie authors must ask themselves some tough questions, among them, can I sell 10 times more books at 99 cents than at $9.99?

For less established authors, a lower price will help draw in readers who might be willing to take a chance on a 99 cent book, as opposed to a higher-priced title. While authors with an established fan base can likely charge more for their work.

MORE EXPOSURE
For those authors whose main concern is getting their book in front of as many readers as possible, the priority should be getting the pricepoint as low as possible. While most online retailers require authors to charge at least 99 cents for each book,

platforms like Wattpad can provide other options for getting readers' attention and building a fan base.

Authors looking to be a little more strategic in how they price their work can enroll in Amazon's KDP Select program. This program allows them to charge a low price for the book (99 cents being the most popular) and offer it for free for specific periods.

Authors can participate in a Kindle Free Book Promotion for a maximum of five days. In order to get the greatest sales impact from the giveaway, authors should get the word out to book blogs and sites that aggregate freebies from around the web. A few examples are:

- Free Book Dude
- Free Kindle Books and Tips
- Indie Book Promo
- Indie Book of the Day
- Kindle Freebies

BiblioCrunch offers a comprehensive, updated list of these sites, newsletters, and Facebook pages.

"We've seen authors who use this list of sites get 20,000 or 60,000 books read right away," says Sattar.

MORE REVENUE

Authors seeking a bit more money for their work should start by looking at the price of other books in the same genre. While romance e-books tend to do best in the 99 cents to $2.99 range, authors writing nonfiction or literary fiction can charge more.

Authors will want to begin at a price under $10 if possible, and test out different pricepoints with short-term promotions. An added motivator for pricing at this level is that retailers will often pay higher royalties for e-books priced between $2.99 and $9.99.

Amazon pays 70% of the retail download price for books in this range, but just 35% for those above or below it.

Authors can expect to earn a return of 60% to 70% through Barnes & Noble, and Kobo within the $2.99 to $9.99 range as well.

Smashwords pays 85% of list price on sales directly through its site, and 60% of list price on sales through other retailers, while BookBaby charges an annual fee, but gives authors 100% of net, keeping no commission.

Once the price is set, authors should make use of promotions to boost revenue. For a Kindle e-book priced at $7.99, run a Kindle Countdown Deal for $4.99. If you are trying to sell it at $4.99, run a promotion at $2.99. As with a book giveaway, these sales should be advertised as widely as possible. In addition to free plugs on websites such as BookBub and Kindle Nation Daily, the author can also consider paid advertising to help get the word out.

Sattar suggests running these promotions no fewer than two days to help them gather steam, and never running them on the weekend.

"If you can get a burst of sales at the lower price, it ups your sales rank for the category," she explains. "That helps your book become a bestseller, and then it can go back to the normal price."

*

Alex Palmer is a freelance journalist and the author of *The Santa Claus Man*.

DIY: Point-of-Sale Programs for Indie Authors
By Alex Palmer

For indie authors looking for more control over sales, greater retail profits, and a connection with readers, point-of-sale programs can be valuable tools.

For most indie authors, selling books online simply means adding a "buy" button to their websites and linking to the online retailer of their choice. However, some self-publishers—looking for more control over sales and greater retail profits—are turning to point-of-sale programs, which allow users to sell directly to consumers via personal websites or at events.

And while POS tools mean more work—authors must handle distribution of print and digital editions themselves—setting up direct sales can also mean higher profits per sale. But before going the POS route, there are a number of challenges indie authors should consider.

TO SELL OR NOT TO SELL
(Note: As of the March 2021 article update, NoRulesJustWrite.com and Ganxy are no longer available.)

Before deciding what sort of POS tools make the most sense, authors should consider whether selling books on their own makes sense at all.

"The greatest success stories I've seen in POS have been nonfiction authors, particularly those who have other offerings and can use the e-book sale to upsell a course or webinar," says C.J. Lyons, a self-published author of 27 novels who runs the *NoRulesJustWrite* blog. "The greatest value comes not from the financial gain from selling the e-book but from the lead capture."

She adds that fiction authors may find the selling of signed copies of their print books as a good source of income. But again the greatest value may not be monetary, but rather from the deeper interaction with fans and increased word-of-mouth.

For those who decide to dive into selling directly from their websites, a number of e-commerce platforms are available. One of the most widely used platforms is e-junkie, which allows authors to set up "buy now" buttons and shopping carts on their websites with transactions handled by PayPal, ClickBank, and other services. E-junkie costs a minimum of $5 per month, with increases based on the number of items sold.

Other options include Ganxy, which helps authors not only with the backend side of selling books, but also with the development of online sales promotion, and Aerbook, which allows authors to sell through social media. Gumroad and Shopify are also popular options among indie authors.

Whatever tools an indie author uses, she must be sure they are simple, flexible, and mobile-enabled.

Still, not everyone is sold on POS tools for indie authors. Joel Friedlander, a book design and self-publishing expert who runs TheBookDesigner.com, suggests authors avoid selling books directly on their websites and instead post a buy button that links to retailer sites.

"This makes quite a bit of sense for indie authors who are already writing, producing, and marketing their books," says Friedlander. "The time and energy it takes to work out these e-commerce platforms, install the necessary code, landing pages, buttons, etc. are not that productive for this group."

Friedlander says the authors he has seen using online point-of-sale services effectively have been nonfiction and how-to authors, who can identify their target audience very specifically and provide books to that market effectively.

EARNING AT EVENTS

In addition to selling directly through websites, indie authors may also want to consider point-of-sale systems for use at events. Tools like Square, Stripe, PayAnywhere, and PayPal Here are making it easier than ever for authors to swipe a book buyer's credit card at a reading or conference via a tablet or smartphone.

These direct sales are ideal for offering special discounts or bundles—such as selling three books for the price of two, or including a piece of merchandise along with a book. For example, Lyons gives her readers a 25% discount off the book's list price and provides them with exclusive material.

But POS sales can present difficulties at readings as well. An author must take local and state sales tax laws into account, which in many places prohibit the selling of anything without a business license.

E-BOOK, AUDIO, AND BEYOND

E-BOOK PUBLISHING: YESTERDAY, TODAY, AND TOMORROW

BY ARTHUR KLEBANOFF

In 2000, I was thinking about how best to address what I was certain would be a new, widely adopted format for digital reading. Backed by partners, I set out to license 100 rights to prominent in-copyright backlist titles from the underlying rightsholders—authors, estates, agents, lawyers—in the United States and the U.K. Titles included *Brave New World* by Aldous Huxley, *1984* by George Orwell, and the best-known works of William Styron and Kurt Vonnegut Jr. (both Random House authors).

Adobe, hoping to discover a new market, loaned us a server. The only market outlet was through an app on Palm Pilots which eventually accessed fewer than 100,000 people among the 10 million Palm Pilot owners in the United States. On opening day, Random House sued us (but not Kurt Vonnegut Jr. and William Styron) for publishing rights they claimed already to own. The front-page-covered litigation enlisted support for Random House from major publishers and support for us from the Authors' Guild and the Association of Authors' Representatives. The federal judge denied Random House's request for an injunction, a decision upheld on appeal with the Second Circuit. The result opened the floodgates in the United States and particularly the U.K. for authors with books published before the mid-1990s to license electronic rights back to their original print publisher or any independent publisher of their choice.

While many had predicted a quick adoption for e-books in 2000, those predictions proved overly optimistic. Devices were primitive and not user friendly. Sony failed with the Sony Reader—Sony had hoped to capture with digital reading what it had lost to Apple with digital music. Barnes & Noble failed with a digital reader. Microsoft failed with a $2,000 tablet—a precursor of the $500 iPad. A gaggle of content companies lost over $1 billion. Amazon learned from others' mistakes and launched Kindle in 2007.

Kindle persuaded publishers and authors to authorize simultaneous release of print and e-books, which satisfied a reader demand for current bestsellers in e-book format. Through alliances with publishers like RosettaBooks, Kindle persuaded prominent backlist authors to release their titles for e-book.

While Adobe, Microsoft, Google, Apple, Barnes & Noble, and others hoped to become important e-book players, Kindle emerged in the United States and the U.K. as the dominant market force. In the library market, large traditional players like Follett and Baker & Taylor were overtaken by upstart independents like Overdrive (now owned by KKR).

Part of the key to Kindle's success was aggressive discounting of e-books—publishers were paid based on the list price. Kindle also launched a corresponding number of price promotions. Since the publishers "shared" the price discount, these offers yielded full margins for Kindle. Today the combination of price promotions and self-publishing represent more than half of the Kindle store sales.

The story behind today's "agency pricing"—the Big Five publishers alone sell on Kindle in a manner where their e-books cannot be discounted—would require its own essay. Suffice it to say that it is a much safer bet that Kindle will continue to expand in consumer service and market share than that any pricing device of any publisher will slow Kindle's growth.

What we know today that we didn't know yesterday:

You can develop a consumer-friendly e-book file no matter how complex the source material. Five+ years ago such a file could cost $15,000 to develop. Today it costs less than $1,500.

A commercial novel with high appeal can sell over 1 million e-books.

A self-published novel priced at $.99 can sell over 1 million e-books.

Some forms of publishing do not yet lend themselves to e-book—illustrated read-aloud children's books, "coffee table" illustrated books.

The hope for a large market for "enhanced" e-books (added sound or video or live links) is so far just hope.

Nearly all of today's publishers in nearly all circumstances have declared e-books a "fundamental" right—and will insist on "bundling" the e-book rights with an initial acquisition. Since all other publishers have the same view, if you want a traditional publisher, that publisher will be publishing your e-book.

All of today's publishers have decided that the "fair" royalty for e-books is 25% of net receipts—except for the (many) publishers who have decided that the fair royalty is even less. This is the case even though Random House imprints started out with their own printed boilerplate paying 50% of net receipts. Because e-books are bundled with the print rights, acquisitions are for life of copyright. For those with a calculator that's author's life plus 75 years with no performance obligation for the publisher. E-books can be kept "in print" with no effort at all.

The number of titles in the Kindle Store has exploded to over 4 million. Kindle has opened stores in 20+ countries. With a computer setting, any English-language title can be offered in English in any of these stores. *The 7 Habits of Highly Effective People* by Stephen R. Covey became #1 in the Kindle stores in Germany and India when promoted. Any translation publisher with a computer setting can distribute titles in the U.S. Kindle store. Consider how many languages offer more than 50,000 titles in the Kindle Store in the United States.

What about tomorrow? As today's young people grow up, the percentage of readers who prefer e-book to print should go up as well. Can anyone compete effectively with Kindle? In the United States, the answer may well be "no" for a very long time. Internationally, Apple, Kobo (owned by Rakuten) and others have nibbled away at Kindle's market share territory by territory.

Will the consumer experience for e-books change? "Yes" based on history. Will "enhanced" e-books develop a market? Perhaps. Will the number of titles available in the Kindle Store continue to grow? Yes. Explode in number? Hard to imagine.

What about e-book devices? Their performance has improved, their price point has come down, but their core audience is usually someone who already owns another e-book device. As the delivery of electronic information diversifies, it is a safe bet that e-books will be a fundamental part of whatever content is delivered to consumers however it is delivered.

When the iPad was first released, its initial television commercials emphasized that the consumer could use it for reading even though the iPad buyer could initially only get an e-book by downloading a Kindle app and buying e-books in the Kindle app—a transaction that captured revenue for Amazon but not for Apple.

In the United States, 3,000+ publishers leading to the Big Five publishers who among them publish 95%+ of all bestsellers in the end lead to Amazon/Kindle for e-books. Stated another way, all e-books roads lead to Kindle for both the reader buyer and the publisher/author seller and all roads probably will for a very long time.

*

Arthur Klebanoff is the Founding Publisher of RosettaBooks. You can view its e-book catalog and its print title catalog (with accompanying e-book editions) at www.rosettaebooks.com.

APA SAYS AUDIOBOOK SALES ROSE 12% IN 2020

BY JIM MILLIOT | JUN 1, 2021

The Audio Publishers Association's annual review of the audiobook market found another year of double-digit sales increases as well as a profound shift in listening habits.

In 2019, 43% of listeners said they most often listened to audiobooks in their car, a percentage that fell to 30% last year when work-at-home orders kept people from commuting to the office. The percentage of people who took part in the APA survey who said home was their preferred listening spot jumped to 55% in 2020, from 43% in 2019.

Despite concerns early in the pandemic that the plunge in commuting would lead to a drop in sales, the APA found that sales from the 27 companies that report results to the APA sales survey increased 12%, to $1.3 billion. The sales gain is in keeping with data from the AAP, whose preliminary figures also show a double-digit increase in audiobook sales.

The consumer part of the survey found that 67% of audiobook consumers said that one of the reasons they enjoy listening to audiobooks is to reduce screen time. Another main takeaway is that parents have been discovering audiobooks as an outlet for their children during the pandemic. The percentage of parents of children ages 17 and younger who say their children listened to audiobooks last year was 49%, up from 35% previously. (The survey measures responses from people 18 and older.)

Audiobook publishers also continued to up the number of titles they produce, with output hitting 71,000 titles last year, up 39% over 2019. Mysteries/thrillers/suspense remained the largest audiobook category, but the APA reported sharp increases in interest for romance, self-help, and business genres.

Other notable findings from the surveys include:

- The percentage of Americans 18 and over who have ever listened to an audiobook is now 46%, up from 44% in 2020.
- vMembership in audiobook services increased, with 38% of listeners indicating they subscribe to at least one such service.
- 56% of audiobook listeners are under the age of 45, up from 52% in 2020.
- 70% of consumers agree audiobooks are a good choice for relaxing.

THE COMING REVOLUTION IN AUDIOBOOK PUBLISHING

BY BILL WOLFSTHAL

Publishers looking for revenue growth in 2022 and beyond will be looking to the audiobook market. According to the Audio Publishers Association, audiobook sales reached $1.3 billion dollars in the U.S. in 2020, an increase of 12% over 2019. According to the APA, it was the ninth straight year of double-digit growth.

Looking back at the book business over the last thirty years, publishers have done well watching for, and well moving into, new channels of distribution to reach more readers and increase sales. In the 1970s and 1980s, shopping malls were the new frontier for publishers. There were dozens of Waldenbooks and B. Dalton stores in many states; and regional chains grew in New England, the Mid-Atlantic, Texas, and California. That bigger marketplace enabled publishers to reach more readers. The partnership gave birth to the era of million-copy hardcover bestsellers. Books like *Yeager, Iacocca, The Clan of the Cave Bear*, and *Lake Wobegon Days* sold in numbers unheard of in previous eras. Some publishers found new markets in specialty chains, selling books through Williams Sonoma, Urban Outfitters, and other chains. Do you remember The Nature Company, the national chain of nature stores that sold gifts and books? Borders then gave birth to the "Superstore" with title counts as high as 75,000 or 100,000. Publishers saw sales grow for backlist and niche books as more titles became available to more readers.

Then Amazon came along, and publishers with deep backlists benefited by having every book available to every reader with a computer. When Amazon launched Kindle in 2006, a new, vibrant method of selling books was built. Every publisher benefited from the e-book boom, especially those who moved quickly to convert their books to the new format and risked offering them at lower-than-expected prices—as low as $1.99.

It's not hard to imagine that publishers see the steadily growing audiobook market as fertile ground for even bigger growth in the coming years. During the sales boom spawned by the 2020–2021 Covid-19 pandemic, when so many were starved for entertainment, book sales grew. For many publishers, audiobooks was a big area of growth. HarperCollins reported their audiobook sales were up 42% in Q1 of 2021, but they were hardly alone. Most of the biggest publishers, and many of the smaller ones have reported growth in audiobook sales greater than both print and e-book sales.

No one can predict what 2022 and beyond will look like, but we know that in 2020 less than 5% of print books were available as audiobooks. That percentage would be much higher if it weren't for the cost of production. Audiobooks have, until recently, required human narration, and that means the minimum cost for production is $2,000–$3,000. The cost is high because it requires a human narrator to read for hours and hours, and then proof listen for hours and hours. The cost can be even more if "star" narration or multiple narrators are used, or if the book has a high page count. (It takes twice as much time to narrate an 800-page book as it does a 400-page book.) But it seems like a technological breakthrough is at hand that will cause an explosion in audiobook production, and revolutionize the audio business.

Multiple companies are rolling out platforms that use artificial technology that creates synthetic narration that provides an enjoyable reading experience. International companies like Speechki, DeepZen, Scribe, and others are beginning to offer publishers the technology that can create audiobooks without a human narrator for as little as 10–20% of the existing cost. These are not the synthetic computer voices we are accustomed to hearing, like Apple's Siri or Amazon's Alexa. These don't sound robotic. Most people might not even recognize that it's not human narration.

Speechki, founded in Russia, has financial backing from Wall Street investor Alan Patricof. His record of supporting companies bringing new technology to market includes America Online and Audible among others. Speechki already offers almost three hundred artificial voices in seventy-two different languages, and that is expected to grow. If Speechki or one of their competitors is successful and the cost of audiobook production drops from $3,000 to as low as $400, the marketplace will change drastically. Speechki is promoting itself as a one-stop shop for publishers. They are providing unit or subscription pricing. They charge the same for an 800-page book as they do for a 400-page book. They are providing proof-listening as quality control, for those publishers who don't have that capability or want to outsource that part of the process.

If costs drop by as much as 80%–90%, publishers will rush to convert hundreds of thousands, even millions, of titles to audio. Suddenly, publishing an audiobook and selling just 100–200 copies would be profitable for large and small publishers alike. Just as it happened with e-books ten years ago, we might expect that the retail price of an audiobook will drop, perhaps dramatically, that publishers will invest more money in promotion and discoverability, and that the number of customers will grow as the price for content is reduced. It's easy to imagine a world where almost every book published would be available on publication in three formats: print, e-book, and audio.

We should not expect the demand for human narration to disappear. Celebrity authors will still narrate their own books. You would not want to listen to a memoir by Barack Obama or Meryl Streep without their narration. Publishers with potential bestsellers and deep pockets won't hesitate to hire the best human talent for their lead titles. Great voice talent will always be a great way to boost attention and sales for audiobooks. What would the Harry Potter audiobooks have been without the talent of Jim Dale? But synthetic narration will allow modest-selling books, and very long books, to be published profitably as audiobooks for the first time. That is just not possible right now with human narration.

Predicting trends in the book business is a notoriously risky enterprise. However, it's easy to recognize that podcasts and audiobooks have become pop culture sensations for the first time in just the last few years. And, if you look back ten years to the shockingly quick acceptance of e-books, it is easy to see why publishers will be looking for ways to produce product to fill the growing demand. We can also expect that Audible, the leading publisher of audiobooks, and its parent company Amazon, will spend aggressively to grow readership, knowing that they will get the lion's share of retailer sales in the market. Just like with e-books, if Amazon builds it, it is likely that customers will come, and publishers will follow. It will happen for the same reason Eddie Sutton said he robbed banks during the depression. That's where the money is!

*

Bill Wolfsthal is a publishing and sales executive with more than three decades of experience selling children's books, fiction and nonfiction, trade and promotional titles, print books and e-books into multiple sales channels for American publishers. He has worked for Harry N. Abrams, Skyhorse, Sterling, and Lyons Press.

PODCASTS: A NEW FRONTIER FOR AUTHORS

BY SCOTT WAXMAN

There is a new frontier for authors in the world of audio. I am not talking about audiobooks, which have been around for decades and have become a crucial revenue stream for publishers. I am talking about podcasts.

What do podcasts mean for authors? Well, up to now, authors have found a platform on two types of podcasts. There are chat shows where an author might appear to promote and discuss a new book (think Tim Ferris's or Joe Rogan's podcasts). And there are author-created podcasts—like *The Shit No One Tells You About Writing* from author Bianca Marais and agents Carly Watters and CeCe Lyra—that focus on the process of writing and publishing.

But there are more opportunities for authors willing to get behind the mic, and compelling reasons for authors and publishers to explore them. I am talking about authors telling stories as narrators. Whether they are reading a wholly original work or an adaptation of an existing one, authors are natural storytellers because they are authentic. Their blood, sweat, and tears have spilled during the creative process, and this kind of commitment and passion comes through in audio.

I always wondered why authors were rarely hired to read their own audiobooks. After all, who better to tell a story than the person who created it? But most often, audio publishers opt for professional actors. Sure, this can make for a smoother listening experience, and in the case of audiobooks, this makes sense as it is typically a straight-ahead read.

But podcasts are quite different. There are sound design, archival audio, multiple interviews, sometimes even actors. In this dynamic world of storytelling, authors can thrive. The voice does not have to be perfect, it just needs to be real. I love hearing the voice behind the writer. They can share their backstory—the story behind the story—and allow listeners into a completely different place, one that is separate and distinct from a book or audiobook. It's also a chance for authors to discover a new voice, their own voice, and a fresh creative self.

From a marketing point of view, podcasting can bring authors a completely new audience. They can then parlay that audience into book sales. In addition, podcasts offer new intellectual property that the author can then exploit for film and television. At Diversion Podcasts, we have worked closely with authors on all of our shows. After all, our background is in book publishing. We look forward to hearing from you about your new projects in all genres of storytelling.

*

Scott Waxman is the CEO of Diversion Publishing Corp. and The Waxman Literary Agency. Scott's company owns the publishing rights to over 2,000 fiction and nonfiction titles and publishes up to 30 original narrative nonfiction books per year. He created Diversion Podcasts to develop new, immersive, episodic audio versions of books that go beyond the traditional audiobook experience.

(14)

DIGITAL PERSPECTIVES

DATA-DRIVEN PUBLISHING

BY KEN BROOKS

Many industries are benefiting from using data in their product development and marketing activities. A widely quoted recent (March 2020) Splunk survey reports that organizations "that place a strategic emphasis on data and have an advanced strategy to extract business value have added 83% more revenue to their topline and 66% more profit to their bottom line in the past 12 months." Since data-driven product development is proving so effective, why are we not seeing a similar trend in publishing?

Many publishing sectors and categories already make use of data in product development. Education publishing uses data to improve efficacy and maintain currency of content. This practice has led to a continuous publishing model now being explored by most higher education publishers. Business information publishing is entirely based on a data-driven continuous publishing framework, which provides current information as soon as it's available. And academic publishers keep a close eye on the most up-to-date research to determine what titles might be attractive in their markets.

Most publishers use data to improve discovery and drive marketing activities. Open Road Media, for example, has built a very interesting business by determining books to acquire based on a profile of their readers and where the company can reliably create a sales lift. While there is an element of acquisition to this, Open Road Media's model is mostly about using data to identify opportunities to boost backlist discovery. And while Ingram Market Insights is not itself a publisher, it is a highly useful tool that many publishers are leveraging to improve discovery and marketing of published titles.

BUT CAN DATA BE USED EVEN EARLIER?

The Bestseller Code (2016, Archer and Jockers) outlined an approach to manuscript analysis to predict whether a work of fiction would become a bestseller or to suggest manuscript alterations to make it a bestseller. This very interesting approach has proven more effective in tailoring movie scripts—as implemented by StoryFit—than in selecting/making bestselling novels. Peter Hildick-Smith's Codex Group, founded in 2004, pioneered book audience research to assist in positioning books still in development and prior to launch. Codex Group has supported successful publication of numerous NYT bestsellers. And Callisto Media's entire publishing program is built on using data to identify unrecognized/underserved categories and publish into them.

It is easy to see that data has been in use in publishing planning for many years, but other than Callisto Media there are no widely known examples of using data to *drive* acquisition.

USING DATA IN ACQUISITIONS

To maximize the value of data a publisher must address several questions:

- How to define a market?
- How to size it?
- How to assess the opportunity—is it underserved?
- How to find titles to meet the needs of that market?
- How to reach the market?

These are all questions that CPG and Technology product managers are familiar with. (NB: This may be why some publishing companies have changed the acquiring editor job title to product manager.)

Historically, target markets have been defined by talented editors who stay current in their areas of specialty and cultivate relationships with key thought leaders. One of the most promising areas for the use of data is to identify growing areas of interest by monitoring social conversations, searches, and trending topics. Dan Lubart of Iobyte Solutions describes a promising approach combining evaluation of relative Amazon category strength over time, a profile of the books and publishers in that category, and share of first-page, book-related search results. Others have taken a similar approach but have applied sophisticated ontological mapping techniques to identify related queries.

Market sizing has often devolved to an initial print run calculation estimating first year and lifetime sales prior to acquisition. More sophisticated methods rely on estimating probable share of the total addressable market (TAM). The most interesting approaches involve looking at growth of category sales growth and sales rank at Amazon, then modeling demand from that data married with trends in correlated features.

This growth-sales rank-trends approach can be used to identify underserved categories by looking at title coverage and distribution of sales among titles on a given topic. The base information is readily available from Amazon, but to take advantage of it a publisher must be able to acquire and publish fast enough to ride the popularity wave. The publishing cycle can't be years, it must be months.

In a February 8, 2020, article on LinkedIn, Callisto Media author Jeff Zafarris offered insight into how Callisto Media does it: They seek out "influencers and experts who can create a quality book" that fulfills the market need. They then couple this with fast speed-to-market and low cost of development and production so that even large errors in market sizing still result in a profitable title.

Which leaves the question of how to reach the market. Fortunately this is becoming a science in understanding market psychographics, the study of where people shop and how to reach them. Key words are determined by book reviews (reflecting *how* people think about the book—as opposed to mining the content of the book itself). Ingram Market Insights provides a comprehensive dashboard on how to optimize discovery and marketing of titles through Amazon.

POTENTIAL APPROACHES

While there are many possible ways to address these questions, a few approaches are readily apparent that integrate answers to all the questions. These approaches include undercutting, branding, fast-follower models, and the more daring "blue-ocean" approach.

Undercutting existing offerings is a time-tested approach with examples ranging from the original introduction of mass market paperbacks, then trade paperbacks and most recently Amazon's $9.99 price point on e-books. It's the underlying principle of executive book summaries and other forms of summary editions that take longer works and synthesize their essential information, usually, but not always, at a lower price point.

Branding is another way to stand out from the competition. This can leverage a corporate brand (Dummies), a series (Captain Underpants), a franchise license (Disney), or an author brand. Advantage|ForbesBooks is an example of this, developing books to support authority marketing campaigns—burnishing the author's reputation as an authority in a particular field—not consumer-driven at all!

If a publisher has fast cycle times, it should be possible to take a "fast follower" approach, publishing additional books in a developing category, or even beating upcoming titles to market via shorter cycle times.

A "blue ocean" approach (named after the 2005 title by Kim and Mauborgne, "Blue Ocean Strategy") involves finding an unknown market and publishing into it. This is what Callisto Media did with Keto diets and Dummies has done with their book on Doodle Dogs.

DATA-DRIVEN PUBLISHING IS BOTH USEFUL AND INEVITABLE

Regardless of publishing sector and category, data is useful in all phases of the publishing process. It is both feasible and beneficial to supplement (not replace) editorial and marketing judgment as a publisher addresses the key questions of publishing. The use of data increases the speed and quality of decisions and can inform an overall strategy. Some strategies, indeed, can only be implemented through a data-driven approach. Becoming a data-driven publisher is not an instantaneous process. But, thanks to services such as Ingram's Marketing Insights and Dan Lubart's Iobyte Solutions, it's not expensive to get started. A data-driven commissioning approach may seem countercultural but it's time for a change. It's crucial to begin now to explore data-driven publishing or risk being left behind by competitors with fully developed data competency.

*

Ken Brooks is the president of Treadwell Media Group, a publishing and operations consulting firm focused on content, product development, and supply chain in the higher education and trade sectors. Prior to Treadwell, he has held positions including Chief Content Officer for the Academic and Professional Learning division of Wiley, Chief Operating Officer of Macmillan Learning SVP Global Supply Chain at McGraw-Hill Education, and senior positions at Cengage Learning, Barnes & Noble, Simon & Schuster, and Random House. Over the course of his career, Ken has founded digital services companies both in the United States and abroad; a public domain publishing imprint; and a distribution-center-based print-on-demand operation and has worked in trade, professional, higher education and K–12 publishing sectors. He holds bachelor and master's degrees in industrial engineering and a master's degree in computer science from Georgia Tech, where he also mentors graduate students in educational technology.

PUBLISHING'S SHIFT TO DIGITAL, DATA, AND DISCOVERY

BY MARY MCAVENEY

Open Road Integrated Media or ORIM (stylized as OR/M and also called Open Road) is a digital media company in New York City that was created by Jane Friedman and Jeffrey Sharp in 2009 with a focus on publishing e-book editions of older works of literature and nonfiction. In addition to its e-book publishing business, Open Road Integrated Media is the parent company of book publisher Open Road Media and content brands Early Bird Books, The Lineup, The Archive, Murder & Mayhem, A Love So True, and The Portalist.

Open Road Integrated Media, Inc. today is a leading technology-driven marketing-as-a-service company serving the media industry. The company acquires the exclusive rights to market, license and sell digital content (principally e-books) to captive audiences. OR/M's automation software allows it to acquire high-quality content and audiences at low cost and activate purchases through marketplace segmentation, data analysis, promotions, and merchandising. It employs 56 in its New York, N.Y., headquarters.

OR/M's marketing services operation (Open Road Ignition) delivers, on average, over 100% uplift in backlist e-book sales. The services also have a positive "halo" impact on print sales of about 45%, and approximately 80% sales increases in selected frontlist titles.

With investment in workflow automation, content and audience acquisition, and data insight tools, OR/M has increased its core business and expanded to other content and product types, as well as extended the business model to allow content owners to use its marketing platform. The principal focus is its proprietary marketing technology within the e-book industry. However, its core competencies and techniques can be readily deployed to other media types.

OR/M's clients are publishers, authors, and agents for whom it markets titles to an engaged consumer base through highly curated, genre-specific websites and industry-leading newsletters.

Successful digital bookselling today requires many times the number of decisions and actions than had been needed traditionally. This means a shift to technology-supported marketing is the only way to effectively resource title management at scale. The number of titles that are published by the industry annually number over one million, and there are hundreds of millions of previously published titles that make up the publishing backlist today. OR/M's technology employs AI—a system that makes the decisions in the way it has been programmed that allows the company to market hundreds of thousands of books quickly and efficiently.

In 2020 and 2021 it became increasingly clear that discoverability is key to the marketing process. OR/M runs several search-engine optimized vertical funnels that bring consumers into their ecosystem. Those consumers become newsletter subscribers, and that reach is a catalyst to discovery at retail and in search engines. As OR/M reaches more readers it triggers search and retail algorithms that improve discoverability for audiences beyond its own. Through this network affect, OR/M has structured a limitless discovery engine for the titles it manages.

As consumers continue to shift to digital for discovery, consideration, and purchase the industry will need to adapt to the changing behavior. The publishing industry has largely been a curator or gatekeeper of content with the largest publishing houses controlling the pipeline to retail and hence consumers. As the market conditions move toward independent search and discovery, the industry becomes more democratized and companies like OR/M that have developed scalable discovery and conversion methodologies will become increasingly critical.

*

Mary McAveney is the Chief Revenue Officer and Chief Marketing Officer at OR/M. A strategic leader with a focus on tech-enabled digital solutions, driving product discoverability and revenue for authors and publishers, her positions have included Vice President Marketing at Simon & Schuster, Vice President Marketing at Zondervan, and Director of Marketing at HarperCollins, as well as numerous consulting positions with media companies, internet start-ups and publishers.

WE NEED TO TALK ABOUT THE BACKLIST

BY THAD MCILROY

This article is a love song to backlist books. Confined to the shadows beneath the bright light of publisher frontlists, these books are too often neglected. But there are many gems on the backlist: books with proven potential and solid profit margins.

WHAT WE TALK ABOUT WHEN WE TALK ABOUT BACKLIST

Every publisher has a picture in their mind when they hear the term "backlist," but it's revealing to consider how definitions can vary in their specifics.

In *The Book Publishing Industry*, noted publishing scholar Albert N. Greco provides about as straightforward a definition as could be imagined: "An old title that continues to sell." In a later work he revised his definition to "an older book (originally released between 9 and 12 months ago) that continues to remain in print."

There are a range of claims as to how recent a title should be in the move from frontlist to backlist. Six months, twelve, a "season." A 2006 *New York Times* article defines frontlist as "titles less than one year old."

Seth Godin, who has authored two dozen books, offers a pithy perspective: "The backlist is the stuff you sell long after you've forgotten all the drama that went into making it."

Another definition leans to the functional: if a book is being advertised or actively promoted by the publisher, it's frontlist. If it's a book that gets continually reordered each time the last copy disappears from the shelf, it's backlist. (This definition, though revealing, fails to embrace publishers' increasing interest in backlist promotion.)

My definition leans toward the nebulous: Backlist is a state of mind. Publishers know when a title is no longer frontlist. They feel it in their bones the moment a bestseller has transitioned, even though it might still be stacked on the front tables in chain bookstores.

WHY BACKLIST MATTERS

Backlist matters for two simple and connected reasons: it's as much as two thirds of what people buy, and it's markedly more profitable for publishers, with better margins and fewer returns from bookstores. Period.

BACKLIST SALES ON THE MARCH

In terms of percentage of sales, NPD reported (via *Publishers Weekly*) that in 2020 "backlist titles accounted for 67% of all print units purchased in 2020, up from 63% the year before. In 2010, backlist accounted for only 54% of all unit sales." Though the sales mix of backlist versus frontlist may be shifting, if even a mere quarter of a publisher's sales come from backlist titles, that's plenty of reason for a continuing focus on the category.

THE LONG TAIL, E-COMMERCE, AND THE BACKLIST

Chris Anderson first described his much-referenced "long tail" theory in *Wired* magazine back in 2004. Its premise for publishers is that the internet makes it worthwhile to distribute and sell just a few copies of a book (once the initial costs of publication have been recovered).

And between e-books and print-on-demand, keeping the long-tail titles available for sale is a cinch. Say what you will about Amazon, it has unquestionably afforded authors and publishers the perfect platform to showcase their backlist titles.

PUBLISHERS TEND TO DISDAIN THE BACKLIST

A publisher's failure to fully embrace its backlist could be mere benign neglect. But is it sometimes something more?

Publishers tend to be judged by the editorial and sales success of their frontlist, rather than the financial performance of their solid, stolid backlist.

> The frontlist is like a drug. Frontlist is sexy, or just plain fun—acquiring new titles and trying to turn them into bestsellers. When people dream of publishing careers, they dream of discovering new authors and transforming them into bestselling Nobel Prize winners—they don't think about goosing the sales of an old book on carpentry or knitting.

Seth Godin again: "It's more exciting, more fun and more hopeful to seek out and launch new books. It's the culture of many industries, particularly ones that are seen as creative."

Mike Shatzkin, writing about backlist a decade ago:

Most publishers "learn" (institutionally) that it isn't worth promoting backlist. To begin with, most publishers aren't staffed to do it: the head counts and working processes of publicity and marketing departments are built around the requirements of "launching" books, not "piloting" them.

John B. Thompson, in his *Book Wars*, noted: "The fiscal demands and incentives of publishing organizations favor short-termism."

Mike Shatzkin again:

In the frontlist negotiation [it's] far more interesting for [publisher sales reps and booksellers] to talk about the future, with the tantalizing promise of "big" books that may catch the public's fancy and sell in large quantity, than to deal with familiar, routine backlist titles that have lost their mystery and excitement.

PRINT-ON-DEMAND AND THE BACKLIST

Print-on-demand (POD) is a 25-year-old technology, though still underappreciated and underutilized by many book publishers. For some time, the problem with POD was quality—just not quite *good enough*, not as good as offset printing; buyers could detect the difference. These days it's plenty good enough for black-and-white books, and even does a good job with the photographs. With four-color books it can fall short, though not by much. Most readers don't notice.

POD is really two different products when supporting the backlist. People often think of it as printing just a single copy of a book to fill a special order. Though the margin is lower on POD books, that becomes secondary if a sale would otherwise be lost.

But POD is also a short-run product, serving a market where offset printing isn't economical, for instances where offset takes too long to meet a bump in short-term demand. (Ingram calls this "just-in-case" printing.)

Today most offset book printers include POD services. Quality and pricing is similar. A variety of considerations go into choosing a short-run service, which are beyond the scope of this article. But one company stands apart from all of the others, not because they're great printers, but because of their enormous distribution network and state-of-the-art logistics. That, of course, is Ingram, which operates POD and book distribution services for publishers large and small, via Lightning Source and IngramSpark.

In his Ingram history, *The Family Business*, Keel Hunt writes "Lightning

Source was beautifully designed to help publishers take advantage of the long-tail phenomenon. . . . Suddenly, it [was] feasible for a publisher to realize the aggregate sales potential of those thousands of 'little' books. . . . By 2020, Ingram's fiftieth year, the Lightning Source digital library included more than eighteen million titles (ready for print-on-demand)."

METADATA AND MARKETING THE BACKLIST

Backlist marketing has one essential characteristic that differs from frontlist marketing. It's the difference between promoting individual titles, one at a time, and promoting a mass of titles with a unified strategy and set of tactics.

Frontlist promotion is mostly art; backlist promotion is mostly science. Frontlist marketing is intimately tailored to each title, each author and each market. Backlist promotion seeks to find a set of common elements that work across a group of titles. Invariably that involves metadata enhancement.

There are a half-dozen published studies describing the impact of improved metadata on book sales. You've probably seen one or more. With each new study, the research methodology becomes more precise and the findings more credible. Just some topline numbers: including all five core descriptive metadata elements—keywords, short description, long description, author biography, and reviews—saw sales three times higher than titles with no descriptive data elements. Titles with just keywords included found their sales increase by more than double.

But sales don't have to double for the effort to be worthwhile. Revisiting the metadata of each title—how much time does that take, what does it cost? Best practices for metadata are still relatively young, and most publishers have not fully embraced them. This shows up particularly in their backlists, where the metadata was formulated before publishers really understood the concept.

The result is that the average backlist title has one or more of the following metadata problems:

1. Poor BISAC code selection, and frequently only one or two codes chosen, rather than the three that most resellers accept.
2. Too few keywords (plus inappropriate and repeated terms).
3. No author page/author bio.
4. Weak book descriptions.
5. No post-publication reviews included with the online listing (only prepublication blurbs, which suffer credibility issues).

There are certainly costs associated with metadata renewal. It takes a trained technician and someone with a flair for copywriting—those are not complementary skills. And it takes some amount of time, perhaps thirty minutes per title, perhaps an hour or more. But you don't have to sell many more copies of that book to get an ROI on the effort.

SOME CLOSING THOUGHTS

Publishers have an obligation to their backlist. The verb "publish," from Latin *publicare*, does not mean to write a book, to edit a book, to design a book, or to print a book. It means "to make public or generally known." The act of publishing is the act of informing the reading public that the book exists. That obligation doesn't cease when a title is no longer new.

*

Thad McIlroy is an electronic publishing analyst and author based in San Francisco and Vancouver, B.C. His site, The Future of Publishing, provides in-depth coverage of the book publishing industry. He is a partner in Publishing Technology Partners and an adjunct professor in the Masters of Publishing Program at Pace University in New York.

METADATA IS THE BOOK

BY THAD MCILROY

I want to believe that 2021 is the year that metadata for books came into its own.

Several years ago most people's awareness of metadata wasn't grounded in books or in publishing, but rather in disclosures of government surveillance of our email and mobile phones.

In those contexts metadata is often defined as "data about data," a definition guaranteed to put an audience into deep sleep.

Book publishing is a small player in the metadata metaverse. And within the book publishing world there are two very separate kinds of metadata: metadata for bibliography and metadata for commerce.

The bibliographic usage of metadata is championed by libraries. Their standards and structures range from Dewey Decimals through Dublin Core to MARC. This metadata is of little value to the commercial needs of book publishers.

ONIX is the standard for e-commerce for books. Yet ONIX is of little interest to libraries. And so, even within the tiny little world of book publishing, metadata is fractured into two camps.

I sometimes argue that metadata is not just *about* the book. It *is* the book. Every chapter title, every factoid, every turn of phrase, every proper noun, all of these are contained within the book, yet, in isolation, are markers to the text of the book. If I mention the Book of Leviticus, I'm clearly referencing the Bible. If I mention Ichabod, I'm probably also referencing the Bible. Unless it's Ichabod Crane from *The Legend of Sleepy Hollow*. This, to me, is metadata.

QUANTITATIVE VS. QUALITATIVE METADATA

Another core distinction within the art of metadata is the division between quantitative and qualitative metadata. "Quantitative" is easy to define: Data that's precise, unequivocal—the book's price, or its ISBN. Either you specify the correct price or you get it wrong. Then the territories where that price applies. And the date(s) the price is valid. Whatever: all of this is quantitative data, even if some of it is text, not numbers. You get it right or you got it wrong.

One standard definition posits that quantitative data is "factual information (such as measurements or statistics)." Yeah, exactly.

With "Qualitative" metadata the text is free-form: for example, the book's description or the author bio. There's not a binary right or wrong.

The qualitative issue is how good (i.e. effective) is your marketing copy? Is it of high enough quality to help sell this book? That's what I mean by qualitative. Possessed of quality. It's not an unreasonable proposition, though in the "data" sense it's all wrong.

Most metadata is based in factual measurements or statistics. So is most metadata for books. But these free-form data fields are a different beast. They are equivocal. Your great book description is my yawn. My fact-filled author bio leaves you wondering, yeah, but what are they really like?

Metadata aside, we know that great marketing copy sells. Copywriters get big bucks. The "data" in these fields is copy, it's advertising. But is it data? It's another curious aspect of metadata for books.

METADATA AND SALES

Pete McCarthy, Director of Consumer Insights at the Ingram Content Group, has been quoted as saying that "Publishers say that they really like metadata, but what they really like is sales." It points to an ongoing challenge within book publishing: Is metadata just a bunch of text and numbers, or is it at the heart of book marketing today?

PROOF THAT METADATA IS UNDERVALUED

In preparing this article I dived into the *Publishers Weekly* Job Zone, searching for jobs that I was certain would demand a familiarity with metadata. If it's true that metadata sells books then why do none of these marketing positions require metadata knowledge?

- Marketing Manager
- Product Marketing Manager
- Senior Marketing Manager
- Publicity and Social Media Coordinator

It gets worse: here are two more job titles posted, both from Big 5 publishers—surely *digital* marketing demands metadata skills?

- Digital and Social Marketing Coordinator
- Digital Marketing Manager

Neither of these mention metadata, not in the job description nor in the desired qualifications.

If we're not expecting metadata knowledge from our managers, no wonder it's still sitting on the back shelves. Until management demands that its managers know how to compete with metadata, metadata will be a good house-keeping afterthought.

Metadata for e-commerce has been sitting in the doldrums for too long now, confined to some kind of bibliographic hell, saddled with the ever vague concept of discoverability. Keywords have been the cry: find the right keywords and you can rule the online universe. Is that all there is? Seven keywords and you're off to the races?

Metadata has been vastly undervalued. I'm here to tell you that metadata is *the* most important part of selling books today. Bar none. Its power should change the way you market books. It can measurably increase your sales. This has been proven.

Publishers have to start approaching metadata as a strategic weapon, not as the digital equivalent of an old library card catalog.

Publishers Weekly started covering metadata 15 years ago (the first article I can find is dated 2002!). "Accurate Metadata Sells Books" is the title of a *PW* article from 2010, 11 years ago. Why, in late 2021, am I still trying to convince publishers that it's true, that metadata sells books?

EDITORIAL MATTERS

Editorial is at the heart of book publishing: if all other factors are equal, the better book will sell more copies. Of course few of the factors are ever equal, and, in publishing, sales and marketing is mostly concerned with trying to tip the precariously balanced scales ever-so-slightly in your direction.

In a world of bricks and mortar the marketing process is well defined and easy to understand: take a good book, seek to influence the conversation via book reviews and the author's presence, and, anticipating some interest, buy your way to prominent retail display, so the book is visible when the educated customer comes calling.

In the online world publishers and authors still seek influence, but, for the most part, can't *buy* prominent display space. It's a Gordian knot. Your book appears most prominently on Amazon because it's selling well despite not appearing prominently on Amazon.

And so achieving prominence becomes a far more multilayered challenge than it was in an exclusively bricks-and-mortar world. Relationships are established digitally; metadata is the grease on the wheel of online connections.

METADATA IS LEFT-BRAINED

Metadata is left-brained, dry, and analytical, and publishing executives are mostly right-brained, creative, and sensitive. They don't understand how metadata really works and, truth be told, they don't want to. They'll settle for the 30,000-foot view, and, more truth be told, from 30,000 feet, metadata *does* look like an old library card catalog.

Up close it looks complicated. Metadata is standards-based, and right-brained people don't like technical standards. Going deep into metadata takes you into the realm of EPUB, HTML, SEO, and ONIX. Yuck. What publishing executive wants to go there?

The other damning thing about metadata is that the #1 reason we need great metadata is to compete on Amazon. And if there's one thing that makes a publishing executive cringe worse than complex technology it's fretting about more effective ways to compete on Amazon. The game is brutal and complex, the rules change all the time, and self-published authors and Amazon imprints keep winning.

In the same sense that the metaphor for metadata can be a library card catalog, the metaphor for competing on Amazon is fighting it out on the shelves at Barnes & Noble, but digitally. Most online shoppers were first trained on bricks and mortar, and it's in Amazon's interest to make its book pages reminiscent of a dusty old bookshop that just installed fluorescent lighting. It's only natural that publishers treat book pages on Amazon as if digitized Barnes & Noble bookshelves.

METADATA IN CYBERSPACE

The unpleasant truth is that while online book pages may appear reminiscent of the Bookshop on Main Street, they are in fact located at the Bookshop in the City of Amazon. OK, yes, the cover still matters—a lot—as do the jacket copy and the blurbs. But there's so much more that happens in Amazon City. There are reader reviews, good ones and bad ones, that signal a book's quality from a customer's perspective, not from a doting friend of the author's. There's a dynamic sales ranking. There are multiple editions on sale side by side: hardcover, paperback, e-book, audio and used. Complementary titles are found below the fold. There's dynamic pricing. On the author's page are videos and links to their blog and to community pages on Facebook, Twitter, and Instagram.

The big hurdle for publishers is understanding that all of this online information, all of these online links, are based in data, dynamic data, metadata.

Metadata has depth and breadth. Metadata should be verbose but accurate. Metadata should emanate outward, linking, constantly linking, to every online waystation that a book buyer might visit.

METADATA IS THE BOOK

In book terms metadata mostly means "information about a particular book." That's all. Simple as that.

Advanced metadata mavens ponder this notion and eventually reach the (by then) obvious conclusion: What information could be more revealing about a book than all of the words in the book? Publishers need to find ways to expose a book's content online so that it can be indexed by search engines.

While publishing will always be grounded in great content, the only way to make that content visible will be via rich metadata linked into smart search systems.

*

Thad McIlroy is an electronic publishing analyst and author based on the West Coast. His site, The Future of Publishing, provides in-depth coverage of the book publishing industry. He is a partner of Publishing Technology Partners and an adjunct professor in the Masters of Publishing Program at Pace University in New York City.

TO CHANGE HOW YOU PUBLISH IN THE DIGITAL AGE, START WITH A QUESTION

Before a publisher launches a digital transformation, it needs staff input

BY BILL ROSENBLATT

When publishers talk with consultants about digital transformation, they are typically looking for some way to transform their businesses from print first or print-centric to digital first or digital-centric. Publishers often assume that the primary task of digital transformation is to find, select, and implement technology solutions, and in parallel to find ways of justifying their costs. But I've noticed that this isn't the case. Instead, the most effective way to approach digital transformation is to ask lots of people a simple question: What would you like to be able to do that you can't do now because it's too difficult or impossible?

If you're a publisher, ask that question to a variety of people in your organization—across different job functions and at levels ranging from individual contributors to top management. Focus on responses that relate to new products and services as well as efficiency of producing existing products and services. No answer is too simple, vague, or off-the-cuff, though you'll want to push for as many specifics and as much quantitative information as possible. You'll get answers ranging from "well, I sort of had this idea . . . " to fully formed business plans crying out for management attention. I've found that the more people you ask, the better, but the magic number before diminishing returns set in tends to be about 20.

Once you receive the responses, you'll need to group them into common elements. You'll probably be amazed at how many common elements there are. They tend to fall into three buckets: people, processes, and technology. Often a simply expressed idea will have many of the same elements as a sophisticated plan—and just as often an idea from one division or workgroup will have much commonality with an idea from another part of the company. You can express each of these elements as capability gaps in people, processes, or technology.

The other important step in compiling the responses is aggregating the business benefits that accrue from filling the gaps. The more quantitative you can be about these business benefits—revenue, cost savings, customer retention, etc.—the better.

As an example, many new product and service initiatives require improvements in content structure and metadata. This entails capabilities in people (skills for creating content structures and metadata), processes (workflow), and technology (editorial systems and content repositories). Small projects of this nature may not move the needle enough to justify investment on their own, but several projects of different sizes aggregated together may. That doesn't mean that you should adopt a one-size-fits-all process or system for all of these initiatives—in fact that is almost always a bad idea—but it does mean that multiple groups can take advantage of the same types of skills, process changes, and tools in different ways.

The magic happens when you present the aggregated results to the stakeholders in your digital transformation initiative. Light bulbs go on over people's heads when they see that they need the same capabilities as people in different parts of the company whom they thought were in completely different businesses. More light bulbs go on when several people who had "small" ideas that they didn't think were worth management attention realize they have different forms of the same idea—or, conversely, when management realizes the various "small" ideas that they've been hearing about can all be implemented using the same set of capabilities.

As a result of this exercise, you'll do two things at once: you'll reach consensus among a diverse group of people on capabilities that the organization needs to add or improve, and you'll have an understanding of the aggregate business benefits that these capabilities can provide. Armed with these two things, you can create an implementation plan that describes the desired capabilities, covers all of the beneficiaries, and comes with a built-in business case to justify investments in people, process changes, and technology solutions.

The first step in creating an implementation plan is a gap analysis. For each of the capabilities you've identified, ask the following: What do you have now?

What do you need? And what is the gap between the two? Does it involve improving an existing org chart, process, or system—or does it require whole-sale replacement?

Once you understand the gaps, you can begin to research and identify ways to fill them. Now is the time to research costs and implementation efforts, because without the context of aggregated business benefits and capability gaps to fill, that information isn't particularly useful. And by the way: any vendor that purports to give you this information before or without that analysis isn't doing you any favors.

Many fancy consulting methodologies are based on these same ideas. Yet the details and formalisms aren't as important as the principles of eliciting ideas from people, seeing what they have in common, and harnessing that commonality to build a vision for a digitally transformed company.

∗

Bill Rosenblatt is president of GiantSteps Media Technology Strategies and a founding partner of Publishing Technology Partners.

A version of this article appeared in the 06/15/2020 issue of *Publishers Weekly* under the headline: Start with a Question.

THE PANDEMIC PUSHED PUBLISHING INTO THE DIGITAL REALM. SO WHAT'S NEXT?

With the digital future arriving early, publishers need to adapt

BY STEVE SIECK

"The future hasn't changed—it's just been accelerated." That's a common take on the pandemic's likely long-term impact, and it rings true. The extent to which white collar workers will return to their offices, students to their classrooms, and all of us to the comfortable privacy of video-less calls remains to be seen. But the forced acceleration of long-evolving trends toward more remote digital access to work, play, and learning activities—via Zoom, Teams, Houseparty, massive online open courses (MOOCs), etc.—seems likely to leave behind a changed societal and business landscape. After all, technology adoption is largely paced by the extent of behavioral change required. And once that change has occurred, there usually is no going back. (See: email, e-commerce, streaming entertainment, etc.)

I'm writing my first Digital Perspectives column from a secluded mountainside 120 miles from New York City. By early March I'd purchased a webcam and USB mic that are now integral to many of my personal, not to mention business, pursuits. Activities that had taken place in on-site group workshops or one-on-one training in New York City have moved, for the most part successfully, to Zoom and the like. Compromises in attention and nonverbal communication have been balanced by gains in convenience, accessibility, cost, and diversity of participants.

So far, though, my relationship to books hasn't changed much. I still do most of my reading on my smartphone and Kindle, still buy print books and have them delivered, and expect soon to be browsing again in local bookstores. So, what does the accelerating shift to virtual modes of work, learning, and community mean for publishers?

At the margins, relative gains in format share by e-books and audiobooks seem likely, given more limited bricks-and-mortar retail options, library purchasing pressures that will result in shifts away from print, and, perhaps, improvements in the e-book reading experience. But greater opportunities for publishers to sustain and grow business in the (post-)Covid era may well stem from the ability to capitalize on newly adopted consumer habits and expectations and newly adopted technologies that can facilitate the marketing of books and their authors, and from the ability to streamline publishing interactions and workflows.

The shutdown of other media and entertainment sectors has sparked some of the most creative responses to the challenges imposed by the pandemic. For example, actors, musicians, and teaching artists are finding the shock of lockdown at least somewhat mitigated by the ability of live performances and training on Zoom et al. to reach larger, more geographically inclusive audiences. And similarly, an early shift to virtual book tours and online book promotion conferences has already begun to expand publishers' marketing reach beyond urban and university centers. Social media initiatives like PRH's "#BooksConnectUs" exemplify the publishing community's opportunities to respond to the isolation borne of lockdowns and social distancing. While it's likely that many booksellers will struggle to survive, publishers now have an opportunity to use the new popularity of videoconferencing and other remote access venues to help fill the consequent vacuum in personalized services to readers.

Concomitant opportunities to modernize the culture and operations of publishing companies, especially by the mainstream trade publishers, could be equally important. The whole idea of a New York City–centric trade publishing industry based on relationships nurtured by long lunches and cemented in Midtown high-rises, already increasingly anachronistic, now seems certain to be more rapidly supplanted. In its place will likely be a more geographically and socially diverse author-agent-publisher ecosystem, enabled by a more expansive communications infrastructure as well as new collaboration and networking norms and tools adopted in response to the pandemic.

A new study by Ithaka S+R of university presses found that "many presses have introduced more process reengineering in the last two months than in the last several years." Educational publishers are moving to expand the availability of digital resources to supplement remote classes, and higher-ed textbook and scholarly publishers in particular are seeking new ways to navigate a shift from teaching by the book to teaching by the platform or MOOC (likely to accelerate and be accelerated by the greater decoupling of courses and campuses).

The scale needed to make serious commitments to post-pandemic virtual community initiatives and invigorate direct-to-consumer distribution models may provide the Big Five with even more advantages, and given the strong probability of diminished resources ahead for other publishers, more industry consolidation is likely. Still, exploiting new digital communications opportunities to foster reader communities in niche markets may help some independent publishers to thrive in the "new normal." Cloud-based services can enable savvy small publishers to develop relationships with readers and get into the direct-to-consumer game much more easily and cheaply than ever.

In a society adapting to increased isolation and decentralization (and perhaps a new recognition of the value of expertise), the role of books in fostering dialogue and bringing together people and ideas can only grow in importance. To ensure that this promise is fully realized in a time of contraction and disruption, publishers should recognize that a more virtual, digital future is not as far away as it used to be and plan accordingly.

*

Steve Sieck is president of SKS Advisors, a consulting firm serving publishers and information services providers, and a partner in Publishing Technology Partners.

A version of this article appeared in the 07/27/2020 issue of *Publishers Weekly* under the headline: Now What?

PART III.
REACHING READERS

⑮

MARKETING, PUBLICITY, AND SOCIAL MEDIA

DISRUPTING THE TRADITIONAL PUBLISHING MODEL

BY JASON KUTASI

In the publishing world, books have long been sold in the same traditional manner with an invisible separation between author, publisher, distributor, retailer, and consumer. With so many hands in the pot, this means authors make less money and consumers pay more.

I did not let these notions get in the way when I made the decision to take a new approach to book publishing and launched Puppy Dogs & Ice Cream. However, even I could not have foreseen just how ready the industry was to break away from its conventional approach and forge a new path forward.

It all started in November 2017 when in its very first month, PDIC blew through its initial inventory of 5,000 children's books. The company's growth continued to skyrocket in 2018 when revenue hit $1.45M with just two titles. We took a look at books on the market and saw an opportunity to grow by delivering books with a purpose—books that teach valuable life lessons children need to read.

The success of Puppy Dogs & Ice Cream came from filling a need. Every family has dozens of books with beautiful art and a great story, but there was a gap in the market. We quickly realized there was an opportunity for us to deliver children's books that sit between traditional educational content and books with an entertaining story. When we started, I would take a lot of customer service calls personally. I really wanted to understand a customer's "why" and overall experience. It's really about the "why." Why should someone buy the book? Why do they *need* to buy the book? We created a bunch of videos and testimonials that pushed our books hard. Our first two books still run today and are still some of our bestsellers, years later.

This new approach of providing quality books with important life lessons for young readers, supported by a direct-to-consumer digital marketing plan, propelled the company's quick takeoff. The company proved the old publishing industry model was ripe for disruption when it sold more than 1.35 million books in 2020 and received more than 365,000 five-star ratings.

I looked at it this way: if an online retailer isn't going to market or run ads for our titles, then they are just acting as a shopping cart to process a sale online. If that's the case, I prefer to process those sales on our own cart and build the one-to-one relationship with the customer.

BREAKING THE PUBLISHING MOLD

The astounding part of PDIC's quick success is that the company didn't set out to disrupt one of the largest industries in the world. It simply wanted a business that was beneficial to authors, bookstores, and customers. Puppy Dogs & Ice Cream was molded by a passion for two things: books and children. They saw an opportunity to share inspirational and beautifully illustrated stories with families.

I don't really think of ourselves as disruptors, but just a publisher who doesn't conform to the old rules of the industry. We didn't do it intentionally. We also didn't invent e-commerce, but simply bolted e-commerce onto a vertical—children's books—that doesn't have the same margins as most e-commerce businesses. I guess we just managed to figure some things out to make direct-to-consumer sales work for kids' books.

PDIC books can be found on Amazon, but that only accounts for about 20% of the company's sales. Currently, the company does not spend one dollar marketing on Amazon.

Amazon does have a lot of reach, but those people are in-market already looking for a book. We get way more reach and scale with Facebook, Google, YouTube, Pinterest, Snapchat, and TikTok than we can get on Amazon.

While that approach is different, the biggest disruption has come in the channel conflict between publishers and retailers. PDIC's direct-to-consumer sales interrupts the traditional publishing industry approach, but I believe the company is nothing but supportive of traditional bookstores.

I don't want anyone to think that running direct-to-consumer means we don't support bookstores. That couldn't be further from the truth. In fact, our discount typically exceeds the industry's standard trade discount because we don't have to pay a distribution fee. So, the combination of our ads and wholesale discounts makes our books really appealing to bookstores.

When a customer walks into a bookstore and recognizes a title from one of our ads, it is beneficial to the brick-and-mortar stores. This is how brand awareness works for all e-commerce products. We are also working on a mapping tool to show customers a list of retailers where they can buy our books, and we are starting with the smallest retailers first. These small bookstores are the ones who could use our help the most.

Also, many people simply prefer to purchase in-store, rather than online. Our own experience and numerous marketing studies have supported this.

BETTER OPPORTUNITIES FOR AUTHORS

PDIC provides support to independent authors who are grossly underrepresented in today's publishing world by offering a direct-to-consumer approach that gets books in the hands of as many children as possible.

When we built our publishing model, we took a look at the pain points authors face today and set about to build a better mousetrap. We realized running a direct-to-consumer business allows us to cut out a lot of middlemen in the industry. This means better royalties for authors and better pricing for consumers.

The company handles all the marketing and publishing costs for the author, not charging a single penny for distribution, printing, fulfillment, or customer service. The authors get an opportunity to sit back and collect a royalty check, providing them the freedom to work on new books.

However, the author benefits from PDIC go beyond royalties. The company tests each and every title with paid ads, before going to print, to give the author the best chance of success. This is about $2,000 in testing authors get free of charge. PDIC also allows authors to send an email to their readers.

I remember the first time we did this. The book was the *Super Tiny Ghost*, and I asked the author if she wanted to email all her readers. She said sure, so that's what we did. The emails she received from people who had actually bought her book were tremendous. She now had a relationship with her readers and the ability to build a tribe.

CONSUMERS VALUE THE CONTENT AND EXPERIENCE

PDIC provides a one-stop shop for parents and grandparents to find quality books that instill lifelong values within their young readers while creating the perfect experience. The company has built an easy-to-use website where customers can shop by age, bestsellers, new releases, and e-books, as well as separated into categories including bedtime stories, social emotional learning, family and friends, inspirational, and more.

We want to publish books with a purpose, books that parents should read with their kids to teach them valuable lessons. Our books highlight topics such as emotional learning, loss, gratitude, and so much more. We strive to make meaningful and educational stories that will help a child grow into the best version of themselves.

In addition to the ease of shopping for children's books with a purpose, customers are given the ability to create that one-to-one relationship with the author that is just not available through the typical publishing route.

It's about creating an incredible experience for the customer. It's about delivering the right kind of content. It's about building a tribe for the authors. It's about the one-to-one relationships between the author and the reader.

*

Jason Kutasi is the founder of Puppy Dogs & Ice Cream, a small, independent children's book publisher based in San Diego, California. They offer an alternative to the traditional publishing model that benefits authors and customers alike. They have a strong belief in supporting American business, and all of their books are printed in the United States.

VOICE LESSONS:
BRAND VOICE FOR PUBLISHERS

BY ALAN SIEGEL

As a pioneer in the business of helping all kinds of organizations connect with their employees, customers, and supporters through a distinctive brand voice, I pay particular attention to the dynamic influence digital media has on brand communications. A recent article in the *Wall Street Journal* discussed the challenges facing Pearson PLC, the leading publisher of educational content, as it transforms into a tech-driven company. It is a perfect example of a company that would benefit from a compelling brand voice. Their new CEO, Andy Bird, pointed out, "While we are continuing to focus on intellectual property, the physical textbook will be replaced by interactive and immersive formats."

With this transformation, the company will provide access to over 1,500 titles with audio, note-taking, highlighting, study cards, flash cards, and other interactive study tools. This heightened engagement will help them cement consumer relationships early on during school and provide a foundation for future growth well beyond graduation. The Pearson+ Program serves college students and then helps them migrate into, and throughout, their careers.

Pearson is redefining what their brand stands for to an expanded audience that has never dealt with them. The challenges they are facing to reposition the company, introduce new technology, and address their commitment to social diversity and social justice provide insight into challenges facing the general publishing community.

BRAND VOICE WORKS AS BRAND GLUE, CRYSTALLIZING STRATEGIES BEHIND IDENTITY.

A fully developed voice drives all communications to project a distinctive personality that reinforces customer interactions. It's a "red thread" running through every touch point, beyond advertising and media, to embrace reputation and crisis management.

When I introduced this concept in a speech in 1980, I noted that the vast majority of communications produced by corporations and government were frequently uncoordinated and fragmented, lacked clarity, and didn't project authenticity. I used a cartoon from the *New Yorker* featuring an executive sitting behind a large desk telling seven or eight of his employees that he wanted "an address that speaks with one voice." Odds are, they were like an orchestra without a conductor, their disparate voices creating dissonance.

I went on to say that to communicate effectively and build a distinctive identity, your brand must develop a voice that is instantly recognizable, generates strong images and associations, and establishes the tone and character of your communications: classic or innovative, glamorous or functional, aristocratic or irreverent, elegant or just simple and down-to-earth—a voice that fuses your language, content, personality, and visual style to convey your personality and culture.

To further understand the potential for this concept I studied hundreds of companies to understand how the most distinctive and successful voices emerged.

The most effective brand voices were generated by powerful visions that were passed down to employees and nurtured by environments designed to project the purpose, positioning, and culture. These visions sprang from many sources—distinctive products, impassioned marketing concepts, the unique perspective and taste of a visionary individual or a strongly defined corporate culture that characterizes an entire organization. The starting point is self-knowledge, where the organization clearly defines what they do, what they stand for that separates them from their competitors, and how to generate supportive behavior from their core audiences.

I emphasized how important it was to recalibrate voice to the right pitch, tone, and volume in an environment where speed, novelty, distraction, and noise rule. Consideration must also be given to personalized communication, providing for two-way conversations, for instant responses to rumors and speculation on the internet and social media, and creating brand communications for expanding digital platforms.

WHO WAS DOING IT RIGHT WHEN I FIRST STUDIED THIS?

ESPN, the dominant sports media company in America that reaches millions of television viewers each week—and this doesn't count the millions who listen to ESPN radio, read ESPN magazine, visit their website, or subscribe to wake-up alerts on their mobile phones. They have established a special connection with sports fans by creating programming that mirrors a conversation in your living room between their anchors and guest commentators.

Their voice is authentic, expert and passionate with an overlay of locker room banter and playfulness. It is driven by the tone and style of their cornerstone television show, *SportsCenter*, and permeates all their communications across all platforms.

They talk with fans, not down to fans. They are serious, but not too serious. They deliver authoritative sports information with humor and personality.

Target, with superstores in 47 states, has built a powerful brand around its positioning of affordable design—what people referred to as discount chic. With their advertising slogan *Expect More, Pay Less*, they transformed their bulls-eye red logo into a lifestyle symbol that is recognized by 96% of American consumers.

Target has built loyalty with the American consumer with its imaginative, forward-looking, youthful, friendly, actionable and socially responsible voice that played a critical role in its success.

Apple built its brand and loyal following by practicing simplicity. Its voice reflects the personality and values of Steve Jobs—brash, exuberant, irreverent. It's crystal clear, speaking for all who work for the company, buy its products, or identify with its values.

Apple's voice is simple, elegant, accessible, brash, exuberant, irreverent and crystal clear. The company doesn't just talk about simplicity, they live and practice it.

WHO IS DOING IT RIGHT NOW?

Warby Parker, the eyeglass provider, uses technology for "virtual try-ons" of eyeglasses, supporting its mission of being fashion-forward, economical, and convenient. It is a practical, helpful reinforcement of its brand voice. Similarly, the company nicely balances low-tech and high-tech experiences, reflecting the reality of life. Their brick-and-mortar shops are filled with books (a lovely nod to eyeglasses facilitating one of life's great pleasures—reading). They even convey their brand voice on the cleaning cloth enclosed with a purchase—by printing the story of the company's origins. By allowing customers to try five pairs of glasses in the comfort of their home and return them postage-free, they are conveying the idea that this is not a one-time transactional relationship. The company encourages back-and-forth commentary, visits, and interactions with its customers.

Warby Parker has found a voice that is fashion-savvy, friendly, helpful, and lighthearted yet grounded. It has turned a prescription into a recipe for success.

SADLY, THE MAJORITY OF BRAND MESSAGES FAIL TO ACHIEVE THE MOST ESSENTIAL TASKS OF COMMUNICATION.

They lack clarity. They pose conflicting messages. They often don't even pay lip service to integrated themes. The most effective brand voice is the result of a singular and powerful vision that is nurtured in environments that encourage innovation and excellence in communication.

Over the last 20 years, the digital revolution has raised the din of marketing communications exponentially, radically altering the messaging environment with its speed, novelty, and noise. Every marketer needs to recalibrate their brand voice to find the right pitch and tone and the ideal volume to be heard. This dynamic has forced organizations to:

- move from one-way communications to a dialogue;
- incorporate personalization, flexibility, and simplicity;
- react instantly to rumor, speculation, and criticism on the internet;
- convert brand communications to proliferating digital platforms;
- build social responsibility into their brand voice; and
- appropriately translate languages for multinational markets.

BRAND VOICE LIVES IN THE RINGS OF A TREE RATHER THAN ITS BARK.

Without the foundation of a compelling brand voice, companies who layer on digital solutions are merely adding veneer rather than substance. In contrast, applying technology in ways that support, extend, and reimagine the underlying brand voice reveal depth. Pearson is adding high-tech functions to its basic offerings—certainly necessary, useful, and practical. However, they would do well to consider the potential to use technology even more adroitly as Warby Parker has. Technology behind the scenes, used to really understand the likes and dislikes of customers, is the most sophisticated evidence of a truly resonant brand voice. When brand voice guides operational and digital strategies, the results are authentic, rooted, and sustainable.

It's past time to clear your throat and raise your digital voice.

*

Alan Siegel is one of the leaders in the global branding business and a pioneer in simplifying business, medical, technical and government communications. He has developed over 250 branding programs for high-profile corporations, educational institutions, and government agencies including Citibank, 3M, the National Basketball Association, Carnegie Mellon

University, and the IRS. His new book, *Voice Lessons*, focusing on how to develop voice programs, will be released by Skyhorse Publishing in 2021.

HOW TO PUBLICIZE BOOKS IN THE 21ST CENTURY? GOOD QUESTION

BY MERYL MOSS

You have written a book and your dream has come true! Writers are a rare and special breed. Whether you write fiction or nonfiction, you are now an author.

Congratulations!

The next part of your journey is fun, exhilarating, validating, and meaning-ful—whether you are ready for it or not. It's that all-important promotion, for which there are several key components to address if you want to be successful and find an audience.

And just a little nugget to consider before we begin: You are not the only one out there trying to get attention for your new book. According to the ProQuest Bowker Report from October 15, 2019, nearly 1.7 million books were *self-pub-lished* in the United States in 2018. That's an astounding increase of 265% in just five years. By 2019, the total number of books published in the United States exceeded 4 million in that year alone—including both self-published books and commercially published books of all types—according to data pro-vided by ProQuest.

So you've got some competition. But not to fret, people buy books—let's just maximize opportunities to increase the odds that they buy yours!

If you work hard and set your sights high on getting the word out to as many readers as possible, you will succeed. You can gain significant attention and traction for your book, but it doesn't happen without dedication, research, and time. Whether you are doing it yourself or with the help of professionals, remember you can only launch your book once, so make the most of it.

FIVE BIG BOOK PROMOTION IDEAS

1. **Book reviews** are very important, for more reasons than you may realize. Of course, a good review in a respected publication will help get the word out, but reviews also can be used as leverage to gain

additional attention—on social media, on your website, on your book's retailer pages, among your friends and colleagues with large followings, and to attract key influencers.

It is essential to start reaching out to reviewers five to six months in advance of the publication date—we call this the runway. Prepublication book reviews in the publishing trade magazines such as *Publishers Weekly*, *Kirkus*, *Library Journal*, *Booklist*, and *Bookpage* are a vital part of the book review process.

Remember:
- It is critical to make sure that on the day your book gets published that four-and-five-star reviews are ready to be posted on Amazon and other online retailers. Asking friends, family, and colleagues is a good beginning to getting the ongoing review machine started.
- No matter how readers hear about your book, they want to know that other readers liked it first before buying it. Go for the five-star reviews.
- The more reviews you have on the online retailers, the better it is.

2. **Book tours and the ever-changing world:** Book tours are arranged with independent and chain bookstores in key markets for readings, talks or panel book discussions. Strong independent bookstores known for having an engaged relationship with readers and robust newsletter lists are approached months in advance for an appearance. The great thing about book tours is meeting booksellers. Booksellers are your conduit to readers. If you make a good connection, they will promote your book before you arrive, in the store while you are there for an event, and way after you leave. Don't miss this golden opportunity to make friends with booksellers. They will be a solid help to you and potentially handsell your book to customers.

Remember:
- When on book tour, make advance contact with the media in each of the cities where events are scheduled.
- Today there is a hybrid approach to a book launch where some events are virtual and others are in person. Book tours are just one component of a book launch.

3. **Media interviews are an important way to get readers to find out about your book.**

   A debut writer should start investigating hometown media first and build from there. Don't be shortsighted about the power of "the local": tell everyone you know, even your dry cleaner, that you have a new book. Your local fans will want to help you—let them.

   There are a variety of media entities to pursue when promoting a new book: radio, television, print, websites, and podcasts. Radio interviews with stations locally and around the country can be the easiest ones to reach and are a great way to publicize a new book.

   Of the many media entities in each city, find out which shows and host match up with your book—that's the first step to being asked to do an interview.

   Remember:
   - Do your research before approaching any producer or host, make sure the show does interviews, and find out what they like to cover.
   - Exploring what a host is interested in personally, where they were educated, and what they like and dislike can also help when pitching your book.
   - Try to listen or watch the program so you know what segments might fit best with your book.
   - Create a sound bite for what your book is about. Practice it so it's perfect.

4. **Online publicity—websites, blogs, and podcasts—**are the new long-lead magazines and are very important. These entities should be cultivated just as you target television, radio, or print for coverage opportunities. When first starting out, you are more likely to secure interest from bloggers. Bloggers have become influencers and may have several channels where they can post about your book. Developing relationships with bloggers, bookstagrammers on Instagram and booktubers on YouTube early in your writing career is an investment in your writing future. Most print publications have an online component which could result in a mention, review, or feature about your book before you get coverage in the print version. Both are great placements. Links are a terrific tool to let others know about your coverage.

5. **Trade shows, literary festivals and speaking engagements—keynotes, panels, webinars are essential and a great way to learn your way around the book industry.** There are events for authors in most states and a few that are national. Since this is your craft, the more you get to know the players in publishing, the more informed you'll be. At trade shows, literary festivals and speaking engagements, try to get yourself on a panel to talk about your craft, process, and area of interest. Speaking engagements at bookstores and libraries, with associations and influencer events, is another key component to learning the new world of which you are now a part. These events are important for making contacts and connections with media, influencers, bloggers and building your social media. Nothing is better for an author than meeting readers.

Say yes to everything that comes your way, be open to the possibilities, and enjoy the ride.

*

Meryl Moss is founder and president of Meryl Moss Media Group, a literary media relations and marketing firm that for 28 years has been promoting and branding authors and their books through media exposure, speaking engagements, social media, and creative marketing solutions. The firm specializes in working with first-time authors, as well as those who are established and looking for a seasoned group of professionals to take them to the next level. Meryl Moss Media Group is proud to work with authors book after book, the best compliment there is.

Like many new ideas, Meryl Moss created BookTrib.com on a napkin. When traditional media outlets started reducing coverage of books and authors, Meryl put a stake in the ground with a website featuring under-the-radar authors who deserved to be noticed and who readers would enjoy discovering—whether debut writers, midlist authors, or even occasional bestsellers. Rather than focus on the household names you read about everywhere, BookTrib.com's mantra is to give voice to those authors that really need to be heard—and read.

THE SOCIAL MEDIA PLATFORM
BY SARAH ELIZABETH HILL

A GROWING AUDIENCE

Right now there are around 4 billion people actively using social media in the world and that number is set to increase by over 10% each year. The rise of social technology has brought with it a rise in audience-building and this has allowed authors and creators of all types to speak directly to their audiences and to build a following through content. Content includes words, images, videos, and more created and posted on social media websites like Facebook, YouTube, Twitter, Instagram, and TikTok. Publishers largely still hold on to the relationships with distributors and retailers, but with social media, authors have suddenly found themselves in the spotlight and able to communicate directly with their readers. And it is not just authors who now communicate online through social media. Publishers, retailers, and readers are all online, competing for the attention of users in the social media algorithms.

THE AUTHOR/FOLLOWER RELATIONSHIP

Authors and prospective authors alike are using social media. Current authors use social media to market their books to their followers—devoted fans who have chosen to see more content from certain accounts. Authors now are compelled to build up the number of followers they have so they can increase awareness and spread the word about release dates, bookstore visits, sales, and more on social media.

DISCOVERY

Aspiring authors also benefit from social media. When a person has a large online presence, it is not uncommon for them to receive multiple offers from book publishers. This is because publishers look at the already-grown audience as a source of built-in book sales, and also because the audience acts as a proof-of-concept for the book idea to publishers.

The proof-of-concept doesn't stop with the audience. Maintaining and growing a social media audience takes a lot of dedication. A dedicated online poster will most likely make a great author as well. Many great authors have been discovered online and some of them even have brought entire markets back to life. For example, Rupi Kaur is well known as one of the first "#instapoets." Kaur's ability to reach poetry audiences through her social media, particularly Instagram, has brought her much success and, along with it, a resurgence in poetry book sales.

For emerging authors the internet is rife with opportunities to grow fans, interact with publishers, and even self-publish. They can test ideas quickly and easily.

CONTENT FOR SOCIAL MEDIA

In this new social media age, online growth is often reliant on posting content regularly. This has forced authors, publishers, and marketers everywhere to expand the original book concept into more pieces of content. Each book becomes its own brand. Animations, graphics, videos, and illustrations—all with the branding of the book in mind—can be created and posted online. Authors and publishers will even take large passages of the book and post them to discuss with the fans and followers, giving readers unprecedented access to the publisher and the author. This online connection with readers and fans has led to the creation of story ideas and crowdsourced book covers.

With fans and readers having more control than ever, many authors and publishers have started to ask online influencers to help in their marketing campaigns. An online influencer is anyone who has a large online following, particularly on social media. For example a book influencer can be a bookstore owner, an author, an avid reader, or a book review blogger. It is common for publishers to now include online influencers on the list to receive advanced reading copies and galleys. If the right influencer posts positive content online about an author or book, it can lead to the book being sold out across the country. Inversely, if the right influencer speaks ill of the book or author, that too can quickly catch wind and impact sales.

AUTHORS ONLINE

For the most part, authors used to be able to live their lives outside of the public eye. This allowed them the freedom to *not* interact with their readers and the public—if they did not want to. Now, with the invention of social media, authors are often "called out," "praised," and/or "questioned" all very publicly. In some cases, public opinion can swing drastically in a short period of time based on the consensus of the online crowd and the current internet ethos. For example, J.K. Rowling, the author of the Harry Potter series, went from a publishing darling and fan favorite with millions of personal followers to experiencing a harsh global backlash after comments she made on Twitter about the transgender community went viral.

There is no question that social media has been a game-changer for publishers, authors, and readers. It has allowed connections between creators and consumers to flourish. And all of these connections have led to many changes to the publishing process and the finished book. One thing is for sure: as platforms and algorithms continue to evolve the book industry will continue to evolve with it.

*

Sarah Elizabeth Hill is the Founder of Bobi NYC social media agency in New York City and is the Co-Founder of Bookstr.com. She has grown audiences into the multiple millions through organic content on various social media channels including Facebook and Instagram.

ALWAYS BE GROWING:
HOW AUTHORS CAN USE SOCIAL
MEDIA TO SELL BOOKS

BY JEN MANN

So, you're a published author now. Congratulations! But whether you're traditionally published or an indie, you might be surprised to find out that you are now the number one member of your marketing team. That's right—unless you're Stephen King, there aren't a lot of dollars coming your way. And if you're indie, you've always known you were footing the bill.

There are tons of different ways you can market your books, but one of the easiest and most affordable ways is by using your social media platform. Plus, don't forget the added bonus that you don't have to leave your house so you can sell books in your PJs!

Before I was an award-winning blogger and a *New York Times* bestselling author, I was a Realtor. My mantra was the famous "Always Be Closing." Now as a writer my mantra is "Always Be Growing." What I mean by that is that you must always be consciously increasing your online platform. Whether you're traditionally published or an indie, your digital platform is absolutely vital to your success, and you can never neglect it. You must feed it, nurture it, and grow it every single day.

I know, I know. I can literally hear you groaning right now. "But Jen, I'm a writer. I just want to write!" I get it. I really do. But unfortunately, I don't know too many successful authors who have the luxury to just sit around and write. Everyone I know is writing and expanding their online reach all at the same time.

I can't tell you how many writers I see who spend an entire year writing a book and doing nothing else and then say, "Okay, *now* I'm ready to work on my platform. Teach me your ways." Sorry, pal, you're too late. You needed to be working on that stuff daily!

When I tell people I'm a full-time writer, they imagine me sitting in a cabin in the woods, drinking tea, writing thousands of words a day that just flow out of me blissfully, and then the book magically becomes a bestseller. They don't understand the amount of work that went on behind the scenes to get me to that point. At this point, writing is a j-o-b for me. I have deadline schedules and weekly word count goals that I stick to. I have a list of tasks that need to be done every single day, and at the top of that list is creating content to build my online presence so that I can then use that platform to generate book sales.

I spend just as much time growing my platform as I do writing. Usually, I work on both throughout the day. I try to post several times a day on my various social media accounts. I have more than one million people across all the platforms following me, but my largest fanbase is on Facebook.

When I started writing back in 2011, there weren't as many social media platforms to choose from. I was the most comfortable on Facebook because I was (and still am) too wordy for Twitter, and Pinterest felt like a place for recipes I'd never make and workouts I'd never do. Over the years I've tried to migrate my readers to Google+, Ello, Slack, MeWe, Snapchat, Instagram, and now TikTok, but my readers just can't quit Facebook. So even though I have a presence across all the sites, Facebook is where I put the bulk of my energy. I think a writer needs a presence everywhere, but they can only do two to three different social media apps well. Pick your strengths and play to those. They can't all be winners.

Social media can feel a lot like work, and I hear a lot of complaints, but it isn't hard as long as you remember the Golden Rule: be authentic and stay true to your brand. I'm always walking a fine line between being myself and staying on brand.

It's important to stay on brand or else you confuse your followers. For instance, one day I got a wild haircut and I felt all warm and fuzzy, so I posted an inspirational quote I'd found on Pinterest. I don't even remember what it was, but I know it was flowery and fluffy and very unlike anything I'd ever posted before. My audience freaked out. Almost all the comments were: "Have you been hacked?" "Jen, are you okay? What's going on?" "Oh, my God, Jen's had a stroke!"

I can be inspirational and flowery and fluffy, but it needs an edge. If I post an article about yoga, it better be people practicing yoga with beer and screaming goats. If I take a picture of a particularly beautiful sunrise, hopefully I literally broke a leg to capture that serene vista and now I have a hilarious story for my next book. All of my motivational speeches use f-bombs like commas.

Do you know what your brand is?

If you don't know what your brand is, ask your readers. Ask them, "What are the three things you think of when you think of me?" That will give you a start. You'll see a pattern and then the trick is to lean into those topics.

That's it. That's all you have to do.

If you don't have any readers to ask, then you have a couple options. You can create your brand from scratch and carefully cultivate it. Everything is incredibly planned out and maximized for the most potential. Your other option is to throw a bunch of spaghetti at the wall and see what sticks. Pay attention to your post and track the likes, comments, and shares. Use your analytics to determine your popular topics.

And sometimes it's a mix of all of these things. When I first started writing, I never posted selfies. I thought no one cared what I looked like and I didn't want any negative comments about my hair. But one day I broke my own rule and put up a selfie. I tell you what, the likes exploded and the (insanely positive) comments poured in. Not only did women not make fun of my hair, they actually asked for a styling tutorial like I was a freaking influencer or something. Now selfies are part of my social media plan, because I learned they get high engagement for me. So if I'm having a good hair day, I'll make a live video, an Instagram post, and a TikTok. I'm not going to waste it!

The one rule I never break is: It can't always be about you, dumb-dumb. Yes, people are following you and want to hear from you, but they don't necessarily want to hear about you and your career. At least not all the time. I try to keep my posts to the 80/20 rule. Eighty percent of the time I'm posting about other things (but still staying on brand) and 20% of the time I'm posting about my products or services. I share entertaining or informative articles from blogs or news sites I respect. I share funny or empowering memes that others have made. I tell stories. I make videos.

I will entertain people all day, but I rarely ask people to buy my book. That is an absolute no-no and this is why: you must think like a reader, not like an author. I follow my favorite authors because I'm interested in what they're working on next or if their latest masterpiece is on sale or if they're going to be signing books in a town near me, but what I really want to know is what kind of dog they have or what titles are in their TBR pile on the nightstand. You know what I don't want to hear? My favorite author barking, "Buy my book!" all day long. That's annoying as hell. I want to connect on a personal level, not be sold to all the time.

It might seem odd for a writer not to mention her books, but I track all my analytics everywhere and I know this works. I've hit the *New York Times* bestsellers list with my traditionally published and independently published books and many of those sales can be attributed to my activity on my robust social media platform. When I engage—in any manner—books sell. There are some days where I just can't be as active on social media as I am normally. Life gets in the way, I'm on a deadline, or I'm just not in the mood to be funny (hello, Coronavirus), and those are the days my book sales are down.

I lied earlier. I said I never yell, "BUY MY BOOK!" but that's not true. If it's book release day all the rules go out the window. When it's release day, it's all promotion all day long. I change all my headers, I make my profile pictures the cover of the new book, and I talk about nothing else but the book. However, I try to always make my sales pitches entertaining or informative for my readers. I share quotes from the book, I share good reviews to encourage sales, and I share bad reviews so we can all laugh together about stupid people who don't get me and my sense of humor. I share excerpts. I make videos, I write articles and place them on other sites. I write a blog post; I send out a newsletter. If I could hire a skywriter, I would. This is when I call in all my favors too. I ask anyone connected to me to help me share the news. I've worked hard to create my community, and release day is when I really put it to good use and make it pay off. I find that because I've been generous with my time and my talents in the past, when release day comes, everyone is happy to help. They're invested in me as a person and they want to help me succeed.

I know this is the point where you're a bit overwhelmed. You're thinking about your lack of time to even write, let alone do social media. I can hear you yelling at me, "I work full-time. I have a family! My precious little free time is spent writing and now you want me to add even more to my plate?"

YES.

But don't worry. It's not as hard as it sounds. I've been in those shoes, so I know how hard it is, but I also know it can be done. When I started writing I was a full-time Realtor, a wife, and a mother of two small children. I didn't know anything about social media. But I learned like everything else, it just takes discipline and something I took from my real estate days: time-blocking. With time-blocking I carve out 30-minute chunks of my day (or evening) where I can work on a task. Sometimes it's moderating one of my private groups, sometimes it's replying to comments on Instagram, sometimes it's creating content for Twitter, sometimes it's writing a blog post.

The first thing you should do is go ahead and claim all your social media channels. It doesn't matter if you don't have any followers yet. They will come. You want them to be able to find you, and the only way that's going to happen is if you've claimed your name.

What name should you claim?

That's a good question. It really depends on your goals and what you want to be known for. This goes back to branding again. When I started this adventure, I was an anonymous blogger who never revealed my last name or shared a picture of myself and didn't know anything about social media and branding. But then I wrote a viral blog post that was read by 1 million people in 24 hours, and that was the push I needed to create social media accounts. I didn't want to claim JEN MANN. In my head, Jen Mann was nobody. No one knew Jen Mann. The viral blog post was written on my blog PEOPLE I WANT TO PUNCH IN THE THROAT, so that was the name I claimed everywhere.

Looking back, it wasn't the wisest decision I made. But it was a decision made completely under pressure and that's what I'm trying to help you avoid. If I'd had more time, I probably would have come up with a suitable pseudonym or a better way to describe myself, because People I Want to Punch in the Throat is a strange mouthful. It's not memorable and it's awkward.

Take some time. Figure out what you want to be known as, because if you do this right, those names are going to define you through a long and winding career.

For social media only, my recommendation is to always go with your name versus a blog or a series name. Ultimately YOU are your brand. Your readers read you, no matter what you write. It's imperative to have a personal account and then if you want other accounts for your popular books or blogs, do that, but make sure you have a personal account too that will link to all these sub-accounts.

And finally, I can't talk about social media without mentioning the trolls and troublemakers you'll inevitably run into. Social media is an excellent tool to give strangers a glimpse into your life. It's where your readers can see and connect to the real you—or at least as much you as you're willing to share with them.

Now, I could write a whole chapter on boundaries, but I won't. I'll just say that social media is a wonderful invention that has brought people together and made the world a smaller place. Going viral on social media literally jump-started the career I'd wanted my whole life, so of course I love it. But I also know it can be a very negative space, so you must always remember that you're in charge. I think of my social media platform as my house. Everyone's invited, but there are rules in my house, and anyone's welcome to stay as long as they follow the rules. But I'm the boss, applesauce. Not only am I the entertainment, I'm also the bouncer at the door who chooses who has access to my house. Just as easily as I let someone in, I will throw them out. I figure no one is allowed to come into my real house and take a dump in the front hall, so why would I let anyone do that in my virtual home?

Basically, if you want a good experience on social media for yourself and your readers, set boundaries and enforce them like a mothertrucker, because fighting with people you want to punch in the throat on the internet is not on your to-do list.

*

Jen Mann is best known for her wildly popular and hysterical blog People I Want to Punch in the Throat. She has been described by many as Erma Bombeck—with f-bombs. Jen is the author of the *New York Times* bestseller *People I Want to Punch in the Throat: Competitive Crafters, Drop-Off Despots, and Other Suburban Scourges* which was a Finalist for a Goodreads Reader's Choice Award. She is also the mastermind behind the *New York Times* bestselling *I Just Want to Pee Alone* series. Her newest book *Midlife Bites: Anyone Else Falling Apart, Or Is It Just Me?* is a humorous guide to exploring the often-overlooked female midlife crisis and will be released in January 2022.

Jen is a married mother of two children whom she calls Gomer and Adolpha in her writings—she swears their real names are actually worse.

CHELSEA APPLE MAKES A CASE FOR BOOKTOK AUTHENTICITY

BY CHELSEA APPLE

I wasn't surprised to discover that Barnes & Noble had created a BookTok page, encouraging readers to "discover the most popular books on TikTok." If anything, I was surprised that more book retailers (and publishers and authors, for that matter) hadn't yet tapped into one of the fastest-growing social media platforms.

I fell down the TikTok rabbit hole during pandemic isolation in May 2020, and for the next seven months I marveled at the creativity, humor, and vulnerability of the platform's millions of content creators around the globe. But, as both a voracious reader and a creative strategist at a literary public relations firm, what interested me most was the BookTok community: hundreds of thousands of readers who dedicate their TikTok accounts to reviewing, recommending, and laughing and crying over their favorite books.

The more time I spent on TikTok, the more certain I felt about two things. First, the app created an immensely powerful opportunity for authors to connect immediately with a staggering number of highly engaged readers. And second, the tools for "success" on TikTok differ from those of any other social media platform.

A recent *New York Times* article, "How Crying on TikTok Sells Books," explores in depth what makes BookTok unique: short-form videos that depict readers' raw tears, anger, and delight over their favorite reads in one minute or less. One BookTok creator who was interviewed suggested that videos in which she is crying get more views. While this may be true, I'd assert that it's not her tears that keep users watching. It's the idea of authenticity behind those tears—viewers getting an unfiltered look at the creator's emotions and thoughts, heightening their sense of connection to the creator.

Authenticity is TikTok's greatest appeal, and its most powerful engagement tool. Users on TikTok are bold in sharing their opinions, emotions, vulnerabilities, insecurities, and imperfections. The content on the app feels more unfiltered, more raw, more real than content featured in other places. As a result, viewers aren't just passively consuming TikTok's content—they're connected to it. Contrast this to Instagram, where heavily filtered, edited, and perfectly curated highlights have become commonplace—and, I would argue, increasingly passé.

So what do authenticity and TikTok have to do with authors? Simply put, authors who are able to authentically present themselves on TikTok will find a vast audience of highly engaged readers who are eager to connect with them and their work. Users on TikTok want to support creators—and they will, if given the opportunity to connect with them.

One of the incredible authors I had the privilege of working with and introducing to TikTok, J. Elle, has plenty of great content—but her reaction to unboxing her novel *Wings of Ebony* is by far her most popular TikTok video, with more than 25,000 views, 6,500 likes, and hundreds of comments (with most saying they've just added *Wings of Ebony* to their TBR or online carts).

Sure, there are tears. But it's her vulnerability, her authentic love and pride for the story she created, that made her engagement and follower count explode. And for the record, *Wings of Ebony* was an instant *New York Times* bestseller.

My advice to authors (and other publishing professionals) who are interested in joining TikTok is this: leave your sales pitches at the door. Tell a story that demonstrates your sincere passion for your work. Be honest about your challenges with your writing. Offer writing advice and unique tips that only industry insiders would know. Celebrate your wins and share your vulnerabilities. Understand that TikTok's algorithm is highly mercurial, meaning that while the "recipe" for going viral is shrouded in mystery, the opportunity to go viral is omnipresent.

And finally, to anyone in publishing who wants to understand TikTok, I would say, use the app! With more than 600 million users, the platform is growing and changing at an astronomic pace—to really "get it," you have to use it. A new generation of readers is creating literary trends faster than ever. They are hungry for books, and freely and eagerly sharing what they love and want from literature. All you have to do is tune in.

*

Chelsea Apple is a creative strategist and content coordinator for Books Forward, a literary PR firm. She helps authors make the most of TikTok and other digital platforms. Learn more at booksforward.com.

A version of this article appeared in the 06/28/2021 issue of *Publishers Weekly* under the headline: No Time for Tears.

16

SALES AND DISTRIBUTION

SUPPLY CHAIN, INFORMATION, AND CURATION

AN INTERVIEW WITH JOSH MARWELL

I see the sales effort as a three-legged stool. The first leg is supply chain, the second is information, which is data and metadata—coming in and going out—and the third is curation. Those elements have always played a part in how books go to market. I've been lucky enough in my career to experience a revolution in all three of those areas, which have really changed the way books are sold in our country.

When I started, publishers weren't very good at shipping books, and nor was it as urgent to get books to customers in the same timeframe as it is today. But there was a revolution in warehousing technology, which extended to the publishers and they became very competitive in terms of being able to ship books on a timely basis.

With data, the first big revolution, which transformed the industry, was POS data becoming available. Of course, now we have BookScan, but POS data really changed the dynamic of selling in because when you didn't have POS basically you loaded books in a big way and over-distributed. POS-driven sales forecasts are one of the key elements in our landscape today. Other digital data—including what's in edelweiss and the metadata and keywords that we send out in the form of electronic feeds have made it very easy for booksellers to understand what books are coming as well as helping consumers easily connect to books of interest to them. Sophisticated analysis of what topics consumers are searching for has revolutionized how we spend our marketing budgets as well as what we publish.

Lastly, curation is sort of the oldest and probably the most central part. When I was growing up, my mother would go to Fox and Sutherland's in

Mount Kisco, N.Y., and Mr. Fox would always put a book into her hands with great enthusiasm, and she would buy it! I still have some in my library today. In those days, the *New York Times* was an important part of the curation for a lot of stores and they devoted shelf display to the *New York Times* bestsellers. And then, of course, Oprah's Book Club happened. There's a direct line from Mr. Fox to Oprah to TikTok today. America has changed and the book business has changed with it.

EXPANDING THE MARKETPLACE

Obviously, you want to have books wherever consumers interface with them, and we're blessed with a wide array of places to showcase our books and market our books. The sales instinct is to put books where people will discover and buy them. Right from the start, from indies to department stores, to super-stores to big boxes to online retailers, Americans have liked to shop for books the way they like to shop for other things. So wherever people are shopping, books have a place in the assortment.

SPECIAL SALES

Special sales is a broad array of different channels including specialty retail stores where books are not the primary focus. Buyers in these stores opt to include books in their assortment for many reasons, not the least of which is the cachet that goes along with carrying a book. They add books that are specific and curated to the kind of store and the clientele they serve. A well-curated book section can help define a store's identity and what it stands for.

INDEPENDENT BOOKSTORES

I think that all things being equal they have survived the pandemic in the last year and a half. They had done a lot of work in terms of shoring up the loyalty of the local communities to their businesses. And people happened to be at home and spending more time locally. It gets back to the curation issue. At the end of the day, having somebody who you know and whose taste you respect recommend a book to you really matters to people. So I think there's a role for that. And in terms of getting excited about new talent and new authors, the indies and librarians are very strong, and the other retailers are also making efforts in that way as well.

LIBRARIES

We have a phrase: If you convince a single person to love a book, you get one reader. If you convince a librarian to love a book, you get a village of readers.

They feel strongly about what they read and like and are willing to share their passion. They have long memories about books they've read ages ago.

BUILDING BUZZ

You have to build buzz, and that gets back to the curation element. You know, our salespeople all read. And they talk about the books amongst themselves. They talk about them with their customers. Our library and marketing people talk about our books. It's building excitement every day. People are always looking for new voices, something new and something distinctive. And then magic happens. Books are talked about in the media. Our marketing and publicity partners are working on getting the books out there in the seasonal roundups. And then—it happens all the time—something just clicks. During the pandemic, people turned to books and connected with books. And now as it started opening up, people are looking for communities where they can hear about books. I think that's one of the reasons why TikTok, or BookTok, has taken off. If you get a book on there, it takes off everywhere. And retailers have been responsive in terms of merchandising these books immediately. I think there's a hunger. During the pandemic, people returned to books and discovered them anew. And now that things have opened up people are hungry to continue and intensify that connection.

THE FUTURE OF THE BUSINESS

The supply chain, which now includes digital books and audio, the POS, data and metadata matrix and the curation and the passion unique to our category are all fundamental keys to understanding our business, and it's helpful to take a step back and look at what's happening now in our industry through those lenses. They play a critical role now, they have made the difference in the past, and will certainly be part of our future.

*

Josh Marwell is the President of Sales at HarperCollins Publishers, a role he has held since 2004. Before joining Harper he worked in sales management at Little, Brown and Saint Martin's Press. He began his career as a field rep in Upstate New York.

PUBLISHING AND THE PANDEMIC
AN INTERVIEW WITH DENNIS ABBOUD

How has the distribution business changed since the pandemic started?
I'd answer that from two vantage points. First, allow me to address the early days of the pandemic, which was generally the period from February through April of 2020. As a backdrop, it's well-recognized that 70% of U.S. consumers have less than a thousand dollars in their savings accounts. During this period, there was a slowdown in discretionary item purchases, including books. I think this was due to numerous factors: First, customers were spending their available funds panic-buying and hoarding household staples and foodstuffs. This was owing to the general trepidation caused by the pandemic, and the fear that ongoing supply of these items would be scarce. Second, mass merchants, warehouse clubs, and grocery stores reappropriated their supply chain resources and promotional space that would otherwise have been available to books, to these types of products.

By way of example, there were books shipped into retailer distribution centers that arrived at stores very late because priority was given to shipping water, paper products, and other commodities perceived to be of higher importance. In some cases, entire displays of spring seasonal books never reached the sales floor because they were trapped within a retailer's supply chain through the end of the season. In addition, some of the largest online retailers shifted their focus in the same way, slowing their receipt and shipment of books, particularly bestsellers, to consumers. As May arrived, a transformation began. The shelter-in-place mandates were instituted around the country, and people began looking for things to do while sheltering. Momentum began to build in subscriptions to streaming services, and sales sharply accelerated in books and educational products.

Customers then came to the realization that they had stockpiled staples and foodstuffs without a material change in consumption of those items, and began to redirect their monetary resources to entertainment options conducive to sheltering in place. Meanwhile, sales of all commodities, especially books, at mass merchants and warehouse clubs were rapidly accelerating due to the supply chain slowdowns at the largest online retailers and the forced closure of most "nonessential" U.S. retail stores, including bookstores. Likewise, mass and club channels were experiencing enormous surges in traffic to their websites and a rapid adoption of "BOPIS," which is retailer shorthand for "buy online and pick up in store." Just as streaming services were abetted by the closure of theaters, mass and club channels were the beneficiaries of the online retailers' bottlenecks and the closure of the "nonessential" retailers, including bookstores. As a result, the mass and club channel's in-store book sales surged to near-record levels, and online book sales increased by several hundred percent, as customers purchased novels, nonfiction books, activity books, workbooks, and other educational products.

In my opinion, two elements of discovery emerged after consumers exhausted their binge-watching on streaming services. First, they rediscovered reading for pleasure and education and realized that they enjoyed it. This has been affirmed in the most recent U.S. Department of Labor Time Use Study, which reported that overall reading time in the United States rose by 21% during the second half of 2020. Second, consumers came to realize that there are attractive and convenient options for buying books outside of online retailers and traditional bookstores.

How do you see the channel mix changing over the next three to five years?
I think the volume in mass, club, and non-online-only channels will persist. Comparable sales increases have been very strong in the mass and club channels during the postvaccination environment of the past several months. I believe that these year-over-year gains are due to the consumers' rediscovery of books and their broad availability within these channels. Also, the mass and club retailers were forced to accelerate improvements to their websites and online fulfillment execution. Another factor is obviously the convenience of buying books in the mass channels, where customers typically shop two or three times weekly. Mass and club retailers are also recognizing the potential of the book category by allocating more space and promotional impetus to books. These efforts have been facilitated by two factors; specifically, the growth of books as a category and the declines in other entertainment categories, such as movies, music, and magazines. Books now comprise 59% of the entertainment category compared to only 35% in 2015. Moreover, books have proven that physical formats can peacefully coexist with digital formats. Today, the book business is 86% physical versus only 8% and 9% for movies and music, respectively.

Obviously, all sales online are going to continue to grow. Online sales of all commodities are projected to increase by 30% by 2024. Likewise, the mass and club channels will continue to grow. Brick-and-mortar bookstores, however, need to focus on two things to grow and stay relevant. The first is capitalizing on their ties to the communities in which they operate. Second, they need to create an enjoyable and experiential destination-shopping experience. For booksellers, this may require some store refreshes, more author events, and frequent promotional events. Localized and experiential marketing by bookstores are the differentiators that can attract customers who would otherwise go online, or to a mass merchant or warehouse club, to make their purchases.

Again, as everyone knows, online is going to continue to grow. I believe, however, that the rate of growth in the book category at pure online retailers is beginning to plateau. Books are arguably the most mature online commodity, insofar as Amazon began selling them in 1994. While many customers already buy their books online, it's very difficult on many websites to discover books and authors that are outside of the *New York Times Best Seller List*. It is also true that more customers discover books in physical retail locations than anywhere else. If customers know what they want, it's quite easy to find it online. If they are browsing, however, the discovery process is much more complex than it is in a local bookstore or a mass or club retailer.

Do you think there's any possibility that POD will ever come to mass merchant places?
At a point in time, ReaderLink partnered with On Demand Books, which had developed the Espresso Book Machine, and successfully leveraged its relationships with its publisher partners to make more backlist titles available to be printed on demand. The program was presented to several retail partners and generated significant interest. Frankly, the pitch was, "Look, Amazon can get you a book the next day, but you can get any book right here in the next five minutes." The general idea was to try to "out-Amazon" Amazon by way of assortment, speed, and convenience. Due to the degree of interest, we shipped Espresso Book Machines to Walmart and Target, and their executive teams were fascinated by them. Then, reality set in. There was pushback on staffing requirements, the need for 220-volt power, the smell of the glue for the bindings, and more. In the end, the program just couldn't get any traction. At one point ReaderLink did have a machine in one of our facilities that was doing CDF orders for Walmart, but the program eventually faded away. As such, I don't think the mass and club channels are quite ready for POD as the technology exists today. POD might become something that works in bookstores, but, to date, the mass channels have been unwilling to make the commitments necessary to support it.

How can brick-and-mortar stores take advantage of the increase in online sales?
With respect to brick-and-mortar retailers' websites, the online shopping

experience isn't quite as frictionless as it is at the pure-play online websites. One of the things that Covid-19 did was accelerate the maturity and importance of mass and club channel retailers' websites. There were huge surges in ReaderLink's CDF book fulfillment operations. To sustain these gains, however, some of the mass and club channel players need to improve their search experience, which includes leveraging better metadata.

In addition, the book category doesn't enjoy its fair share of online promotional activity. Targeting books via email blasts or onsite promotions with a regular cadence would substantially build book sales at the mass and club accounts. Another growth-driver would be making book recommendations as a companion to nonbook items in the online shopping cart. This could be a home run for both the website operators and the publishing industry. By way of example, if a customer buys a car seat, they could be presented with some age-appropriate baby books. If they buy an air fryer, present them with an air fryer cookbook that could be sold with the device. This type of cross-merchandising strategy has not been leveraged to its full potential.

Are the changes in business practices—virtual author tours and conferences, online sales calls, working from home for at least some days a week—things that you think will become permanent?

Virtual author tours enable an author to reach a much broader audience than they could with a single store appearance. That said, the book industry needs to do a better job of monetizing those events. ReaderLink has been working with a company called Talk Shop Live, where authors have an opportunity to interact with their social media and email fan bases, as well as book buyers generally. The key differentiator is that there is a buy button where the book can be purchased instantly without leaving the Talk Shop Live site. This enables the author to speak directly to their fan base, and build up hype, excitement, and enthusiasm about their book. Meanwhile, all a customer needs to do is click, and they can buy the book during the session. It's powerful when there's a two-way interaction that humanizes the author and makes them accessible in a somewhat intimate way to their biggest fans. With the buy button on the screen, it enables a purchase to be made in real time. This program has gotten some great traction, and we are expecting it to grow as a meaningful source of revenue for the foreseeable future.

As far as online conferences go, I believe they lack the personal connection, camaraderie, and intimacy of in-person meetings. Good things tend to happen when you get smart and like-minded people together. Live conferences spark creativity and create something of a community, where the industry acts more like a body, rather than each enterprise operating in its own vortex.

As far as what's happening with the work landscape, I think there are going to be lasting work-life changes that will be attributable to the pandemic, or at least where adoption was accelerated by the pandemic. Some were nascent. Many companies were experimenting with telecommuting, but now it's become more accepted, and everyone from the employee to the employer has gotten more comfortable with the concept of remote work. I think many companies in our industry, including ReaderLink, are launching telecommuting policies concurrent with their planned return-to-work strategy. The pandemic taught us that working from home can still be productive, and it has paved the way for broader adoption of telecommuting. That said, I still think there needs to be a physical location presence, or a "mothership," if you will.

One of the reasons things worked well during the pandemic was because employees were already affiliated with their company and their coworkers. It becomes more difficult to sustain that level of productivity when trying to onboard people on a remote-work basis. Likewise, I think it's harder to build affiliation with coworkers, and the company generally, without a place to converge.

As far as online sales calls go, I think they can be effective to an extent. That said, there's a benefit to seeing and touching the product. I'm something of a book lover, and I get a visceral reaction when I pick up a leatherbound classic book or get to press the button on a child's sound book. I also think that there's a person-to-person connection that occurs when parties meet face-to-face. Salespeople, their relationships, and the consultative expertise that they can provide can be a differentiator when there's a large population of books that need to be curated into an actionable product assortment cohort.

Does consolidation of the publishers concern you? Do you have any acquisition plans yourself? How do you see consolidation impacting your business going forward?

I think consolidation in virtually all industries is inevitable. There's a common theorem around something referred to as "the rule of three," which holds that in any major industry, three players will eventually scale and become dominant. The publishing industry has had a big six, then a big five, and may eventually have a big four, or even a big three. If that market position is used to build scale and efficiency, it can be a good thing. If it's used to be abusive to smaller parties in the value chain, not so much. So far, there's been a healthy outcome from most of the consolidation activity that's occurred in recent years. At ReaderLink's scale, consolidation among publishers isn't a source of great concern. That said, I have heard that there are authors, agents, and other constituencies who have some anxiety over prospective publisher consolidations. I presume time will tell whether their concerns are valid.

With respect to acquisitions by ReaderLink, we are always seeking out opportunities to give us a chance to leverage our scale and to better serve our customers and publishing partners. The fact that we've been acquisitive, operate well, and have achieved scale is what has strengthened our company and allowed it to remain viable when over 450 industry cohorts have perished. As such, we will continue to look at acquisitions that make sense.

Any thoughts on B&N and Amazon? Both have publishing businesses as you do. How do you see your publishing business evolving and changing over the coming years?

I see our publishing business as adjunctive and complementary to our distribution business. Our goal is to use our POS database, where we collect daily store-level data from tens of thousands of stores, to inform our product development process. At times we'll see trends emerge before anybody else. If there isn't quality product to build on the trend, we'll step up and produce something to fill that gap. We always do the right thing by our customers, so we don't look to bump any publisher's product off store shelves to the extent that it belongs there. That said, in many cases we can build a product that's competitive and a good option for an account to consider, and we let the market determine whether it succeeds or fails.

We're getting good distribution, and we've had great growth in our publishing business. It has more than doubled since we entered the business in 2015. Amazon's publishing business has principally been a vehicle to support authors or content that Amazon has chosen to exploit. I think it's a great idea for them, because they have a plethora of self-published authors on their platform. In theory, they can bring more of those self-published authors, like L.J. Ross and Amanda Quick, to market. Factually, however, many book retailers perceive Amazon as a principal competitive threat and don't want to support titles from Amazon Publishing. We've had customers come to us and say they don't even want their vendors to use Amazon's web services. They're that vehemently opposed to doing anything that aids and abets Amazon.

Over the years, Amazon Publishing has acquired books from some mainstream authors like Patricia Cornwell and Dean Koontz. But from my observation, I think that when authors sign on with Amazon, it becomes something of a Faustian bargain. They've committed themselves to counting on Amazon to advance their fortunes. Although Amazon has a mighty platform, I'm not sure that these authors wouldn't have been better served by distribution across a more diversified bookseller universe, but that's just my opinion.

As far as Barnes & Noble goes, I think that James Daunt is a very talented leader. I've met him, and I think he's very smart. Unfortunately, he's up against years of underinvestment in the B&N stores. As I said earlier, in my humble opinion, shopping in bookstores has to be experiential. People shop at retailers like Lululemon for the experience, not for the opportunity to spend $100 on a pair of yoga pants they could get at Target for $20. I don't think Barnes & Noble can effectively compete on price against the mega-retailers, be it online or offline, because the mega-retailers offer books as a category that's ancillary to everything else they sell. Barnes & Noble is a bit of a one-trick pony that isn't going to win on price. They have to win on experience.

I learned that lesson when I was in the grocery business early in my career. If Coca-Cola wanted to put a hurt on 7 Up, they didn't discount Coca-Cola, they discounted Sprite. This was because Sprite was less than 5% of Coke's business, but Sprite was directly competitive with 7 Up's *sole* business. Barnes & Noble is facing a similar situation. They simply are not going to win a price war. They need to make people *want* to go there. The things we mentioned earlier, like store events, author signings and community involvement can be their differentiators. That said, the stores also really need some capital investment to be thought of as pleasant places to spend time. It is hard to attract customers with dirty carpets, threadbare furniture, and chipped laminate on the café tables.

It seems like they're buying smaller and smaller quantities thinking that they can transform the returnability side of the business and not return books. What do you think of that?
I've heard that, and, from what I understand, they've done that reasonably successfully in the U.K. What I don't know is if they're buying less and selling less, or if they're buying less and selling the same amount. I think there's a pretty significant distinction there. If you're buying less and selling less, I don't know if that's such a great thing, but if you're buying less and selling the same amount, it could be a home run.

Do you think the higher interest in book buying and reading during the pandemic will last?
I do, actually. ReaderLink didn't experience the softness that affected the broader industry last year because of the "essential-business" customer base we have. What's remarkable to me is that we've been in a post-vaccine world for the last few months, and our sales haven't tapered off. The sales in the overall industry are up nicely, but they're comparing against the periods when bookstores were shut down and things were generally in chaos. Our most recent monthly comparisons

are against strong sales periods from the prior year and we're still up double-digits. We're pretty optimistic about it. We believe that millions of people have been reintroduced to reading and it's sticking. I also think the period where things slowed down online and bookstores were closed raised awareness that the mass and club channels were convenient and low-priced places to buy books.

More and more publishers are moving into non-book-related product. They're moving into puzzles and then moving into games and moving into calendars. But do you see an expansion in that area in terms of ReaderLink?

Our publishing company does produce some products like that. We're trying to fill a need that's in the marketplace. Certainly, when Covid-19 hit, workbook sales went off the charts. Coincidentally, Printers Row Publishing Group, our publishing division, happened to have millions of workbooks on the water, and we were able to bring them to market quickly to address the demand. Likewise, activity books like adult coloring, word search, sudoku, and craft titles really took off as people were looking for things to do once they had binge-watched all they could find on the streaming services. Line extensions are always going to be a part of the business. If it's not us doing it—meaning the publishing community—it's going to be somebody else. That said, line extensions won't ever be *the* business. By and large, our industry will remain a content-driven business, with branded content, written by people you recognize.

Where do you see future growth for books in mass-market channels?

The mass-market channels are going to continue to grow. If you look at the book category, it's one of the few categories in retail that is actually "under-retailed." If you want to buy apparel, think of what your options are. There's everyone from Talbot's to Hot Topic, to Gap, American Eagle, to Kohl's to whomever. There are many thousands of apparel stores. Same thing with household goods, furniture, and food. In the book category, however, there only two meaningful chain retailers and the independent bookstores. In my mind, I think that leaves the mass and club channels, where customers already shop several times weekly, as the oasis in the book desert to meet those needs. So, yes, I am bullish on the future of books in the mass and club channels.

*

Dennis E. Abboud is President, Chief Executive Officer, and Chairman of the Board of ReaderLink, LLC.

SELLING TO BRICK-AND-MORTAR STORES

BY BILL WOLFSTHAL

For generations, when book lovers went shopping for new books, they thought of independent bookstores. Today the book trade is much more than local bookstores. Online sales, mostly Amazon, are the biggest part of the book market in the United States, but brick-and-mortar stores still represent a significant portion of sales and revenue for publishers and authors. The market is complicated and the buying process confusing, but the success of any book may be up to which outlets stock a title.

Most stores plan their buying months before publication, and most purchases are made "returnable," meaning that the store or chain can return the books for credit or refund to the publisher. If you are publishing a book in September or October in time for the Christmas season, presentations to buyers are made to the biggest chains six or more months before publication and to other stores at least two or three months prepublication. Every store chooses books based on one single analysis. Will it sell in my store?

A chain or store can only stock a book if it believes it will sell. That's how they stay in business. So, a buyer will want to know: Has the author been published before? Did his or her last book sell well? Does the author have a platform like a website or a large social media following? Will the author be interviewed on national television? Does the book have a great cover? If the buyer believes the book has a good chance of selling, he or she will stock it, mostly 1–2 in a location, sometimes 10–20, sometimes 100–200 (if they expect it to be a runaway bestseller). If the buyer does not think customers will be interested, he or she will not stock the book and wait to see if any customers request it. That is not unusual. It's true for the vast majority of books. According to ProQuest Bowker Report, the total number of books published in the United States in 2019 exceeded 4 million—including both self-published books and commercially published books of all types. That means all stores need to be very selective in their choices.

Mass-merchandise outlets, or big-box stores, represent a large percentage of brick-and-mortar book sales. Costco, Target, Walmart, Sam's Club, BJ's Wholesale, and others all carry books. However, their title selection is far, far smaller than that of any traditional bookstore. Where a bookstore might carry 10,000 or even 50,000 titles, a big-box store might carry just 100 or 200. That means there is a huge competition between publishers and authors for placement.

Big-box stores focus mostly on *New York Times* bestselling authors and popular cookbooks and the most well-known children's books. These accounts can only stock the biggest of the biggest, because they are expecting huge weekly sales for each book in each location. Think Pioneer Woman cookbooks, Dr. Seuss children's books, Disney and *Star Wars* titles, brand-name novelists like James Patterson and Margaret Atwood, renowned authors like Michael Lewis and Ta-Nehisi Coates, and politicians like Barack Obama. The major publishers have whole sales teams who focus on just these accounts. Smaller publishers working with distributors also have representation selling these accounts. Self-published authors rarely have access to mass-merchandise retailers.

Most orders from these major accounts are placed through the major national book distributors: Readerlink Distribution Services, Ingram Content Group, and Baker & Taylor. The rewards of success are great. Orders can be for 2,000 or 5,000 or 10,000 copies of a title or series. The risk is great, too. Books are mostly sold to these accounts on a returnable basis. Returns average between 30%–50%, but it is not unheard of for a publisher to receive 80% returns if a book or series does not sell as well as expected.

It was not too long ago, before the age of Amazon and big-box stores, that large chains of bookstores were kings of the mountain in book sales. From the 1970s through the turn of the century, chains like B. Dalton, Waldenbooks, Borders, and regional chains like Crown and Lauriat's claimed the lion's share of the book market. Readers and publishers loved them. A book lover could head to the local mall and find the latest bestseller. A publisher's sales representative could meet with a buyer and place a title in 300 or 1,000 locations. Those days have passed. Barnes & Noble and Books-A-Million are now the last two remaining national book chains.

Barnes & Noble, with over 600 stores nationwide, was bought in 2019 by Elliott Management, the company that owns the Waterstones chain in the U.K. The CEO, James Daunt, has committed to reimagining the chain for the 21st century with new store layouts and new systems of purchasing. He wants to give more control to store managers to do what's best for books and readers in each store. Almost every trade publisher has a representative working with

Barnes & Noble to stock their titles. And Barnes & Noble has always been interested in carrying a wide selection of books from the largest publishers, independent publishers, and even strong self-published titles.

Now that store managers are playing a role in title selection, it may become even easier for little-known authors to have their books stocked at Barnes & Noble. Authors of all kinds can visit their local B&N and talk to staff about arranging to have their book stocked or to host a reading or a signing. Barnes & Noble continues to host big-name and local authors for reading and signing events. They are good for sales, and maybe even more important, they can offer authors a platform to create publicity opportunities with local media. Authors must be willing to promote events, because the store will want the author's family, friends, and fans to attend.

Books-A-Million, or BAM, operates over 250 stores in 32 states. These stores tend to be more rural than B&N, and their selection reflects their readership— less academic, more popular, more categories like gardening and hunting/fishing, lower-priced books. Headquartered in Birmingham, Alabama, BAM is the right place for a wide range of books that you might not find at Barnes & Noble or more literary independent bookstores.

That brings us to independent bookstores. It always seems that indie bookstores are looked upon as some kind of endangered species. However, reports of their death seem greatly exaggerated, as Mark Twain might say. First it was chain stores, then it was Amazon that threatened the life and health of local, independent bookstores. Then the Covid-19 pandemic came, and shoppers stayed home. Yes, some stores have closed, but others have survived and are flourishing. They are more than just a place to buy books. They are a home away from home for book lovers, authors, and their communities. If you visit BookPeople in Austin, Texas; The Strand in New York, New York; Elliott Bay Book Company in Seattle, Washington; Politics & Prose in Washington, D.C.; Northshire Bookstore in Manchester Center, Vermont; or Powell's Books in Portland, Oregon; and hundreds of others, you will find tens of thousands of books to choose from, staff that is passionate about reading and books, author events, couples on dates, parents with children, and a place where readers come together for books and community. Almost all are members of the American Booksellers Association. Traditional book publishers have sales representatives who call on these bookstores in person, by phone, or (more recently) by video.

Self-published authors will find a friend in the manager and staff at your local store. If you send your friends and family to ask for your books there, the store is likely to order it or stock it. Keep in mind, though, for most titles in these stores, they will only keep 1–3 copies in stock at any time. Keeping sales high and inventory low is essential to the financial health of every retailer.

*

Bill Wolfsthal is a publishing and sales executive with more than three decades of experience selling children's books, fiction and nonfiction, trade and promotional titles, print books and e-books into multiple sales channels for American publishers. He has worked for Harry N. Abrams, Skyhorse, Sterling, and Lyons Press.

SPECIAL SALES

BY BILL WOLFSTHAL

When most people think of book sales, they think of Amazon online and their local bookstore, but the world of book sales is much broader than that. Have you ever seen a book in a chain like Cracker Barrel, T.J.Maxx, or Dollar General? Have you ever been given a book when making a purchase of another product? Have you bought a book on how to make summer cocktails or at your local beach gift shop? The answer is probably yes, and you know that these "special" sales are a significant part of the book market.

Most publishers have a team dedicated to selling books into nontraditional book outlets and refer to them as the special sales or special markets department. Special sales are very much category driven. Fiction and serious works on academic subjects rarely do well in these markets. What does? Illustrated books of all kinds: children's books, cookbooks, photography books, woodworking and crafting books, books on gardening or raising chickens, and any book that can be given as a gift for Mother's Day, Father's Day, Halloween, Christmas, or another holiday.

The good news about special sales is that, unlike most book trade sales, they are almost always nonreturnable. That enables publishers and self-published authors to offer a better price to these customers with less worry about books being returned for credit or refund. Also, nontraditional outlets can bring books to consumers who may not regularly surf Amazon for books or visit their local bookstore.

There are tens of thousands of gift shops and special retailer shops in every city and town in America. They can be reached through sales representatives who sell gift products, and many sell books along with their clothing or jewelry or dishware lines. Publishers work with these "gift reps" on a commission basis. Anne McGilvray and Co., Inc. has developed into the largest network of sales representatives selling books into the gift market. They sell many publishers with large lists of gift books, including Hachette Book Group, HarperCollins, Penguin Random House, Simon & Schuster, Chronicle Books, Harry N. Abrams, and more.

Whether you are selling with an established sales rep or on your own, there is a wide variety of gift shops to sell to. Do you have the right book for a gift shop? Might your lobster cookbook be right for gift shops in Maine? Yes! Might your book on how to pan for gold be right for gift shops in Northern California? Yes! Every museum or aquarium in America has a gift shop. The New England Aquarium might be interested in your ABC book that features whales and dolphins. The John Wayne Birthplace Museum might be interested in your book on classic Westerns. Just don't expect even a local gift shop to stock your novel or business book. Though Event Network in San Diego handles book buying for over 100 museums and aquariums throughout the United States, most buy independently. Most are members of either the Museum Store Association or the Association of Zoos and Aquariums, or both.

Selling books one gift shop at a time is important to special sales, and orders are often for $100–$500 each; but chain stores are a different and sizable opportunity for nontraditional book sales. They can order thousands or even tens of thousands of copies of a title. A wide variety of non-bookstore chains across the United States represent books among their product mix, including Ollie's Bargain Books, Five Below, Dollar Tree, Dollar General, T.J.Maxx, Marshall's, Tractor Supply, and more. However, they are looking for very specific subject matter and very aggressive pricing. They are providing great pricing to their customers in their selection of products, and that includes books.

They may want books that might normally sell for $14.99 to $24.99 at a cost low enough for them to sell them for $1.99–$4.99. They might want books in just the right format to fit their racks and displays. It is rare that they buy just one book from a publisher. They are looking for a series or line of books that can be bought in bulk. To sell these accounts, it is (with few exceptions) necessary to reach critical mass in a category. They are looking for five or ten children's titles or cookbooks at time, not just one title. This market, while exciting and important for many publishers, is difficult for self-published authors to access.

There was a time, in the days before Amazon, that mail-order catalogs were a sizable channel for book sales. Those days are mostly gone. Still, some mail-order catalogs like Edward Hamilton Booksellers, Inc., and newer "flash" sites like Zulily and Groupon can move hundreds or thousands of the right title. However fertile ground for publishers, these accounts can be difficult for self-published authors. They, too, like the chains, want to work with suppliers who can supply a steady flow of books, not just one title.

Most larger publishers also have a "premium" department within their special sales team. This sales rep or team of reps works to have corporations or organizations buy books. Sometimes these groups buy books as a premium or bonus purchase. "Send us proof of purchase of six boxes of Cocoa Puffs and we'll send you a free children's coloring book." "Come to our career seminar, and we'll give you a book on how to write a stellar résumé." "Donate to the ACLU and we will send you a free copy of the U.S. Constitution." "Buy our food dehydrator and the box will include a book of tips and tricks and recipes."

Prospecting for these kinds of deals is difficult but not impossible. Of course, established publishers have the advantage of name recognition and a range of titles, with brand names, to offer. But self-published authors sometimes have just the perfect book or a personal connection at just the right organization or corporation. These sales are usually made at 40% to 80% off retail depending on circumstance and quantity. And they are almost always nonreturnable. It is an advantage to be able to offer these customers the option to customize the books they purchase. Maybe a nonprofit wants their logo on the book cover. Maybe a company wants to include a letter from their CEO as a preface. Maybe a company wants their product on the cover. Be ready to do that, if the order is big enough for an entire print run.

*

Bill Wolfsthal is a publishing and sales executive with more than three decades of experience selling children's books, fiction and nonfiction, trade and promotional titles, print books and e-books into multiple sales channels for American publishers. He has worked for Harry N. Abrams, Skyhorse, Sterling, and Lyons Press.

THE DISTRIBUTION BUSINESS

BY JED LYONS

The sales and distribution of American books didn't change much from the nineteenth century until World War II. Until then, book publishers' sales reps took orders from booksellers and shipped the books from their own warehouses. The story goes that, Richard Simon, cofounder of Simon & Schuster (and the father of singer Carly Simon) came up with the idea of allowing booksellers to return books for credit during the war years. That change and increasingly sophisticated logistics requirements led smaller publishers to outsource their sales and distribution needs beginning in the 1970s.

The first company formed to sell and distribute others' books was Independent Publishers Group (IPG). Based in Chicago, the company was founded in 1971 by college professor Kurt Mathews. His sons run the business today. Following on its heels in 1976 came Publishers Group West (PGW) in Berkeley, California, founded by Charlie Winton. In 1980, Eric Kampmann started Kampmann & Company, and in 1986, Stan Plotnick and I founded National Book Network (NBN) as a subsidiary of the Rowman & Littlefield Publishing Group. NBN remains a wholly owned subsidiary of Rowman & Littlefield today. These and several smaller distributors handled the sales and distribution needs of thousands of small and large book publishers throughout the 1970s, 1980s, and 1990s.

The cottage industry that relied on a handful of distributors began to attract the attention of larger publishers, as well as Ingram, a major book wholesaler based in Lavergne, Tenn. Simon & Schuster and other big houses discovered they could defray operating expenses by signing up outside clients to fill their cavernous warehouses. Ingram entered the fray with Ingram Publishers' Services.

By the early 2000s, the distribution business was getting more competitive as new players jockeyed for position and distribution fees declined. By then Kampmann had gone into bankruptcy and PGW's new parent, Advanced Marketing Services, also went bankrupt, taking PGW down with it. A start-up publisher, Perseus, scooped up PGW and soon built the largest distribution business in the industry. When Perseus's publishing business was sold to Hachette in 2016, Ingram bought the distribution business. It now boasts more than 600 publisher clients and is the largest business of its kind in North America. Today, in addition to Ingram, there are several major book publishers that distribute for other publishers. IPG and NBN, the last of the firms that started the industry back in the '70s and '80s, remain the only independently owned book distributors still actively selling and distributing other publishers' books.

The 2020 pandemic caused some disruption to the book distribution business, but only because so many independent stores and customers were forcibly closed. Distribution companies in most states were allowed to continue to operate, so the only change was a much lower level of volume processed. Those levels recovered in 2021, and book sales have rebounded in ways most distributors could only have dreamed of a year ago. The book distribution business—physical books and digital books—is resilient and in it for the long haul.

*

Jed Lyons is the president and CEO of Rowman & Littlefield.

THE PUBLISHER/DISTRIBUTOR
RELATIONSHIP
AN INTERVIEW WITH MICHAEL PERLMAN

CHOOSING A DISTRIBUTOR

The key factors to consider when choosing a distributor are the concepts of flexibility, access to the company, engagement, and expectations. Do you see eye to eye? Do you get along? How is it going to look to work with them? This can be tough to determine early on, but that's why there are a lot of conversations that take place. The number that's been bandied around is sometimes 18 months from start to finish—from the first conversation to signing a contract. You want to get to know into whose hands you're putting your entire business.

Flexibility comes down to: What are the publisher's needs and what is the distributor able and willing to do? Everybody looks at it a little differently, and there is no right or wrong answer. Some people will say, "I only do X." Others will say, "Oh, I'll do X, Y, and Z." And if the publisher values X, Y, and Z— great. If the publisher doesn't, if they just want X, they go with that. I would also determine some sort of table stakes. What does the sales force look like? What do the operational requirements look like? What do their relationships with the major retailers look like? How often does someone accept orders from Amazon? How often do they ship to Amazon? What's their level with Amazon and what does that really mean for me in my every day? Some of it may not matter to certain types of publishers and some of it may.

There's something to be said for the distributor having access to the retailers and for a publisher having access to all levels of a distributor. They need to have somebody, or a group of people, where, if something really goes wrong, or if a publisher or distributor thinks something has gone wrong, there are people at the other company who can engage and respond and either do something or talk them off the ledge.

THE ROLE OF THE DISTRIBUTOR

My goal is to add value to the publisher, and that can happen in various ways.

I really believe a big part of the role of a distributor is making things easier for the publisher, trying to remove as many monkey wrenches as you can from their day to day processes. Every switch we may make might be a little ripple for us, but it could be a much bigger ripple for different-sized publishers, and we need to be cognizant of that.

I don't want to create problems where they don't exist. For example, if retailers require books in their distribution centers and their stores 10 days before on-sale, then I have to go to the publishers to say I need books X days before to make that work. But do I need to go to them and say I need four times as long as that? Well, no. I'm creating a problem there. You want to be realistic and honest, but you want to try and keep the headaches to a minimum.

Your core competency as an independent publisher is publish, market, publicize, and get the books to me. But if you manage your warehouse and manage the number of days it takes to get to Amazon, manage the relationship with Amazon, and manage the shipping efficiency because of this truck shortage, all of a sudden this turns into 30 or 40% of your time—unless you somehow can increase the number of hours in a day or you stop sleeping.

There certainly are still publishers out there of varying sizes who are doing it themselves, either with small warehouses or printers. But there are efficiencies to pick up with a distributor as well as making use of the relationships they have with a broad swath of accounts.

A distributor must have an adequate number of people to talk to the publishers. And by "talk to," I mean personal relationships. The publishers have to feel like there are people there to talk to them—to talk about their publishing program, about what's working, about expectations.

If a publisher has the expectation that their 18th-century Amish woodworking book, which could be a very beautiful book, belongs in Walmart, you better set that straight upfront. Once again, expectations are key, and we need to be realistic and honest.

You want to have a partner who will engage you in that manner when appropriate, when that's right. Depending on the publisher's business, sometimes those things come up and sometimes they don't, sometimes everything's fine. But when things are out of whack, a distributor should be a sounding board when you need one.

Before you change distributors—or stop doing it yourself, if you're doing it yourself—you should ask for a lot of references. You should talk to a lot of people. This can be a tough conversation to have, but I would even go back to the distributor and bring up the things that have come up. Have a real conversation. And if you aren't able to do that with your potential new distributor, how is the relationship going to work down the road?

One of the best ways to decide whether or not a distributor is likely to be appropriate for your company is to talk to publishers who have left that distributor, find out why they left, and see if some of those reasons might apply to you.

No two publishers are alike. Part of the fun that I've had with distribution is all the different categories and all the different publishers, and fundamentally I believe having more books in our bag by category helps. We've seen growth recently in the gift category, for example. Not only because we've signed up more gift publishers, but because in the start we had a tough time getting face time with the gift commission groups and those accounts. We didn't have anything for them. As we built up that bag, they had to look. And then eventually they wanted to look.

For a long time, there has been a question of being overburdened. But I've always felt that more is better. And as we continue to grow, we have different levers we can pull—more client managers, more operations people, and more sales reps by channel.

The biggest issue right now, which is the same for everyone, is dealing with the global supply chain problems and keeping up with any sort of demand: printers, shipping, containers. It's a perfect storm, and it isn't stopping any time soon.

MANAGING EXPECTATIONS AND PRIORITIZATION

Someone could say, "I need to be able to call down to your warehouse and stop a shipment." Or, "I need to be able to call down at 4 p.m. and get something out within 10 minutes." It's important to be able to say, "Look, I can't do that. There are a lot of things I can do and let's walk through them. What's the goal? What are you trying to accomplish? Let's discuss how we might accomplish that in a different manner." Sometimes you figure out a way to do it. Sometimes you don't, but at least you went through the exercise and tried to figure it out.

That's back to flexibility, sensibility, engagement. Everybody thinks everything is important. It comes down to prioritization.

We all have to figure out what is really life and death, right? It's not just money. We are going to try and figure out a way to solve everything we can. Sometimes we won't be able to, but we're always going to at least talk about it. The talking could be 10 seconds, 10 minutes, 10 hours, whatever. Use the example of asking a publisher for their lead titles for the season. Of course, every book is important. That doesn't mean that if you've got five lead titles, I forget the other titles. But if you focus on everything, you end up focusing on nothing.

Michael Perlman has worked at Simon & Schuster for over sixteen years and is the Vice President and General Manager of Simon & Schuster Publisher Services. Prior to that he worked at Client Distribution Services, which was acquired by Perseus in 2005.

THE WORLD IS READING
INGRAM CONTENT GROUP

ngram Content Group ("Ingram") connects readers with content in all forms. By providing comprehensive services for publishers, retailers, libraries, and educators, Ingram makes content distribution seamless and accessible. Ingram's technology and innovation are revolutionizing global content distribution.

Ingram knows and specializes in content distribution at every point in a book's life, from creation, assembly, and production to distribution, discovery, and storage. Ingram's suite of services includes: print on demand / "virtual distribution," full-service sales and distribution, digital asset management and distribution, digital marketing services, library services, digital learning, self-publishing, content customization, and wholesale services. Each Ingram platform and service is powerful on its own, but when combined and utilized within Ingram's unmatched global distribution network and industry expertise, the power is even greater.

Ingram's extensive services connect authors, publishers, booksellers, libraries, educators, and readers all over the world.

Lightning Source®, Ingram's Print on Demand solution, is a better way to meet customer demand and potential sales without the costs of overprinting and excess inventory. This service allows publishers and authors to print only what they sell and creates a clear path to capturing more sales while lowering overhead. Aside from being an efficient and cost-effective way to print high-quality books, print on demand is also incredibly flexible. From order to production to fulfillment, Ingram has publishers covered with direct-to-publisher options, wholesale solutions, global distribution, and custom publishing.

Global Connect is Ingram Content Group's global network that enables your titles to be available and printed directly in more markets around the world. Our Global Connect partners will show your titles as available for that particular market and they will print them as orders come in from their local channels and retailers. Publishers simply make a title available for the market by adding the relevant market pricing and Ingram handles the rest.

Ingram's **CoreSource** platform allows publishers to archive, manage, and streamline digital asset management and distribution through a single, powerful platform. With tens of thousands of audio titles, CoreSource has become one of the largest providers of audiobook content to the industry. Designed to help publishers realize the full potential of any digital content distribution, CoreSource provides a single point to submit digital content and metadata, allowing files to move swiftly and safely to many business partners.

Marketing Insights is a tool to assess how well publishers' titles are positioned for discovery and sale online. It measures signals like metadata health, availability, and consumer demand. Marketing Insights recommends actions to increase discoverability and conversions based on algorithms focused on the full marketing funnel—from metadata analysis to retailer positioning, to consumer activity.

Ingram Distribution Services is a family of brands that offers publishers full-service solutions that span sales and distribution across all categories and gives publishers the broadest reach possible. Backed by unsurpassed sales and marketing support, Ingram combines the power of five great distribution brands under one roof.

- **Ingram Publisher Services®** provides publishers with a trusted distribution network, a sales team of passionate book lovers and access to leading e-book and print-on-demand technologies.
- **Consortium Book Sales and Distribution** distributes high-quality books to the world, including fiction, nonfiction, popular culture, politics, children's/parenting, poetry, and art/photography titles.
- **Two Rivers Distribution®** offers global distribution and flexible, customized solutions for category-leading independent publishers. With bestselling titles spanning a wide variety of genres, there's a title on Ingram's list for every reader.
- **Publishers Group West®** aims to create bestsellers in all categories by providing full-service distribution, complete digital conversion services, and marketing expertise. Publishers Group West is devoted to building a diverse editorial mix and ensuring that captivating titles reach readers.

- **Ingram Academic Services®** is geared toward meeting the needs of academic publishers and university presses. Ingram Academic provides publishers with resources to advance scholarship in their communities and around the world through customized services from Ingram. These services include warehousing, print-on-demand network, digital asset management services and metadata management system, as well as far-reaching sales representation. Ingram Academic pairs all of this with state-of-the-art marketing services.

IngramSpark® is an award-winning self-publishing platform, offering indie authors and publishers the ability to publish print and e-books. Access to IngramSpark's global distribution allows self-published authors to make their book available to 40,000+ retailers and libraries—both in stores and online.

Ingram's Wholesale Services gives book retailers every advantage with solutions designed to fit their unique needs, access to a huge inventory, and dedicated support. With programs, services, and promotions exclusively for booksellers, Ingram is here to help get more books into the hands of more readers around the world.

Ingram Library Services delivers innovative systems, expertise, and precise assistance in acquiring, developing, and maintaining a library's collection. Ingram helps librarians through a vast title selection, easy-to-use search and ordering tools, collection analytics, and customized cataloging and processing. Expert collection development services from MLS-degreed librarians coupled with Ingram's inventory helps position libraries for the future.

Tennessee Book Company | Class Gather is Ingram's textbook depository that provides Tennessee schools with a central source of supply at the lowest costs and with the fastest service possible. They are the K–12 academic products division of Ingram Content Group. As a distributor for many educational publishers, Tennessee Book Company sells only to state-certified boards of education, individual public schools, private and parochial schools, learning centers, teachers, and several retailers acting in the capacity of schoolbook dealers. In addition to supplying state-adopted materials, the company also sells Advanced Placement, special education, and other non-basal materials for all subject matter areas from kindergarten through 12th grade, including college-level products and trade paperbacks. Tennessee Book Company includes ClassGather, a digital hub that allows districts to easily manage and deploy their publishers' digital content into their Learning Management System.

THE STATE OF THE REMAINDER BOOK BUSINESS

BY MIKE PAPER

To get an understanding of the current state of the remainder book business, it's important to first understand the history of this end of the publishing industry.

When we opened our first store in 1993 it was designed to be a full-service, frontline bookstore. As fate would have it, a B&N opened up directly across the street from us six months later. We were still new to the business, and undercapitalized. Our sales were cut in half by the second day of the superstore's opening. After a year, we terminated our lease and moved across town into a huge below-grade basement-type location. In order to fill the shelves, we purchased a truckload of store returns or "hurts" from a local distributor. It turned out that the basement location and bargain books were a perfect fit. We soon limited our frontline titles to bestsellers and a new arrivals wall, with the rest of the store focused on bargain books.

I didn't know it at the time, but this was the "Golden Age" of the bargain book business. Publishers were anxious to unload their hurts and remainders at any price. Large picture books could be purchased by the pound for pennies on the dollar. Anyone with an account could call up almost any publisher and purchase great books at very inexpensive prices. Publishers seemed to be happy to be able to dump their books and have them quietly go away so as not to hurt their frontline sales. You couldn't help but make a profit.

At some point in the early 2000s, with the rise of the internet, things started to change. At this point, we were in the wholesale business as well, selling excess inventory to other booksellers. With the rise of Amazon, it became even easier to become a bookseller. We were selling pallets of books to local residences all over the country. They would break down the pallets and list everything online. We even sold pallets to our plumber and electrician as payment. The bargain book business was exploding.

Within a few years publishers became aware that their hurts were in high demand. They were much better for internet sellers than remainders because they were a mix of titles with smaller quantities and had more current publishing dates. Actual remainders, by contrast, were usually sold as a full quantity of what was left after the book sales had tapered off. Distributors also realized the demand for hurts and set up exclusives with many publishers. What used to be a call to any publisher for an order soon became getting in line with a distributor for hurts. The prices also started to go up quickly to the point where most "part-time" sellers were driven from the market. Publishers also started to limit what books were sold as hurts and started to pulp many of their returns.

Fast-forward to 2021 and the business seems light-years away from when we started back in 1993. When we started wholesaling books back in the early 2000s, most of our business was done by breaking down hurts and selling them to independent booksellers across the country as well as the occasional sale to the chain bookstores, B&N, BAM, and Borders. Today, our customer base has changed almost 180 degrees. Most of our customers are value retailers that sell books alongside other items such as pet supplies, clothes and home furnishings. They are not interested as much in the latest Tom Clancy novel or World War II history title as they are in an attractive cookbook or kids' board book. Most of what we purchase today are remainders by the title in large quantities to be sold as smaller quantities to larger retailers. They require us to—for a fee—repack, sticker, sort and label much of what we ship out today. We used to come back from a trade show with 200 orders. Today we might come back with 30 orders worth several times as much as the 200 we used to take.

From a personal note, I felt it was much more enjoyable to deal and haggle with 200 independent customers rather than 30 larger ones. I also enjoyed picking up the phone and dealing and negotiating with dozens of publishers. Today it's more of poring over spreadsheets and reviewing samples. I guess I'm just showing my age.

*

Mike Paper is the owner of Bradley's Book Clearance.

SELLING DIRECT-TO-CONSUMER

BY SARA DOMVILLE

The benefits of selling direct-to-consumer go back to the days of the negative-option book clubs. The clubs drove significant sales volumes and gave niche-vertical-enthusiast companies opportunities to publish profitable titles. The sheer volume of sales added thousands of units to an initial print run—albeit at a high discount, but often at a higher hardback price. The demise of those book clubs was challenging at the time but gave publishers a new opportunity to connect directly with consumers with significant financial and consumer insight upside. As in any industry, publishers must exceed the expectations of customers. Direct contact gives us the chance to learn what is important to our readers. And with that knowledge, we are better able to anticipate what may resonate in the future.

We live in an ever-changing world, and the pace of change quickens every year. Of course, consumer expectations are especially relevant for the publishing industry, as we must anticipate the needs of the market 12 to 18 months in advance if we hope to commission the right content and develop a remarkable package prior to launch. Direct contact with our readers opens the door for us to listen and learn from them and thus set up the market in advance.

Naturally there are exceptions. But even bestselling fiction from high-profile authors still demands connecting with readers, community building, sharing new titles, and potentially developing additional valuable revenue streams. If we rely solely on third parties, we will never know who our customers are, and we will never learn what makes them select our titles.

Also critical is understanding that our readers need choice—not just in what they read, but in what format they read and how they purchase. We must offer our consumers the chance to purchase books in the channels they choose and in every format that matters to them. We must be channel-agnostic so that we can produce content that resonates. But our content also needs to be discovered and subsequently purchased in all formats as one-time use is surely not enough. Raising all boats in all channels is of paramount importance.

As a book publishing executive, it has always been my goal to prioritize the "4 Cs": content, community, curation, and commerce. These all are inter-connected, as having a direct connection to your consumers enables you to add content offerings and thus new revenue streams to further enhance your business, which subsequently ensures that you produce the very best content. If we look at book content as highly valued yet format-agnostic material, we can quickly imagine new revenue streams—including, for example, curricula for different types of B2B and B2C events, partnerships, sponsorships with other top brands, TV, or video content production, etc. All of this boosts the bottom line and enables publishers to become media powerhouses and grow their businesses, which drives the ability to further invest in the content team and the rest of the company.

Developing a media brand that has a clear mission and a reputation for quality content with diverse revenue streams will no doubt take a company from good to great. Enabling your expert staff to think creatively across all formats provides them with new opportunities for growth and the ability to get involved in emerging revenue streams. And it increases the likelihood of a bestselling book. Collaboration creates a snowball of creativity throughout the business. The power of *everyone* running in the same direction—rather than an elite few—is deeply rewarding. Ideas from everyone are encouraged; the best ideas come from collaboration at every level—from the consumer to the editorial, sales, production, and finance teams. As we know, it takes a village to produce and sell great content. And the diversity of thought, experience, and culture lead to a more sustainable community and successful financial, personal, and cultural outcomes.

Subscriptions are arguably the most attractive direct-to-consumer model for any publisher as they offer an opportunity to have regular income—"money whilst you sleep"—giving financial stability and consistency unlike the other business, which can have ups and downs in an ever-present volatile mar-ket. Again, quality content is paramount, as is ensuring that your subscrip-tion-model business also enables regular consumer connection. Amazon has showed its expertise here, with Amazon Prime membership extending across an incredible number of citizens throughout the world. So valuable is the sub-scription model that they have constantly added perks to exceed our expecta-tions. Delivery speed is second to none: free movies, TV shows, e-books. It's all added value that becomes an invaluable offer to all. Clearly matching this level of service is challenging for many competitors, but challenges drive innova-tion, and we have certainly seen huge innovation since the Covid-19 pandemic forced us to think differently. Nothing gives more joy than seeing independent stores thrive and adapt to change in such unprecedented circumstances. Their consumer-focused commerce, content knowledge, and curation truly set them apart.

We all have strengths. We just need to focus on those and develop our unique selling points to build the 4 Cs. Social media and digital initiatives constantly gather pace and sophistication at every turn as our consumers demand more and more. It is not good enough to be on the target, we need to be on each individual bull's-eye to win and become the remarkable companies that we all can be.

So, let's challenge ourselves to think of direct-to-consumer as a key tool in our publishing tool kit to be successful. We need to understand how our audience is evolving and how to exceed expectations with diverse and desired content. We must break through the noise and reach out to share why our content is valuable. And we need to create the best possible content. We must be channel-agnostic and partner with others across every commercial channel. We want a diverse and innovative culture throughout our organizations, and we want to be open to change in order to adapt to the marketplace. By supporting all sales channels, we want to add new products and services to offer alternative revenue streams as we build out our respective brands.

Most of all, we must treasure the relationship with our consumers. We need to build trust and always treat consumers as we would like to be treated ourselves. Take the high road, collaborate with everyone, and create an inclusive and dynamic culture, and the rewards will follow. I have learned that it is okay to be vulnerable, and certainly we are only as good as the talented individuals we work with. The most innovative person may be the new person just joining the organization. Mistakes happen, but the ability to pivot and learn from them is invaluable. I encourage you to focus on how to make working directly with your consumers work for your respective organizations. I have certainly never regretted doing it, as it enables you to more clearly manage your own destiny.

*

Sara Domville is a media executive with a proven track record for creating and developing new revenue streams through mutually beneficial innovative partnerships. She is the chief revenue officer at America's Test Kitchen and formerly president of F+W, a content and e-commerce company. She has launched many new businesses, including Digital Book World.

THE PROMOTIONAL
PUBLISHING BUSINESS

BY JEANETTE LIMONDJIAN

WHAT IS PROMOTIONAL PUBLISHING?

Promotional publishing really got its start in the 1930s when two companies—Harlem Book Company, founded by one of my mentors, Norman Blaustein, and Outlet Book Company, started by Nat Wartels and Bob Simon—began selling overstocks and remainders into nontraditional marketplaces. Both companies started by selling remainders mostly through markets like department stores such as Gimbels, for example. From the 1930s through the early 1980s, all department stores had major book departments. The problem with remainders was that there were never enough titles and, more importantly, never enough of the titles that sold well. Eventually, the need for more priced-to-sell books led to the organic growth of the reprint business, starting with simple reprints of successful remainders and eventually evolving into creating books in-house and making purchases of attractively priced coffee table books, children's books, popular literary classics, and something called "special imports" from packagers and publishers primarily in the U.K. and Europe. This was the beginning of "promotional publishing."

By the mid-1930s, Nat Wartels also started a trade publishing company, Crown Books, and a mail-order company, Publishers Central Bureau, which began with remainders and overstocks and eventually extended into any value-driven area of publishing.

In the 1960s, there was Marboro Books, which dedicated itself to more serious and academic remainders and special reprints purchased from the U.K., both in their stores and in an extensive mail-order business. Marboro was purchased by Barnes & Noble in 1979 to kick-start Barnes & Noble's own mail-order company. Also, in the 1960s Doubleday began dedicating a section of their bookstores to off-price hardcover coffee table books and offering special editions of their regular trade hardcovers. This section would also be filled with what the book industry called "White Sales"—books that were offered to booksellers at very deep discounts on an annual or semiannual basis.

THE GOLDEN AGE OF ILLUSTRATED PUBLISHING

Paul Hamlyn started in the book business in the 1960s and was dedicated to producing quality illustrated books at affordable prices. His focus was always on producing books by price point and packing these books with as much heft, illustrations and well-written text as the price point could tolerate. Also, like Outlet and HBC in the thirties, he focused on selling to more nontraditional retailers like supermarkets. At the time, Hamlyn wanted to give a wide berth to carriage trade bookstores and what they stood for and was more interested in democratizing bookselling and book buying, something that Barnes & Noble would later be dedicated to.

In time, most trade publishers around the world would expand their frontlists with more and more illustrated books purchased from packagers. This interest in illustrated books led to more promotional publishing. Well-priced illustrated books sold to both trade publishers and promotional book companies in the late 1970s and hit their stride in the 1980s. Again, promotional publishers and packagers took a page from Paul Hamlyn and published by price point. In other words, the *subject* of the book did not dictate how many pages a book would be, but rather the price point would dictate the number of pages, illustrations and words a book would have. It is important to remember that a book with an affordable price point did not in any way lessen the quality of its content.

BARNES & NOBLE'S PROPRIETARY PUBLISHING BUSINESS

Before I can explain how Barnes & Noble's proprietary publishing business came about, I need to express my lifelong mission and ideas of book buying and bookselling, reading, and a bit of retailing 101:

- Reading is an addictive process.
- Book buying can be a feel-good purchase and an aspirational one at the same time.
- Enticing a first-time book buyer with a purchase of an affordable book in a comfortable, non-threatening environment will most likely initiate the desire for more books.
- Eventually, as the desire for more books increases, the purchases become more random and the possibility of buying a full-price book becomes inevitable.
- In any retail setting, the main aim is to entice the customer to buy something and open their pocketbook. Once it's open, the opportunity to sell more is a foregone conclusion. Affordably priced books provide the encouragement.

So, for me, it began with the Sales Annex. The Sales Annex was Barnes & Noble's first foray into popular off-price bookselling. The Sales Annex also had park benches, shopping carts and bathrooms! All intended to extend the customers' visit and make the overall experience fun and comfortable. In the beginning, the primary inventory was overstocks, hurt books, returns, close-outs, and remainders—not only from trade publishers but also from university presses. It also had promotionally priced trade books by taking a page from the book clubs and selling the weekly *New York Times* bestseller list at deep discounts, which, for a while, seriously confused the book industry. Barnes & Noble then started selling promotionally priced mammoth books, nick-named "doorbusters," positioned strategically in the stores in large skids like supermarket endcaps. This was the beginning of Barnes & Noble's proprietary business. At first, all that was wanted were doorbusters: books such as *Webster's Dictionary*, *The Columbia Encyclopedia*, and *The Rand McNally World Atlas*. The success of these books would lead to the development of an enormously large, pervasive, in-house proprietary publishing program that stayed mostly anonymous. Throughout the years, customers had no idea what the source was of the books they bought. Their purchases were spontaneous, impulsive, and motivated by a perceived value both in price and quality.

At the beginning of our publishing journey, big remainder purchases were becoming harder to find. Barnes & Noble began to need many more books to feed the hungry book-buying public. Once again, promotional publishing houses helped fill our retail footprint.

Soon, after a series of successful *New York Times* full-page bargain books ads for which I wrote some copy, I was tasked with starting Barnes & Noble's mail-order catalogs. Again, we started with remainders and overstocks. Within a few years, Barnes & Noble purchased Marboro Books, which not only had retail stores but also an extensive mail-order business focusing on more serious bargain-priced books and would provide us with the necessary back-end mechanics for mail-order fulfillment. As the mail-order business grew, we had a familiar problem: a lack of quality bargain books. We solved this problem in three ways:

1. by purchasing promotional books from the likes of Outlet, W.H. Smith, Bookthrift, and others;
2. by buying and selling full-price backlist, mostly academic paperbacks as well as general nonfiction;
3. by beginning our hardcover reprint business based on sales of bargain books in the catalog as well as sales of the full-price

paperbacks. One amazing book we found was *The Gentle Art of Verbal Self-Defense* by Suzette Haden Elgin, a remainder that had done extremely well and was out of print. Amazingly, the rights were available. By the time I left Barnes & Noble in 2010, what was once a remaindered and out-of-print book, had gone on to sell well over a million copies in our retail stores.

So began the Dorset Books program, which was sold mostly via mail order. The focus was mainly academic and serious mainstream backlist titles. Our first reprints were licensed from Penguin Books and Farrar, Straus and Giroux. However, there were some hardcover reprints that were allowed to sell whole-sale via our Marboro Books division. Which was a wonderful footnote to our mission to democratize book buying and bookselling as these books were sold to independent bookstores. Eventually, 60% of each catalog would be full-price paperbacks; another 30% would be reprints. Barnes & Noble had accidentally tapped into the needs of a starving and serious book-reading public that could not get their books easily and certainly not from Dalton's or Walden's since their book assortments were limited to 25,000–30,000 SKUs, which pretty much cut out most academic books. This interesting discovery would be confirmed by other metadata and would make a convincing argument for the future creation of the big, 100,000-plus-title Barnes & Noble stores.

Our foray into full-price paperbacks also fed our reprint business and began to convince publishers that special hardcover editions would not affect the sales of their successful paperbacks. Eventually, that would be our argument that both editions could co-exist in our stores without cannibalizing the trade paperback sales. Our need for more reprints led to our exploring the libraries of every publisher we could. We focused first on British publishers—mostly academic publishers with large backlists—and began to reprint many books for the mail order and wholesale businesses. This would change once Barnes & Noble bought B. Dalton and our dominant interests became more mainstream. By this time, the Barnes & Noble mail-order business had reached 25 catalogs a year. When Barnes & Noble bought B. Dalton my job shifted to full-time proprietary publishing and I was originally tasked with finding 25 blockbuster proprietary titles a year. So began our trips to the international book fairs: Frankfurt and London. This would eventually lead us to become, for a time, the largest purchasers of co-editions in the world and most trade publishers would limit the number of packages and illustrated books they published.

At our first few fairs, packagers and overseas publishers were befuddled by our presence and very few gave us the time to meet with them. Many said,

"You are a retailer, we sell to the American publishers. Just buy from them." But a few met with us that first year and suffice it to say they became very important partners in the years to come.

Eventually there were breakthroughs. One of them had to do with the regimen of publishers' seasonal purchasing—in other words, timing. At the time, all publishing was based on seasons, and many times an illustrated book would need co-editions in order to be able to go to press. Barnes & Noble did not have seasons and could buy books at any time. On one occasion at the London Book Fair, an offer was made to us by an English publisher. Our purchase led to blockbuster sales. The only reason we got the chance to buy the book was timing. The book was being considered by Oxford University Press, but they would not commit in time for the printing. We agreed to buy the book and join the print run. Because Barnes & Noble worked on sharper margins than trade publishers, it meant that we had the chance to sell more copies in less time and require more reprints sooner. The name of this book was *100 Great Archeological Discoveries,* and it went on to sell over 100,000 copies. English publishers were also happy to sell to Barnes & Noble because Barnes & Noble reprinted rapidly which allowed the publisher to satisfy smaller foreign commits in the next season by running these smaller co-editions on our larger reprint. That would turn out to be a very good reason to sell to Barnes & Noble in the first place and soon many more books were sold to us, with that principle in mind. This became another model of how to buy illustrated books that were originally destined for the trade market based on the timing needs of the packagers and U.K. and European publishers and thereby raising the quality of the books we sold.

The other interesting breakthrough in our proprietary program was a commitment to selling illustrated books on serious subjects. We started to align ourselves with English publishers who had terrific black-and-white content. We found a small English publisher specializing in the mind, body, and spirit category and began to support their creating illustrated editions of these books. Barnes & Noble committed to purchasing hardcover editions to be sold at affordable prices, while, at the same time, the publisher sold full-price trade paperback editions. They were successful and so were we. Many of the books we partnered on sold well over half a million copies each at affordable prices, which probably led to a faster development of this subject category.

We also partnered with an English packager that focused on military books and to this day is still a major contributor to Barnes & Noble. The key to our success was always to actively suggest to our proven partners possible directions these projects could go based on our knowledge of the vast Barnes &

Noble sales metadata. Before Barnes & Noble, these books would have been sold to specialty publishers who then sold them at very high retail prices and in much smaller quantities. Barnes & Noble made these titles available at promotional prices which no doubt added to the in-store traffic and also allowed us to sell other books to this specialist customer base.

Our continued success led us to align ourselves with terrific U.K. and European illustrated publishers and we began to buy the co-edition rights to North America. Such partnerships also led to our encouraging the creation of various books based on subjects that had done or were doing well for us. It turned out that these books ended up being successful worldwide on a co-edition basis.

All of our success with these publishers encouraged us to be more focused on getting the trade publishers in America and the U.K. to allow us to do special proprietary promotionally priced editions of successful paperbacks. This also led to us doing leatherbound literary collections from major trade publishers. This program exists to this day. As our proprietary publishing business grew, the need for more in-house publishing skills led to the purchase of Friedman Books.

At the end of the day, the enormous success of Barnes & Noble's proprietary business had to do with the following:

- Finding quality content to sell at the right price and producing quality books. In other words, authoritative content, great design and terrific production values. This turned out to be a winning strategy and irresistible selling points to customers. All of which led to most of out first printings reprinting many times.
- Not limiting ourselves to what we were comfortable in publishing but trying to appeal to every type of reader. I would call it publishing from the sublime to the ridiculous. But what was "ridiculous" and what was "sublime" depended on the buyer—another aspect out of democratizing the bookstore and taking a page out of Paul Hamlyn's hymn book. Eventually, maybe the buyers would buy both types of books!

THE FUTURE OF PROMOTIONAL PUBLISHING

The period from the 1980s to the early aughts began the great technological change in book production. Books could be digitally created faster, printed using digital printers' files, reprinted, and updated easily. All of this led to creating and printing books at a cheaper price and not being required to do mega print runs. These technological advances would lead to the great expansion of illustrated books.

Ironically, the marketplace for promotionally priced illustrated books began to shrink in the biggest markets. In the last 10–15 years, the Borders bookstores closed, and physical books were momentarily shunned in the face of e-readers (my conviction at the time was that e-readers represented a massive but momentary diversionary interest as a new techy object and that the interest would eventually settle into a place in the book business—but not the primary place. I remember saying: "Physical books are here to stay!"). But at the time, e-readers dominated the front of store at Barnes & Noble and the footprint for promotionally priced illustrated books was reduced. For a while, price clubs continued to dominate as the major sales source.

Finally, as Barnes & Noble's dominance in promotionally priced illustrated books diminished, trade publishers began to gradually own that space again. And yet, we face a shrinking of the promotionally illustrated bookselling footprint in the price clubs as well and so, there is now a search for other venues.

*

Jeanette Limondjian began her career on the founding team of Barnes & Noble, becoming a key executive in the retail and publishing divisions. She was tasked with opening the innovative, groundbreaking Sales Annex; started the Barnes & Noble mail-order division and helped to start the Barnes & Noble proprietary publishing division which grew to be, for a period of time, one of the largest publishers of illustrated books in the world.

In 2011, Jeanette started Shelter Harbor Press, a publishing company dedicated to creating soundly written and beautifully illustrated books that provide an introduction to serious nonfiction subjects through the art of storytelling. One series has gone on to sell nearly a million copies and has been translated into 20 languages.

LICENSING AND SUBSIDIARY RIGHTS

A SHORT HISTORY OF BOOK CLUBS

BY DENISE MCGANN

When they launched in the 1920s, direct-mail book clubs were very popular and remained so throughout the twentieth century. Glossy come-ons in the form of direct mailings lured readers with hard-to-resist offers such as five books for $1. Once you became a member, you were obligated to purchase a certain number of books each year and needed to opt out of automatic shipments of monthly selections—a model known as negative option. At their peak, the two largest books clubs had over 9 million members combined. The two main clubs—Book of the Month Club and the Literary Guild—were general interest but spawned what were dubbed "specialty clubs," which catered to certain genres and hobbies, such as Mystery Guild, History Book Club, The Good Cook, Crafter's Choice, and more.

BOOK OF THE MONTH CLUB

Harry Scherman was a mail-order copywriter at J. Walter Thompson in 1916 when he, with a group of friends, created a new way to distribute literature by publishing small-format editions of public domain titles that ultimately sold via direct mail and were marketed in conjunction with Whitman Chocolates. The Little Leather Library, as it was called, was highly successful and sold 30 million copies of 30 classics in five years.

In the early 1920s, most books were sold in bookstores, which were primarily located in big cities. This left much of the country without an outlet to purchase books. Scherman saw an opportunity to employ the model he had developed for the Little Leather Library to distribute new titles to potential customers across the United States. The new Book of the Month Club would have a panel made up of authors, journalists, and editors select the best books each month. By convincing readers they were getting titles selected by experts, BOMC was able to persuade subscribers to sign up for a membership that included a commitment to purchase a certain number of books each year. By 1927 there were over 60,000 members and within 20 years that number had grown to 550,000.

Being selected by the esteemed judges was a coup, especially for unknown or first-time authors; J.D. Salinger's *The Catcher in the Rye* became a bestseller as a result. Renowned classics such as *Gone with the Wind*, *The Grapes of Wrath*, and *To Kill a Mockingbird* owe their fame, in part, to being BOMC selections. As budgets for solicitation of new members grew, books featured in mailings and ads also saw a boost in bookstore sales.

Over the years, the judges had less and less influence over selections, as marketing and analytics took over. In 1994, the decision was made to eliminate the judges. The judges' panel was briefly reincarnated in 2005 but quickly disbanded.

In 1977, Book of the Month Club was acquired by Time Inc. Specialty clubs included Quality Paperback Book Club, the History Book Club, the Money Book Club, the Good Cook, Crafter's Choice, and Children's Book of the Month Club.

THE LITERARY GUILD

In 1927, The Literary Guild of America was founded by Harold Guinzberg and Samuel Craig to compete with Book of the Month Club.

The Literary Guild was purchased by Doubleday Publishing in March 1929. The stable of specialty clubs grew from Doubleday Book Club (featuring hardcover editions of paperback romances, among other genres) to include Science Fiction (founded in 1953), Military, Fireside Theater (founded in 1950), Mystery Guild, and Large Print.

Both companies operated on a negative-option model, which meant books were automatically shipped unless members opted out—an accepted but unusual method of gaining sales through no action on the consumer's part. The large clubs printed their own editions in smaller formats and on different paper, which allowed them to offer discounts of up to 40% off the publisher's retail price. Warehouses were in the bucolic-sounding Camp Hill, Pennsylvania (Book of the Month Club), and Garden City, New York (Doubleday Book Clubs), and employed hundreds of local residents. Not solely relying on publishers' offerings, the Literary Guild also had a proprietary publishing program that created exclusive titles such as *First Ladies of the U.S.* and a collection of specially designed volumes of Shakespeare's works.

In the heady 1980s, the two big clubs competed for rights to new titles by bestselling authors such as Robert Ludlum, Tom Clancy, Stephen King, and Anne Tyler via bidding wars that could reach over $1 million. BOMC, with a larger male membership, was considered the more literary club than Literary Guild, which featured more commercial fiction. Some of the top-performing Literary Guild titles were by authors such as Danielle Steel and Barbara Taylor Bradford.

Doubleday & Company, including the book clubs, was purchased by Bertelsmann in 1986. Bertelsmann, a German company, had a successful worldwide book club business with over 35 million subscribers, and had long wanted to break into the U.S. book club business. This deal allowed them to do just that.

At their peak, BOMC had 4.5 million members and Doubleday Direct had 4.8 million members across all their clubs and reportedly sold almost 20% of all books in the United States. Amazon, which launched in 1994 as an online bookseller, would change all that. There were also smaller book clubs run by Rodale, Meredith, Newbridge, and Watson-Guptill that were ultimately acquired by the larger clubs or dissolved.

BOOKSPAN

In March 2000, to offset operating costs and gain economies of scale, the two leading clubs joined forces. Book of the Month Club and Literary Guild, along with the smaller specialty clubs, became Bookspan. Total membership across the new entity was now approximately 8 million, with about $900 million in annual revenues. The joint venture between Time Warner and Bertelsmann lasted until 2007 when Bertelsmann bought out Time Warner and took over sole ownership.

During this time, several initiatives were launched, including special-interest clubs for Spanish-language, Jewish, and conservative readers. In addition to these, an online business called Zoomba and an International Book of the Month were tested, both without success.

As Amazon's business grew, the book clubs suffered. No longer did consumers have to rely on these old-school direct-mail book clubs—with their monthly catalogs and automatic shipments—to learn about new titles at discounted prices. Amazon offered all of that, and more, without a commitment or membership.

In 2008, with declining membership and the sale of its U.S. book clubs,

Bertelsmann sold the entity known as Direct Brands, which included Bookspan and Columbia House (the music club), to Najafi Companies, an investment group.

In 2012, Najafi sold Bookspan to Pride Tree Holdings. In 2015, Book of the Month Club was relaunched with a different target audience—young women in their twenties and thirties—and featuring books by less well-known authors chosen to appeal to this new demographic. From all reports, this has been successful in rejuvenating Book of the Month Club and making it relevant again. The large number of specialty clubs have been narrowed down to eight and include Science Fiction, Mystery Guild, Doubleday Book Club, and the Literary Guild.

Different book club models have emerged led by Oprah Winfrey's now occasional selections of books she recommends. Other celebrities have gotten into the game, including Reese Witherspoon and Jenna Bush. These are not the traditional member-based book clubs, but they have the same effect of creating bestsellers.

The newest traditional membership book club is Literati, which launched in 2020 and features clubs curated by experts such as Steph Curry, Roxane Gay, Richard Branson, and others.

So the traditional direct-to-consumer book club lives on, although on a smaller scale. Given the plethora of new books published every year, some readers still value having titles selected for them by like-minded people they admire and respect. While Amazon continues to be the world's largest bookseller, it does not offer this curation option—yet.

*

Denise McGann is a 25-year veteran of book clubs, with stints at Doubleday Direct, Meredith's *Better Homes & Garden* book clubs, Book of the Month Club, and Bookspan.

BOOK SCOUTING

BY MARIA B. CAMPBELL

Scouting is hard to define in a few sentences. Since I have been scouting for decades, I will try to explain it below, focusing on a scout's role in the American publishing landscape. Let's start with what it is not: agenting or translating. A scout does not work for American publishers or agents. A scout does not buy or sell. Rather, a scout works as a consultant to entities (usually international publishers, producers, studios, and streamers), advising clients on which American books to acquire and publish in their marketplace and/or adapt for TV or film. Remuneration for a scout is usually based on an annual retainer paid by clients reflecting the size of their markets and scope of the work.

I founded my own scouting company, Maria B. Campbell Associates, in 1987. Prior to that, I worked as a scout based in Mondadori's New York office and then in the Rizzoli offices above the bookstore on 57th Street, steadily taking on clients in different countries. Fast-forward to 2021: the company represents 25 international publishers, for which we scout English language and international adult and children's books. I opened a London office in 2015 to expand the company's footprint in Europe (pre-Brexit), and we now have ten languages in-house between the New York and London offices. My interest has always been how books travel into a multitude of languages, and we scout every language that we can read. As of 2016, the company is also the global book scout for Netflix.

Working with some of the most distinguished publishers in the world—market leaders in their respective countries—has been a privilege and has enabled me to enjoy some of their successes with scouted books. American authors ranging from Donna Tartt to Colson Whitehead, Walter Isaacson, Patricia Cornwell, and John Grisham have found excellent homes among my clients. On the film side, scouting *Jurassic Park* for Amblin, Steven Spielberg's company, was great fun. The genius of Steven Spielberg is that he saw it not only as a great film but an entire business including sequels, amusement parks, and merchandise. Netflix has a policy of not discussing acquisitions, which means the books scouted for them will remain our secret forever!

There is no school for scouts, but a few qualities help: a love of reading (speed-reading is especially handy) languages, connectivity, and travel, plus curiosity, stamina, and flexibility. In my case, growing up between New York and Italy with Italian as my first language was a great boon. Studies in Paris were wonderful. One of my favorite things in life has always been connecting people. Add books to this and that, for me, has been the foundation of scouting. My own experience has reflected an ever-growing interest in scouting books from all over the world.

Scouting has changed enormously in the course of my career. I started communicating with Mondadori, my first client, by telex! Manuscripts were photocopied and sent by post, messengers were essential, and the phone a lifeline. Fast-forward to the internet, computers, electronic transmission of manuscripts, iPhones, text messages, FaceTime, Google, and now Zoom. When I first started scouting, there were a handful of scouts, and now there are dozens working all over the world. The Frankfurt Book Fair was in two halls—one German and one international. The American publishers brought the "hot commercial books" to the fair and international publishers vied for them. First the ABA, then London became the Spring rights fair for publishers. Decades later, publishing has become both more local and global, except for the United States, which continues to be primarily American with a 3% translation rate.

It is hard to predict how scouting, much less publishing, will evolve after the Covid-19 pandemic. It is a quintessentially social business, and this has made the last 15 months especially difficult. Zoom calls lack intimacy, spontaneity, creativity, and a sense of community, all of which can help foster the easy exchange of ideas. But the ability to communicate with our clients throughout the world at 8 a.m. or 9 p.m. across time zones has been a positive development, as has the opportunity for people who normally would not go to the book fairs and junior staff to be a part of the conversation.

We have all learned how to work remotely, and some scouts will never return to an office. How entry-level scouts will learn, grow, and expand their connections is still terra incognita! Perhaps with the global content of streamers like Netflix, stories will not be as local as they have been. A Swedish or French series can capture the imagination of people all over the world. If they are based on books, the market for international books could expand. Audiobooks and podcasts are increasing all over the world and creating more ways to tell stories that can be scouted. With Trump gone, American books have more oxygen and can travel better. Fiction writers have also come out of hibernation to deliver new novels. As long as writers write and books are published in whatever form, scouting will continue. Connecting stories, be they fiction or nonfiction, to people is the backbone of scouting. Whether we communicate our discoveries by fax or by supersonic videoconferences via our avatars, I think there is a role for us in the publishing. The only real barrier is a failure of imagination!

*

Maria B. Campbell is the founder and president of Maria B. Campbell Associates, Inc. and Maria B. Campbell Associates UK Ltd. A graduate of Smith College, Maria began her career in publishing as an assistant to the editorial representative in the New York office of Arnoldo Mondadori Editore, the Italian publisher. In 1987, Maria formed Maria B. Campbell Associates and year by year expanded her roster of international clients. Maria was one of the founding board members of Words Without Borders and the treasurer of PEN America, where she served on the executive committee for ten years. She is currently on the boards of the Center for Fiction and for Pilobolus, an internationally acclaimed dance company, renowned for its unique, diverse collaborative performances.

WHO'S SCOUTING WHOM 2021: A *PUBLISHING TRENDS* GUIDE TO LITERARY SCOUTS

* = Includes children's/YA, ital = Children's only	UK/Australia	Germany	France	Italy	Spain (S), Portugal (P), Latin America (LA)	Brazil	The Netherlands	Scandinavia: Sweden (S), Denmark (D), Norway (N), Finland (F)	Asia: Japan (J), China (C), Korea (K), Taiwan (T)	Other Countries; Film/TV Literary Scouting in the U.S.
Baker Literary Scouting, Inc. (212) 641-0782 jon@lbscout.com	Oneworld (UK)	DuMont	Albin Michel				AW Bruna, Signatuur		Beijing Media Time (C)	Alexandra Group and Europa (Hungary), Hello Sunshine (film/TV), Media Res (film/TV), Miramax (film)
Maria B. Campbell (212) 679-4700 mviguet@mbcbook.com	Little, Brown Book Group* (UK), *Hachette Children's Book Group* (UK)	S. Fischer *Verlag**	Fayard, *Livre de Poche, Hachette Romans*	Mondadori*	Penguin Random House Grupo Editorial* (S, P, LA)	Companhia das Letras*/ PRH Brazil	Veen Bosch & Keuning (Atlas Contact, Alfabet, Business Contact, Zomar & Keuning*, Luitingh-Sijthoff* Kosmos, Ten Have, Omniboek, AnkHHermes, Kok Boekencentrum*)	Albert Bonniers, Wahlström & Widstrand, *Bonnier Carlsen,* Forum (S), Otava* (F), Politikens* (D), Gyldendal* (N)	Tuttle Mori Agency* (J), Minumsa (K), ThinKingdom* (C)	Psichogios* (Greece), AST* (Russia); Modan/Keter* (Israel), Libri Publishing Group* (Hungary), Marginesy (Poland), Netflix*
Linda Clark (212) 348-5515 linda@lindaclark.net					Roca* (S)				Shinchosha (J)	Czarna Owca (Poland), Timas (Turkey), ABC Television Group/ABC Studios, ABC Signature, ABC Freeform (formerly Disney Family)

* = Includes children's/YA, *Ital* = Children's only	UK/Australia	Germany	France	Italy	Spain (S), Portugal (P), Latin America (LA)	Brazil	The Netherlands	Scandinavia: Sweden (S), Denmark (D), Norway (N), Finland (F)	Asia: Japan (J), China (C), Korea (K), Taiwan (T)	Other Countries; Film/TV Literary Scouting in the U.S.
Del Commune Enterprises (212) 226-6664 *ldelcommune @dcescouts.com*	Penguin Group (UK)	Rowohlt Verlag	Fleuve Editions, 10/18, Pocket	Gruppo editoriale Mauri Spagnol			Modernista Group (S)			
Erin Edmison Peter Harper (646) 684-3029 *erin@edmisonharper.com peter@edmisonharper.com*	Pan Macmillan/ Picador Australia	Hanser (Hanser Berlin, Hanserblau, Zsolnay/ Deuticke); Nagel & Kimche	Editions Gallimard	Feltrinelli	Anagrama (S)	Editora Todavia	Maven Publishing, Ambo|Anthos	Natur & Kultur (S), Gads Forlag (D)	Beijing Huazhang (China Machine Press) (C)	Redrum Productions
KF Literary Scouting (212) 691-8079 *kelly@kfscout.com*	Scribe Publications	Hoffman Und Campe Verlag, *HarperCollins Germany*	Calmann Levy, Editions Kero, *Editions Milan, Bayard Editions*	Il Saggiatore	Ediciones Urano* (S, LA), *Presenca* (P)	Grupo Editorial Record*	Xander Uitgevers, *Blossom Books*	Mondial Forlag (S), Aula & Co (F)	United Sky New Media* (C)	Publicat* (Poland), Eksmo* (Russia)
Alanna Feldman Scouting (949) 400-9161 *alanna@afscouting.ccm*	Orion Publishing Group (UK)	HarperCollins Germany	Sonatine, Le Cherche Midi	HarperCollins Italia*						New Regency Productions

Who's Scouting Whom 2021: A Publishing Trends Guide to Literary Scouts (contin.)

* = Includes children's/YA, *Ital* = Children's only	UK/Australia	Germany	France	Italy	Spain (S), Portugal (P), Latin America (LA)	Brazil	The Netherlands	Scandinavia: Sweden (S), Denmark (D), Norway (N), Finland (F)	Asia: Japan (J), China (C), Korea (K), Taiwan (T)	Other Countries; Film/TV Literary Scouting in the U.S.
Aram Fox (212) 563-7365 aram@aramfox.com	HarperCollins, Fourth Estate, William Collins, HQ/Harlequin* (UK)	Piper* & Berlin Verlag, Ullstein Buchverlage	Belfond	Bompiani*	Libros del Asteroide (S, LA)	Sextante/Arqueiro*, Intrínseca*	Overamstel uitgevers (Carrera, Hollands Diep, Horizon, Lebowski, The House of Books)			Disney Channel
Franklin & Siegal (212) 868-6311 todd@franklinandsiegal.com	Hodder & Stoughton*/Sceptre, Hodder Studio, John Murray Press/Two Roads, Quercus/riverrun (UK)	Heyne*, Karl Blessing, *cbj*	Flammarion, autrement, Pygmalion, J'ai lu, *Nathan*	Sperling & Kupfer*/Frassinelli	Grupo Planeta* (S, P, LA)	Planeta Brasil*	Unieboek Spectrum, *Van Goor, Van Holkema*, Prometheus	Lindhardt & Ringhof (D), *Carlsen* (D), WSOY*, Bazar, Minerva, Docendo (F), Southside Stories/Lavender Lit* (S)	Hayakawa (J), Citic (C), China Times (T)	Litera* (Romania), 21. Szazad (Hungary), Egmont* (Bulgaria), Yedioth/Miskal* (Israel), Universal, Paramount TV
Simone Garzella (917) 482-8409 sg@sgbookscouting.com	Penguin Random House Australia, Blackstone	Mare	Hugo & CIE*	SEM, Aboca	Alfaomega* (S), Saida de Emergencia* (P), Audible* (S, LA)	Saraiva, Melhora-mentos*, Audible*		Volante* (S), Minerva (F)	Business Weekly Publications (T), Guandcheng (C)*	Arab Scientific Publishers* (Arabic), Kobiece Illuminatio* (Poland), Euromedia* (Czech Republic), Ikar* (Slovakia), Klidarithmos* (Greece)

Who's Scouting Whom 2021: A Publishing Trends Guide to Literary Scouts (contin.)

* = Includes children's/YA, *Ital* = Children's only	UK/Australia	Germany	France	Italy	Spain (S), Portugal (P), Latin America (LA)	Brazil	The Netherlands	Scandinavia: Sweden (S), Denmark (D), Norway (N), Finland (F)	Asia: Japan (J), China (C), Korea (K), Taiwan (T)	Other Countries; Film/TV Literary Scouting in the U.S.
Liz Gately Book Scouting (718) 643-6553 liz@lizgately.com	Headline (UK)	Suhrkamp, *Oetinger & Dressler*	HarperCollins France	Piemme*	Maeva* (S), Leya* (P)	Editora Nacional	Meulenhoff Boekerij		The English Agency (J), Horizon (C), Munghak-dongne (K)	Nemira* (Romania), Lumen* (Croatia), Tchelet* (Israel), Agora (Poland), Sony Pictures Television
Sanford Greenburger (212) 206-5600 jbowers@sjga.com		Beck, dtv, *dtv junior*	Buchet Chastel, Phébus, Noir sur Blanc, Notabilia	*Il Castoro*	V&R*	V&R*		*Alvilda*	Discovery 21 (J), Beijing Huaxia Winshare Books Co., Ltd.*/Tiandi Press* (C)	Editoria RAO* (Romania), Bard* (Bulgaria), Maxim* (Hungary)
Jana-Maria Hartmann (312) 358-3099 jana@jmhscouting.com		Aufbau Verlag	Editions du Seuil		Trini Vergara Ediciones (S, LA)	Trama/Nova Fronteira	Nieuw Amsterdam	Jentas (S, D)		Muza (Poland)
Rachel Hecht | Children's Scouting (212) 658-0217 rachel@rachelhecht.com		*Ravensburger*	*Gallimard Jeunesse*	*DeA Planeta*	*Anaya Infantil y Juvenil*	*Globo Livros*	*Moon (Overamstel Uitgevers)*	*Alvilda (D), Vigmostad & Bjørke (N)*		*Kinneret Zmora Dvir Publishing House (Israel), Zysk i-Ska (Poland), Alexandra Publishing (Hungary), Fred Rogers Productions, Hello Sunshine Kids + Animation*

Who's Scouting Whom 2021: A *Publishing Trends* Guide to Literary Scouts (contin.)

* = Includes children's/YA, *Ital* = Children's only	UK/Australia	Germany	France	Italy	Spain (S), Portugal (P), Latin America (LA)	Brazil	The Netherlands	Scandinavia: Sweden (S), Denmark (D), Norway (N), Finland (F)	Asia: Japan (J), China (C), Korea (K), Taiwan (T)	Other Countries; Film/TV Literary Scouting in the U.S.
Bettina Schrewe (212) 414-2515 *bschrewe@bschrewe.com*	PRH: Cornerstone, Ebury, Transworld, Vintage, Penguin *Random House Children's*	Verlagsgruppe Penguin Random House	Laffont*	Rizzoli*, Fabbri*	Alianza	Rocco*	De Bezige Bij, Cargo, *Gottmer*	Norstedts, Bromberg, *Rabén & Sjögren, B. Wahlströms* (S), Gyldendal* (D), Cappelen Damm* (N), Tammi* (F)	Crown* (T), Dook* (C)	Matar (Israel), Patakis* (Greece), Foksal* (Poland), Euromedia* (Czech Republic), Ikar* (Slovakia), Central Publishing* (Hungary), Alma* (Lithuania), Bookzone* (Romania), Fraktura (Croatia), Penguin Random House* (Canada), River Road (film)
Jane Starr (212) 421-0777 *jane@janestarr.com*	Allen and Unwin*, Murdoch Books, Atlantic Books	Bastei Lübbe, Eichborn, LYX	Michel Lafon*	Newton Compton Editori*			Uitgeverij De Fontein*	Vigmostad & Bjoerke (N)	Japan Uni Agency* (J)	Vulkan Publishing* (Serbia)

Who's Scouting Whom 2021: A *Publishing Trends* Guide to Literary Scouts (contin.)

* = incl des children's/YA, *Ital* = Children's only	UK/Australia	Germany	France	Italy	Spain (S), Portugal (P), Latin America (LA)	Brazil	The Netherlands	Scandinavia: Sweden (S), Denmark (D), Norway (N), Finland (F)	Asia: Japan (J), China (C), Korea (K), Taiwan (T)	Other Countries; Film/TV Literary Scouting in the U.S.
Thompson Associates (212) 254-1502 *mat@mathompson.com*	Pan Macmillan/ Picador/ Bluebird/ Mantle (UK)	Kiepenheuer & Witsch	Presses de la Cité	Neri Pozza		Globo Livros	HarperCollins Holland		Beijing Xiron (C), Bookie Publishing (K), Commonwealth Magazine Publishing (T)	Kinneret Zmora (Israel), Baltos Lankos (Lithuania), Zysk-i-Ska (Poland), Lira Publishing (Hungary), Metaichmio Publications (Greece)
Barbara Tolley & Associates (212) 647-1800 *bt@btolley.com*	Bonnier Publishing UK	Kein & Aber, *Arena*	JC Lattès, Le Masque, *Albin Michel Jeunesse*	La Nave di Teseo, Baldini & Castoldi		HarperBrasil	Singel Uitgeverijen (Athenaeum, De Arbeiderspers, De Geus, Nijgh & Van Ditmar, Volt), *Leopold*	Gummerus* (F)	Tatsumi* (J)	

Licensing and Subsidiary Rights | **543**

ADAPTATION ADORATION: WHY HOLLYWOOD STILL LOOKS TO THE BOOK

BY DEREK BRITT

For a film and television producer, the greatest thrill of all is to be struck with an inspiration so shuttering that you have no other choice but to pursue it. And pursue it you do. Thus beginning the laborious, nerve-inducing and adrenaline-fueled process of creation. But, there is a formula to it all, and the producer who sets out failing to prepare is, as they say, preparing to fail. The TV and movie business is a balancing act. It is one that, surprisingly, places the "concept" far down on the list of assets, and forces creatives to think like risk managers. This is why producers rely on the process of "packaging."

Packaging is the way of adding risk-mitigating assets to a concept, to ensure that it is solid and liability-free, that a studio or network (or financier) has to say "yes." None of this is as stimulating or creative as the actual filmmaking process, but it's the best way to ensure your project gets made. And isn't that the point? While getting an original concept through the gauntlet of development hell is not impossible, it is no comparison to the sheer power of an adaptation.

Let's imagine a perfect film/TV package, which happens in the development phase, far before the script is ever finalized or the studio/network has given the greenlight. This ideal package might include the attachment of an Academy Award–winning director, an A-List actor, a funding model, a successful production company, and of course powerful IP (intellectual property). The IP, if strong enough, may actually lead the package.

Today, IP comes in many shapes—anything from a million-follower podcast, to a blog or a YouTube account, to a Tony-winning play, an off-off-off Broadway play, or an award-winning documentary. But, truth be told, the holy grail of IP is and has always been a bestselling book.

Over the past century of TV and cinema, many of the great stories that have shaped our culture and opened our eyes have in fact been adaptations. To name a few: *The Godfather, To Kill A Mockingbird, The Color Purple, The Lord of the Rings, American Psycho, Pride and Prejudice, 12 Years a Slave, Life of Pi, Gone with the Wind, Brokeback Mountain, The Handmaid's Tale, Harry Potter, Game of Thrones, Forrest Gump, American Psycho, Silver Lining's Playbook, The Girl With the Dragon Tattoo, The Queen's Gambit,* and *Moneyball.* The list of acclaimed adaptations is long.

A book adaptation provides the producer with readily available material, attention to detail, character development, settings, subplots, arcs, and an entire world. In the case of bestsellers like *Harry Potter,* the book has an immediate domestic, and/or international fanbase, and details you just can't make up (unless your initials are J.K.). For everyone involved, including talent, crew, studio, the book gives them a sense of the project and its infinite potential. For the studio, the opportunity for merchandising, promotion and international recognizability is paramount when vetting which movie or series to pursue and fund.

But not all books need to be bestsellers. In the case of *Forrest Gump,* by no means a bestseller, the producer fell in love with the character of Forrest, and "had to make this movie." But the original book had sold about 10,000 copies and taken its place on a dusty shelf until the adaptation received six Academy Awards, propelling the original novel to sales of over a million copies. It's a fairytale ending for many authors and publishers. A book sits dormant for years, becomes a hit adaptation, and get rereleased as a bestseller.

It's apparent that global bestsellers like *The Girl With the Dragon Tattoo* are a no-brainer for adaptation, but now more than ever, the search for lesser-read books is of great value. In the same way that DJ's dig for hidden gems in a record store, producers and studios scour to find incomparable stories—preprint, on the shelves, or lost in the stacks. Relationships between producers, authors, and publishers should be paramount. It is a hand-in-hand relationship that should be as natural and symbiotic as that of a director and cinematographer or writer and editor.

We truly are fortunate to live in an era where quality storytelling, nonfiction and fiction, longform and short, book, television, film and documentary, is regarded with such appreciation. It's also a time when the studios and streaming outlets are going all-in with their pursuit for the best in high-end entertainment.

For the writer, always be thinking: "How would this book adapt into a screenplay?"

For the screenwriter, always be thinking: "How would this idea work as a novel?"

For the studio, always be thinking: "What books may not have performed, but could be our next *Forrest Gump*?"

For the publisher, always be thinking: "Every book we have has the potential to be a cinematic masterpiece in the right hands."

*

Derek Britt is a Peabody Award–winning producer and director.

HOW PUBLISHERS CAN FIND
THE ROI FROM RIGHTS

BY BILL ROSENBLATT

All publishers need to manage rights. But what value does effective rights management have to a publisher—beyond the obvious value of legal risk avoidance? This question has gone largely unanswered. Publishers say they want to improve their rights management capabilities, but they often don't invest in new systems. The Book Industry Study Group found this out back in 2017: it did a survey that revealed that while the majority of respondents saw value in improved rights management, only 40% had plans to make investments in the coming three to five years.

The question has always been the same: How much is a better rights management system really worth? Senior management wants quantitative evidence of ROI, but such evidence has been hard to come by; most of it has been anecdotal. This question takes on more urgency as rights-related revenue— permissions, digital licensing, audiobooks, foreign rights, and so on—becomes a bigger piece of many publishers' overall revenue.

Last summer, BISG commissioned my firm to undertake a study to find the financial benefits of rights management, to get credible and useful estimates of ROI. To do this, we worked with the BISG Rights Committee to create "ROI buckets" that we could assign to specific outcomes from implementations of new or upgraded rights management systems and processes. We learned about these from a series of in-depth interviews with rights executives from more than a dozen publishers and literary agencies, large and small, across most segments of the industry.

We settled on eight buckets, five on the incremental revenue side and three on the cost efficiencies side. We worked with interviewees to quantify the benefits they were seeing and put them into each of the buckets. The results were published in October 2020 as a report that's available on BISG's website (free to BISG members).

We found that though specific rights management applications vary from one segment of publishing to another, the financial benefits outweigh publishers' investments in rights management systems by a wide margin across the board. Here are just a few highlights of the findings:

- A midsize trade publisher was able to increase licensing revenue from 8% to 15% of total revenue over a period of five years, a gain in the low millions of dollars.
- A small agency has been able to complete more deals with its existing staff and increase annual revenue by 10%–15%.
- Another midsize trade publisher used its rights management system to examine data on audiobook deals to determine their profitability. It discovered that it could increase total annual revenue by 3%–4% by bringing audiobook production in-house.
- A large STM publisher started using an online licensing agency and saw a multimillion-dollar increase in permissions sales, equivalent to what it would earn from an in-house staff of 15 at about half the cost.
- A large educational publisher is able to avoid paying for about 10% of the tens of thousands of assets that it licenses in per year, by using a rights management system to track the assets and the rights being licensed. This saves it several million dollars per year.

In addition to these data points—and many others—we found some particularly promising use cases in each segment. For trade publishers, the most beneficial use cases included increased subrights sales through data analysis to determine optimum pricing, and self-service web portals for increased efficiency in permissions sales. For agencies, the best use cases were more capacity to do foreign rights deals and increased cash flow through automated payment reminders.

Three general themes emerged from our analysis. One was the power of data analysis: having lots of data about rights deals leads to better decisions on where to focus sales efforts and how to get the best prices. Another was that it's important to look at rights management capabilities as sources of incremental revenue through capacity expansion instead of merely as cost reduction. The third was the increasing criticality of third-party licensing agencies as rights become a bigger part of overall revenue: licensing agencies enable faster expansion, usually at a much lower cost.

We also measured ROI as percentages of publishers' overall revenue. The biggest percentages were at literary agencies, where investment in modestly priced rights management systems led to high-single-digit percent increased revenue. Among the largest publishers, higher ed publishers experienced the most benefit, but even the large trade houses saw benefits that added up to millions of dollars per year. In many cases, the benefits on the revenue side outweighed the benefits on the cost-savings side by an order of magnitude.

Rights managers know that what they do is increasingly important to their companies' bottom lines. Now they have some quantitative evidence to bring to senior management in support of investment in better systems and processes.

*

Bill Rosenblatt is president of GiantSteps Media Technology Strategies and a founding partner of Publishing Technology Partners.

A version of this article appeared in the 03/22/2021 issue of *Publishers Weekly* under the headline: Finding the ROI from Rights.

(18)

PRODUCTION AND MANUFACTURING

THE WORLD OF PRINTING AND PRODUCTION: THEN AND NOW

BY LINDA PALLADINO

In 1977, when I started my first job in publishing as a production assistant, the world of printing and production was entirely different from what it is today. Publishing was a world of mechanical boards, Schaedler rulers, picas, and ruby lith. Production was an opportunity to get into the nitty-gritty of how to bring an author or illustrator's vision to life. Throughout my career, I have had the good fortune of working with some of the best and brightest in our industry. And over time, I learned a lot from both the printers and in-house production people who took me under their wing.

Back then, publishing, and production in particular, was an entrée into the creative book-making process. Most of my colleagues were focused on editorial, marketing, or publicity positions—production was not a career that anyone knew about—but I reveled in the craft of making a physical book, in exploring the various creative ways of bringing the work to life. And I've never regretted pursuing a career in production, even as so much of the process has changed.

When I started, there were many printing companies in the United States, both large and small—American Book Stratford Press, Dunenewald, Horowitz Rae, The Mazer Corporation, The George Banta Company, Bookbinders in New Jersey, United Litho, General Offset, Colonial Press, Von Hoffman Press, Book Press, Arcata Graphics, World Color, Cenveo, R.R. Donnelley and Sons, W.A. Krueger, Deridder Thurston, Carton Craft, Webcrafters, Quebecor, Command Web, Freisens, Maple-Vail, Transcontinental, Malloy

Printing, Hess, Danner Press/Press of Ohio, C.J. Kriebel, Victor Graphics, Edwards Brothers, and Thomson-Shore, to name a few. Each printer specialized in the different types of books published by various publishers. Some printers specialized in educational books—workbooks, hardcover textbooks, overhead transparencies, and mimeographs. Other printers specialized in 1/c novels, and still others focused on children's books—four-color hardcovers, paperbacks, board books, and novelty books. As a production assistant just starting out, I was fascinated to learn all about book printing and the world of book printers.

In the late 1960s and into the 1970s, type was transitioning from hot metal to computer-generated. Prepress houses had cameras to shoot mechanical boards. They used filters—magenta, cyan, yellow, and black—to shoot four-color artwork and then output to film. The film was then used to create the four pieces needed to print four-color titles. The four-color process was an interesting combination of science and art, and achieving quality results was a delicate balancing act that required a good amount of skill.

In the early 1980s, scanners (Scitex) replaced cameras for doing prepress. Companies like Black Dot Graphics, Stevenson Litho, Schwak, York Graphics, TSI, NEC, Color Associates, American Color, and Carey Color invested in this expensive equipment. But as the industry grew, newer, and cheaper high-end scanning equipment was developed that replaced the Scitex system. These high-tech scanners helped to expand the color range even further. Chromalin contact proofs replaced color keys. Chromalins gave way to Kodak approvals, which were largely replaced by Epsons.

Prepress evolved over the years with the advent of digital prepress software and electronic files, which were used to print books. Aldus's PageMaker was purchased by Adobe in 1994 and became the primary design program used by the publishing industry. Adobe then lost market share to QuarkXPress, which had launched in 1992. In 1999 Adobe came out with a design program called InDesign to compete with Quark, and in the years since InDesign has overtaken Quark to become the standard now used by designers across the publishing industry.

When it came to printing, Heidelberg started manufacturing offset presses in 1962, and by the early 1970s offset printing had come into its own. High-quality four-color printing was done on a sheetfed press, which had better registration. But good registration depended on proper registration of the film from which plates were created. The large (77-inch) sheetfed presses made it hard to maintain good registration. Lack of tight registration of the film and plates, combined with paper stretch, made good registration challenging. Most sheetfed presses had four to six men running the press. Adjustments to ink were made with a wrench that opened the channels that controlled the flow of ink to the press.

Web printing came into play in the late 1970s. The web presses were huge and filled several football field–size areas in a plant. Heat-set web printing was relatively new; most webs until this time were what were referred to as "cold-set," meaning the ink was left to dry on its own. With heat-set presses, ovens were added to dry the ink as the paper sped through the web at a fast pace.

The presses required as many as 10 people to run them and, again, the controls were more mechanical.

In 1995, the computer-to-plate process eliminated the need for film and print registration issues were, for all intents and purposes, eliminated along with it. High-quality four-color printing was easier to achieve and maintain. With this came computer-controlled panels from which the color could be adjusted.

Up until the late 1970s book printing was primarily done in the United States. However, in the late 1970s several overseas plants—South China Printing Co., Tien Wah Press, Wing King Tong, Singapore National Printers (now Toppan Leefung) Excel, and Siravitana to name a few—started producing work for publishers. The pioneers who started to explore these plants and their capabilities—Ava Weiss, Art Director at Greenwillow, Ricki Levinson, and Dave Zabel Production from Dutton—began to travel to Asia to use these printing plants. They were in Hong Kong. High-quality four-color sheetfed 40-inch presses printed four-color children's hardcovers.

In the 1990s in the United States you had Berryville Graphics, Worzalla Printing, Horowitz Rae, and United Litho, Bookbinders in New Jersey, Lake Book, and General Offset, who specialized in four-color thin-cased hardcover picture books. Phoenix Graphics launched Rockway, which focused on kids' books. The goal was to compete with Asian manufacturing.

Overseas printing for specialized children's books evolved. As the industry changed, Horowitz Rae, Bookbinders, and other plants were no longer viable. Quality, good customer service, and new equipment with low labor costs encouraged the move of children's books printing overseas. Children's publishing moved to the overseas print platforms in Asia due to the ability to produce board books, lift-a-flap books, touch-and-feel as well as high-quality, four-color, thin hardcovers, many of which required hand labor. Costs were rising in parts of Asia, so plants moved to China, which became the manufacturing hub for many industries.

The print infrastructure in China has grown significantly with an explosion of plants that could produce the wide variety needed for children's books due to a low-cost labor pool for hand assembly and dedicated craftsmanship that was developed over many years. Printing had deep, centuries-old roots in China.

I still remember my first trip to Asia, in 1995, to see the grand opening of the new Tien Wah plant in Singapore. Many of my colleagues from book publishers around the world and the United States were invited to see the new plant, which had state-of-the-art equipment. Ink was fed from a central location to the presses. High-speed binding lines were delivering books. A huge export business grew and flourished.

In the United States, it was a different story. Mergers and acquisitions over the years led to less competition. Some of this was driven by the advent of the first e-book readers in 1998. Many saw this as the demise of book printing. Mergers and bankruptcies became the story as the book printing industry consolidated. Many of the storied, family-owned companies were bought by competitors—many of which were decommissioned to remove excess print capability.

Educational publishing, which had been a major part of the print business, saw their business move to digital. Demand continued to shrink, and printers were no longer investing in new equipment. Eventually, this led to a small number of 1/c printers that printed hardcover novels and paperbacks. The four-color printing pool of printers became smaller and smaller. Very few specialized in thin four-color hardcover and paperback books. Most focused on books with high page counts that were easier to bind. This led most children's printing to move permanently overseas due to lower costs and accessible hand labor for labor-intensive products. Equipment at most plants dated back to the 1970s and 1980s. New investments in equipment were limited to a small number of new presses.

In Asia, printers have always focused on investing in new presses, binding lines, and casing-in lines. They have kept up to date with investments in their core business. Smaller printers have consolidated or closed. Yet China has the firepower and maintains its status as one of the largest exporters of books to publishers.

2020 was a year that changed the fate of book publishing and with it printing. During the pandemic, bookstores and schools closed. Publishers were faced with declining sales and a bleak future. However, after the initial shock of lockdown, sales of printed books grew and grew. Children were remote learning, and adults adopted new lifestyles. Sales of home décor, self-improvement, cooking, gardening, timely nonfiction, and children's books all grew.

The print industry is seeing the kind of resurgence that hasn't been seen in years. We are finally seeing more and more investment in new printing presses, binding lines, casing-in machines.

The industry I know and love is in a renaissance as people rediscover the joys of a well-printed book.

*

Linda Palladino has spent her career working in production for the children's books divisions of several New York publishers. In 2003 she became Director of Production for Random House Children's Books, the world's largest children's trade publisher, and was promoted to V.P., Director of Production in 2008 and Senior Vice President in 2019. Linda and her team are responsible for producing books for the division's line of premier authors, illustrators, brands, and licensed characters. She works closely with her department to position Random House Children's Books as a company that sets the standard in innovative, environmental and sound business practices.

Linda is past President of the Bookbinders' Guild of New York. Linda has participated in and served on various industry educational seminars and committees including Women in Production, which awarded her the Luminaire Award. She currently serves on the Goddard Riverside NY Publishing Executive Committee.

A NEW NORMAL IN BOOK MANUFACTURING

BY MATT BAEHR

A s we can all attest, 2020 was a year like no other. Once the pandemic hit, many book manufacturers scrambled as their businesses were thrown upside down. Certain customers saw huge upticks, while other markets went silent. Manufacturers had to move staff and equipment around to aid in social distancing. They had to put new sanitation procedures in place and figure out protocols if a staff member became ill. Toward the end of the year, we saw trade book sales rise, giving many hope.

Into 2021, it became clear that "the new normal" was anything but. The supply chain has been ravaged as supply cannot meet demand. Staffing shortages are affecting every industry. As mills converted machines to packaging grades to meet the demand there, fine book papers are seeing inventories at the lowest levels ever. The education market continues to print fewer textbooks as the push toward digital continues.

Over the last few years, the push toward print-on-demand and just-in-time inventory has left publishers not able to meet the new demand. Manufacturers are seeing an uptick in order sizes as publishers work toward making sure they have enough of their titles in stock. Digital printing adoption continues to take hold, but traditional offset book manufacturers are still seeing high demand. For all manufacturers, looking at various ways to automate production lines has become paramount.

Even though many predicted that the printed book would have been a thing of the past by now, growing book sales prove that to be a myth. E-book sales have been trending down, with various print book segments showing significant growth. As I speak to people and tell them what I do for a living, almost all of them go out of their way to tell me that they prefer reading a physical book. They love the feel of the paper, highlighting passages, dog-earing their place, and even the smell of a book. No matter how fast the adoption of digital, nothing can replace what a printed book can offer.

As we move forward, book manufacturers will look to meet today's demand by maximizing the efficiencies of their current technologies while adopting new automation and other technical advances. In the short term, output will be limited by factors outside the control of manufacturers: supply chain issues, labor market issues, and paper availability. Ideally, those issues will be rectified in the next 12–18 months, ushering in a new age for book manufacturing.

*

Matt Baehr is the Executive Director of the Book Manufacturers' Institute (BMI), a not-for-profit trade organization that supports book manufacturing leaders in their work to drive the promotion, efficiency, and growth of book markets for readers and educators in North America.

BMI BOOK MANUFACTURERS

Since 1933, BMI has provided tremendous value to its member companies and others associated with the book manufacturing industry. BMI member companies (see below) range from full-service book manufacturers to those specializing in the digital print market, specialty binderies, component printers, packagers, equipment manufacturers, and suppliers of a variety of materials and services.

Bethany Press International, Inc.
6820 West 115th Street
Bloomington, MN 55438
952.914.7404
Email: plarson@bethanypress.com
Website: www.bethanypress.com

Book Printing Capabilities: Web Offset, Sheetfed Offset, Digital Toner
Cover Finishing: Foil Stamping, Embossing, Spot UV, Film Lamination, Specialty (Raised, Glitter, Gritty Matte, etc)

Bookmasters, Inc.
30 Amberwood Parkway
Ashland, OH 44805
419.281.5100
Email: bgospodarek@btpubservices.com
Website: www.bookmasters.com

Book Printing Capabilities: Web Offset, Sheetfed Offset, Digital Inkjet, Digital Toner, Print-on-Demand (POD)
Binding Types: PUR, Layflat Adhesive, Smyth Sewn, Side Sewn, Spiral Binding, Wiro Binding, Case Bound—Flat Backed, Case Bound—Round Backed, Case Bound—Headbands, Case Bound—End Sheets, Printed Paper Casemaking, One-Piece Material Casemaking, Three-Piece Casemaking
Cover Finishing: Foil Stamping, Embossing, Spot UV, Film Lamination
Finishing Capabilities: Ribbons, Round Corner, Folded Flaps
Industry Specifications: MSST (Textbooks), Library Binding
Environmental Certification: Paper Related (FSC, SFI, EPFC), Soy Based Ink
Other Certifications and Memberships: PIA Member

Books International

22883 Quicksilver Drive
Dulles, VA 20166
Email: d.hetherington@booksintl.com
Website: www.booksintl.presswarehouse.com

Bound to Stay Bound Books

1880 West Morton Road
Jacksonville, IL 62650
217.245.5191
Email: rsibert@btsb.com
Wesbite: www.btsb.com

Book Printing Capabilities: Digital Inkjet, Digital Toner
Binding Types: PUR, Side Sewn, Case Bound—Flat Backed, Case Bound—Round Backed, Case Bound—End Sheets, Three-Piece Casemaking
Industry Specifications: Library Binding
Other Certifications and Memberships: Certified Library Binder

Bridgeport National Bindery, Inc.

662 Silver Street, P.O. Box 289
Agawam, MA 1001
413.789.1981
Email: brucej@bnbindery.com
Website: www.bnbindery.com

Book Printing Capabilities: Digital Inkjet, Digital Toner, Print-on-Demand (POD)
Cover Finishing: Foil Stamping, Film Lamination
Finishing Capabilities: Ribbons
Industry Specifications: Library Binding, Edition Binding
Other Certifications and Memberships: Certified Library Binder

Cameron France Investment CPI Group

98-102 rue de Paris
Boulogne-Billancourt, Ile de France 92100
330156000000
Email: mbaldwin@cpi-print.com
Wesbite: www.cpi-print.com

With 16 factories spread out over five countries, CPI is one of the major players in the printing market in Europe. We produce books and printed documents for major publishing houses, large industrial groups and service companies, and administrative bodies.

With an impressive heritage—a rich industrial past, featuring prestigious printers such as Firmin-Didot in France (1713), Ebner & Spiegel in Germany (1817) or Mackays in the United Kingdom (1857)—CPI is the first European printer to have invested in digital inkjet printing. Today, at the heart of the transition to digital, we combine our industrial power with innovative computerised solutions to create even more value for our customers.

CPI is a French group founded in 1996 and is privately owned.

Book Printing Capabilities: Web Offset, Sheetfed Offset, Digital Inkjet, Digital Toner, Print-on-Demand (POD)
Binding Types: PUR, Notchbound Adhesive, Smyth Sewn, Side Sewn, Spiral Binding, Wiro Binding, Case Bound—Flat Backed, Case Bound—Round Backed, Case Bound—Headbands, Case Bound—End Sheets, Printed Paper Casemaking, One-Piece Material Casemaking, Three-Piece Casemaking
Cover Finishing: Foil Stamping, Embossing, Spot UV, Film Lamination
Finishing Capabilities: Ribbons, Round Corner, Rough Front, Folded Flaps, Guild Edge Finishing
Environmental Certification: Paper Related (FSC, SFI, EPFC)
Other Certifications and Memberships: ISO Certified

Command Web Offset/Bind-Rite Robbinsville
Secaucus, NJ 7094
201.863.8100
Email: smerson@commandcompanies.com
Website: www.commandcompanies.com

Copywell
60 Creditview Road
Woodbridge, Ontario L4L 9N4
705.321.9604
Email: jdhood@copywell.com
Website: www.copywell.com

Book Printing Capabilities: Web Offset, Sheetfed Offset, Digital Inkjet, Digital Toner, Print-on-Demand (POD)

Binding Types: PUR, Side Sewn, Wiro Binding, Case Bound—Flat Backed
Cover Finishing: Foil Stamping, Embossing, Spot UV, Film Lamination
Finishing Capabilities: Folded Flaps
Industry Specifications: MSST (Textbooks)

D&L Press

2434 South 24th Street
Phoenix, AZ 85034
602.448.3108
Email: brad@dandlpress.com
Website: www.dandlpress.com

The 58-year-old family owned and operated company has focused on trade commercial printing and now over the last 15 years has been an on-demand book printer. We have top customer relationships and pride ourselves on being a quality producer of paperback books. Also capable to provide author or publisher support materials in bookmarks, postcards and a variety of other specialty products for them to choose from.

Book Printing Capabilities: Digital Toner, Print-on-Demand (POD)
Binding Types: PUR, Spiral Binding
Cover Finishing: Spot UV, Film Lamination
Other Certifications and Memberships: PIA Member

Dekker Bookbinding

2941 Clydon Avenue S. W.
Grand Rapids, MI 49509
616.538.5160
Email: chrisd@dekkerbook.com
Website: www.dekkerbook.com

District Photo, Inc.

10501 Rhode Island Avenue
Beltsville, MD 20705
301.937.5300
Email: badams@districtphoto.com
Website: www.districtphoto.com

Book Printing Capabilities: Digital Inkjet, Digital Toner, Print-on-Demand (POD)
Binding Types: PUR, Layflat Adhesive, Smyth Sewn, Wiro Binding, Case Bound—Flat

Backed, Case Bound—Headbands, Case Bound—End Sheets, Printed Paper Casemaking, One-Piece Material Casemaking, Three-Piece Casemaking
Cover Finishing: Foil Stamping, Embossing, Spot UV, Film Lamination, Specialty (Raised, Glitter, Gritty Matte, etc)

Gasch Printing

1780 Crossroads Drive
Odenton, Maryland 21113
301.362.0700
Email: jupton@gaschprinting.com
Website: www.gaschprinting.com

Full-service, all digital book printer specializing in fast, reliable schedules
Book Printing Capabilities: Digital Inkjet, Digital Toner, Print-on-Demand (POD)
Cover Finishing: Foil Stamping, Film Lamination
Industry Specifications: MSST (Textbooks)
Environmental Certification: Paper Related (FSC, SFI, EPFC)

HF Group

1010 N. Sycamore Street
North Manchester, Indiana 46962
260.982.2107
Email: jheckman@hfgroup.com
Website: www.hfgroup.com

HF Group has remained dedicated to quality and service to our printing, binding, library, digitization, and conservation clients since 1821. Clients include publishers, book distributors, many of our nation's oldest and most prestigious research libraries, museums and archives.

Some of our specialties include:
Printing & Binding, Prebinding, Library Binding, Digitization, Edition, Textbook Rebinding, Enclosures and Conservation.

Book Printing Capabilities: Digital Toner, Print-on-Demand (POD)
Binding Types: PUR, Notchbound Adhesive, Layflat Adhesive, Side Sewn, Case Bound—Flat Backed, Case Bound—Round Backed, Case Bound—Headbands, Case Bound—End Sheets, Printed Paper Casemaking, One-Piece Material Casemaking
Cover Finishing: Foil Stamping, Embossing, Film Lamination

Finishing Capabilities: Ribbons
Industry Specifications: MSST (Textbooks), Library Binding, Edition Binding
Other Certifications and Memberships: Certified Library Binder

Independent Publishers Group
814 N. Franklin Street
Chicago, IL 60610
312.337.0747 x 280
Email: clarkmatthews@ipgbook.com
Website: www.ipgbook.com

Book Printing Capabilities: Digital Toner, Print-on-Demand (POD)
Cover Finishing: Film Lamination

Kingery Printing
3012 South Banker Street
Effingham, Illinois 62401
800.743.5151
Email: steves@kingeryprinting.com
Website: www.kingeryprinting.com

Lake Book Manufacturing Inc.
2085 N. Cornell Avenue
Melrose Park, IL 60160
708.345.7000
Email: dan@lakebook.com
Website: www.lakebook.com

Book Printing Capabilities: Web Offset, Sheetfed Offset
Binding Types: PUR, Notchbound Adhesive, Layflat Adhesive, Smyth Sewn, Side Sewn,
    Case Bound—Flat Backed, Case Bound—Round Backed, Case Bound—Headbands,
    Case Bound—End Sheets, Printed Paper Casemaking, One-Piece Material Casemaking,
    Three-Piece Casemaking
Cover Finishing: Foil Stamping, Embossing, Spot UV, Film Lamination, Specialty
    (Raised, Glitter, Gritty Matte, etc)
Finishing Capabilities: Ribbons, Round Corner, Rough Front, Folded Flaps, Guild Edge
    Finishing
Environmental Certification: Paper Related (FSC, SFI, EPFC), Soy Based Ink

Lakeside Book Company

99 Park Avenue 14th Floor
New York, NY 10016
844.572.5720
Email: dave.mccree@lsccom.com
Website: www.lsccom.com

Book Printing Capabilities: Web Offset, Digital Inkjet, Digital Toner, Print-on-Demand (POD)

Binding Types: PUR, Notchbound Adhesive, Layflat Adhesive, Smyth Sewn, Side Sewn, Spiral Binding, Wiro Binding, Comb/Cerlox Binding, Case Bound—Flat Backed, Case Bound—Round Backed, Case Bound—Headbands, Case Bound—End Sheets, Printed Paper Casemaking, One-Piece Material Casemaking, Three-Piece Casemaking

Cover Finishing: Foil Stamping, Embossing, Spot UV, Film Lamination

Finishing Capabilities: Ribbons, Round Corner, Rough Front, Folded Flaps, Guild Edge Finishing

Industry Specifications: MSST (Textbooks)

Environmental Certification: Paper Related (FSC, SFI, EPFC)

Other Certifications and Memberships: Union Certified, ISO Certified, PIA Member

Lehmann Bookbinding

97 Ardelt Avenue
Kitchner, ON N2C 2E1
519.570.4444
Email: lisa@lehmannbookbinding.com
Website: www.lehmannbookbinding.com

Binding Types: PUR, Notchbound Adhesive, Layflat Adhesive, Smyth Sewn, Side Sewn, Case Bound—Flat Backed, Case Bound—Round Backed, Case Bound—Headbands, Case Bound—End Sheets

Cover Finishing: Foil Stamping, Embossing

Finishing Capabilities: Ribbons

Industry Specifications: Library Binding, Edition Binding

Other Certifications and Memberships: Certified Library Binder

Marquis Book Printing

350 Rue des Entrepreneurs
Qu√©bec, Qu√©bec G1M 1B3
855.566.1937

Email: info@marquisbook.com
Website: www.marquisbook.com

Book Printing Capabilities: Web Offset, Sheetfed Offset, Digital Inkjet, Digital Toner,
  Print-on-Demand (POD)
Binding Types: PUR, Notchbound Adhesive, Layflat Adhesive, Smyth Sewn, Side
  Sewn, Spiral Binding, Wiro Binding, Case Bound—Flat Backed, Case Bound—
  Round Backed, Case Bound—Headbands, Case Bound—End Sheets, Printed Paper
  Casemaking, One-Piece Material Casemaking, Three-Piece Casemaking
Cover Finishing: Foil Stamping, Embossing, Spot UV, Film Lamination, Specialty
  (Raised, Glitter, Gritty Matte, etc)
Finishing Capabilities: Ribbons, Round Corner, Rough Front, Folded Flaps
Industry Specifications: Library Binding, Edition Binding
Other Certifications and Memberships: CANOPY Member

Mercury
2332 Innovation Way, Building 4
Rochester, NY 14624
585.458.7900
Email: cschamberger@mercuryprint.com
Website: www.mercuryprint.com

Phillips Graphic Finishing LLC
150 Arrowhead Drive
Manheim, Pennsylvania 17545
717.653.4565
Email: andyh@pgfinish.com
Website: www.pgfinish.com

Binding Types: Notchbound Adhesive, Spiral Binding, Wiro Binding
Cover Finishing: Foil Stamping, Embossing
Finishing Capabilities: Round Corner

Publishers' Graphics, LLC
131 Fremont Street
West Chicago, Illinois 60185
630.221.1850
Email: nlewis@pubgraphics.com
Website: www.pubgraphics.com

Publishers Storage & Shipping, LLC
660 S. Mansfield Street
Ypsilanti, MI 48197
734.487.9720
Email: mseagram@pssc.com
Website: www.pssc.com

Publishers Storage and Shipping is a service business specializing in book storage and order fulfillment for publishers. Offering end-to-end service solutions for all your inventory management needs. For over 40 years, PSSC has offered fulfillment and logistics expertise in both domestic and worldwide supply chains. Our state-of-the-art facilities and premiere customer call center provide the highest standard of service to you—our partner. Smart Solutions for a Smarter World.

R & R Bindery
499 Rachel Road
Girard, IL 62640
217.627.2143
Email: alan.mcintire@rrbindery.com
Website: www.rrbindery.com

Book Printing Capabilities: Digital Toner, Print-on-Demand (POD)
Binding Types: PUR, Side Sewn, Spiral Binding, Case Bound—Flat Backed, Case Bound—Headbands, Case Bound—End Sheets, One-Piece Material Casemaking
Cover Finishing: Foil Stamping, Embossing, Film Lamination
Finishing Capabilities: Ribbons, Round Corner, Folded Flaps
Industry Specifications: Edition Binding

Stromberg Allen and Company
18504 West Creek Drive Suite 100
Tinley Park, Illinois 60477
773.847.7131
Email: bill@strombergallen.com
Website: www.strombergallen.com

Superior Packaging and Finishing
1 Federal Drive
Braintree, Massachusetts 2184
781.820.9243

Email: jay@sbpack.com
Website: www.superiorpackagingandfinishing.com

Tara TPS
245, Sanjisuk-gil
Paju-si, Kyunggi-do
82319392027
Email: andy@taratps.com
Website: www.taratps.com/eng

The Maple Press Company
Box 2695
York, PA 17405
717.764.5911
Email: jimw@maplepress.com
Website: www.maplepress.com

Book Printing Capabilities: Web Offset, Sheetfed Offset, Digital Toner, Print-on-Demand (POD)
Binding Types: Notchbound Adhesive, Smyth Sewn, Case Bound—Flat Backed, Case Bound—Round Backed, Case Bound—Headbands, Case Bound—End Sheets, Printed Paper Casemaking, One-Piece Material Casemaking, Three-Piece Casemaking
Cover Finishing: Film Lamination
Finishing Capabilities: Ribbons, Rough Front, Folded Flaps

Thomson Reuters—Core Publishing Solutions
610 Opperman Drive
Eagan, MN 55123
763.326.5562
Email: tim.hughes@thomsonreuters.com

TPS Enterprises, Inc./Total Printing Systems
PO Box 375
Newton, IL 62448
618.783.2978 x 346
Email: rick@tps1.com
Website: www.tps1.com

Book Printing Capabilities: Digital Inkjet, Print-on-Demand (POD), Digital Toner

Binding Types: PUR, Notchbound Adhesive, Layflat Adhesive, Side Sewn, Spiral Binding, Wiro Binding, Comb/Cerlox Binding, Case Bound—Flat Backed, Case Bound—Headbands, Case Bound—End Sheets, Printed Paper Casemaking, One-Piece Material Casemaking, Three-Piece Casemaking

Cover Finishing: Foil Stamping, Embossing, Spot UV, Film Lamination, Specialty (Raised, Glitter, Gritty Matte, etc)

Finishing Capabilities: Ribbons, Round Corner, Folded Flaps

Environmental Certification: Paper Related (FSC, SFI, EPFC)

Other Certifications and Memberships: PIA Member

U.S. Government Printing Office

732 North Capitol Street, NW

Washington, DC 20401

202.512.0593

Email: jlanne@gpo.gov

Website: www.gpo.gov

Versa Press, Inc.

1465 Spring Bay Road

East Peoria, IL 61611

309.822.8272 x 170

Email: mkennell@versapress.com

Website: www.versapress.com

Versa Press is a family-owned business located in East Peoria, Illinois. We are a leading manufacturer of trade, religious, educational, medical, university, and commercial publications.

Throughout our history, we have provided exceptional value and customer service through our experienced staff and their superior printing craftsmanship. At Versa Press, we're proud to offer a wide range of services for every step of the book printing process. From full prepress capabilities including proofing and computers-to-plate, to one, two, and four color text printing, and up to five color cover printing, to binding and shipping—we strive to deliver the best book possible.

Book Printing Capabilities: Sheetfed Offset, Digital Inkjet

Binding Types: PUR, Layflat Adhesive, Smyth Sewn, Case Bound—Flat Backed, Case Bound—Round Backed, Case Bound—Headbands, Case Bound—End Sheets, Printed Paper Casemaking, One-Piece Material Casemaking, Three-Piece Casemaking

Cover Finishing: Embossing, Foil Stamping, Spot UV, Film Lamination, Specialty (Raised, Glitter, Gritty Matte, etc)
Finishing Capabilities: Ribbons, Round Corner, Folded Flaps
Industry Specifications: MSST (Textbooks), Edition Binding
Environmental Certification: Paper Related (FSC, SFI, EPFC), Soy Based Ink

Vicks Lithograph & Printing Corp
Attn: Dwight E. Vicks III
Yorkville, NY 13495
315.272.2455
Email: dwight@vicks.biz
Website: www.vicksbiz.com

Book Printing Capabilities: Web Offset, Sheetfed Offset, Digital Toner, Print-on-Demand (POD)
Binding Types: PUR, Layflat Adhesive, Spiral Binding
Other Certifications and Memberships: PIA Member

Wallaceburg Bookbinding & Mfg. Co. Ltd.
Attn: Suzanne Wiersma PO Box 533
Marine City, MI 48039
800.214.2463
Email: swiersma@wbmbindery.com
Website: www.wbmbindery.com

Binding Types: Notchbound Adhesive, Case Bound—Round Backed, Case Bound—Headbands, One-Piece Material Casemaking
Cover Finishing: Foil Stamping, Embossing
Finishing Capabilities: Ribbons, Round Corner
Industry Specifications: Library Binding
Other Certifications and Memberships: Certified Library Binder

Walsworth Publishing Company
306 North Kansas Avenue
Marceline, MO 64658
660.456.4299
Email: jim.mead@walsworth.com
Website: www.walsworth.com

Book Printing Capabilities: Web Offset, Sheetfed Offset, Digital Toner
Binding Types: PUR, Notchbound Adhesive, Layflat Adhesive, Smyth Sewn, Spiral Binding, Case Bound—Flat Backed, Case Bound—Round Backed, Case Bound—Headbands, Case Bound—End Sheets, One-Piece Material Casemaking, Three-Piece Casemaking
Finishing Capabilities: Ribbons, Round Corner, Folded Flaps
Environmental Certification: Paper Related (FSC, SFI, EPFC)
Other Certifications and Memberships: PIA Member

Wert Bookbinding
9975 Allentown Road
Grantville, PA 17028
800.344.9378
Email: gary@wertbookbinding.com
Website: www.wertbookbinding.com

Book Printing Capabilities: Digital Toner, Print-on-Demand (POD)
Binding Types: PUR, Notchbound Adhesive, Layflat Adhesive, Smyth Sewn, Side Sewn, Case Bound—Flat Backed, Case Bound—Round Backed, Case Bound—Headbands, Case Bound—End Sheets, Printed Paper Casemaking, One-Piece Material Casemaking, Three-Piece Casemaking
Cover Finishing: Foil Stamping, Film Lamination
Finishing Capabilities: Ribbons, Round Corner, Folded Flaps
Industry Specifications: MSST (Textbooks), Library Binding, Edition Binding
Environmental Certification: Paper Related (FSC, SFI, EPFC), Soy Based Ink
Other Certifications and Memberships: Certified Library Binder

Worzalla, Inc.
3535 Jefferson Street
Stevens Point, WI 54481
715.344.9600
Email: jfetherston@worzalla.com
Website: www.worzalla.com

Book Printing Capabilities: Web Offset, Sheetfed Offset
Binding Types: PUR, Notchbound Adhesive, Layflat Adhesive, Smyth Sewn, Side Sewn, Case Bound—Flat Backed, Case Bound—Round Backed, Case Bound—Headbands, Case Bound—End Sheets, Printed Paper Casemaking, One-Piece Material Casemaking, Three-Piece Casemaking

Cover Finishing: Foil Stamping, Embossing, Spot UV, Film Lamination, Specialty (Raised, Glitter, Gritty Matte, etc)

Finishing Capabilities: Ribbons, Round Corner, Rough Front, Folded Flaps, Guild Edge Finishing

Industry Specifications: MSST (Textbooks), Library Binding, Edition Binding

Environmental Certification: Paper Related (FSC, SFI, EPFC), Soy Based Ink

Other Certifications and Memberships: ISO Certified, PIA Member

BOOK PRODUCERS ARE CREATIVE PLAYERS

BY RICHARD ROTHSCHILD

Book producers are some of the most valuable players on the creative side of the publishing industry today. They have earned this distinction for their mastery of one type of book in particular—namely, the "complicated" book, which is just about any book that involves more than a straightforward, single-author text. Complicated books include all manner of highly illustrated, elaborately designed, or multiauthored titles, such as how-to books, coffee table books, reference books, textbooks, cookbooks, and more. Quietly, these books make up the backbone of the publishing business.

Creating complicated books is a labor-intensive craft that often involves teams of writers, editors, designers, illustrators, photographers, researchers, and other specialized talent whose separate contributions must be integrated into a seamless whole. Sometimes it means executing a highly elaborate design, or even incorporating nonprint materials such as CDs, juggling balls, or other merchandise into a final product. Often it means working closely with an outside organization to shape a custom, one-of-a-kind title for a special event. Book producers make it their business to devote the focused time, energy, and attention necessary to bring these projects to fruition.

But the book producer's mastery of complicated books goes well beyond mere execution. Book producers are visionary as well, conceiving and developing the books that they create. They are able to pull together the necessary ingredients to see these visions through. Books created by producers—"packaged books"—cover all the essential subjects: art, medicine, cooking, history, parenting, gardening, sports, popular culture, self-help, and more. They cover the spectrum of publishing markets, including trade, mass market, educational, juvenile, professional, and reference. And every year some of the most impressive and lucrative titles on the market are packaged books.

Book producers bring their products to market through deals with book publishers. For the most part, producers make these deals based on proposals they have developed and written themselves, selling the publication rights to a book before starting work. This sale, in turn, finances the book's creation.

Depending on the particular arrangement, the book packager may deliver to the publisher anything from an edited manuscript to printer-ready files to finished books—and the publisher takes the project from there. Marketing and distribution are virtually always the publisher's responsibilities.

WHY PUBLISHERS USE PACKAGERS

Book packagers can expand a publisher's list with titles they can't get anywhere else—books or projects that literary agents cannot offer to publishers and that publishers themselves generally cannot execute in-house. And yet without such complicated books, publishers' lists would be missing many remarkable—and lucrative—titles.

Packaged books generally make their way onto publishers' lists in one of two ways:

- Editors may acquire original submissions from packagers. Like agents, packagers routinely submit book proposals to publishers. As a rule, these constitute some of the smartest ideas around. For this reason, it makes sense to get on a packager's submission list.
- Editors may hire packagers to develop and execute in-house ideas. Packagers are quite willing to help shape editors' ideas into viable projects. Teaming up with a packager is often the only way editors can transform solid in-house ideas into actual books. It's also an excellent way for publishers to exploit their own corporate brands. Book packagers fill many different niches. Each company has its own areas of expertise and working style.

The professional, comprehensive approach of book packagers ensures that these complicated projects will be completed in a timely and efficient manner. We invite you to peruse the American Book Producers Association Member Directory (https://abpaonline.org/find-book-producer/) to get a fuller picture of who we are, what we do, and the many ways we can work with the publishing community.

*

Richard Rothschild is president of the American Book Producers Association. The ABPA was founded in 1980 as the trade association for independent book producers, also called packagers, in the United States and Canada. Members of this rapidly growing profession produce, from concept through bound books, a wide variety of titles for publishers, nonprofits, corporations, and others.

ABPA BOOK PRODUCERS

The Book Shop, Ltd.
7 Peter Cooper Road #7G, New York, NY 10010
Nancy Christensen Hall, President
tel: 917.388.2493
fax: 917.534.1304
nancy@thebookshopltd.com
www.thebookshopltd.com
member since: 2008

The Book Shop, a full-service book producer founded in 2008, produces illustrated adult nonfiction titles, as well as juvenile educational books, kits, and innovative novelty formats.

Subjects of special interest include fashion, art, food and wine, science, culture, education, body decorating, and travel, as well as how-to books on a wide variety of different crafts and origami themes.

Bright Futures Press
911 Reedy Creek Road, Cary, NC 27513
Diane Lindsey Reeves, Publisher
tel: 919.637.0194
dreeves@brightfuturespress.com | www.brightfuturespress.com
member since: 2020

Author and book producer Diane Lindsey Reeves has spent many years and lots of ink turning ideas into creative multi-title book series that target specific age and grade levels, meet common core learning standards, and help kids learn and grow. Most recently, her company, Bright Futures Press, collaborated with Cherry Lake Publishing to respond to the growing national trend of early career exploration by creating and producing books that help students figure out what they want to be when they grow up. This middle grade career exploration collection features 61 titles over six distinct, interactive series that include:
- *Choose a Career Adventure* (8 titles)
- *Emerging Tech Careers* (8 titles)
- *Find Your Future in STEAM* (5 titles)

- *Get a Job* (6 titles)
- *Soft Skills Sleuths* (8 titles)
- *World of Work* (16 titles)

Bright Futures Press has also worked with publishers that include Films for the Humanities, Infobase Publishing, Prentice Hall, Sourcebooks, and Zondervan. Current interests include creative nonfiction, middle grade fiction with nonfiction twists, and projects with digital components.

Connected Dots Media LLC
57 Post Street #913, San Francisco, CA 94104
Leslie Jonah
tel: 415.235.9360
leslie@connecteddotsmedia.com | www.connecteddotsmedia.com
member since: 2013

Connected Dots Media specializes in full-color illustrated books with expertise in cooking, art, design, gardening, lifestyle, and children's media. Services include concept and editorial development, art direction, and design to finished books. We delight in working with publishers and corporate clients to create content-rich, visually stunning books.

UPCOMING AND PUBLISHED TITLES:
Amazing Edible (Mostly) Experiments (Quarry); *Bee & Me* (Accord); *Everyone Loves New York* and *Everyone Loves Paris* (TeNeues); *Feed Your People* (PowerHouse); *Floret Cut-Flower Garden Book.* (Chronicle Books); *The Flower Workshop* (Ten Speed Press); *The Joy of Watercolor* (Running Press); *Love Found* (Chronicle Books); *Meaningful Arrangements* (Chronicle Books); *The Model Bakery Cookbook* (Chronicle Books); and *The Small Pleasures of Paris* (Chronicle Books).

Connections for Kids, LLC
Burnt Hills, NY 12027
Heather E. Schwartz
tel: 518.429.5168
heather@connections-for-kids.com | www.connections-for-kids.com
member since: 2019

Connections for Kids was founded in 2016 to produce Connections, a magazine-style publication focused on STEAM subjects for students in grades 3–5 in New York's

Capital Region. The company's growth into book packaging takes advantage of founder Heather E. Schwartz's background working with educational publishers including Scholastic, Capstone Press, Lerner Publishing Group, Lucent Books, and Teacher Created Materials. Authoring credits include licensed titles for Disney, Sesame Street, Time for Kids, and the Smithsonian, as well as content production for National Geographic Kids, Discovery Girls, Kids Get Arthritis, Too (the Arthritis Foundation), and NASA. Services include (but are not limited to) concept and editorial development, authoring, editing, hi-lo, leveling, art direction, project management, and quality control.

Facts That Matter, Inc.
N2826 Wildwood Dr., Lake Geneva, WI 53147
Les Krantz, Principal
tel: 262.348.0883
Les.krantz@factsthatmatter.com | www.factsthatmatter.com
member since: 2020

For 30 years we have been creating and producing trailblazing nonfiction books for major English-language publishers in the U.S. and the U.K. They comprise over 50 large to medium-size publishing houses, our "co-publishers." Among them are Simon and Schuster, HarperCollins, Macmillan/St. Martins, Hachette, Penguin Random House, and others.

For some books, we and our co-publishers bring in yet another partner, a leading organization that's known for its authority on a particular subject. Recent ones include the Associated Press, the Smithsonian, and the BBC. These and many other important organizations put their imprint on a selective group of our titles, allowing our company and our co-publishers to distribute and market leading books in many subject areas.

Focus Strategic Communications, Inc.
15 Hunter Way, Brantford, Ontario, Canada N3T 6S3
Adrianna Edwards, Ron Edwards, Directors
tel: 519.756.3265
aedwards@focussc.com; redwards@focussc.com | www.focussc.com
member since: 2002

Established in 1988, Focus Strategic Communications Inc. is a North American full-service book packaging firm, providing complete book production development and production, from original concept to finished product, both print and digital.

Focus is innovative in assembling tailored and creative teams of experts to develop and produce superior products, on time and on budget. We provide hands-on, personal service designed especially for your needs. When you hire us, you get the full and special attention of the principals. Our track record, impeccable reputation, and over three decades of experience speak for themselves. Also, we're really nice!

Focus specializes in children's nonfiction books for the trade, library, and classroom markets, as well as educational materials such as K–12 classroom books and teacher resources. Our curriculum experts guide clients in the best approaches to the CCSS, NGSS, and other standards.

Focus attends and exhibits at numerous tradeshows in North America and around the world—from London to Frankfurt, from Cape Town to Beijing.

GGP Publishing, Inc.

PO Box 635, Larchmont, NY 10538
Generosa Gina Protano, President/Owner
tel: 914.834.8896
GGProtano@GGPPublishing.com | www.GGPPublishing.com
member since: 2020

GGP Publishing, Inc., is a full-service development house or packager firm founded in 1991. We offer services from concept to finished electronic files/bound books to online distribution or for any one step of this publishing process. We specialize in educational publishing from K–12 to college/university to adult education. We have a niche in the writing, development, editing, and production up to finished electronic files/bound books of textbooks and trade books for the study of foreign languages such as French, German, Italian, Latin, Portuguese, and Spanish. We also translate complete/partial programs or cluster of books from English into any of these languages or from any of these languages into English, edit the translation for publication, and set the edited translation into book form up to finished electronic files/bound books.

Besides our specialization in educational publishing, we also attend to the development, editing, art/design, and production of different genres within the trade-book market both for publishing houses as well as individuals who wish to self-publish. We have produced novels, memoirs, and books in the field of religion, psychology, and culinary arts among others. We have a special interest in memoirs, and are looking to publish many more of them!

SELECT TITLES

The Family Jewels (GGP Publishing, 2018); *Practical Spanish Grammar: A Self-Teaching*

Guide, Self-Teaching Guide Series (John Wiley, 1997) & *Advanced Spanish Grammar: A Self-Teaching Guide, Self-Teaching Guide Series* (John Wiley, 1997); *You Already Know Italian* (McGraw-Hill, 2006) & *Spanish in Plain English* (McGraw-Hill, 2009); *Sentieri: Attraverso l'Italia Contemporanea, PE & TE* (Vista Higher Learning, 2011) & *Juntos: Uno, PE & TE* (Pearson Prentice Hall, 1997); *Elements of Literature/Spanish Resources, Grades 6–12* (Holt, Rinehart & Winston, 2001)

Girl Friday Productions

231 Summit Ave. E, Seattle, WA 98102
Kristin Mehus-Roe, Director of Publishing Partnerships
tel: 206.524.4257
kristin@girlfridayproductions.com | www.girlfridayproductions.com
member since: 2016

At Girl Friday, we do things a little differently. We build around a core in-house team of editorial professionals who, collectively, have worked on nearly every type of book in the industry. We stay nimble through an international network of vetted design and editorial freelancers with expertise in specialty genres. Every book we produce is led by a staff specialist who assembles the perfect team for that individual title. It's a model that allows for greater flexibility, unsurpassed quality, and total creative control.

OUR SERVICES:

Because of our unique model, we're able to develop a project from concept to bound books or take on discrete parts of the production process. Our current publishing partners engage Girl Friday in a variety of ways: some ask us to take full ownership of their titles, including developmental editing and author management, and others prefer that we white label their production services.

OUR TEAM:

We don't just "manage" projects; our traditionally trained production editors get inside their books. Our editorial, design, and photo research teams have worked with licensors including CBS Paramount, Lucasfilm, and the Audrey Hepburn Children's Fund, and with deluxe formats.

OUR WORK:

Since 2006, we have worked with clients to create beautiful books that tell compelling stories. Anything but niche, we are as comfortable with self-help and sci-fi as we are with cookbooks and children's. Whether you need outside "back office" support or a traditional book producer, GFP provides the relationship and quality you're looking for through a modern service model.

Green Typewriter Creative

Kelli Chipponeri, Founder & Creative Director

tel: 646.483.8891

kelli@greentypewritercreative.com | www.greentypewritercreative.com

member since: 2021

Green Typewriter Creative specializes in the ABCs of storytelling: Acquisition Development, Book Making, and Content Creation. Established in 2018 in San Francisco, GTC is a West Coast, full-service book producer specializing in children's physical and digital content. Titles produced include: *Dots & Spots* (Walter Foster Jr., 2020); *Sam & Sofia's Scooter Stories* (Little Passports, 2020); *The Kids on the Bus* (Chronicle Books, 2020); *Tiny T. Rex and the Very Dark, Dark* (Chronicle Books, 2020); *Tiny T. Rex and the Impossible Hug* (Chronicle Books, 2019).

Indelible Editions

62 Summit Street, Ground Floor Brooklyn, NY 11231

Dinah Dunn, Principal

tel: 917.414.7449

Dinah@IndelibleEditions.com | www.IndelibleEditions.com

member since: 2020

Established in 2019, Indelible Editions produces compelling, illustrated nonfiction for children and adults, including ancillary such as calendars, journals, and planners.

SELECTED TITLES:

Mental Floss's Amazing Facts Calendar (Andrews McMeel, 2020); *Midlife, No Crisis* (Indelible Editions, 2021); *The Curious Kid's Guide to the Awesome 50 States* (Shelter Harbor Press, 2021); *The Curious Reader: A Literary Miscellany of Novels and Novelists* (Weldon Owen International, 2021); *CheeseSexDeath presents The Cheese Bible: Scriptures for Blessing Your Body with Cheesus* (Abrams Books, 2021)

Jan Hartman Books

PO Box 319, 21 Back Road, Brooksville, ME 04617

Jan Hartman, Principal

tel: 202.338.5535

jan@janhartmanbooks.com | www.janhartmanbooks.com

member since: 2020

Jan Hartman Books is an independent book editor and packager, creating original and branded content with authors, organizations, and publishers. Offering comprehensive editorial, illustration, and project management services, Jan has over 30 years' experience in book publishing across more than 200 titles. She is known in the industry for recognizing trends and publishing creative and vibrant books of unsurpassed beauty and design. Jan's mission is founded in making books of merit, value, and distinction.

If you are an author, Jan works with you to develop your ideas, create a distinctive package, and conceive works that tell compelling stories. If you are a publisher, she works with you the same way you do an independent editor, literary agent, or packager. If you are a company or institution, Jan develops a strategic publishing plan that advances your distinct story to accomplish your goals.

As Princeton Architectural Press' program director of the acclaimed Campus Guide series of North America's leading colleges, universities, and academies, Jan partnered with schools from Yale and Princeton to Amherst and Williams, UVA, Penn, MIT, Stanford, and others. She established publishing partnerships with nonprofits such as the Beverly Willis Architecture Foundation, Beatrix Farrand Society, and The Historic New Orleans Collection.

SELECTED TITLES:

Revolutionizing Organic Farming in the 21st Century (Downeast Books and MOFGA, 2021); *The Groundbreakers: Women Who Changed Architecture* (Princeton Architectural Press, 2021); *The Official Guide to the Houses of Downton Abbey* (Princeton Architectural Press, 2022); *The Conservatory: Gardens Under Glass* (Princeton Architectural Press, 2020); *Visualizing Nature: Essays on Truth, Beauty and Life* (Princeton Architectural Press, 2021).

Jenkins Group, Inc.

1129 Woodmere Ave., Suite B, Traverse City, MI 49686
Jerrold R. Jenkins
tel: 231.883.5365
fax: 231.933.0448
jrj@bookpublishing.com | www.jenkinsgroupinc.com
member since: 2018

Jenkins Group specializes in the publishing of high-quality books for first-time and veteran authors, corporations, and organizations worldwide. Our custom solutions fit a variety of budgets and publishing timelines. We work in all genres of book publishing including business, fiction, nonfiction, children's, and corporate anniversary, among others.

Don't know where to start? We pride ourselves on being able to provide every book-publishing service you could need. From ghostwriting, manuscript development, editing, illustration, cover design and proofreading, to printing, binding, shipping and e-book conversion and audiobook production, our comprehensive menu of services will make sure you have all of the expert knowledge you need to make your book a success.

Since 1988, the publishing professionals of Jenkins Group have been focused on just one goal: to make your vision, our mission.

Jennifer Barry Design

229 Tamalpais Rd., Fairfax, CA 94930
Jennifer Barry, Principal
tel: 415.342.0337
jbarry@jenniferbarrydesign.com | www.jenniferbarrydesign.com
member since: 2020

Jennifer Barry Design produces distinctive illustrated books and graphic design for publishing and corporate clients. A former publisher and creative director for HarperCollins in San Francisco, principal Jennifer Barry brings a rare combination of visual, editorial, and marketing creativity to her wide-ranging work. With more than 30 years in the design and publishing worlds, Jennifer Barry has designed and art directed hundreds of illustrated books on subjects ranging from food and photography to nature and winemaking. Working collaboratively with writers, editors, photographers, designers, and stylists, Jennifer Barry Design creates unique and award-winning books, managing projects from conception to completion.

SELECTED TITLES:

Gather: Casual Cooking from Wine Country Gardens (Jennifer Barry Design Books, LLC, 2021); *Tupper Ansel Blake: Forty Years of Wildlife Photography and Conservation* (Marsh Island Press, 2020); *Pecans: Recipes & History of an American Nut* (Rizzoli, 2019); *Wine Country Table* (Rizzoli, 2019); *Stone Edge Farm Kitchen Larder Cookbook* (Rizzoli, 2019); *Silver Oak Cookbook* (Rizzoli, 2016); *Savoring Simi: Since 1876* (Simi Winery, 2016); *Margrit Mondavi's Vignettes* (Robert Mondavi Winery, 2015); *Bee Happy!—Wit and Wisdom for a Happy Life* (Andrews McMeel, 2014); *Almonds: Recipes, History, Culture* (Gibbs Smith, 2014); *Down to Earth: A Seasonal Tour of Sustainable Winegrowing in California* (Wine Institute, 2014); *Carla's Comfort Foods* (Atria Books, 2014); *Stone Edge Farm Cookbook* (Stone Edge Farm Winery, 2013)

Literary Productions

631 North Stephanie Street, Suite 700, Henderson, NV 89014

Kirk Kazanjian, President and Editorial Director

tel: 213-255-5540

kirk@literaryproductions.com | www.literaryproductions.com

member since: 2021

Literary Productions has been described as a super literary agency, mega-author incubator, first-rate publicity and marketing firm, multimedia creator and mammoth idea factory, all combined into one company.

Working closely with our expert authors—including celebrities, business executives, medical professionals, master chefs, leading brands and some of the world's top social media influencers—Literary Productions develops popular nonfiction books in such categories as business, personal finance, real estate, politics, self-help, history, food, health, fitness, religion, travel, sports, biographies, parenting, pets, popular reference, cookbooks, children's, young adult and more.

We develop all of our book concepts in-house and partner with carefully-selected authors to bring them to life. We then find the best publishers around the world to print and distribute our books—often in multiple languages—and oversee the entire development process.

We are intimately involved in all aspects of making each book a success—from crafting marketing plans to leading omnichannel publicity efforts in order to ensure that every title generates maximum attention and sales, both at the launch and for years to come. We also turn some of our titles into TV shows and ancillary products around the world.

Literary Productions is led by our Founder, President and Editorial Director, Kirk Kazanjian. Kirk has personally written dozens of bestselling books and is also an experienced literary agent and marketing expert. In addition, Literary Productions has a team of editors, ghostwriters, designers and foreign/subsidiary rights agents working to develop and market our books worldwide.

SELECTED TITLES:

Exceeding Customer Expectations (Crown Books); *The Making of Dr. Phil* (Wiley); *The Bear Necessities of Business* (Wiley); *Driving Loyalty* (Crown Books); *The Online Millionaire* (Wiley); *Countdown to Your Perfect Wedding* (Macmillan)

MTM Publishing

435 West 23rd Street, #8C, New York, NY 10011

Valerie Tomaselli, President

tel: 212.242.6930

vtomaselli@mtmpublishing.com | www.mtmpublishing.com

member since: 2003

MTM Publishing produces high-quality books for trade, library, and educational publishers and for individuals, organizations, and institutions. We are the exclusive publishing rep for the Baseball Hall of Fame, helping them to develop books and placing them with publishing companies in all markets. Our works have garnered over twenty citations, including:

- VOYA, Perfect Ten List 2016, *Major Nations in a Global World* (2015)
- NCSS/Children's Book Council Notable Social Studies Trade Book for Young People, *Massacre of the Miners* (2015)
- Choice Outstanding Academic Title, *The Princeton Companion to Atlantic History* (2014)
- ALA's Dartmouth Medal, honorable mention, *Encyclopedia of Journalism* (2008)

SELECTED TITLES:
CHILDREN'S AND YA:
Know Your Food nonfiction series (Mason Crest, 2018); *Drug Addiction and Recovery* nonfiction series (Mason Crest, 2017); *Horrors of History* narrative fiction series (Charlesbridge Publishing, 2012–2015)

CULTURE, ART, AND DESIGN:
Women in the Literary Landscape: A Centennial Publication of the WNBA (C&R Press, 2018), *Grounds For Sculpture: A Living Legacy* (The Sculpture Foundation, 2013), *Baseball: 100 Classic Moments in the History of the Game* (DK, 2000)

HISTORY AND POLITICS:
The Making of the Modern World nonfiction series (Mason Crest, 2017); *The Princeton Companion to Atlantic History* (Princeton University Press, 2015); *Debates on U.S. Health Care* (Sage Publications, 2012)

Oomf, Inc.
420 West 24th Street, New York, NY 10011

Mark Shulman, Director

tel: 212.807.1385

Mark@Oomf.com | www.Oomf.com

member since: 2002

Oomf, Inc. is the author, designer, and packager of many original children's books. We create quality nonfiction, picture books, preschool, educational, novelty, activity, merchandise, and licensed titles for a whole lot of leading publishers. We produce adult humor, trivia, and gift titles as well.

There is no single look or style at Oomf, Inc. Generally our books come from original concepts and inspirations, though we also enjoy developing or co-developing a publisher's new book ideas. We can also quickly provide concepts and text, which publishers develop in-house. (Our background in advertising and publishing helps us pursue concepts that sell.)

Oomf, Inc. titles are known for their original themes, superior art, quality writing and design, intelligence and/or humor, and a few unique twists. There is almost always an educational element, and it is almost always hidden away where our readers won't realize. Please inquire about our many unpublished concepts. We prefer they be published.

OUR SKILLS & SERVICES:

We provide original, complete books in any genre.
We create original books for any existing series.
We develop any publisher's new concepts.
We work with publishers to create new concepts.
We deliver finished manuscripts.
We rewrite or re-work works in progress—text, art, concept—or ghostwrite whole books.
We work closely with literacy specialists for just-right content at any reading level.
We provide creative direction and editorial services.
We help promote, market, and otherwise add value after the book is complete.
. . . which is why we have so many satisfied publishing partners.

Peachtree Publishing Services, LLC

259 Highway 74 N, Suite 4, Peachtree City, GA 30269
Christopher Hudson, President
tel: 770.631.9073
chris@peachtreeeditorial.com | www.peachtreepublishingservices.com
member since: 2020

Peachtree Publishing Services focuses on titles developed for the faith-based and Christian market. We offer a full suite of publishing services and manage complex projects for the world's leading Christian book publishers.

SELECTED TITLES:

99 World-Changing People Influenced by the Bible (Museum of the Bible, 2018); *That's So Weird! 101 Fun and Fascinating People in the Bible* (Museum of the Bible, 2018); *KJV Promise Study Bible* (Barbour Publishing, 2019); *KJV Study Bible Atlas Edition* (Barbour Publishing, 2020); *The Book of Esther: Bible Word Search* (TheBiblePeople, 2020); *Mark: Hidden Bible Pictures Activity Book* (TheBiblePeople, 2020); *Jesus Every Day Devotional Guides by Candace Cameron Bure* (DaySpring, 2020); *David Jeremiah Bible Studies* (Thomas Nelson, 2020)

Pinafore Press

109 East 35th Street, Savannah, GA 31401
Janice Shay, Principal
tel: 912.547.5212
janices434@icloud.com | www.pinaforepress.com
member since: 2020

I'm a book packager specializing in illustrated books, children's books, and memoirs. I handle all production up to the point of printing.

SELECTED TITLES:

The Twisted Soul Cookbook: Modern Soul Food with Global Flavors (Rizzoli, March 2021); *Italy Is My Boyfriend: A Memoir* (Post Hill Press, 2020); *Old Southern Cookery* (Globe Pequot, 2020); *California Cooking & Southern Style* (Skyhorse, 2020); *Welcome to Buttermilk Kitchen* (Gibbs-Smith, 2020); *Cocktail Italiano* (Skyhorse, 2019); *Sallie Ann Robinson's Kitchen* (University of Florida Press, 2019)

Plan B Book Packagers

32 Tuliptree Road, Thorold, Ontario, Canada L2V 0A6
Rosie Gowsell Pattison, Creative Director
tel: 289.362.2811
rosie@planbbookpackagers.com
www.planbbookpackagers.com
member since: 2009

Plan B Book Packagers is a trusted producer of engaging and vibrant books. We work closely with publishing clients, institutions, and nonprofits to create quality products from concept development to finished books. Our specialty is reference, edu-trade, and trade nonfiction for the child and adult market, and we are known for our research, design, and attention to detail. Plan B understands the demands of contemporary publishing schedules and workflows. We also provide part-work services including design, editorial, production, photo research, and fact checking.

Print Matters Productions Inc.

23 Waverly Place, 6B New York, NY 10003
Richard Rothschild
tel: 917.620.9440
Richard@PrintMattersInc.com | www.PrintMattersInc.com
member since: 2004

Print Matters is an independent book producer specializing in illustrated nonfiction. We create books, e-books, and online content for publishers, corporations, nonprofits, and individuals. Making complex topics accessible and inviting is our forte, and we love working with clients to develop concepts.

Print Matters combines creative bookmaking with cutting-edge technology, offering a full menu of writing, development, editing, project management, design, manufacturing, and distribution solutions. We are happy to completely produce a book from proposal through printer-ready files or provide a la carte services.

As a boutique firm, we tailor our services to the content, schedule, and budget needs of each project. We excel at the personal touch, providing clear and consistent communication throughout the process. We also bring to the table abundant experience turning around projects in need of TLC.

SUBJECTS:

- media tie-ins
- performing arts
- design and visual arts
- health and fitness
- cooking and food
- gay and lesbian
- history
- science and technology

SELECT TITLES:

Organic: Farmers and Chefs of the Hudson Valley (powerHouse Books); *American Inventors: A History of Genius* (Time-Life Books); *Social Progress and Sustainability*, 10 volumes (Mason Crest); *The Pure Joy of Monastery Cooking* (Countryman Press); *L.L. Bean Ultimate Book of Fly Fishing* (The Lyons Press); *Color Your Life: How to Design*

Your Home with Colors From the Heart (St. Martin's Press); *Top Careers in Two Years*, 11 volumes (Ferguson Publishing); *The How Not to Die Cookbook* (Flatiron Books)

ROBIE LLC

1172 Park Avenue, 8C, New York, NY 10128
Robie Rogge, President
tel: 212.427.5328
Robie.nyc@gmail.com | www.Robieproducts.com
member since: 2013

ROBIE LLC is a company established in 2012 to create, refresh, and extend products for clients in the United States and England. ROBIE LLC sells concepts, complete manuscripts, or finished designs to publishers and to novelty companies for their production and sales distribution. Clients include Clarkson Potter, Chronicle, Abrams, Laurence King, Little Simon, Museum of Modern Art, Race Point, C & T Publishing, Thames & Hudson, Kikkerland, Fred and Friends, and NPW.

Among ROBIE's successes is a series started with *Do One Thing Every Day That Scares You*, which now includes four other published titles, with over 600,000 copies in print. Four more books are scheduled for the series. Novelties include a book that forms a beehive when opened and has two attached bees, a one-minute diary with a sand-timer, and a book with prompts to practice good deeds, with heart-of-gold stickers for completion.

Rock Scissors Paper Press

432 John Joy Road, Woodstock, NY 12498
Bill Luckey
tel: 212.861.1560
wluckey@aol.com | www.rockscissorspaperpress.com
member since: 2017

Rock Scissors Paper Press is a creative book packager serving the trade book industry. We fuse innovative concepts, inspired writing, and talented graphic illustration as we develop books that enliven visual and tactile sensibilities. Our titles are both juvenile and adult in content, and both traditional and digital in format.

SELECTED TITLES:
JUVENILE:
Labs Love Leaping Long Linguini; Through the Doggy Door; You Need a Haircut

Scout Books & Media

Peter Stuyvesant Station, Post Office Box 365, New York, NY 10009
Susan Knopf
tel: 646.535.4741
fax: 646.478.9279
susan@scoutbooksandmedia.com | www.scoutbooksandmedia.com
member since: 2011

Scout Books & Media is an independent book packager, brand developer, and publishing consultant. Our creative commitment is to unite accomplished authors; skillful and inspired illustrators; experts in research, photo curation, and fact-checking; talented art direction and design; successful sales and marketing professionals; and high-quality and efficient manufacturing solutions.

WE SPECIALIZE IN:

Children's fiction, nonfiction, and reference
Chapter books, readers, informational books, and tween pop culture
Board books and book-plus/novelties
All categories, including: animals, nature, science, mysteries, and space
Adult nonfiction
Memoirs, gift and impulse, journals, cooking, science, space, and politics

WE PARTNER WITH:

Publishers of all kinds, including trade, mass, clubs, and educational
Individuals, organizations, and brands

OUR CLIENTS INCLUDE:

Time Inc. Books, Scholastic, Quarto, Bearport Publishing, Rowman & Littlefield, Kids Can Press, Barnes & Noble

We can bring you original ideas or take your ideas and bring them to life. No project is too big or too small, and no schedule is too tight. Let's team up!
SCOUT BOOKS & MEDIA—GOOD BOOKS, MADE WELL.

Shelter Harbor Press

603 West 115th Street, Suite 163, New York, NY 10025
Jeanette Limondjian
tel: 212.864.0427
fax: 212.316.6496

jeanette@shelterharborpress.com | www.shelterharborpress.com
member since: 2013

Shelter Harbor Press, established in 2012, is a growing specialty packager and small publisher, specializing in high-quality trade reference books, new age packs and gifts, and novelty titles suitable for the international market. Successful titles include the Ponderables series: *Mathematics, The Elements, Physics, Philosophy, Engineering, Biology,* and *Psychology.* In 2019, two new titles will be added to the series: *Earth Sciences* and *Astronomy.*

Shelter Harbor Press is dedicated to publishing STEM titles and introduced a new Math series entitled Inside Mathematics in 2017, starting with the publication of *Numbers: How Counting Changed the World* and *Algebra to Calculus: Unlocking Math's Amazing Powers.* In 2019, a third title will be published called: *Geometry: Understanding Shapes and Sizes.*

Shoreline Publishing Group

125 Santa Rosa Place, Santa Barbara, CA 93109
Jim Buckley, President/Editorial Director
tel: 805.564.1004
jbuckley@shorelinepublishing.com | www.shorelinepublishing.com
member since: 2001

So here's the thing.

You're looking for a book producer (okay . . . "packager") who can deliver your product on time and on budget, and can do so with style, verve, and good humor.

You're looking for a company that can handle just about any size project (and probably has . . . we've made more than 500 books and we've been doing this for almost 20 years).

You're looking to work with people who understand every part of the process, from soup to nuts and everything in between. (We write, we edit, we design, we do photo research, we print: It's like a menu, just pick what you need.)

You're looking, to be perfectly frank, for us. (And make sure to read to the end to find our special ABPA Directory offer!)

Shoreline Publishing Group has worked with dozens of major national publishers to create everything from board books to reader series, from sticker books to coffee table books. We've worked with Scholastic, DK, Reader's Digest, Penguin, Time Inc., National Geographic Kids, and many more publishers.

Sports is certainly our specialty. We've worked with publishers to create dozens of books with Major League Baseball, the National Football League, and Major League Soccer, along with many non-licensed sports titles.

We're not all about sports, though. As a nonfiction illustrated children's book packager, we have produced books on history, science, geography, animals, robots, and something called *The World's Biggest Everything*, which really covered it all.

We love to talk about new projects (special ABPA Directory offer: Free Brainstorming!!) Drop us a line. We'd love to meet you.

Spooky Cheetah Press

33 Glendale Drive, Stamford, CT 06906
Stephanie Fitzgerald
tel: 203.357.1160
stephanie@spookycheetah.com | www.spookycheetah.com
member since: 2002
Spooky Cheetah Press is a full-service book-producing company specializing in high-quality illustrated books and continuity series in a wide range of subject areas.

Founded in 1998, Spooky Cheetah Press has built a reputation for bringing the highest standards of quality, excellence, and innovation to published product development. From shapes and colors to motorcycles and Muppets, Spooky Cheetah's catalog features a wide array of nonfiction topics in a broad range of formats.

Stoney End LLC

6103 Stoney Hill Road, New Hope, PA
Christopher Navratil
tel: 415.378.3548
cknavratil@gmail.com
member since: 2019

Publishing consultant and book producer, focusing primarily on illustrated gift, lifestyle, pop culture, and children's activity books, guided journals, book-plus kits.

SELECTED TITLES:

Secrets of Modern Calligraphy (Bluestreak Books, 2018); *A Little Taste of Cape Cod: Recipes for Classic Dishes* (Bluestreak Books, 2017); *Foraged Art* (Bluestreak Books, 2018); *Career Dreams: An Essential Workbook for Finding Your Passion and Purpose* (Bluestreak Books, 2018); *Ru Paul's Drag Race Paper Doll Book* (Bluestreak Books, 2017); *The Not So Subtle Art of Being a Fat Girl* (Bluestreak Books, 2017)

Tandem Books Inc.

480 6th Ave #205, New York, NY 10011
Ashley Prine, Creative Director/Co-founder
tel: 718.908.1405
ashley@tandem-books.com |
www.tandem-books.com
member since: 2020

Tandem Books provides a unique cross-section of creativity and practicality to publishers across the country. We're a services team that acts a bit like a book packager and a bit like an extension of your own in-house team. We can help you get books to the printer, whether they're from one of our proposals or a project you already have on your list.

SELECTED TITLES:

Friendsgiving (Running Press / Hachette Book Group, 2020); *Beautiful Salads* (Quarto Publishing Group, 2020); *In Focus: Sacred Geometry* (Quarto Publishing Group, 2020); *Crayola: Create It Yourself* (Black Dog & Leventhal / Hachette Book Group, 2020); *Knit a Hat* (Abrams, 2020); *History Channel: The Civil War* (Meredith, 2020); *Fargo* (Little Brown / Hachette Book Group, 2019); *History Channel: The American Mafia* (Meredith, 2019); *In Focus: Numerology* (Quarto Publishing Group, 2019); *All You Need Is Love . . . and Pets* (Sterling Publishing, 2019); *The Burn Cookbook* (Grand Central & Lifestyle / Hachette Book Group, 2018); *In Focus: Palmistry* (Quarto Publishing Group, 2018); *Unicorn Your Life* (Sterling Publishing, 2018); *History Channel: The Search for Alien Life* (Time Inc., 2018); *Make Every Day Beautiful* (Sterling Publishing, 2018); *Genius Jokes* (Quarto Publishing Group, 2018); *101 Do-It-Yourself FaceMasks* (Countryman / W.W. Norton and Company, 2017); *The New York Times Book of Crime* (Sterling, 2017); *Unsinkable: The History of the Boston Whaler* (Quarto Publishing Group, 2017); *You Will Never Have This Day Again* (Sterling Publishing, 2017); *A to Z for Your V* (Quarto Publishing Group, 2017)

Terri Wright Design

120 West Los Olivos Street, Santa Barbara, CA 93105
Terri Wright, Designer/Producer/Consultant
tel: 805-729-3549
hello@terriwright.com | www.terriwright.com
member since: 2020

Terri Wright is a book designer and content producer with over 30 years of experience and hundreds of titles to her credit. From children's books, coffee table books, fine special and limited editions, to complex educational textbooks, manuals, directories, and catalogs, Terri Wright Design brings concepts to life and delivers outstandingly beautiful, award-winning products.

In today's world of changing technology, Terri Wright Design collaborates extensively with experts in media, sound, musical composition, songwriting, and animation. Utilizing collaboration and innovation, this design model adds dimension beyond the printed page, resulting in quality e-books, audiobooks, and interactive 21st-century models.

Managing projects from concept to completion, Terri Wright Design creates cutting edge visual experiences where words, photographs, illustrations, and media, whether printed on paper or viewed on a device, allow publishers, independent authors, artists, institutions, museums, and other organizations the freedom to create integral emotional and timeless works in any medium.

SELECTED TITLES:

Eagle vs Bear: Adventures of a Child Cub (EvB Media); *The Wild Herd: A Vanishing American Treasure* (Val de Grace Books); *Medical Animation & Illustration Sourcebook 32*, (Serbin Creative for Assoc. of Medical Illustratiors); *Directory of Illustration 36* (Serbin Creative); *Walter S. White: Inventions in Mid-Century Architecture* (Art, Design & Architecture Museum, University of California, Santa Barbara); *Orchid Stories: Stories of Hope and Love Inspired by Orchids* (Bella by Rolinda Ltd.)

Weller Smith Design, LLC

59 Molyneaux Road, Valley Stream, NY 11580
LeAnna Weller Smith, Principal
tel: 646.594.5742
leanna@wellersmithdesign.com | www.wellersmithdesign.com
member since: 2020

Weller Smith Design is a multidisciplinary design studio that works with individuals, as well as publishers, to design, produce and publish beautiful, high-quality books. We specialize in cookbooks, coffee table books, and personal development–style books, but also have a wide range of styles that can work with most publishing projects. We can also help define an author's niche, brand, or platform, and can help them to launch with a website, marketing materials, and more. We welcome partner opportunities as well.

SELECTED TITLES:

The Ultimate Cookie Handbook (Self-published by Tessa Arias, 2020); *Beautiful Booze* (The Countryman Press, 2020); *The Little Book of Support for New Moms* (The Countryman Press, 2020); *Cooking with Miss Quad* (The Countryman Press, 2019); *Asian Paleo* (The Countryman Press, 2019); *Clean Cocktails* (The Countryman Press, 2017)

WonderLab Group, LLC

26 Quincy Street, Chevy Chase, MD 20815
Jennifer Emmett, Founder
tel: 301.523.4233
jennifer@wonderlabgroup.com | www.wonderlabgroup.com
member since: 2020

WonderLab Group is a custom content creation and editorial services firm specializing in publishing, audio, and digital content in the areas of children's nonfiction and STEM. We focus on developing programmatic and 360° content to build nonfiction brands and franchises that promote science and inspire curious kids.

We are experts in the kids and family nonfiction space. Collectively we have over 50 years of experience at National Geographic Kids and other publishers. We draw upon an extensive network of best-in-class kids nonfiction content creators primarily based in the Washington, D.C. area.

We have edited *New York Times* bestsellers and nonfiction franchises with millions of copies sold. We believe mixing science and imagination sparks curiosity and leads to lifelong learning.

SELECTED TITLES:

Real World Math series (Scholastic, 2021); *Nature Numbers* series (Scholastic, 2022)

TYPESETTING

BY TYLER M. CAREY

The process for producing or "typesetting" a book has changed dramatically over the past 50 years. Once handled almost exclusively with heavy, industrial machinery, in the 1980s a move to using personal computers and desktop publishing software to generate printer files became common. This allowed for a lower financial barrier to entry in the typesetting industry, prompting the rise of individual entrepreneurs (once called "desktoppers") providing these services and ultimately the global book production businesses we see today, with many of today's firms headquartered in India. Increasingly, vendors that provide typesetting services additionally help further upstream with editorial services like copyediting, or even with content development and illustration.

These days, a book is typically written and then developmentally edited in Microsoft Word. Once the language in a book meets both the author's and publisher's expectations, the book is then sent to a copy editor. These copy editors—usually freelancers or supplied by a vendor to the publisher—use Track Changes in Microsoft Word to keep track of any spelling, syntax, grammar, or style changes that they make to the manuscript. An author or the publisher generally reviews to accept or reject individual changes and then send the final manuscript files off to their production department or typesetting vendor. The typesetter—or sometimes the copy editor—will "tag" the manuscript with styles that will be used to better present the content once it is typeset.

The typesetter—or "compositor"—generally works in partnership with a designer who may be responsible for creating solely the cover or also the interior design of the book. A book's design usually takes into consideration what typefaces are used on the cover of the book, whether the publication is fiction or nonfiction, whether the book is for children or adults, and finally the spacing of text on the page to allow the book to "cast off" or match expectations for the number of pages the book will be once printed. The design is generally created as a template or set of design files in Adobe InDesign, although other typesetting systems like 3B2 and LaTeX may be used for particular content types published in the academic and scholarly publishing markets.

The compositor then takes the final, copyedited manuscript from Microsoft Word and typesets or "pours" that text into the design files that exist in InDesign. While continued upgrades to InDesign have made it a lot easier to have a tagged manuscript automatically update to reflect the proper design once it is loaded into InDesign, the compositor still has a lot of work to do. They inspect the sample pages for things like paragraphs that "break" in visually unappealing ways like having an individual final line from a paragraph appear at the top of a page, or an introductory line appear on its own at the bottom of a page. While these types of typography decisions may sound like needless perfection to those not involved in the publication process, the ability to present a "balanced" page makes for easier reading by the consumer and for a more aesthetically appealing book. The compositor uses many skills and approaches to modify the text and spacing on the page to make things fit and create as appealing a typeset page as possible.

Once the compositor has set initial pages—called "First Pass" or "1P" in publishing—another compositor or proofreader typically reviews them to ensure styles were applied properly, before they are sent to the publisher and/or author for review. These pages are presented as PDF files, and the author or publisher are encouraged to mark up the pages to indicate any changes. These revisions, called "author alterations" or "AAs," allow the author or publisher to make any changes to the final language that would improve the book at this stage. Authors are not encouraged to make substantial rewrites, in the hopes that that was done before final copyediting. Should a publisher note any editorial errors like a misspelling, those are marked as an "editorial alteration" or "EA" so that they can be tracked to find out how they were missed earlier in the process. While in the past most edits were made on paper pages that were shipped to the compositor so they could apply changes, the industry standard is to have authors and publishers either use markup tools like those in Adobe Reader or to supply scanned copies of printed pages that had been written on.

The compositor then takes these marked-up changes, applies them to the pages, reviews the final pages again, and sends them back to the publisher for approval or further revisions. This process of sending "second pass"/"2P" can move into 3P, 4P, and more depending on how much the publisher wishes to change the content before asking the compositor to issue "final printer files." These final files are PDFs that are generated to the specifications of the printer being used for this title. The publisher often has these final printer files proofread once more before transmitting to the printer. They will also ask to have "blues" or samples from the printer provided, so that they can see the content on paper to approve before going to press. Why all these last-minute checks? If a publisher has thousands of copies of a book printed and then finds a substantial error they missed, they may need to have the inventory of books destroyed (or "pulped") and pay to have the book printed again. Many publishers would live with a stray comma or minor typo and fix those when they go to future printings of the book, but might need to replace or repair the print run if a book was issued with a missing chapter in the printer files, issues with the printing of art in a book, or some other substantial error.

Finally, the compositor will generate ePub files based on the final text in the printer files. These are sometimes generated in tandem with the printer files, but usually done sequentially so that any final edits have been applied and the ePub files are ready at the first pass of ePub file generation. InDesign allows compositors to export ePub3 files, but many typesetting operations customize that process to apply the publisher's requirements ranging from how page numbers are handled in a digital medium to the alt text and accessibility that many e-reading devices allow for these days. With advances in technology, accessibility guidelines continue to evolve to support new ways of serving content to those who may not be able to read the text on a Kindle, iPad, or other device. By extensively checking ePub3 files on devices or with custom software, typesetters can ensure the digital experience for an ePub3 version of the typeset book is optimized. From there, publishers often have their typesetters also generate XML, webPDF, and other file formats as needed for all of their distribution channels.

Want to know more? The *Chicago Manual of Style* has a section called "How Books and Journals Are Produced," which dives into alternate workflows and approaches. Talking to your typesetting partner may give you ideas as to how they are solving your particular production challenges for other clients they support. With the dozens of different workflows used in the industry, chances are good that someone has handled something similar to your own needs before.

*

Tyler M. Carey is the Chief Revenue Officer of Westchester Publishing Services. Westchester has been serving the publishing industry since 1969 and is the only U.S. employee-owned company focused on editorial, design, composition, and digital conversion services. The company's offerings include project management, copyediting, composition, art services, design, ePub creation, fixed-layout ePub creation, and other services for book, journal, and white paper publishers. In the education space, Westchester's subsidiary Westchester Education Services provides services as far upstream as content development, illustration, and working with learning management systems. Representative clients include Harvard University Press, W.W. Norton, The MIT Press, ABC-CLIO, Macmillan, and Bloomsbury. Westchester has offices in Danbury, Connecticut, Dayton, Ohio, Stratford upon Avon, U.K., and New Delhi and Chennai, India.

THE BOOK PRINTING INDUSTRY THROUGH AN ONGOING COVID-19 LENS

BY CHRIS KURTZMAN

Assessing the book printing industry at this particular moment in time is a curious exercise. Pre-pandemic growth projections notwithstanding, it's evident to anyone living through the last 18 months that the impacts of Covid-19 have left a mark. As we at CJK Group look at all facets of our industry, it's impossible to ignore how some things have changed, and may likely be forever changed.

IN THE MIRROR OF THE BOOK PUBLISHING INDUSTRY

Since book printing is the outcome of book publishing, we need only look to the activity in the publishing realm to gauge our own role as book printers.

Book publisher consolidations continue, as the "Big Five" is poised to become the "Big Four" with the prospective sale of Simon & Schuster to Penguin Random House. PRH dominates the top spot by a wide margin. As these publishing giants gain mass through consolidations, winning work from the top houses becomes a more significant print victory.

Regarding consolidations, as goes book publishing, so goes book printing; as our own CJK Group acquisitions attest. In 2020, we acquired Quad's Kentucky book printing facility, adding bench strength to our other book-producing Sheridan plants in Minnesota, Wisconsin, and Michigan, as well as Kentucky's venerable clientele. (In a related side note, CJK Group also acquired content service assets in 2020 from Cenveo Publisher Services and Cenveo Learning, merging them with Sheridan's content service offerings to form KnowledgeWorks Global Ltd., online services that indeed support the book and publication industries.) In 2019, we absorbed the assets of Thomson-Shore, and in 2018, we acquired Dickinson Press and Kingsport Book assets. Despite the high-profile attempted merger of Quad and LSC Communications in 2019—denied as a result of the Department of Justice's antitrust ruling—printing company consolidations do continue.

Aside from the big commercial publishing houses, self-publishing or indie publishing houses represent a fast-growing segment, popular with independent authors who want to circumvent commercial publishers and book agents and get their books in the marketplace quickly and cost-effectively. Most often, this work is produced as shorter run, on digital presses.

READING THROUGH THE QUARANTINE

The book business in 2020 uniquely reflected not only reactions and needs resulting from the pandemic, but a proliferation of political and social justice bestseller reads in an intensely charged election season amid ongoing and escalating civil unrest.

As we saw schools and universities implement learn-from-home policies, K–12 instructional materials and higher educational course materials understandably took a dip, but as most of the nation sheltered in place, books for leisure (and magazines) were on the rise. Common themes that saw a spike: self-help, cooking, crafts, religion, and lifestyle titles.

Interestingly, even pre-pandemic, the popularity and demand for print books has been on the rise. Surveys have indicated that a growing number of younger readers—from millennials to Gen Z—prefer the reading experience of print over pixel.

The question going forward is, how much of this book embrace, helped along by unprecedented circumstances, will stick?

SUPPLY CHAIN NIGHTMARES AND THE LABOR CRISIS

In stark contrast to a healthy book business and increased demand, printers—indeed the world at large—have been stymied by lack. For printers, it's currently a critical shortage of paper as a result of closing paper mills, a deliberate redirect in the type of paper a mill produces, or the elimination of certain stocks, raw pulp and chemical scarcity, and transportation woes.

While the transport situation isn't quite as dire as it was several months ago (at the height of the crisis this past spring, recall the blocked *Ever Given* container ship stuck in the Suez Canal), containers still sit in ports all over the world with limited resources to unpack and transport their goods, holding everything from appliances to soon-to-be-out-of-season merchandise hostage. And as they sit, the eventual cost to move the goods continues to increase. Many projections indicate this scenario isn't going away anytime soon.

The final piece of this dilemma is labor. Nationally, we face a labor shortage on so many fronts. As printers, we know that our ability to meet our customers' deadlines is absolutely dependent on receiving our raw materials—and enough raw materials—when we need them (both a supply and labor/transportation issue), and delivering the finished product to our customers on time. We have all been challenged by a lack of labor to serve the transport industry.

In the manufacturing world, labor is also a critical issue, as businesses do their best to court new hires and bring a younger generation to the force amid an economy struggling to rebound and restaff. Printing companies of course are no exception.

THE IMPACT OF DIGITAL

Digital printing and print on demand have been gaining in popularity in the book world for quite some time. Publishers have found that shorter print runs give them better control over inventory costs, and as digital print grows, so do the wide array of solutions digital best fits, from fulfilling backlist and out-of-print titles to producing advance reader copies and book signing shipments to limited edition compilations to versioned or regional printings. The distribute-and-print model—allowing publishers to print books in various locations around the world dependent on readership/audience location—is also growing as a smart, cost-effective solution that saves or dramatically minimizes shipping costs. And POD in general supports quicker turns when tighter deadlines must be met.

Printing companies like ours have reacted to the demand by investing in and expanding our digital platform. Five of our eight facilities run multiple digital presses in addition to our sheetfed and web presses.

COVID-19 CONTINUES

At this writing, the Delta variant is surging. A few months ago, the nation and much of the world saw light at the end of the tunnel. That encouraging glimpse is now being replaced with questions, a spike in cases and hospitalizations, and a reimposition of masking and social distancing mandates occurring business by business, and state by state. CJK Group and many others in our industry were able to continue production uninterrupted through Covid-19 by diligently adhering to restrictions and practicing good hygiene. While no one looks forward to having to adopt those practices again for the long term, it's exactly what we'll do in order to serve our customers.

PRINT PROJECTIONS

With more than half of 2021 behind us, it's still no easy task to see the trajectory of the book printing business given all its associated impactors and ongoing conditions. Comparing 2020 to 2019, the American trade book market showed a healthy 9.7 % gain.

Coming into 2021, book printers are enjoying continued growth, despite the paper and labor scramble to keep up with demand. Covid-19 remains the biggest factor, presenting the biggest questions. One of the more thoughtful articles on the topic cites a study done by NPD BookScan showing book printing growth projections for 2021 ranging anywhere from 2% to 8%.

For our part at CJK Group and our Sheridan print facilities, we are committed to the health and future of book publishing, and truthfully, we've learned a lot from this unique and challenging season. We remain resilient, agile, and ready to deliver the needs of an equally resilient book publishing industry.

*

Chris Kurtzman is the CEO of CJK Group, Inc. CJK Group's Sheridan print facilities are located in Brainerd, Minn.; Brimfield, Oh.; Chelsea, Mich.; Grand Rapids, Mich.; Hanover, N.H.; Hanover, Penn.; Madison, Wis.; and Versailles, Ky. CJK Group's KnowledgeWorks Global Ltd. content service facilities are located in Boston, Mass.; Richmond, Va.; and Waterbury, Vt., in the United States; Bengaluru, Chennai, Mumbai, and Noida in India; and London in the United Kingdom. For more information, visit cjkgroup.com.

THE EVOLUTIONARY PATH OF POD

BY CHRIS KURTZMAN

P rint-on-demand—or POD—is by definition both efficient and expedient. While the process has been widely available for over two decades, some intriguing foreshadowing for a print-on-demand automated workflow can be found in mid-twentieth-century American science fiction, in a magazine titled *Galaxy*, which imagined "high-speed facsimile machines which would produce a book to your order, anywhere in the world." By the early 1990s, digital presses, introduced by Indigo, were a reality, and their debut into our industry, as many of us recall, was revolutionary.

POD ECONOMICS 101

Likely the most significant and compelling rationale for POD is the impact it has on inventory management. Publishers who have struggled with demand for obsolete or out-of-print titles and back issues know the pain (and expense) of building and maintaining a physical inventory to accommodate a dribble of requests, weighing warehousing and fulfillment costs against often anemic demand. It can be a zero-sum game, at best.

The economics of POD, then, requires balanced consideration. While on its face, the POD product carries a unit cost that eclipses that of the traditionally printed product, the benefit of eliminating back inventory and the costs associated with its management and fulfillment far outweigh the POD unit cost.

EVERYWHERE IT NEEDS TO BE

POD's applications are myriad, with new applications emerging all the time. From zero-inventory management of backlist titles to one-off print copies of online-only publications to supplying a few copies for conferences, advance reader copies, or even first printings of books and journals, the uses continue to grow. Yet, another stand-out benefit of POD is that it allows publishers to print in different regions—closer to their readerships—with the added benefit of freight savings, which can be quite substantial. This distribute-and-print model works particularly well in the books arena.

SHERIDAN'S UNIQUE APPROACH

Our flagship Sheridan facility in Pennsylvania was an early adopter of print-on-demand, installing their first Kodak iGen POD press in 2004, which produced perfect-bound journals for a few high-profile clients. Today, we've grown from that single iGen to a fleet of toner and inkjet presses across five of our eight facilities—a variety of HPs, Timsons, Kodaks, and an ever-growing battery of binders, folders, casemakers, and other in-line equipment. Indeed, we see the potential to continue to expand our significant digital footprint.

In 2009, we envisioned and built a platform that facilitates our proprietary automated workflow for our clients, which we named Sheridan Select. It's become the premier—and preferred—POD workflow in the publication and book markets. All files received through the Sheridan Select portal are automatically stored in our electronic warehouse, making repeat orders an incredibly simple process. It features zero-touch ordering through sophisticated data signal solutions that reduce or remove transactional costs. It's an extremely user-friendly environment. And, our turnaround times are among the best in the industry.

Today, Sheridan Select's unique capabilities permit not only digital/inkjet print-on-demand, but extend to sheetfed and web work as well. The uses for Sheridan's Select system are diverse and growing all the time. We handle first printings of books and journals, and, of course, Sheridan Select facilitates a zero-inventory model as well as a back-issue-management approach. Even backlist titles can be made available as an endless virtual inventory; older titles need never go out of print.

We handle Advanced Reader Copies, POD catalogs, and print requests for online-only titles. We have also developed a synergy with another proprietary Sheridan-developed technology—Sheridan Connect, our e-commerce solution, which allows publishers' users to purchase content in a secure shopping cart environment, be it an e-book or a printed book. All printed content is processed POD, seamlessly and immediately, through Sheridan Select.

We happily serve many markets with our POD offering, including some of the most recognizable STM, academic, trade, and education publishers in the world. We also facilitate global distribute and print models, sole-sourced through Sheridan to strategically selected global print partners.

GROWTH ON THE HORIZON

The digital print industry at large has not only taken off over the decades, the growth projections are staggering. The 2019 Smithers report *The Future of Digital Print: Long-Term Strategic Forecasts to 2029* offers a global forecast indicating a 65% increase over the course of the decade. Package printing, books, and other graphic print products represent the major growth areas. New advances and technologies in the digital realm are also projected to grow.

While POD was envisioned as a "book of one" solution decades ago, its uses and benefits continue to evolve and broaden. Our vision of POD sees convenience and broad accessibility as the trajectory by which we configure our future offerings—always streamlining, simplifying, and refining a powerful web-to-print environment that is the epitome of convenience, expedience, and service.

*

Chris Kurtzman is the CEO of CJK Group, Inc. CJK Group's Sheridan print facilities are located in Brainerd, Minn.; Brimfield, Oh.; Chelsea, Mich.; Grand Rapids, Mich.; Hanover, N.H.; Hanover, Penn.; Madison, Wis.; and Versailles, Ky. CJK Group's KnowledgeWorks Global Ltd. content service facilities are located in Boston, Mass.; Richmond, Va.; and Waterbury, Vt., in the United States; Bengaluru, Chennai, Mumbai, and Noida in India; and London in the United Kingdom. For more information, visit cjkgroup.com.

MORE PRICE HIKES HITTING THE PRINT INDUSTRY

Spiraling costs of raw materials, freight, logistics, and
procurement due to pandemic-related restrictions have
resulted in soaring prices

BY TERI TAN | JUL 23, 2021

One supplier after another in the print industry has announced price hikes in recent months. All of them attributed the hikes to the spiraling costs of raw materials, freight, logistics, and procurement due to pandemic-related restrictions.

German press manufacturer Heidelberg and its rival Koenig & Bauer have both increased the prices of their equipment. Soaring input costs, including steel rebar and computer chips, prompted their decisions. The three major printing-plate makers—Agfa, Kodak, and Fujifilm—likewise cite sharp spikes in the cost of aluminum, silver, and packaging materials as the cause of their price increases.

Ink companies are not slow to take action either. EFI is hiking prices for its inkjet inks and supplies in Europe. Flint, Huber, and Sun Chemical are doing the same for their inks, coatings, and adhesives for their North American market. Shortages of raw materials to make the inks—pigments, resins, vegetable oils, and petrochemicals, for instance—have exerted pressure on their manufacturing overheads.

Paper companies have also had their turn: Sappi Europe is increasing the price of its coated and uncoated woodfree grades by up to 10% and its packaging and specialty products by about 11%. Mitsubishi HiTec Paper Europe is applying a 5% increase to all of its coated inkjet papers.

In China, major paper companies, such as Shandong Chenming Paper and Shandong Sun Paper, are raking in profits, but they had to suspend paper production for printing and writing grades for short periods early this year due to the high cost of raw materials. Prices for wood pulp have risen about 25% in 2021, while fuel and energy costs are escalating.

After the Chinese Ministry of Ecology and Environment banned the import of waste paper in January, the short supply of raw materials for papermaking became even more acute. Beijing's latest plastic restriction order, in turn, sends consumers and companies rushing to switch to paper packaging, thereby increasing pressure on its already stressed paper-based food packaging and packing bags supply. Paper prices have been rising since mid-2020, and there is no sign of a downward trend as yet.

So falling supply meets rising demand equals price increases. Add unpredictable supply-chain disruptions in different spots of the globe, due to the pandemic and sporadic outbreaks, and the situation worsens for players in the print manufacturing industry.

(19)

LIBRARIES

AMERICAN LIBRARY ASSOCIATION: 2021 STATE OF AMERICA'S LIBRARIES SPECIAL REPORT: COVID-19

The following chapters are excerpted from American Library Association's *2021 State of America's Libraries Special Report: Covid-19*, released in April 2021. The full report can be found at bit.ly/soal-report-2021.

Introduction: Libraries Serve as "First Restorers"

Julius C. Jefferson Jr., ALA President, 2020–2021

Excerpt from American Library Association's *2021 State of America's Libraries Special Report: Covid-19*, page 4.

In 2020, libraries of all types stepped up to meet the needs of their communities as they responded to the impacts of Covid-19, a national financial crisis, and social unrest. They were at the center of some of our nation's most consequential work, including supporting accurate counts in the U.S. Census, fighting political disinformation, and facilitating free and fair elections.

Libraries also extended necessary lifelines to community members facing job losses, health-care crises, and remote work and learning during an unprecedented and uncertain time. As we assess the state of America's libraries, we find 2020 was a year when library professionals answered the call to serve amid multiple emergencies and a year when library workers again proved to be essential "first restorers" or "second responders."

It also proved to be a year of opportunity, as libraries kept Americans connected in ways that brought our communities closer. Buildings may not have been open, but libraries were never closed.

I was lucky enough to see this work in action myself when I embarked on a national virtual tour meant to understand the needs of libraries on the ground. What I saw was awe-inspiring, even for someone like me who has spent decades in the profession.

At the Cambria County Library in Johnstown, Pennsylvania, for instance, workforce development programs, services, and local partnerships supported patrons with finding jobs and building careers. At the time of my visit with them, the state's unemployment rate was 16%, and the library's career center was essential for residents seeking economic advancement, digital literacy, and professional certifications.

Rural communities across the country faced and continue to confront tall hurdles to connect residents often scattered over large geographic areas. In Zanesville, Ohio, the Muskingum County Library's parking lot was filled most days with families, jobseekers, telecommuters, and students taking advantage of free Wi-Fi to participate in Zoom meetings, distance learning, job interviews, and telemedicine appointments.

From the Midwest to the Southwest (and everywhere in between), people who didn't have access to reliable, affordable broadband internet found themselves on the wrong side of the digital divide. In 2018, the Federal Communications Commission estimated that more than one in three residents living on tribal land lack access to broadband. During the pandemic, rural New Mexicans used the Jemez Pueblo Community Library's parking lot to access Wi-Fi, and librarians there helped community members with unemployment and stimulus forms and even auto license renewals.

Social justice is an issue that is close to my heart, and as the nation faced a racial reckoning, the work of our libraries as centers for engagement and community dialogue came into sharper focus. The John Brown Watson Memorial Library at the University of Arkansas at Pine Bluff, a historically Black university, takes its role in preserving history that is not always visible in white institutions very seriously. In Oakland, California, community programming like the Father Circle, a nonjudgmental family setting where fathers can share their feelings, and bike repair workshops that resist gentrification and support youth entrepreneurship are just two examples of the countless ways libraries demonstrate their commitment to diversity and community empowerment.

Of course, we can't speak of the past year without acknowledging the significant role of school librarians in supporting their communities" remote learning needs. In Texas, I met creative and innovative librarians like those at Castleberry Independent School District's Grab & Go Library, who provided families with activity packs so they could create and learn at home, and at Dallas's Franklin Middle School, who distributed laptops to students when in-person learning was cut short by lockdown orders.

In Hawaii, school librarians had to be flexible long before coronavirus made remote learning the default for students across the country. School librarians at Kamehameha Schools told me students are offered three modalities of learning—traditional in-class instruction, distance learning, and a blend of both—because some of the students travel as far as 68 miles just to get to school.

As we move into the future, I realize that 2020 was not the first time librarians and library workers have been challenged. Yet libraries are still standing. Read on for more about how these fundamental institutions are serving our communities during a most unusual time. And I hope you'll join me in advocating for their success.

Wi-Fi and Broadband Access

Excerpt from American Library Association's *2021 State of America's Libraries Special Report: Covid-19,* page 12.

In the pre-Covid-19 era, America's 16,557 public library locations provided critical digital infrastructure to their communities. For many, the library's computers were their personal computers. Libraries offered internet hotspots to borrow, promoted digital literacy through specialized training, and assisted careers by allowing job seekers to access crucial online information.

Throughout the pandemic, the library's role as a digital provider widened. The American Library Association (ALA) recognized the importance of libraries as broadband service points early in the crisis. In a March 2020 statement, the ALA Executive Board recommended that "libraries can and should leave their Wi-Fi networks on even when their buildings are closed wherever possible."

During the pandemic, libraries such as the rural Marathon County (Wis.) Public Library and the suburban Cuyahoga County (Ohio) Public Library compensated for closures by making their Wi-Fi networks accessible to patrons outside the building. Library users could sit in or near their cars and tap into the networks with laptops or smartphones, as long as they maintained six feet of social distance from passersby.

The Leominster (Mass.) Public Library took it one step further, installing mobile hotspots at the local senior center and veterans' center.

Santa Fe (N.M.) Community College and Pima (Ariz.) Community College played a vital role during the pandemic for students and communities that didn't have reliable internet access. They purchased and lent out hundreds of laptops and dozens of portable Wi-Fi hotspots. Expanded Wi-Fi also allowed students to safely access the internet outside closed buildings from the parking lot or other outdoor spaces.

The bookmobile, the classic vehicle for library outreach, reinvented itself as a conveyor of broadband to communities in need. Williamsburg (Va.) Regional

Library parked its bookmobile outside schools, grocery stores, and community centers, while the Topeka and Shawnee County (Kans.) Public Library deployed its bookmobiles as Wi-Fi hotspots to a local mobile home park and a correctional facility.

INEQUITIES LAID BARE

But even as libraries responded to the call, inequities in allocation were exposed—gaps that would affect communities in need of broadband during the pandemic for access to digital collections, e-government services, legal information, distance learning, telemedicine, and other essential community services.

The Covid-19 outbreak exacerbated these inequities. About 25% of Americans lack high-speed internet access at home, according to a June 2019 study by the Pew Research Center. Roughly 33% of rural Americans lack home broadband access.

In a September case study of two tribally owned and operated networks, the ALA Public Policy and Advocacy Office reported that barely half of Native Americans living on tribal lands had access to high-speed internet. Six tribal libraries and two schools in six pueblos in north-central New Mexico aggregated their demand and built two 60-mile fiber-optic networks. During the pandemic, tribal libraries stepped up significantly to form partnerships to connect diverse populations with broadband.

In Washington, D.C., lawmakers proposed several bills to address broadband needs, including the Health and Economic Recovery Omnibus Emergency Solutions (HEROES) Act, passed by the House in May, which would have provided $2 billion for hotspots and other devices for library patrons and K–12 students. This bill was never brought up for consideration in the Senate.

LEARNING GOES VIRTUAL

When learning moved online, school libraries like those in the Leander (Tex.) Independent School District became tech hubs for teachers and students. There, librarians helped guide teachers during the initial weeks of the pandemic, sitting in on staff meetings, helping set up Google classrooms and Zoom calls, answering copyright questions, and curating digital resources.

"Everyone in the school turns to you," when dealing with computers and setting up online learning, said Four Points Middle School librarian April Stone. "Librarians stepped in to help teachers navigate those new tools and shift what they were doing physically versus virtually. We were always on the front lines for campus tech anyway, and it's the librarians helping not only navigate Zoom, but also best practices on how to use the tools."

When its physical locations closed, the Florida State University (FSU) Libraries demonstrated the crucial educational role academic libraries play on their campuses. It began providing electronic resources, online instructional support, open education resources, online tutoring, and other remote services. FSU librarians also helped instructors identify digital, open, and primary-source resources to use in remote teaching.

Meanwhile, advocates called for the Federal Communications Commission to boost broadband connectivity during the pandemic to help school libraries. FCC Commissioner Jessica Rosenworcel recommended the FCC expand its E-Rate program, a subsidy created in 1996 for K–12 schools. She warned that without action students nationwide could be locked out of their virtual classrooms.

How We Read in 2020

Excerpt from American Library Association's *2021 State of America's Libraries Special Report: Covid-19*, page 17.

Libraries in 2020 saw a significant shift in borrowing habits as e-book usage soared. OverDrive, a major distributor of e-books, audiobooks, and streaming video to libraries, reported that its clients worldwide collectively loaned out more than 289 million e-books, a 40% increase from 2019. The company attributed this shift to the pandemic. After all, no-contact e-book lending is the perfect way to get content from a safe social distance.

Digital book borrowing reached record highs, with readers in 102 public library systems each checking out 1 million or more e-books. Twenty-nine of those systems hit that mark for the first time.

With buildings closed to the public, libraries accelerated or adopted plans to issue digital library card ("eCard") offerings. Sarasota County (FL) Libraries, for example, were able to create and launch their eCard within a few weeks of branches being closed to the public.

In March, with 86 locations closed to the public, the Los Angeles County Library offered temporary digital library cards, valid for 90 days. The cards enabled access to all of the library's digital offerings—e-books, audiobooks, magazines, movies, TV, homework help, and online classes.

HIGHLIGHTING COMMUNITY HEROES

Faced with the challenge of celebrating Library Card Signup Month in September, librarians at the Gail Borden Public Library District in Elgin, Illinois, decided to turn the annual campaign into a way to honor Hometown

Heroes who worked on the front lines during the Covid-19 outbreak. The library collected their photos and added superhero capes and face shields to the images. The heroes, along with "Secret Superhero Words," were posted on the front windows or entrances of local businesses that were participating in a socially distanced scavenger hunt in which each Superhero Word directed people to such virtual library services as "eAudiobooks" or "streaming."

Librarians also performed heroic deeds in making sure community members in need had access to resources. Jayanti Addleman, director of library services at the Hayward (Calif.) Public Library, worked with staff to streamline the process for registering for a library card online, paying particular attention to eliminating barriers for undocumented individuals. She also oversaw the distribution of hundreds of tablets, hotspots, and other devices to help bridge the digital divide. Moreover, she secured funding for a new bookmobile to meet the needs of those residents who lacked transportation and could not take advantage of curbside pickup.

CURBSIDE PICKUP AND CURBING LATE FEES

With buildings closed or users uneasy entering them, curbside pickup became popular, and libraries got creative promoting this service that is more often associated with retail shopping. Donning a cowboy hat and aviator sunglasses and adopting the persona of Curbside Larry, Harris County (TX) Public Library's Program Production Specialist John Schaffer delivered a pitch in the style of a bombastic used car salesman, touting the library's curbside services in a video that attracted more than 50,000 views on YouTube, as well as mentions in *Texas Monthly* and *Southern Living*.

Even before the pandemic, libraries were going fine-free. Library fines "present an economic barrier to access of library materials and services," according to an American Library Association resolution adopted in 2019, and the pandemic urged many districts to action. Since March 2020, 91 of the Urban Libraries Council's roughly 160 member libraries have opted to go fine-free.

*

American Library Association (ALA) is the foremost national organization providing resources to inspire library and information professionals to transform their communities through essential programs and services. For more than 140 years, ALA has been the trusted voice of libraries, advocating for the profession and the library's role in enhancing learning and ensuring access to information for all. Visit ala.org/ for more information.

THE TOP 10 LIBRARY STORIES OF 2020

PW looks back at the library stories that captivated the publishing world this year—and what they portend for 2021

BY ANDREW ALBANESE | DEC 11, 2020

1. Covid-19 Closes America's Libraries

We can reliably count on a major event to top this list each year. But nothing compares to the Covid-19 pandemic that has so far claimed some 300,000 American lives, and in March forced a historic nationwide mass closure of public spaces, including libraries.

On February 29, Washington's King County reported what was then believed to be the nation's first death from Covid-19—a man in his 50s, in Kirkland. Two weeks later, on March 13, the King County Library System closed its buildings to the public—all 50 libraries, serving some 1.4 million residents in the Seattle area. Just days later, on March 17, the American Library Association, for the first time in its history, issued a memo recommending that all libraries across the nation close to the public.

"Libraries almost never close. We're usually the last to close during a crisis," King County librarian Lisa Rosenblum told *PW* in May, adding that at first the idea of a months-long, indefinite closure was at first almost unthinkable to her. "In the beginning, I thought, 'Okay, maybe we'll have to close for a week or two,' which is a long time for a library. But eventually, I realized I had to totally rethink everything. And part of my rethinking was to plan as if we were not going to be open again for a really, really long time—because otherwise, we would keep thinking we were just going to go back to pre-pandemic service. And that's just not going to happen."

In recent years, observers have argued that if public libraries didn't already exist in America we probably wouldn't be able to invent them. In the wake of the Covid-19 crisis, the question facing libraries today is: Can we reinvent them?

So far that reinvention means services like curbside pickup, and limits on patron visits. It means ensuring library workers have appropriate workspace and personal protective equipment, and reconfiguring the library itself: less furniture, more distance between computer stations, hand sanitizer stations, spit guards, and plexiglass dividers. It means contactless checkout, new cleaning procedures, 72-hour materials quarantines, and efforts like OCLC's Project Realm, which has shared important research on how long the virus can live on different surfaces.

And it means more digital services. A scan of the national headlines on any given day shows libraries reporting sharp rises in digital engagement, including e-books and other digital resources as well as online storytimes, author events, and Zoom book clubs.

In a May 28 editorial, New York Public Library president Anthony Marx wrote that Covid-19 has exposed the need for "radical" change in America's libraries. But however our public libraries may evolve post-pandemic, one thing is clear: as we seek to recover from this historic global health crisis, we're going to need them more than ever.

"We now have millions of people who are feeling isolated and stressed and out of sorts," Eric Klinenberg, author of the acclaimed 2018 book *Palaces for the People* told *PW* in early May. "I think the pandemic has magnified the importance of the public library in American community life. This is a moment in our history where we are going to need public spaces like never before, and there simply is no other place that has such capacity to bring people together."

2. Library Workers Take a Stand

As Covid-19 forced the nation into an unprecedented lockdown in March, librarians did what they always do: they jumped in to help. But as an idealized narrative of selfless hero librarians began to take root in the national media in the early days of the pandemic, the reality on the ground was far more grim: too many librarians and staff working without the proper protective equipment and safety precautions, terrified of becoming sick, facing uncertainty and economic ruin as layoffs and furloughs mounted, with some library workers even being ordered to redeploy from their closed libraries to shelters, makeshift testing facilities, or other frontline, high-risk jobs in their communities.

In a widely shared article on the *Book Riot* website in April, Kelly Jensen, a former librarian, sounded the alarm. "For institutions ranked among the most trustworthy and beloved," Jensen wrote, "it's shameful how the individuals who comprise libraries are treated as disposable."

But amid the rising fear and deadly uncertainty that came with the early days of the pandemic, library workers organized and effectively shifted the focus to issues of worker safety and well-being. The movement started with a #CloseTheLibraries campaign in early March that raised critical awareness of the dangers facing library workers in the early days of the outbreak. That effort soon expanded into two more campaigns—#ProtectLibraryWorkers, which advocated for the safety and fair treatment of library employees; and #LibraryLayoffs, which created a crowdsourced list of rising number of library layoffs and furloughs across all types of libraries.

"The flipside of all of these feel-good pieces on digital story time, backyard summer reading, and boosted Wi-Fi signals in the parking lot is library workers forced to do jobs they never signed up for [and] scolded for their attempts to fight for their well-being," wrote Massachusetts-based librarian Callan Bignoli, a prominent voice in the movement, in a May editorial in *Library Journal*. "It's time to say, 'not anymore.'"

In fact, librarians point out, workplace stress is a problem that long predates the Covid-19 crisis. In a groundbreaking 2018 journal article, Rutgers University librarian Fobazi Ettargh coined the term "vocational awe" to describe how the public library's ever expanding mission to serve their communities too often ignores the the health of the librarians and library workers who have traditionally found it difficult to advocate for their own safety and well-being.

With the virus surging again, serious questions and problems remain. But library workers have now shown they can effectively organize around a powerful principle: that the public library's commitment to serve its community cannot come at the expense of the health, safety, and physical and mental well-being of library staff.

"This pandemic has highlighted the fact that library workers need as much training in collective action and self-advocacy as they do in lobbying for library funding," wrote Meredith Farkas in the November/December issue of *American Libraries*. "This kind of collective organizing requires a willingness to look beyond our institutions and traditional hierarchies, but the collective influence we wield can create powerful positive change."

3. Black Lives Matter
On May 25, the world watched in horror the footage of a Minneapolis police officer coldly kneeling on the neck of an African American man named

George Floyd for an agonizing eight minutes and 46 seconds, killing him. And with the anger, outrage, and protests that followed has come a long over-due acknowledgement of just how deeply embedded systemic racism is in the U.S.—including in our public libraries.

Equity, diversity, and inclusion are of course core values for the library profession. And in the wake of public protests this summer, libraries nationwide stepped up and did a lot of good. Many libraries moved swiftly to provide racial and social justice collections and other resources to their communities, for example, and many offered safe spaces in their communities for conversations on race and equity. Efforts to aid those discussions were assisted by publishers and other service providers, who made e-book and digital audio collections and titles available with no holds, including bestselling titles like Ta-Nehisi Coates's *Between the World and Me*; Robin DiAngelo's *White Fragility: Why It's So Hard for White People to Talk About Racism*; and Ibram X. Kendi's *How to Be an Antiracist*.

Beyond the public-facing resources and programs, librarians also committed to taking a hard look at their owns institutions as well. A historically white profession that has struggled to diversify its ranks, the library profession is now confronting issues within their organizational cultures, and committing to do the work needed to become truly anti-racist institutions. "It's true that libraries, publishers, and schools and colleges work for the betterment of society," wrote R. David Lankes, director of the Information School at the University of South Carolina, in a July 10 *PW* column. "But as part of that society, we have also played a role in sustaining its worst elements. The crises we face today—in public health, in our economy, and in confronting the structural racism in our society—demand that we rethink everything, including what we've always considered virtuous institutions."

A June 26 statement from the American Library Association also acknowledged the profession's fraught history with race: "We recognize that the founding of our Association was not built on inclusion and equity, but instead was built on systemic racism and discrimination in many forms. We also recognize the hurt and harm done to BIPOC library workers and communities due to these racist structures," the statement reads. "We take responsibility for our past, and pledge to build a more equitable association and library community for future generations of library workers and supporters."

Recent headlines in our divided nation suggest the road ahead will have its pitfalls. For example, when the Douglas County Public Library in Nevada briefly posted a draft statement of support of the Black Lives Matter movement for discussion on the library website this summer, it led to a swift, ugly backlash. And the county sheriff offered a particularly headline-grabbing response: "Due to your support of Black Lives Matter and the obvious lack of support or trust with the Douglas County Sheriff's Office," the sheriff wrote in a public letter to library leaders, "please do not feel the need to call 911 for help." In an equally shocking coda, rather than standing up for the library, the library's board, over the objections of the library director, later voted to spend up to $30,000 of the library's scarce resources to investigate the library's initial BLM statement.

But there's positive news out there, too. In September, backed by city officials, the Iowa City Public Library released a new 2021–2023 strategic initiative that made headlines for including concrete measures to address equity, diversity, and inclusion issues. "Everybody needs to be willing to have hard conversations," ICPL director Elsworth Carman told *Library Journal* reporter Lisa Peet in a recent article. "To say, OK, I'm not an expert but, I want to try to fix it. I'm going to talk about it. I'm going to try to get there."

4. Macmillan Defends, Then Abruptly Ends Its Library E-book Embargo

On the morning of January 25, at the 2020 ALA Midwinter Meeting in Philadelphia, Macmillan CEO John Sargent thoroughly frustrated a hotel meeting room full of librarians with his defense of the publisher's controversial two-month embargo on new release e-books in libraries. Over 90 minutes, Sargent insisted that the rapid growth of library e-book lending was creating an "imbalance in the publishing ecosystem." He told librarians that he would reassess the effectiveness of the embargo around March or April, but until then the embargo was staying.

Then the pandemic hit. In a March 17 announcement, Macmillan abruptly ended the embargo. Just like that a contentious two-year battle was over. "There are times in life when differences should be put aside," Sargent offered as an explanation, in a short memo to librarians.

The embargo's end was welcome news for librarians, who at the time were shifting their print spending to their digital collections to serve readers in the wake of physical library closures. The change was good business for Macmillan, too, which couldn't afford to be the one major publisher not selling new release e-books to libraries during a period in which most libraries had suspended their print purchases.

Still, coming nearly two years after Macmillan's unilateral "test" embargo on new releases from its Tor imprint started the controversy, the sudden ending left a lot of questions unanswered. Does Macmillan still see library e-books causing "an imbalance" in the marketplace? Might the publisher return to the embargo after the pandemic has ended? As they have from the beginning, Macmillan executives declined to comment on the matter. And thus the company's library e-book embargo ended much like how it began—with a frustrating lack of transparency and communication.

Of course, it wouldn't be 2020 without one more twist: in September, longtime Macmillan CEO John Sargent announced that he would be stepping down at the end of 2020, to be replaced by Don Weisberg, president of Macmillan's U.S. Trade division. And what that change portends for Macmillan's future approach to the digital library market is now the subject of intense speculation.

Over the years, the library community had come to regard Sargent himself as one of the most implacable skeptics of library e-book lending. With Sargent out of the picture, librarians in 2021 will be curious to learn whether Macmillan's reticent approach to the library e-book market will be continued by its new leadership.

5. Covid-19 Pushes Library E-book Lending to Record Levels

As evidenced by the battle over Macmillan's library e-book embargo, the library e-book market has long been a source of tension between publishers and librarians, marked by shifting access restrictions and high prices that librarians have long warned are unsustainable. But in March, as librarians necessarily shifted their spending from print to digital in the wake of the pandemic, a number of publishers eased pricing and restrictions on library e-books. The result? A historic surge in digital lending.

"Every single day we are crossing into new record territory," Steve Potash, CEO for OverDrive, the leading e-book provider for libraries, told *PW* in March. "I think digital library lending and services are being elevated to a new plateau. It's obviously not going to grow at this pace consistently. But it's going to the next level."

Library leaders across the nation have backed Potash up, reporting massive increases in digital circulation through the summer. "In April, May, and June, our digital circulation was up 40%, 46%, and 42% over 2019," said Carmi Parker, a committee member for the Washington Digital Library Consortium, a coalition of 46 libraries in Washington State which manages digital access for its members. The neighboring King County Library System, one of the nation's biggest and busiest library systems and a perennial leader in digital circulation prior to the pandemic, reported a 42% increase in March through August 2020 over the previous year.

Librarians have spoken for years about their desire to introduce more patrons to their digital collections. But not under these circumstances. And now, librarians worry that the speed of this massive, virtually overnight digital shift has left them vulnerable. What happens when the pandemic is finally behind us? If the library e-book market simply returns to its pre-pandemic state—in which publishers unilaterally raise prices and change terms without negotiation or even consultation—and digital demand remains dramatically higher, as is expected, how will libraries manage?

"We've revamped our website to highlight our digital content, and people are responding," *PW* columnist and White Plains (N.Y.) Public Library director Brian Kenney told *PW* in March. "We are bringing a lot of people online, and it's turning out to be a good experience for them. My guess is that many will want to stay there."

Indeed, the uneasy feeling shared by many librarians is that the pandemic may have necessarily changed the course of the digital library market during this annus horribilis, but the underlying dysfunction in the marketplace has still not been addressed. For libraries, the question heading into 2021 is whether publishers and librarians will take the experience of this extraordinary year to finally chart a new, stable, and sustainable course for e-books and digital content in libraries.

"When you think about some of the comments that have been made by publishers, it's clear that libraries are still not really seen as a player in the market," Kelvin Watson, director of the Broward County (Fla.) Public Library told *PW* in May. "What I think this pandemic has done for some publishers, if not all, is shine a light on the library's role in the market."

Meanwhile, in a sign that there may be progress made in the digital library market in 2021, Amazon Publishing has confirmed that it is in talks with the Digital Public Library of America (DPLA) to make Amazon-published e-books available to public libraries.

Such an agreement would be a breakthrough, as Amazon Publishing currently does not make its digital content available to libraries—an exclusion that librarians have loudly criticized for years. Neither Audible's digital audio titles nor titles from Amazon's KDP program are part of the discussion, but gaining access to Amazon Publishing e-books would still be a step forward for libraries. And landing Amazon for the DPLA Exchange, the DPLA's nascent e-book platform, would be a major coup for DPLA. After all, to license Amazon Publishing titles, libraries would have to use the DPLA Exchange, and to access them patrons would need to deploy the SimplyE app (a free, open source e-reader app developed by the New York Public Library)—meaning library users would not have to go through Amazon to access the titles.

At press time, both parties say talks are still ongoing, and that a pilot program could launch in early 2021.

6. Publishers Sue the Internet Archive

In last year's top 10, we questioned whether the events of 2019 suggested the Internet Archive might soon find itself in court over its nine-year-old program to scan and lend PDF copies of print books. Sure enough, on June 1, 2020, four major publishers—Hachette, HarperCollins, John Wiley & Sons, and Penguin Random House—filed a copyright infringement lawsuit over the program in the Southern District of New York, coordinated by the Association of American Publishers.

The suit is not a surprise. Publishers and author groups have long bristled over the Internet Archive's program to acquire print books, scan them, and then lend the DRM-controlled PDF copies in lieu of the print books under an untested legal theory known as controlled digital lending. Still, despite a few warning shots fired in 2019, a lawsuit against the IA didn't appear imminent.

But then, in April, IA leaders made a fateful decision: with libraries and schools across the nation shuttered by the pandemic and their physical book collections largely unavailable, the IA decided to make its collection of some 1.4 million scans temporarily available for multi-user access.

Specifically, under a controversial program known as the National Emergency Library, the Internet Archive temporarily removed the one-copy/one-user rule governing its e-book lending program, known as the Open Library. Users would still have to sign up and borrow the e-books, but there would be no holds list. The announcement of the National Emergency Library garnered national headlines. And the program almost certainly exhausted what little forbearance publisher and author groups had maintained for the IA's book scanning program over the years.

Among the court filings, the publishers' complaint makes clear they are not focusing on the National Emergency Library program (which IA leaders voluntarily shut down shortly after the suit was filed). Rather, the suit challenges the fundamental legality of the IA's scanning and lending program itself. The publishers specifically decry what they see as the "purposeful collection of truckloads of in-copyright books to scan, reproduce, and then distribute digital bootleg versions online." In announcing the suit, AAP executives cast the Internet Archive as thieves in league with the "largest known book pirate sites in the world." Among the remedies requested, the publishers' suit seeks damages, and to destroy all infringing IA scans.

Author and president of the Authors Guild Douglas Preston also backed the suit, accusing the Internet Archive of hiding behind a "sanctimonious veil of progressivism," in a statement of support. "The Internet Archive hopes to fool the public by calling its piracy website a library," Preston opined. "But there's a more accurate term for taking what you don't own: it's called stealing."

But in its July 28 answer to the suit, IA lawyers firmly rejected those characterizations. Far from a "pirate" site where illegal digital editions are freely distributed, IA lawyers say the program is designed to function like a traditional library—the print books from which the scans are made are legally acquired; only one person can borrow a copy at a time; the scans are DRM-protected to prevent copying and enforce lend limits; and the corresponding print book from which the scan is created is taken out of circulation while the scan is on loan (and vice versa) to maintain a one-to-one "own-to-loan" basis. And, IA founder Brewster Kahle has pointed out, the scanning wouldn't be necessary if publishers sold PDFs of books to libraries.

"With this suit the publishers are saying that in the digital world [libraries] cannot buy books anymore. We can only license them, and under their terms," Kahle said at an online press conference this summer. "We say that libraries have the right to buy books and preserve them and lend them, even in the digital world."

The parties have agreed to a schedule that would have the case ready for trial by November 2021. And while the case raises some interesting legal questions, the more fundamental question may be this: Deep into the streaming age, 13 years after the commercial e-book market took off and more than four years since the Google Books lawsuits ended after 11 years of litigation, how are we still fighting over low-quality PDFs of older, mostly out-of-print books?

7. Canadian Publisher Calls Public Libraries a "Net Harm" to Literature—Librarians Clap Back

It's an age-old question: How do public libraries impact the book business? This summer, one independent publisher in Canada caused an uproar after he took to the pages of a major newspaper to offer a controversial opinion.

In a nearly 3,000-word July 25 *Globe and Mail* opinion piece provocatively titled "Overdue: Throwing the Book at Libraries," Kenneth Whyte, the publisher of Toronto-based indie Sutherland House Books, pinned blame for the troubles of Canada's independent bookstores and publishers on public libraries. The "crux of the matter," Whyte argued, is that libraries rely on "pimping free entertainment to people who can afford it," concluding that all "the genuine good" libraries do "is to some extent made possible by being a net harm to literature."

The article was widely shared on social media, though comments on the article suggested few people agreed with Whyte's thesis. And as you would expect, librarians were also eager to respond.

On July 27, Mary Chevreau, president of the Canadian Urban Libraries Council (CULC), submitted a reply essay to the *Globe and Mail* opinion editor. And what happened next came as a surprise, CULC officials told *PW*: the paper apparently declined to publish the essay. So, CULC turned to *PW*, which published the librarians' response in full on July 31. The piece quickly went viral, racking up nearly 10,000 likes on Facebook over the first weekend of its publication.

In her essay, Chevreau cited evidence—including a fresh Booknet Canada survey—which showed library users are in fact book buyers. And she reminded readers that the library enterprise is grounded in something more profound than commerce.

"Public libraries are a democratic institution that are critical in a civil society," Chevreau wrote. "More and more, they are playing a crucial role in empowering citizens to thrive in today's changing world by providing the essential tools, connectivity and information in all its forms. And most importantly, libraries are committed to providing equitable access to the widest range of human knowledge, experience, and ideas. That includes John Grisham, and Jesmyn Ward."

The episode recalled the media firestorm over a 2018 *Forbes* article—which was later retracted—in which a Long Island University economics professor argued that Amazon should replace public libraries. And, as happened in 2018 with that piece, rather than dent the public's support for libraries, Whyte's editorial has rallied it.

8. Two State Bills Propose "Parental Review Boards" for Public Libraries—and Jail for Librarians Who Defy Them

In January, free speech and library advocates sounded the alarm over a bill proposed in Missouri that sought to establish "parental review boards" in public libraries as a condition of state funding. According to the bill's text, these boards would have the power to decide which "age-appropriate" materials could be made accessible to minors within the library. But the most shocking provision: librarians who refuse to comply with the board's decisions would be subject to fines and up to a year in prison.

Specifically, House Bill 2044, the Parental Oversight of Public Libraries Act (or POOPLA, as one sharp-eyed commenter dubbed it) would establish five-member boards, elected by a simple majority vote at local town meetings.

"The main thing is I want to be able to take my kids to a library and make sure they're in a safe environment, and that they're not going be exposed to something that is objectionable," said the bill's sponsor, state legislator Ben Baker, in a February interview with the local KOAM News. Baker later conceded that the bill was motivated in part by the popularity of Drag Queen Story Hour events in libraries and bookstores around the country.

In a statement, James Tager, deputy director of free expression research and policy at PEN America, offered a different take on the bill. "This act is clearly aimed at empowering small groups of parents to appoint themselves as censors over their state's public libraries," he observed.

Curiously, just weeks after the Missouri bill was introduced, a clone of the very same bill surfaced in the Tennessee legislature, ramping up concerns of a nationally coordinated, state-by-state effort. And while the bills have failed to advance so far, library and free speech organizations remain wary that these kinds of bills could once again show up in 2021.

"The belief that a small group of parents know what is best for every family in their community denies the very real fact that each community is made up of families and individuals with diverse beliefs, identities and values," reads a February 20 statement from ALA, which has registered its strong opposition to the bills and continues to monitor the situation. "ALA supports the right of families and individuals to choose materials from a diverse spectrum of ideas and beliefs."

9. Library Leaders Praise Senate Confirmation of Trump's Pick to Lead IMLS; Trump Then Renews His Bid to Eliminate the Agency

It's almost hard to fathom, but 2020 kicked off with a bit of good news for the library community. On January 9, the Senate easily confirmed Kansas City (Mo.) Public Library executive director R. Crosby Kemper III to be the new director of the federal Institute for Museum and Library Services (IMLS).

The vote came just weeks after Trump nominated Kemper in November 2019—warp speed for a nonjudicial appointee in the Senate. "Confirming a new IMLS director so quickly shows the high regard in which elected leaders hold libraries as places of opportunity for all Americans," ALA president Wanda K. Brown said in a statement at the time, praising Kemper as "the right leader for IMLS at the right time."

But Kemper's confirmation was a short-lived moment of comity between the Trump administration and the library community. Just weeks later, the Trump administration for a fourth straight year proposed the permanent elimination of the IMLS—and with it virtually all federal funding for libraries.

Fortunately for library supporters, lawmakers have consistently rejected the Trump administration's recommendations to slash federal library funding, and have instead responded by increasing the IMLS budget each year. But what will happen with federal library funding going forward remains an open question.

On the positive side, the Biden administration will almost certainly end Trump's four-year string of proposals to end federal library funding. At the same time, veteran political observers warn that GOP lawmakers always seem to rediscover their opposition to government spending when a Democrat is in the White House. And even as the nation seeks to recover from what has been a devastating pandemic, many observers expect that will be the case again.

All of which makes the year-round advocacy work of library supporters as important as ever in 2021 and beyond. As Kathi Kromer, associate executive director of ALA's Public Policy and Advocacy Office in Washington, D.C., has observed, libraries were successful in defeating Trump's proposed cuts to federal library funding over the last four years because library supporters have consistently "made it a point to remind their elected officials of the importance of libraries in their community."

In 2021 and beyond, that kind of year-round advocacy will remain the recipe for success.

10. Tracie Hall Becomes the ALA's First African American Woman to Serve as Executive Director

In January, the American Library Association named Tracie D. Hall its new executive director, the first African American woman to serve in that post in ALA's 143-year history. Hall officially took the reins on February 24 from the retiring Mary Ghikas, who had served since longtime executive director Keith Michael Fiels stepped down in July 2017.

In a May interview, Hall told *PW* that being the first African American woman to lead ALA, one of the nation's largest professional associations, was a meaningful milestone—but one she has had little time to reflect on. Just days after her appointment was announced, ALA revealed to its membership that the organization was facing a serious financial shortfall. Then came the Covid-19 pandemic, forcing ALA to recommend for the first time in its history that the nation's libraries close. And a week after that, ALA announced the cancellation of its in-person ALA Annual Conference—a key revenue driver for the association. It was the first time since 1945 and the end of World War II that ALA had not held an in-person annual conference.

It's fair to say that no ALA executive director has faced a more challenging set of circumstances at the outset of their tenure than does Hall. As if ALA's full-scale reorganization wasn't a tall enough order, the public library itself is being reimagined in the wake of the pandemic, and a social justice and racial awakening. Oh, and Hall's first year was an election year that highlighted the nation's fractured political culture fueled by fake news, conspiracy theories, and alternate realities.

Hall has outlined a bold vision for ALA. "One of the Association priorities that really stands out is to expand our membership and stakeholder base," she told *American Libraries* in an interview following her appointment. "Reaching a broader base is key. I want those committed to universal literacy; to closing the school achievement gap or the wealth gap; to ending mass incarceration; to diversity, equity, accessibility, and inclusion; to environmental and community sustainability; and more, to see the Association as among the premier leaders and partners in that work. Getting there must begin with listening, observing, and assessing [ALA's] needs and opportunities."

*

A version of this article appeared in the 12/14/2020 issue of *Publishers Weekly* under the headline: The Library Stories of 2020.

SELLING TO LIBRARIES

BY BILL WOLFSTHAL

Books and libraries go hand in hand like peanut butter and jelly, but libraries are not just depositories that loan books out to their patrons. The modern library in the United States provides access to computers and Wi-Fi, a place for communities to gather, a safe and educational space for parents and their children, and more. For the book publishing community, libraries represent a significant marketplace and source of revenue.

There are over 125,000 public, academic, and school libraries in the United States. According to some estimates, they represent a market for books in the billions of dollars. They buy print books and loan them, and they make e-books available to patrons. Every publisher needs some of that market. Those not selling to libraries miss out on a significant channel of distribution. But no two books are the same. No two publishers are the same. No two library systems are the same. There is no single marketing plan or strategy for the school and library market that suits every publisher or every book.

Libraries, just like bookstores, want the most popular books in their collections. Public library patrons want to borrow the most popular bestsellers, so libraries will want to have them on hand. School libraries will want to have the most talked about and exciting new children's books to get their students reading. Academic libraries will want the most important research and reference titles available for both their students and professors.

When publishers launch "big" books each year, they make sure that the school and library markets know they are coming. Libraries find out about books the same way everyone else does, through reviews, advertising, promotion, and word of mouth. General review coverage will push libraries to add titles to their collections. If a book is reviewed in the *New York Times* or the *Wall Street Journal* or featured by Reese Witherspoon's book club or on *60 Minutes*, local libraries will want it on hand to fill demand by their patrons.

Having a book reviewed in the publications librarians read is the best and most cost-effective way to sell books into the library market. Each issue of *Publishers Weekly*, *Library Journal*, and *Booklist* (the review organ of the

American Library Association) contains many reviews. *Publishers Weekly* alone reviews over 9,000 titles a year. These publications are read by many in the library community, including the decision makers, usually the "acquisition librarian." Get a "starred" or rave review in one of those magazines, and libraries will want your book. It could mean 100 extra books sold, 1,000 copies, or even more.

Each publication has very specific guidelines on how and when to submit a book for review. You will need to produce advance reading copies (ARCs) to allow reviewers to read the book pre-publication. And you will need to follow their submission guidelines carefully. Do not miss their deadlines, or you will lose any chance of review. There are other useful publications as well, including *Kirkus Reviews, Foreword, Choice,* and more. The more publications you submit to, the more opportunities you have for reviews and outreach. *School Library Journal* is probably the most important review publication for children's books. Other publications of note for children's books include *Horn Book* and *Voya.*

Whether or not you are getting reviews in library publications, you may also want to advertise to the library market. If you are trying to create a national bestseller and have a large advertising budget, don't just advertise on Google and Facebook or in the *Boston Globe* or the *Washington Post.* Use some of that money to reach librarians by advertising in *Publishers Weekly, Booklist, Library Journal, School Library Journal,* and other publications librarians read. Space advertising is available, and so are e-blasts or events or newsletters that reach acquisition librarians.

Publishers often build a direct relationship with the library community. Many have a newsletter (or multiple newsletters) that go out regularly to librarians. Children's book publishers focus on children's acquisitions librarians at both public and school libraries. Publishers of adult books focus on the public library market. Publishers of more academic lists focus on academic and "special" libraries.

All the larger publishing houses, and many of the small and midsize houses, also reach librarians through trade shows. The most important is the American Library Association Conference and Exhibition, an annual opportunity to promote your books to librarians. The ALA also has a midwinter meeting attended by publishers and librarians. The costs of those shows can be a deterrent, but if you are serious about making the library market a significant part of your business, you need to be there—with your staff, through a distributor, or through a partnership of some kind.

There are some public library systems that are so big that publishers large and small try to cultivate relationships with them. They are the systems with dozens of branch locations that can, and do, order dozens or even hundreds of copies of a popular title that is in high demand. The biggest systems include the New York Public Library, the Queens Public Library, the Cuyahoga Public Library System, the County of Los Angeles Public Library, the Chicago Public Library, and the Miami-Dade Public Library System.

Libraries normally do not buy directly from publishers. Most have a contract with a book wholesaler who provides them with books at an agreed-upon discount and with the special services they need. So, in addition to promoting your books, you need to make sure your book or books are available through the major distributors. Baker & Taylor is the largest wholesaler of books to public libraries. A very large percentage of books bought by libraries from publishers of all sizes go through Baker & Taylor. In 2016, B&T was bought by Follett Corporation. Follett is the largest distributor of books to K–12 schools in the United States. So, if you want to reach the library market, you need to make sure that your title or titles are carried by Baker & Taylor and/or Follett. There are other wholesalers serving the library market, albeit on a smaller scale. They include Ingram Book Company, Brodart, Bookazine, Midwest Library Services, and others.

If you are self-publishing or selling through a distributor or if you are an author negotiating with a publisher, you will want to know whether or not your partner can reach the library market. Ask them: "Do you sell to Baker & Taylor?" and "How do you promote your books to the library market?" These are questions that a good partner can answer easily. An unclear or incomplete answer may mean your partner can't reach this important market with your book.

Most publishers, large and small, employ a combination of tactics, from reviews and advertising to advance reading copies to newsletters and trade shows to reach the library market. In some channels of distribution, you might have one customer buy 1,000 copies of a title. In this market, it might be 1,000 libraries buying one copy each. Organized and steady outreach is required, but the results are important to publishers, to authors, and to readers.

*

Bill Wolfsthal is a publishing and sales executive with more than three decades of experience selling children's books, fiction and nonfiction, trade and promotional titles, print books, and e-books into multiple sales channels for American publishers. He has worked for Harry N. Abrams, Skyhorse, Sterling, and Lyons Press.

PART IV.
THE YEAR IN
PUBLISHING

NEWS AND FINANCE

A YEAR UNLIKE ANY OTHER

BY JIM MILLIOT AND ED NAWOTKA

E ven before the coronavirus struck the U.S. in March, and the killing of
George Floyd by Minneapolis police led to widespread calls for new social
justice efforts, there were signs that 2020 would be industry-changing for
book publishing and bookselling.

The year began with the January publication by Flatiron Books of *American
Dirt* by Jeanine Cummins. The novel, in which a bookseller from Mexico flees
to America with her son to escape a drug cartel, soon became a lightning rod
as its critics said it was an inaccurate and stereotypical depiction of Mexico
and Mexicans; Cummins came under attack for appropriation, as she is neither
Mexican nor an immigrant. Flatiron canceled part of Cummins's tour, apolo-
gized for mistakes in the publishing process, and hired Nadxieli Nieto, editor
and former program director of literary awards at PEN America, as editor-at-
large to acquire upmarket and literary fiction, nonfiction, and YA, with a focus
on work by Latinx and BIPOC authors.

In early March, scores of employees at Hachette Book Group staged a walkout
to protest the acquisition of Woody Allen's memoir, *Apropos of Nothing*. The
employees were angered that HBG's Grand Central Publishing division had
made the deal despite longtime accusations that Allen had molested his adopted
daughter, Dylan Farrow, when she was seven years old. Allen has denied those
charges. After first standing by the decision to publish the book, HBG executives
ultimately dropped the title, which Skyhorse Publishing later published.

On June 8, about 1,300 workers across book and media industries, most of
them junior staffers, took action to protest the deaths of Floyd and "the many
other Black lives lost to racist violence in America," according to a statement

released by the organizing group. The action was a response to emails CEOs of the Big Five publishing companies sent to their employees addressing the continuing protests and the current political climate—statements the group considered inadequate in addressing issues of white supremacy, racist capitalism, and the killings of Black people at the hands of police.

The problems with the lack of diversity in publishing were further highlighted by the social media campaign #PublishingPaidMe, which revealed the inequities in advances paid to Black authors compared to white writers by encouraging writers to publicly share the advances they received. Though there was some debate about what #PublishingPaidMe actually quantified, it was generally acknowledged that authors of color have received lower advances than white authors.

As in the case of Flatiron with the *Dirt* backlash and HBG with the outcry over the Allen memoir, many publishers did in fact respond to the various calls for greater diversity, equity, and inclusion efforts. Penguin Random House US acknowledged that, though the company has made progress in diversifying its workforce and the types of books it publishes, it must do more on both counts. After conducting an analysis of the demographics of its employees, PRH announced a host of actions it was undertaking to diversify its publishing ranks and to publish more books by people of color. Hachette Book Group also reviewed the diversity of its workforce and authors, and shared the report with employees as the basis for setting goals for hiring more diverse staff and publishing more diverse voices. HBG also created Legacy Lit, a new imprint that will focus on books by BIPOC writers, which is headed by Krishan Trotman.

Among new executives hired by the big houses were journalist Dana Canedy, named publisher of Simon & Schuster's adult publishing group, succeeding Jonathan Karp, and Lisa Lucas, executive director of the National Book Foundation, appointed senior v-p and publisher of PRH's Pantheon and Schocken Books imprints.

Publishers also responded to demands that they raise starting salaries, which, among other things, would make it more economically feasible for BIPOC and others from marginalized or low-income communities to consider a career in publishing. Of the Big Five, all but HarperCollins announced they have, or are planning to, lift entry-level salaries to at least $40,000. A handful of independent publishers also raised entry-level wages, including Beacon Press and Grove Atlantic.

The fight for racial and social justice led to a boom in sales of books about race, much of which was funneled through the approximately 130 Black-owned and African American–focused bookstores in the U.S. The rush led to many of the most popular titles, such as Beacon's *White Fragility*, which sold over 850,000 print copies, and *How to Be an Antiracist* by Ibram X. Kendi, which sold over 770,000 copies, going out of stock and leaving many booksellers unable to fulfill many orders for several weeks.

The surge in demand revealed what Black booksellers have been telling publishers for years: there simply are not enough books in print or titles available to meet the needs of BIPOC readers. Several booksellers benefited both from sales and the renewed attention. Mahogany Books in Washington, D.C., saw a 400% increase in sales for June 2020 over June 2019, and sold 100,000 books in the 45 days after Floyd's death. Marcus Books, one of the country's best-known and oldest Black bookstores, founded in 1960 in San Francisco and now located in Oakland, had been struggling financially early in the year and had turned to GoFundMe to raise cash, eventually netting $261,000. Numerous new Black-owned bookstores opened this year, including Semicolon in Chicago and Fulton Street Books & Coffee in Tulsa, Okla., while several more, such as Niche Book Bar in Milwaukee, are in the works.

UPENDING INDUSTRY NORMS

As important as activism was to forcing industry changes, the coronavirus also left an indelible mark on trade publishing, in some cases accelerating trends that were already gaining momentum. Online sales surged, e-book sales rebounded, and digital audio sales continued to grow at double-digit rates while sales through bricks-and-mortar bookstores tumbled. Through October, bookstore sales were down 31% compared to the same period in 2019. In contrast, after giving publishers a scare by cutting book orders at the beginning of the pandemic to focus on essential items such as medicine and household staples, Amazon enjoyed record sales throughout the year. Amazon had total sales of $96 billion in the third quarter, up from $70 billion for the same period in 2019, and the fourth quarter is expected to be the best sales period in the company's history.

With auspicious timing, Bookshop.org launched in January, to try to counter Amazon by offering independent bookstores an improved online commerce hub. After many bookstores were forced to close in early spring due to pandemic-related lockdowns, Bookshop provided an online option for their customers. Profits from sales at Bookshop support expansion of the site, including abroad (the site launched in the U.K. in November), and are funneled back to affiliate independent bookstores. The site has sold more than $50 million in books. "We've earned $10,162,000 for bookstores this year, including direct store sales and our profit pool," said CEO Andy Hunter. "Our next profit pool distribution will happen in January, when we'll distribute over $2 million to stores." As of late December, 1,000 stores had signed up as affiliates in the U.S.

Bookshop's success was part of a larger online shift at indie booksellers. Digital audio bookseller Libro.fm reported a 48% increase in bookstore partnerships last year over 2019, and now works with 1,321 stores. The number of units sold jumped by 200% over 2019, Libro.fm said.

Barnes & Noble was looking to revive its fortunes under the leadership of new CEO James Daunt when 2020 began. The national lockdowns forced B&N, at one point, to close all but a handful of its locations. Daunt used the forced closures as an opportunity to refurbish many of its stores. Book buying at the chain was also changed, with the company shedding numerous buyers at its corporate offices in favor of granting many of its more than 625 stores more autonomy in buying front- and backlist titles that suit their local communities. Another focus of the company is streamlining its supply chain and reducing overstock and returns. Daunt said that local engagement is the key to winning customers away from competitors, and this must be done both in stores and at home, which can be done digitally and through better delivery options, such as curbside pickup, which proved especially popular when stores were closed to in-store browsing. Daunt expected to finish 2020 with sales no more than 20% below those of 2019.

The coronavirus also led to large numbers of employees leaving central offices to work remotely. While both employees and employers thought the shift would be temporary—some initial return-to-the-office targets were after Memorial Day—few employees were back by year-end. A *PW* survey conducted in late November assessing the impact of Covid-19 on work policies found that 375 (93%) of the 404 publishing employees that responded said they have worked remotely at some point this year—and of those who have, 360 (96%) said they continue to do so.

CONFERENCES MOVE ONLINE

The pandemic also forced most domestic and international book fairs and conferences to either cancel or hold online events rather than the traditional in-person meetings. The London Book Fair was the first major book fair to be canceled, in March. After scores of exhibitors began canceling their plans to attend, organizers called off the event one week before it was scheduled to take place.

Other events followed, including the Bologna International Children's Book Fair, which had originally moved its event from March to May, then shifted to holding a virtual event exclusively. Among the many international conferences that shifted to a virtual format were those in Beijing; Gothenburg, Sweden; Guadalajara, Mexico; Madrid; and Moscow. The Frankfurt Book Fair, which canceled all in-person events, drew more than 1.5 million viewers for its online events. Of the major global book fairs, only the Sharjah International Book Fair in November managed to host an in-person professional fair, albeit a very small one.

Reed Exhibitions, organizers of BookExpo and BookCon, held some online panels in late May after a plan to conduct a delayed live event in New York City's Javits Center became untenable, as the city had become an epicenter of the virus's outbreak in the U.S. in late spring. In late November, Reed announced it was "retiring" the two shows for 2021. Reed said it hoped the shows could return in a reimagined format at some point. The announcement did not surprise many industry members, since Reed had been trying for a number of years, with limited success, to develop an event that would meet the varied needs of the book world.

Most book business insiders contacted by *PW* expressed little interest in returning to the same version of BookExpo, but nearly all hoped some type of annual event could be created. BookExpo originated in 1901 as the American Booksellers Association convention. The ABA added trade exhibits in the mid-1940s, and Reed bought control of the show in the early 1990s. At its height, BookExpo attracted about 30,000 attendees, but attendance had trended down for years.

Two of the biggest industry players, Ingram and Penguin Random House, expressed support for a new event. "We are certainly sad to see the retirement of BookExpo, but know that our industry will find new ways for our colleagues to come together—perhaps in ways that haven't even yet been imagined," said an Ingram spokesperson.

Markus Dohle, PRH worldwide CEO, said the company "looks forward to working with our industry partners to explore a newly imagined event where we all can come together to celebrate books and their essential role in our society and culture."

PRH AGREES TO BUY S&S

In most years, the news that the country's largest trade publisher was acquiring the third-largest one would have overshadowed all other events. But 2020 was not an ordinary year. Following the March decision by Simon & Schuster's parent company, ViacomCBS, to place the publisher up for sale, Penguin Random House and its parent company, Bertelsmann, emerged the winner, acquiring S&S for $2.175 billion. Among the companies PRH beat out for S&S was the country's second-largest trade publisher, HarperCollins. Pending approval by regulatory authorities, the purchase is expected to be completed in the middle of 2021.

Several industry organizations raised concerns about the purchase, citing fears of more consolidation in the industry, with the country's largest trade publisher buying one of its largest rivals to form a company with revenue of about $3 billion. Both the Authors Guild and the American Booksellers Association called for the Department of Justice to investigate the purchase.

For its part, PRH said it does not expect any antitrust issues to arise. Markus Dohle said the U.S. book market remains highly fragmented and that even since the Penguin–Random House merger eight years ago, new publishing companies have been formed and continue to grow. Dohle said that when the time comes to integrate S&S and PRH, S&S will retain its editorial independence, while current S&S CEO Jonathan Karp and COO Dennis Eulau will join PRH.

THE TRADE LOSES TWO CEOS

The trade publishing industry had not seen a change among CEOs at the Big Five since Michael Pietsch took over at the Hachette Book Group for David Young in 2013. Under very different circumstances, Simon & Schuster and Macmillan Publishing got new CEOs in 2020.

In early May the industry was shocked by the news that CEO Carolyn Reidy had died of a heart attack at age 71. Reidy had worked at S&S since 1992, and had been CEO since 2008. During her tenure, she steered the company through the Great Recession, publishing's digital disruption, and a slow-growth sales environment to keep it a commercial and critical success. Employees and colleagues alike spoke of Reidy's love of the publishing business and her affection for her staff. Dennis Eulau pointed to Reidy's "rare combination of business acumen and creative genius that made her a once-in-a-lifetime publishing executive." Reidy was succeeded by Karp, who had been president and publisher of Simon & Schuster Adult Publishing since 2018.

In September, Macmillan Publishing stunned the industry with the announcement that its longtime CEO, John Sargent, would be leaving the company at the end of the year. In making the announcement, Macmillan's parent company, Holtzbrinck, said Sargent's departure was due to "disagreements regarding the direction of Macmillan." Don Weisberg, president of Macmillan US Trade, was named to succeed Sargent as CEO of the worldwide trade group, while Susan Winslow, general manager of Macmillan Learning, was appointed to head that division as president.

Despite all the year's turmoil, 2020 held one final surprise for trade publishing: sales are likely to be up over 2019. Unit sales of print books were up 7.8% over 2019 at outlets that report to NPD BookScan, with two weeks left to go in the year. The AAP reported that through October, sales of adult books in all formats were up 9.1% over the same period in 2019 at publishers that supply data to its StatShot program, while sales of children's/young adult titles rose 4.2%.

*

A version of this article appeared in the 01/04/2021 issue of *Publishers Weekly* under the headline: A Year Unlike Any Other.

NOTABLE PW PUBLISHING
STORIES OF 2021

New Report Explores 'Engagement' with Books, Digital Media
By Andrew Albanese | Feb 19, 2021

A new report released this week is being billed as the first study to capture critical data about how consumers "engage" with books within a "connected media ecosystem" that includes video games, TV, and movies.

The report, *Immersive Media & Books 2020,* is the most ambitious project yet from the Panorama Project, the cross-industry research initiative chartered in 2018 by leading digital library vendor OverDrive. Drawing on data from more than 4,300 "pre-qualified" respondents, surveyed from September through November of 2020, the report offers one of the most comprehensive looks at consumer media consumption and behavior in the e-book age, with demographic data broken down into three age groups, five U.S. regions, and seven racial/ethnic groups.

The study was designed and carried out by professors Rachel Noorda, Ph.D., and Kathi Inman Berens, Ph.D., faculty members of the Portland State University graduate program in Book Publishing, with financial support from OverDrive, the Book Industry Study Group, the American Library Association and the Independent Book Publishers Association.

The study's focus on consumer "engagement" with books—vs. "reading" behaviors—is a key distinction.

"To capture the wide range of things people do with books, we researchers asked people how many books they engaged per month, rather than how many books they read," explains the executive summary. "Reading for entertainment is still the #1 reason people buy books: 50% of survey respondents said that was their top reason to engage with a book. But that leaves a wide swath of book engagement behaviors—50%—that the industry could probe. This study provides the data to do so."

Engagement with books can run the gamut, researchers found, including people who check out materials from the library but don't always read or watch them, people who give books as gifts, buy them to collect or display, and people who dip into a book for reference, whether for work, school, or a hobby.

In terms of demographics, the report found strong book buying patterns among Black and Latinx millennials, labeling "men, millennials, and non-white people of all generations" as groups to pay attention to. "They engage with more books than middle-class baby boomer women, except in the context of book gifting," the report concluded.

The data also revealed interesting engagement patterns in the age of digital media, including multitasking. Some 61% of e-book readers and 70% of audiobook listeners reported multitasking when engaging with these book forms. "Our data support broadening the notion of what constitutes immersive attention," the authors conclude. "Immersion does not mean only the deep, uninterrupted concentration we associate with reading printed books or playing video games. Immersion can also happen while multitasking. The data support a more nuanced view of how entertainment products and formats feed different types of attention."

Among the report's other key findings: "avid" book engagers (those who engage with more than four books per month) are "equivalently active" across other media, which presents an opportunity for publishers to consider how books might benefit from cross-media discovery. The report also finds that book discovery is "context-agnostic and highly distributed." For example, the largest category of discovery—recommendations from friends—accounts for just one fifth of the survey population illustrating that there "are many ways people discover books and thus there are many ways to reach potential book buyers, borrowers, and gifters."

The report found that libraries, bookstores, and online channels "mutually reinforce" each other. Some 75% of respondents reported having library cards, with 30% saying they will choose to buy the book rather than wait when a book is stuck on a long holds list at the library. Also notable, more library card holders are buying books during the Covid-19 crisis (in all formats) than the general survey population. And activities like author events at libraries, browsing library shelves, and browsing online library catalogs, all lead to new book discovery.

When it comes to the Covid-19 crisis, the authors acknowledge that it has played a role in shaping consumer behavior in 2020, but how much of a role will be pulled more into focus over time.

"Over 2021 and beyond, the world will see whether new book engagement behaviors developed during the pandemic will persist beyond it," the report states. "Our study is proposed to be longitudinal; as we gather survey data going forward, the robust snapshot in this report will be contextualized by new answers to deliberately repeated questions, shedding light on new directions and behaviors the publishing industry should watch."

Method of Book Discovery

Amazon's recommendation algorithm
Recommendations from booksellers
Recommendations from librarians
Other
Bestseller lists (New York times, USA Today, Publishers Weekly, Amazon, etc.)
Review/book lists on book-related websites (Amazon, Audible, Barnes & Noble, Goodreads, etc.)
Recommendations on social media (Facebook, Instagram, Twitter, Reddit, YouTube, etc.)
Recommendations from family
Favorite author
Recommendations from friends

■ All ■ Preferred

SOURCE: IMMERSIVE MEDIA & BOOKS 2020

Note: Each respondent was first asked to select all of their methods of book discovery and then asked to select one preferred method.

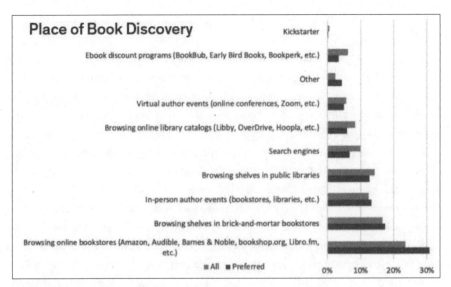

Place of Book Discovery

Kickstarter
Ebook discount programs (BookBub, Early Bird Books, Bookperk, etc.)
Other
Virtual author events (online conferences, Zoom, etc.)
Browsing online library catalogs (Libby, OverDrive, Hoopla, etc.)
Search engines
Browsing shelves in public libraries
In-person author events (bookstores, libraries, etc.)
Browsing shelves in brick-and-mortar bookstores
Browsing online bookstores (Amazon, Audible, Barnes & Noble, bookshop.org, Libro.fm, etc.)

■ All ■ Preferred

SOURCE: IMMERSIVE MEDIA & BOOKS 2020

Note: Each respondent was first asked to select all of their places of book discovery and then asked to select one preferred place.

*

A version of this article appeared in the 02/22/2021 issue of *Publishers Weekly* under the headline: Looking at Book Engagement.

Book Biz Closes Out an Unexpected 2020

By Jim Milliot | Apr 2, 2021

Last week Penguin Random House reported that it had a 23.3% increase in profits in

2020 over 2019 on a 4.6% gain in revenue, capping a remarkable year for America's five biggest trade publishers that report financial results. Despite the disruptions caused by the pandemic, all five had annual increases in both earnings and sales. Higher sales of e-books and digital audiobooks and solid gains of backlist titles helped drive the revenue and profit gains. Online sales also rose in the year, offsetting soft sales through bookstores due to pandemic-induced lockdowns.

According to PRH parent company Bertelsmann, PRH US had a particularly good year and drove the overall gains for the publisher. PRH US accounted for just over 58% of PRH's total revenue, or roughly $2.59 billion. In 2019, the U.S. represented 56% of PRH revenue (about $2.2 billion).

Worldwide, Bertelsmann said PRH benefited from strong sales of e-books and digital audiobooks, as well as from more online sales. The publisher's top title was Barack Obama's *A Promised Land*, which sold more than 7.3 million copies worldwide across all formats. Distribution sales increased 7% in the year.

PRH worldwide CEO Markus Dohle said that in 2021 the publisher will continue to use many of the strategic approaches it used last year, aligning its resources in sales, marketing, and publicity more "with a marketplace increasingly dependent on the online, e-commerce, and digital channels. Online optimization will help us grow our backlist sales significantly." He added that PRH will continue to invest in its supply chain, promising that the company "will steadfastly remain a loyal and reliable partner to physical bookstores."

Lagardère Publishing was the only one of the reporting publishers to post a revenue decline in 2020, but that 0.4% dip was for the company's worldwide business. In the U.S., sales increased 3.9% from 2019, and Hachette Book Group accounted for 29% of Lagardère's total revenue, or about $839 million. In the U.S., sales gains were led by Stephenie Meyer's huge bestseller *Midnight Sun*, as well as a number of titles connected with the Black Lives Matter movement. HBG also benefited from higher sales of e-books and downloadable audiobooks, as well as the acquisition of 1,000 children's titles from Disney Publishing Group early in the year.

HarperCollins saw sales in 2020 rise 7.9% over 2019, while profits jumped 33.2%. After a mixed start to the year, HC had a strong finish, with revenue in the final six months of 2020 up 18.3% over the second half of 2019. The big finish was led by what parent company News Corp termed a "historic" fourth quarter. HC revenue increased 23% in the three months ended December 31, and EBITDA (earnings before interest, taxes, depreciation, and amortization) soared 65%. News attributed the increase to trends that had been occurring for much of the final half of the year: strong backlist sales and strong digital sales, which rose 15% in the fourth quarter alone.

Like HarperCollins, Simon & Schuster closed out 2020 on a strong note, with sales up 17% in the final quarter over the last three months of 2019, reaching $252 million.

S&S CEO Jonathan Karp said a range of titles performed well in the period. For the full year, all formats had gains over 2019, and total digital sales accounted for 28.5% of S&S's revenue. The company also had solid sales through mass merchandisers, including Walmart and Target, and sales to Amazon were also up.

Overall, the S&S adult division had a great year, Karp said—especially in nonfiction, where the publisher had one of the year's biggest bestsellers, Mary J. Trump's *Too Much and Never Enough*, and where other Trump-related titles performed well. Sales in the children's division were flat. International sales were up, led by good results in Canada, the U.K., and Australia.

The Houghton Mifflin Harcourt Books & Media division turned an operating loss in 2019 into a profit last year, with sales up 6.5%. The company attributed the revenue gain largely to licensing agreements, including a new $9.6 million deal for an undisclosed series. HMH's deal with Netflix earned the publisher $3.4 million last year.

Operating Performances 2019–2020
(in millions)

HarperCollins

	2019	2020	Change
Total Sales	$1,687.0	$1,821.0	7.9%
EBITDA	$208.0	$277.0	33.2%
Margin	12.3%	15.2%	–

Houghton Mifflin Books & Media

	2019	2020	Change
Total Sales	$180.0	$191.7	6.5%
Operating income	(8.1)	4.2	NM
Margin	NM	2.3%	–

Lagardère Publishing

	2019	2020	Change
Total Sales	€2,384.0	€2,375.0	-0.4%
Recurring EBIT	€220.0	€246.0	11.8%
Margin	9.2%	10.3%	–

Penguin Random House

	2018	2019	Change
Total Sales	€3,636.0	€3,802.0	4.6%
Operating EBIT	€561.0	€691.0	23.3%
Margin	15.4%	18.2%	–

Simon & Schuster

	2019	2020	Change
Total Sales	$814.0	$901.0	10.7%
OIBDA	$127.0	$141.0	11.0%
Margin	15.6%	15.6%	–

SOURCE: COMPANY REPORTS, PUBLISHERS WEEKLY

Book sales were relatively flat in the year, HMH said. Sales in both the adult and children's groups were down from 2019, and the company blamed bookstore closures and delays in releasing certain new frontlist titles.

Prospects for the five companies are decidedly mixed. S&S and HMH Books & Media will all but certainly finish 2021 as part of PRH and HC, respectively. (HC agreed to buy HMH trade last week) Prior to announcing the deal for HMH, News executives said that, though they expect trends in reading and book buying to remain strong, they are worried about difficult fourth-quarter comparisons. That concern should be lessened with the HMH purchase.

Lagardère executives expressed some caution about the year, explaining it isn't clear if the opening up of different entertainment venues and restaurants will affect the time people spend reading.

*

A version of this article appeared in the 04/05/2021 issue of *Publishers Weekly* under the headline: Closing Out an Unexpected 2020.

Trade Publishing Segment Shines in a Flat 2020
By Jim Milliot | Feb 25, 2021

In a result no one in publishing would have predicted last spring when Covid-19 first hit the U.S., book publishing sales finished 2020 flat with 2019 based on year-end figures supplied by 1,354 publishers to AAP's StatShot program. The two major trade categories, adult books and children/young adult, had gains of 12% and 6.4%, respectively, while the two big educational segments saw declines.

With many public schools teaching remotely for long stretches of last year, sales of K-12 instructional materials fell 19.6% in 2020 compared to 2019. Sales of higher educational course materials declined 4.3% last year as many colleges and university turned to hybrid instruction, which changed buying habits by students.

In the adult books segment, sales of both print and digital formats rose in the year. Hardcover sales had the largest increase, up 18.9% over 2019. They were helped by a strong December, during which sales, boosted by big sales of Barack Obama's *A Promised Land*—which had a $45 cover price—rose 25.8%. Trade paperback sales increased 7.8% in the year, while mass market paperback sales dipped by 2.5%.

The downloadable audio format had another great year, with sales up 15.3%. Its share of all adult sales inched up to 10.3% in 2020, from 10% in 2019. E-books had their strongest performance in several years, with sales rising 11% over 2019, but since print sales had a bigger annual increase, e-books' share of adult sales fell slightly, to 17%, from 17.2% in 2019.

PUBLISHER SALES BY CATEGORIES, 2019–2020

(\$ in millions)

CATEGORY	2019	2020	CHANGE
Adult Books	\$4,914	\$5,502	12.0%
Children & Young Adult Books	\$2,283	\$2,430	6.4%
Religious Books	\$640	\$667	4.2%
Professional Books	\$613	\$619	1.0%
K–12 Instructional Materials	\$3,168	\$2,547	-19.6%
Higher Educational Course Materials	\$3,001	\$2,872	-4.3%
University Presses	\$48	\$49	2.2%
All other	\$70	\$65	-6.6%
Total	\$14,739	\$14,753	0.1%

SOURCE: AAP STATSHOT

In the children/YA category, digital sales in the year skyrocketed but still remained a relatively small part of overall revenue. E-book sales jumped 70.5% in the year and accounted for 5.5% of category sales, while downloadable audio sales increased 37% and accounted for 2.8% of revenue. The board book format had a great year, with sales up 18.2% and accounting for 7.9% of overall sales. Hardcover sales increased 5.6%, while paperback sales rose 3.2%.

The year-end numbers are a solid recovery from April and May, when disruptions to the supply chain caused the AAP to note that gross sales were experiencing deep declines—all while acknowledging that net sales were faring better because of a steep drop in returns. (AAP calculates net sales by deducting returns from gross sales.) Many in the industry were bracing for a flood of returns once the supply chain improved, but excessive returns never materialized. For the year, total returns were down 20.2% compared to 2019, with returns in both trade segments each down by about 20%.

Later this year, the AAP will issue estimates for total industry sales, which combines StatShot figures with projections for companies that do not report data to the association.

*

A version of this article appeared in the 03/01/2021 issue of *Publishers Weekly* under the headline: Trade Shines in Flat Year.

The Surge of Print Books Sales Continues
Unit sales of print books jumped 29% in 2021's first quarter
By Jim Milliot | Apr 9, 2021

Unit sales of print books rose a remarkable 29.2% in the first quarter of 2021 over the same period in 2020 at outlets that report to NPD BookScan. Though some of that gain was due to the slump in sales that occurred in mid-March last year, most of the increase was due to the surge in book buying that began last spring and carried over into 2021. All six major categories tracked by BookScan had double-digit increases, and all four print formats posted gains.

Units rose 24.6% in adult nonfiction, the industry's largest category. Sales in the home and gardening subcategory, which began to take off late last April, remained strong into the first quarter of 2021, up 54.1% in the period. Sales of general non-fiction increased 44.7%, while sales in the self-help and biography/autobiography/memoir areas rose 38.8% and 35.7%, respectively. The long-awaited revival in travel books has not arrived yet, with unit sales down nearly 25%.

Print sales of adult fiction increased 34.7% in the quarter. Graphic novels led the way, with sales soaring almost 146%. Big gains were also seen in fantasy (up 48.4%), science fiction (40.6%), and romance (29.9%).

Sales in the juvenile fiction category jumped 39.6%. The smallest increase was in the SF/fantasy/magic subcategory, where units still rose 20.7%. The largest gain came in animal books, with print units jumping 64.7%.

The juvenile nonfiction category—the first segment to show big sales gains last year as parents flocked to buy educational materials for children who were stuck at home after schools closed—had a relatively modest 11.7% increase in the first quarter. Unit sales fell in two of last year's most popular nonfiction subject areas: sales of education/reference/language books declined 15.6%, and sales of games/activities/hobbies titles slipped 2.3%. All other subcategories within juvenile nonfiction were still posting better-than-double-digit increases through the end of March, led by biographies/auto-biographies, where sales were up 40.1%.

In young adult, fiction sales jumped 62.8% and nonfiction rose 42.9%. Two back-list books led the gains in YA fiction: *We Were Liars* by E. Lockhart sold more than 155,000 copies and Adam Silvera's *They Both Die at the End* sold over 140,000 copies.

The top sellers

While backlist sales remained strong in the quarter, two new releases took the top spots: Dav Pilkey's *Mothering Heights (Dog Man #10)* was #1, selling more than 411,000 copies in just two weeks on sale, and Kristin Hannah's *The Four Winds*, published in early February, sold almost 390,000 print copies. A third new title that cracked the top 10 list was Sanjay Gupta's *Keep Sharp*, which sold more than 245,000 copies.

In addition to the strong showing by the new Dog Man book, the juvenile fiction segment benefited from higher than usual sales of Dr. Seuss titles, with four in the top 10. Interest in Seuss books rose this winter when Dr. Seuss Enterprises, which oversees the author's estate, said it would stop printing six books written between 1937 and 1976 because of concerns that the titles portrayed people in hurtful ways. (None of the six have had meaningful sales in years.)

The Hill We Climb by Amanda Gorman, published March 30, was the #12 title in the quarter, selling about 214,000 copies in its first week. Gorman read the poem at the inauguration of President Joe Biden.

UNIT SALES OF PRINT BOOKS FIRST QUARTER, 2020-2021
(in thousands)

	2020	2021	CHANGE
Total	158,033	204,710	29.2%
Category			
Adult Nonfiction	66,439	82,382	24.6%
Adult Fiction	28,964	39,015	34.7%
Juvenile Nonfiction	15,868	17,720	11.7%
Juvenile Fiction	38,870	54,263	39.6%
Young Adult Fiction	4,233	6,891	62.8%
Young Adult Nonfiction	654	934	42.9%
Format			
Hardcover	43,254	58,889	36.1%
Trade Paperback	88,829	111,556	25.6%
Mass Market Paperback	8,938	10,201	14.1%
Board Books	10,004	14,119	41.1%

SOURCE: NPD BOOKSCAN

*

A version of this article appeared in the 04/12/2021 issue of *Publishers Weekly* under the headline: The Surge Continues.

How Ingram Content Group Became a $2 Billion Company

By Jim Milliot | Apr 16, 2021

In its first year, 1970, the Ingram Book Co. had sales of $1 million and employed 18 people, but by 2020, its successor, the Ingram Content Group, had revenue topping $2 billion. That is just one nugget that publishing insiders (and other readers) will find in *The Family Business: How Ingram Transformed the World of Books*, set to be released April 20 by West Margin Press, an Ingram subsidiary.

Written by journalist (and onetime Ingram spokesman) Keel Hunt, *The Family Business* chronicles Ingram Content Group's 50-year evolution from the Ingram Book Co.—formed to house the Tennessee Book Co., which Bronson Ingram bought in 1964 for $245,000—to the country's largest book wholesaler, largest print-on-demand company, and largest independent book distributor.

As a 50-year chart of its revenue shows, ICG did not have steady annual growth. Indeed, the company has had its ups and downs, reflecting trends in the entire trade book business. Ingram enjoyed sustained growth from about 1990–2000, fueled in part by the expansion of bookstore chains. Growth temporarily peaked in 2000 at about $1.5 billion, dipping because of changes in the retail market, then started to rebound in 2005. The company rode the financial roller-coaster through 2015, through the digital evolution of the book business. However, ICG has had very strong gains since 2016, as the various initiatives begun by John Ingram took hold.

Hunt divides up the financial performance of ICG into two broad periods—1970 through 1995, and 1996 through 2020—to show how new services have driven the company's expansion. In 2005, new businesses accounted for 13% of total revenue and legacy businesses accounted for 87%. In 2020, new businesses accounted for 64% of revenue and legacy businesses 36%.

Two of the most important additions to ICG were Lightning Source and Ingram Publisher Services. Lightning Source began life in 1997 as Lightning Print under the direction of Y.S. Chi and Larry Brewster with the goal of printing as few as one copy at a time in contrast to the runs of tens of thousands of copies done by offset presses. Lightning Print produced its first book in January 1998 and at the end of that year had only 1,500 titles in its library. With the support of John Ingram, the company persevered, but Lightning Source didn't turn its first annual profit until 2004.

By 2020, Lightning Source had more than 18 million titles in its inventory and had developed the Guaranteed Availability Program (GAP), which helps publishers when they have trouble meeting demand because of problems with offset printing. According to *The Family Business*, that was the case in 2020, due to pandemic-induced supply chain disruptions. Demand for the GAP service "shot through the roof" last spring, Hunt writes, and GAP produced 400,000 books in June. In the week of June

26, five of the top 10 titles on the *New York Times'* nonfiction bestseller list "were supplied primarily by GAP," he noted.

Ingram Publisher Services shipped the first books from its first customer, Applewood Books, in March 2005, but Ingram's first attempt to enter the distribution business was in the late 1980s with Publisher Resources Inc. PRI was kept separate from Ingram's core operations, and the combination of that separation and the perception that it wasn't offering enough value to publishers led to the steady dismantling of the division, which was closed in 2003. The lessons learned from PRI, however, helped Phil Ollila create IPS.

That distribution operation took a major leap forward in spring 2016 when ICG bought the Perseus distribution business, which had annual sales of about $300 million. Hunt quotes John Ingram as saying that with the purchase, "the center of gravity for the Ingram Content Group shifted from wholesale to publisher services."

Another new business that has helped ICG expand in recent years is IngramSpark, the company's self-publishing operation. Launched in 2013, a key attribute of IngramSpark is its easy access to Lightning Source, which allows indie authors to quickly print as many, or as few, copies of their books as they want. Originally overseen by Robin Cutler, IngramSpark had more than $100 million in sales in 2020, had published more than seven million books, and was adding 4,000 new books each day.

An attempt at online bookselling

Although expansion into a range of digital services, including the 2005 creation of the digital asset management system CoreSource, helped to increase ICG revenues, not all innovations succeeded. One such effort was Ingram Internet Support Services (I2S2). Begun in 1996, it was an attempt to start an online bookselling platform that could be used by independent bookstores, and Ingram would benefit by handling shipping to customers directly from its warehouses. Faced with intense discounting pressure on books from Amazon, however, Ingram gave up the idea in less than a year.

John Ingram said the company's experience with I2S2 gave ICG the knowledge it needed to create a viable third-party distribution system and helped the company build a fulfillment business that now, according to Hunt, represents "a sizeable fraction of Ingram's business."

The blockbuster deal that wasn't

In addition to providing a look at ICG's different businesses, *The Family Business* sheds light on some of publishing's most pivotal moments, including the failed acquisition of the Ingram Book Group by Barnes & Noble in 1998 and 1999. According to the book, the idea for the purchase came from B&N owner Len Riggio during a brainstorming session among B&N executives and Ingram brass. John Ingram was intrigued by the proposal because it came at a time when consolidation among both its retail customers and publisher partners was putting pressure on the company's traditional wholesale business. In addition, John Ingram was concerned that B&N and Borders would expand their own supply networks and was increasingly worried about the rapid growth of online bookselling.

Riggio made an initial offer of $450 million, but before accepting, Ingram talked to three other potential buyers: Borders, Amazon, and Bertelsmann, which at the time was in the process of buying Random House. The overtures pushed the B&N offer up to $600 million. Then strenuous opposition from many parts of the book business, especially independent booksellers, led the FTC to oppose the deal, and the plan was dropped.

Hunt writes that John Ingram suspected that part of Riggio's intent in making the proposal was to keep Ingram Book Company out of Amazon's hands and deprive the upstart of an efficient distribution operation. But as the regulatory process dragged on, "it became clear that Amazon was going to build more of their own warehouses, rather than buy Ingram," John Ingram told Hunt. "I think B&N became less interested."

The collapse of the deal was a "heavy blow to John," Hunt writes, but it made him more determined to find ways to expand the company and to create a new version of the Ingram Content Group.

*

A version of this article appeared in the 04/19/2021 issue of *Publishers Weekly* under the headline: How Ingram Content Group Became a $2 Billion Company.

Saluting HMH, a Storied Trade Publisher
The former head of HMH trade remembers a feisty and proud house, now gone
By Gary Gentel | Jun 18, 2021

I came to the trade division at Houghton Mifflin in fall 2003 as senior v-p of trade sales, at the tail end of the Lord of the Rings movie trilogy. The French conglomerate Vivendi had purchased Houghton a few years earlier, taken it private, and had sold it to a consortium of bankers and investors at a huge loss. Vivendi was the first, but it wouldn't be the last disastrous foreign investor in what had historically been the highly profitable U.S. education business. Meanwhile, the trade division was coming off an outstanding three-year run thanks to Tolkien—perhaps the best in its long and storied history.

The longevity of HM (founded in 1832) isn't unique among publishing houses, but it was certainly a source of pride inside the division and within the larger corporation. There was a deep respect for the history, close attention to the present, and a vision for the future. In other words, it was a company that knew what it was about: educating and entertaining children and adults. But dark clouds were forming on the horizon.

The education marketplace had been a cash-rich business for decades, with much higher margins than those in the consumer business. Educational spending was slowly but steadily rising in these years, which attracted investor attention. In short, the industry was ripe for takeover and consolidation. Investors began leveraging these cash-rich businesses, taking on what they thought was manageable debt and looking for synergies across their acquisitions.

In December 2006, Riverdeep Holdings purchased Houghton Mifflin. One year later, Riverdeep purchased the educational and consumer publisher Harcourt Education and created Houghton Mifflin Harcourt. Both purchases were highly leveraged. In need of cash to service its enormous debt, Riverdeep sold the trade imprint Kingfisher to Macmillan, and shortly after, sold the college division to Thompson Learning (now Cengage).

It was in this environment that I was asked to take over as president of the trade division in fall 2007. A year later, the Great Recession roiled the economy and educational spending plummeted. After a tumultuous and difficult year of painful cost cutting, the trade division was put up for sale in 2009. Offers were made, but a deal was never struck. Through several debt restructurings, and a few turnovers in the corner office, the company went public in 2013.

In 2015 HMH made a cash purchase of Scholastic's EdTech business, but the financial pressures in the education business continued. In 2018, the standardized testing division, Riverside, was sold. In fall 2020, more than 500 employees were laid off. Once HMH made the decision to transition into a primarily digital company, it was only a matter of time before what was called HMH Books and Media (Trade) was sold to continue paying down the debt.

I retired as president of the trade group in summer 2016. For all its ups and downs, the 13 years I spent at HM(H) were the best years of my career. Working with the best authors, illustrators, and the highly committed and engaged staff brought out the best in all of us. I knew, when I was asked to head up the division in 2007, that I was only the latest traveler among a long continuum of extremely talented and dedicated people who had come before me. I was no more nor less important than any of those who made up the fabric of a place like Houghton. I sensed from my first day there that this place was different. It was intangible, but you could feel it. It was special. I reminded myself daily not to screw it up.

And now, it's gone. Yes, the HMH logo will appear on the spines and copyright pages of books and audios for a short while, but the proud and feisty trade publisher we all loved and adored is no more, with the brand to be used by the digital technology company. HMH is now part of history, another merger story, among so many in publishing.

During my 40-plus years in the book business, I've experienced my share of mergers and acquisitions, but this one especially hurts. For those of us who have recent experience at HMH, and those who are long gone from HM, it's a sad day. Seeing this iconic publisher disappear—a home to so many throughout the centuries and decades—is a punch to the gut.

But wow! I am so proud of all we accomplished. What a publishing legacy HMH leaves behind. That, at least, makes me smile.

*

Gary Gentel was president of the HMH trade division from 2007 until his retirement in 2016.

A version of this article appeared in the 06/21/2021 issue of *Publishers Weekly* under the headline: Saluting a Storied Publisher.

High Costs, Services Disruptions Plague Book Biz Supply Chain
By Jim Milliot | Jul 7, 2021

Truck driver shortages, widespread port congestion, and skyrocketing container costs are among the biggest challenges facing the book industry supply chain for the rest of the year and into 2022, panelists on a July 6 BISG webinar looking at freight and shipping issues agreed.

Book International's v-p of global business development David Hetherington said that, in all his time in the book business, he has never seen such pressure building in the supply chain as is happening now. He predicted that things could get worse as more buying shifts online and more packages need to go directly to consumers' homes.

Hetherington, along with Ryan Forbes of Readerlink and Susie Scally of the international logistics firm Meadows Wye, also agreed that now is not the time for publishers to negotiate with trucking companies or the major delivery services. The lack of freight capacity is a real issue, Forbes said, and companies don't need to yield on price. It is estimated, for example, that there is now a truck driver shortage totaling to 60,000. Trucking firms are also having difficulty sourcing large trailers to move books, Forbes explained.

Scally focused her remarks on the international markets, noting that while it is difficult getting timely shipments out of China, "congested ports are everywhere." Complicating delivery times, Scally added, is that even when goods reach a U.S. port, the infrastructure isn't in place to speed shipments to domestic locations. Observing that shipping companies have managed to jack up the price of containers, Scally said that publishers need to deal with the reality that the cost of transporting books is extremely high and that they need to be ready to "pay the bill" and not bicker over price. Scally added that she doesn't see the costs of containers ever going down to pre-pandemic levels.

All three speakers also said that it is important for publishers to see what is happening in the publishing supply chain in the context of the entire American economy. The U.S., Forbes noted, is working through a year's worth of pent-up demand that is intensifying competition for shipping and freight services among all sectors, Forbes said.

The three speakers also agreed that publishers need to make adjustments to their supply chains. "While challenges are significant, many are surmountable—but changes to the supply chain are mandatory," Hetherington said.

Making some suggestions on how the business should adjust, Hetherington said publishers need to look more closely at the benefits of domestic digital printing, emphasizing that publishers—given the escalating costs of shipping and freight—should pay more attention to lowering the total cost of ownership rather than unit costs. He also urged publishers to shorten their supply chains as much as possible, and suggested that publishers ship to customers directly from their manufacturer whenever possible.

Bookshop.org Continues to See Strong Sales
By Ed Nawotka | Jul 8, 2021

Online bookseller Bookshop.org is on track this month to surpass $15 million returned to independent bookstores since the company began in 2019. That figure is in addition to the $250,000 it donated to Binc's "Survive to Thrive" campaign. "It is a milestone we are anticipating surpassing by the end of July," Andy Hunter, CEO of Bookshop.org, said.

Sales have reached $29 million this year, including tax and shipping, and are up 17% for the first half of 2021 compared with 2020. That increase comes despite an expected decline in sales compared to a year ago since April, when most bookstores around the country began to reopen for normal business. In the April-June period, sales were down 20% from the comparable time in 2020, less than the 30% drop that Hunter had been expecting. "Last year, June was very busy for us, particularly with the huge sales of antiracist books with the Black Lives Matter protests happening around the country. This year is more like a normal June."

The site currently hosts 1,100 bookstores, with 400 using Bookshop exclusively for their e-commerce and another 700 that use it in addition to their own e-commerce solutions. Notably, among the top 10 highest-earning bookstore sites on Bookshop, six are Black-owned bookstores, Hunter said. Of the sites top-selling books, several are multicultural and diverse titles, including *How the Word Is Passed* by Clint Smith (Little, Brown), *Somebody's Daughter* by Ashley Ford (Flatiron), *Yoke* by Jessamyn Stanley (Workman), and *Crying in H Mart* by Michelle Zauner (Knopf), *The Other Black Girl* by Zakiya Dalila Harris (Atria) and *Long Division* by Kiese Laymon (Scribner).

"Our bestseller list does not look like the typical list," Hunter said. "It reflects the diversity and iconoclastic nature of the community we serve."

The site launched in the U.K. last year and in Spain earlier this year. Now, the focus is on improving the user experience in the United States, Hunter said. Among the plans are to allow bookstores to sell merchandise and sidelines, allow in-store pick up and, eventually, fulfill directly from a bookstore's own stock. "Ultimately, we want bookstores to succeed and our goal is to help them capture more e-commerce," Hunter said. To help promote Bookshop.org, Kimberly Sneed recently joined the company as chief marketing officer. Sneed served as director of brand strategy and partnerships at Penguin Random House from 2012 to 2015.

In addition to bookstores, Bookshop.org has some 26,000 affiliates, such as magazines, media outlets and influencers, which generated $8 million in sales in 2020. "Oprah, *Time*, the *Atlantic*, are all selling books through us," Hunter said, adding, "a year ago they all would have linked to Amazon, but we pay twice as much as Amazon does for affiliate sales."

Addressing competition, Hunter said he wants to see Barnes & Noble succeed, but sees Amazon as a rival—one that is vulnerable in certain ways. "There is more awareness than ever of the damage Amazon can do to communities and the book ecosystem," said Hunter. "There is more antitrust activity happening around Amazon and a social awakening among consumers about how they spend their money and trying to do it in a socially conscious way. Consumers know they are creating the future with how they spend their money."

Print Book Sales Soar in Year's First Half
By Jim Milliot | Jul 9, 2021

In the first half of 2020, unit sales of print books surprised many in the industry by posting a 2.9% increase over the same period in 2019 at outlets that report to NPD BookScan, overcoming a slump in sales in early spring following the onset of the Covid-19 pandemic. Print sales finished 2020 up 8.2% over 2019, and that strong performance continued into 2021, with units jumping 18.5% in the first six months over the comparable period in 2020. With the exception of the juvenile nonfiction category, all the major publishing categories had double-digit sales increases in the first half of the year. Backlist had the strongest gains, up 21.4%, but frontlist sales were also solid, rising 12.4%.

The increase in the first half of 2021 was led by the adult fiction category, where units rose 30.7%. The top seller in the category was Kristin Hannah's *The Four Winds*, which sold more than 558,000 copies since its release in early February (see "2021 Bestselling Print Books [So Far]"). The other top sellers in adult fiction were a mix of new releases and backlist titles. *Where the Crawdads Sing* by Delia Owens took two spots on the category bestseller list: the trade paperback edition sold more than 294,000 copies following its publication at the end of March, while the hardcover edition was #20, selling nearly 151,000 copies.

The big story in adult fiction was the strength of the graphic novel format. Unit sales soared 178.5% in the first half of the year, rising to 16.2 million copies sold, making graphic novels the second-largest adult fiction subcategory. Graphic novels made up nearly 20% of adult fiction unit sales in the first six months of 2021, compared to 9.3% last year.

Viz Media was one of the big beneficiaries of the graphic novel boom. Kohei Horikoshi's *My Hero Academia, Vol. 26* was the top adult graphic novel in the first half of the year, selling more than 90,000 copies. Other volumes in the Academia line also sold well, including volume two (about 82,000 copies sold) and volume one (81,000 copies). *Demon Slayer: Kimetsu No Taiba, Vol. 1* by Koyoharu Gotouge, also published by Viz, sold more than 82,000 copies. A title published by a company other than Viz, *Attack on Titan, Vol. 1* by Hajime Isayama, published by Kodansha, sold nearly 88,000 copies.

YA fiction sales had the largest gain among all the major categories in the first half of 2021, with units up 48.8%. The jump came despite tough comparisons to the first half of 2020, when Suzanne Collins's Hunger Games prequel, *The Ballad of Songbirds and Snakes*, sold more than 887,000 copies, making it the bestselling book in the period. This year's top-title in the category was *They Both Die at the End* by Adam Silvera, which sold nearly 331,000 copies. First published in December 2018, *They Both Die* was propelled up the charts by exposure on BookTok, a forum that lifted sales of a number of YA titles this year.

Juvenile fiction sales rose 17.8% in the first six months of 2021, and the category had the most popular book in the period. *Mothering Heights (Dog Man #10)* by Dav Pilkey sold more than 867,000 copies, and Pilkey's *Cat Kid Comic Club* sold almost 370,000 copies.

Adult nonfiction unit sales rose 15.6% in the first half of the year, driven by increases across most subcategories. Sales of self-help books had the largest gain, up 32.1%, followed by business and economics books, up 24%, and home and gardening and general nonfiction, which both had increases of just over 22%. Only two areas had sales declines: humor, where sales fell 17.4%, and crafts/hobbies/antiques/games, where sales dipped 1.2%. The #1 title in the category was *The Hill We Climb* by

Amanda Gorman, the book version of the poem she read at President Biden's inauguration, which sold more than 455,000 copies.

In the first six months of 2020, the juvenile nonfiction category had the strongest sales gain over the first half of 2019, with print units up 25.5%, as demand for books geared toward helping parents educate and entertain their children at home soared. Sales in the category were expected to decline this year, but the drop has been mild, with sales down 3.2% compared to the first half of 2020 (and sales are up substantially from the 27.5 million copies sold in the first half of 2019). Sales of education/reference/language books, the second-largest subcategory within juvenile nonfiction, fell the most, down 26.5%. Sales of social history/sports/people/places titles, the largest juvenile nonfiction subcategory, rose 2.7%. The biggest gain came in social situations/family/health titles, where sales increased 46.2%.

Unit sales throughout the first half of 2021 have shown continuous weekly increases compared to 2020, but sales gains have become smaller. In the first quarter, sales of print books were up 29% over the first quarter of 2020, a margin that has shrunk in the second quarter to about 8%. Some publishers have expressed concern over how the balance of 2021 will play out, as reading and book buying face more competition from forms of entertainment that were unavailable during Covid lockdowns. Others are betting that the rise in reading will remain for some period of time. There are still six months left to see who is right.

UNIT SALES OF PRINT BOOKS, 2020–2021
(in thousands)

	2020	2021	CHANGE
Total	326,449	386,689	18.5%
Category			
Adult Nonfiction	133,859	154,764	15.6%
Adult Fiction	62,692	81,923	30.7%
Juvenile Nonfiction	35,130	34,009	-3.2%
Juvenile Fiction	77,524	91,304	17.8%
Young Adult Fiction	9,861	14,670	48.8%
Young Adult Nonfiction	1,636	1,947	20.6%
Format			
Hardcover	91,023	112,360	23.4%
Trade Paperback	187,047	219,615	17.4%
Mass Market Paperback	18,651	19,605	5.1%
Board Books	19,044	22,123	20.1%

SOURCE: NPD BOOKSCAN

A version of this article appeared in the 07/12/2021 issue of *Publishers Weekly* under the headline: Half-Year Print Sales Soar.

Print Book Sales Could Grow by 2% This Year—Or by 8%

By Jim Milliot | Jul 22, 2021

Few people in the industry have been willing to venture a prediction on how the book business will finish 2021, but in a July 21 presentation on industry print unit sales through the first half of the year, NPD BookScan analyst Kristen McLean laid out three possible scenarios. All outcomes assume that the rapid gains in print unit sales the industry has posted so far this year will slow in the last six months of 2021.

Indeed, McLean noted that, since the end of what she called an historic first quarter, the year-to-date growth rate has lost about one point per week; in other words, growth was up 29% at the close of the first quarter and ahead 18% at the end of the second quarter. At present, she said, sales appear to be steadily gliding back to a more normal performance.

If that is the case and sales run even with 2020 for the balance of the year, print unit sales will finish 2021 with an 8% gain over last year. If sales return closer to 2019 levels—which means a decline in sales in the last months of the year compared to 2020—sales would still finish the year ahead up 2% over 2020. The fastest growth rate, at 10% for the year, will be possible only if higher infection rates result in more lockdowns and stay-at-home orders, she said. Publishing "performed well with people at home," McLean said in explaining why lockdowns may be good for the industry. She noted that she believes the 10% increase to be the least likely scenario, predicting that unit sales will finish the year with gains between 2% and 8%.

The biggest wild card factor, she said, is the future course of the virus, as there is still much uncertainty about how Covid-19 will impact the country. The ongoing pandemic has led to higher-than-normal differences in book sales among various geographic areas, she noted, which complicates how sales will continue to perform.

Prior to making her prediction, McLean reviewed trends through July 3, in which sales were up 18.4% above last year. Two of the biggest drivers of sales in the period came from graphic novels and young adult fiction. Half of the increase in graphic novel sales came from manga, McLean said, attributing the growth in part to streaming services, which have featured a number of shows based on manga stories.

The gains in young adult, McLean said, were given a huge boost by #BookTok. BookScan began to see videos about people's favorite books posted on the platform at the end of the year, and that trend has continued into 2021. The increase in manga sales and YA is good for the industry in the long and short runs, McLean noted, since it means publishing is attracting younger readers.

And while backlist continues to sell exceptionally well in 2021, frontlist sales picked up in the second quarter, gaining 3 points of market share from backlist. Still, at the end of the first half of 2021, backlist still accounted for 69% of print units sold.

*

A version of this article appeared in the 07/26/2021 issue of *Publishers Weekly* under the headline: Where Will 2021 Sales Land?

BOOK BIZ SAW LITTLE M&A IN 2020, WITH SOME BIG EXCEPTIONS

BY JIM MILLIOT | JAN 15, 2021

The economic uncertainty caused by both the pandemic and the presidential election limited merger and acquisition activity in 2020, but there were still a number of significant transactions. The most dramatic move, of course, was Penguin Random House's November 25 announcement that it had agreed to acquire Simon & Schuster for $2.175 billion—the biggest trade book deal in American publishing history. PRH expects to complete the acquisition sometime around the middle of this year.

ViacomCBS announced early in 2020 that it was looking to sell S&S, but it paused negotiations when the pandemic hit in March. Discussions heated up in early fall as ViacomCBS looked to close the deal before the end of the year. That pattern can be seen in overall deal announcements in 2020: a smattering of acquisitions were announced early on, while the summer saw a dearth of deals before transactions picked up in the fall.

The only book-publishing-related acquisition that was completed in July and August was CJK Group's purchase of a printing plant that Quad/Graphics had put up for sale after its agreement to buy LSC Communications was terminated. Quad completed its exit from the book printing business in November with its sale of two other facilities to Bertelsmann Printing Group USA. The pandemic contributed to the challenges the country's largest book printer, LSC, faced after the merger with Quad was called off, and in April LSC filed for Chapter 11 bankruptcy. In September the private equity firm Atlas Holdings was named the winner in the auction to buy LSC's assets, and that deal was completed in December.

The biggest transaction in the digital area was investment firm KKR's purchase of OverDrive from Rakuten USA, a subsidiary of Japan's Rakuten Inc.

The deal was announced the day after Christmas in 2019, but the closing, originally scheduled for the first quarter of last year, did not occur until June. Last week OverDrive reported that 2020 was a record year for digital audio and e-book lending in public libraries and schools. In addition to OverDrive, KKR owns RBmedia, one of the largest independent publishers and distributors of audiobooks. RBmedia made its own mark in 2020, getting into the audio dramatization business with the purchase of AudioGraphics.

Among the more significant transactions between publishers in early 2020 was Hachette Book Group's purchase of more than 1,000 children's titles from the Disney Book Group. The combination of bestselling and award-winning titles, including backlist and new books, became part of Little, Brown Books for Young Readers, which is overseen by executive v-p and publisher Megan Tingley.

Shanghai-based Trustbridge Global Capital increased its presence in the worldwide children's book market with its purchase of Walker Books, the U.K. parent company of Candlewick Press. The Walker purchase was Trustbridge's third significant acquisition involving American children's publishers, following its 2018 purchase of Peachtree Press and its 2016 acquisition of Holiday House.

MERGERS & ACQUISITIONS, 2020

Date	Buyer	Target	Notes
Jan. 2	The Experiment	Appletree Press	Health and lifestyle titles
Jan. 2	Mango Publishing	Yellow Pear Press	Lifestyle and regional titles
Feb. 4	Phaidon	Monacelli Press	400 Illustrated titles
Feb. 6	Hachette Book Group	Disney Book Group	1,000+ children's backlist and new books
Feb. 26	Riverdale Avenue Press	Circlet Press	170 titles
Mar. 11	RBmedia	GraphicAudio	Audio dramatization titles
Apr. 1	HarperCollins	Egmont divisions	HC bought Egmont book groups in Germany, Poland, and the U.K.
May 8	Arcadia Publishing	River Road Press	Regional titles
May 12	Trustbridge	Walker Books	Includes Candlewick Press
June 9	KKR	OverDrive	The private equity firm completed the purchase of the digital distributor to libraries and schools
July 2	QK Group	Quad/Graphics book plant	Facility in Versailles, Ky.
Sept. 2	Hachette UK	Laurence King Publishing	U.K. publisher of lifestyle and adult coloring books
Sept. 3	Abrams	Cameron + Co.	Photography, lifestyle, and children's titles
Oct. 7	Private investors	Rittenhouse Distributors	Medical distributor
Nov. 3	Bertelsmann Printing Group USA	Quad/Graphics book plants	Facilities in Fairfield, Pa. and Martinsburg, W.Va.
Nov. 13	Chronicle	Wild + Wolf brands	Toys and games from the U.K.-based publisher
Nov. 25	Bertelsmann	Simon & Schuster	The PRH parent company agreed to buy S&S for $2.175 billion
Nov. 25	Deep Vellum	Dalkey Archive	Books in translation
Dec. 1	Red Ventures	Lonely Planet	The digital platform bought the print and digital publisher
Dec. 7	Atlas Holdings	LSC Communications	The private equity firm bought the country's largest book manufacturer

SOURCE: PUBLISHERS WEEKLY

Covid-19 delayed some deals last year, but Houghton Mifflin Harcourt's announcement in November that it is placing its trade group up for sale guarantees that at least one major acquisition will take place in 2021. How active M&A will be in the year depends on the course of the pandemic and the economy. David Lamb, partner at Book Advisors, said he believes the market will be quiet in the early going but should pick up in the second half of the year as the different players get more clarity about where their businesses are headed.

*

A version of this article appeared in the 01/18/2021 issue of *Publishers Weekly* under the headline: A Roller-Coaster Year for M&A.

NOTABLE PW MERGERS AND ACQUISITIONS STORIES OF 2021

Japan's Media Do Buys Firebrand

By Jim Milliot | Feb 2, 2021

Quality Solutions/Firebrand Technologies has been acquired by Media Do International, the U.S. subsidiary of Tokyo-based Media Do Ltd. Fran Toolan, who founded the company in 1987 as a provider of technology support to publishers, will stay on as CEO for a minimum of three years.

As Quality Solutions expanded the scope of its offerings to include digital distribution and marketing, Toolan rebranded Quality Solutions as Firebrand in 2007. He acquired the digital galley service, NetGalley, in 2008. Media Do, one of the largest e-book distributors companies in the world, has been NetGalley's partner in Japan since 2016.

"Firebrand and NetGalley have never been stronger as companies, and I believe that becoming part of the Media Do Group ensures continuity for our customers and opportunities for our team for many years to come," Toolan said in a statement. Toolan told *PW* he doesn't expect to see any changes in Firebrand's day-to-day operations.

"We are very pleased to bring Firebrand and NetGalley into the Media Do family," said Daihei Shiohama, CEO of Media Do International, in a statement. "We have long respected the works of the Firebrand Group, and are very excited about the prospects of working closely with them in the future."

RBMedia Acquires Spain's Booka

By Ed Nawotka | Feb 11, 2021

RBmedia, parent company of Recorded Books, has acquired Booka, a Barcelona-based audiobook publishing company, and its full catalog of Spanish language titles. The company has been in business since 2015 and has recorded and published books in both English and Spanish from a variety of bestselling authors, such as Juan Gómez-Jurado, Fernando Gamboa, Jorge Magano, and Marc Reklau.

In addition to publishing audiobooks, Albert Codina Llorens, the founder of Booka, is also leading audiobook producer in Spain, producing for both Penguin Random House and Planeta, and it is retaining its professional services audio production business.

Troy Juliar, chief content officer for RBmedia, underscored that audiobook sales are increasing across the world, particularly in the Spanish language. "With Booka as a cornerstone, we will build our Spanish-language audio publishing to include premier global properties—both fiction and nonfiction—while also capturing the distinct local and regional authors required to serve all Spanish listeners," he said.

Albert Codina Llorens, founder of Booka, said, "I built Booka's audio catalog over the years with great care. Putting it in the hands of RBmedia was the right choice for me and for my authors. I can trust that the titles will be widely sold around the Spanish-speaking world under good terms, in all markets, and with all resellers. I know RBmedia has big plans to increase this part of their business."

According to the most recent report from the e la Federación de Gremios de Editores de España, audiobooks still account for less than 1% of book sales in Spain.

HarperCollins to Acquire HMH Trade

By Jim Milliot | Mar 29, 2021

No one in the industry was surprised last week when HarperCollins emerged as the buyer for Houghton Mifflin Harcourt Books & Media, the sixth-largest trade publisher in the U.S. Ever since HC and its parent company, News Corp, lost out to Bertelsmann's Penguin Random House in its bid to buy Simon & Schuster last November, HC was seen as the favorite to acquire the HMH trade operation, which parent company HMH put up for sale last fall. The biggest question mark was what the purchase price would be. The answer is $349 million in cash.

HMH trade had 2020 revenue of $192 million, giving the deal a multiple of 1.8 times revenue; by comparison, PRH is paying $2.175 billon for S&S, roughly 2.4 times its 2020 revenue of $901 million. S&S has been consistently more profitable than HMH trade and has a much bigger footprint in all areas of the industry, but analysts see the $349 million price as fair, given that in the ever-consolidating trade book business, there are few companies remaining that can significantly move the financial needle for a publisher looking for meaningful growth. The HMH purchase will keep HC firmly entrenched as the country's second-largest trade publisher, with revenue of about $2 billion.

At the old News Corp, HC was a smaller part of the conglomerate, which included television and movie studios. But those properties were spun off in 2013 into Twenty-First Century Fox, and HC is much more important to the current News Corp; it has been called one of the three pillars of the company's growth by CEO Robert Thomson. In 2014, about a year after the corporate split, HC paid C$455 million for Harlequin, which had revenue of C$398 million in 2013 (giving it a sale multiple of 0.9 times revenue, much lower than what HC is paying for HMH) and operating income of C$52 million (11 times earnings). And under CEO Brian Murray, HC has largely delivered for News—including last year, when it had a record-shattering fourth quarter, with sales up 23% and profits jumping 65% over the fourth quarter of 2019.

To keep growing in what is, overall, a generally flat trade market, publishers need to make acquisitions, and in an interview with *PW*, Murray called HMH a great fit with HC. Murray said HC is in a much better position to exploit HMH rights and content than the trade publisher was able to do as part of an educational publishing company. "There is much more opportunity [for HMH] being part of another trade publisher," Murray said. He noted that in previous acquisitions, such as with the purchase of Harlequin, newly acquired operations were able to take advantage of HC's international presence and other partnerships to grow outside of their core markets, and he believes that will be the case with HMH.

Murray is particularly excited about HMH's backlist of 7,000 titles, which according to News generated about 60% of HMH's revenue last year. "There is no other catalog like it," Murray said. He also pointed to the company's media production operation. In 2020, licensing revenue generated about $13 million for HMH, a figure that includes $3.4 million from a long-term agreement with Netflix for rights to its *Carmen Sandiego* property. HMH's ties to the film, TV, and streaming world could help HC properties find new partners.

Meanwhile, HC's audiobook operations will help HMH's audio business. HMH only began doing its own digital audio production in 2019, and Murray said that as rights previously sold by HMH expire, HC will keep them in-house.

In addition to boosting HC's sales, the integration of HMH, News Corp said, should allow it to find annual cost savings of $20 million. That same $20 million cost savings target was achieved following HC's acquisitions of Thomas Nelson and Harlequin, which both occurred during Murray's tenure as CEO.

Murray said HC will not start integrating HMH until after the deal closes, but he has had a chance to talk with the various HMH teams and thinks bringing the publisher on board will be straightforward. "HMH fits like a glove," he said.

While News said it hopes to complete the sale by June 30, there is a potential complication—the ongoing government review of PRH's purchase of S&S. The HC purchase is not nearly the size of PRH's acquisition, but until regulators are finished with the review of the S&S deal, the HMH review could be stalled.

*

A version of this article appeared in the 04/05/2021 issue of *Publishers Weekly* under the headline: HC Will Buy HMH Trade for $349 Million.

Francisco Partners to Acquire VitalSource from Ingram

By Calvin Reid | Apr 15, 2021

Ingram Content Group has reached an agreement to sell VitalSource, its digital learning platform, to Francisco Partners, a global investment firm specializing in technology. The acquisition is expected to close by the summer pending the usual regulatory approvals.

The platform was acquired by Ingram in 2006 and was among the early efforts of the book industry to begin the transition to the use of digital learning materials in the classroom. Since its acquisition by Ingram, the VitalSource platform has expanded the range of digital course materials it offers and the platform now delivers digital learning products to more than 16 million users around the globe.

The sale is seen by both Ingram and Francisco Partners has a way to accelerate VitalSource's growth. Francisco Partners senior operating partner Paul Ilse said, the firm is excited about "the opportunity to invest in VitalSource during its next phase of growth and look forward to leveraging our education technology investment expertise to further transform the business."

Kent Freeman, long-time Ingram executive and president of VitalSource, said "this acquisition is a great fit for our business, for our team, and for our customers and partners. It ensures that we will be able to expand our efforts to deliver affordable and impactful learning solutions for students and professionals."

Investment Firm in Deal with RosettaBooks

By Jim Milliot | May 4, 2021

MEP Capital has made an investment in RosettaBooks in a deal that gives MEP ownership of Rosetta's e-book catalog while leaving operations at Rosetta unchanged. The deal is similar in nature to a firm acquiring the rights to a musician's catalog.

Arthur Klebanoff, founding publisher and CEO of Rosetta, will continue to oversee all parts of the company, including the frontlist trade program distributed by Simon & Schuster and the backlist e-book catalog that MEP Capital has backed. Michelle Weyenberg remains director of marketing, and Emily Proano continues as distribution manager. "Authors will see no change in how things are operated," Klebanoff said.

The financial support of MEP will allow Rosetta to expand marketing efforts for its e-book catalog and make selective acquisitions of e-book titles. Observing that there are far fewer e-book rights for sale than when he started Rosetta in 2001, Klebanoff said that some opportunities still exist, pointing to plans to release a couple of new Winston Churchill e-books. The Rosetta backlist now comprises more than 700 e-books, including titles by authors ranging from Ray Bradbury to Winston Churchill.

"We see RosettaBooks as a trailblazer in rights management in the e-book publishing world, and are happy to be working with them," said Andrew Kotliar, partner at MEP Capital. The company invests in various intellectual property opportunities, and has made investments in companies working in such areas as music, film and television, and digital media.

Klebanoff said Rosetta will continue publishing new print titles, primarily in the area of business thought leadership, and will also continue publishing titles for the Mayo Clinic.

Rosetta was advised on the deal by the boutique investment bank Sonenshine Partners and the media law firm Franklin Weinrib Rudell & Vassallo. Marshall Sonenshine, chairman of Sonenshine Partners, serves as chairman of RosettaBooks, and was a founding partner at the publisher, along with Klebanoff and Rafael Pastor, a media CEO and investor.

HarperCollins Completes Purchase of HMH Trade
May 10, 2021

HarperCollins, the second-largest trade publisher in the U.S., has completed its acquisition of Houghton Mifflin Harcourt Books & Media. HC, which is owned by Rupert Murdoch's News Corp, agreed to buy the HMH trade division in March for $349 million.

In a letter to employees, HC CEO Brian Murray acknowledged that "many" decisions need to be made over the coming months surrounding the acquisition. Still, he noted that he has outlined an initial, temporary organizational plan that will be kept in place until a new, permanent structure has been conceived.

Under that structure, Ed Spade, who took over as head of HMH trade following the departure of Ellen Archer last November, will report to Murray. On the editorial side, Deb Brody, v-p and publisher for HMH Adult Trade, will report to Liate Stehlik, president and publisher of the Morrow Group. Cat Onder, senior v-p and publisher of HMH Books for Young Readers, will report to Suzanne Murphy, president and publisher of HarperCollins Children's Books.

In other appointments, Scott Simpson, HMH's director of distribution, will report to John Reindl, HC's senior v-p of warehouse and fulfillment for North America. The customer experience, global supply, and inventory planning teams will now report to Larry Nevins, HC's executive v-p of operations. The rest of the HMH Books & Media leadership team will continue to report to Spade.

"Like HarperCollins, HMH has a long and storied history of publishing award-winning authors," Murray wrote, adding that he believes that "there are many outstanding titles—from children's classics to contemporary fiction and lifestyle works—that can benefit from our combined experience and global reach." He continued: "I look forward to working closely with Ed and the entire HMH Books & Media team to see how we can share best practices for the mutual benefit of our combined organizations. We will continue to provide additional information about the transition as we work together to integrate our businesses."

Despite some thoughts that the ongoing review of Penguin Random House's pending purchase of Simon & Schuster may delay approval of the HMH acquisition, the deal was approved quickly. The PRH-S&S deal is still expected to be completed sometime this year.

Kakao Entertainment Acquires Radish Reading App
By Calvin Reid | May 11, 2021

Radish, a mobile reading app offering serialized bingeable genre fiction, has been acquired by Kakao Entertainment, the entertainment media arm of Korean internet platform Kakao, in a transaction valued at $440 million. The Radish board and shareholders have approved the acquisition, which is expected to be finalized in June.

Under the terms of the agreement, Radish will maintain the autonomy of its brand and the management of its day-to-day operations. Radish founder and CEO Seungyoon Lee will stay with the company and continue to direct its operations. Lee will now also serve as global strategy officer of Kakao Entertainment. The acquisition will add Radish's content and its fast-growing North American fan base to Kakao Entertainment's IP platform of webtoon digital comics, novels, video, TV/movies, musical performance and more.

Lee said the acquisition will "take our business to the next level in this ever-evolving industry. We are excited about the growth opportunities for Radish, not only expanding our fan base but exploring new business opportunities as well. We will be utilizing Kakao Entertainment's wide-ranging value chain to further exploit Radish's original content."

Founded in 2016, Radish is modeled after reading platforms in Korea and China. The app offers short serialized fiction, including such genres as romance, sci-fi, paranormal, LGBTQ, horror and more. The site offers early chapters for free and a micro-payments option that allows readers to open additional episodes quickly. The site's content is produced TV-style.

Kakao Entertainment CEO Jinsoo Lee said that Radish "has found enormous success with fast-paced, original mobile content and undergone dramatic growth with a ten times increase in annual revenue last year. With the combination of Kakao's expertise in the IP business and Radish's strong North American foothold, we are excited about what we can achieve together."

RBmedia Buys M-H Professional Audiobook Business

By Jim Milliot | May 11, 2021

RBmedia has acquired the audiobook publishing business of McGraw-Hill Professional, a subsidiary of McGraw-Hill. According to Troy Juliar, chief content officer for RBmedia, the purchase adds about 400 business audiobook titles to the company's catalog. Under the deal, RBmedia bought M-H Professional's previously published works and obtained the rights to publish audio editions of all new M-H Professional books, which Juliar expects to amount to 40 books annually.

"We are excited to participate more fully in the rapidly expanding audiobook category by partnering with RBmedia," Scott Grillo, president of McGraw-Hill Professional, said in a statement. "Leveraging RBmedia's unique abilities in spoken audio will help us reach business and trade professionals and all those striving to advance their education or careers."

RBmedia, which was created in 2017 after the acquisitions of multiple pre-existing audiobook companies, has steadily expanded its audio business's book holdings, which now comprise roughly 5,000 titles. Juliar said that the trove of titles will permit the company to expand beyond the trade market into such areas as education and training. McGraw-Hill Professional's catalog of business, lifestyle, technical, and professional titles includes such international bestsellers and classic business titles as *Crucial Conversations* and *SPIN Selling*.

John Shea, chief product and marketing officer at RBmedia, said the company has been growing in line with the overall industry increase in the digital audiobook sector, which amounts to about 15% annually. The company saw a sales surge earlier this year after Netflix's *Bridgerton* became a streaming hit, boosting sales of RBmedia's audiobooks for Julia Quinn's Bridgerton book series. The company also owns the rights to *Nomadland*, and the audiobook for that title had a sales bump of its own after the film adaptation on the title won Best Picture at this year's Academy Awards.

M-H is not the first acquisition for RBmedia this year; earlier in the year, it bought the Barcelona-based audiobook publisher, Booka. Juliar didn't rule out more acquisitions in 2021.

Barnes & Noble's Owner Buys Paper Source

By Jim Milliot | May 12, 2021

Elliott Investment Management, the private equity firm that owns Barnes & Noble, has reached a definitive agreement to acquire the assets and business operations of Paper Source. One of the country's largest stationery and gift retailers, Paper Source filed for bankruptcy in March.

In its release announcing the planned purchase, Elliott said B&N CEO James Daunt will oversee both B&N and Paper Source. Elliott added that while the two businesses will operate separately, "considerable opportunities exist for mutually beneficial retail partnerships." In the announcement, Elliott also gave a vote of confidence to Daunt, writing that B&N "has enjoyed a strong performance since its acquisition by Elliott in September 2019, overcoming a number of pandemic-imposed challenges."

At the time of its bankruptcy filing, Paper Source operated 158 stores. Plans now call for the retailer to run about 130 outlets. The company also has a wholesale division, Waste Not Paper by Paper Source.

In a statement, Daunt called Paper Source "a wonderful brand," and promised to help Paper Source's management team "accelerate the brand's strategic growth initiatives." He added that the opportunities for Paper Source and B&N to work together are "tremendously exciting for both businesses."

Clarivate to Buy ProQuest for $5.3 Billion

By Jim Milliot and Andrew Albanese | May 17, 2021

In a huge deal in the library and information publishing world, London-based Clarivate has agreed to acquire ProQuest for $5.3 billion. The purchase price includes $4.0 billion in cash plus $1.3 billion in equity. Clarivate is buying ProQuest from the private equity firm Cambridge Information Group, and other partners including Atairos.

The acquisition is expected to be completed in the third quarter, at which time Andrew Snyder, chairman of ProQuest and CEO of Cambridge Information Group, will become vice chairman of the Clarivate board.

Based in Ann Arbor, ProQuest is an information and technology company that delivers content and technology solutions to over 25,000 academic, corporate and research organizations in more than 150 countries, including services like ProQuest One Academic, Ebook Central, and ProQuest Dissertations & Thesis. The company had 2020 revenue of $876 million and earnings of $250 million. Following the acquisition, the combined Clarivate total revenue will be between $1.79 billion and $1.84 billion.

In a release, company officials said the combination of ProQuest content and products with Clarivate's Web of Science platform would create "a leader in research and innovation information and workflow" solutions across colleges and universities, research institutions, and corporations. "Through this combination, ProQuest will be enabled to better serve the evolving needs of our customers by providing end-to-end solutions to our customers faster than we could on our own as well as expanding our global reach beyond our current capabilities," Matti Shem Tov, CEO of ProQuest, said in a statement.

Readerlink Acquires Activity Publisher Dreamtivity

By Karen Raugust | May 21, 2021

Readerlink Distribution Services has acquired the Dreamtivity brand and assets from Retail Centric Marketing, which is based in Franklin, Tenn. Dreamtivity will become an imprint of Readerlink's San Diego-based publishing arm, Printers Row Publishing Group, and will continue to operate from its current location with its existing team, including cofounders Chad Wiggins and Beth Peters.

Simon Tasker, executive v-p, general manager, and group publisher of Printers Row, said Dreamtivity's coloring and activity books, arts and crafts products, and strength in the value channel fill gaps in Printers Row's list and knowledge base. "We're hiring their expertise," he said. "We love what they're doing, and we can add our resources to help them leverage their business even more."

Licensing is one area where both Tasker and Peters see opportunities for synergies. Both Dreamtivity and Printers Row, especially under its Studio Fun imprint, have strong licensing programs. They work with some of the same licensors, including Disney, Nickelodeon, and Mattel. Dreamtivity also brings new licenses to Printers Row, notably Crayola, for which it makes sun catchers, canvas art, and art kits. With the Crayola brand, Tasker said, "they have the ability to expand outside the book department and get product throughout the store."

Dreamtivity's price points, distribution, and formats complement those of Printers Row, which specializes in higher-end formats such as book-plus, collections, and sets sold through mass and club channels. This will enable the combined company to work with their common licensors on broader programs. "We'll be able to make a bigger impact by publishing across more formats and having a whole program at retail," Peters says.

Both companies have developed proprietary content that could be shared. "They can take our content, break it down, and put it in the value channel, and we can take theirs and bring it into the clubs," Tasker explained.

"This makes so much sense from a synergistic standpoint," Peters said. "We'll be able to really strengthen our distribution as well as grow our licensed business." Readerlink's distribution arm services nearly 100,000 retail locations across the U.S.

Private Equity Firm to Buy McGraw-Hill for $4.5 Billion

By Jim Milliot | Jun 16, 2021

Eight years after it bought McGraw-Hill Education for $2.4 billion, Apollo Global Management has reached an agreement to sell the company to another private equity firm, Platinum Equity, for $4.5 billion. The proposed purchase comes about a year after MH and Cengage called off their merger following opposition from the Justice Department.

When Apollo acquired the publisher, MHE had revenue of about $2 billion; in the fiscal year ended March 31, 2020, company revenue was $1.58 billion and it had an operating loss of $135.3 million, with EBITDA (earnings before interest, taxes, depreciation and amortization) of $372.9 million. Results for fiscal 2021 have not been released, but for the nine months ended December 31, 2020, revenue fell 5.4%, to $1.22 billion; still, the company posted net income of $118 million, up from a loss of $28.3 million. EBITDA in the nine months rose 6.4%, to $439.9 million.

In announcing the deal, the parties emphasized the increase in digital sales over the last eight years, which have risen from about 25% of total revenue to approximately 60% now. To get there, MHE made six digitally-focused acquisitions.

Following the completion of the acquisition, which is expected to occur this summer, MHE will continue to be led by CEO Simon Allen and his leadership team. Allen said he is looking forward to working with Platinum to accelerate MHE's digital growth.

Open Road Buys U.K.'s Bloodhound Books

By Jim Milliot | Jul 27, 2021

Open Road Integrated Media has acquired Bloodhound Books, a U.K.-based publisher of e-books and print titles. Founded in 2014 by Betsy Reavley and Fred Freeman, Bloodhound has a backlist of about 600 fiction titles, and has sold approximately six million copies of its books worldwide. Among its top-selling authors are Keri Beevis, Valerie Keogh, Dreda Say Mitchell, Jeneva Rose, and Rob Sinclair.

According to the purchase announcement, the Bloodhound editorial, production, and commissioning teams will be integrated into Open Road's existing company structure, and the Bloodhound name will continue to be used in all markets. Founders Reavley and Freeman will continue to head the company.

Reavley said that by becoming part of Open Road, Bloodhound's titles will gain better access to new markets, both in the U.S. and internationally. For Open Road, the deal brings additional content it can sell to its base of consumers. "The acquisition of Bloodhound Books is demonstrative of the evolution of the publishing industry," Open Road CEO Paul Slavin said in a statement, "and the opportunity for publishers and authors to align more directly with consumer interests and habits."

Open Road, which now describes itself as a marketing tech company, markets and sells its own titles and those of its partners and clients to some 3 million consumers.

Hachette Book Group Will Acquire Workman Publishing for $240 Million

By Jim Milliot | Aug 16, 2021

The biggest trade publishers continue to get larger: Hachette Book Group has entered into a "binding commitment" to acquire one of the industry's largest and most unique independent publishers, Workman Publishing. HBG, backed by its parent company, Lagardère, is paying $240 million for Workman, which had sales of $134 million last year. The deal is expected to be completed by the end of September.

In making the announcement, HBG CEO Michael Pietsch called Workman "a brilliant publisher, the most creative in the industry," that pioneered the method of combining images and information in a distinct way. That approach has led to such hugely successful franchises as the What to Expect and Brain Quest series as well as Page-a-Day calendars.

When the acquisition is completed, Workman Publishing will become HBG's eighth publishing group, comprising the imprints Workman, Algonquin, Algonquin Young Readers, Artisan, Storey Publishing, and Timber Press. (The publisher has about 300 employees scattered across offices in New York City, Chapel Hill, N.C., North Adams, Mass., and Portland, Ore.) The new group will be led by Workman Publishing's current CEO, Dan Reynolds, who will report to Pietsch and join HBG's executive management board. Carolan Workman, executive chair and president of the company—who has been heading the publisher since 2013, following the death of her husband, company founder Peter Workman—will retire following the completion of the deal.

In an interview with *PW*, Reynolds said finding a new owner for the company, founded by Peter Workman in 1968, had been in the works for a few years. Reynolds said Carolan Workman's "#1 priority in finding a new home for the company, even over price, was the security of our employees, and we have found that with Hachette. They understand what makes us tick."

Pietsch told *PW* that, given that most of Workman's most popular books and products have been developed in-house, HBG would be "crazy" to interfere with the company. "They have a unique culture," Pietsch said.

HBG and Workman fit together in many business ways. Workman is backlist-driven, with Reynolds saying that at some of its imprints, 70% to 80% of revenue is generated by its backlist. Despite acquisitions and organic growth, HBG has continued to look for ways to expand its backlist, and Pietsch praised the quality and depth of Workman's roughly 3,500-title backlist.

With its unique approach to publishing, Workman has maintained it own sales force, and has sold its line far beyond bookstores. Both Reynolds and Pietsch said that they see a big opportunity in reaching those markets with a broader list from the combined companies.

Another practical reason for the deal, Reynolds said, is that it costs a good deal of money to invest in the type of publishing Workman does. Freed from the distraction of maintaining its own infrastructure, he said, Workman could devote its full attention to developing new products.

CENSORSHIP OF BOOKS: HISTORICALLY AND IN 2021

CENSORSHIP ON THE RISE WORLDWIDE

BY ED NAWOTKA | AUG 06, 2021

Since the start of the Covid pandemic, there's been a rise in instances of government censorship of books around the world. In October 2020, the International Publishers Association released a 106-page report, "Freedom to Publish: Challenges, Violations and Countries of Concern," that outlined 847 instances of censorship in a host of countries, including France, Iran, Serbia, and the United Kingdom, as well as the United States. According to the report, in 55% of those instances, the censorship was undertaken by government authorities. The report is downloadable from the IPA website.

Since that report was issued, efforts to censor books have continued. In July, the Hungarian government imposed an $830 fine on the distributor of the Hungarian translation of Lawrence Schimel's children's book *What a Family!*, citing a law that bans the depiction of homosexuality and gender reassignment in material aimed at minors. The book tells the story of two families with young children—one with two fathers and the other with two mothers.

That incident follows another in Hungary, in October 2020, when a member of parliament put a copy of *Meseorszag mindenkie* (*A Fairy Tale for Everyone*), which also features LGBTQ characters, through a shredder. "So the publisher reprinted it as a board book" said Schimel, whose book had the same Hungarian editor.

Schimel, an American living in Madrid, has published dozens of LGBTQ-themed works for children and adults. "It's important for all families, not just those who are LGBTQ, to see and read these books which show just how normal these families are," he said. *What a Family!* is now sold in Hungary with a sticker, warning readers that it depicts families "outside the norm." It was originally published as two books in Spanish, and Orca Book Publishers is releasing it as two books in the U.S. in September.

Russia led the way in overt European LGBTQ censorship with the passage of its "anti-LGBTQ propaganda" law in 2012. Today, LGBTQ books are routinely suppressed there, and those that make it to market are sold with warning stickers.

"The campaigns by the populist governments in Europe, such as in Hungary and Poland, against the LGBTQ community are in direct violation of the principles of inclusion and the celebration of diversity," said Michiel Kolman, chair for inclusive publishing at the IPA. He noted that in Poland, several towns have declared themselves LGBTQ-free zones, forcing LGBTQ residents to move, while in Hungary the transgender community was first targeted, and after that the broader LGBTQ community.

"The policies manifest themselves through censorship of books and other media that directly contradict the freedom-to-publish mission of the IPA," Kolman told *PW*. He added that the Hungarian laws are likely an effort to deflect attention from the country's dismal economic and Covid-19 track record.

Following the news of the attack on Schimel's book in Hungary, the IPA, the Federation of European Publishers, and the European and International Booksellers Federation all reaffirmed their support for Hungarian publishers and readers, and their solidarity with LGBTQ communities in Hungary.

BELARUS AND CHINA CLAMP DOWN

Also in July, the government of Belarus moved to dissolve the local branch of PEN after the freedom of speech organization released a report showing 621 instances of human rights violations, including arrests and imprisonments, against culture workers in the first six months of 2021. Suzanne Nossel, CEO of PEN America, was among those around the world who issued a statement in support of PEN Belarus. "When a government silences and stomps on its writers, it reveals a level of shame and decay that leaders are aiming to hide, but instead only expose," Nossel wrote. "Belarus' leaders may think they can suppress the truth by muzzling those who dare tell it, but the story of the will of the people and the scale of brutal repression will find its way to the world.

We stand in solidarity with the writers of PEN Belarus and are determined to ensure that their vital voices are heard and their rights to express themselves vindicated." As recently as last week, a dissident journalist from Belarus who disappeared was found dead in Ukraine.

Nossel told *PW* that this type of activity is an attempt by authoritarian governments to control the narrative, both at home and abroad, in a world where information is fast moving, freely available, and difficult to suppress. She cited China and the closures of bookstores and publications that express dissent in Hong Kong as particularly egregious examples of censorship. "[The Chinese] are reaching down to destroy the remnants of any challenge to their authority," she said. "For organizations like PEN, fighting this is an ongoing battle."

Nicholas Lemann, director of Columbia Global Reports, a publisher that offers short books on hot political and social justice topics, noted his house has been vigilant in covering the rise of authoritarianism, the curtailing of press freedoms, and China. In May, Columbia Global Reports published *The Politics of Our Time* by John Judis, a one-volume contemporary history of populism, nationalism, and socialism.

Lemann, the former dean of the Columbia School of Journalism, said he routinely gets reports from former students about the rise in persecution of journalists. "In recent years, I have heard more and more often from journalists in India about Narendra Modi and in Brazil about Jair Bolsonaro and what they are doing to limit press freedoms," he noted. "At the turn of the millennium, we thought that the triumph of the American economic system inextricably went along with the triumph of the American freedom of expression system. And we thought these would be globalized. Well, that didn't happen," Lemann said.

It has long been known that the Chinese government keeps a close eye on which books are distributed there and maintains control of the issuing of ISBNs. Officially, censorship is not a state policy. Publishers have long held that if a book does not become too popular or influential in China, it will be tolerated. But unofficial policy is flexible, and recent trends have shifted toward a narrowing of what is considered acceptable. For example, there's been a crackdown in recent years on what can be published on China's wildly popular writing websites, such as China Literature, and works that are deemed too "salacious" have been removed. Last year, Fang Fang, who lives in Wuhan and published a blog about the early days of lockdown during the pandemic, was vilified by the government. Her blog entries were collected into the book *Wuhan Diary*, published by HarperCollins.

In July, the Chinese government outlawed foreign direct investment in education companies. The law is aimed at companies that offer tutoring to Chinese students—a business that has ballooned to an estimated $100 billion per year. The law is likely to impact numerous foreign education publishers that have invested hundreds of millions of dollars in the sector. "The government is operating with the idea that liberal Western ideas may be damaging the children," Nossel said.

Different countries have different means of controlling book publication and exerting censorship. In Turkey, authorities require that any book sold in bookstores has a government "banderol"—a sticker testifying to its "authenticity." The government claims this is necessary to combat piracy, but in effect it acts as a means of regulating publishers.

In Venezuela, officially, publishers can publish anything—but they may not be able to acquire paper and ink to print certain books. The same happens in Russia, where a printer might suddenly become reticent to produce a potentially objectionable book for fear of government blowback.

IPA FIGHTS FOR THE FREEDOM TO PUBLISH

The IPA maintains a committee that monitors freedom-to-publish issues around the world and presents an annual award, the Prix Voltaire, honoring courageous publishers that have faced oppression. To reinforce its mission to support global publishing during the pandemic, the IPA also recently launched a program to promote publishing, dubbed INSPIRE (International Sustainable Publishing and Industry Resilience). Two of the tenets of the program's charter are maintaining that "freedom to publish is a prerequisite for diversity, creativity, prosperity, tolerance, and progress" and that "copyright and freedom to publish are mutually reinforcing fundamental rights that are essential to the practice and preservation of political culture, education, scholarship, and socioeconomic development." The charter has garnered signatures from more than 100 organizations around the world, including *Publishers Weekly*.

"Many countries have introduced special laws to deal with the Covid-19 crisis," said Kristenn Einarsson, chair of the IPA's Freedom to Publish committee and former managing director of the Norwegian Publishers Association. "There is a growing concern that these might be maintained in the future, after the crisis has ended, and that some of them could be used to limit the freedom to publish and freedom of expression."

Einarsson said in some authoritarian states, censorship can be internalized and become self-censorship. "The same fears that can affect publishers and lead them to self-censor can also infect authors, booksellers, and librarians. In the end, if these fears delay or stop the creation or publication of such reports and works, then it is we, the readers, who are deprived. Any discussion about what should be published is of course welcomed, but it is important that publishers stand firmly to defend the publishing of all that they deem worthy of publication, even—and perhaps especially—if those works challenge the boundaries established by the society they operate in."

*

A version of this article appeared in the 08/09/2021 issue of *Publishers Weekly* under the headline: Censorship on the Rise Worldwide.

CANCEL CULTURE

BY ALAN DERSHOWITZ

One dictionary recently selected "cancel culture" as "the word of the year" because "it has become, for better or worse, a powerful force."[1] The most famous United States dictionary, Merriam-Webster, has posted a lengthy description in its section "Words We're Watching," which are "words we are increasingly seeing in use but that have not yet met our criteria for entry." According to Merriam-Webster, "Cancel is getting a new use." Whereas in previous usages, canceling referred to canceling an object, such as an event or a subscription, now:

> canceling and cancel culture has to do with the removing of support for public figures in response to their objectionable behavior or opinions. This can include boycotts or refusal to promote their work. In the latest use of the word, you can cancel people—in particular, celebrities, politicians, or anyone who takes up space in the public consciousness. To cancel someone (usually a celebrity or other well-known figure) means to stop giving support to that person. The act of canceling could entail boycotting an actor's movies or no longer reading or promoting a writer's words. The reason for a cancellation can vary, but it usually is due to the person in question having expressed an objectionable opinion or having conducted themselves in a way that is unacceptable, so that continuing to patronize that person's work leaves a bitter taste.

Merriam-Webster then goes on to explain the origin of the term:

> The idea of canceling—and as some have labeled it, cancel culture—has taken hold in recent years due to conversations prompted by #MeToo

---

1   *Australian Macquarie Dictionary*, December 2019. The Committee's Choice & People's Choice word of the Year 2019, December 9, 2019, available at https://www.macquariedictionary.com/au/resources/view/word/of/the/year.

and other movements that demands greater accountability from public figures. The term has been credited to Black users of Twitter, where it has been used as a hashtag. As troubling information came to light regarding celebrities who were once popular such as Bill Cosby, Michael Jackson, Roseanne Barr, and Louis C.K.—so come calls to cancel such figures. The cancellation is akin to a canceled contract, a severing of the relationship that once linked a performer to their fans.[2]

There are some who still argue, in the face of overwhelming evidence to the contrary, that the entire phenomenon of cancel culture is an exaggeration concocted by the right to discredit the left.[3] I leave it to the readers, after reviewing the evidence, to decide for themselves.

CANCEL CULTURE CONTEXT AND CREATIVITY

One of the great dangers of cancel culture is that it stifles creativity. Intellectuals are terrified about being canceled if speculations made years earlier are wrenched out of context and become weaponized in the war against political incorrectness. My friend and teaching colleague, Steven Pinker, is a perfect example of this dangerous phenomenon.

When Steve and I taught together, he was well known for his creativity, ingenuity, and willingness to explore controversial ideas. Indeed, one of the courses we taught together was called "Taboo." It focused on issues that cannot be discussed and debated in today's universities. I don't know whether recordings were made of our classes, but I do know that we threw out ideas in order to encourage students to think, challenge, and come to their own conclusions. It would be easy for a current canceler to wrench out of context some statements each of us made in the course of this didactic exercise. The students back then loved the course, especially its focus on taboo ideas. But today's cancelers might very well assume that every idea that was thrown out for discussion represented our carefully thought-through, definitive opinions on controversial subjects. That would be a serious mistake, as the cancelers well know but ignore in the interest of deploying their weapon against those whom they disapprove.

Pinker and I were both tenured professors who did not fear university reprisals for expressing controversial views. Indeed, one of the people we invited

---

2   *Merriam-Webster*, available at https://www.merriam–webster.com/words-at-play /cancel-culture-words-were-watching.
3   See Osita Nwanevu, "*The Cancel Culture Con*," *New Republic*, September 23, 2019.

to the class was the president of Harvard, whom we both criticized openly. In retrospect, it seems that the treatment accorded President Lawrence Summers was one of the opening salvos in the cancellation campaign. He was forced to resign—an early form of cancellation—for speculating out loud about some of the reasons why women have not achieved the same level of success in STEM as men. Whether he was right or wrong about what he said should make no difference in a university setting. If he was wrong, his ideas should be refuted in the open marketplace. Instead, he was canceled as president of Harvard. A cartoon in a local paper illustrated the double standard applied to cancellation even back then. It portrayed Summers pleading for his job and saying: "I didn't mean that women are intellectually inferior. I meant that Israel is an apartheid country. Now can I have my job back?"

The *Boston Globe* quoted me as comparing the tribulation of Summers to the "Trial of Galileo":

> "In my 41 years at Harvard, I have never experienced a president more open to debate, disagreement, and dialogue than Larry Summers," wrote Dershowitz, adding that "professors who are afraid to challenge him are guilty of cowardice."
>
> Dershowitz noted that he disagreed with Summers's comments last month that innate differences might help explain why more men than women are top achievers in science and math, but he defended the university president's right to raise the proposition.
>
> "This is truly a time of crisis for Harvard," he wrote. "The crisis is over whether a politically correct straitjacket will be placed over the thinking of everybody in this institution by one segment of the faculty."[4]

Among Summers's other defenders was Professor Pinker, who argued that the empirical issue raised by Summers should be "determined by research, not Fatwa."

The firing of Summers was an early manifestation of what has become cancel culture, but the situation has gotten worse over the past 15 years.

Young professors and students trying to survive today's cancel culture will be deterred and disincentivized from saying anything that might come back to haunt or cancel them in years to come. Cancel culture has no statute of limitations. It goes back to the earliest days of a person's career.

---

4   Marcella Bombardieri, "Some Professors Back Harvard's Summers," *Boston Globe*, February 17, 2005.

There are those who are now trying to cancel Professor Pinker for views he has expressed over his long and distinguished career. I tend to agree with many of his views, but even if I did not, I would defend his right to be controversial and to ask difficult questions whose truthful answers may be politically incorrect.

The attempt to cancel or at least de-platform him reflects another disturbing consequence of the cancel culture: its negative effect on centrist liberals is greater than on right-wing conservatives. This disparity results from the reality that right-wing conservatives have their own large constituency, which will continue to invite them to present their views, regardless of cancel culture. These include conservative universities, such as Liberty University, as well as conservative think tanks, talk radio, podcasts, and TV stations. But there are few, if any, comparable outlets for centrist liberals who have been canceled, especially since cancel culture has its greatest impact on campuses and liberal venues.

Even leftists are sometimes canceled by those to the left of them, as illustrated by a recent story in the *New York Times*. Professor Adolph Reed, who is a Black Marxist scholar at the University of Pennsylvania, was invited to speak to the Democratic Socialists of America's New York City chapter. Professor Reed planned on arguing that the left's focus on the disproportionate impact of Covid-19 on Blacks undermined multiracial organizing. Throughout his distinguished career, Professor Reed has argued that race is an overstated concept and that the focus should rather be on class in a deeply unjust society. This position was offensive for some. They argued that Professor Reed's downplaying of racism was "cowardly and cedes power to the racial capitalists." So the Democratic Socialists of America canceled his talk.[5]

A crowning irony of cancel culture was when 150 public intellectuals, professors, and writers wrote a letter protesting cancel culture[6] and did not include me among the signatories, despite my long history of defending freedom of speech, my extensive publications, and my 50 years as a professor. The only reason I was not asked to sign—while others far-less accomplished and well-known were asked—is that I have been canceled even by those who organized the letter opposing cancel culture. Nevertheless, the substance of the letter reflects my views.

---

5   Michael Powell, "A Black Marxist Scholar Wanted to Talk About Race. It Ignited a Fury," *New York Times*, August 14, 2020.
6   "A Letter on Justice and Open Debate," Harper's Magazine (October 2020 issue), available at https://harpers.org/a-letter-on-justice-and-open-debate/.

CANCEL CULTURE AND THE MEDIA

An example of how a false and defamatory media report can result in the cancellation of a good person who has done excellent work over a lifetime is what happened to Linda Fairstein, a former prosecutor and bestselling author. Fairstein was the chief prosecutor in the Central Park Five case, which may well have resulted in an injustice and erroneous convictions. Reasonable people could disagree about whether she was in any way responsible for the miscarriage of justice, but Netflix simply made up a "series of facts" that were totally untrue. They portrayed her as having led the initial investigation at the scene of the crime and making decisions that impacted the rest of the case. The truth is that Fairstein had not even been assigned to the case at that time. But, because it was shown on Netflix, it was believed to be true by large numbers of people, and Fairstein was canceled.[7] She was forced to resign as a trustee of Vassar College, and book contracts, appearances, and awards were rescinded. She became a pariah among the woke and progressive cancelers. She is now suing Netflix for defamation, as am I.

I am suing because Netflix broke its promise to me that if I gave them all the documentation proving that I never met my false accuser, they would present this evidence on the air. I was interviewed by Netflix and I laid out the evidence in detail. I also provided them with tapes, emails, and other indisputable documentation, all of which they deep-sixed and never put on the air. Instead, they presented my false accuser as a credible woman with no evidence of lack of credibility. It was this mendacious Netflix series, called *Filthy Rich*, that resulted in my cancellation or de-platforming among many in cancel culture.

Another example is the cancellation of Woody Allen. I was one of Mia Farrow's lawyers in her lawsuit against Allen. I don't know, of course, whether Allen did anything illegal or improper with Mia's daughter, Dylan. But the matter was thoroughly investigated back when the accusation of wrongdoing was made. The Yale New Haven Hospital investigated and found that "It is our expert opinion that Dylan was not sexually abused by Mr. Allen. Further, we believe that Dylan's statements on videotape and her statements to us during our evaluation do not refer to actual events that occurred to her on

---

7   See, e.g., Noah Goldberg, "Central Park Five Prosecutor Resigns from Vassar Board After Student Outcry," *Brooklyn Eagle*, June 4, 2018. The article also mentions that "In 2018, Fairstein—now a writer of mystery novels—won an award from the Mystery Writers of America. After backlash about her role in the Central Park Five Case, the organization decided to rescind the award."

August 4th, 1992."[8] The matter receded from public view for many years, and Allen continued to make his films. Then came the #MeToo movement and cancel culture. With no new evidence, Allen was canceled. His book and film contracts were violated. He, too, became a pariah, though the evidence suggests he may have done nothing wrong. The accusation became the conviction, and cancel culture kicked in.[9]

*

Alan Dershowitz is one of the most celebrated lawyers in the world. He was the youngest full professor in Harvard Law School history, where he is now the Felix Frankfurter Professor of Law, Emeritus. The author of numerous bestselling books, from *Chutzpah* to *Guilt by Accusation* to *The Case Against Impeaching Trump* to *The Best Defense* to *Reversal of Fortune* (which was made into an Academy Award–winning film) to *Defending Israel*, Dershowitz has advised presidents and prime ministers and has represented many prominent men and women, half of them pro bono.

---

8   Woody Allen was not charged then or since with any sexual impropriety. See also, Moses Farrow, "A Son Speaks Out," May 23, 2018, available at https://mosesfarrow .blogspot.com/2018/05/a-son-speaks-out-by-moses-farrow.html.
9   His memoir was published by a different publisher and his film will be shown in the United States in late September 2020.

PUBLISHING VS. CANCEL CULTURE

BY DAN KOVALIK

We live in strange times. Members of the liberal intellectual class who used to rightly mock and decry the banning of books are themselves the ones calling for books to be banned and censored. While this is often being done in the name of social justice, there is little just about this.

Oftentimes, the cries for books not to be published center not around the content of the books themselves but around the alleged misdeeds of the authors. We saw this recently with publishing house revolts against the publication of Woody Allen's autobiography, Mike Pence's memoir, and Blake Bailey's biography of Philip Roth. In each of these cases, young staffers called upon their publishing company not to print these books because they decided that the authors should not be rewarded with a publishing deal, and the money that goes with it, in light of their moral deficiencies. They also argue that if their own publishing houses reject these authors, the authors can just go down the street and have someone else print their books. And so, the reasoning goes, this does not really amount to book banning after all.

I think that the argument that people we view to be reprehensible should not be rewarded with a hefty book advance is certainly an appealing one. The problem, however, is that the failure to publish an important work, and I think all of the books I mention are important in their own way, punishes not only the author, but also the public who might be denied the opportunity to read these books and to make up their own minds about the authors and their works. This issue is most pronounced in the case of the memoir of Woody Allen because he defends himself therein against the very (hotly contested) allegations upon which the canceling of his book is premised. Aren't members of the public entitled to read his defense before making up their minds that he is guilty?

I would submit that the young people fortunate enough to have jobs in publishing have no right to assume the role of judge and jury of all the authors who come to them. And they don't have the right to assume the role of executioner of their works. Many controversial people author books that have incredible social value. Indeed, I would dare say that controversy and social value often go hand in hand.

There are many who might argue, for example, that Mumia Abu-Jamal—a man convicted by a jury of his peers of killing a policeman in cold blood—has no right to be published. However, Mumia continues to claim his innocence, and many in the public believe he is innocent. Mumia has become a prolific author, focusing on issues related to social justice, thanks to the courage of some publishing companies to publish his works over the strenuous objections of the family of the slain officer. And that is as it should be, I would argue. And I am sure that those calling for the cancellation of Woody Allen, Blake Bailey, and Mike Pence would agree with me in this instance, only showing how tricky and even dangerous it is to start down the road of morally judging every would-be author.

Moreover, the claim of these self-righteous cancelers that they are really not banning any works because someone else is going to publish them anyway does not hold up. First of all, if they truly believe that they are merely kicking the can down the road, then their moral stance really isn't much of one. They are simply asking for someone else's hands to be dirtied—not exactly a victory for virtue.

But of course, I suspect that the would-be censors understand that if they succeed in getting their own publishing house to cancel a book that it will most likely not be published by someone else. And the chances of this happening is growing as the publishing industry continues to be consolidated further and further. At last count, there are now only four major publishing companies. This means that the chances for an author to have their book published after being canceled at one company is shrinking. And while the famous authors discussed herein have a better chance of landing on their feet, lesser-known authors who may be canceled have little chance.

The other authors in danger of losing publishing rights are the long-dead ones who no longer bring in much money but who have written classic works that are now being banned in schools and libraries. If enough of these institutions ban such books—for example, *Huckleberry Finn*, *To Kill a Mockingbird*, *The Scarlet Letter*, and *Fahrenheit 451*, just to name a few—then there is a good chance that publishers will simply stop printing them. We would then be in danger of losing great works of literature because, in these instances, some people find some of the content therein to be objectionable. And they find the content objectionable because the books were written in different times with different mores and norms that may seem antiquated now. The idea that we cannot still learn from such works, and indeed gain insight about the times in which they were written and about how much progress we have made since then, seems the height of ignorance and hubris.

And that is what troubles me most about this new move among the liberal elite to ban works of literature and art. This impulse comes from a place of presumed moral superiority to those who have come before them, as if our current norms and way of doing things simply popped out of nowhere and aren't the product of years of struggle and human progress, which we should be proud of, but which we must also build upon.

The impulse to cancel also comes from a naïve notion that it is only the righteous and virtuous who can make great and beautiful works of art. In fact, history shows that it is usually quite the opposite—that it is the damaged and flawed and pained who are able to weave their suffering and imperfection into beauty. And it is beauty that comes from such dark places, which to me is the most precious and wonderful to behold.

*

Dan Kovalik is the author of *Cancel This Book*, the critically acclaimed *The Plot to Scapegoat Russia*, *The Plot to Attack Iran*, *The Plot to Control the World*, *The Plot to Overthrow Venezuela*, and *No More War* and has been a labor and human rights lawyer since graduating from Columbia Law School in 1993. He has represented plaintiffs in ATS cases arising out of egregious human rights abuses in Colombia. He received the David W. Mills Mentoring Fellowship from Stanford Law School, has appeared on Fox News's *The Ingraham Angle*, has written extensively for *HuffPost* and *CounterPunch*, and has lectured throughout the world.

RECALLING A FREE SPEECH LANDMARK

BY CHRISTOPHER M. FINAN | MAY 21, 2021

In May 1953, 25 publishers and librarians met at a country club in Westchester County, N.Y., to create the "Freedom to Read Statement." The Cold War between the United States and the Soviet Union was at its peak. Americans who were considered disloyal were being fired based on the books they read, the music they liked, and the art that hung on their walls. In Oklahoma, librarian Ruth Brown was dismissed for subscribing to the *Nation*, the *New Republic*, *Soviet Russia Today*, the *Negro Digest*, and *Consumer Reports*.

The authors of the "Freedom to Read Statement" explained that they were responding to the growing popular sentiment "that our national tradition of free expression is no longer valid; that censorship and suppression are needed to counter threats to safety and national security." Librarians at the American Library Association convention in June adopted the statement overwhelmingly. The *New York Times* called it one of "America's outstanding state papers" and joined the *Washington Post* in publishing the full text.

We are living through another age of deep ideological division. Many people sincerely believe that the best way to fight ideas they consider dangerous is to deny them an airing—or as we now say, "a platform."

Book publishers are once again under intense pressure to engage in censorship. And I don't use that word carelessly. Censorship involves more than the government suppression that is banned by the First Amendment. Private companies play a critical role in protecting free speech.

Many people in publishing are unhappy with their employers and rightly complain about the lack of diversity at all levels of the industry. They also strongly object to their companies publishing books that they believe are harmful, even dangerous. Amplified by vocal support on social media, these critics are having an impact. Contracts have been canceled. Books have been withdrawn from publication.

At a time when a new civil rights movement is demanding an end to centuries of injustice, it is easy to lose sight of the importance—and fragility—of the freedom to read. This freedom is actually a recent development in American history. The battle to read what we want began in the 1920s and won its major legal victories in the '50s and '60s.

If we are to preserve this crucial liberty, we must continue to defend the principles set forth in the "Freedom to Read Statement":

1. "It is in the public interest for publishers and librarians to make available the widest diversity of views and expressions, including those that are unorthodox, unpopular, or considered dangerous."
2. "Publishers, librarians, and booksellers do not need to endorse every idea or presentation they make available. It would conflict with the public interest for them to establish their own political, moral, or aesthetic views as a standard for determining what should be published or circulated."
3. "It is contrary to the public interest for publishers or librarians to bar access to writings on the basis of personal history or political affiliations of the author."
4. "It is the responsibility of publishers and librarians, as guardians of the people's freedom to read, to contest encroachments upon that freedom by individuals or groups seeking to impose their own standards or tastes upon the community at large."
5. "It is the responsibility of publishers and librarians to give full meaning to the freedom to read by providing books that enrich the quality and diversity of thought and expression. By the exercise of this affirmative responsibility, they can demonstrate that the answer to a 'bad' book is a good one, the answer to a 'bad' idea is a good one."

The claim that the best answer to bad speech is more speech seems naive to many of us who have seen the power of social media to spread misinformation and outright lies. But the publishers and librarians who gathered in Westchester readily acknowledged the perils of free speech: "We do not state these propositions in the comfortable belief that what people read is unimportant," they wrote. "We believe that what people read is deeply important; that ideas can be dangerous; but that the suppression of ideas is fatal to a democratic society."

As the statement concludes: "Freedom itself is a dangerous way of life, but it is ours."

*

Christopher M. Finan is the executive director of the National Coalition Against Censorship and the author of *From the Palmer Raids to the Patriot Act: A History of the Fight for Free Speech in America.*

A version of this article appeared in the 05/24/2021 issue of *Publishers Weekly* under the headline: Recalling a Free Speech Landmark.

Talking About Censorship and Publishing
The NCAC's executive director says conversation is needed to bridge divides
By Christopher M. Finan | May 28, 2021

Can we talk?

In last week's *Publishers Weekly*, I summarized the principles of "The Freedom to Read," a statement essential to the ethical foundation of the library and publishing community since 1953. The statement did more than expound principles: It committed the signatories to fight for them.

Today this commitment is being questioned by people within the library and publishing communities. Many do not believe that publishers should release books that express dangerous ideas or books that are written by bad people. They reject the idea that the best answer to a bad book is a good one.

How are we to resolve these differences? So far, there have been Twitter debates. Petitions have been circulated. There has been a lot of talk about harmful books, but much less about how demands for suppression conflict with the commitment to publish a broad range of ideas. There has been little dialogue and almost no give-and-take. Yet there is strong evidence that conversation works, if not to fully resolve differences at least to build greater interpersonal understanding and lower the temperature of conflict, opening the way to further communication.

The National Coalition Against Censorship has some experience in this area. In 2017, building on groundwork by the American Booksellers Association, we launched a pilot program, the Open Discussion Project, that sought to bring liberals and conservatives together in independent bookstores to discuss the issues that divide them. This seems even more foolhardy today than it was four years ago, but we did our homework. We learned that political polarization was not new. Researchers had identified the problem in the 1970s, and nonprofits have been trying to find a solution ever since.

There were some encouraging results from experiments with groups that were small enough to let the members get to know one another. They developed empathy, making it possible for them to discuss their differences.

We were surprised by the large turnout at the initial meetings in the six stores participating in the pilot. We had hoped that the groups would be small, but 80 people showed up at the first meeting at Gibson's Bookstore in Concord, N.H. The pilot established that many people are eager to engage with those who hold different views—not to punish or convert them but to find a place where they can discuss their differences.

While we were unable to proceed with a national rollout of the program, two of the stores continue to hold meetings and others are considering restarting their groups. The Bipartisan Book Club, which began at Politics and Prose in Washington, D.C., includes liberals, conservatives, and libertarians. Now operated by its members, the club meets every six weeks to discuss books that present different perspectives. The topics include policing, gender identity, social cohesion, capitalism, antifa, and diversity.

More evidence of success is the response to Nadine Strossen's book *Hate: Why We Should Resist It with Free Speech, Not Censorship.* As the president of the ACLU from 1991 to 2008 and a prominent defender of civil liberties, Strossen has always had a busy speaking schedule. But between the publication of her book in May 2018 and the beginning of the pandemic, she made more than 300 appearances, mostly to talk about hate speech.

Though Strossen often speaks to junior high and high school students, many of her events were on college campuses where activists were organizing against racism. Instead of fearing the wrath of students, she urged those who had invited her to actively reach out to students who disagree with her. Many did attend speeches and rejected her argument that restrictions on hate speech are ineffective, but other students were convinced by her argument that the best way to fight hate is to continue to organize and protest against it.

There is so much that is encouraging about our new age of protest and its promise for eliminating the injustices suffered by people of color, women, and members of the LGBTQ community. Inevitably, this has put pressure on all of our major institutions to change. It is particularly difficult for publishers, who must balance their desire to be more inclusive with a commitment to promote free expression.

To maintain this balance, we must commit ourselves to talking about the problem. NCAC is ready to do whatever it can to help. My email is chris@ncac.org.

∗

Christopher M. Finan is the executive director of the National Coalition Against Censorship and the author of *From the Palmer Raids to the Patriot Act: A History of the Fight for Free Speech in America*.

A version of this article appeared in the 05/31/2021 issue of *Publishers Weekly* under the headline: Talking About Censorship and Publishing.

BESTSELLERS, PRIZEWINNERS, AND BOOK FAIRS

THE BESTSELLING BOOKS OF 2021 (SO FAR)

BY JOHN MAHER | JUL 9, 2021

The first six months of 2021 saw sales of adult fiction buoy overall print book sales week after week. Still, there was only one runaway bestseller in the first half of the year, and it's a children's book: the 10th installment in Dav Pilkey's Dog Man series, *Mothering Heights*, which topped the year-to-date children's overall bestseller list and has sold upwards of 867,000 copies since its March 23 release.

Another kids' book, Dr. Seuss's perennial bestseller *Oh, the Places You'll Go!*, placed second overall, selling more than 584,000 print copies. This marked an increase of roughly 200,000 copies compared to the book's sales last year at this time, when graduation ceremonies were not being held in person. (The decision by Dr. Seuss Enterprises, announced in March, to stop publishing six of the late author's titles over what the AP called "racist and insensitive imagery," also gave Seuss sales a boost.) Of the top five children's bestsellers this year to date, three are by Seuss and two are by Pilkey.

The Four Winds by Kristin Hannah was the top-selling adult title in the first half of 2021, and its roughly 558,000 copies sold made it the third-biggest bestseller overall. *Four Winds* was followed on the adult list by backlist bestseller *The Boy, the Mole, the Fox and the Horse* by Charlie Mackesy, which pushed around 544,000 copies. Amanda Gorman's *The Hill We Climb*, the book version of the poem she read at the inauguration of President Biden, sold nearly 456,000 copies—a massive number for any poet—and placed third. And though adult fiction sales were up 30.7% in the first six months, Matt Haig's *The Midnight Library* was the only frontlist title other than *Four Winds* to crack the top 10 in the adult segment, selling nearly 357,000 copies.

In the YA segment, Leigh Bardugo has had a banner year, with three of her Grishaverse novels placing in the top 10 and selling a combined total of roughly 421,000 copies. Her books have benefited from the Netflix film *Shadow and Bone*, which was adapted from Bardugo's book of the same name. Adam Silvera had the top seller in YA with *They Both Die at the End*. The novel, like a number of other YA titles, benefited from exposure on BookTok.

The takeaway is that there have been no real surprises on the bestseller lists in 2021, unlike last year, when sales for several juvenile nonfiction books (such as *My First Learn-to-Write Workbook*) skyrocketed as parents scrambled to buy educational titles for their children, and when numerous books on race and social justice hit the lists following the murder of George Floyd. No Trump exposés have made the lists either, unlike in the past few years, though many books on the former president's administration will be released in the second half of 2021.

As these lists indicate, backlist continued to sell well in the first half of 2021, just as it did in 2020. Half of the top 10 adult titles were published before 2020, and such obvious perennial bestsellers as George Orwell's *1984* (#18) were accompanied on the list by less-heralded backlist backbones such as psychiatrist Bessel van der Kolk's exploration of PTSD, *The Body Keeps the Score* (#12).

Adult

RANK	TITLE	AUTHOR	IMPRINT	UNITS
1	The Four Winds	Kristin Hannah	St. Martin's	558,479
2	The Boy, the Mole, the Fox and the Horse	Charlie Mackesy	HarperOne	543,522
3	The Hill We Climb	Amanda Gorman	Viking	455,603
4	Atomic Habits	James Clear	Avery	396,007
5	The Four Agreements	Don Miguel Ruiz	Amber-Allen	379,642
6	The Midnight Library	Matt Haig	Viking	356,964
7	Greenlights	Matthew McConaughey	Crown	318,896
8	The Song of Achilles	Madeline Miller	Ecco	304,133
9	Where the Crawdads Sing	Delia Owens	Putnam	294,397
10	The Women of the Bible Speak	Shannon Bream	Broadside	292,138
11	Keep Sharp	Sanjay Gupta	Simon & Schuster	282,953
12	The Body Keeps the Score	Bessel van der Kolk	Penguin Books	275,377
13	A Promised Land	Barack Obama	Crown	274,533
14	Sooley	John Grisham	Doubleday	257,099
15	Untamed	Glennon Doyle	Dial	244,142
16	The Invisible Life of Addie Larue	V.E. Schwab	Tor	234,208
17	Caste	Isabel Wilkerson	Random House	231,102
18	1984	George Orwell	Signet	230,763
19	Burn After Writing (pink)	Sharon Jones	TarcherPerigee	222,958
20	Later	Stephen King	Hard Case Crime	217,315

Children's

RANK	TITLE	AUTHOR	IMPRINT	UNITS
1	Mothering Heights (Dog Man #10)	Dav Pilkey	Graphix	867,397
2	Oh, the Places You'll Go!	Dr. Seuss	Random House	584,469
3	Cat Kid Comic Club	Dav Pilkey	Graphix	369,848
4	Green Eggs and Ham	Dr. Seuss	Random House	334,633
5	One Fish Two Fish Red Fish Blue Fish	Dr. Seuss	Random House	333,392
6	Rowley Jefferson's Awesome Friendly Spooky Stories	Jeff Kinney	Amulet	329,134
7	The Very Hungry Caterpillar	Eric Carle	Philomel	322,222
8	I Love You to the Moon and Back	Hepworth/Warnes	Tiger Tales	310,701
9	Grime and Punishment (Dog Man #9)	Dav Pilkey	Graphix	304,147
10	The Deep End (Diary of a Wimpy Kid #15)	Jeff Kinney	Amulet	302,598

YA

RANK	TITLE	AUTHOR	IMPRINT	UNITS
1	They Both Die at the End	Adam Silvera	Quill Tree	330,840
2	We Were Liars	E. Lockhart	Ember	276,107
3	Midnight Sun	Stephenie Meyer	Little, Brown	194,114
4	Shadow and Bone	Leigh Bardugo	Square Fish	179,542
5	The Outsiders	S.E. Hinton	Speak	134,722
6	The Twisted Ones (Five Nights at Freddy's Graphic Novel #2)	Scott Cawthon et al.	Graphix	131,698
7	A Good Girl's Guide to Murder	Holly Jackson	Ember	129,453
8	Siege and Storm	Leigh Bardugo	Square Fish	120,778
9	Six of Crows	Leigh Bardugo	Square Fish	120,405
10	The Giver	Lois Lowry	HMH	115,345

*

A version of this article appeared in the 07/12/2021 issue of *Publishers Weekly* under the headline: 2021 Bestselling Print Books (So Far).

NOTABLE PW PRIZEWINNERS AND AWARDS STORIES OF 2021

Louise Glück Wins 2020 Nobel Prize in Literature; New Collection to Publish Next Year
By John Maher | Oct 8, 2020

The 2020 Nobel Prize in Literature was awarded on October 8 to the American poet Louise Glück, "for her unmistakable poetic voice that with austere beauty makes individual existence universal."

Glück will give her Nobel lecture in the United States due to coronavirus travel restrictions, according to the permanent secretary of the Swedish Academy, the body that awards the prize. After receiving the Award, in a short phone conversation with a representative of the Academy, Glück said her first thought upon hearing the news was "I won't have any friends, because most of my friends are writers." She added: "It's too new. I don't know really what it means. It's a great honor, and of course there are recipients I don't admire, but then I think of the ones that I do."

Glück's current publisher, Farrar, Straux & Giroux, will go back to press on all her books following the announcement, although the press did not cite specific numbers. In addition, FSG president and publisher Jonathan Galassi, Glück's editor, said that a new collection of poetry, *Winter Recipes from the Collective*, is due to be released next year, although a date has not been decided upon.

Glück, a former U.S. poet laureate, is considered one of the foremost voices in American poetry, and is the author of 14 collections—her first, the appropriately titled *Firstborn*, with New American Library in 1968, then nine books with Ecco, followed by four with FSG starting in 2006. In 1985, she won the National Book Critics Circle award for *The Triumph of Achilles* and, eight years later, was awarded the Pulitzer Prize (and the William Carlos Williams Award) for *The Wild Iris*, perhaps her best-known collection.

Her other collections include *Vito Nova* 1990), *Proofs and Theories* (1994), *Meadowlands* (1996), *Ararat* (2000), *Averno* (2006), *The Seven Ages* (2007), *Poems 1962-2012* (2012), and *Faithful and Virtuous Night* (2014). In addition, Glück has published two chapbooks and two essay collections, 1994's *Proofs and Theories* and

2017's *American Originality*. In her call with the representative of the Academy, Glück suggested *Averno* or *Faithful and Virtuous Night* as good entry points to her oeuvre for first-time readers.

Glück has received the Academy of American Poets' Wallace Stevens Award, the American Academy of Arts and Letters Gold Medal in Poetry, the National Humanities Medal, and dozens of other honors. Born in New York City in 1943 and raised on Long Island, she attended Sarah Lawrence College and Columbia University, and now lives in Cambridge, Mass., and teaches at Yale University.

The award comes only four years after Bob Dylan, another American, won the Nobel Prize in Literature, and many pundits were skeptical that an American would be named a laureate again so soon. After all, the drought between wins for Americans prior to Dylan was nearly a quarter-century long, as Toni Morrison had previously been the most recent American to be named Nobel laureate, in 1993. Galassi, for one, was certainly as surprised as he was elated.

"It's very deserved, and her work has innate translatability—she's already been translated in a number of countries, and I think there will be a lot more of that," Galassi said. "And I think we're going to have a lot more readers for Louise. Her work is deeply poetic and literary, but also deeply sensical and direct. It's like you hear your inner voice when you read her."

The poet Daniel Halpern, who, in his tenure as publisher of Ecco, published Glück's work for more than 30 years, was also both stunned and thrilled. "It's such a great choice," he said. "You never know what the Swedish Academy is going to do. I didn't think they would go back to America so quickly, but it's really a righteous award, and a beautiful one. They picked one of the best poets writing in the world."

Ecco published Glück from 1975 until 2006, when she moved to FSG. "I think that, from her first book, it was clear to me that she was going to be one of the most important poets in America," Halpern said. He added: "It has to do with the way she schemetizes the world—it's definitely her voice and that language, which is unmistakable. I don't think you'd ever not recognize a Louise Glück line if you'd read it."

This year's prize was awarded after two years of turmoil for the Swedish Academy. The suspension of the 2018 prize ceremony until 2019 came as the awards body was mired in a complex controversy surrounding sexual harassment and other issues that saw a mass exodus from its ranks. And last year, when two prizes were awarded, the selection of Austrian writer Peter Handke, an apologist for Serbian-led genocide during the Bosnian War in the 1990s, spawned a controversy of its own.

This year's award, Galassi speculates, might soothe critics of the Academy for the time being. "I think it's a really great Nobel Prize in that it's really about literature—it's not politicized, and it's sort of a return to a calmer, more considered award than we've had," he said. "There was a lot of turbulence around the Nobel for quite a while, and this is the kind of award that makes a lot of sense."

In the announcement, a representative of the Swedish Academy said that Glück "won early acclaim as one of the most prominent poets in American contemporary literature," describing all of her collections as "characterized by striving for clarity, childhood and family life; the close relations to parents and siblings is a thematic that has remained central with her. Even if the autobiographical background is significant," the Academy representative continued, "Glück is not to be regarded as a confessional poet. She seeks the universal, and in this, she takes inspiration from myth and classical motifs. The voices of Dido, Persephone, or Eurydice are masks for a self in transformation, as personal as they are universally valued."

In her work, which is filled with "the topic of family life, austere but also playful intelligence, and a refined sense of composition," Glück regularly employs "ordinary diction in her poetry," the representative said. "We encounter almost brutally straightforward images of painful family relations without a trace of poetic ornament. Louise Glück's voice is unmistakable. It is candid and uncompromising, and it signals that this poet wants to be understood. But it is also a voice full of humor and biting wit. This is a great resource when Glück treats one of her great topics, radical change, where the leap forward is made from a deep sense of loss." He added: "She writes oneiric, narrative poetry recalling memories and travels, only to hesitate and make a halt for new insights. The world is disenthralled only to become magically present once again."

Callender, Miri, Choi, Payne and Payne, and Yu Win 2020 National Book Awards
By John Maher | Nov 18, 2020

"This is our night," author Jason Reynolds, the host of the 71st National Book Awards, told his audience from his ceremony headquarters in Washington, D.C. "I know there's so much going on in the world, but this is still our night, and it's a big deal."

Indeed, the event was historic: the first-ever all-virtual National Book Awards, with a live-streamed broadcast free and open to all, and the fifth and final ceremony to be headed by executive director Lisa Lucas, who will leave the National Book Foundation in January for a new position as publisher at Pantheon and Schocken. Despite the challenges from both an impending change in leadership and the ongoing Covid-19 pandemic, the NBF pulled out all the stops—from tribute videos to graphic animation to live award acceptances via Zoom—to ensure the event made as big a splash as ever, even at its uncharacteristically brisk pace.

First up during the evening were the lifetime achievement prizes, including the Literarian Award for Outstanding Service to the American Literary Community, awarded to late Simon & Schuster publisher Carolyn Reidy. In a tribute video, Reidy's former authors and industry colleagues paid tribute to a world-class publisher.

"The first thing I thought of when we lost Carolyn Reidy was that she was a reader," author Rachel Kushner said. "She ran this huge company, she knew everybody in the publishing world, she knew intricately how it works. But she was a *reader*." Oren Teicher, the former head of the American Booksellers Association and the recipient of last year's Literarian Award, said: "I just can't imagine anybody more deserving than Carolyn Reidy to receive this recognition. The contributions she has made to the book business and more broadly to the literary landscape in America are just unparalleled." Author Walter Isaacson added that to his mind, "Carolyn's legacy is understanding how to move the publishing industry into each new age that comes along."

Stephen Reidy, Reidy's widower, was "tremendously honored" to accept the award on behalf of his late wife, "with whom I have been sharing books and reading since we were 19 years old, when we had our first conversation, and it was about a book." Reidy, he continued, "believed that authors and publishers, through the power of the words and the books, do not just reflect our culture, but help to create it." He added: "I think she was proudest of being a publisher because, as she said, 'in publishing, we are the shepherds of this gift of the book.'"

The evening's other lifetime achievement honor, the Medal for Distinguished Contribution to American Letters, was presented by author Edwidge Danticat to author and Publishing Certificate Program at the City College of New York cofounder Walter Mosley, making him the first Black man to ever receive the award. "It has been more than 30 years since I have embarked on the path that writing conjures out of almost nothing, a path wrought in the mind, a mind that is too small to contain the full scope of a project and has within it, like language itself, the full scope of experience of our species," Mosley said in accepting the award, after listing off dozens of Black men of letters—from Ralph Ellison to Randall Kenan—without whom, he said, he could not be here today. "There's a great weight hanging over the reception of an award when the underlying subject is 'the first Black man to receive,'" he said. "I prefer to believe that we are on the threshold of a new day, that this evening is but one of 10,000 steps being taken to recognize the potential of its nation."

Following Mosley's acceptance, the Foundation aired a video in support of the Black Lives Matter movement and narrated by last year's awards host, LeVar Burton. Through the video, the Foundation pledged its commitment to Black literature, and promised to be "a literary community as life-giving and rich and as varied as the stories we tell. A community of which we can all be proud. A community which unequivocally understands why Black lives matter, and that there is no American literature without the voices of the disenfranchised, the undocumented, the marginalized, and the unheard."

Lucas then joined the ceremony, which doubles as the Foundation's biggest yearly fundraiser, live from the children's room at the main branch of the Los Angeles Public Library. "One book, we know, can change a life, and these books, we also know, will impact the world for years to come—every single one of them," she said, noting that, despite this year's challenges, the Foundation has doubled down on its mission by, for instance, distributing more books to young people and the imprisoned than ever. Still, Lucas said, the Foundation can't keep up its mission without funding: "I'm just a girl standing here in a ball gown and a pair of crocs in a library asking you to love books with money."

Following a video showing the scope of the Foundation's work, David Steinberger, chair of the Foundation's board of directors, said his farewells to Lucas. "When I was thinking back this week about everything you accomplished, I just kept coming back to that day when you first told me that we might be able to get books to kids in some public housing authorities—you called them book deserts," he said. "The research is clear that if you do nothing more than just get books in the home of a child, that child's chances in life just got a whole lot better. And now here we are, just a few years later, and thousands and thousands and thousands of books have somehow made their way into the homes of thousands and thousands and thousands of kids. If that's not making a difference in the world, I don't know what is."

After showing live shots of some of the viewers on Zoom across the U.S., the broadcast turned to the awards portion of the evening. The awards announcements were held live—all but the award in Translated Literature, which was pre-recorded due to the variation in time zones among the authors and translators—with custom-made animations narrated by a handful of celebrities introducing the finalists and the chair of each judging panel announcing the winner. Winners were fed in live from "Zoom rooms," or virtual green rooms, to make their acceptance speeches.

First, Joan Trygg, chair of the Young People's Literature judging panel, announced that Kacen Callender was the winner of the 2020 National Book Award for Young People's Literature for *King and the Dragonflies* (Scholastic Press).

"I know I'm not the only one who believes that these next generations are the ones that are meant to change everything," Callender said, upon accepting the award. "Young people already have changed the world in so many ways, and it is an honor and a privilege to be given a platform and the opportunity to help in their guidance through the power of story."

Next, Dinaw Mengestu, chair of the Translated Literature panel, announced that the winner of the 2020 National Book Award for Translated Literature was *Tokyo Ueno Station* by Yu Miri and translated from the Japanese by Morgan Giles (Riverhead Books).

"I am so happy Morgan Giles translated *Tokyo Ueno Station* into English," Miri said. "It is a shame that we can't be together on stage right now. I'd like to give her a high five and a hug." Miri added that she lives in Minamisōma, a city only 16 miles north of the Fukushima Daiichi Nuclear Power Plant that exploded in March 2011, and where she ran a bookstore at that time. "I would like to share this joy with the people of Minamisōma," she said, noting that they suffered from many hardships after the nuclear disaster, including the consequent tsunami and earthquake. "This is for you."

Then Layli Long Soldier, chair of the judging panel for Poetry—which Reynolds said he calls, with a somewhat cheeky reverence, "the piano of literature"—announced that *DMZ Colony* by Don Mee Choi (Wave Books) was the winner of the 2020 National Book Award for Poetry.

"Poetry and translation have changed my life," Choi said upon accepting the award. "For me, they are inseparable. The International Women's Network Against Militarism have taught me to think critically about translation," she continued, noting that a handful of "wonderful small and independent presses have generously published my translations of Korean feminist poets and translation-related writings." She added: "It is more important than ever that we engage in the non-predatory, idle labor of writing and reading poetry and translation."

Following poetry, Terry Tempest Williams, chair of the Nonfiction judging panel, announced that the winner of the 2020 National Book Award for Nonfiction was *The Dead Are Arising: The Life of Malcolm X* by Les Payne and Tamara Payne (Liveright).

"Since beginning the journey to finishing *The Dead Are Arising*, we've seen how Malcolm X has influenced people internationally. Today, we see the youth all over the world continue to embrace him because his message still rings true," said Tamara Payne, accepting the award on her own behalf and on the behalf of her late father. "I want to thank my father, Les Payne, for committing to this enormous work and making it his life's work, and for bringing me on as his copilot."

Finally, Roxane Gay, chair of the Fiction judging panel, announced that the winner of the 2020 National Book Award for Fiction was *Interior Chinatown* by Charles Yu (Pantheon).

"I prepared nothing, which tells you about how realistic I thought this was," Yu said. "I have had goose bumps several times tonight. There's not many reasons for hope right now. But to be here, hearing about some of these books, having read some of them, going on to read more of them, it is what keeps me going. And I hope this community can sustain other people in the same way." He added: "This seems about right for 2020. Pretty sure this is a simulation."

To close out the night, John Darnielle, the two-time novelist, lead singer of the band The Mountain Goats, and one of the judges from this year's Translated

Literature panel, broadcast in from his home in Durham, N.C., with a rendition of "This Year," the group's most famous song—and one that likely resonated with viewers the world over. "I am gonna make it through this year," Darnielle sang, "if it kills me."

LeVar Burton Named Inaugural PEN/Faulkner Literary Champion
By John Maher | Feb 2, 2021

LeVar Burton, the actor and longtime host of *Reading Rainbow*, has been named the inaugural PEN/Faulkner Literary Champion, a new annual commendation that will "recognize devoted literary advocacy and a commitment to inspiring new generations of readers and writers," the PEN/Faulkner Foundation said in a release. Burton will be honored in a virtual celebration on May 10, when this year's PEN/Faulkner Award winner—its 40th—will be announced.

"I come from a family for whom service to others is the highest possible calling," Burton said. "Whatever efforts I have made toward advancing the cause of literacy, give honor to my mother, Erma Gene Christian, my first teacher and from whom I have inherited my love for books and reading. As we move forward out of a time when alternative facts and mendacious propaganda shaped public opinion, the work you do through the PEN/Faulkner Award, and your committed investment in DC schools, has never been more important. I couldn't be more honored to be the inaugural PEN/Faulkner Literary Champion."

In addition, the longlist for the 2021 PEN/Faulkner Award for Fiction has been announced:

- *Bestiary* by K-Ming Chang (One World)
- *Dear Ann* by Bobbie Ann Mason (HarperCollins)
- *Disappear Doppelgänger Disappear* by Matthew Salesses (Little A)
- *The Knockout Queen* by Rufi Thorpe (Alfred A. Knopf)
- *Mother Daughter Widow Wife* by Robin Wasserman (Scribner)
- *Nine Shiny Objects* by Brian Castleberry (Custom House)
- *The Office of Historical Corrections* by Danielle Evans (Riverhead)
- *Scattered Lights* by Steve Wiegenstein (Cornerpost)
- *The Secret Lives of Church Ladies* by Deesha Philyaw (West Virginia University Press)
- *Transcendent Kingdom* by Yaa Gyasi (Alfred A. Knopf)

Three judges chose the 10 titles from a group of 419 novels and short story collections submitted by more than 170 publishing houses; the books were all written by American authors published in the U.S. Finalists will be announced in early March.

Eight Writers Awarded $165,000 Windham-Campbell Prizes
By Ed Nawotka | Mar 22, 2021

The winners of the 2021 Windham-Campbell Prizes have been announced. Eight writers, who are being honored for their literary achievement or promise, will receive $165,000 each to support their work.

The prize is administered by Yale University, where the papers of the prize patrons Donald Windham and Sandy Campbell are housed in the Beinecke Rare Book & Manuscript Library. There is no shortlist and the judges are not named. Two awards are given in each of the following categories: drama, fiction, nonfiction, and poetry.

The winners are Dionne Brand (Canada/Trinidad and Tobago), Kate Briggs (United Kingdom/Netherlands), Nathan Alan Davis (United States), Renee Gladman (United States), Vivian Gornick (United States), Michael R. Jackson (United States), Canisia Lubrin (Saint Lucia/Canada), Natalie Scenters-Zapico (United States).

2021 Audie Award Winners Announced
By John Maher | Mar 23, 2021

The Audio Publishers Association hosted the 26th annual Audie Awards virtually last night, making them open to the public for the first time.

The event, hosted by John Leguizamo, saw *Piranesi*, by Susanna Clarke and narrated by Chiwetel Ejiofor (Bloomsbury), take home the 2021 Audiobook of the Year award. *Clap When You Land*, by Elizabeth Acevedo and narrated by Acevedo and Melania-Luisa Marte (HarperAudio), won the 2021 Young Adult Audie Award.

"The reading is a triumph of tone," Jennifer Egan, who judged the Audiobook of the Year category with fellow authors Tommy Orange and David Sedaris, said of *Piranesi*, calling the audiobook "one of the best readings of contemporary literature that I have ever listened to." Orange added: "When the book got darker and more thrilling, and as the mystery at the center of the novel was revealed, Chiwetel Ejiofor moved the story along beautifully."

Melissa de la Cruz, who judged the Young Adult Audie Award category with Jerry Craft and V.E. Schwab, said of *Clap When You Land*: "The narration of this title brought the story to life in a rich and luscious manner." Schwab added: "The dual narration was powerful, as was the execution of the novel-in-verse component, which could be felt in the pacing and choices made by the two narrators. It was a perfect balance of writing and narration."

The 2021 Audie Award Winners are as follows:

Audiobook of the Year
Piranesi by Susanna Clarke, narrated by Chiwetel Ejiofor (Bloomsbury PLC)

Audio Drama
Doctor Who: Stranded 1 by Matt Fitton, David K. Barnes, Lisa McMullin, and John Dorney, performed by Paul McGann, Nicola Walker, Hattie Morahan, Rebecca Root, Tom Price, and Tom Baker (Big Finish Productions)

Autobiography/Memoir
The Autobiography of Malcolm X: As Told to Alex Haley by Malcolm X as told to Alex Haley, narrated by Laurence Fishburne (Audible)

Best Female Narrator
The City We Became by N.K. Jemisin, narrated by Robin Miles (Hachette Audio)

Best Male Narrator
The Autobiography of Malcolm X: As Told to Alex Haley by Malcolm X as told to Alex Haley, narrated by Laurence Fishburne (Audible)

Business/Personal Development
The Gift: 12 Lessons to Save Your Life by Dr. Edith Eva Eger, narrated by Tovah Feldshuh (S&S Audio)

Faith-based Fiction and Nonfiction
Fierce, Free, and Full of Fire, written and narrated by Jen Hatmaker (Thomas Nelson)

Fantasy
The City We Became by N.K. Jemisin, narrated by Robin Miles (Hachette Audio)

Fiction
Such a Fun Age by Kiley Reid, narrated by Nicole Lewis (PRH Audio)

History/Biography
His Truth Is Marching On: John Lewis and the Power of Hope by Jon Meacham, with an afterword by John Lewis, narrated by J.D. Jackson (PRH Audio)

Humor
A Very Punchable Face, written and narrated by Colin Jost (PRH Audio)

Literary Fiction and Classics
The Death of Vivek Oji by Akwaeke Emezi, narrated by Yetide Badaki and Chukwudi Iwuji (PRH Audio)

Middle Grade
The Good Hawk by Joseph Elliott, narrated by Fiona Hardingham and Gary Furlong (Brilliance Publishing)

Multi-voiced Narration
Clap When You Land by Elizabeth Acevedo, narrated by Elizabeth Acevedo and Melania-Luisa Marte (HarperAudio)

Mystery
Fair Warning by Michael Connelly, narrated by Peter Giles and Zach Villa (Hachette Audio)

Narration by Author or Authors
More Myself, written and narrated by Alicia Keys (Macmillan Audio)

Nonfiction
Fire in Paradise by Alastair Gee and Dani Anguiano, narrated by T. Ryder Smith (Recorded Books)

Original Work
When You Finish Saving the World by Jesse Eisenberg, narrated by Finn Wolfhard, Kaitlyn Dever, and Jesse Eisenberg (Audible Originals)

Romance
Dirty Letters by Vi Keeland and Penelope Ward, narrated by Andi Arndt and Jacob Morgan (Brilliance Publishing)

Science Fiction
The Deep by Rivers Solomon with Daveed Diggs, William Hutson, and Jonathan Snipes, narrated by Daveed Diggs (S&S Audio)

Short Stories/Collections
The Chekhov Collection of Short Stories by Anton Chekhov, narrated by Richard Armitage (Audible Studios)

Spanish Language
El laberinto del fauno by Guillermo del Toro and Cornelia Funke, narrated by Luis Ávila (PRH Grupo Editorial México)

Thriller/Suspense
When No One Is Watching by Alyssa Cole, narrated by Susan Dalian and Jay Aaseng (HarperAudio)

Young Adult
Clap When You Land by Elizabeth Acevedo, narrated by Elizabeth Acevedo and Melania-Luisa Marte (HarperAudio)

Young Listeners
The Overground Railroad by Lesa Cline-Ransome, narrated by Shayna Small and Dion Graham (Live Oak Media)

NBCC Award Winners Announced in Emotional Ceremony
By Ed Nawotka | Mar 25, 2021

In a virtual ceremony on March 25, the National Book Critics Circle announced the winners in six categories for its annual awards honoring the best books of the previous publishing year. Books published by Harvard University Press won two of the awards, while books published by Big Five publishers won the remaining awards.

The winners in each category are as follows:

- Autobiography: *Minor Feelings: An Asian American Reckoning* by Cathy Park Hong (One World)
- Biography: *Stranger in the Shogun's City: A Japanese Woman and Her World* by Amy Stanley (Scribner)
- Criticism: *Marking Time: Art in the Age of Mass Incarceration* by Nicole Fleetwood (Harvard UP)
- Fiction: *Hamnet* by Maggie O'Farrell (Knopf)
- Nonfiction: *Island on Fire: The Revolt That Ended Slavery in the British Empire* by Tom Zoellner (Harvard UP)
- Poetry: *Here Is the Sweet Hand* by francine j. harris (FSG)

In addition, Raven Leilani won the John Leonard Prize for a first book, judged by voting members of the NBCC, for her novel *Luster* (FSG). As previously announced, the $1,000 Nona Balakian Citation for Excellence in Reviewing went to Jo Livingstone, a staff writer at the *New Republic*, and the Ivan Sandrof Lifetime Achievement Award went to the Feminist Press, which celebrated its 50th anniversary last year.

During the ceremony, which was streamed online, authors were visibly moved and used the occasion to remark on recent events. In her acceptance speech for the John Leonard Prize, Leilani said that the award came after a year that surpassed her "wildest dreams," but also contained "insurmountable grief."

Jo Livingstone said that they found hope in other writers, as we appear to be "living through the end of the world." Jamia Wilson, former editor and publisher of Feminist Press—who moved to Random House in January—noted: "Research studies have shown the person most likely to read a book in any form today is a college-educated Black woman." She added that she was reminded of "how important it was to be doing this work today." This moment was followed with a montage of literary luminaries, including Molly Crabapple and Michelle Tea, honoring the press as Bikini Kill's "Rebel Girl" played.

Maggie O'Farrell dedicated her award to the late Knopf editor Sonny Mehta. francine j. harris, moved to tears by her win, cited the lasting influence and mentorship of previous generations of Black women poets, and noted the passing of poet Adam Zagajewski earlier this week.

The most intense moment came when Cathy Hong Park, visibly moved at winning, dedicated her award to the eight people murdered in Georgia last week. "This is for their families, and this is for all of the Asian women, the women in the sex industry, in the service industry, the migrant workers, the factory workers, the mothers and daughters who have come from homelands riven by empire, who have labored and struggled and died in the shadows of American history," she said. "Your hardship and spirit will not be in vain. We will remember you. We will fight for you. Your lives are not expendable. You will be remembered."

David Varno, president of the board of the NBCC (and *PW*'s fiction reviews editor), remarked: "This culmination of a year of reading was a joyous and deeply moving occasion, from the intimate readings by thirty of the finalists to the emotional and powerful acceptance speeches from the winners, all of whose work demonstrates literary excellence and cultural and political relevance."

Deesha Philyaw Wins 2021 PEN/Faulkner Award

By John Maher | Apr 6, 2021

The Secret Lives of Church Ladies by Deesha Philyaw (West Virginia University Press), a debut short story collection, has won the 2021 PEN/Faulkner Award for Fiction.

"In *The Secret Lives of Church Ladies*, her masterful debut collection of stories, Deesha Philyaw speaks in the funny, tender, undeceived voices of her title characters, who have more in common perhaps even than they know, from love to loss to God," this year's judges, Charles Finch, Bernice L. McFadden, and Alexi Zentner, wrote in a prepared statement. "In the group portrait that emerges, Philyaw gives us that rarest and most joyful fusion—a book that combines the curious agility of the best short fiction with the deep emotional coherence of a great novel."

Philyaw's book, which was a finalist for the 2020 National Book Award for Fiction last year, was selected from among 419 eligible novels and story collections by American authors published in the U.S. during 2020 and submitted by 170 publishing houses. Philyaw is also the co-author, with her ex-husband, Michael D. Thomas, of *Co-Parenting 101: Helping Your Kids Thrive in Two Households After Divorce* (New Harbinger).

Gay, Wang, Ehrenreich, Hartman Win at 2021 PEN Lit Awards

By Calvin Reid | Apr 8, 2021

The PEN Literary Awards, presented this year in a virtual ceremony, awarded poet Ross Gay the $75,000 PEN/Jean Stein Book Award for *Be Holding: A Poem* (University of Pittsburgh), a book-length lyrical tribute to the great basketball player Julius Erving and much more. Michael X. Wang's *Further News of Defeat: Stories* won the $25,000 PEN/Bingham Short Story Prize, and Barbara Ehrenreich won the $15,000 PEN/Essay Award for her career-spanning collection *Had I Known: Collected Essays* (Twelve).

In addition, Saidiya Hartman was awarded the $10,000 PEN/Galbraith Nonfiction Award for *Wayward Lives, Beautiful Experiments*, a groundbreaking history of radical queer black women (Norton). Jonathan Slaght won the $10,000 PEN/Wilson Science Writing Award for *Owls of the Eastern Ice: A Quest to Find and Save the World's Largest Owl* (Farrar, Straus, Giroux), an acclaimed record of a scientific quest and a devotion to nature.

These are among the 18 literary prizes and fellowships awarded during a polished virtual ceremony. Last year's gala event, held at Town Hall in Manhattan, was one of the last in-person literary awards events held before the pandemic shut down public gatherings. This year's virtual event, hosted by Harlem-born and -raised Broadway actor Kara Young, opened with a moody black and white video montage resembling the opening of a *Saturday Night Live* broadcast that spotlighted Young (as well as the band featured during the ceremony and its wonderful singer, Alicia Olatuja) as she makes her way through the darkened streets of New York. Like many online ceremonies over the last year, the ceremony appeared to combine live and recorded segments.

Across its list of 18 literary awards, and fellowships, the PEN Literary Awards honors writers, translators, and playwrights, and presents $380,000 in prize money. Other winners announced during the event include Asako Serizawa's short story collection *Inheritors* (Doubleday), which was awarded the $10,000 PEN Open Book Award for an exceptional book by an author of color; Kawai Strong Washburn's *Sharks in the Time of Saviors* (MCD), which received the $10,000 PEN/Hemingway Award for a debut novel; and Amy Stanley's *Stranger in the Shogun's City: A Japanese Woman and Her World* (Scribner), which received the $5,000 PEN/Weld Award for Biography. Emma Ramadan received the $3,000 PEN Translation Prize for her work translating Abdellah Taïa's novel *A Country For Dying* from the French.

Despite the remote and displaced nature of virtual ceremonies, during which the winners, located all around the country, accept their prizes in spare rooms ("I'm in my bedroom in a cocktail dress," Amy Stanley said after her win) and home libraries stacked with books, the awards still had great emotional impact on the winning authors. Short story winner Michael Wang said: "My goal as a Chinese American writer is to separate the politics of the country from the people. China is still a country of rural communities that are rarely explored by the U.S. media. I hope my fiction bridges that gap a little so that we as Americans have a better idea of the Chinese people and not just the politics surrounding them."

And Stein Book Award winner Gay said his book is "not only so much desire but this practice, the practice of understanding that we are made of each other; and I mean the trees, the microbes and the breeze." He cited the works of authors Christina Sharpe, Saidiya Hartman, Susan Sontag, and Toni Morrison as being critical to his writing process, as well as the voices of "Allen Iverson, Donny Hathaway's voice, my friend Don Belton. Had these voices not been with me, I just don't think I could have finished this book."

2021 Whiting Award Winners Announced

By John Maher | Apr 14, 2021

The 10 winners of the 36th Whiting Awards, each of which comes with a $50,000 prize, were announced on April 14 in a virtual ceremony. The event featured a keynote by former U.S. Poet Laureate Tracy K. Smith, who won a Whiting in 2005, and readings by each of the winners.

This year's winners are:

- Joshua Bennett, for poetry and nonfiction
- Jordan E. Cooper, for drama
- Steven Dunn, for fiction
- Tope Folarin, for fiction
- Donnetta Lavinia Grays, for drama
- Marwa Helal, for poetry
- Sarah Stewart Johnson, for nonfiction
- Sylvia Khoury, for drama
- Ladan Osman, for poetry
- Xandria Phillips, for poetry

"In a year of singular difficulty, these writers accessed joy, honoring past voices in their own family histories, and in the culture," Courtney Hodell, director of literary programs, said in a statement. "To a striking degree, they move fluidly across restrictive genre borderlines to create a vibrant picture of new writing in this country."

The Whiting Awards are given annually to writers of drama, fiction, nonfiction, and poetry. They are designed, according to the Whiting Foundation, "to recognize excellence and promise in a spectrum of emerging talent, giving most winners their first chance to devote themselves full-time to their own writing, or to take bold new risks in their work."

L.A. Times Book Award Winners Announced
By Ed Nawotka | Apr 19, 2021

The 41st annual Los Angeles Times Book Prizes were awarded in a live-streamed virtual ceremony last Friday. The awards are presented in 12 categories; 56 books were shortlisted overall.

"The pandemic has upended every single aspect of our lives, but I suspect many of you will agree with me that it's only deepened our appreciation for the solitary pleasure of reading," said Boris Kachka, books editor of the *Los Angeles Times*, who hosted the virtual event. "[Reading] is solitary but of course it's communal, too, because in reading we communicate with socially-distanced writers and all their characters, real or invented. We may isolate, but as long as we have books we are never isolated."

Joining Kachka in announcing the awards were several of the judges for the prizes, including Tananarive Due, who judged the Ray Bradbury Prize for science fiction; Jenny McPhee, judge for the fiction prize; and Angie Wang, judge for the graphic novel/comics prize.

The 2020 Book Prize winners are as follows:

- Art Seidenbaum Award for First Fiction: Deesha Philyaw, *The Secret Lives of Church Ladies* (West Virginia University Press)
- Biography: William Souder, *Mad at the World: A Life of John Steinbeck* (Norton)
- Christopher Isherwood Prize for Autobiographical Prose: Andrew O'Hagan, *Mayflies* (Faber & Faber)
- Current Interest: Isabel Wilkerson, *Caste: The Origins of Our Discontents* (Random House)
- Fiction: David Diop and Anna Moschovakis (translator), *At Night All Blood Is Black: A Novel* (FSG)
- Graphic Novel/Comics: Bishakh Som, *Apsara Engine* (Feminist Press)
- History: Martha S. Jones, *Vanguard: How Black Women Broke Barriers, Won the Vote, and Insisted on Equality for All* (Basic Books)
- Mystery/Thriller: S.A. Cosby, *Blacktop Wasteland* (Flatiron Books)
- Poetry: Victoria Chang, *Obit* (Copper Canyon Press)
- Ray Bradbury Prize for Science Fiction, Fantasy & Speculative Fiction: Stephen Graham Jones, *The Only Good Indians* (Gallery/Saga Press)
- Science & Technology: Sara Seager, The Smallest Lights in the Universe: A Memoir (Crown)
- Young Adult Literature: Ibi Zoboi and Dr. Yusef Salaam, *Punching the Air* (Balzer + Bray)

In addition to the book prizes, Leslie Marmon Silko was honored with the Robert Kirsch Award for lifetime achievement and the Book Industry Charitable Foundation (Binc) received the Innovator's Award.

The Book Prizes awards ceremony precedes the Los Angeles Times Festival of Books, which started April 17 and will run through April 23.

Mellon, Flamboyan Foundations Launch Fellowship for Puerto Rican Writers

By John Maher | May 12, 2021

The Andrew W. Mellon Foundation and the Flamboyan Foundation's Arts Fund have jointly established the Letras Boricuas Fellowship, which will support emerging and established Puerto Rican writers of fiction, nonfiction, poetry, and children's literature. Each of the 30 fellowships will come with an unrestricted $25,000 grant, with the first 15 writers to be announced this November.

The fellowships are open to Puerto Rican writers living in Puerto Rico and from across the diaspora in the United States. Applications may be submitted in either Spanish or English. The deadline is June 20.

"The literature of Puerto Rico—poems, memoirs, fiction, nonfiction, and creatively mixed genres—is an open window into Puerto Rico's rich and complex cultural lineages, on the island and in diaspora," Mellon Foundation president Elizabeth Alexander said in a statement. "Mellon's program initiative and funding in Puerto Rico was one of my first commitments when I came to lead the Foundation, and we are now thrilled to partner with our friends at the Flamboyan Foundation to fund the Letras Boricuas Fellowship."

Carlos Rodríguez Silvestre, executive director of Flamboyan, added: "We can't think of a better way to honor the rich heritage and diversity of Puerto Rican literature in the archipelago and the diaspora than creating a fellowship that lets writers do what they know how to do best. Our Flamboyan Arts Fund recognizes the existing lack of support for this particular sector and the absence of funding opportunities for them in Puerto Rico and abroad."

Since 2018, the Mellon Foundation has committed more than $11 million in funding to support the arts and humanities in Puerto Rico, with the Flamboyan Foundation providing more than $10 million of its own in the wake of hurricanes María and Irma. The two foundations also worked jointly in response to the Covid-19 pandemic to provide $1 million in emergency relief to 89 art organizations and 450 individual artists in Puerto Rico in 2020.

Congratulations to Our 2020 BookLife Nonfiction Prize Winner!

Author Sabreet Kang Rajeev has won the grand prize for her memoir, *Generation Zero.*

By PW Staff | May 28, 2021

Selecting the grand prize winner for the BookLife Prize is always a difficult decision. After careful consideration, BookLife has chosen *Generation Zero* by Sabreet Kang Rajeev as the winner for the 2020 BookLife Prize in Nonfiction. The memoir was ultimately chosen from among four finalists in each of the following categories: Self-Help/Relationships, Memoir/Autobiography, Inspirational/Spiritual, and Business/Personal Finance.

Here's what the judge said about Kang Rajeev's powerful memoir:

"In *Generation Zero*, Sabreet Kang Rajeev explores not just the South Asian immigrant experience, but the weight of having disappointed her father by being born a girl and the toxicity of so-called "positive stereotypes" that kept her working class family in a kind of hiding and shame. The particular beauty of this book lies in its contradictions and intersections, as Kang Rajeev empathically depicts the heroism and nobility of her immigrant parents, despite having carried the burden of feeling unwanted due to her gender. Both timely and timeless, the once 'voiceless' Kang Rajeev's incredibly intimate voice is a gift."

—Gina Frangello

Stay tuned for a profile piece on Sabreet Kang Rajeev and *Generation Zero* to run in the May 31 issue of *PW* and on the BookLife and *PW* websites.

Join us in congratulating Sabreet!

Erdrich, Diaz Among 2021 Pulitzer Prize Winners
By John Maher | Jun 11, 2021

This year's virtual Pulitzer Prize ceremony, held on June 11, honored five books spotlighting the lived experiences of people of color in the United States from multiple perspectives.

Louise Erdrich won the 2021 Pulitzer Prize in Fiction for *The Night Watchman* (Harper), which *PW* called a "stirring tale of a young Chippewa woman and her uncle's effort to halt the Termination Act of 1953." Natalie Diaz won the Poetry prize for *Postcolonial Love Poem* (Graywolf Press), which *PW*'s starred review described as studying "the body through desire and the preservation of Native American lives and cultures, suggesting that to exist as a Native in a world with a history of colonization and genocide is itself a form of protest and celebration."

The Pulitzers award three books in nonfiction categories yearly. The winner in General Nonfiction is *Wilmington's Lie: The Murderous Coup of 1898 and the Rise of White Supremacy* by David Zucchino (Atlantic Monthly Press), which *PW* called, in its starred review of the title, "a searing chronicle of the November 1898 white supremacist uprising in Wilmington, N.C., that overthrew the municipal government." The late Les Payne and Tamara Payne won the Pulitzer Prize in Biography for *The Dead Are Arising: The Life of Malcolm X* (Liveright), which our starred review called "an extraordinary and essential portrait of the man behind the icon." The winner in History is Marcia Chatelain for *Franchise: The Golden Arches in Black America* (Liveright), giving Liveright, a Norton imprint, two of the five wins this year.

ON THE HEELS OF BLOWOUT SUCCESS, U.S. BOOK SHOW ANNOUNCES 2022 DATES

BY CHRISTI CASSIDY | JUNE 3, 2021

NEW YORK—June 1, 2021—The U.S. Book Show is celebrating the success of its inaugural year. With 6,299 registrants, including nearly 1,000 members of the media, and 150+ exhibitors, *Publishers Weekly*, the virtual show's producers, are pleased to announce the show will go forward next year, scheduled for May 24–26, 2022.

The producers anticipate hosting a hybrid show next year consisting of a mix of virtual and in-person programming, exhibits and networking. This year's show, which ran from May 25–27, 2021, was virtual only and drew an international audience.

"The U.S. Book Show achieved its goal of reaching all quadrants of the publishing industry," said Cevin Bryerman, CEO and publisher of *Publishers Weekly*. "The target market of booksellers, librarians and media, including book reviewers, were given an intimate, front-row seat to the big books of Fall 2021. It is that insider experience that we will optimize next year in serving the core publishing community."

The show aimed to "create buzz" about the most anticipated books of the fall and to "connect the community" with professional development panels and virtual networking built in to the virtual environment. Attendance surged at the opening keynote speech by Oprah Winfrey and for a conversation with the actor Keanu Reeves about his forthcoming graphic novel. *PW* Editors' Picks panels across all genres hosted the publishers' editors talking about their big fall books.

Keynote and other notable speakers included Ijeoma Oluo, author of *So You Want to Talk About Race* and the forthcoming *Be a Revolution*, who opened Adult Books Day; the Pulitzer Prize–winner Anthony Doerr (*All the Light e Cannot See*); Senator Elizabeth Warren, who opened Children's Book Day; Bravo's *Top Chef* host Padma Lakshmi in conversation with her editor, Tamar Brazis; Stevie Van Zandt, who did a live interview with his editor, Ben Greenman, and audience Q&A; and the bestselling children's book author Brian Selznick, who closed the show.

Press coverage came from the *New York Times*, AP, *Washington Post Book World*, *Oprah Daily* and more, in addition to global trade coverage in *Publishing Perspectives*, *The Bookseller*, *Library Journal*, *BookBrunch* and others.

All content—speeches, industry and buzz panels, author panels and exhibit halls—are available for show attendees and new registrants on-demand through August 31, 2021, at the U.S. Book Show digital platform.

Websites:
U.S. Book Show: **https://usbookshow.com**
BuzzBooks.com: **https://buzzbooks.com**

FAREWELL TO BOOKEXPO

BY JIM MILLIOT

The first ABA convention I attended was in 1980 in Chicago, and at that show—and in all the others I've attended since then—people always found something to complain about. In my early years, the convention was four days over the Memorial Day weekend, and, needless to say, the most common complaints were that the show was too long, and, "Why does it need to be held over Memorial Day weekend?!" (Answer: when the show was started by the American Booksellers Association in 1947, many stores were closed for the holiday weekend.) Years later, when Reed tried to shoehorn it into two days, people griped that it was too short.

When the ABA owned and ran the show, up until 1994–'95, booth location was a hotly contested issue. It was such a source of friction that one year, executive director Bernie Rath asked me to attend a meeting as a neutral observer to vouch that the booth drawing was on the up-and-up.

At one point, the size of booths became the subject of much debate, as the major houses engaged in an arms race to see who could build the biggest. The brief period culminated in the creation of what many termed "Randomland," a huge exhibit that featured all of Random House's imprints, which were then under the control of Alberto Vitale. Cooler heads eventually prevailed and those large booths became much smaller, as most large houses augmented their booths with private rooms on the show floor.

The name of the show went through several changes, morphing from the ABA Convention and Trade Show to BookExpo America shortly after Reed bought it, to just BookExpo in 2016, when Reed execs felt that shortening the name of the fair would expand its geographic appeal.

Where to hold the show was another source of irritation. For many years it moved to different cities, and in its heyday, it was so big that only a few cities had conference centers large enough to accommodate the crowds. But eventually people became tired of the travel, and publishing executives argued that they could save money if the show was held in the same city every year, which would allow them to use the same booths (with a few tweaks) at subsequent shows. So show organizers picked the convention-friendly town of Chicago.

After four happy years there starting in 1995, the industry consensus was that going to the City of Big Shoulders every year was boring, so BEA went back on the road with talk of implementing a rotation of Chicago–West Coast city–East Coast city. After a 10-year effort of shuttling between cities and a rather disastrous Los Angeles event in 2008, BEA arrived in the Big Apple for what would be its last stand. The big New York trade houses, which were by then footing most of the BEA bill, were happy to have the show in their backyard, where they could save money on T&E (well, maybe not that much savings on E), but many out-of-towners complained that the cost of attending a New York show was too high.

BEA was also dogged by complaints about attendance. While most of the complaints took the position that there were not enough booksellers and librarians at the show, others thought there were too many people there who didn't belong, such as bloggers and would-be authors. And I think it was after my fifth show that I began hearing what is now the familiar refrain from publishers, "We don't write orders anymore."

So now, will people complain enough that the show will come back in some form? I hope that they do, and I hope the powers that be can agree on an event that works for everyone so that the world's largest book market won't be left without a place to come together. BookExpo was never perfect, but I am reminded of the Joni Mitchell lyric, "You don't know what you've got till it's gone." BookExpo was never paradise, but it was better than a parking lot.

*

A version of this article appeared in the 12/07/2020 issue of *Publishers Weekly* under the headline: Letter from the Editor.

BOOK FAIRS AND FESTIVALS

(Editor's note: The following list has been adapted from PW*'s "Select Conferences, Fairs, and Festivals in 2020" by Gilcy Aquino.)*

January
ABA Winter Institute
Albuquerque Comic Con
Angoulême International Comics
   Festival
AniMore
Atlanta Comic Convention
Cairo Book Fair
Çukurova Book Fair
International Kolkata Book Fair
Jaipur Literature Festival
New Delhi World Book Fair
Shoff Promotions Comic Book Show
Wizard World Portland

February
Amelia Island Book Festival
AniMangaPOP
C2E2
Casablanca Book Fair
Emirates Airline Festival of Literature
Feria Internacional del Libro La Habana
Lahore International Book Fair
Lit & Luz Festival of Language
PubWest
Riga Book Fair
San Francisco Writers Conference
San Miguel Writers Conference
Savannah Book Festival
Taipei International Book Exhibition
Tempo di Libri
Vilnius Book Fair

March
AWP Conference & Bookfair
Bangkok International Book Fair

Bologna Children's Book Fair
Book Lovers Con, Nashville
Deckle Edge Literary Festival
Foire du Livre de Bruxelles
History Book Festival
Left Coast Crime
Lehigh Valley Book Festival
Leipzig Book Fair
London Book Fair
North Texas Teen Book Festival
Palm Beach Book Festival
Salon du Livre de Paris
SleuthFest
South by Southwest
New Orlean Book Festival
Southern Kentucky Book Fest
Tech Forum and E-bookcraft
Tennessee Williams/New Orleans
   Literary Festival
Texas Library Association Conference
Tucson Festival of Books
UW–Madison's Annual Writers'
   Institute
Virginia Festival of the Book
Wizard World
The Write Stuff Writers Conference

April
Abu Dhabi International Book Fair
Alabama Book Festival
Alexandria International Book Fair
Arkansas Literary Festival/Six Bridges
   Book Festival
Bogotá International Book Fair
Buenos Aires Book Fair
Calgary Expo

Chicago Humanities Festival Springfest
Eurasian International Book Fair
Festival Neue Literatur
IBPA Publishing University
Idaho Writers Guild Pitchfest
International Book Festival Budapest
L.A. Times Festival of Books
Newburyport Literary Festival
Norwescon
Quebec International Book Fair
San Antonio Book Festival
Sant Jordi Festival
The Self-Publishing Conference
Sharjah Children's Reading Festival
Strokestown International Poetry
   Festival
Tehran International Book Fair
Tulsa Lit Fest
Unbound Book Festival
WonderCon
YALLWest Book Festival

May
Anime Central
Bay Area Book Festival
Biographers International Organization
   Annual Conference
Book World Prague
BookCon
BookExpo
Bookfest
ECPA Leadership Summit
Feira do Livro de Lisboa
Florida Writing Workshop
Gaithersburg Book Festival
Hawaii Book & Music Festival
Hay Festival Wales
Hudson Children's Book Festival
International Arsenal Book Festival
Literary Hill BookFest
LitUp
Madrid Book Fair
Malice Domestic
Miami Writers Institute
New York Rights Fair
Nonfiction Writers Conference

Pennsylvania Writers Conference
The Prince George's Book Festival
Romance Slam Jam
St. Petersburg International Book Fair
Tbilisi International Book Fair
Thessaloniki Book Fair
Turin International Book Fair
Venezuela International Book Fair
Warsaw International Book Fair

June
ABA Children's Institute
ALA Annual Conference
Association of Jewish Libraries Annual
   Conference
Bronx Book Festival
Brooklyn Comic Con
Chuckanut Writers Conference
Istanbul International Literature
   Festival
Lit Crawl Boston
Nantucket Book Festival
PePcon: The Print + ePublishing
   Conference
Printers Row Lit Fest
Queens Book Festival
Queen's Park Book Festival
The Santa Barbara Writers Conference
Sarah Lawrence College Writing
   Institute
Seoul International Book Fair
Squam Writes Retreat
Why Reading Matters

July
Anime Expo
Book Passage Mystery Writers
   Conference
Comic-Con International
Fiction at Its Finest Festival
Hero Hype
Hong Kong Book Fair
International Book Fair of Lima
Northwest Book Festival
Otakon

Paraty International Literary Festival
(FLIP)
PoetryFest
Read Up, Greenville
Santiago Book Fair
ThrillerFest

August
Beijing International Book Fair
Book Passage Travel Writers and
Photographers Conference
Ghana International Book Fair
Killer Nashville
Melbourne Writers Festival
Mississippi Book Festival
National Book Festival
Nepal International Book Fair
Romance GenreCon
Writer's Digest Conference
Writers at Woody Point

September
AJC Decatur Book Festival
Amman International Book Fair
Bloody Scotland
Bookmarks Festival of Books and
Authors
Brooklyn Book Festival
Burlington Book Festival
California Independent Booksellers
Alliance Discovery Show
Digital Book World Conference + Expo
Dragon Con
Feira do Livro do Porto
Göteborg Book Fair
Harbor Springs Festival of the Book
Indonesia International Book Fair
International Fair of Intellectual
Literature
Kentucky Women Writers Conference
Kerrytown BookFest
Komiket
Lviv International Book and Literature
Festival
Nairobi International Book Fair
New American Festival

New England Independent Booksellers
Association Fall Conference
Open Book Cape Town
Pacific Northwest Booksellers
Association Tradeshow
South African Book Fair, Johannesburg
Southern Independent Booksellers
Alliance Discovery Show
Transylvanian Book Festival
Unicorn Writers Conference
The Village Trip
Word on the Street

October
2019 Neustadt Lit Fest
Antwerp Book Fair
Brilliant Baltimore
Bienal do Livro
Boston Book Festival
Bouchercon
Brattleboro Literary Festival
Bucks County Book Festival
Dodge Poetry Festival
Florida Writers Association Annual
Conference
Frankfurt Book Fair
Geneva Book and Press Fair
The Heartland Fall Forum
Helsinki Book Fair
High Desert Book Festival
Istanbul Book Fair
Krakow International Book Fair
Krasnoyarsk Book Culture Fair
LIBER International Book Fair
Lit & Luz Festival of Language,
Literature, and Art
Litquake
Mountains and Plains Independent
Booksellers Association Fall
Conference
New Atlantic Independent Booksellers
Association Fall Conference
New York Comic Con
Rainbow Book Fair
RomCon
Southern Festival of Books

Texas Book Festival
Texas Teen Book Festival
Twin Cities Book Festival
Vancouver Writers Fest
Wisconsin Book Festival

November
Anime NYC
Bibliotéka Bratislava
Dublin Book Festival
ECPA Publishing University and Art of
   Writing Conference
Festival Albertine
Gaudeamus Book Fair
Guadalajara International Book Fair
Interliber
International Children and Young
   Adults Book Fair (FILIJ)
Malta Book Festival

Miami Book Fair
NCTE Annual Convention
Salon du Livre de Montréal
Shanghai International Children's Fair
Sharjah International Book Fair
Slovenian Book Fair
Tampa Bay Times Festival of Reading
Vienna International Book Fair
Wordstock: Portland's Book Festival
YALLFest

December
Con+Alt+Delete
International Belgrade Book Fair
Jeddah International Book Fair
Moscow Non/Fiction Book Fair
Più Libri Più Liberi (Rome Book Fair)
Pula Festival of Books and Authors
Sofia International Book Fair

㉓

THE FUTURE OF PUBLISHING

BY MICHAEL PIETSCH

Well, hell! If anyone had any unresolved doubts about whether book publishing has a bright future, the global pandemic brought extraordinary proof that our business is one for the ages. The heads of major publishing companies have filled the press recently with reports of having reached more readers than ever before. Their ebullience is well founded: Book publishing has been stress-tested by an epochal disruption that severed us from offices, routines, friends and family, and that temporarily closed thousands of book retailing outlets nationwide. And while Covid-19 has brought untold loss, grief, and isolation in the U.S. and globally, our industry has not just survived but thrived. What has the past year-plus of disruption and success revealed?

The clearest and most heartening lesson is: *Books are essential. Truly.* In all times, and especially in difficult ones, a book is the best source of information, of reassurance, of entertainment, of education, of escape, of transformation. People isolated for long stretches by the pandemic reached out for connection—and a book remains one of the simplest and richest ways ever created of connecting deeply with another mind.

A second lesson is: *Readers will find the books they want.* We create books in multiple formats, and sell them through many types of retailers, in order to reach readers whatever their reading or shopping preferences. People understand that there are many places to buy and ways to experience books, and when favored venues were closed, they found books wherever they remained available—in e-book form, as downloaded audios, at online retailers, and at mass-merchant stores that were permitted to remain open as sellers of essential goods.

And a third, most unexpected lesson is: *Publishing is portable.* Infected with chronic we've-always-done-it-this-way-itis, publishers have long carried the overhead of big-city offices, expensive travel and entertainment bills, in-person events, book fairs, and other customary ways of operating. We have been profitable enough that we haven't been pressured into learning that we could accomplish much of our work through online communications, digital marketing, and remote-working capabilities that have long been available. Working from home, freed from onerous commutes, without in-person sales calls, publicity pitches, sales conferences and trade shows, publishers have opened their minds at last to new and in many cases more effective ways of working.

Extrapolating from these lessons and other trends, publishing's future looks strong. The unforeseen changes brought by the pandemic make predictions going very far into the future seem foolhardy. So here are a few thoughts on what we might expect to see in the near term.

Authors will continue to want publishers. Self-publication options are more abundant and easier to use than ever, and self-published books constitute a vast, largely unreported volume of purchases and reads. Most writers will nonetheless continue to prefer finding publishers to self-publishing when they are able to do so, for the financial and professional support publishers provide and the opportunity of fully accessing the complex marketplace of physical and digital retailers. Publishers provide advance payments against future royalties, professional editing, copy editing, design, and legal services, copyright protection, manufacturing, warehousing, and, most important, selling, marketing, publicity, and distribution. It is a unique combination of financial support and professional outreach that self-publishing can't come close to replicating.

Revenues will grow. Pandemic effects brought significant revenue growth for publishers in 2020 and 2021. We can't expect this to continue once normal lives resume, and as the pandemic recedes we will likely see some decline. But after that, we should expect our business to continue the steady growth we saw in the years preceding the pandemic, as the generation of readers raised on the bumper crop of superb children's books in recent decades emerge as dedicated and adventurous adult book buyers.

Consolidation isn't over. As the business continues its steady growth, as top-selling books continue to sell more copies, and as retail sales and wholesaling are concentrated in the hands of fewer, bigger companies, the financial dynamics that turned the Big 6 into the Big 5 will continue to motivate large publishers to keep acquiring, just as smaller publishers will continue facing pressures that make them consider selling.

Online sales will keep growing. Online sales of print books have been increasing steadily for years, and with recent growth in downloadable audio offsetting declining e-book sales, the result is that more than half of all book purchases are made by someone at a computer, phone, or tablet rather than in a store. The pandemic introduced even more readers to the habit of getting books delivered to their doors or devices, and they are likely to continue ordering online when there is a particular book they know they want. Publishers will keep improving their online and digital marketing capabilities to drive online and in-store purchases, and will take the opportunity of developing more direct connections with book buyers to sell more books themselves. And retailers will continue to improve their online and omnichannel experiences with their customers.

Print books are here to stay . . . I love talking about how powerfully the experience of reading inheres in the delivery system of the printed book. Book buyers clearly agree: in recent years they bought print books over e-books by more than four to one from major publishers. E-books and audiobooks have their unique pleasures and are perfect for certain times, places, and kinds of reading. But for the most deeply immersive experience, having the writer's stream of words rendered into a beautiful and lasting physical object is a perfect and complete embodiment of that mind-to-mind communication.

. . . and so are bookstores. As long as readers want printed books, shopping for those books in the sanctum of a bookstore will continue to be a singularly pleasing experience. People who love reading love the experience of curated discovery offered in a storeful of books, uniquely organized by in-store staff who are passionate and knowledgeable about the books and authors they are selling. The brick-and-mortar book superstore may have been made largely redundant by online stores that stock every book in print, but smaller bookstores, both chains and independents, will endure based on selection, display, community-centeredness, and personality.

New marketing skills will become essential. Book marketing has always involved influencing established media and retail gatekeepers, and those relationships and skills continue to be essential. An interlocking set of skills, for reaching the world congregating ever more massively online, has grown equally necessary. Trending topics blow up fast, and our ability to speedily join and influence social media conversations will become even more crucial. In a world where Barnes & Noble's top-selling books are often driven by TikTok videos, publishers will develop new and constantly evolving skillsets. And the accumulation of data about reader's desires, affinities, preferences, and habits will inform skills and tactics for marketing particular books to particular readers at particular moments, across entire front- and backlists, beyond the new-title mindset that has long been most publishers' focus.

Important work on diversity, equity, and inclusion will continue. The painful and necessary reckoning about race that publishers began during the summer of 2020 has had some tangible early results. Publishers have stated the ethical, creative, and business need for change, and have acknowledged that the efforts they'd made in years past to employ and retain more people from underrepresented backgrounds were not nearly as successful as they need to be. Many have made commitments to reach staffing levels more reflective of the nation's population and to bring more employees of color into leadership roles, and several have begun publicly reporting their statistical progress. They have committed to acquiring more books by traditionally underrepresented writers and investing in multicultural marketing strategies to reach a broader diversity of readers. Some worry that these early efforts will fade; we should expect publishers to hold themselves accountable by prioritizing these essential initiatives in order to achieve measurable results for employees and for readers.

Publishing houses will spread out. There was a time when major publishers needed to be in New York—that's where the media outlets they rely on for publicity and marketing were based, where their corporate parents were headquartered, where the literary agents who represented the writers they worked with lived. All those factors still matter, but as technology has made it possible to create and nurture relationships with less reliance on in-person connections, major publishers recognize that in theory they could now be based anywhere. In practice, they are likely still to have New York headquarters, but also to open more employment hubs and smaller offices in other locations. As employers everywhere try out hybrid work arrangements, with employees in offices a few days a week rather than full time, publishers will look for benefits including lower overhead, increased racial and ethnic diversity, connection with regional literary and cultural scenes, and bringing more varied worldviews and life experiences into their work community. This decentralization will come with serious issues including how to establish connections among colleagues, inculcate culture, and foster career advancement, and it will take significant work to keep the strong identities and sense of mission that publishers prize.

Publishers will listen more and communicate more. For centuries, publishers have benefited from a stream of entry-level employees willing to put in years working long hours for relatively low pay, for the pleasure of working with writers and among book-loving colleagues. As expectations have changed and social media offers every employee a microphone, publishers are hearing more loudly than ever before how their employees feel about their jobs, work/life balance, career development, the company's position on social and environmental issues, its commitment to diversity, and much more. Publishers will listen more and communicate more, making the company's ethics and business goals more public, and work harder to make sure that the talented people who choose to work in publishing find it a place they want to stay and grow.

I've always been optimistic about our business, despite the challenges and stresses of bringing thousands of books each year into an ever-changing marketplace. And I don't mean, in this optimistic prognostication, to ignore that there are major concerns confronting our industry: the relentless, escalating assault on copyright waged by well-funded representatives of the major technology companies, new state laws aiming to regulate e-book sales to libraries, the printing and supply-chain bottlenecks confounding publishers for the past several years, the challenges that unlimited subscription models pose to author and publisher. Our business, like our world, grows more complex each year, and the questions before us are ever more sophisticated ones. But my optimism holds. The partnership between writers and publishers is profound and essential, and I feel certain that it is more than strong enough to support our finding a rewarding future together.

*

Michael Pietsch has been CEO of Hachette Book Group since 2013. Before that he was Publisher of Little, Brown and Company and an editor at Harmony Books and Scribner. He started in publishing as an intern at David R. Godine, Publisher, in 1978, and has never looked back.

"DIY: Point-of-Sale Programs for Indie Authors" by Alex Palmer | copyright © BookLife LLC

"APA Says Audiobook Sales Rose 12% in 2020" by Jim Milliot | copyright © PWxyz LLC

"To Change How You Publish in the Digital Age, Start with a Question" by Bill Rosenblatt | copyright © PWxyz LLC

"The Pandemic Pushed Publishing Into the Digital Realm. So What's Next?" by Steve Sieck | copyright © PWxyz LLC

"Chelsea Apple Makes a Case for BookTok Authenticity" by Chelsea Apple | copyright © PWxyz LLC

"How Publishers Can Find the ROI from Rights" by Bill Rosenblatt | copyright © PWxyz LLC

"More Price Hikes Hitting the Print Industry" by Teri Tan | copyright © PWxyz LLC

"The Top 10 Library Stories of 2020" by Andrew Albanese | copyright © PWxyz LLC

"A Year Unlike Any Other" by Jim Milliot and Ed Nawotka | copyright © PWxyz LLC

"New Report Explores 'Engagement' with Books, Digital Media" by Andrew Albanese | copyright © PWxyz LLC

"Trade Publishing Segment Shines in a Flat 2020" by Jim Milliot | copyright © PWxyz LLC

"Book Biz Closes Out an Unexpected 2020" by Jim Milliot | copyright © PWxyz LLC

"The Surge of Print Books Sales Continues" by Jim Milliot | copyright © PWxyz LLC

"How Ingram Content Group Became a $2 Billion Company" by Jim Milliot | copyright © PWxyz LLC

"Saluting HMH, a Storied Trade Publisher" by Gary Gentel | copyright © PWxyz LLC

"High Costs, Services Disruptions Plague Book Biz Supply Chain" by Jim Milliot | copyright © PWxyz LLC

"Bookshop.org Continues to See Strong Sales" by Ed Nawotka | copyright © PWxyz LLC

"Print Books Sales Soar in Year's First Half" by Jim Milliot | copyright © PWxyz LLC

"Print Book Sales Could Grow by 2% This Year—Or by 8%" by Jim Milliot | copyright © PWxyz LLC

"Book Biz Saw Little M&A in 2020, with Some Big Exceptions" by Jim Milliot | copyright © PWxyz LLC

"Japan's Media Do Buys Firebrand" by Jim Milliot | copyright © PWxyz LLC

"RBMedia Acquires Spain's Booka" by Ed Nawotka | copyright © PWxyz LLC

"HarperCollins to Acquire HMH Trade" by Jim Milliot | copyright © PWxyz LLC

"Francisco Partners to Acquire VitalSource from Ingram" by Calvin Reid | copyright © PWxyz LLC

"Investment Firm in Deal with RosettaBooks" by Jim Milliot | copyright © PWxyz LLC

"HarperCollins Completes Purchase of HMH Trade" | copyright © PWxyz LLC

"Kakao Entertainment Acquires Radish Reading App" by Calvin Reid | copyright © PWxyz LLC

"RBmedia Buys M-H Professional Audiobook Business" by Jim Milliot | copyright © PWxyz LLC

"Barnes & Noble's Owner Buys Paper Source" by Jim Milliot | copyright © PWxyz LLC

"Clarivate to Buy ProQuest for $5.3 Billion" by Jim Milliot and Andrew Albanese | copyright © PWxyz LLC

"Readerlink Acquires Activity Publisher Dreamtivity" by Karen Raugust | copyright © PWxyz LLC

"Private Equity Firm to Buy McGraw-Hill for $4.5 Billion" by Jim Milliot | copyright © PWxyz LLC

"Open Road Buys U.K.'s Bloodhound Books" by Jim Milliot | copyright © PWxyz LLC

"Hachette Book Group Will Acquire Workman Publishing for $240 Million" by Jim Milliot | copyright © PWxyz LLC

"Censorship on the Rise Worldwide" by Ed Nawotka | copyright © PWxyz LLC

"Recalling a Free Speech Landmark" by Christopher M. Finan | copyright © PWxyz LLC

"Talking About Censorship and Publishing" by Christopher M. Finan | copyright © PWxyz LLC

"The Bestselling Books of 2021 (So Far)" | copyright © PWxyz LLC

"Louise Glück Wins 2020 Nobel Prize in Literature; New Collection to Publish Next Year" by John Maher | copyright © PWxyz LLC

"Callender, Miri, Choi, Payne and Payne, and Yu Win 2020 National Book Awards" by John Maher | copyright © PWxyz LLC

"LeVar Burton Named Inaugural PEN/Faulkner Literary Champion" by John Maher | copyright © PWxyz LLC

"2021 Audie Award Winners Announced" by John Maher | copyright © PWxyz LLC

"NBCC Award Winners Announced in Emotional Ceremony" by Ed Nawotka | copyright © PWxyz LLC

"Deesha Philyaw Wins 2021 PEN/Faulkner Award" by John Maher | copyright © PWxyz LLC

"Gay, Wang, Ehrenreich, Hartman Win at 2021 PEN Lit Awards" by Calvin Reid | copyright © PWxyz LLC "2021 Whiting Award Winners Announced" by John Maher | copyright © PWxyz LLC

"L.A. Times Book Award Winners Announced" by Ed Nawotka | copyright © PWxyz LLC

"Mellon, Flamboyan Foundations Launch Fellowship for Puerto Rican Writers" by John Maher | copyright © PWxyz LLC

"Congratulations to Our 2020 BookLife Nonfiction Prize Winner!" by PW Staff | copyright © PWxyz LLC

"Erdrich, Diaz Among 2021 Pulitzer Prize Winners" by John Maher | copyright © PWxyz LLC

"U.S. Book Fair Announced for 2022" | copyright © PWxyz LLC

"Farewell to BookExpo" by Jim Milliot | copyright © PWxyz LLC

SUBSCRIBE TO *PUBLISHERS WEEKLY* AT YOUR EXCLUSIVE PW ALMANAC RATE

Stay connected to important industry news and the buzz around the very best upcoming books

YOUR *PUBLISHERS WEEKLY* SUBSCRIBER BENEFITS START IMMEDIATELY:

- **Weekly issues:** 175+ prepublication book reviews in every issue, industry news
- **Digital edition access.** Read the interactive digital version issue on Saturday and get the latest news first. Available for your desktop, tablet, and phone
- **Announcements Issues.** Spring & Fall Children's & Adult round-ups of what's coming
- **Subscriber-Only premium website access.** Breaking news, expanded Bestsellers lists, 350,000+ book reviews, author interviews, feature spotlights, and more

START YOUR IMMEDIATE ACCESS TO PW AT YOUR EXCLUSIVE PW ALMANAC RATE

PUBLISHERSWEEKLY.COM/ALMANAC